The Psychology
of Health and
Health Care

The Psychology of Health and Health Care

A CANADIAN PERSPECTIVE

SECOND EDITION

Gary Poole
University of British Columbia

Deborah Hunt Matheson
Malaspina University College

David N. Cox
Simon Fraser University

PEARSON

Prentice
Hall

Toronto

National Library of Canada Cataloguing in Publication

Poole, Gary, 1950–
    The psychology of health and health care : a Canadian
perspective / Gary Poole, Deborah Hunt Matheson, David N. Cox.—2nd ed.

Includes bibliographical references and index.
ISBN 0-13-143366-0

    1. Medicine and psychology. I. Matheson, Deborah Hunt, 1966– II. Cox, David Neil, 1947–
III. Title.

R726.7.P66 2005   610'.1'9   C2003-906565-0

ISBN 0-13-143366-0

Vice President, Editorial Director: Michael J. Young
Acquisitions Editor: Ky Pruesse
Executive Marketing Manager: Judith Allen
Associate Editor: Patti Altridge
Production Editor: Martin Tooke
Copy Editor: Imogen Brian
Proofreader: Michelle Harrington
Production Coordinator: Patricia Ciardullo
Page Layout: Heidi Palfrey
Photo Research: Amanda McCormick
Art Director: Mary Opper
Cover Image: Getty Images/Imagebank

Photo credits begin on page 493, which constitutes a continuation of the copyright page.

Statistics Canada information is used with the permission of the Minister of Industry, as Minister responsible for Statistics Canada. Information on the availability of the wide range of data from Statistics Canada can be obtained from Statistics Canada's Regional Offices, its World Wide Web site at http://www.statcan.ca, and its toll-free access number 1-800-263-1136.

2 3 4 5   09 08 07 06 05 04

Printed and bound in the United States.

For our families:

Marsha, Colleen, and Graeme Poole

Owen and Wyatt Matheson

Susan, Kelsi, Kieran, and Dylan Cox

Contents

Preface   xv

Acknowledgments   xvii

Chapter One   The Development of the Field   1

What Is Health Psychology?   3

The Development of Health Psychology As a Discipline   5

    The Early Stages of Health Psychology's Development: Applying the Principles of Behaviourism to Health   5

    Health Psychology Expands to Include Cognition and Personality Factors   7

    More Attention Is Paid to the Ways People Cope   8

    The Introduction of Psychoneuroimmunology: Finding Links between Psychological and Biological Processes   9

    Summary   9

Why Has Health Psychology Come into Prominence?   10

    Changing Profiles of Illness and Health in Canada   10

    Multiple Perspectives Are Needed to Understand Health and Health Statistics   12

Health Psychology Today   13

    A Biopsychosocial Approach to Health   13

    Prominent Theories in Health Psychology   15

Working in Health Psychology   26

    Clinical and Counselling Psychologists Working in Health Psychology   27

    Research Careers in Health Psychology   27

Key Terms   28

Chapter Two   Stress and Coping   29

Issues of Definition   31

The Physiology of Stress   35

    The General Adaptation Syndrome   37

Cognitive Transactional Models   38

The Role of Personality in Stress and Coping   41

Coping   43

    East and West: Now the Twain Shall Meet   46

    Relaxation   48

Behaviour Therapy and Cognitive Therapy   49

The Relaxation Responses: A Personal Guide   51

Key Terms   53

Chapter Three   Psychoneuroimmunology   55

The Importance of Psychoneuroimmunology to Health Psychology   57

An Introduction to the Immune System   57

How Immune-System Function Is Measured in Psychoneuroimmunological Research   59

Counting Cells to Measure Immunocompetence   60

Functional Tests of Immunocompetence: Measuring Cells in Action   60

Methodological Issues in the Measurement of Immune-System Function   62

Research in Psychoneuroimmunology: Providing Evidence for a Biological Link between Psychology and Health   64

The Effect of Stress on Immune Functioning   64

The Effect of Mood on Immune Functioning   70

Personality and Cancer   80

Social Support and Immune Functioning   80

Proposed Biological Mechanisms to Explain Why Psychological States Affect the Immune System   82

Future Directions for Psychoneuroimmunological Research   83

Key Terms   84

Chapter Four   Communication in Medical Settings   85

Perceiving and Interpreting Symptoms   87

Seeking Medical Care   90

Delaying Medical Care   91

Physician–Patient Interaction   94

Basic Models of Physician–Patient Interaction   95

Physician–Patient Communication   99

Adhering to Medical Advice   108

Assessing Adherence   108

Frequency and Cost of Non-Adherence   109

What Factors Predict Adherence?   110

Improving Patient Adherence   112

Health Outcomes   115

Key Terms   116

Chapter Five   Hospital Stays and Medical Procedures   117

The Hospital As a Distinct Culture   119
    A Hospital Patient's Loss of Control   121
    How Patients Cope with the Hospital Culture   125
    The Role of Nurses in Hospital Culture   125
    Patient-Centred Care: An Ideal in the Hospital   128
The Psychological Impact of Medical Procedures   129
    The Psychology of Mammography   129
    The Psychology of Magnetic Resonance Imaging   131
Day Surgery   134
In the Hospital   135
    The Emergency Department   135
    Recovering from Surgery   136
    The Intensive-Care Unit   138
    Discharge   141
    Palliative Care   143
Key Terms   145

Chapter Six   The Health Care Provider   146

Physicians   148
    Why People Choose a Career in Medicine   149
    Medical School   150
    Physicians' Emotional Involvement in Their Work   153
    Physicians and Stress   154
Gender Issues in Medical Practice   158
    The "Feminization" of Medicine   158
    Male and Female Physicians' Perceptions of Themselves, Their Work, and Their
        Careers   158
    Gender Differences in the Provision of Patient Care   159
Nursing   161
    The Nature of Modern Nursing   161
    Stress in Nursing   162
Other Health Care Professionals   167
    Physical Rehabilitation and Physiotherapists   169
    Technologists   171
A Final Word   172
Key Terms   172

Chapter Seven   Health Promotion   173

The Development of Health Promotion in Canada   175

    The Goals of Health Promotion in Canada   177

    Health Promotion Mechanisms   179

Improving Health Promotion by Applying Principles of Psychology   182

    Prominent Theories in Health Psychology Applied to Health Promotion   182

    The Social Psychology of Health Promotion   183

    The Elaboration Likelihood Model of Persuasion   183

    Fear Appeals: An Example of Health Promotion by the Peripheral Route   184

    The Application of Other Social-Psychological Principles to Health Promotion   189

The Precede–Proceed Model   191

Assessing the Effectiveness of Health Promotion Programs   193

Key Terms   194

Chapter Eight   Health and Physical Activity   195

The Nature of Physical Activity   197

Physical Activity and the Five Components of Health   200

    Rates of Physical Activity   200

The Five Forms of Physical Activity   202

Psychological Benefits of Physical Activity   202

    Physical Activity and Sense of Self   203

    Physical Activity and Cognitive Functioning   207

    Physical Activity and Mood   208

Physical Benefits of Physical Activity   209

Adherence to Physical Activity   211

Psychological Factors Affecting Performance in Exercise and Sport   212

    Relaxation   213

    Self-Talk   214

    Imagery   215

    Goal-Setting   216

Physical Activity and Injury   216

Key Terms   221

Chapter Nine   Health-Compromising Behaviours   222

Substance Abuse   224

    Smoking   224

    Alcohol Use   234

Illicit Drug Use   238

Unsafe Sexual Behaviours   241

Obesity   242

    Biological Factors That Contribute to Obesity   244

    Psychosocial Factors That Contribute to Obesity   246

    Sociocultural Factors That Contribute to Obesity   246

    Prevention and Treatment of Obesity   248

    Pharmacological Treatment of Obesity   249

    Behavioural Treatment of Obesity   249

    Surgical Treatment of Obesity   250

Eating Disorders   251

    Biological, Cultural, and Psychological Contributors to Eating Disorders   252

    Treatment for Eating Disorders   254

Key Terms   255

Chapter Ten   Pain   257

The Significance of Pain   260

Pain Perception   261

Theories of Pain   262

    Gate Control Theory   262

    Neuromatrix Theory   264

Neurochemical Basis of Pain and Pain Inhibition   265

Acute versus Chronic Pain   266

Psychosocial Factors and Pain   270

    Gender Differences   270

    Cultural Differences   272

The Measurement of Pain   272

    Psychophysiological Measures   273

    Behavioural Assessment   273

    Self-Reports of Pain   274

    Assessing Pain in Infants and Children   278

    Assessing Pain in Older Adults   279

Pain Control Techniques   280

    Pharmacological Control of Pain   280

    Surgical Control of Pain   281

    Transcutaneous Electrical Nerve Stimulation   282

    Acupuncture   283

    Physical Therapy   285

Massage   285

Relaxation   285

Distraction   287

Biofeedback   288

Hypnosis   288

Multidisciplinary Pain Management Programs   290

Key Terms   292

Chapter Eleven   Chronic and Life-Threatening Illnesses   293

Cancer   295

Physical Problems   297

Psychological Distress   298

Cancer Treatment   300

Helping People Cope with Cancer   304

Diabetes   307

Diabetes and Psychological Distress   308

Helping People Cope with Diabetes   310

Diseases of the Cardiovascular System   311

Psychological Distress in Cardiovascular Disease   311

Helping People Cope with Cardiovascular Disease   313

HIV and AIDS   315

Psychological Distress and HIV/AIDS   316

Helping People Cope with HIV and AIDS   316

Other Chronic Conditions   317

Quality of Life   318

The Tradeoff between Duration and Quality of Life   319

Quality of Life As a Subjective Phenomenon   320

Death and Dying   321

Patients' Reactions to Death   321

Bereavement and Grief   322

Key Terms   323

Chapter Twelve   Health and the Internet   324

What Is the Internet?   326

Search Engines   327

Patterns of Internet Use   327

Examples of Health-Related Resources Available on the Internet   327

Medical Articles and Reports 328

Services 330

Health Initiatives and Health Promotion 330

Surveys 331

Support 331

Assessing the Quality of Health Information on the Internet 331

Usability 333

Accessibility 334

How People Process Information from the Internet 335

Implications of Internet use for Individual and Public Health 336

Patient–Physician Relationships 336

Practitioners' Use of the Internet 340

Hospital Web Sites 342

Equality of Access 342

The Challenges of Using the Internet Effectively 343

Health-Related Uses of the Internet in the Future 344

Key Terms 344

Focused Module A   Conducting Research in Health Psychology   345

Focused Module B   Epidemiology: What Can Be Learned from the SARS Outbreak in Canada?   355

Focused Module C   Complementary and Alternative Medicine   359

Focused Module D   Medical Sociology   364

Focused Module E   Aboriginal Health   369

Focused Module F   A Sampling of Canadian Research in Health Psychology   373

Glossary   384

References   404

Index   481

Photo Credits   493

Preface

The writing of a textbook provides an excellent learning opportunity. In writing the first edition of *The Psychology of Health and Health Care: A Canadian Perspective,* we became familiar with a wider range of health-related topics and literature than we ever had in using other people's books. With the writing of the second edition, we have continued to learn.

One important lesson has been that the preparation of a second edition can be every bit as challenging as a first edition. The second time around, a host of new questions arise, such as: Are the topics covered still relevant? Has thinking changed regarding any of the topics covered? What new research has emerged since the first edition? Should new topics be added? Answering questions such as these often took us right back to the beginning of our work. Health psychology continues to be a growing field. Moreover, as a discipline, it is expanding to interface with other disciplines. In so doing, the relevant literature expands accordingly. The second edition of *The Psychology of Health and Health Care: A Canadian Perspective* features hundreds of new references. More than ever before, the medical literature, as found through sources like *Medline*, provides rich sources of research on biopsychosocial issues. We believe this indicates the maturation of health psychology, and the increased influence of the social sciences on health care.

Other important questions that must be asked when writing a second edition of a textbook address the book's structure and writing. Are the chapters in the right order? Are there better ways of organizing this material? Can we help students better understand concepts by representing them differently? In answering these questions, we have relied considerably on colleagues from across the country who have taught with our book. As a result of their feedback, and the experience we gained from using the book in our own courses, we have made some very noticeable changes to the structure of the book.

This book contains the rather bold claim that it has been written from "a Canadian perspective." What exactly do we mean by this? It does not mean simply writing *behaviour* instead of *behavior* or proudly proclaiming, as many of us do, "I AM CANADIAN." There is much more to it than this. Most psychological theories developed in the United States cross the border quite well; however, when it comes to health and health care, our geography, demography, history, and health care system make Canadians unique. While writing both editions of this book, we found it surprisingly easy to capture this uniqueness. As a country, Canada does a very good job of documenting the health of its citizens. Statistics relevant to that documentation are found throughout the book. Some examples can be found in chapter 1 in our introduction to the field, in chapter 7 where we discuss health promotion, in chapter 11 on chronic and life-threatening illnesses, and in focused module E on Aboriginal health.

While writing this book, it was also gratifying to be able to confirm that Canadians are very active in research that goes beyond descriptions of our health to explore factors affecting it. Again, this research is discussed throughout the book. To get a sense of this, turn to focused module F, where we list many examples of health psychology research conducted at Canadian universities and in health care settings.

HOW BEST TO USE THIS BOOK

The second edition of *The Psychology of Health and Health Care: A Canadian Perspective* is organized into chapters and *focused modules*. Chapters are the traditionally used organizational elements. Focused modules might be new to you. The chapters of this book present topics that are commonly found in most health psychology textbooks. Stress and coping, communication in medical settings, pain, and chronic and life-threatening illnesses are examples of such topics. However, *The Psychology of Health and Health Care: A Canadian Perspective* also contains chapters on some topics typically covered in less detail. Examples include psychoneuroimmunology, health promotion, health and physical activity, and health and the Internet.

Instructors are invited to use the book's chapters as they fit their educational context. For example, nursing and medical students may want to focus more on chapters such as Psychoneuroimmunology, Communication in Medical Settings, Hospital Stays and Medical Procedures, The Health Care Provider, Pain, and Chronic and Life-Threatening Illnesses.

Health psychology is essentially an applied discipline and each chapter of our book opens with a vignette intended to provide students with a realistic context for what they are about to read. In this way, we begin each chapter with an applied focus. Students will also find case studies throughout the book. In addition to the analysis we provide, students can discuss these case studies in lectures or seminars.

The focused modules are intended to provide material for still more learning contexts. Most of these modules cover topics that pervade the entire book. Research Methods in Health Psychology; Epidemiology; and Aboriginal Health are good examples. The focused modules are long enough to introduce a topic reasonably well, yet short enough to be assigned as reading for tutorials or online discussions.

We hope that the focused modules will make the book even more flexible to use. Our conversations with instructors from across the country taught us that each has his or her own particular areas of emphasis. In some institutions, Aboriginal health is given considerable attention. In others, research methodology is an integral part of every course in the psychology curriculum. In still others, health issues are approached from multidisciplinary perspectives, and so people majoring in a field like psychology must be familiar with the language and concepts of more macroscopic disciplines like sociology.

Hence, each of these is featured in a manageable focused module that can augment the chapters or be assigned for tutorials or other discussion forums.

We decided to end the second edition with a focused module that provides a sampling of Canadian research in health psychology. When we grouped these references by province and put them together in one module, we were struck by their number and diversity. This impression was underscored by the fact that this is a very limited list, and for the most part, it features papers published since 2000. Students who wish to pursue the health field at a graduate level need to know that Canada provides many opportunities for them. We hope that they will look through this list and come to the conclusion that Canada is very active in health psychology research. This continues to be the most persistent conclusion we have drawn in writing both editions of *The Psychology of Health and Health Care: A Canadian Perspective.*

Acknowledgments

We are very grateful for the help we received from Sean Benay, who provided a very careful reading of our first edition, and from Caroline Murphy of the University of British Columbia, who pointed us in the right direction regarding the content for Chapter 12, Health and the Internet. We also continue to be very grateful to Peter Gibson for sharing and updating his remarkable story with us in Chapter 8. For their feedback on the first edition, we would also like to thank Lois Hunt, Dennis Krebs of Simon Fraser University, Tina Niwinska, Jody L. Bain of the University of Victoria (who also offered commentary on the new edition), British Columbia, Kathleen A. Martin Ginis of McMaster University, Dean Tripp of Queen's University, and Angie MacKewn of the University of New Brunswick.

Pearson Canada and the authors would like to thank the following individuals for their reviews during the development phase of this title: Linda Hatt of Okanagan University College, Cameron C. Muir of Brock University, and Melady Preece of the University of British Columbia.

Gary Poole

Deborah Hunt Matheson

David N. Cox

chapter one

The Development of the Field

CHAPTER OUTLINE

What Is Health Psychology?

The Development of Health Psychology As a Discipline

The Early Stages of Health Psychology's Development: Applying the Principles of Behaviourism to Health

Health Psychology Expands to Include Cognition and Personality Factors

More Attention Is Paid to the Ways People Cope

The Introduction of Psychoneuroimmunology: Finding Links between Psychological and Biological Processes

Summary

Why Has Health Psychology Come into Prominence?

Changing Profiles of Illness and Health in Canada

Multiple Perspectives Are Needed to Understand Health and Health Statistics

Health Psychology Today

A Biopsychosocial Approach to Health

Prominent Theories in Health Psychology

Working in Health Psychology

Clinical and Counselling Psychologists Working in Health Psychology

Research Careers in Health Psychology

KEY QUESTIONS

1. What is health psychology, and what other terms are used to describe the work conducted in this area?
2. How has health psychology developed over the years?
3. Why has the field of health psychology grown rapidly in recent years?
4. What is meant by a biopsychosocial approach to health?
5. What are some of the prominent theories used in health psychology?
6. What sorts of career opportunities are available in the field, and what training is required for them?

The British Columbia Cancer Agency's Vancouver Centre is a very active place. People are coming and going all the time. Many are coming in for treatments, in many cases staying only for the day. Some arrive with family members or friends; others are driven by volunteers. Many others come to the centre for consultations. And in the background, research, both biomedical and psychosocial, is a constant and vital part of the picture.

As you can imagine, all this requires a considerable administrative machine. At places like the BC Cancer Agency, good organization can help people live longer and happier lives.

The Vancouver Centre is a hive of offices, hospital rooms, meeting spaces, waiting areas, and other facilities. Today, a health psychologist arrives at the centre for a regular research meeting. The discussion will focus on funding sources, as it often does. These meetings are usually held in the second-floor boardroom, which looks deceptively like any room in a downtown office building. Today, however, the meeting is in a room on the fifth floor, a floor with hospital rooms. The elevator doors open to reveal a very frail woman being weighed on a scale. She has lost her hair, and is very thin, making it difficult to ascertain her age. She is helped off the scale and back to her room. For the health psychologist, the switch from the second to the fifth floor means much more than spending a bit longer on the elevator. It allows for a glimpse beyond the impersonal talk of funding and research, and provides a vital reminder of the real people all health professionals serve.

This encounter serves as a very important reminder for the health psychologist. We can talk about the politics and strategy of obtaining research funding; we can design studies, being careful to plan for adequate sample sizes and citing the appropriate theory; and we can publish our papers. However, what matters most are the people whose lives are affected by the things we study. Above all, health psychology is an applied discipline, and the woman being helped on and off that scale reminds all of us in the field of our ultimate responsibility.

CASE 1-1	**Matters of the Heart**

Alan was admitted to hospital with classic symptoms of a heart attack, though that wasn't how he was explaining his chest pain, difficulty breathing, and profuse sweating. He had been suffering from a cold for the past week and he thought the virus had flared up badly. However, Alan was wrong. Tests revealed an *infarct*, or tissue that has died because of a lack of oxygen. Other tests showed the reason for the infarct. A coronary artery was completely blocked. In fact, so were two others— not the stuff of viruses. Alan was advised that he needed emergency bypass surgery.

WHAT IS HEALTH PSYCHOLOGY?

After reading Case 1-1, ask yourself what might have caused Alan's heart attack. From the case study, we might conclude that the cause was the arterial blockage, and this would certainly be correct. But is that *all* that caused it? Why did bypass surgery like Alan's become so common in the latter half of the twentieth century? Did millions of people in North America develop blocked coronary arteries because of some colossal biological coincidence? No. To understand Alan's heart attack and the growth industry that bypass surgery has become, we must look beyond biology. We must consider psychological causes, such as Alan's outlook on life, his lifestyle, and his stress level. We must consider sociological causes, such as the nature of his employment as well as his social network. Finally, we must consider environmental causes, such as the air he breathes.

Not only is this collection of causes relevant to Alan's heart, it is, indeed, at the heart of this book. In this first chapter, we want you to develop an appreciation for the fact that an understanding of health is best achieved by a partnership between medical and social science. We will explore, in detail, the contributions of the social science of psychology to this understanding.

Clinical psychologists have long recognized that there are psychological consequences associated with ill health. Conversely, there are physical consequences associated with many psychological disorders. It wasn't until the 1970s, however, that psychologists from other non-clinical subdisciplines began to recognize that there were many ways psychological principles could be applied to health and health care.

It was out of this recognition that the fields of behavioural medicine and ultimately health psychology emerged. There were a range of terms introduced as names for the new discipline linking psychology and health. All these terms can be somewhat confusing, because some psychologists use them interchangeably while others believe they refer to distinctly different subcategories. We will begin our investigation of the field's development by trying to sort out some of the different names that have been used as labels.

The first formal definition of the field used the term **behavioural medicine**. The term was defined at the Yale Conference on Behavioral Medicine in 1977 and improved upon the following year by the Academy of Behavioral Medicine Research. Here is their definition:

> Behavioral medicine is the interdisciplinary field concerned with the development and integration of behavioral and biomedical science knowledge and techniques relevant to the understanding of health and illness, and the application of this knowledge and these techniques to prevention, diagnosis, treatment and rehabilitation (Academy of Behavioral Medicine Research, 1978).

This definition stressed an integration of biomedical and behavioural approaches.

Other terms have been proposed to deal with various components of the relationship between psychology and health. Over time, the more all-encompassing term **health psychology** emerged, for which Matarazzo proposed the following definition:

> Health psychology is the aggregate of the specific educational, scientific and professional contributions of the discipline of psychology to the promotion and maintenance of health, the prevention or treatment of illness, and the identification of etiologic and diagnostic correlates of health, illness, and related dysfunction (Matarazzo, 1980).

Notice that this definition includes not just maintenance of health but also treatment of illness. Health psychology, then, is the compilation of all that psychology has to offer to the diagnosis and treatment of illness as well as people's attempts to maintain health and well-being. In this context, the word *health* means more than just the absence of illness. As far back as the 1940s, the World Health Organization promoted the notion that being "healthy" also means being able to enjoy a desired quality of life in terms of physical, mental, and social functioning.

We can apply this notion of health to Alan, who has just had a heart attack. We can, with some accuracy, assess the extent of his tissue damage. However, what will it take to help Alan be *healthy* again, and what does this mean? If we adopt the World Health Organization's definition of health, our role as health psychologists becomes clearer. We must help Alan return to a level of functioning that restores his sense of quality of life. This may include addressing his fears of having another heart attack, helping him change his approach to life so that it is less hostile, and helping him develop the conviction that these changes are possible.

In this example, and in Matarazzo's definition of health psychology, we form an image of psychologists working at the interface of medicine and psychology. This work has been recognized by the Canadian Psychological Association in its creation of a section on Health Psychology, and by the American Psychological Association through its creation of Division 38, the Division of Health Psychology.

Another term common in the field is **psychosomatic medicine**, according to which a particular medical complaint is viewed as being the result of an underlying chronic emotional conflict that ultimately surfaces in the form of physiological symptoms. Specific symptoms are linked to particular kinds of conflicts. Probably the most well-known example of this relationship between psychological conflict and physical symptoms is the understanding that essential hypertension (high blood pressure) is connected to an inability to express feelings of anger in an appropriate manner.

As you might expect, psychotherapy is the treatment of choice in such cases because it aims to provide insight into the impact that unresolved conflicts are having on a particular individual's life. It is hoped that insight will be accompanied by symptom reduction. However, treatment of medical disorders based on this approach has not been successful. In comparison, treatment in behavioural medicine is focused on addressing the individual's current *behaviour*, which is viewed as being strongly influenced by learning. Symptoms are considered to be important in their own right and the emphasis is on defining them in observable and measurable terms.

In summary, there are many terms that are used to describe the work done by psychologists working in health-related areas. Some focus on behavioural interventions, some on enhancing people's abilities to maintain their own health. All these terms relate to the same process—the application of psychological principles to the understanding of and improvement of our health.

THE DEVELOPMENT OF HEALTH PSYCHOLOGY AS A DISCIPLINE

When health psychology first emerged as a field, the *Annual Review of Psychology* began publishing articles summarizing the evolving state of the new discipline. First there was Neal Miller's 1983 article on behavioural medicine (Miller, 1983). This article was followed by a number of reviews over the years. Some of the more comprehensive include those by Krantz, Grunberg, and Baum, who reviewed the field in 1985, Rodin and Salovey in 1989, Cohen and Herbert in 1996, and Baum and Posluszny in 1999. Taken collectively and in combination with other important reviews, these articles provide a good overview of how the field has developed, especially in terms of the topics given prominence over the years. By looking at the highlights of each article, we will get a sense of the field's development.

The Early Stages of Health Psychology's Development: Applying the Principles of Behaviourism to Health

In 1983, Neal Miller reviewed the state of the field in an article entitled "Behavioral Medicine: Symbiosis between Laboratory and Clinic." In this article, Miller traced the development of the biomedical perspective on illness, starting with the invention of the microscope and moving to the development of **germ theory**, which is based on the discovery that many illnesses were caused by the activity of microorganisms such as bacteria. From germ theory came the refinement of antibiotics to fight these germs. The biomedical perspective was now in full flight, realizing considerable success by reducing illnesses to a cellular level and treating them with medicines.

At least two important developments resulted from these discoveries. First, the success of antibiotics brought about a change in the profile of life-threatening illnesses. Germs were replaced by lifestyle as the number one killer. Second, an emphasis on technical aspects of medicine came to replace a consideration for emotional factors in health. The paradox is that the technical medicine so revered for its success in treating germ-based conditions, was useless against health problems caused by lifestyle and other psychosocial factors.

When behavioural medicine emerged, it did so in response to these two factors. It was called *behavioural medicine* because of the emphasis placed on the link between *behaviour* and health. This emphasis was consistent with the theoretical stance adopted by some of the field's pioneers, such as Neal Miller. Miller was a **behaviourist**, which means that he believed that most behaviour was learned, rather than innate.

People adopting a behavioural perspective believe that our health is affected primarily by what we *do* rather than what we *think*. You will see later in this chapter how this perspective contrasts with theories forwarded in the 1970s and '80s, such as the health belief model, which emphasizes the way that our thinking can affect the decisions we make. In recent years, though, there has been a resurgence of behaviour-based approaches, causing some to label the 1990s "the decade of behaviour" (Smith, Kendall & Keefe, 2002).

In Miller's article, the key issues of the day were explained using the language of behaviourism. For example, Miller identified *non-compliance* with medical regimens as an important problem. He explained it in terms of what he called a **gradient of reinforcement**. By this, he meant that the greater the lag time between behaviour and reinforcer, the weaker the behaviour would be. Non-compliance could be explained in these terms because the reinforcement for following a medical regimen was often delayed. When we exercise, we don't suddenly get fit. High blood pressure doesn't drop to a normal range after one low-sodium meal. These benefits take time to realize. Behaviourists call this time lag between behaviour and reinforcer **delayed gratification**. Returning to our case study, Alan would have to contend with problems of delayed gratification as he recovered from his heart attack and tried to change his behaviour and thinking.

There is research support for the delayed gratification explanation of Miller's concept of non-compliance. Specifically, we know that compliance rates are higher for regimens bringing about a rapid reduction in symptoms than they are for those in which improvement takes longer. Lowest of all are compliance rates for conditions that are **asymptomatic**—conditions not accompanied by palpable symptoms or sensations (Buckalew, 1991).

For example, the delayed gratification theory helps explain why significantly more people will follow instructions to take an antibiotic to relieve them of a painful ear infec-

Hostility, as identified by the Type A Behaviour Pattern, can take the form of road rage.

tion than will change their lifestyle to reduce hypertension. According to the behavioural explanation, this is because taking the antibiotic is reinforced almost immediately by pain relief; however, lifestyle changes for the usually asymptomatic condition of high blood pressure are reinforced by longer life expectancy, which is far less immediate. This problem is further compounded by the fact that behaviours worsening hypertension, such as eating a high-fat diet, are immediately reinforced—these foods taste good. Miller provided a similar analysis to explain why it is hard to quit smoking cigarettes.

Miller addressed a number of other conditions, including alcohol abuse, obesity, stress, and the Type A behaviour pattern. At the time of Miller's article (1983), it was believed that the entire constellation of attributes identified by the Type A pattern were linked to heart disease. These included time urgency, achievement orientation, and hostility. Large-scale studies, such as the Framingham study, published around the time of Miller's article, showed that people exhibiting the Type A pattern were generally at greater risk for coronary heart disease (CHD) (Haynes, Feinleib, & Kannel, 1980). More recent work, however, has shown that hostility is the trait most reliably linked to CHD (Dembroski & Costa, 1988).

Health Psychology Expands to Include Cognition and Personality Factors

Shortly after Miller's article, Krantz and colleagues (1985) published another major review that identified a number of key areas in which health psychology had made contributions and more research was needed. By the mid-1980s, psychologists were working with physiologists and others to identify the mechanisms whereby stressful environments put people at risk for health problems. Further, Miller's behavioural perspective had been expanded to include the study of cognitive and personality factors predisposing some people to view a situation as being stressful that others may not.

At the same time, psychologists were studying ways that stress could be reduced. For example, social support had grown as a significant area of study, as had therapeutic interventions such as *cognitive restructuring*, aimed at changing people's stress-prone interpretations of events (for a review, see Matarazzo et al., 1984).

Closely related to these investigations was the study of the relationship between behaviour and cardiovascular health. The link between cigarette smoking and disease had been sufficiently established, so the next logical step was to study the psychology of smoking. To this end, studies looked at when people (usually young people) started smoking (Kozlowski, 1979; Pomerleau, 1979), how their habit was maintained (Kozlowski & Herman, 1984), and why smoking cessation programs were less successful than they might be (Schachter, 1981).

Following the work of Miller, Krantz and colleagues took a more detailed look at the Type A construct introduced in the late 1950s when two cardiologists identified behaviour patterns that they claimed were more common among their cardiac patients than in the general population (Friedman & Rosenman, 1959). They called this the Type A Coronary Prone Behaviour Pattern. The Type A construct generated a considerable number of studies in the 1970s and early 1980s. Some of these studies supported the assertions of Friedman and Rosenman; others did not. We will review the balance of these findings in chapter 2 in our discussion of stress and coping. For now, it is important to understand that the Type A construct proved to be an important catalyst for general research attempting to link psychology with health.

Eating disorders was another topic that rose to prominence in the 1980s, specifically obesity, anorexia, and cachexia (malnourishment). Obesity was studied from biological, behavioural, and social perspectives; today we call this a *biopsychosocial approach*, discussed later in the chapter. In their discussion, Krantz and colleagues addressed the problem of maintaining a healthy weight. Anorexia was also looked at from a biopsychosocial perspective.

Finally, Krantz and colleagues continued the study of compliance by introducing perspectives other than behaviourism. The study of compliance was very important historically for a number of reasons. First, the work of Howard Waitzkin in the United States (Waitzkin, 1985), Philip Ley in Great Britain (Ley, 1977), and others showed that communication between physicians and their patients often lacked clarity and relevance. Through this work, physicians discovered that their impression of an interview with a patient could be quite different from that of the patient. Specifically, less information was being conveyed and patients' understanding of that information was poorer than physicians realized. Communication in medical settings continues to be an important topic in health psychology (see chapter 4).

The study of compliance was also important because it led to a more in-depth study of the patient–physician relationship. Indeed, the term "compliance" has come under fire because of its implication that the physician–patient relationship is unidirectional (DiMatteo, 1991). Some analysts criticized the expectation that the physician should give the orders and patients should passively follow them.

More Attention Is Paid to the Ways People Cope

Four years after the review paper by Krantz and colleagues, Rodin and Salovey (1989) published another review of health psychology. At that time, further work was being done to investigate dispositional, or personality, variables as well as the relationship between thinking and health. Social support and health promotion continued to be topics of importance.

Some new topics had emerged by 1989. For example, research attention was being paid to the ways in which people *coped* with illness and everything that went along with it, such as hospital stays and the impact of illness on relationships with others. Consistent with the investigation of dispositional variables, health psychologists were attempting to identify **coping styles**—patterns in the ways people deal with difficult situations.

One good example is Suzanne Miller's notion of *monitors and blunters* (Miller, 1980). **Monitors** are information seekers. **Blunters** are information avoiders. The coping style of each type is consistent with their desire for receiving or avoiding information. This is just one example of how people differ in the ways they cope with illness and the challenges it brings. We will look more closely at these and other coping styles in chapter 5 when we talk about hospital stays and medical procedures, and again in chapter 11 in our discussion of chronic and terminal illness.

Another topic that continued to be prominent from the time of Miller's review was substance use and abuse. The analysis moved away from the addictive properties of the substance to the cognitions and behaviours of the addicted. Combined with this was a study of the possibility of a genetic predisposition to substance abuse.

The Introduction of Psychoneuroimmunology: Finding Links between Psychological and Biological Processes

In 1996, Cohen and Herbert summarized the state of health psychology by focusing exclusively on **psychoneuroimmunology (PNI)**. This is the study of the relationship between our psychological state and the functioning of our immune system, a relationship alluded to by Miller in 1983 and studied in more detail in recent years. The breakthrough in this area came with the development of techniques to quantify the status of our immune systems (called **immunocompetence**) through blood tests and saliva samples. This advance made PNI extremely important because it provided an opportunity for health psychology to produce empirical proof of hypothesized relationships between mind and body.

In truth, PNI was introduced well before the mid-1990s. In fact, a prominent book on the subject was published in 1981 (Ader, 1981). Our knowledge of PNI has been significantly advanced by a number of researchers since then. One of the more prolific is Janice Kiecolt-Glaser, who has been publishing extensively in the area of PNI since the mid-1980s. She has looked at such diverse psychological states and situations as marital conflict (Kiecolt-Glaser et al., 1987a) and caregiving for patients with Alzheimer's disease (Kiecolt-Glaser et al., 1987b) in terms of their effects on the immune system. We present a detailed examination of PNI in chapter 3.

The most recent *Annual Review of Psychology* article to summarize the field is that of Andrew Baum and Donna Posluszny (1999). Their paper provides an excellent overview of the ways in which all the major relevant topics since Miller's 1983 article have coalesced and evolved into what health psychology is today. They cover the following topics, all of which are discussed in the chapters that follow: stress and health (chapter 2), health-enhancing and health-impairing behaviours (chapter 9), and behaviours related to seeking and consuming health care (chapters 6, 7, and 9).

Summary

By comparing these major reviews of health psychology, we can see that the actual topics being studied have changed much less than the ways in which these topics are viewed. From the strong behavioural roots of Miller and others, we have expanded to include theories featuring a more cognitive approach. Today, health psychologists employ interventions that combine behavioural and cognitive theories, evidence of which we will see in this book.

The research in health psychology continues to proliferate, though questions have been raised as to whether the work is building upon itself to create a body of knowledge or just going off madly in all directions with few interconnections being made among studies (Belar, 1997). We have reached the point in health psychology where we have established that tangible links exist between numerous psychological phenomena and physical health. The next step is to hone and test interventions to affect these phenomena in order to increase well-being and save time, money, and lives. If health psychology is to thrive, or indeed survive, as a field, it must reach this level of accountability.

WHY HAS HEALTH PSYCHOLOGY COME INTO PROMINENCE?

Health psychology is an established field. The Health Psychology section of the Canadian Psychological Association (CPA) is one of the association's larger sections. According to the CPA web site, membership has remained stable for the past few years at approximately 200 members (CPA web site, 1999, www.cpa.ca). There are many reasons for the importance of the Health Psychology division, not the least of which are the changes in health and illness patterns in this country and elsewhere in the second half of the twentieth century.

Changing Profiles of Illness and Health in Canada

One important reason for the prominence of health psychology as a discipline can be demonstrated by comparing mortality statistics over the course of the twentieth century. This reveals that the major causes of death today are quite different from those of just 50 or 100 years ago.

At the turn of the century, the most common cause of death in North America was acute, infectious disease, namely, respiratory diseases such as influenza and pneumonia (Sexton, 1979) (see Figure 1-1). By 1950, the leading cause of death in Canada had become circulatory diseases (heart and cerebrovascular disease). Cancer had become the second leading cause, ahead of respiratory diseases (Wilkins, 1995). This was still true at the end of the century (Public and Population Health Branch of Health Canada, 2000).

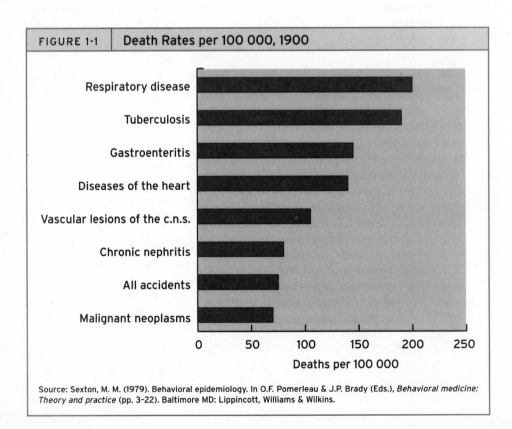

| FIGURE 1-1 | **Death Rates per 100 000, 1900** |

Source: Sexton, M. M. (1979). Behavioral epidemiology. In O.F. Pomerleau & J.P. Brady (Eds.), *Behavioral medicine: Theory and practice* (pp. 3-22). Baltimore MD: Lippincott, Williams & Wilkins.

When psychologists look at this change, they focus on the *preventability* of these diseases. Some time around the middle of the twentieth century, lifestyle replaced microbiology as our major source of life-threatening toxins. Hence the rationale for behavioural medicine, which, as we have seen, is concerned with the relationship between health and behaviour. A comparison of 1950 and 1993 death rates in Canada reveals a dramatic 57 percent drop in deaths from circulatory disease, a trend that continued to the end of the century. Much of this decline can be attributed to lifestyle change, which is, in many ways, a psychological phenomenon. It is very possible that lifestyle change will be the most pressing challenge Alan from our case study will face as he approaches life after his heart attack.

According to Statistics Canada, 56 percent of men and 58 percent of women report that they exercise regularly. This means that they engage in vigorous activities such as calisthenics, jogging, racquet sports, team sports, dance classes, or brisk walking for a period of at least fifteen minutes at least three times per week. Only 21 percent of men and 22 percent of women say they rarely exercise. Figure 1-2 shows the percentage of men and women reporting regular exercise across various age groups. While this graph indicates a slight decline in exercise rates as people age, it is perhaps more noteworthy that Canadian seniors are maintaining exercise rates that are not remarkably below those of people in early adulthood. The result is improved cardiovascular health for all ages.

Activity level is one aspect of lifestyle relevant to health. Cigarette smoking is another. In Canada in 2001, 54 percent of smokers over the age of 25 were planning to quit smoking, either in the next six months or in the near future (Health Canada, Canadian Tobacco Use Monitoring Survey, 2001). If you have ever tried to quit smoking or make some other significant and lasting change to your lifestyle, it is likely that you encountered

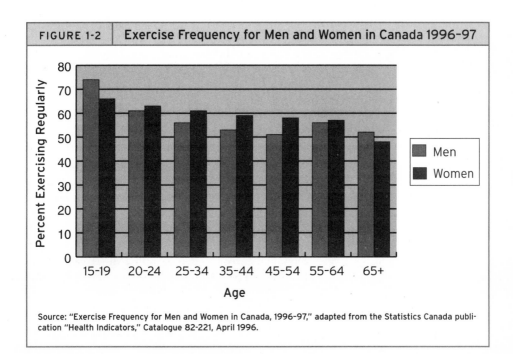

| FIGURE 1-2 | Exercise Frequency for Men and Women in Canada 1996-97 |

Source: "Exercise Frequency for Men and Women in Canada, 1996-97," adapted from the Statistics Canada publication "Health Indicators," Catalogue 82-221, April 1996.

some psychological barriers along the way. You had to *learn* new behaviours and *unlearn* old ones. You had to *believe* that you were capable of making the change, and other people may have been involved who made the change easier or harder. Even from this brief analysis, we can see that learning theory, cognitive psychology, and social psychology are very relevant to lifestyle change, which has become an integral part of our health and wellness in the new millennium.

Alan will be encouraged to learn new ways of thinking and behaving that will result in reduced stress, greater relaxation, and improved fitness. These changes will also have a social component, as family and friends will be called upon for support.

Multiple Perspectives Are Needed to Understand Health and Health Statistics

2

Another reason for the growth of health psychology is that it provides helpful ways to understand the statistics describing our health. For example, male deaths from cancer in Canada rose over 35 percent in the second half of the twentieth century (Wilkins, 1995; Public and Population Health Branch of Health Canada, 2000). Which perspective provides us with the best way to respond to this new reality in ways that will affect that statistic? Biomedical research may focus on the biology of **malignant neoplasms**, which are cancerous growths that may be treated by radiation and chemical therapy. This is a valuable perspective, but is there more to the story? Just as we discovered when talking about Alan's heart attack, there are additional perspectives that will help us better understand cancer statistics.

Perhaps we can learn something further by looking at the *types* of cancer that account most for this 35 percent increase. When we do, we find that lung cancer showed the greatest increase, accounting for nearly one-third of all male cancer deaths in 1993 in Canada. The next sharpest increase was in prostate cancer, which accounted for about one-eighth of male cancer deaths in the same year (Wilkins, 1995).

These data indicate that there is more at work than a random and unfortunate growth of neoplasms. Lung cancer is linked to a behaviour—smoking. Psychologists can make valuable contributions to the modification of this behaviour from what they know about attitude change, persuasion, and addiction. They can help reduce the number of smokers and thus reduce death rates resulting from lung cancer.

There is even more to this picture, however, than can be captured within biomedical and psychological perspectives. Environmentalists may argue that increases in lung and prostate cancer rates have resulted from breathing toxic air and eating foods containing chemicals that are potentially **carcinogenic**, or cancer causing. From this perspective, the field of **medical geography** has developed. Clearly, some environments are healthier than others; medical geographers study these differences.

Thus far, we have identified biomedical, psychological, and geographical perspectives used to understand cancer deaths, and we still haven't exhausted our list of useful perspectives. For example, we also know that there are **demographic differences** in the health of Canadians—differences that depend on culture, affluence, employment status, gender, and so on.

When asked, the majority of Canadians report that they are in good health. In the provinces, 63 percent of residents gave this rating to their health. In a study of residents in the Yukon and Northwest Territories, 69 percent of non-aboriginal residents rated their health as very good or excellent; however, only 47 percent of the aboriginal residents of the Northwest Territories called their health very good or excellent (Diverty & Pérez, 1998). We must be cautious when comparing health statistics across cultures. Nevertheless, data such as these invite further study of cultural and demographic differences in diet, social support, the use of medical services, and many other factors. If Alan is a member of a culture in which high-fat foods are common, he will find it harder to adopt a heart-healthy lifestyle. Cultural factors are studied by **medical anthropologists** and demographic factors are studied by **medical sociologists** and **epidemiologists**.

The patterns of illness and health are changing in Canada. Also, there has been a change in emphasis from cure to prevention. To understand these changes and to improve health and health care, we need to acquire the knowledge of many disciplines. This is the essence of the **biopsychosocial approach** (Engel, 1977). As the term implies, this model considers biological, psychological, and social factors affecting health. We will take a close look at this approach in the next section. At this point, it is important to understand that psychology has much to offer in our attempt to understand as much as we can about health and illness.

HEALTH PSYCHOLOGY TODAY

In this section, we will begin by introducing the most fundamental assumption of the field, as captured by the biopsychosocial approach. We'll then look at what this approach means for psychologists working in health care settings. From there, we'll move to an overview of prominent theories in the field today and conclude with a look at what people with training in health psychology actually do.

A Biopsychosocial Approach to Health

It is essential to understand that good and poor health can be attributed to a multitude of causes. Further, these causes are varied enough that they cannot be understood from any one perspective, whether in medicine or the social sciences. The biopsychosocial approach to health takes all of these various perspectives into account, acknowledging that biological, psychological, and social factors combine to influence our health.

The term *biopsychosocial* refers to three major perspectives on the causes of health and illness. As we move from the biological to the psychological to the social, we move from a microscopic perspective to a macroscopic one. For example, we can study cancer at a *biological*, cellular level by analyzing neoplasms (new growths), at a *psychological* level by assessing patients' coping abilities and correlations between stress and immune function, and at a *sociological* level by identifying government policies that affect environmental toxins or hospital regulations that affect the nature of treatment.

Why Is a Biopsychosocial Approach so Important? Health psychologists believe that no medical condition exists that can be fully understood from one perspective alone. Mortality statistics make it clear that many life-threatening conditions are preventable, in some cases by inoculation, in others by lifestyle changes, and in others by government policies such as seatbelt legislation. Only the biopsychosocial approach encompasses all these levels.

Even the common cold has psychological and sociological causes. Our immune systems are affected by our psychological state (for a review, see Cohen and Herbert, 1996), so we are more likely to catch a cold when we have endured something stressful, and we often catch colds from other people with whom we interact at work and in other social settings.

What Are the Implications of the Biopsychosocial Approach for Health Psychologists?   Today, the adoption of the biopsychosocial approach demands clear communication among health care practitioners and social scientists as well as a mutual respect for the potential contributions each can make to health and health care. It makes no more sense for a physician to downplay psychological factors affecting patients than it does for psychologists to say that viruses, tissue damage, and neoplasms are of little consequence.

Clear communication between practitioners and social scientists requires mutual understanding. This doesn't mean that social scientists must have all the knowledge of a physician or that physicians must be trained psychologists, but it does require a mutual appreciation for each other's potential contributions to the understanding of health and illness. For a number of reasons, however, achieving this mutual appreciation can be difficult. One important reason for this stems from the different ways in which health care professionals are trained.

Medical practitioners are trained primarily in the **biomedical model**. According to this model, as the name implies, health is best understood in terms of our biology. Students of this model are taught that it is precise and concrete. The concreteness of the model might make it easier to understand; however, it is a daunting task to learn enough human biology to be able to practise medicine. The time required often results in the exclusion of other models of health and well-being. It stands to reason that the dedication required to cope with the reams of material presented in medical school demands a strong belief in the efficacy of the biomedical model.

The end result, understandably, is that most medical school graduates are firmly entrenched in that model. Other approaches, for example those from the social sciences, seem much less precise and far too abstract by comparison. Psychosocial causes can't be viewed under a microscope or measured directly via blood tests or a CT scan. This abstractness can affect a physician's view of the credibility of disciplines like health psychology.

For their part, psychologists have their own set of beliefs specific to their discipline that are not always considered legitimate by people outside the field. For example, psychologists are trained to believe that behavioural phenomena can be reliably measured, that correlations as small as .3 can be meaningful, and that there are attributes shared by large groups of people that go beyond how many kidneys or lungs they have. As part of their training, psychologists are sensitized to the *psychological impact* of events on our lives.

The different emphases in training produce graduates with different perspectives. This is well illustrated by health psychologist Robin DiMatteo, who describes a tour a physician gave her through their intensive care unit (ICU). The physician was justifiably excited by the recent acquisition of new equipment for the ICU. Dr. DiMatteo, on the other hand, had her attention drawn in different directions:

> I remember feigning interest in the newly acquired machinery, little of which I understood, and I congratulated everyone on this up-to-date facility. But as I looked around to where the loved ones of the intubated people were waiting, I tried to catch a glimpse of their faces. My concern was not with the tremendous technical advances in the intensive care unit (ICU). As a psychologist, my

focus was on the loved ones of those in the ICU, people who were suddenly forced to have their lives revolve around the ICU, where they waited day after day for some news that their child, spouse, relative, or friend might survive and someday be normal again (DiMatteo, 1995, p. 217.)

The point of this example isn't that the physician was misguided in his focus on the new equipment in the ICU. Rather, it is that there are many phenomena needing attention in a place like the ICU. Robin DiMatteo and other health psychologists provide expertise that fills in other pieces of the puzzle implied by the biopsychosocial approach.

As we mentioned earlier, the biopsychosocial approach grew, in part, from a change in the causes of life-threatening illnesses. Psychological and behavioural factors became more significant. From this, it became clear that there were psychological causes and consequences associated with *many* aspects of our health, not just those that resulted in mortality statistics.

Prominent Theories in Health Psychology

In this chapter, we are attempting to tell the story of health psychology. We began by defining what health psychology is. We then looked at how it developed from its early years and why it has grown so rapidly. We then looked at the overarching model in modern health psychology—the biopsychosocial approach. Now it is time to look into the "tool kit" of today's health psychologists. In it, we will find a number of very useful theories they use to help them understand health issues and help people recover from illness or injury and stay healthy. Our list of theories will not be exhaustive at this point. Rather, we will talk about some of the more prominent theories in the field to give you a sense of the work health psychologists do in research and intervention. We return now to Alan who, as you will see in Case 1-2, is home from the hospital and has been put on a rehabilitative plan for his recovery.

CASE 1-2	Alan Revisited: The Road Back

Alan spent five days in the cardiac care unit of the hospital. His moods swung between fear and frustration. He certainly didn't want another heart attack, but he had a business to run and countless other responsibilities. The people in cardiac care didn't seem to appreciate this. They kept telling him to try and relax—easy for them to say.

Now that he was home convalescing, it was even harder to "relax." He had so much to do and think about. On top of it all, the cardiologist had given him a bunch of pills to take and a strict diet to follow. And then there was the Healthy Heart program at the hospital that he was expected to start attending on a weekly basis. He had been asked to rethink his life's priorities, change the way he ate, and start the Healthy Heart program. Would Alan do all these things? It is an important question, since Alan's life might depend on it. The theories we look at in this section will help us predict the answer.

The Health Belief Model   One of the most well-developed and useful contributions psychology has made to the understanding of health is the **health belief model** (Becker, 1974; Rosenstock, 1974). As such, it represents a good entry point for our exploration of the psychological component of the biopsychosocial approach. A "health belief," as the term implies, is something we think to be true concerning our health. For example, we might believe that a low-fat diet will improve cardiovascular health or that modern medicine can cure most ailments. There are many different health beliefs.

The health belief model starts with the reasonable assumption that health behaviours are explained by our health beliefs. This is a good start, but we really need to know *which* specific health beliefs are most closely linked to behaviour if the model is to be of value.

The health belief model is valuable because it identifies a manageable number of relevant, measurable types of health beliefs that often do a reasonable job of predicting health behaviour. In its most basic form, the model focuses on two beliefs—the belief that a health threat exists and the belief that a given course of action will affect the threat.

Social psychologists have learned that beliefs don't exist in isolation (see for example, Harvey, 1997; Schroder, 1971). Rather, they co-exist interdependently in *belief systems*. Consistent with this, the health belief model expands to include several other beliefs that influence these two basic ones concerning health threat. Specifically, our belief about the existence of a health threat is influenced by the extent to which we believe we are personally vulnerable to that threat as well as by our beliefs about the severity of the consequences.

Here is an everyday example. When the weather channel reports a 100 percent chance of rain on a day when you must go outdoors, you know you are personally vulnerable to rain, but the *consequence* isn't particularly severe, so you don't believe a threat exists. On the other hand, if you read that one in three people will get cancer, you develop a belief regarding the likelihood that you could be that one (personal vulnerability), as well as a belief regarding how bad it would be to get cancer (severity of consequences). These beliefs affect your perception of threat and, in turn, affect your cancer-preventing behaviours, such as using sunscreen.

There are two types of beliefs that influence the fundamental confidence you have that a course of action will *reduce* a threat. First, there is something called an **efficacy belief**. This refers to the extent to which you think a course of action (e.g., a preventive behaviour or treatment) will actually work. Second, there is a **cost-gain belief**. This refers to your assessment of the costs (e.g., effort, discomfort, embarrassment, or inconvenience) associated with this action compared to the benefit of the behaviour to your health. For example, if someone believes that the gains of exercise seem distant and minor compared to the costs such as effort and short-term fatigue, then exercise behaviour is unlikely.

Table 1-1 outlines the health belief model and contrasts the beliefs of two people (Person A and Person B). In this case, the model is being used to predict condom usage. At the top of the table, we begin with the two general beliefs in the existence of a threat and in the possibility that a behaviour can affect the threat. Beneath that, specific beliefs related to these general beliefs are listed. The next two rows provide examples of those related beliefs for each of these fictitious people.

Person A believes himself to be somewhat vulnerable and also that the consequences of contracting acquired immunodeficiency syndrome (AIDS) are severe (i.e., fatal). He also believes that condoms work and that the costs of using them are outweighed by the benefits. As a result, Person A uses condoms. In contrast, Person B feels little vulnerabil-

TABLE 1-1	The Health Belief Model Applied to Condom Usage			
General Belief	A health threat exists		A behaviour will affect the threat	Result
Related Beliefs	Beliefs regarding personal vulnerability to the threat	Beliefs about the severity of the consequences	The belief that a course of action will actually work or not	The assessment of the costs and benefits associated with this action	
Person A	*"I could get AIDS."*	*"AIDS is a fatal disease."*	*"Using condoms will greatly reduce my chances of getting AIDS."*	*"I get embarrassed when I buy condoms, but they will reduce the risk of getting AIDS."*	Condoms are used
Person B	*"Other people might get AIDS but I won't."*	*"With new drugs, AIDS isn't as life-threatening as it once was."*	*"Condoms don't always work."*	*"I feel very embarrassed when I buy condoms and using them ruins sex."*	Condoms are not used

ity, doesn't think AIDS is necessarily fatal, does not believe in the effectiveness of condoms, and thinks the personal costs of using them are high. Not surprisingly, this person doesn't use condoms.

The beliefs in this example have been intentionally polarized to make the contrast clear. In reality, a person may hold a range of beliefs working together in such a way that prediction of behaviour is more difficult. For example, a woman might believe that she could get cervical cancer and that it could be fatal. She might think the costs of screening are low but lacks confidence in the accuracy of the Pap test used in the screening, so she doesn't think the behaviour will work. What could we predict here? Perhaps sporadic Pap tests? It is difficult to be certain.

And what about Alan? The health belief model can help us predict the likelihood that he will attend the Healthy Heart program. To start, we would need to know if Alan believes he is vulnerable to a second heart attack and, if so, whether he thinks its consequences would be severe. In fact, he does believe that people who have had a heart attack are at increased risk for a second one and that people are much less likely to survive a second one than they were their first. Now we move to his beliefs regarding the behaviour that is supposed to affect that threat—the Healthy Heart program. We already know that he has considered the costs of attending. He is busy and thinks it will be inconvenient. And what about his efficacy belief? Does he think the program will reduce the threat of a second heart attack? If he does, then he might attend. The problem is that he must *keep attending*, therefore his beliefs in the efficacy of the program must be strong enough to keep him going.

Health Beliefs and Health Values   The health belief model attempts to predict behaviour using a person's specific beliefs regarding two main topics—the existence of a threat and the effectiveness of a particular behaviour to reduce the threat. There is one more important factor to consider, however. This is the extent to which the person values good health. Even if a person's beliefs would appear to predict a certain behaviour, such as condom use or screening for cancer, the behaviour will not follow unless the person values his or her health.

It may be difficult to imagine that there are people who don't place a high value on their health. However, research indicates that people do vary in terms of their health values. To understand this, we must view values as being relative to each other. For example, an adolescent might value health to a certain extent, but he or she might value group acceptance more. This person might take up smoking, in spite of the fact that it compromises health, to achieve the more valued outcome of group acceptance.

It is also possible that some people can *afford* to place health values high on their list while other people must be more concerned with basic survival. This does not mean, however, that people living in poverty do not value their health. A study of homeless women, for example, found that health and self-respect were two commonly held values (Rosengard, 2001). *Gender differences* also exist regarding health values. Women tend to value their health more than men do (Felton, Parsons, & Bartoces, 1997). Clear reasons exist, then, for individual differences in health values. These differences are important to consider because research has shown that the health belief model is most predictive for people who place a high value on their health (Lau, Hartman, & Ware, 1986).

How Well Does the Health Belief Model Predict Behaviour?   If the health belief model is to be useful, it must do a better-than-chance job of explaining and predicting health-related behaviour for those individuals who place a relatively high value on their health. For health psychologists, it is important to investigate the model's utility because the model has the potential to make significant contributions to the biopsychosocial understanding of health and illness. Given this importance, it is not surprising that a great deal of research has been conducted over the years testing the ability of the health belief model to explain and predict behaviour in a wide variety of health-related contexts, from youth cigarette smoking (Li et al., 2003) to osteoporosis prevention (Silver Wallace, 2002).

One area in which the health belief model has been used extensively is in AIDS-risk-related behaviours. DiFranceisco and colleagues (1998) used the health belief model to predict whether gay/bisexual men would complete a small-group program in HIV-risk reduction. The health belief model has also been used to explain some of the variance in sexual risk behaviours among college students, such as having multiple partners and being intoxicated or high during sexual encounters. It was less helpful, however, when it came to predicting condom usage for this group (Lollis, Johnson, & Antoni, 1997).

Some studies have produced more encouraging results than others when it comes to the ability of the health belief model to predict HIV-risk behaviour. Differences of opinion regarding the usefulness of the health belief model could be attributed to differences in the way the beliefs are measured and in just what it is that is being predicted. Specifically, some researchers use the model to predict behaviour, such as dropping out of a prevention program, while others use it to predict intention to engage in or avoid a particular behaviour. For example, some researchers (e.g., Smith & Stasson, 2000) argue that the health belief model can be used to explain differences in people's *intention* to practise safe sex. Taken in sum, the research using the health belief model in AIDS-related contexts appears promising, but it cannot be used exclusively to explain differences in sexual behaviour putting people at risk for HIV infection.

The health belief model has also been used extensively in predicting behaviours associated with screening for cancer. In general, these behaviours can be analyzed reasonably well using the health belief model, given that important issues of perceived vulnerability and belief in the value of early detection fit well within the model. The model is far less than perfect in this context, though, because of other psychological factors. Perhaps the most notable is the role that *emotion* plays in cancer screening. People might believe in the accuracy of a given screening technique and see cancer as a threat. However, they might not want to know if they have cancer (Cameron, 1997). Such a discovery would constitute too great a cost of the behaviour (e.g., Millar, 1997).

Focus on Research 1-1	**Checking Yourself Out**

Roger Katz, Kelly Meyers, and Jennifer Walls (1995) have conducted research on cancer awareness and self-examination practices in young men and women. Their objective was to test the usefulness of the health belief model in predicting whether college students would practise self-examination (SE) for breast or testicular cancer.

To test this, 178 college men and women completed a series of questionnaires, including the Testicular Cancer Awareness Survey (completed by the men) and the Breast Cancer Awareness Survey (completed by the women). Personality scales were also completed, including measures of health locus of control, perceived social support, and hypochondriasis.

The researchers found that women were more fearful of developing breast cancer than men were of developing testicular cancer. Consistent with this perception of vulnerability, women were significantly more likely to practise SE. Thirty percent of women practised SE compared to 19 percent of the men. Fear of cancer and confidence in doing the SE correctly were significantly correlated with actually practising SE. Women were better informed about breast cancer than men were about testicular cancer, however those practising SE were not necessarily those with the most knowledge.

The authors concluded that the health belief model is supported by their data to the extent that fear of cancer (vulnerability beliefs) and confidence in ability (efficacy beliefs) help predict SE. Since this research was conducted, more recent studies have questioned the efficacy of breast self-examination as a way to reduce breast cancer mortality (Thomas, et al., 2002).

We have introduced the health belief model in this first chapter because it is a good example of the way in which psychological constructs can be applied to our understanding of health and health behaviour. It is a model that continues to be widely used and refined, with research going into the improvement of measurement tools and appropriate applications (for a review, see Strecher, Champion, & Rosenstock, 1997). We will return to the health belief model in chapter 7 when we discuss health promotion.

According to the Health Belief Model, this person feels vulnerable to SARS, thinks it is serious, and believes that wearing a surgical mask will reduce his chances of contracting SARS at a Toronto Blue Jays game.

TABLE 1-2	**The Health Belief Model Applied to the Decision to Have Back Surgery**			
General Belief	**A health threat exists**		**A behaviour will affect the threat**	**Result**
Related Beliefs	Beliefs regarding personal vulnerability to the threat	Beliefs about the severity of the consequences	The belief that a course of action will actually work or not	The assessment of the costs and benefits associated with this action	
Stan	*"I definitely have a back problem."*	*"I am in pain. I can't work and I can't enjoy my life."*	*"Surgery will correct this problem."*	*"I'm nervous about the possibility of being paralyzed but the risk is low."*	Stan chooses surgery

The health belief model was derived from other theories in social and cognitive psychology designed to predict behaviour from beliefs. Two of these related theories, the *Theory of Reasoned Action* and its relative, the *Theory of Planned Behaviour*, have been applied directly to health-related thinking and behaviour.

The Theory of Reasoned Action   The **Theory of Reasoned Action** (Ajzen & Fishbein, 1980; Fishbein & Ajzen, 1975) shares a number of things in common with the health belief model, while adding some other considerations. As we explain the theory, it will be helpful if you can appreciate these similarities and differences. One important assumption of the Theory of Reasoned Action is that behaviour is preceded by *intention*. Alan will not attend the Healthy Heart program until he *intends* to do so. Thus, understanding the link between thinking and intention is an important step to understanding how beliefs lead to behaviour.

The two main elements of the Theory of Reasoned Action are a person's attitudes toward a behaviour and the person's beliefs regarding other people's thoughts about the behaviour. It is this introduction of other people's beliefs that most strongly differentiates the Theory of Reasoned Action from the health belief model. In the language of the theory, other people's beliefs help us to develop **subjective norms**—what we think other people want us to do.

According to the Theory of Reasoned Action, we consider our attitudes toward a behaviour and our subjective norms to determine our *intention* regarding the behaviour. As in the health belief model, we have related beliefs to consider for each of these two main elements of the Theory of Reasoned Action. Specifically, our attitudes toward a behaviour are influenced by our beliefs regarding the *outcomes* it will bring about and the extent to which we *value* that outcome.

Subjective norms are composed of beliefs regarding what others think we should do and the extent to which we are motivated to go along with these people. To put all this together and apply the theory to health, we will look at Table 1-3.

TABLE 1-3	The Theory of Reasoned Action				
General Beliefs	**Attitudes toward the behaviour**		**Subjective norms**		**Result**
Related Beliefs	Belief that the behaviour will produce a given outcome	The value placed on the outcome	Beliefs regarding what other people think regarding the behaviour	Motivation to do what other people think should be done	
Person A	"Surgery will relieve the pain in my back."	"I would love to be pain free again."	"My friends and family think I should have the back operation."	"I want my friends and family to know I have the courage to have the operation."	Surgery chosen
Person B	"Surgery might not work. There's no guarantee."	"Being pain free isn't really possible. Everyone lives with some degree of pain."	"My wife thinks I should try bed rest before risking surgery."	"My wife is usually right."	Surgery not chosen

Table 1-3 charts two people facing a decision regarding treatment of back pain. Person A believes that the surgery will work, so he sees a connection between the behaviour (surgery) and the outcome (pain relief). He values a pain-free existence. His friends and family are in favour of surgery and he wants them to have a favourable impression of him. These beliefs lead to a decision to choose surgery.

In contrast, Person B is not convinced of the efficacy of the surgery, nor does he place as high a value on being pain free. His subjective norms oppose surgery; namely, his wife favours exercise over surgery and he values his wife's opinion. Consistent with these beliefs, surgery is not chosen.

As we did with Table 1-1 in relation to the health belief model, in Table 1-3 we have presented two people with diametrically opposed views. In reality, our beliefs are more mixed than this. We may really want to engage in a health-related behaviour (be it surgery, a low-sodium diet, etc.) but find that our friends are opposed to it. The process by which we *choose* the people whose opinions to consider can also be quite complicated (Kahneman & Miller, 1986). For example, we take into account such things as friendship and how similar they are to us. This is part of the social component of the biopsychosocial approach.

How Well Does the Theory of Reasoned Action Predict Health Behaviour?

Modern research has used the Theory of Reasoned Action to address many of the same phenomena as the health belief model has been applied to. Thus, we find studies testing the power of the Theory of Reasoned Action for predicting HIV risk and prevention behaviours (for a comprehensive review, see Crepaz & Marks, 2002) and cancer screening behaviours (e.g., Barling & Moore, 1996). The Theory of Reasoned Action has also been applied to an understanding of exercise behaviour (e.g., Olson & Zanna, 1987).

In a scan of the literature, we see that the Theory of Reasoned Action does a good job of predicting behaviours related to HIV and AIDS prevention. The addition of social norms tends to increase its predictive power over that of the health belief model. For example, Morrison and colleagues (2000) found that the Theory of Reasoned Action worked well to predict both intention and actual condom use among high-risk heterosexual teens.

In terms of cancer screening behaviour, the Theory of Reasoned Action predicts the intention to do self-examination (breast and testicular) very well (Moore, Barling, & Hood, 1998). The theory has also been used to explain differences in women's intentions to be screened for cervical cancer via a Pap smear test (Barling & Moore, 1996).

The Theory of Planned Behaviour The predictive power of the Theory of Reasoned Action is generally improved with the addition of the notion of **perceived behavioural control** (Millstein, 1996). In other words, beliefs about the effectiveness and costs of a given behaviour are augmented by beliefs about one's ability to actually carry off the behaviour. This is consistent with the thinking of Fishbein and Ajzen, the psychologists who proposed the theory in 1975. In fact, Fishbein and Ajzen developed a hybrid theory that included perceived behavioural control, and named it the **Theory of Planned Behaviour** (Fishbein & Ajzen, 1975).

The only difference between the two theories is the addition of the belief that the person is actually capable of performing the behaviour. "Can I really quit smoking?" "Can I go through with the operation?" These are questions about perceived behavioural control. The answer must be "Yes" for the Theory of Planned Behaviour to predict that intention will follow belief.

The Theory of Planned Behaviour can be a powerful tool to help explain variation in health-related intention and behaviour. For example, Johnston and White found that the theory helped predict binge drinking among university students (Johnston & White, 2003). In other words, the elements of the theory combine to correlate significantly with adolescents' reports of intention to drink, though the authors propose some expansions of the social norms construct to include measures of self-identity and one's tendency to identify with the group providing the social norms. As one might expect, the Theory of Planned Behaviour has been used as widely as the Theory of Reasoned Action to analyze a wide range of behaviours, including condom use and drinking and driving (Armitage, Norman, & Conner, 2002).

How can the Theory of Planned Behaviour help us predict whether Alan will attend the Healthy Heart program? To answer this question, consider each of the elements of the theory. First, like the health belief model, there are Alan's beliefs regarding the efficacy of the program and the value he places on not having another heart attack. Then there are the subjective norms. Would other people want him to go to the program? For example, his wife might really encourage him to attend, or she might see it as an unnecessary inconvenience, as Alan does. Also, we must know whether Alan is motivated to do what his wife thinks he should do, or whether he would rather assert his independence and either not go or go in opposition to her wishes. Finally, there is perceived behavioural control. Does Alan really believe that he can do the things the Health Heart program will expect of him in terms of exercise, diet, tests, and so on? According to the Theory of Planned Behaviour, the answers to these questions will determine whether Alan intends to go to the program.

Beliefs about Personal Control: Locus of Control and Self-Efficacy Social psychologists would not be surprised to find that we learn more about health behaviour by taking control beliefs into account. It was, after all, back in the late 1950s that Phares (1957) introduced the notion of **locus of control**, the extent to which we believe the events in our lives are controlled internally by us or externally by outside forces. This construct was refined by Rotter (1996) and a scale was devised to measure it.

Our beliefs regarding control can affect our behaviour. We choose different courses of action depending upon whether we believe we have the power to affect outcomes or that we are helpless. As demonstrated by the Theory of Planned Behaviour, control beliefs specific to health behaviours play a role in determining that behaviour. Given this relationship, it would make sense to develop a scale that measured health-specific control beliefs. This is what Wallston and colleagues did when they created the **Multidimensional Health Locus of Control Scale (MHLC)** (Wallston, Wallston, & DeVellis (1978). Designed in the 1970s, the scale is still widely used today in studies that have attempted to find correlations between thinking and health behaviour. There have been over 500 studies published in the past 10 years using health locus of control as a variable.

This 18-item scale presents a series of straightforward statements intended to assess the extent to which people think their health is under their control, under the control of such factors as luck or fate, or under the control of "powerful others" such as physicians and other health care staff. People's scores on these three dimensions (internal, external, and powerful-other) are correlated with health-related behaviour.

Some of the best applications of the MHLC have been in settings in which people must be motivated to comply with a program or to overcome adversity. For example, locus of control is related to diabetics' ability to control their diabetes (Surgenor et al., 2000); people with an internal orientation control their diabetes better. It is also related to physical functioning among people who are in rehabilitation to be able to return to work (Wiegmann & Berven, 1998). In their study, Wiegmann and Berven found that people with higher scores on the internal and powerful-other dimensions showed the most improvement. Similarly, people with spinal cord injuries have been shown to make better life adjustments if they have an internal orientation (Krause, Stanwyck, & Maides, 1998).

Because of studies like these, health psychologists generally view an internal orientation to be a good thing. Yet, there are other important issues to consider before we try to convince everyone to adopt this orientation. These issues relate primarily to the realities of being sick.

For many people, being sick means giving up a certain amount of control over their lives. This is especially true for hospitalized patients who find themselves in what sociologists call a **total institution**—a place in which almost all of a patient's behaviours are controlled by hospital staff. This is compounded, of course, by the fact that most illnesses wrestle some control away from us by confining us to bed or otherwise restricting our activities.

Given these realities, how reasonable is it for health psychologists to encourage an internal orientation in their clients? This is an important question, because an overemphasis on internal control in the face of strong external factors can be stressful. It can also be upsetting if the patient takes personal responsibility for disease progression or recovery rates that might, in truth, be beyond his or her control.

With this in mind, Newsom and colleagues looked at the relationship between perceptions of control and symptoms of depression among people with recurring cancer (Newsom, Knapp, & Schulz, 1996). One important assumption of this study was that we don't simply have a set of general control beliefs; they also come in a number of specific forms. For example, we have beliefs about what should be blamed for cancer, the extent to which onset can be prevented or controlled, or to what degree symptoms and side effects can be controlled. The researchers found that, over an eight-month period, depression among patients with recurrent cancer was significantly related to what they called **onset control**—the greater the patient's belief that the onset of the illness could have been controlled or avoided, the greater the depression when it recurred.

This depression could develop from a number of different thoughts. It may stem from a sense of **learned helplessness**, in which the patient despairs that his or her situation cannot be remedied no matter what he or she does. It may also be related to **self-blame**, the patient's belief that somehow he or she is personally responsible for the illness. Though little current research has been conducted on the nature of self-blame in cancer patients, one study (Malcarne, Compas, Epping-Jordan, & Howell, 1995) did find that self-blame was *not* related to control beliefs, though it was related to psychological distress. Presumably, then, while self-blame is a problem for those coping with cancer, it is not necessarily the result of an internal orientation. We'll have more to say about control beliefs in chapter 2 when we look at stress and coping.

The Stages of Change Model   When we look at the topic of health promotion in chapter 7, we will see that an important challenge for health psychologists involves helping people make changes to their lives. In many cases, these changes involve aspects of lifestyle, as we have seen with Alan in Cases 1-1 and 1-2. In others, changes are forced upon us by illness, accident, or aging. Because change is such a major topic, a model that describes the ways people go about effecting change (or not) would be most helpful.

The **stages of change model** provides just such a description (Prochaska & DiClemente, 1983; 1986). In this model, change is broken down into six stages: precontemplation, contemplation, action, maintenance, termination, and relapse. Though these stages are simple enough to comprehend, they can be very valuable as a way to understand health behaviour and, in particular, behaviour involving a lifestyle change. One of the most common applications of the Stages of Change Model is to smoking cessation. The people in the precontemplation stage have not thought about quitting and see no need to do so. People in the contemplation stage may have some symptom or nagging thought that has them considering quitting. In the next stage, they take action. Perhaps they see their physician, or use patches, or make a pact with a friend. If the action works, then they must maintain their non-smoking behaviour. Eventually, after three years or more of abstinence, they would be considered in the termination stage (Gilpin, Pierce & Parkas, 1997).

One of the most valuable contributions of the model is the acknowledgment of relapse as a stage rather than as failure. This allows the person to deal with a bout of cigarette smoking as something that is part of the process, rather than as a sign that the entire lifestyle change has failed. They can then get back into the maintenance stage, rather than starting over.

Focus on Canadian Research 1-1	Stages of Change and Support for Government Quit-Smoking Programs

Researchers at the University of Toronto have applied the Stages of Change Model to assess smokers' and former smokers' knowledge of the health consequences of smoking (Cohen et al., 2002). They hypothesized that the higher a person's stage in the model, the more knowledge the person would have regarding health consequences.

Remember that current smokers will be placed at one of three stages when it comes to quitting smoking: precontemplation, contemplation, or preparation. Former smokers, on the other hand, could be placed at either of three different stages: action, maintenance, or termination. (Relapse was not included in this study.)

Cohen and colleagues provided operational definitions of each stage and then collected survey data from 846 people in Ontario to determine their knowledge of the health consequences of smoking. They asked questions about such things as smoking and lung cancer,

chronic bronchitis, pregnancy complications, heart attacks, and environmental tobacco smoke. They did not stop there, however. They also reasoned that smokers' or former smokers' positions on the Stages of Change Model would be related to their attitudes toward and support for government legislation regarding tobacco control measures. To test this, they also asked questions about these attitudes.

The researchers did indeed find that the further along the Stage Model the person is placed, the more knowledge the person has regarding health consequences. This was particularly true for the current smokers, who showed greater knowledge on seven of eight knowledge questions the further they were along the three stages that applied to them. For the former smokers, this increase in knowledge across the stages applied to only two of the knowledge questions. The Cohen group also found that attitudes toward tobacco control

(continued on next page)

and support for government control measures increased along the stages of the model.

These findings are interesting for at least two reasons. First, the study has implications for the health promotion programs designed to help people quit smoking. We will look closely at health promotion in chapter 7. It is simplistic to assume that smokers are not recep- tive to stop-smoking messages. Rather, precontemplative smokers are most likely to be unreceptive. Also, people in this category are the least well informed regarding health consequences. Secondly, this study extends the Stages of Change Model. The model was originally intro- duced to help explain *behaviour*. Cohen and colleagues have used the model to help understand *cognition*.

Summary of the Models   You may have wondered, as you read through these theo- ries, just how well they apply across different cultures. For example, the notion of inter- nal locus of control tends to make more sense to people who have been raised in **indiv- idualist** rather than **collectivist** cultures (Hart & Poole, 1995; Triandis et al., 1988). Individualists focus on independence and self-reliance, whereas collectivists see them- selves as part of a greater whole in which one's individualism is less important than alle- giance to the group.

The Theory of Reasoned Action and the Theory of Planned Behaviour have been test- ed with Latin American, English-speaking Caribbean, and South Asian participants (Godin et al., 1996). The conclusion was that the Theory of Planned Behaviour was more useful in these three cultures than the Theory of Reasoned Action, even though these cultures would be considered more collectivist than most Western cultures. This would suggest that the Theory of Planned Behaviour's inclusion of a measure of perceived control was still useful for cultures in which the orientation was more collectivist.

This brief introduction to some of the major theories and models common to health psychology was presented to give you an idea of some of the ways psychological theory has been applied to health and health care. The theories and models presented in this chap- ter grow, for the most part, from a cognitive perspective, with their focus on people's thought processes, attitudes, and beliefs. Of course, there are many other theories, some with a stronger behavioural emphasis, others more humanistic or psychodynamic. We will be referring to such models and theories throughout the remaining chapters of this book. We invite you to think critically about their utility and about ways in which they could be further developed to be even more useful.

WORKING IN HEALTH PSYCHOLOGY

Health psychology is a field that offers a number of interesting career opportunities. The vast majority of these require a graduate degree, usually a PhD. There are two main paths you can take when preparing for a career in health psychology. One is to be trained as a clinical or counselling psychologist. The other is to be trained as a researcher.

Clinical and Counselling Psychologists Working in Health Psychology

Clinical and counselling psychologists require different training and perform different roles in health psychology. Clinical psychologists must have either a master's or doctorate degree, depending upon the province or territory in which they are practising. The Canadian Psychological Association has recommended that all clinical psychologists hold a PhD. Clinical training usually involves a year of internship and, in some jurisdictions, students must pass a certification exam to be considered clinical psychologists.

Counselling psychologists do not require a PhD, though some will have one. The certification process for counselling psychologists tends to be less rigorous than for clinical psychologists. In fact, in some jurisdictions, no formal training is required to call oneself a counsellor. It is usually the case, though, that counsellors working in health settings have formal training at least at the master's level.

Clinical health psychologists work with people who are experiencing psychological problems that are either the result of illness or a cause of it. They may work with cancer patients who are suffering from depression, or breast reconstruction patients who are grappling with issues related to self-image. They may also work with people who suffer from anxiety and, as a result, are dealing with psychosomatic disorders. These are just a few of the types of people who benefit from a clinical health psychologist's intervention.

Clinical health psychologists might be employed by hospitals or they might work in private practice. Their salaries tend to be quite good, in keeping with what one might expect for a person with an advanced degree and considerable training who is dealing with challenging psychological issues related to health.

Counselling psychologists work with people in similar circumstances. For example, a counselling psychologist might work with a family in which a member is seriously ill. Another might work with someone who is recovering from an injury or illness and is trying to integrate back into work and society. As is the case with clinical health psychologists, there is plenty of work for a skilled counselling psychologist working in health-related settings. Their salaries tend to be somewhat lower than those of clinical psychologists, though they can still do very well financially. Similar work might also be conducted by people in other helping professions, such as social work.

Research Careers in Health Psychology

Not all people working in health psychology have clinical training. Some are trained in other fields, such as social or developmental psychology, and they apply the theories of those disciplines to health and health care. Indeed, some of the major theories we introduced earlier in the chapter were forwarded by social psychologists. A good example is the Theory of Reasoned Action developed by Fishbein and Ajzen. Instead of providing clinical services, psychologists from these other areas conduct research and consult with health professionals regarding aspects of health care delivery.

Most people conducting research in health psychology hold academic appointments at universities, though some are employed by other institutions such as hospitals and cancer agencies. Most hold doctoral degrees. Those working in universities combine their research duties with teaching and other academic responsibilities. Of course, clinical work and research are not mutually exclusive; many people do both, within private practice, institutional appointments, or university positions.

KEY TERMS

asymptomatic (p. 6)

behavioural medicine (p. 3)

behaviourist (p. 5)

blunters (p. 8)

biopsychosocial approach (p. 13)

biomedical model (p. 14)

carcinogenic (p. 12)

collectivist cultures (p. 26)

coping styles (p. 8)

cost-gain belief (p. 16)

delayed gratification (p. 6)

demographic differences (p. 12)

efficacy belief (p. 16)

epidemiologists (p. 13)

germ theory (p. 5)

gradient of reinforcement (p. 6)

health belief model (p. 16)

health psychology (p. 4)

immunocompetence (p. 9)

individualist cultures (p. 26)

locus of control (p. 23)

learned helplessness (p. 24)

malignant neoplasms (p. 12)

medical anthropologists (p. 13)

medical geography (p. 12)

medical sociologists (p. 13)

monitors (p. 8)

multidimensional health locus of control scale (MHLC) (p. 23)

onset control (p. 24)

perceived behavioural control (p. 22)

psychoneuroimmunology (PNI0) (p. 9)

psychosomatic medicine (p. 4)

self-blame (p. 24)

stages of change model (p. 24)

subjective norms (p. 21)

theory of planned behaviour (p. 22)

theory of reasoned action (p. 20)

total institution (p. 24)

chapter two

Stress and Coping

CHAPTER OUTLINE

Issues of Definition

The Physiology of Stress
   The General Adaptation Syndrome

Cognitive Transactional Models

The Role of Personality in Stress and Coping

Coping
   East and West: Now the Twain Shall Meet
   Relaxation
   Behaviour Therapy and Cognitive Therapy
   The Relaxation Responses: A Personal Guide

KEY QUESTIONS

1. Take some time to write down your definition of the two terms used in the title of this chapter—*stress* and *coping*. What do these terms mean to you?

2. What are the major sources of stress in your life at present? A major source of stress does not necessarily need to be a major event such as a car accident; it may involve something less significant, although important to you, such as having recently received a speeding ticket.

3. What are the coping strategies you use most frequently in your life? It will be obvious to you that some of these strategies are more appropriate or more effective than others are.

4. Each one of us tends to have characteristic behavioural responses that indicate stress is overwhelming us. Typical behaviours include nervous tics, nail biting, accident proneness, unusual mannerisms, absent-mindedness, increased alcohol consumption, changes in eating and sleeping patterns, and inappropriate emotional reactions. Take a moment to think about the signs that indicate stress is beginning to get the best of you.

It is thousands of years ago and a young man wakes up to prepare for the coming day. He is well rested, as he fell asleep the previous night with the setting sun and slept uninterrupted until the warmth of the new day woke him. He is a hunter and soon he goes forth, spear in hand, in search of prey. He is optimistic, as he has a feeling that today he will be successful. However, as he crosses the brow of a hill he unwittingly disturbs a large tiger feeding on a freshly killed deer. It is angry at being disturbed and moves aggressively toward the hunter. He has little time to prepare himself. There is no opportunity to flee and so he prepares to fight the advancing animal. His body immediately begins to respond in a manner designed to allow him to optimize his skills as a hunter. He experiences a pounding in his chest as his heart beats faster and his blood pressure rises, increasing the blood supply to the areas that need it. Muscles in his arms and legs tense in preparation for action. His breathing is rapid, providing more oxygen to his system. He grits his teeth, his pupils are dilated and all his senses are heightened. His emotions race in anticipation of the battle ahead, and he vacillates rapidly between fear and excited anticipation. Perspiration covers his body but most noticeably on the palms of his hands and the soles of his feet. He is not aware that this improves his grip on the spear and his bare feet cling to the smooth rock beneath him. He is ready. Suddenly the tiger turns and walks away, perhaps intimidated, but we will never know. The young hunter slumps to the ground, exhausted and relieved. Although it seems like a long time, he realizes that only a short time has passed. He goes in search of a cool, mountain stream in which to wash the sweat from his body and quench his thirst. After doing this he will get back to his work.

It is many, many years later and a young business executive is awakened by his alarm. He hits the snooze button but his relief lasts only 10 minutes. He snaps to attention, realizing that he is now running late. He was out until 12:30 last night at a social function and, although he understands that it is important for his work, he wishes he had not had so much to drink and had got home earlier. He rushes to shower and shave and in his haste cuts his chin badly. Blood from the cut stains the shirt he had planned to wear and the replacement he finds is not a good colour match, but there is nothing he can do. Leaving his apartment, he runs to his car through heavy rain only to discover that he left his briefcase inside. Once on the road he aims for Starbucks for his morning dose of caffeine, the first thing he will ingest today. He arrives to find a long lineup but the alternative, a commute without coffee, is not an option he would even consider. This is the first of approximately 20 cups of coffee he will have today and he wants it to be a good one. His impatience is visible and he curses under his breath at the woman at the head of the line who is having the difference between a latte and a mocha explained to her and then has the audacity to order a pound of ground coffee beans as well. As he leaps back into his car, grande latte and chocolate croissant in hand, he spills coffee on his pants.

A heavy rush hour is endured by riding the bumper of the car in front of him and yelling at those around him who seem oblivious to his sense of urgency. His cell phone appears to be glued to his ear. Periodically, he has to slam on his brakes in order to avoid rear-ending the vehicle ahead of him. He has difficulty finding a parking spot and, after running through the rain again, arrives at his office 45 minutes late for an important meeting. His boss tells him not to bother coming into the meeting and suggests, in a somewhat sarcastic manner, that he should attend instead to some of the accumulated work on his desk. As he curses again, he pours himself another coffee and sneaks a jelly doughnut from a box in the coffee room. Sitting down to his desk he is aware that his heart is racing, he is sweating profusely, his jaw is clenched, he is grinding his teeth, his breathing is rapid and shallow, and a muscle-tension headache is beginning. He is angry, frustrated, and worried by his boss' response to his lateness. His confidence has been shattered, and he is having difficulty focusing on the tasks in front of him. His motivation for his work has decreased dramatically. He longs to return home and curl up in his bed but knows this is not a possibility if he wants to keep his job. There is nowhere to go. The abundance of sweat on his hands and feet will not find expression in the gripping of a spear and a sureness of step on smooth rocks. Rather, it results in embarrassingly sweaty palms and socks that give off an increasingly unpleasant odour as the day progresses. The tiger in front of him is made of paper.

ISSUES OF DEFINITION

In this text, we provide many definitions for the terms we use. This is to ensure clarity with regard to the meaning of the concepts presented. There is usually considerable agreement concerning the correct definition for a particular term. However, with regard to the topics of this chapter, **stress** and **coping**, this is not the case. In our "Key Questions" we asked you to write down how you would define these terms. If we compared your definition with those of others reading the same chapter, we would expect that there would be considerable variability. Individual definitions would be highly personalized and reflect the uniqueness of a particular individual's life experiences.

Brannon and Feist (1999) compare the concept of stress to that of love—everyone appears to know what it means, the role it plays in their lives, and they are sure they know it when they feel it. We have a commonsense understanding of these terms. When someone tells us they are feeling stressed we identify with what they are feeling because we believe we have experienced similar feelings. Many of us would describe ourselves as being "experts" in the field. We have attained a high level of competency through one of the acknowledged avenues by which this can occur—personal experience.

A similar vagueness exists with regard to how we define coping. To say we "cope with stress" is a highly individualized statement that also reflects the variability of human experience. It is obvious that there is no "right" way to cope with stress; there are different ways. My stress is not your stress, and my coping strategies are not yours. We do not experience stress in a similar way. The questions are many. Is all stress a bad thing, or should positive events such as getting married or having a child be viewed as stressful? How much more stressful is it to lose a close relative than to receive a speeding ticket?

Are the strategies one person uses to cope applicable to another individual's world? Can particular coping strategies actually increase the stress we experience? Why do we continue to use coping strategies that appear to be quite ineffective? It seems we are describing two phenomena that appear to have meaning, like love, only in the eye of the beholder. Given the number of times we use the terms *stress* and *coping* in describing our daily activities, it is remarkable how little consensus exists as to how to define them.

Our opening vignette, which presented our version of an age-old tale, reminds us that stress and coping are concepts that have always existed. Only recently, however, have they been the object of research and systematic efforts at conceptualization. What we are struggling with here is what Smith (1993) has described as **stress literacy**. He considers this an issue of considerable importance, as the alternative is confusion. He suggests that the "popular culture provides volumes of conflicting bits of stress wisdom" (p. 5). For example, is it better to face your problems or ignore them? Do we perform better when we are "psyched" up or when we are relaxed? The contradictions are many, and Smith suggests that the first step in the process of "stress literacy begins with a useful definition of stress" (p. 6).

One might expect that, in the empirical world, this issue would be somewhat clearer; however, even in that context considerable confusion seems to exist. Haan (1993) addresses this concern directly. She believes that those involved in the investigation of stress and coping are "handicapped by a lack of consensus on the meaning of these terms. The concept of stress is used and understood by laypersons, but its scientific study has proven difficult" (p. 256). Haan also suggests that this same level of controversy and confusion is attached to the meaning of coping. She argues that if we would acknowledge "that our knowledge of stress arises from common, shared understandings and not from objective reality, the insight would be liberating" (p. 260).

This lack of consensus has led some researchers to question whether the concept of stress is worth retaining (Pearlin, 1993). Pearlin believes that the very nature of stress dictates that it can be many things and that it is a diffuse, multidimensional phenomenon that cannot be reduced to one element. Our efforts should be directed toward examining the interconnections between its multiple dimensions. This process is proceeding slowly, as it requires an interdisciplinary focus that is difficult to bring about. Pearlin laments that "firmly and actively engaged in his chosen research, each investigator is convinced that the manifestation of stress that he is examining represents 'real' stress" (p. 305). Pearlin argues that we should continue to work on the concept of stress but do so in an interdisciplinary fashion. It will be interesting to observe whether or not the kind of paradigm shift he considers necessary occurs in the future.

Aldwin (1994) acknowledges that stress is a somewhat amorphous concept, but argues that the term should be retained. She writes that "stress refers to that quality of experience, produced through a person-environment transaction, that, through either overarousal or underarousal, results in psychological or physiological distress" (p. 22). DiMatteo and Martin (2002) conclude that as the concept of stress has developed and become more popular it has also become more imprecise.

Hans Selye, the originator of the biological concept of the term *stress* (see Focus on Canadian Research), defined it as "the nonspecific result of any demand upon the body, be the effect mental or somatic" (1993, p.7). He also recognized that, for most people, stress is viewed as a negative experience that they equate with *distress*. To counter this position, he coined the term *eustress* to reflect a positive stressful, experience. **Eustress** (like its related word *euphoria*) is a state of physical and psychological well-being that is associated with increased motivation and the acceptance of challenge. The ultimate expression of this positive state is found in the title of the book by the Canadian physician Peter Hanson, *The Joy of Stress* (1986). Selye argued that what is essential is a sense of balance; that we function best when stress is used to produce an optimal level of arousal. The implication is that too little stress can be as harmful as too much, that distress can result from being over- *or* understimulated. Selye believed that "stress is the spice of life" (1974, p. 83).

Lazurus and Folkman (1984) and more recently Lazurus (1999) have provided us with descriptions of stress and coping that have received wide acceptance in the field. Stress is described in terms of a relationship that exists between a "person and the environment that is appraised by the person as taxing or exceeding his or her resources and endangering his or her well-being" (p. 21, 1984). An individual's cognitive appraisal of a situation will determine the level of stress he or she will experience. Coping is defined as "constantly changing cognitive and behavioral efforts to manage specific external and/or internal demands that are appraised as taxing or exceeding the resources of the person" (p. 141).

Focus on Canadian Research 2-1	A Great Canadian

Hans Selye has been described as "the grand master of stress research and theory." Born in Vienna in 1907, Selye lived and worked in Montreal for 50 years until his death in 1982. He first used the term *stress* in 1936 to describe the non-specific result, either mental or physical, of demands placed on the body. It is interesting to note that close to 40 years later, Selye indicated that if his English had been better at the time, he would probably have chosen the word "strain" to describe this response. He had taken the idea of stress from the field of physics where it describes the force exerted by one body against another. The response to this tension is strain and, as what Selye was describing was a response, he acknowledged that he probably should have used this term. Rather than correct him, we have adjusted our definition to fit his model. You might try to substitute the word "strain" for "stress" and experience how awkward this sounds even

(continued on next page)

though it may be more appropriate. For example, how does "I feel so strained today," "the strain of life," or "I've had a very strainful day" sound to you?

Selye initially observed a consistent pattern of responses in rats when these animals were exposed to diverse noxious stimuli. He called this a "stereotypic response," which he had first become aware of in human patients some 10 years earlier (the "general adaptation syndrome" or "biologic stress syndrome") and for which he now had experimental evidence. He also identified an initial "alarm reaction" in which the organism's defences were activated. If the organism survived this initial attack, Selye identified an adaptive phase or rebound effect that occurs, which he called the "the stage of resistance." Eventually, if the demands on the organism were of sufficient severity or length, a "stage of exhaustion" occurred.

In 1956 Selye published his best-selling book, *The Stress of Life*, in which he translated the concept of stress for the layperson. Selye dedicated his life to the study of stress and wrote over 1700 articles and 39 books on the topic. He was a scientist, trained as both a physician and an endocrinologist. He served as a professor and director of the Institute of Experimental Medicine and Surgery at the University of Montreal. He also served the non-scientific world through texts such as that mentioned above and *Stress without Distress* (1974), which he wrote to help us better understand the impact of the stress response on humans throughout the lifespan. He was made a Companion of the Order of Canada, the highest honour this country can bestow upon an individual. He has been described as a "Canadian resource to the world."

Central to our understanding of stress are the contributions of Walter Cannon. In 1939, he introduced the concept of **homeostasis**, which describes the body's attempt to maintain a stable internal state. This is a dynamic physiological response on the part of the body to the demands of the environment. The body seeks balance, and stress presents a challenge to homeostasis. It was Cannon who articulated the concept of the **fight-or-flight response**. The fight or flight response involves a complex autonomic reaction in preparation for emergencies. The sympathetic nervous system and hormones secreted by the adrenal glands interact in an adaptive response developed through evolution. It is this response that allows us to cope with potential attacks from a threatening world. In the vignette we presented at the start of this chapter, we observed two individuals, separated by thousands of years, responding to threat in their world with essentially the same physiological response even though the behavioural options available to them were quite different.

Cannon (1939) expressed concern about the implications for physical illness through the continuous activation of the fight or flight reaction in response to the chronic pressures and demands of the contemporary world. The actions implied by the term "fight or flight" are simply not always appropriate in the contemporary world. In fact, to engage in either of these responses in today's world could have disastrous consequences. Our young businessman could neither fight nor flee. He had to sit at his desk while his body experienced the same physiological responses that his ancient brother had. The stomach churns, the muscles tighten, the heart pounds, the blood pressure soars, the teeth grind, hyperventilation occurs, sweat flows, and the emotions run wild. It is not difficult to understand how the continual stimulation of this response could eventually result in physical illness.

A challenge to the universality of the fight or flight response has recently been put forth by Taylor et al (2000) who propose that, although the physiological component of this response may be common to both males and females, the behavioural component in females is better described as "tend and befriend." The implication is that the female response to stress has evolved according to natural selection principles in order to increase the likelihood of survival of both the self and offspring. Tending is associated with nurturant activities and befriending involves establishing social networks This attachment–caregiving response in females may be triggered by neuroendocrine responses to stress. This theory is described as "a biobehavioural alternative to the fight-or-flight response (Cannon, 1932), which has dominated stress research for the past five decades and has been disproportionately based on studies of males" (p. 422).

Rice (1999) describes three distinct meanings attached to stress. The first has to do with external causes. These are the environmental demands placed upon us that cause us to feel stressed. As such, these should be described as *stressors*, rather than *stress*. It is in response to these external stressors that we invoke coping strategies to reduce their impact. The second meaning of stress is concerned with subjective responses and refers to the interpretive mental state of the individual. It allows us to react cognitively to diminish, augment, or distort the impact of external events. We can create our own stress.

The intuitive sense that stress is somehow "all in our minds" has been expressed by writers and philosophers throughout history. Epictetus said some two thousand years ago that, "Humans are not disturbed by events, but by the view they take of them." Shakespeare wrote in Hamlet that, "There is no such thing as good or bad, but thinking makes it so." Milton suggested in Paradise Lost that, "The mind is its own place, and in itself can make a Heaven of Hell, a Hell of Heaven." Mark Twain commented, "I am an old man and have known a great many troubles—but most of them never happened."

Rice (1999) points out that even though stress is a very subjective experience, we frequently use physical terms to explain the impact of stress. We speak of being on the "edge" of a breakdown, of feeling the "weight" of the world, of not being sure that we can cope with "the pressure" or of "exploding" if we are exposed to any more stress. The third definition of stress focuses on the body's physical response to events in the manner described by Selye and Cannon. Regardless of our personal views of what stress feels like, the fact is that stress imposes a physiological challenge, which if prolonged can result in a decreased capacity to cope physiologically (Rice, 1999).

THE PHYSIOLOGY OF STRESS

There are two major components of the physical response to stress—the **nervous system** and the **endocrine system**. The nervous system comprises two divisions, the **central nervous system** and the **peripheral nervous system**. The former is composed of the brain and the spinal cord. The latter is made up of the somatic nervous system and the autonomic nervous system, which is further divided into the sympathetic and parasympathetic nervous systems. The physiology of stress features a highly complex response that begins when an individual perceives a (real or imagined) threat.

The stress response begins with the **hypothalamus**, which is located in the central core of the brain. It initiates the stress response in both the nervous system and the endocrine system. The hypothalamus helps maintain homeostasis in the body through its many regulatory functions. It controls activities such as eating, drinking, and sexual behaviour, all of which are greatly affected by stress. The activities of the hypothalamus increase arousal in the sympathetic nervous system in the form of the previously described fight-or-flight response (Cannon, 1939). The physiological changes we described in the initial vignette now occur. The heart beats faster and blood pressure increases at the same time as peripheral blood vessels, in areas such as the hands and feet, constrict to ensure sufficient blood supplies for the brain and skeletal muscles. Stored fats and glucose flow into the bloodstream to provide fuel for necessary actions. Respiration rate increases and the bronchial tubes dilate to help increase oxygen flow for the metabolism of fuel. Pupils dilate to allow more light to enter the eyes and improve vision. The efficiency of the process is demonstrated when non-essential activities, such as digestion, decrease.

As a part of this response, the hypothalamus causes the **adrenal medulla**, located above the kidneys, to secrete catecholamines, which contain the hormones adrenaline and noradrenaline. Catecholamines affect the response of the sympathetic nervous system, and the level of these two hormones increases with the severity of the stress. Adrenaline has a powerful impact on heart function and blood pressure. Presumably it is this experience that finds expression in the phrase "adrenaline rush." It is interesting that this phrase is usually viewed in positive terms as something that people seek. We even go so far as to ascribe an addictive quality to it by describing people who purposefully seek the physiological "high" that adrenaline brings as "adrenaline junkies." These sensation-seekers may engage in extreme activities that presumably initiate the fight or flight response and the flow of adrenaline. It is interesting to note that the actions of adrenaline and noradrenaline are different. The former is fast acting and increases with mental stress; the effect of the latter is more prolonged and increases with physical activity (Rice, 1999).

Also involved in the stress response is the **limbic system** of the brain, which adds an element of *emotion* to the response that goes beyond the identified dimensions of fight or flight. The feelings associated with the limbic system include aggression, anger, fear, anxiety, sexual arousal, and pain. The **reticular formation** is a complex system running through the middle of the brain stem that performs several functions in the stress response. It serves as a communication network that filters messages between the brain and the body. This is most important when we consider the impact that the brain's perception of psychosocial stressors can have on physical systems in the body. The reticular formation receives input from all of the sensory systems and can influence which sensory information is processed or blocked.

Such selectivity results in increased efficiency in the system, which can become apparent to us in quite dramatic ways. For example, in high-arousal situations we may find ourselves remarkably able to selectively attend to a specific task while ignoring irrelevant distractions. A basketball player, given the opportunity to win a game by sinking a last-second foul shot, is able to focus his attention on the front rim of the hoop. He is not distracted by the noise of the crowd and the purposeful movement of those behind the basket, who will go to considerable extremes in an attempt to get his attention to waiver. We find that during an exam we can block all distractions and become completely absorbed in the task. Parents notice that they are able to selectively attend to the sounds of their children above all other noises. We develop the ability to attend to what matters and to ignore the rest. The reticular formation also serves an important role in modulating the brain's levels of arousal or alertness in preparation for action.

In contrast to the **sympathetic** nervous system, the **parasympathetic** component of the autonomic system is activated by the hypothalamus to re-establish homeostasis in the system and to promote the reconstructive process following a stressful experience. It is associated with a relaxed state in which the heart rate slows and blood pressure drops. Muscle tension decreases and respiration is slow and easy. In essence, the fight-or-flight response is neutralized.

The endocrine system responds to stress more slowly than does the nervous system, but the effects associated with it can persist for weeks. The **pituitary gland**, which is located in the brain close to the hypothalamus, is described as the "master gland" because of its controlling effect on other glands. Most of the hormones secreted by the pituitary gland have an indirect impact on stress. The most important of these is adrenocorticotropic hormone (ACTH), which acts on the adrenal glands and is eventually involved in the release of up to 30 stress hormones (Smith, 1993).

The **adrenal cortex** secretes glucocorticoids and mineralocorticoids. One of the former is cortisol, an important stress hormone that provides energy to the system through the conversion of stored protein and fats to glucose. If stress is prolonged, glucocorticoids can adversely affect the body's ability to resist disease and recover from injury. Cortisol levels are often used as an index of stress. Aldosterone is an important mineralocorticoid that regulates minerals in the body during stress by increasing blood pressure.

The **thyroid gland** functions in the stress response by producing thyroxine, which increases the release of fatty-acid fuels that are metabolized in the stress process. Elevated thyroxine levels increase blood pressure and respiration rate. Mental processes are also affected, in that individuals feel more anxious or agitated. The **pancreas**, which lies close to the stomach, secretes insulin and glucagon as a function of blood sugar levels. The former serves to decrease blood sugar by storing it, whereas the latter stimulates increases in blood sugar, which is an energy source during times of stress.

The indication is that the autonomic nervous system responds rapidly in response to stress and the endocrine system responds somewhat slower, although its impact usually continues much longer. Acting together, these two systems provide a physiological response to stress that can be both adaptive and potentially maladaptive.

The General Adaptation Syndrome

Initially, Selye conducted research on laboratory animals. He observed that animals exposed to chronic stress demonstrated physical distress that included organic pathology and ultimately death. This work and that of others, such as Brady's work on executive monkeys (Brady, Porter, Conrad, & Mason, 1958), resulted in Selye's conceptualization of the **General Adaptation Syndrome (GAS)** (Selye, 1956). This is a three-stage response of the body to stressors. In the initial phase, the body goes into **alarm** as it mobilizes its defences against the stress. This involves many of the processes involved in the fight-or-flight response. As our own experience will confirm, this acute response is often enough to allow us to deal successfully with the impact of a stressor and to allow homeostasis to be re-established.

If a source of stress moves from acute to chronic, the body enters the second phase of adaptation, which Selye called **resistance**. Here the body mobilizes its resources over an extended period of time. Initially, the individual will appear as normal. If the stress continues for too long, however, the body's resources are depleted and resistance decreases. The result of neurological and hormonal changes can be what Selye described as **diseases of adaptation**. These include problems such as cardiovascular disease, hypertension, peptic ulcers, bronchial asthma, and increased risk of infection.

The body's resources to resist stress are clearly finite. Eventually, if the stressor is too severe or continues for too long, the body enters what Selye called **exhaustion**. This is an endpoint at which the body's ability to resist the stressor breaks down, possibly resulting in death if a return to homeostasis is not possible.

Criticisms of Selye's theory centre on its narrowness as it is concerned only with physical responses to stress and does not take into account psychosocial factors influencing the human stress response. This emphasis may have derived from his initial work with animals, and his critics suggest that he neglected those cognitive processes unique to humans (Brannon & Feist, 2000).

Other biologically based models have been proposed to explain our ability to resist the impact of stress. One emphasizes genetic influences that may predispose an individual to be at increased risk for specific diseases or to display vulnerabilities or reductions in resistance that may be expressed under certain conditions. Closely linked to this is the **stress-diathesis model** that examines the interaction between the environment and heredity, often referred to as *nature versus nurture*. This model proposes that there may be predisposing factors present in an individual that determine whether or not a physical effect is experienced in the presence of stressful events. Thus, an individual with a genetic predisposition for a particular condition may never display signs of the predisposed problem if he or she is not exposed to the precipitating stress. However, high levels of stress may extend the limits of invulnerability even in those who are genetically robust. There is a sense of adaptability to the model. It makes us think of phrases that relate to a "survival of the fittest" mentality. The implication is that stress forces an individual to adapt and evolve or run the risk of being selected out. Certainly many of us, when we consider our own vulnerability to disease, are quick to blame or applaud our genes. We boast to others that we will never develop cardiovascular disease no matter how much we abuse our body through environmental stressors such as a poor diet or lack of exercise, as we are blessed with "good genes." We develop an inappropriate sense of invulnerability. The stress-diathesis model (or diathesis-stress model, as Grossarth-Maticek and Eysenck call it) is also discussed in chapter 3 in our examination of psychoneuroimmunology.

COGNITIVE TRANSACTIONAL MODELS

Selye's popularization of the idea of stress can't be underestimated. It's hard to imagine where we would be today without the contributions he made to the field. He brought us a long way in a very short time. However, as we indicated, his theory may be limited by its reliance on physiological processes based on an animal model of behaviour. In this regard, it fails to take into account those higher level cognitive abilities that are distinctly human and allow us to interpret our vulnerability to a particular stressor both now and in the future. Compared to Selye's model, **cognitive transactional models** of stress hold more appeal for psychologists. As indicated by the definition provided by Lazarus and Folkman earlier in this chapter, these models emphasize the relationship existing between individuals and their environment and the appraisal individuals make of that relationship. Personal **cognitive appraisals** determine whether or not an event will be perceived as stressful. These are based on an individual's unique social learning history. Of relevance here are temporal concerns, because what is psychologically or physically threatening at one time may not be at another.

Lazarus and Folkman (1984) describe the process of cognitive appraisal as one that is "largely evaluative, focused on meaning or significance, and takes place continuously during waking hours" (p. 31). They distinguish between three kinds of appraisal influencing the coping process: **primary appraisal, secondary appraisal**, and **reappraisal**. They acknowledge that these are somewhat unfortunate terms, as one form of appraisal (e.g., primary as compared to secondary) is neither superior to nor precedes the other.

Primary appraisals are concerned with the initial evaluation of a situation. Three kinds of primary appraisal are identified—**irrelevant, benign–positive**, and **stressful**. The first involves a cognitive process by which an event is appraised to have no implications for the individual's well-being, it is simply irrelevant and requires no response. Benign–positive appraisals involve outcomes appraised to be positive and that may increase well-being. They are associated with pleasurable emotions such as happiness, joy, or love. The only demand benign–positive appraisals place on the individual is the awareness that these feelings will end.

There are three types of stressful appraisal—**harm/loss**, **threat**, and **challenge**. Harm/loss appraisals involve significant physical or psychological loss such as might be experienced in a serious illness or the loss of one's job. Threat involves the anticipation of situations of harm or loss. When an individual has experienced harm/loss, threat is involved, as it has implications for the future. Perceptions of threat allow one to anticipate and prepare for the impact of an event. Challenge appraisals involve events perceived to be stressful, but the focus is one of positive excitement and anticipation of the potential for growth contained in the situation. Having to speak in front of a class may be perceived as very threatening by a person with anxiety about public speaking and as an opportunity to test one's public-speaking abilities by an individual who has worked on these skills. Clearly, threat and challenge may be experienced in the same situation. The confident speaker may experience some threat in the speaking opportunity, which is expressed in the form of anxiety and some fear, however the dominant emotions are confidence and anticipation. The overall emotional tone is positive and the individual actively employs available resources to prepare to meet the demands imposed by the presentation.

Secondary appraisal is concerned with a person's evaluation of his or her ability to cope with a situation. After the initial evaluation of the nature of the event, which is *primary appraisal*, options are considered. As Lazarus and Folkman (1984) make clear, this is not simply an intellectual exercise. It is "a complex evaluative process that takes into account which coping options are available, the likelihood that a given coping option will accomplish what it is supposed to, and the likelihood one can apply a particular strategy" (p. 35). They point out that this is very similar to the distinction Bandura (1985) makes between outcome and efficacy judgments. Bandura states that "efficacy and outcome judgments are differentiated because individuals can believe that a particular course of action will produce certain outcomes, but they do not act on that outcome belief because they question whether they can actually execute the necessary activities" (1985, p. 392).

The interaction between the secondary appraisals of coping options and the primary appraisals of the situation determines the emotional reaction to the event. If the consequences of an event are important to the individual, considerable stress may be experienced if they believe they do not have the ability to cope with the event; a state of helplessness may result. Conversely, *challenge appraisals* are more likely to result when an individual feels in control of the situation, even if this means overcoming extreme adversity. We are all aware of individuals who, when faced with a devastating situation such as an illness or loss of a relationship, articulate their efforts to cope in very positive ways. They describe the challenge of *confronting* through their own behaviour what others would perceive as overwhelming odds. They know they may not ultimately have an outcome others would consider desirable, but they focus their attention on elements of the situation that are under their control. For example, they may talk of the challenge of coping with pain, either physical or psychological, to the best of their ability while recognizing that there are elements of the situation that are outside their control and will have to run their course. Even though a situation may appear hopeless they search for challenges.

Reappraisal is a continuous experience in which existing appraisals are changed or modified on the basis of new information. Reappraisal simply follows an earlier appraisal of an event and results in a new appraisal. What may vary is the direction of the outcome of the appraisal. For example, an irrelevant situation may now be perceived in terms of threat, or a harm/loss situation may now be appraised as a challenge. Lazarus and Folkman (1984) also identify what they call a *defensive reappraisal*. They describe this as a self-generated coping strategy in which an attempt is made to reinterpret past events more positively, or to view current threats or losses as being less threatening.

Also of importance in the cognitive appraisal process is the concept of **vulnerability**, which reflects the adequacy of an individual's resources. This is a concept that, like so many in this area, is defined in the context of a relationship. With regard to physical issues it is possible to think of vulnerability only in terms of resources. A physical injury can increase vulnerability to further injury. However, deficiencies in resources will result in a psychological vulnerability only when it threatens that which is valued by the individual. Therefore, an individual may have resource deficiencies but not experience vulnerability, as the deficiencies do not threaten areas that are important to them.

This model also identifies **person** and **situation** variables that influence appraisal. The impact of these variables is in the determination of the salience of an event, an individual's understanding of the event, the consequence of an event, and, ultimately, the outcome of a particular encounter (Lazarus and Folkman, 1984). Person and situation variables are interdependent and involve transactions between the individual and their environment. The person variables of importance are **commitments** and **beliefs**. Commitments are concerned with what is important to an individual. They influence appraisal by determining the importance of a particular encounter and will affect the choices made to achieve a desired outcome. They interact with concepts we discussed in the context of primary appraisal, such as challenge, threat, benefit, or harm, to determine whether an individual will engage in or avoid an encounter. Beliefs are pre-existing notions that determine the meaning given to the environment. They can be both personal and cultural. Their impact, which is often difficult to observe, is most obvious when there is a sudden change in the belief system.

Numerous factors influencing the appraisal process have been identified. **Novelty** refers to an individual's previous experience with a situation. **Predictability** identifies characteristics of the environment that can be learned or discerned. Predictability allows an individual to prepare for an event and therefore reduce the stress involved. Of more relevance to appraisal, particularly in humans, is the concept of **event uncertainty**, which involves issues of probability. The observation is that high levels of uncertainty can be extremely stressful. Temporal situational factors are also important in stress appraisal. **Imminence** concerns the interval during which an event is being anticipated. It is usually the case that the more imminent an event, the more intense the appraisal. **Duration** refers to the period during which a stressful event occurs. The implication is that the longer the duration, the more stressful the event. This concept is reminiscent of Selye's General Adaptation Syndrome in which the duration of stress plays an important role; continued exposure to stress compromises resistance and leads ultimately to exhaustion. **Temporal uncertainty** is concerned with the stress involved in *not knowing* when an event will occur. A final concern here relates to the *timing* of stressful events in the context of the life cycle. This suggests that there are appropriate or "usual" times for events to occur in one's life. If these expectations are violated, it may result in the event being appraised as more stressful by some individuals. We have a sense of an order that we move through in our lives, and this master daytimer allows us to develop expectations and prepare for events. When the timing is wrong, normal life events become sources of stress. We can all think of people who have been affected by life events in this way. It may be the couple who has children later in life, or the athlete whose career is brought to an abrupt end due to injury, or perhaps it is the person who is finally able to attend university after 25 years in the workplace.

The model developed by Lazarus and his colleagues views stress as a complex, dynamic process in which an individual's experience of stress is determined by their own unique cognitive appraisal of the event and their coping abilities.

THE ROLE OF PERSONALITY IN STRESS AND COPING

The idea that personality may be related to stress and coping is very appealing. If it were possible to prove that a particular disposition or set of personality traits predisposed an individual to a specific disease, then, given the stable, enduring qualities of personality, it might be possible to predict disease and intervene to reduce risk. There are several ways these interactions might occur (Rice, 1999). A specific personality profile might cause a specific disease to develop, as is the case with Type A personality and coronary heart disease. A second possibility is that a particular disease process could cause a particular personality profile as when depression results following diagnosis of a serious illness. The third possibility is that personality affects or filters the response to an illness. One individual receiving the news of a serious illness may respond in an optimistic and active manner compared to another who responds passively and pessimistically. In the fourth possibility, personality interacts with the disease process in a feedback loop that affects the individual's physiology and may influence the disease process itself. Ultimately, the question centres on whether there are a set of personality traits that predict behaviours such as smoking or alcohol use or disease processes such as cancer or coronary disease.

The most extensively studied set of personality traits in connection with disease is the **Type A behaviour pattern**. This personality type was first identified by two cardiologists, Friedman and Rosenman, in 1974. They described a type of individual they saw frequently in their medical practice who they felt was at a much higher risk for cardiovascular disease. Such an individual displays a sense of time urgency, is impatient, is very competitive, and can be aggressive and hostile. This is a person who does not relax. He or she displays behavioural characteristics such as rapid, explosive, clipped speech; frequent interruptions of another speaker; speech hurrying techniques (e.g., nodding the head while another person speaks), vehement reactions to time impedance; emphatic one-word responses; and pointing a finger to emphasize speech.

These individuals stand in comparison to Type B individuals, who give the impression of being relaxed and calm, are less competitive, are not overly reactive to time impediments, and rarely display hostility. Very strong empirical support has emerged for the suggestion that Type A behaviours are linked to an increased risk for coronary disease. Indeed, this set of behaviours has been identified as a risk factor for all forms of morbidity (Yakubovich, Ragland, Brand, & Syme, 1988). However, some inconsistencies in the findings have led to a search for the toxic core of Type A behaviours. This work initially identified the components of hostility and anger to be the crucial elements. Wright and colleagues (1988) expanded it to describe a multi-causal pathway that identifies Type A behaviour in combination with family history, lifestyle risks, and anger as being the core risk factors. Williams et al., (2000) report that individuals with high anger scale scores have a greatly elevated risk of heart attack in comparison to those with low scores. Also of interest is work summarized by Smith and Ruiz (2002) that identifies **social dominance** as a risk factor for coronary disease that is independent of hostility. Social dominance is described as "a set of controlling behaviours, including the tendency to cut off and talk over the interviewer" (p. 552).

Being able to identify the risk factors of coronary heart disease increases the likelihood of designing successful interventions that may be able to modify or eliminate the destructive behaviours (Straub, 2001). These could involve a variety of activities ranging from making philosophical decisions about one's lifestyle, training in relaxation techniques, to specific behavioural management programs. The latter are designed to help people learn to do things like retrain emotions such as hostility and anger, take control of their environment through techniques like time management, engage in problem solving, begin an exercise program, develop communication skills, and manage their diet. You might find it relevant at this point to read Peter's Story in chapter 8 of this book. Peter is an example of an individual who would have been described as a Type A individual prior to having a heart attack. After surviving this scare he became involved in a hospital-based behavioural retraining program and has made significant lifestyle changes that have resulted in remarkable improvements in his health.

It is interesting to note that programs designed to change maladaptive behaviours are not usually described in terms of coping but instead reflect the other side of the relationship. They are usually described as being programs in "stress management." This suggests that it is easier to sell the concept of *stress* than of *coping*. The term "stress management" permeates our culture to such an extent that it is hard to think of it being otherwise. We are taught to "manage" our stress rather than to cope. This sounds like an active, dynamic, even aggressive response to the situation by which we will overwhelm the stress. Coping, on the other hand, suggests a more passive, reflective stance. To say that you are going to a stress management workshop implies that you are still in control of your situation and are learning techniques to help you maintain your position. A workshop in coping suggests that things have deteriorated for you and you are seeking help.

COPING

This discussion of the Type A behaviour pattern and its modification provides a transition into a discussion of specific coping behaviours. Sarafino (1998) states that as individuals make the "effort to neutralize or reduce stress, coping activities are geared toward decreasing the person's appraisal of or concern for this discrepancy. Thus coping is the process by which people try to manage the perceived discrepancy between the demands and resources they appraise in a stressful situation" (p. 133). These efforts may not necessarily improve the person's situation. As Rice (1999) points out, it has not always been clear whether we are talking about the process or outcome of coping. He cites research by Rudolph, Dennig, and Weisz (1995) that identifies three components of coping. They distinguish between a **coping response** and a **stress response**. The former is an intentional physical or mental act that is initiated in response to a stressor. It can be directed toward either external events or internal states. The latter is defined as "any response that reflects a spontaneous emotional or behavioral reaction to stress, rather than a deliberate attempt to cope" (p. 329). The objective of a coping response, which is usually to reduce the impact of stress, is described as a **coping goal**. The specific or actual outcomes of a coping response are called **coping outcomes**.

Lazarus and his colleague suggest that coping can serve two functions (Lazarus & Folkman, 1984). One, **problem-focused coping**, is concerned with changing the situation by defining the problem, looking at alternative solutions, evaluating the implications of the alternatives, and choosing the best one to act on. It is a rational approach and in this way is similar to problem solving. However, it also includes solutions that are inward focused as well as those directed at the environment. In our daily existence we use problem-focused coping strategies frequently as we take action to reduce the demands placed upon us. Students who feel overwhelmed with assignments may seek out the professor to discuss how they can reduce the impact of their workload. As part of this process, they might focus on what material to study, using time management to plan their study time more efficiently and reorganizing their approach to prepare for the exams. Two types of problem-focused coping have been identified—proactive coping and combative coping (Aspinwall & Taylor, 1997). In proactive coping, potential stressors are anticipated and acted on in advance to either prevent or decrease their impact. In combative coping, an unavoidable stress is reacted to in a manner designed to help cope with the stress. For example, the relaxation technique described at the end of this chapter can be used as a combative coping skill to help deal with muscle tension.

Emotion-focused coping refers to controlling emotional responses to an event. This could consist of using cognitive processes such as avoidance or minimization to decrease emotional distress, or conversely using techniques to increase emotional intensity, as one might do in preparation for an athletic competition. Some forms of emotion-focused coping change nothing about the objective situation. They only change the manner in which an event is perceived and, as such, constitute reappraisal. One's emotional response to a situation can be regulated both through behavioural and cognitive strategies. Cognitive strategies change the way we think about a situation. There is a tendency to use emotion-focused coping when the individual believes there is nothing that can be done to change the stressful situation. It is indicated (Lazarus & Folkman, 1984) that problem-focused and emotion-focused coping strategies can be used at the same time and can either facilitate or impede one another in the coping process.

In their efforts to cope with stress, people call upon the **personal resources** available to them to help prevent the potential for stressful events and to help them cope with stressful situations as they occur. The first of these personal resource mechanisms is **social support**. We discuss social support on a number of occasions in this book. In times of stress we have all experienced the benefits of social support received from friends, family, and institutions such as social agencies, the health care system, and the church. As an example, it is reported that 80 percent of Americans believe prayer can have a positive impact on the course of an illness (Levin & Puchalski, 1997). We are also aware that we ourselves provide assistance to family and friends when they are stressed. That we can turn to others and they to us is an expectation of the human condition, and, as a first line of defence, it is a highly effective and widely used resource. Social support takes different forms. **Emotional support** refers to being cared for and loved; **informational support** is the advice and information made available to us concerning a particular event; and **tangible support** is the direct aid or services we receive to assist us in coping with stress. Each of these forms of support will be more relevant at different times in the coping process. However, it is clearly the *perception* of social support rather than the *objective situation* that is most important (Coyne, Aldwin & Lazarus, 1981).

Social support is believed to exert its effect on stress in one of two ways (Cohen & Wills, 1985). The **stress-buffering hypothesis** suggests that social support has an indirect effect and acts as a buffer to protect individuals from the negative effects of stress. This means that when people are exposed to stress, the social support they receive from others serves to buffer and therefore reduce the impact of the event. Social support acts between the event and the recipient or between the response to the stress and the outcome. This means that the effect of social support should be most noticeable at higher levels of stress and that it should have little impact on the effect of stress at lower levels. Alternatively, social support may have direct effects that are independent of stress and serve to enhance an individual's general sense of well-being and self-esteem. This, in turn, may increase one's sense of control, decrease anxiety, and increase health-promoting behaviours; all of which help to reduce stress.

Kaplan, Sallis, and Patterson (1993) suggest that more complex models will ultimately be required to explain the relationship between social support and the impact of stress. One possibility is a direct-effect model incorporating the functional effects of the social support system (which may affect health either positively or negatively). These researchers "would expect that close, caring relationships would play a stronger role in reinforcing health behavior and in enhancing use of the healthcare system. At the other extreme, social isolation might contribute to disconnection with services, poor nutrition, and inadequate responses to emergency" (p. 145). It is clear that lack of social support is a risk factor for disease. For example, social support is reported to be as important a risk factor for cardiovascular disease as is cigarette smoking, diet, and physical activity (Kaplan, Sallis, & Patterson, 1993).

Another factor that may influence a person's ability to cope with stress is his or her sense of **personal control**. The sense of being in control of a situation appears to reduce the impact of stressful events. As Bandura (1985) has indicated, one's sense of control over events can be achieved either behaviourally, by taking actions to reduce stress; or cognitively, by believing in one's ability to control the impact of stressful events. Bandura points out that it is important to distinguish between these two forms of control, as the relationship between actual and perceived coping efficacy is often not perfect. He states that "there are many competent people who are plagued by a sense of inefficacy, and many less competent ones who remain unperturbed by impending threats because they are self-assured of their coping capabilities" (p. 440).

Behavioural control has been demonstrated to greatly reduce the impact of stressful events. To have behavioural control over an event increases one's sense of predictability, which reduces stress. With regard to cognitive control, it has been demonstrated that individuals who believe they can effect control over stressful events will be less affected physiologically and behaviourally than those who believe they have no personal control over the situation.

The role of perceived behavioural and cognitive control over stressful events is of great importance to the emerging field of **positive psychology**, which encourages psychologists to use fewer negative or problem-focused frameworks and to focus more on effective human functioning (Sheldon & King, 2001). Fundamental to this new interest is the concept of **resilience** which Masten (2001) describes as "a class of phenomena characterized by good outcomes in spite of serious threats to adaptation or development" (p. 228). Research in this area attempts to understand better the process by which resilience is fostered. Masten argues that positive emotions can have a powerful undoing effect on negative emotions and that individuals should be encouraged to cultivate positive emotional experiences to help them cope with stress and adversity (Fredrickson, 2001). Lyubomirsky (2001) discusses cognitive and motivational strategies that have been demonstrated to increase happiness and reduce the impact of stress. These include developing positive perceptions of one's self, learning to derive positive meanings from negative experiences, using humour and faith, not engaging in self-rumination, and using social comparison selectively in a manner designed to protect one's sense of well-being.

Social support and personal control are resources that increase one's ability to cope with stress. However, at times such resources are unavailable or insufficient to cope with high levels of stress. At these times, it is often necessary to seek the assistance of techniques that have been specifically developed to help people cope with stress either directly or indirectly. It is important to recognize that these are techniques that are considered adaptive, compared to strategies such as alcohol or drug use that, although effective in the short-term, are not adaptive and ultimately increase stress. Although these are coping techniques, they are often labelled **stress management techniques**.

Some of the most widely used and effective interventions against stress are the various **relaxation techniques** that have been developed throughout history. These are strategies based on a very simple principle; that we can not be relaxed and tense at the same time. It is the antidote to the fight or flight response, which is under the control of the sympathetic nervous system, whereas the relaxation response is under the control of the parasympathetic nervous system. In a relaxed state, the heart slows, blood pressure drops, breathing is slow and easy, and muscle tension decreases. This response, described as **hypometabolic**, is the opposite of the **hypermetabolic** fight or flight response. These responses reciprocally inhibit one another. One of the implications of understanding this inhibitory process is that it may allow us to gain some control over the autonomic nervous system, which has long been considered an involuntary system; that is, outside of volitional control. Demonstrations of physiological control by highly trained yogis in India provided early support for this possibility. A series of studies carried out by Western scientists on some of these individuals further expanded our understanding of physiological control.

East and West: Now the Twain Shall Meet

Since the mid-1960s, Western society has shown an increased interest in Eastern philosophies and meditative disciplines. This enthusiasm, shared by many, has largely focused on techniques designed to promote psychological and physical well-being; it therefore forms an important component of the stress and coping literature. Many researchers have been intrigued by accounts of powers of control often difficult for us to comprehend (Brunton, 1972; Murray, 1980; Yogananda, 1946). In the "Yoga-sutras" of Patanjali, written in the fourth or fifth century AD (Woods, 1966), a lengthy discussion is given on how one can attain "supernatural powers." In his translation of these writings, Woods states that "these supernatural powers are to be accomplished by constraints. And constraint is the combination of fixed-attention and of contemplation and of concentration" (p. 205). Brunton, in a book first published in 1934, describes his travels to discover a "secret" India. He speaks of a culture described under the generic term of *Yoga* that "proffers benefits to mankind as valuable in their own way as any proffered by the Western sciences. It can bring our bodies nearer the healthy condition which nature intended them to possess; it can bestow one of modern civilization's most urgent needs—a flawless serenity of mind" (p. 6).

Naranjo (1971) describes how our concern for personal development has caused us to "turn a respectful gaze to the wisdom of the remote past and to the wisdom of the East that we once thought obsolete and superceded" (p. 3). The philosopher Harvey Cox suggests that the "mystics and contemplatives have served as the guardians of that uniquely human realm called interiority" (1973, p. 93). He believes that our renewed interest in this realm represents a survival instinct intended to turn our attention from without to within.

Our fascination with these traditions is significant, as it has caused us to question our understanding of the mind–body interaction. Our ability to control physiological processes was challenged by reports of individuals who made claims such as being able to control or even stop their heart, to survive lengthy pit burials, to regulate their body temperature, or to permit penetration of the skin without bleeding. It is quite reasonable to suggest that it was these early investigations that provided the foundation for many of the stress-management techniques we practise today. Techniques such as biofeedback and many of the secular relaxation strategies we use today are firmly rooted in the belief that we can regain control of physiological variables previously thought to be outside our control.

Therese Brousse was a pioneer in this field. In 1935 she took a crude, portable electrocardiograph to India to record attempts by yogis to achieve voluntary control of cardiovascular activity. One of her published records indicates that for one individual heart potentials and pulse waves, recorded from the radial artery, decreased almost to zero and remained there for several seconds. Over 20 years later, Wenger, Bagchi, and Anand (1961) returned to India with more sophisticated equipment to record cardiovascular activity in four individuals (including one who had previously been investigated by Brousse) claiming to be able to slow or stop their heart.

It was clear from the investigators' results that these individuals did not directly control the functioning of their heart; rather, evidence suggested that they used striate muscle control to produce changes in circulatory patterns. These yogis used a technique called the Valsalva manoeuvre, which involves an increase in muscle tension in the abdominal and thoracic muscles, closure of the glottis, and development of intrathoracic pressure. The effect is to interfere with venous return to the heart, so that heart sounds are diminished and masked by muscular sounds, and the radial pulse seems to disappear. The increased sophistication of the equipment in the study by Wenger and colleagues indicated that normal cardiac activity continued to occur. The results Brousse had reported were an artifact of the crude recording techniques she used and did not take into account the impact of the Valsalva manoeuvre. It is interesting to note that although these individuals did not stop their hearts, they did demonstrate a remarkable level of muscular control.

Anand and Chhina (1961) carried out a similar investigation with three yogis who claimed to be able to stop their hearts. Rather than supporting their claim, the electrocardiogram (EKG) indicated that their heart rate actually increased while the yogis held their breath. This finding is supported by accounts of research done on Swami Rama at the Menninger Foundation (Luce & Peper, 1971). Physiological recordings indicated that when Swami Rama "stopped" his heart, his heart rate actually increased to approximately 300 beats a minute over a period of 17 seconds. This sudden atrial fibrillation, a dangerous cardiac condition that prevents the necessary volume of blood from being pumped to the body, would normally render a person unconscious and, if continued, would soon lead to death. Apparently the Swami was intrigued by this result, as he indicated that when he did this he experienced a "fluttering" in his chest. It is also reported that he was able to produce a temperature difference of 10 degrees between two spots on his hand.

An interesting extension of this work was done by Anand, Chhina, and Singh (1961a) who conducted experiments on Sri Ramanand Yogi while he was sealed in an air-tight box for two periods of eight and ten hours. The data indicated that he was able to reduce his oxygen intake and carbon dioxide output beyond his requirements under basal conditions. Even when breathing air with decreased oxygen and increased carbon dioxide content, his heart rate did not increase, nor did his respiratory activity increase or deepen. The electroencephalograph (EEG) indicated brain waves suggestive of early stages of sleep, despite there being no evidence that he actually slept.

EEG measures can also be used to assess the ability to maintain attention without being distracted. Anand, Chhina, and Singh (1961b) used EEG to test the assertion that during meditation highly trained yogis are oblivious to external stimulation. They examined four such individuals and found that they were indeed able to achieve this state. The yogis did not demonstrate the expected blocking of the EEG alpha waves in response to stimulation during meditation. Two of the subjects kept their hands immersed in cold water for 45 to 55 minutes with no apparent discomfort. During this experience, they displayed persistent EEG alpha wave activity, which is associated with a state of wakeful relaxation. Swami Rama, while at the Menninger Foundation, experimented with EEG recordings and is reported to have produced alpha and theta waves with ease. The latter are slow waves associated with sleep states. He is also said to have entered a state he called "yogi sleep", which appeared, on the basis of the EEG, to be much like deep sleep, and yet was able to repeat, almost verbatim, statements made to him during this state upon awakening 25 minutes later. Luce and Peper (1971), commenting on these findings, stated that "our idea of a 'normal' EEG is based upon the particular, limited, habitual use that a person makes of his brain. Swami Rama's agile and controlled transitions from one state of consciousness to another would, no doubt, be considered abnormal" (p. 43).

It is this final point that is important. As indicated earlier, this research raised questions about what our physiological and psychological limitations really are. When we think of stress and coping, we often think of physiological and psychological processes that are out of our control. It is our opinion that research such as that just described has considerable significance as it resulted in the development, over a very short period of time, of highly effective techniques oriented more to the Western mind and lifestyle. The impact of these techniques on our ability to regain control of our lives and effectively cope with stress has been profound.

Relaxation

There are many different relaxation techniques. The most popular of these is **progressive muscular relaxation (PMR)**. It originated in the 1930s with Edmond Jacobson, who spent the next 50 years of his life developing the technique. The literature abounds with the many variations on Jacobson's original relaxation strategies, with the most widely cited being that of Bernstein and Borkovec (1978) (we provide you with the opportunity to practise this technique through instructions provided at the end of this chapter). Another method, autogenic training, is an imagery-based relaxation technique developed in Europe by Schutz and Luthe (1959). As a result of his interest in transcendental meditation, Herbert Benson developed a secular form of meditation, which he described as being based on achieving the "relaxation response" (1975). Although there are many different relaxation techniques, they share many similar features. To a large extent they require a quiet, undisturbed setting, where one can sit passively, usually with eyes closed, and allow the muscles to completely relax. It is of major importance that patterns of deep, rhythmical breathing be observed, although variations on breathing are often used.

Meditation has been used throughout history to reduce stress. There are literally thousands of different forms of meditation practised throughout the world. Again, they usually share common features such as positioning and attention to the *process* of thought rather than its *outcome*. There are differences in approach, particularly as many of these forms of meditation are based on religious belief systems. A system that has greatly influenced Western culture is **transcendental meditation (TM)** a technique of meditation introduced by Maharishi Mahesh Yogi in the late 1950s. He adapted a system of meditation developed initially for monastic practice to a Western lifestyle. An international organization supports those involved in the technique, and provides follow-up courses and training. A very important aspect of TM is the extensive body of empirical research that has accumulated regarding the efficacy of the meditative practice. Although there are concerns about some of the research methodology, a consistent picture emerges indicating that the practice of TM has a beneficial physiological and psychological impact on an individual, and that its benefits accrue with time (Dillbeck & Orme-Johnson, 1987; Alexander et al., 1994). Techniques such as this have important implications for stress and coping.

Biofeedback is another technique that has received significant attention with regard to the possibility of modifying physiological processes. It involves recording physiological measures with electronic instruments that provide immediate information or feedback concerning the subject's physiological state. The implication is that, since it has been shown that we can exercise conscious control over aspects of our physiology, this feedback would allow us to make beneficial alterations where necessary. The enthusiasm for this procedure came from several areas. One was the interest in the control of autonomic activity observed in India. Another was the study of the control of cortical activity among practitioners of Zen in Japan (Hirai, 1974; Kasamatsu & Hirai, 1963; 1966). Many of these individuals displayed the ability to control their EEG readings, which were considered to reflect various states of consciousness. It was hoped that biofeedback could be used to manipulate these states, particularly as they relate to the experience of relaxation and perhaps "higher" states of consciousness. This thinking encouraged the research of individuals such as Kamiya (1968; 1969), who suggested that this was indeed possible. Another line of research began with Miller and DiCara who reported that laboratory animals were able to achieve control of their autonomic responses, specifically cardiovascular activity, through reinforcement by way of feedback (Miller, 1969; Miller & DiCara, 1967).

These findings led to the extensive development of biofeedback technology aimed at controlling physiological variables such as muscle tension, heart rate, blood pressure, brain wave activity, and skin temperature. For example, electromyography (EMG) has been widely used to record and modify muscle tension in specific muscle groups in the body. Temperature control of blood flow has been examined in the context of migraine headaches and Raynaud's disease (Blanchard & Haynes, 1975; Green, Green, & Walters, 1972). The initial enthusiasm for biofeedback was considerable, however this enthusiasm has since been tempered by realistic evaluations of its efficacy. It appears that many of the effects attributed to biofeedback have more to do with the general state of relaxation, or the relaxation response, experienced during the procedure than the specific feedback provided (Straub, 2001). This development has been disappointing, particularly given the promise the technique held for teaching people to regain control of their physical and psychological state and thereby effect important changes in their lifestyle.

Behaviour Therapy and Cognitive Therapy

In the fields of behaviour therapy and cognitive therapy, a wide array of strategies have been developed that have direct relevance for coping with stress. For example, Wolpe (1958) developed the technique of **systematic desensitization** to help people cope with fear and anxiety. It is based on the principle of reciprocal inhibition between the sympathetic and parasympathetic nervous systems and recognizes that anxiety and relaxation are incompatible responses. The client is initially trained in a relaxation technique, and then asked to construct an anxiety hierarchy of events that elicit increasing levels of anxiety. The client is then asked by the therapist to imagine or visualize these events from the least to the most anxiety-arousing. The technique assumes that imagining the feared event results in significant anxiety. Our ability to create high levels of stress as a function of our thinking is a fundamental principle underlying our discussions in this chapter. Through cognitive exposure to the feared situation we enter into the process of *desensitization*. At the point at which the anxiety attached to imagining a particular event becomes unpleasant, the client is encouraged to use relaxation to decrease arousal. The process of pairing these two inhibiting responses can lead to a significant reduction in the stress associated with the situation, whether it be undergoing a medical procedure such as an MRI or an injection, flying on an airplane, giving a public talk, or writing an exam. It is clear that a crucial component of this process is the repeated exposure to the feared situation, which ultimately leads to fear reduction (Newman et al., 1994).

Modelling is another procedure that can be used effectively to reduce stress associated with fear-provoking situations. Bandura (1985, 1997), who has described this process in detail, points out that most human behaviour is learned through the observation of models. We acquire cognitive skills and new behaviours through observing others. The influence of a model can serve to instruct, inhibit, disinhibit, facilitate, enhance environmental effects, and arouse emotions. Individuals can learn to cope with stressful situations by observing models. The process is very similar to that of desensitization in that observing a model coping well with an anxiety-provoking situation reduces the fear of that situation.

In **participant modelling**, the individual observes a model coping with the anxiety-evoking situation. The individual is then encouraged to imitate the model and engage in the behaviour while receiving reassurance from the model (Ritter, 1968). The model may also be presented symbolically through videos or films. This procedure has been used very effectively by Melamud and her colleagues to help reduce children's anxieties about hospitalization and medical procedures (Melamud & Siegal, 1975). It has also been used with adults to prepare them for the stress of aversive medical procedures. Bandura argues that modelling is an effective intervention because it increases the individual's sense of self-efficacy (1995).

In **cognitive restructuring**, maladaptive, stress-producing cognitions are identified and replaced with ones that are more appropriate. The most well-known approach to cognitive restructuring is based on the work of Ellis, who developed *rational emotive behaviour therapy* (REBT) (Ellis, 1962, 1977). Ellis believes that it is our beliefs about events, not the events themselves, that create stressful emotional reactions. The sequence proceeds in the following manner—an event occurs, it is interpreted irrationally, and negative emotions and inappropriate behaviours occur. Ellis has identified specific logical errors that form the basis of this irrational thinking, such as over-generalization, catastrophizing, and absolute thinking. To reduce the stress of the experience, it is necessary to identify the thoughts that are based on irrational beliefs, challenge the irrational beliefs, and replace them with thoughts based on rational beliefs. Rational emotive behaviour therapy has been used effectively in managing stress-related emotional states such as anxiety, anger, fears, and depression; as well as in dealing with behavioural concerns such as Type A behaviour and obesity.

The work of Beck is similar to that of Ellis in its emphasis on helping people to modify distorted cognitions (Beck, 1963, 1976). Beck describes his approach as *cognitive therapy*. Although it was initially developed to treat depression, cognitive therapy has now been applied to a wide variety of psychological problems. It differs from REBT in encouraging people to identify their dysfunctional beliefs and then to put these beliefs through a process of hypothesis testing, or what Beck calls "collective empiricism," to test their validity.

The final behavioural technique we will consider here is based on the work of Meichenbaum and is appropriately called **stress inoculation training** (Meichenbaum, 1977, 1985). This is a package of procedures designed to help people cope effectively with stressful events. Initially, individuals are asked to examine how they conceptualize stressful events and are taught that they can be reconceptualized in less stressful ways. They are encouraged to view coping as a process in which they can prepare for, confront, and cope with stressful events. In the second phase, they learn and rehearse coping strategies such as relaxation training, problem solving, and self-reinforcement. In the third phase, this reconceptualized approach, both cognitive and behavioural, is applied to relevant situations. This can be done initially through imagery and role-playing and then applied gradually to situations eliciting increasingly higher levels of stress. Like so many cognitive and behavioural strategies, stress inoculation training has been applied with success to a wide variety of problems within the health psychology realm.

BOX 2-1	Medical Crisis

Crisis is described as a situation in which an individual perceives a stressor as being insurmountable. When crises occur, we often find ourselves totally unprepared to deal with the threat and loss of control such events imply. The manner in which a crisis is precipitated (e.g., timing and nature of the event) is considered to be important in determining how stressful it will be (DiTomasso & Kovnat, 1994, p. 329). Various cognitive factors will also determine how stressful a crisis will be; these include unrealistic beliefs and assumptions, cognitive distortions, biased recall and perception, self-efficacy, lack of information, and the cognitive triad identified by Beck, which includes a negative view of self, world, and future (p. 330). The behavioural factors that will influence the stress of the crisis are a lack of coping strategies, negative coping, lack of social support, and the inability to access support (p. 331).

In response to a crisis, DiTomasso and Kovnat describe a number of cognitive–behavioural interventions that can be used to help a patient cope. They include forming a working relationship with the patient, identifying the disturbing aspects of the crisis, emphasizing the patient's strengths, setting mutually acceptable goals, identifying dysfunctional cognitions, emphasizing realistic thinking, using graduated task assignment, using behavioural rehearsal, inoculating the patient against negative factors, setting homework assignments, and providing reinforcement (p. 332). As DiTomasso and Kovnat point out, medical training has historically focused on the physical components of crisis; as a result, physicians are not prepared to deal with the psychosocial concerns of their patients. It is only recently that we have become concerned with the implications of the severe stress experienced by individuals in such crisis situations. The cognitive and behavioural interventions described in this chapter are clearly important in the coping process.

As we bring this chapter to a close, we thought that after speaking so much about stress and coping, we should give you the opportunity to experience the benefits of relaxation for yourself. So, read on.

The Relaxation Responses: A Personal Guide

You can have someone else read the procedure to you, you can make a tape of it, or you can commit it to memory and take yourself through it. We'll provide you with a general overview and the specifics of the technique. It's based on the original procedure developed by Jacobson in the 1930s and subsequently modified by Bernstein and Borkovec (1973) and Bernstein and Given (1984). The basic principle of the procedure is learning to identify the sensations associated with muscular tension and relaxation through tensing and then relaxing different muscle groups in the body. It's important to realize that learning relaxation skills is like learning any other skill—no one else can do it for you, it's not a matter of desire, it's a skill that needs to be learned. This means learning the technique and practising it.

You will be asked to tense a specific muscle group initially to become aware of what muscle tension feels like and to be able to compare it to the experience of relaxation. As well, if the muscle group is tensed prior to relaxation a greater reduction in muscle tension will occur upon relaxation.

Rest in a comfortable position such as in a recliner or lying down with support for your head and spine. Do not cross your legs or arms, and try to minimize body movements. Close your eyes so as to be less aware of your external surroundings and loosen any tight items of clothing. During the relaxation session, breathe slowly and regularly. Tense each muscle group for 5 to 7 seconds and relax it on cue for 30 to 40 seconds. If you have a tape of the procedure or someone is guiding you through it, a cue word such as "tense" can be used to signal the beginning of the tension phase and "relax" to signal the relaxation phase.

The tension phase need not be extreme and should not involve any pain to the muscle. If you feel pain or cramping, shorten the period of tension. You only need to tighten the muscles, not strain them. At the beginning of the relaxation phase, you should focus your attention on the sensations attached to the reduction in tension and the increase in relaxation in the muscles.

It's usual to relax each muscle group twice, although it's not inappropriate to continue the tension/relaxation sequence in a particular muscle group several times until a desired depth of relaxation is obtained. There are many variations on the sequence and methods used; the following is one example. As you practise and develop your relaxation skills, it's important to remember that you do not need to try to relax, you just let it happen. Increased effort is not the key to success; rather, you need to take a passive stance, let go, and enjoy the experience.

1. Dominant hand and forearm: make your hand into a tight fist, then relax.

2. Non-dominant hand and forearm; make your hand into a tight fist, then relax.

3. Dominant upper arm: bend your arm at the elbow and bring your hand toward your shoulder, then relax.

4. Non-dominant upper arm: bend your arm at the elbow and bring your hand toward your shoulder, then relax.

5. Forehead: raise your eyebrows and wrinkle your forehead, then relax.

6. Eyes: close your eyes tighter, then relax.

7. Lower face and jaws: clench your teeth and tighten the corners of your mouth, then relax.

8. Shoulders: raise your shoulders as if to touch your ears, then relax.

9. Chest: take a deep breath and hold it, then relax.

10. Abdomen: tighten the stomach muscles, then relax.

11. Legs one: point your toes downward, away from your body, then relax.

12. Legs two: bring your toes upward, toward your body, then relax.

13. Scan your body for residual tension: if tension is experienced in a muscle group, repeat the tension/relaxation sequence for that muscle group.

14. Take some time to enjoy the feelings of relaxation in your body.

15. You can end the session by counting backwards from five to one, becoming more alert as you count down. When you get to one, open your eyes.

The procedure will take approximately 30 minutes. You should practise the technique regularly for optimal effectiveness; twice a day would be ideal. When you begin to learn a relaxation procedure, it's best to do so in a setting that is quiet and comfortable, where distractions are minimal, and in which you are not likely to be disturbed. This may require some preparation on your part, but it will make it easier to focus your attention on learning the technique. As you become more skilled at relaxation, you'll want to generalize the learning experience to those places in your life where relaxation is most needed (e.g., your workplace, a performance activity, social situations). As you become more familiar with the relaxation experience, as indicated by greater levels of relaxation both during and outside the relaxation sessions, you can cut out the tension phase of the sequence and focus only on the relaxation of the muscle. Increased familiarity with the sensations of relaxation will make it unnecessary for you to have the feeling of tension to compare them to.

With time, you'll be able to combine muscle groups in obvious ways. For example, the four-group procedure involves the following groups: 1) hands and arms; 2) head; 3) chest, shoulders, and abdomen; and 4) legs. Combining muscle groups will reduce the time of the procedure to under 10 minutes. Eventually, you should be able to achieve a relaxed state simply by recalling the sensations of the relaxed muscle groups together with deep breathing and a cue word such as "relax" or "let go." Ultimately, you should be able to achieve this relaxed state simply through a countdown in combination with deep breathing. When you have arrived at this level, you will have achieved the desired skill level. You should continue to practise and use this skill. It is a powerful resource for coping with stress.

KEY TERMS

adrenal cortex (p. 37)

adrenal medulla (p. 36)

alarm (p. 37)

beliefs as person variables (p. 40)

benign-positive appraisal (p. 39)

biofeedback (p. 48)

central nervous system (p. 35)

challenge appraisal (p. 39)

cognitive appraisals (p. 39)

cognitive restructuring (p. 50)

cognitive transactional models (p. 38)

commitments as person variables (p. 40)

coping (p. 31)

coping goal (p. 43)

coping outcomes (p. 43)

coping response (p. 43)

diseases of adaptation (p. 38)

duration (p. 41)

emotion-focused coping (p. 43)

emotional support (p. 44)

endocrine system (p. 35)

event uncertainty (p. 41)

eustress (p. 33)

exhaustion (p. 38)

fight-or-flight response (p. 34)

general adaptation syndrome (GAS) (p. 37)

harm/loss appraisal (p. 39)

homeostasis (p. 34)

hypermetabolic (p. 45)

hypometabolic state (p. 45)

hypothalamus (p. 36)

imminence (p. 41)

informational support (p. 44)

irrelevant appraisal (p. 39)

limbic system (p. 36)

meditation (p. 48)

modelling (p. 49)

nervous system (p. 35)

novelty (p. 40)

pancreas (p. 37)

parasympathetic (p. 37)

participant modelling (p. 50)

peripheral nervous system (p. 35)

person variables (p. 40)

personal control (p. 44)

personal resources (p. 44)

pituitary gland (p. 37)

positive psychology (p. 45)

predictability (p. 40)

primary appraisal (p. 39)

problem-focused coping (p. 43)

progressive muscular
   relaxation (PMR) (p. 48)
reappraisal (p. 39)
relaxation techniques
   (p. 45)
resilience (p. 45)
resistance (p. 38)
reticular formation (p. 36)
secondary appraisal (p. 39)
situation variables (p. 40)
social dominance (p. 42)
social support (p. 44)

stress (p. 31)
stress-buffering
   hypothesis (p. 44)
stress-diathesis model
   (p. 38)
stress inoculation training
   (p. 50)
stress literacy (p. 32)
stress management
   techniques (p. 45)
stress response (p. 43)
stressful appraisal (p. 39)

sympathetic (p. 37)
systematic desensitization
   (p. 49)
tangible support (p. 44)
temporal uncertainty (p. 41)
threat appraisal (p. 39)
thyroid gland (p. 37)
transcendental meditation
   (TM) (p. 48)
Type A behaviour pattern
   (p. 41)
vulnerability (p. 40)

chapter three

Psychoneuroimmunology

CHAPTER OUTLINE

The Importance of Psychoneuroimmunology to Health Psychology

An Introduction to the Immune System

How Immune-System Function Is Measured in Psychoneuroimmunological Research
Counting Cells to Measure Immunocompetence
Functional Tests of Immunocompetence: Measuring Cells in Action
Methodological Issues in the Measurement of Immune-System Function

Research in Psychoneuroimmunology: Providing Evidence for a Biological Link between Psychology and Health
The Effect of Stress on Immune Functioning
The Effect of Mood on Immune Functioning
Personality and Cancer
Social Support and Immune Functioning

Proposed Biological Mechanisms to Explain Why Psychological States Affect the Immune System

Future Directions for Psychoneuroimmunological Research

KEY QUESTIONS

1. What is the relationship between our psychological states and our health?

2. Why is the study of psychoneuroimmunology so important to the work of health psychologists?

3. How does the immune system work to fend off infection?

4. How can researchers assess the effectiveness of someone's immune system?

5. What proof is there that the immune system is affected by psychological states and life circumstances?

6. What are the biological mechanisms linking these psychological states to our immune system?

Lori's last exam was scheduled for December 11. She was flying home the next day. Lori was really looking forward to being home for a while, but she expected she would spend the first few days with a bad cold or maybe the flu. Lori was a third-year student who was experienced with final exams and flying home, but didn't know why she got sick every year after final exams.

Was there something about being home that made Lori sick? That didn't seem likely. She got along well with her family and loved her parents' cooking. Maybe it was the airplane. She had heard about "bad air" on planes. But Lori played university volleyball and flew with the team all the time without ever getting sick.

Could it be the exams? That seemed more likely, since Lori often got sick right after April finals too, and she didn't fly home until mid-May. Lori finally concluded that writing exams somehow affected her immune system.

Lori is not alone. Many university students get sick either during or just after exams. Indeed, research has shown that immune system functioning suffers during exam time (e.g., Glaser et al., 1993). Glaser and colleagues measured immune-system functioning in medical students one month before an exam period and then again on the last day of that exam period. They found significant declines in a number of indicators of **immunocompetence**—the extent to which our immune system is functioning properly to ward off microorganisms that invade our bodies. More recently, researchers have found that self-hypnosis and massage therapy can actually reduce these exam-related effects on the immune system by reducing stress (Gruzelier et al., 2001; Kiecolt-Glaser et al., 2001; Zeitlin et al., 2000).

This sort of research raises a number of important questions for students of health psychology. How is immunocompetence assessed in studies like this? What biological mechanisms link a psychological state such as stress to immune-system functioning? How strong is this link? These are some of the key questions addressed by **psychoneuroimmunology (PNI)**, which is the study of the relationship between psychological states and the functioning of the immune system.

The term *psychoneuroimmunology* is best understood by dividing it into its three component parts. Our psychology (*psycho*) affects nervous-system functioning (*neuro*) which, in turn, affects our immunity to disease (*immunology*). In this chapter, we will study the immune system and learn how research has discovered a link between this system and a number of psychological states. We begin with an explanation of why PNI is so important to the discipline of health psychology.

THE IMPORTANCE OF PSYCHONEUROIMMUNOLOGY TO HEALTH PSYCHOLOGY

In chapter 1, we traced the development of health psychology from its roots. Many of the people participating in this early development cautioned that, while health psychology held considerable promise, it would be essential to avoid extravagant and unsubstantiated claims regarding what was known and what could be achieved in terms of improving health through psychological interventions. One very important piece of the puzzle missing in those days was empirical proof that psychological states were directly linked to biological processes. Psychoneuroimmunology has uncovered that piece.

Not only does PNI research provide much needed information linking psychology and health, it also provides data in a form that makes sense to people whose training is biomedical in nature. As such, PNI research represents an invaluable bridge between social scientists and health care providers, and increases the credibility of health psychology in the eyes of health care providers.

When David Spiegel and colleagues discovered that women attending breast cancer support groups had average survival rates that were almost twice those of women who were not randomly assigned to such groups, people in the medical community took notice (Spiegel, Bloom, Kraemer, & Gottheil, 1989). The next step was to identify a biological mechanism that would explain this link between social support and survival; this is the ongoing job of PNI research. This interdisciplinary research features teams consisting of people with a knowledge of the biology of immune functioning and others with an understanding of psychosocial factors.

AN INTRODUCTION TO THE IMMUNE SYSTEM

The immune system is designed to monitor the invasion of microorganisms in the body and prevent their spread and growth by eliminating them. **Microorganisms** come in many different forms. In terms of the immune system, the relevant forms include bacteria, viruses, parasites, and fungi. These invading microbes are called **antigens**. The term *antigen* is generally used to refer to any microorganism that is foreign to our physiology. If these antigens have the potential to cause disease, they are called **pathogens**.

The immune system is our guard against infection and the growth of cells associated with disease. Infection, if confined to a defined site, is called **localized infection**. If it remains in one area but sends toxins to other parts of the body, it is called a **focal infection**. If it spreads to affect a number of areas of the body at once, it is called a **systemic infection**. The immune system's first line of defence is the skin and mucous. Most antigens are stopped here. This is why people who suffer serious burns are at risk for fatal infection. The skin's ability to prevent the invasion of large numbers of dangerous pathogens is compromised, and the internal components of the immune system aren't able to deal with such a massive invasion. These internal components of the immune system work by producing cells that are designed to attack antigens and eliminate infected cells.

In this section, we will provide a basic introduction to these immune-system cells in order to help you make sense of psychoneuroimmunology research that assesses the number and efficacy of these cells.

When our immune system detects an antigen, it acts in one or more ways to eliminate it. This action can be specific or non-specific in nature. As the terms imply, **specific immunity** refers to protection against a particular antigen. This immunity is acquired some time after birth and is the result of prior exposure to the antigen, either by having contracted the disease or by having received an inoculation giving the body a non-toxic dose of the antigen. This is called **acquired immunity**.

Specific immune function is the result of acquired immunity. There are three hallmarks of this functioning—memory, specificity, and tolerance (Seymour, Savage, & Walsh, 1995). **Immune-system memory** refers to the ability of certain immune system cells to adapt to an antigen and to "remember" the antigen when it encounters it again and work to eliminate it. Not only will it recognize the antigen, it will also react much more explosively upon this subsequent exposure to it. If you have had chicken pox, you probably won't get the disease again. This is because your immune system has a *memory* for the virus causing chicken pox. It is for this same reason that we are more susceptible to certain diseases when we travel to exotic destinations. We increase our chances of encountering a pathogen (in the drinking water, for example) for which we have no memory. By contrast, the water doesn't bother the locals, because they have cells (B lymphocytes) that have a memory for the pathogen, and they produce the antibody to deal with it before it causes any trouble. **B lymphocytes** produce antibodies that attack antigens. It is these B lymphocytes that produce antigen-specific antibodies for specific, acquired immunity. Antitetanus antibody is an example. A particular kind of B lymphocytes, called **memory B cells**, develop a memory for a specific antigen after being exposed to it and act only on that antigen by producing antibodies and immunoglobulins. The production of these antibodies is sometimes called **seroconversion**.

An important point to realize is that the process involved in this form of immunity takes time. In fact, it takes B lymphocytes five or more days to generate specific antibodies (Maier, Watkins, & Fleshner, 1994). Fortunately, in most cases the immune system generates antibodies faster than the antigen can multiply. You may wonder why the body doesn't just keep an ample supply of these specific antibodies on hand for immediate response to the antigen. The answer is that there are many millions of different antigens and the body can't keep a plentiful stock of the antibody required for each. Instead, it keeps a small stock of each and relies on the B lymphocytes to generate an ample number when called upon to do so, which is what takes the time. Fortunately, memory B lymphocytes allow this process to occur more quickly if we are re-exposed to the antigen. This is how the inoculations we receive before travelling work. They present the body with small dosages of a given pathogen so that we can produce antibodies and develop a memory for the pathogen. That way, if we do encounter the pathogen when travelling, our immune systems can produce cells quickly and deal with it while we lie on the beach.

Specificity means that not only will the B lymphocyte remember this antigen, it will respond to this antigen *only*. Having chicken pox does not make you immune to the mumps. **Tolerance** means that these cells will not react to the body's own cells—what is called "the self," in the language of immunity. Instead, immune cells react only to antigens, which are recognized as "non-self."

Non-specific immunity differs from specific immunity in that it relies on a system we are born with. It works in a number of different ways. In one process, the immune system creates chemicals (called **antimicrobial substances**) that kill antigens. One result of this process that can be seen by the naked eye is inflammation. An infected cut will usually become inflamed because fluids carrying white blood cells enter the area, making it red as the fluids build up. In other words, inflammation is an indication that an immune system is working.

However, B lymphocytes need help to produce antibodies. This help comes from T lymphocytes called **helper T cells**. These helper cells produce substances called **interleukins**, referred to generally as *cytokines*, that speed the division of B lymphocyte cells. When you read PNI research, you will often encounter references to things like interleukin-1 or interleukin-2. Interleukin production is a measure of immunocompetence. These helper T cells are also referred to in the literature as CD4. Interleukin-6, for example, is called a *proinflammatory*, because it aids in immune responses that result in inflammation. Our immune system also needs an "off switch" so that antibodies aren't produced unnecessarily after the antigen has been destroyed. This is the job of **suppressor T cells** (sometimes referred to as CD8). B cells and T cells work together to maintain immunity.

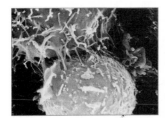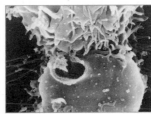

A t-cell in action. In the first photo, the t-cell makes contact with the antigen. In the second, it creates holes in the antigen by hitting it with protein. In the third, little is left of the antigen.

Lymphocytes, then, are important components of the immune system. They include B cells, T cells, and **natural-killer (NK) cells**. Natural-killer cells have the specific job of "seeking and destroying" cells that are infected, cancerous, or altered in some other way. The rapid and efficient production of lymphocytes is essential to immunocompetence—the effective functioning of the immune system.

HOW IMMUNE-SYSTEM FUNCTION IS MEASURED IN PSYCHONEUROIMMUNOLOGICAL RESEARCH

One of our main objectives in presenting this section on measuring immune-system function is to help you develop a familiarity with the language used in PNI research, without which the research can be very confusing to read. With this objective in mind, we will focus on the *language* of PNI research as well as the *processes* involved in assessing immune-system function. The *dependent variable* in an experiment is the variable we are measuring to determine if our treatment or manipulation has had any effect. In PNI research, dependent variables take the form of measures of immunocompetence. The manipulation, or *independent variable*, is usually some psychological state. This can be naturally occurring, as was the case with the stress caused by Lori's exams in our opening example, or it can be experimentally induced by putting people through stressful experiences or presenting them with stimuli aimed at eliciting positive moods such as happiness.

We know that immune-system function involves the production and activity of specific cells. It stands to reason, then, that we should measure immunocompetence by somehow counting the number of these cells and by subjecting them to antigens to see how well they work. This is, indeed, the basic approach to measuring immunocompetence in PNI research. It sounds simple, but, for several reasons, it is actually quite complex. First, there are a number of places throughout the body where immune-system cells are located, such as the tonsils, appendix, small intestines, spleen, and bone marrow. This makes it difficult to just go to the source and measure activity. Instead, we must assess cellular activity in the bloodstream or mucous. Second, there are a variety of forms this cellular activity can take, and these operate independently of each other. So it is possible that a psychological state might influence one aspect of immune functioning and not another. This means that researchers must assess a number of immune-system cellular functions to ascertain the potential impact of a situation or mood state. It also means that two studies assessing the impact of the same psychological variable, such as exam stress, might come to different conclusions depending on which aspect of immune functioning is being assessed—that which fights off colds or that which kills tumour cells, for example.

Counting Cells to Measure Immunocompetence

You have learned that immune-system function is dependent upon the system's ability to produce, or *proliferate*, cells to do its work. We have also said that one simple way of measuring immunocompetence is to count these cells (typically white blood cells) as they exist in the bloodstream. This cell counting is called an **enumerative assay** and is common in PNI research. In studies using cell counts, you will see lymphocyte measures taken from blood samples, counting such white blood cells as NK, T, and B cells. Researchers look for two things in these counts—a minimum number of cells for adequate immune function; and a balance between various cell types, such as different types of T cells (Herbert & Cohen, 1993).

In general, the better the immune system functions, the higher these counts are. Studies using cell counts will often report lower cell counts in blood samples taken from groups of individuals who have been exposed to a stressor, such as an exam.

Functional Tests of Immunocompetence: Measuring Cells in Action

Counting cells can be informative, but it is even more important to try to assess the immune system *at work*. This is what **functional tests of immunity** do (Cohen & Herbert, 1996). We can perform these functional tests inside the body, though this can be difficult because it is hard to localize the sites of the immune system. However, we can also measure cell functions by *removing* them from the body and incubating them with other cells to see how the immune-system cells respond. Functional tests performed on cells outside the body are called *in vitro* tests. Those performed inside the body are called *in vivo* tests.

In vitro tests of immunocompetence start with a blood sample that is combined with a substance called a **mitogen**. A mitogen is a substance that stimulates immune-cell activity as though the immune cell were acting against an invading cell, or antigen. Three of the most common mitogens used in PNI research are concanavalin A (Con A), phytohemagglutinin (PHA), and pokeweed mitogen (PWM).

A PNI study might say "People whose interactions with others were less confrontational showed greater lymphocyte proliferation in response to PHA." Translated, this means that blood samples taken from people who differed in the amount of confrontation they experienced in their interactions with others were incubated with PHA. From this, it was discovered that the blood of people whose interactions were less confrontational produced more lymphocytes when put with PHA. Other studies using this general design might substitute Con A or PWM as the mitogen, or they might run a number of tests (or *assays* as they are sometimes called) using two or more different mitogens. In these studies, you will see data reported separately for each mitogen.

Natural-killer cell activity is also measured through *in vitro* techniques. Because NK cells perform a "seek and destroy" function, their activity is measured by exposing NK cells to diseased cells, usually tumour cells. For this reason, PNI research linking psychological variables to cancer often measures NK cell activity.

After exposure, NK cells are assessed in two ways. In one, *proliferation* is measured through cell counts taken after the introduction of tumour cells. In the other, NK cell *effectiveness* is assessed by measuring the destruction of the tumour cells. In PNI literature, this second method is often called an **NK cell cytotoxic activity assay**. This process of killing tumour cells is called **NK cell lysis** because to *lyse* a tumour cell means to destroy it. PNI researchers, especially those dealing with cancer, might talk of "a decrease (or increase) in NK cytotoxic activity," or "a significant effect on NK cell lysis." It is important to note that NK cells aren't the only immune-system cells capable of cytotoxic activity. However, they are the most commonly measured in PNI studies involving cancer. In this type of research, data reporting cytotoxic activity or cell lysis relates to the search for a link between psychosocial factors and cancer.

There are also a number of *in vivo* functional tests of immunocompetence. Here, we will look at two of the more common types. One takes advantage of the fact that almost everyone carries herpesviruses. The other uses injections of small dosages of antigens.

Herpesviruses are somewhat unique in that, once you have been exposed to one, you carry it with you for life. The virus usually stays in such small quantities that you don't experience any symptoms, but it is there all the same. There are many different types of herpesviruses, from cold sores to Epstein-Barr virus. One reason you don't have to spend much time worrying about herpesviruses is that your immune system does the worrying for you. It produces antibodies (Ab) whose job it is to "flag" herpesviruses for destruction, thus keeping their numbers under control. Herpesviruses will multiply when the immune system is suppressed, thus creating the need for more Ab. Therefore, we can determine immunocompetence by measuring Ab. Be careful when you read studies that use this measure, though. The more suppressed the immune system, the more herpesviruses, and thus the more Ab. This means that, when herpesvirus-specific antibodies are being measured, the *higher* the Ab count, the *poorer* the immune-system function.

Researchers can also introduce an antigen into the body and measure the specific Ab activity meant to deal with that intrusion. In these studies, small quantities of an antigen are introduced by injection. After this is done, there are two ways to measure immune-system activity. In the simplest, the skin is observed at the site of the injection. If the immune system is working properly, there should be swelling and redness. Remember that inflammation is a sign of a properly functioning immune system.

The second way involves counting antigen-specific Ab produced in response to the injection. This can be done through blood samples or mucous secretions that are measured most often in the saliva. One antibody commonly measured in the saliva or mucous is called sIgA, which stands for *secretory* or *salivary immunoglobulin A* antibody. Because it exists in saliva and mucous, it represents one of the body's first lines of defence against antigens (Tomasi, 1971). But measuring salivary sIgA isn't always as easy as it sounds. What happens when we want to measure sIgA levels during times of stress? Many people experience "dry mouth" at these times; that is, they don't produce much saliva.

These, then, are other *in vivo* tests that measure Ab production to assess immunocompetence. Be careful when you read these studies, though. It is easy to get confused about the meaning of Ab counts, because they have opposite meaning depending upon whether the count is herpesvirus-specific or is in response to an injection. In herpesvirus studies, higher Ab counts indicate *immunosuppression*. An increase in that virus comes about because of suppression of the immune system. This means that an increase in Ab has come about because of a *poor* immune system that can't keep herpesvirus counts down. In the case of injection studies, more Ab indicates *better* immunocompetence. In these studies, the antigen is introduced into the body. This means that Ab is being produced by a *competent* immune system that is dealing with an invading antigen.

Methodological Issues in the Measurement of Immune-System Function

As you read through the preceding section on measurement, did you wonder just *how* these blood samples were taken, and *when*, given that the independent variable in much PNI work is often stress related? Can we casually draw blood from someone who is in the middle of an argument with his wife or studying for final exams? Hardly. In PNI research, a sophisticated knowledge of measurement techniques and biological processes is needed. Measurement of immune functioning is intrusive and it requires skill. Certainly, conducting research in psychoneuroimmunology is not without its challenges.

Short-Term versus Long-Term Effects   In PNI research, an important distinction must be made between short-term and long-term effects. In laboratory research, it is common for a participant to be subjected to an **acute stressor**, which is to say one that is immediate in its duration and proximity. The effects of this acute stressor are then measured through blood samples taken just before, just after, and then again some time (minutes to hours) after the stressor has been introduced. Studies of this nature measure the quick reactivity of the immune system. As we will see in the next section, when we look at specific studies in PNI, short-term changes in immune-system function occur quite commonly in the face of these acute stressors. This leads to the conclusion that our immunocompetence fluctuates over the course of a day in response to daily hassles. It remains to be determined, however, whether these short-term fluctuations can increase our susceptibility to disease.

Not all psychological variables occur on an acute basis, however. Trait anxiety, job stress, marital problems, loneliness, and many other facts of life are *chronic*, or long-term. Their effects are more like a constant hum than a single blast. Psychoneuroimmunological research designed to measure the effects of chronic stressors cannot rely on well-controlled laboratory environments. Instead, field research must be conducted that studies people exposed to these stressors and compares their immune functioning to those who are not exposed. It is much more difficult to ascertain definitive cause-and-effect relationships in these studies because there are so many other variables in field work that cannot be controlled for.

One reason to emphasize the short-term versus long-term distinction is that some research has found that immune-system function is actually temporarily *improved* in the face of acute stressors. The body reacts with what Hans Selye (1976) called **resistance**, a set of physiological responses that allow us to deal with the stressor (refer back to chapter 2 for more on Selye's theory). The important question is, do these short-term responses take their toll on the immune system in the long run? Most researchers in the field would say that they do. Conversely, it is possible that some events, such as expressing emotion, might show detrimental short-term effects on immune functioning but result in improved functioning over the long-term. The important point here is that short-term immunologic effects of some psychological variables may be *opposite* to long-term effects.

Immune-System Function Takes Many Forms   As we mentioned earlier, there is no single accepted measure of immunocompetence. This is because the immune system does its job in a variety of ways depending on the nature of the antigen. Also, external factors and the internal states accompanying them will have different effects on the immune system depending on what those factors are. Finally, as is the case with all biological systems, there are individual differences between people in the ways their bodies respond to these factors.

For these reasons, PNI studies often report a multitude of dependent measures. This makes the work more difficult to wade through if you are a student of the field, but it also makes the findings more valid in that multiple measures increase the likelihood that an affected immunologic process will be identified.

Statistical Significance versus Clinical Significance   In any scientific endeavour, researchers need to be aware that data might be statistically significant without being clinically or socially significant, and vice versa. This fact is of great relevance to PNI studies aimed at determining if an aspect of the immune system has been affected by a person's psychology.

To prove that some aspect of immune functioning has been *affected,* we must be able to show that the difference in cell count or cytotoxic activity between groups of subjects is large enough not to have occurred by chance. In such a case, the results are said to be *statistically significant*. This means that there is less than a one-in-twenty chance that the differences detected would occur without the experimental manipulation. Applied to PNI research, statistical significance means that some psychological factor causes real immunologic effects.

Statistical significance may be scientifically important, but is it *clinically* important? In other words, do the statistically significant differences mean that people are actually more or less likely to *get sick*? Or are the differences, though statistically detectable, too small to affect our susceptibility to illness? These are very important questions for PNI research, because it is entirely possible that our statistical tests are more sensitive to cellular differences than our bodies are.

In a concise review of some important PNI research, Kiecolt-Glaser and colleagues (2002a) observe that, "…future work should identify and examine immune measures that are directly relevant to particular health conditions" (p. 451). In other words, some studies show that psychosocial factors can make us sick or well, and others show that these factors can affect the immune system at the cellular level. What we need more of are studies that do *both*; that is, measure symptoms and immune functioning concurrently.

Such studies are difficult to carry out for a multitude of reasons. If we want to study the link between immunocompromise and illnesses such as cancer that take a relatively long time to develop, then we must take our measurements regularly, on a longitudinal, prospective basis. This means that we must start with participants who are well, follow them over a long period, take regular assays, and compare the results for those who get sick and those who do not. This work isn't impossible to do, but it is expensive, intrusive, and fraught with the problem of extraneous variables that can account for health differences.

One way to get around these problems is to expose healthy people to antigens and psychological factors in the same study. Then we can observe the progression of symptom display while we monitor immune functioning. In studies that follow this approach, volunteers are exposed to a cold virus or similar pathogen, and disease course is monitored for a two- or three-week period following exposure. During that time, some of the volunteers in the study go through a stressful life event such as an exam period.

RESEARCH IN PSYCHONEUROIMMUNOLOGY: PROVIDING EVIDENCE FOR A BIOLOGICAL LINK BETWEEN PSYCHOLOGY AND HEALTH

In the following overview of PNI research, we have organized the studies according to the psychological factors measured. Some, such as mood, state anxiety, and short-term stress are acute in nature. Others, including personality factors such as cynical hostility, coping styles, and social support, are more chronic or long-term. As you read through the summary of these studies, keep in mind the methodological issues discussed in the previous section. We have tried to select studies that are not only representative of the field of PNI but that also use dependent measures and terminology consistent with those introduced earlier in this chapter. If you get confused at any point as you read this section, refer back to our explanations in the section entitled "How Immune-System Function is Measured in Psychoneuroimmunological Research."

The Effect of Stress on Immune Functioning

In the example we presented to open this chapter, you read about Lori, a university student who got either a cold or the flu regularly just after exams. The assumption is that the stress of exams increased Lori's susceptibility to these illnesses by compromising her immune system. Students' immune functioning before, during, and after exams has been studied for some time in health psychology (e.g., Jemmott et al., 1983; Kiecolt-Glaser, 1999; Wadee et al., 2001). The general finding has been that symptom complaint goes up at these times, and that cellular measures of immune response indicate immunosuppression.

Some of these students will catch a cold or flu after final exams are over because their immune systems have been compromised by stress.

Before we can link stress to disease using PNI research, we need at least a working definition of stress. For this purpose, we will use a simplified version of the definition forwarded by Lazarus and Folkman (1984), who define stress as an aversive condition in which the demands of a situation are perceived to be greater than our ability to cope with them.

The scientific study of the relationship between stress and disease was initiated in 1964 with the publication of a study by Solomon and Moos entitled "Emotions, Immunity and Disease: a Speculative Theoretical Integration." Since that time, a large number of studies have linked various types of stressors to a wide variety of diseases (see, for example, Bowler, 2001).

In the laboratory, volunteers have been exposed to acute, short-term stressors such as having to make speeches or perform mental tasks under time pressure. At the same time, their immune functioning was monitored. Using designs such as these, researchers can learn about the immediacy with which a stressor can affect immune functioning. Such studies have discovered that, while it may take days for the immune system to react to an antigen, it takes as little as five minutes for a stressor to inhibit the ability of the immune system to respond effectively (Herbert et al., 1994). Laboratory studies have also shown that the effect of stressors on immune functioning is stable over time for a given individual, leading to the conclusion that there are dispositional or personality factors that influence the extent to which a stressor affects immunity (Wadee et al., 2001). For example, laboratory research has demonstrated that people differ in their physiological reactivity to a stressor, as measured by cortisol levels. Not surprisingly, highly reactive people show the greatest incidence of such things as upper respiratory infections in the face of real-life stressors (Cohen et al., 2002).

In addition to laboratory studies of the effects of acute stressors, other work has investigated chronic, long-term stress as it occurs in real life. Boscarino (1997) conducted a 20-year follow-up of 332 Vietnam veterans who had presented symptoms of post-traumatic stress disorder (PTSD). He compared their health to 1067 veterans who did not suffer from PTSD. Post-traumatic stress disorder was reasoned to be evidence of severe stress exposure.

Boscarino discovered that the veterans who had suffered from PTSD were significantly more likely to suffer from a wide range of medical problems, including circulatory, digestive, musculoskeletal, and metabolic ailments. The worst problems were nervous-system disorders, which PTSD veterans were 2.47 times more likely to suffer from than non-PTSD vets; and non-sexually transmitted infectious diseases, which they were 2.14 times more likely to contract. Two aspects of this study are particularly impressive. First, Boscarino controlled 14 other factors that could account for increased susceptibility to illness, including substance abuse, hypochondriasis, age, and smoking history. Controlling for external variables such as these greatly increases the validity of attributing the higher odds of suffering from this wide variety of illnesses, in large part, to the effects of the stress exposure. Second, the long range of the follow-up (20 years) demonstrated that severe stress exposure can have long-term effects.

Many studies have demonstrated the potential long-term effects of stress on immunity. For example, a study of people living near the Three Mile Island nuclear disaster site almost ten years after the accident found more antibodies to herpesviruses than those living elsewhere in a demographically matched control-group (McKinnon et al., 1989). (Remember that increased antibody to herpesvirus is a result of an increase in herpesvirus numbers, indicating immunocompromise.) And research on clusters of symptoms experienced by veterans of the Gulf War has also implicated the immune system (Ferguson & Cassaday, 1999). These authors hypothesize that the illnesses commonly experienced by these veterans (sometimes called Gulf War Syndrome, or Syndromes) are associated with the production of interleukin-1. The authors also hypothesize that these conditions persist, in part, because of classically conditioned associations triggered by such stimuli as smells and tastes.

More recent research has shown that immune function is affected by exposure to natural disasters. Survivors of Hurricane Andrew in the United States showed disruption in their sIgA counts (Rotton & Dubitsky, 2002), and those who lived through an earthquake in Northridge, California showed a positive correlation between immunocompromise and degree of distress experienced up to four months after the quake (Solomon et al., 1997).

In another study of real-life stressors and their effect on general health and the immune system, Kiecolt-Glaser and colleagues (1987a) took multiple measures of immune functioning from women who were recently divorced or separated (within the past year). They found that these women had significantly poorer functioning on five of the six immune-system measures compared to women who were neither divorced nor separated. In a subsequent study of men, it was found that those who initiated the divorce reported better health than those whose partner had initiated it (Kiecolt-Glaser et al., 1988).

It is clear from this collection of work that stress affects health through the immune system, both in acute and immediate ways as well as on a long-term basis. We turn now to a discussion of the link between specific illnesses and stress.

Stress and Upper Respiratory Infection   Many people doing PNI research believe that, of all the medical conditions brought on or worsened by stress, **upper respiratory**

infection (URI) might be the most common. Upper respiratory infection refers to a collection of common illnesses such as colds, coughs, flu, and bronchitis. This is the category that Lori's illness in our opening example would fall into. If you have ever developed sniffles and sneezes or a nagging cough during or after exams, you may well have been a walking demonstration of the well-established relationship between stress and URI.

In an early study, people were tracked for six months and asked to report traumatic life events and daily hassles, the two most commonly identified sources of stress in our lives (Graham, Douglas, & Ryan, 1986). At the same time, these volunteers were monitored for URI episodes. It was discovered that those people experiencing high levels of life-event and daily-event stress suffered more and longer bouts of URI than those people not experiencing stressful events.

Field studies such as this one are important because they are clearly applicable to the realities of our daily lives. However, they also feature less than optimal experimental control. That is, we can get self-report measures of the intensity of the stress being experienced, but we can't control the event. As such, we can't know for sure whether we are dealing with the kind of events most people would find stressful, or if we have a volunteer who is particularly vulnerable to stress. Is the variable a *situational* one that might affect most people the same way, or is it a *dispositional* one that can only be generalized to certain types of people? Some might argue that it doesn't matter—if a person reports stress, then there is stress. Stress is thus seen as an entirely subjective experience. The fact that immune functioning clearly fluctuates with self-reports of stress supports the view that these subjective reports are a legitimate way of assessing stress for the purposes of PNI research.

Some people are more prone to stress than others. From the perspective of PNI, we should be able to learn something about the effects of stress by studying the URI experiences of these types of people. This is just what La Via and his colleagues (1996) set out to do. They studied 14 people with generalized anxiety disorder, a disorder characterized by excessive and chronic apprehension about a wide variety of aspects of one's life, such as work, family, and social contacts.

People with generalized anxiety disorder experience greater impact from stressful events, or in the language of stress research, their **stress-intrusion scores** are high. La Via and his team measured stress intrusion in these 14 people using the Impact of Events Scale. To measure immune functioning, they took *in vitro* measures of lymphocyte activity and kept track of the number of URI-related sick days the subjects reported. They began by confirming that the people with generalized anxiety disorder had higher stress-intrusion scores. The researchers discovered that the anxiety group had less lymphocyte activity and almost three times more sick days than a control group. In fact, the anxiety group averaged 24.8 URI sick days in a 12-month period, compared to only 9 days among the non-anxious control participants. Finally, they were able to show that lymphocyte activity was correlated with URI sick days and with stress intrusion.

A potential problem with field studies is that researchers cannot control the amount of antigen participants are exposed to. For example, it might well be that, in times of stress, people turn to others for help, thus increasing their exposure to people who might be infected with cold or flu viruses. That is, stress could increase the likelihood of URI, not because of immunosuppression, but because of increased exposure to others who were infected. Support for the immune system explanation is supplied by the finding that people with larger and more diverse social networks are actually less likely to develop colds after being exposed to a cold virus in a controlled laboratory setting (Cohen et al., 1997).

Another way to gain even more control over antigen exposure is to do laboratory experiments in which volunteers are given controlled dosages of viruses and have their course charted over a period of time. Cohen, Doyle and Skoner (1999) used this technique in the study described in Focus on Research 3-1.

Focus On Research 3-1

A Virus up Your Nose

Intriguing research findings about the links between perceived stress and susceptibility to the flu led researchers Sheldon Cohen, William Doyle, and David Skoner (1999) to try identify the biological mechanism through which stress affects immune function and subsequent health. Field studies in which people's stress levels are measured while they are being monitored for the development of upper respiratory infection (URI) have the advantage of *external validity*, which means that the results can be generalized to real-life settings because the studies were conducted in these settings. The downside to these studies, though, is that control is relinquished. For example, researchers don't control the intensity of the stress-inducing stimulus, nor do they control exposure to viruses that cause URI. Researchers doing field work aren't so concerned about controlling stress-inducing stimuli because the researchers consider stress to be a subjective phenomenon that is best measured by self-report. It is the *perception* of stress that matters, not some objective measure of the intensity of the stimulus that brought on the stress.

Control of exposure to antigens is another matter. It is very possible that stress causes people to either seek out the company of others or hide away from them. In either case, exposure to viruses is significantly affected. For this reason, a number of studies have adopted a methodology whereby they intentionally expose volunteers to controlled dosages of URI-related viruses. These are called **viral challenge studies**.

In one viral challenge study, 55 participants were exposed to a safety-tested clinical dose of influenza A via nasal drops. To control exposure, participants were quarantined from one day prior to exposure to seven days afterwards. Self-reports of symptoms were collected and mucous weights were calculated. Immune functioning was measured by assaying cytokine activity. Participants also completed the Perceived Stress Scale, and a number of demographic variables were controlled for.

For all participants, upper respiratory symptoms increased sharply from onset to Day 2, then gradually dissipated for the remainder of the quarantine period. Symptom severity, as measured by self-reports of symptoms, mucous weights, and nasal secretions was significantly correlated with perceived stress. The viral challenge approach used in this study proves that stress-related increased susceptibility to upper respiratory infection can't be explained solely by increased exposure to viruses at times of stress.

Thus far, we have assumed that stress works alone to influence URI. In the language of statistics, we have assumed a *main effects* model. However, while main effects models allow us to isolate a factor to determine its unique contribution to illness, they also over-simplify the realities of health and well-being. Stress rarely works in isolation. Instead, it *interacts* with other factors such as social support, demographics, and personality.

In recognition of this fact, Miyazaki and colleagues (2003) have investigated the possible moderating effects of social support. Their predictor variables were perceived stress *and* perceived social support. They found that social support did help reduce the harmful effects of stress on the immune system. In particular, social support was positively correlated with NK cell production.

At least one study has found that *positive* life events can also increase vulnerability to URI (Evans, et al., 1997). University students were asked to complete the Life Experience Survey as well as other measures such as personality and stress experience. They were then monitored for just over six weeks for URI episodes, which were verified with body temperature readings. It was discovered that positive life events were most closely related to URI, independent of personality measures or health-related behaviours. This means that we need to consider the effect of *any* major event, not just the negative ones, when conducting PNI research.

What can we conclude about the extent to which stress puts us at risk for upper respiratory infection? Certain types of stress do affect specific aspects of immune functioning. In particular, major life event stress often results in immunosuppression. If a person is exposed to a respiratory virus at the same time, it is likely that the person will get sick. These stressful events don't all have to be recent, though they probably have an additive effect if several of them "pile up" over time.

Stress and Autoimmune Disease   For people with autoimmune diseases their own immune system becomes their worst enemy. These diseases cause the immune system to produce antibodies that attack the body's own tissue. In other words, the system fails at one of its hallmarks—*tolerance*. Autoimmune diseases include rheumatoid arthritis, insulin-dependent diabetes, and multiple sclerosis.

Research indicates that stress can put people at greater risk for contracting these diseases and for suffering more once they have contracted them (Homo-Delarches et al., 1991). What we don't know is *how* stress causes the immune system to react against the body's own tissue. On a more positive note, relaxation and hypnosis have both been shown to be effective in reducing the pain of arthritis, as has the use of analgesic medication (Gay, Philippot, & Luminet, 2002). Potential exists, therefore, for these therapies to be applied successfully to other autoimmune diseases as well.

Stress and Cancer   A great amount of research on the relationship between stress and cancer exists in the health psychology literature. However, most of these studies discuss the stress brought on by cancer rather than the possibility that the cancer was brought on by stress. One researcher who provides a notable exception is David Spiegel, who presents a convincing argument that the immune system is the means by which stress can cause cancer.

In our explanation of how the immune system works, we pointed out that natural-killer (NK) cells were primarily responsible for seeking out and destroying abnormal cells. This function makes NK cells crucial in the body's ability to remain cancer free. Numerous *in vitro* studies have clearly established the relationship between stress (and other psychological factors) and NK cell activity (Herbert & Cohen, 1993). This relationship has been directly applied to breast cancer research (Andersen et al., 1998).

David Spiegel and colleagues (1998) reviewed the literature on the impact of major life stressors on the progression of cancer. Two studies found a positive relationship between severe adverse life events and cancer growth. In one (Ramirez et al., 1989), breast cancer patients with relapse had experienced significantly more of these events than had a group of matched patients who were in remission. In fact, patients who had experienced a family death or job loss were more than five times as likely to have had a relapse. In the other study (Geyer, 1991), women who had seen a physician to have a breast lump diagnosed were monitored for eight years. It was found that women who developed malignancies had experienced more stressful life events. More recently, Stone and colleagues have shown that stress is positively correlated with prostate-specific antigen (PSA) counts, though the biological mechanisms linking stress and PSA are not clear (Stone et al., 1999). PSA counts are used as a diagnostic tool for prostate cancer.

Other research has failed to find these links. A study of 204 breast cancer patients found no relationship between severe life events and relapse (Barraclough et al., 1992). In contrast to the Ramirez study, Barraclough used a prospective design, in which stressful events were measured *before* rather than *after* relapse.

These mixed findings indicate that the progression of cancer is not always adversely affected by major life stressors. One reason for this might be that the immune system cannot detect all tumour types. Spiegel and colleagues (1998) also point out that the cause-and-effect relationship between immune-cell activity and cancer progression isn't one-way. That is, while compromised immune systems may put the body at greater risk for tumour growth, the presence of cancerous cells may also bring on immunosuppression. Spiegel and colleagues (1998) conclude that "the role of stress in immunosuppression and tumor progression may be central to *potentiating* existing tumor rather than *initiating* primary carcinogenesis" (p. 679). In other words, stress may worsen existing cancer but not make a person more susceptible to getting it. Further investigation is certainly warranted.

Hans Eysenck spent much of the latter part of his very distinguished career studying the relationship between psychological factors and two types of disease—cancer and coronary heart disease. Much of this work focused on personality factors that Eysenck believed put people at risk for these health problems. Eysenck's interest in personality isn't surprising, since there is a close relationship between our personalities and how stressful we perceive situations to be.

In one study, Eysenck and colleagues (1989) identified a number of personality types that were hypothesized to be at varying degrees of risk for illness. Type 1 personality is typified by the belief that happiness is determined by nearness to an object or person that is highly valued emotionally. Any situation that prevents this nearness is very stressful; thus Type 1 people are more prone to stress. (Grossarth-Maticek, Eysenk, & Vetter, 1998). Eysenck and his colleagues contend that Type 1 people are more susceptible to cancer. We will be discussing the relationship between personality and cancer later in this chapter.

The Effect of Mood on Immune Functioning

Our body's physiological responses to stress may be adaptive in the face of the stressor, but in the long run, they compromise our immune system. It is the *arousal* associated with stress that puts strain on our bodies. What effect, if any, do the opposite feelings associated with *under*-arousal, such as depression or sadness or loneliness, have on our immune system?

We have seen in our discussion of stress and immunity that so-called major negative life events affect immunity. One reason for this is that these events are stressful. But another reason may relate to the impact of these events on our mood (or *affect*), as they often elicit strong, unpleasant emotions, such as depression, sorrow, anger, grief, and helplessness. A clear example of such a life event is the death of a loved one. Most health psychologists believe that coping with a seriously ill loved one brings on *stress*. Coping with their death, on the other hand, brings on *negative mood*. This is why studies that measure immune functioning of a caregiver when the loved one is very ill and then again if the loved one dies allow us to differentiate between stress and mood in terms of their impact on our immune systems.

An early study (Irwin et al., 1987) measured immune functioning in three groups of wives: 1) wives whose husbands were in good health; 2) wives whose husbands were being treated for lung cancer that had spread to other parts of the body; and 3) wives whose husbands had died from lung cancer up to six months previously. They discovered that this third group was the most depressed and also had the poorest immune functioning. A similar study of men whose wives were dying of breast cancer found that lymphocyte proliferation was better in pre-bereavement husbands than among those in the group whose wives had died (Schleifer, 1983).

But because the stress of caregiving and the depression associated with bereavement can both compromise immune functioning, we cannot always assume that bereaved spouses will always be at higher risk. More recent work (Glaser et al., 2000) studying those caring for spouses with dementia found opposite results. Immune function was better in those whose spouses had died than in those who were still providing care for living spouses. It may be that the nature of dementia helps to explain this apparently contradictory finding; that is, caring for a spouse with dementia may be both stressful and depressing.

Longitudinal work supports the conclusion that depression compromises the immune system. Having discovered that almost 25 percent of hospital patients had abnormally high depression scores, a group of researchers set out to measure the relationship between this depression and mortality. They measured depression in 454 people when they were admitted to hospital (Herrmann et al., 1998), and then monitored them for the next 22 months. Fifteen percent of them died. The strongest predictors of mortality were then identified through statistical analysis. After the expected variables of age and the nature of the illness that brought them to the hospital in the first place, depression scores taken upon admission were the best predictors of mortality. When the other factors were controlled for, it was discovered that people scoring high in depression were over three times as likely to die as those scoring low (see Figure 3-1).

Depression increased mortality risk for all types of patients, regardless of their age or sex. However, depression had its strongest impact on patients with cardiopulminary disease, which is consistent with research showing that depression increases mortality risk after myocardial infarction (heart attack) (see for example, Glassman & Shapiro, 1998). Herrmann and colleagues also found that depression increased mortality risk for patients with hematological diseases and cancer.

These studies linking mortality rates and mood provide an important first step, but because they do not measure immune functioning, we can't conclude from them that the

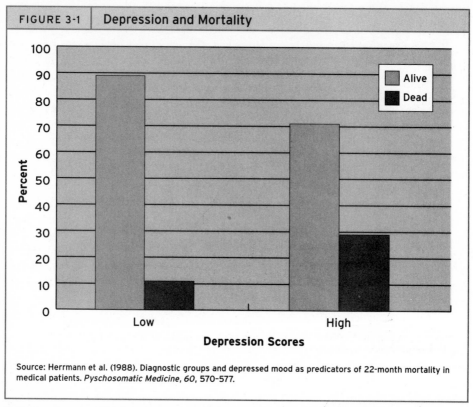

FIGURE 3-1 | Depression and Mortality

Source: Herrmann et al. (1988). Diagnostic groups and depressed mood as predicators of 22-month mortality in medical patients. *Pyschosomatic Medicine, 60,* 570–577.

Patients who scored high on a measure of depression were more than three times as likely to die within the next 22 months.

link is due to immunocompromise. Other research testing the hypothesis that the relatively short life span of sIgA makes it more susceptible to daily mood fluctuations has shown that certain components of the immune system do fluctuate along with mood. (Stone et al., 1987). To test this, people were monitored for just over eight weeks. Three times per week they completed checklists of adjectives describing mood. Their responses were divided into positive and negative moods. Two weeks prior to all this, they started to ingest a harmless antigen. It was discovered that negative moods suppressed immune function and positive moods improved it (see Figure 3-2). More recent work has hypothesized that cytokines, specifically Interleukin-6 (IL-6) may provide the pathway between mood and health (Kiecolt-Glaser et al., 2002b).

Negative Mood and Upper Respiratory Infection   One of the conceptual problems encountered when studying negative mood is that it can be difficult to distinguish between mood and personality characteristics. In other words, we must be sure that we are dealing with a "person who is down" rather than a "downer of a person." In the language of psychology, we are talking about a distinction between **states**, which are short-term conditions, and **traits**, which are enduring characteristics. This distinction might be particularly relevant if one of your dependent measures were symptom reporting, because increased reporting could just as easily be an indication of chronic complaining as of genuine symptom experience.

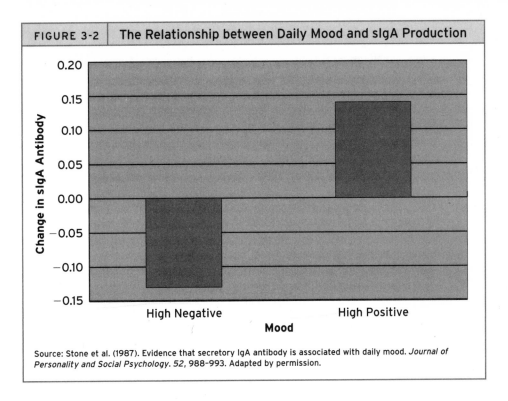

FIGURE 3-2 | **The Relationship between Daily Mood and sIgA Production**

Source: Stone et al. (1987). Evidence that secretory IgA antibody is associated with daily mood. *Journal of Personality and Social Psychology. 52,* 988–993. Adapted by permission.

A study by Cohen and colleagues (1995) made the distinction between state- and trait-negative affect, including anxiety, anger, depression, and fatigue. The main purpose of the study was to sort out whether negative states or negative traits had more influence on the development of colds and flu.

At the start of the study, blood samples were taken to establish baseline measures of specific antibody levels. The participants were then exposed to either a cold or influenza virus by way of nasal drops (another viral challenge study). Measures of state- and trait-negative affect were also taken at the start of the study. To do this, participants filled out a scale called the Profile of Moods States (POMS). They did this twice—once for how they have felt in the past 24 hours (state) and once for how they felt generally (trait).

The participants were then quarantined in hotel rooms for the duration of the study and their URI symptoms were monitored daily, via assessments of nasal secretions and self-reports of symptoms. Finally, a second blood sample was taken four weeks after exposure to the virus.

The researchers wanted to know to what extent were symptom severity and frequency related to negative affect. The answer is interesting, because it underscores the importance of drawing a distinction between state and trait affect. Both state- and trait-negative affect were correlated with symptom reporting; however, only state-negative affect was correlated with objectively confirmed symptoms. This means that higher state-negative affect at the outset of the study predicted the actual symptoms a person would experience upon exposure to a virus. It also means that people high on trait-negative affect reported symptoms that could not be verified objectively.

This illustrates why we have to make the distinction between personality and state in this work. Interestingly, people who scored high on trait-negative affect didn't start complaining about symptoms until they actually started experiencing some. They therefore weren't simply inventing them. Instead, their *cognitive bias*, as it is called, took the form of a *misinterpretation* of sensations once they started to feel the symptoms of a cold or the flu. The authors suggest that this misinterpretation is due to an inability to accurately discriminate between real symptoms and other sensations, rather than to an oversensitivity to actual URI symptoms.

At least three important points must be noted concerning the design of this study. First, the authors demonstrated statistically that state-negative affect and trait-negative affect are different things. Second, in their design they did not correlate antibody proliferation with symptoms. This means that we can only infer that the high state-negative affect people had compromised immune systems, though it is arguably a reasonable inference in this case. Third, this study used a *prospective* design, starting with healthy individuals and charting their course. This is important because the relationship between mood and URI is bidirectional (Hall & Smith, 1996).

Negative Mood and Cancer   At the beginning of this section on negative mood, we showed that depression was a significant predictor of a number of illnesses, including cancer. Here, we will take a closer look at the possibility that negative moods such as depression, hopelessness, and pessimism increase the risk of getting cancer or of surviving the disease for shorter lengths of time. Of course, all research in this area must be prospective in nature. A diagnosis of cancer is depressing for most people. As such, we know about that causal direction. What we need to know is the extent of the other direction—the impact of depression in causing or accelerating cancer.

Prospective studies in this area take one of two forms. Researchers may begin with cancer-free people, measure their levels of negative mood, then monitor them for cancer onset; or they may assess the moods of people with cancer and then monitor the *progression* of their cancer. In this latter type of study, researchers have to be careful to control for type of cancer and severity at the outset of the study to be able to make meaningful comparisons among people regarding survival.

Interest in the relationship between mood and cancer progression was fuelled in the 1960s when Arthur Schmale identified what he and George Engel called the "giving up–given up" complex (Schmale & Engel, 1967). This term referred to the accelerated rate of decline they observed in cancer patients after these patients gave up hope for survival. Because these observations were anecdotal rather than empirically manipulated, it is difficult to sort out cause and effect. Evidence for causal links between mood and cancer came some 15 years later from a study in which cancer-free participants were monitored for 17 years to assess the extent to which depression predicted cancer deaths (Shekelle et al., 1981).

In this large prospective study of male employees at the Western Electric Company, over 2000 cancer-free men were administered a battery of psychological tests, including the Minnesota Multiphasic Personality Inventory (MMPI), in the 1950s. The MMPI is a comprehensive measure that is often used in the diagnosis of psychological disorders. Its subscale measuring levels of depression provided the main independent variable for this study. Once the study began, the men were given annual physical exams for each of the next 11 years. Then, 17 years after the start of the study, mortality statistics were collected from the sample.

It was discovered that men who showed evidence of clinical depression on the MMPI were 2.3 times as likely to have died of cancer at some point in the 17 years covered by the study than those who didn't (see Figure 3-3). This effect was independent of age, cigarette smoking, use of alcohol, family history of cancer, occupational status, or type of cancer contracted. Further, depression was not related to any other cause of death. These results were replicated in a follow-up study 20 years later (Persky, Kempthorne-Rawson, & Shekelle, 1987).

More recently, researchers have discovered that pessimism, independent of depression, is related to decreased survival rates among younger people who already have cancer (Schulz et al., 1996). A study involving patients who were receiving palliative radiation treatment for either recurrent or metastasized cancer showed that, for patients aged 30 to 59 years, pessimism was a significant predictor of mortality, regardless of type of cancer (see Figure 3-4).

Here again we run into the difficulty of distinguishing between a psychological state and a personality trait. We all feel pessimistic from time to time (state) but that doesn't mean that we are *pessimists* (trait). This study does not lead to the conclusion that pessimists are more likely to get cancer for two reasons. First, the design did not begin with cancer-free participants. Second, pessimism was conceptualized more as a state than a trait.

In summary, it is safe to say that depression and other negative mood states are related to increased risk of contracting cancer and of dying from it once it is contracted. It is

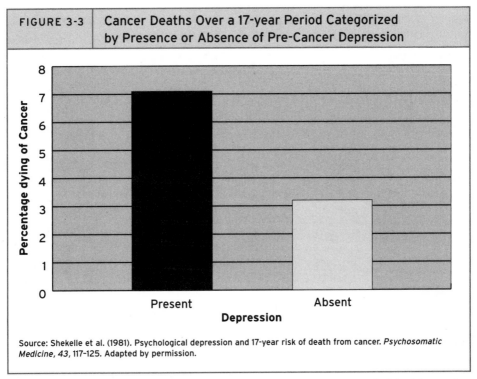

| FIGURE 3-3 | Cancer Deaths Over a 17-year Period Categorized by Presence or Absence of Pre-Cancer Depression |

Source: Shekelle et al. (1981). Psychological depression and 17-year risk of death from cancer. *Psychosomatic Medicine, 43*, 117-125. Adapted by permission.

In a 17-year prospective study, physically healthy men who showed signs of clinical depression at the start of the study were 2.3 times more likely to die of cancer.

also likely that immunocompetence provides one explanation for these increased risks. It has been suggested that cancers related to viruses such as Epstein-Barr would be more susceptible to mood fluctuation than would cancers that are induced by chemical carcinogens, such as lung cancer (Kiecolt-Glaser, et al., 2002a).

However, immunocompetence doesn't provide the whole explanation; we must remember that negative mood states are related to a number of other behavioural phenomena that can affect the experience of cancer, especially its progression. People who are experiencing depression or hopelessness are less likely to follow medical regimens and to generally take care of themselves. Also, they tend to sleep poorly and have less energy (Jenkins, 1996). So it would be an oversimplification to say that the fact that negative mood compromises the immune system is the sole reason that negative mood is associated with increased cancer risk. But whatever the actual mechanisms involved, health psychologists, counsellors, and others working in a psychosocial capacity with cancer patients must pay close attention to patients' moods and work to help patients be optimistic and hopeful.

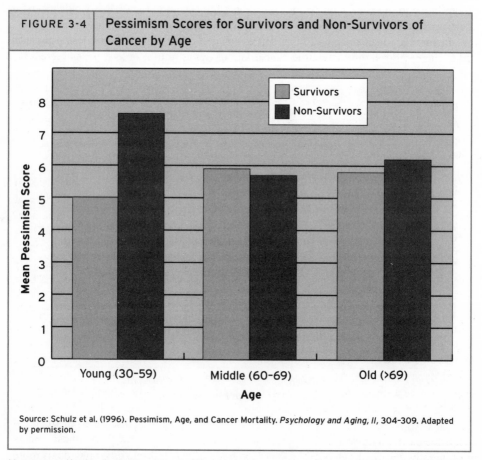

| FIGURE 3-4 | **Pessimism Scores for Survivors and Non-Survivors of Cancer by Age** |

Source: Schulz et al. (1996). Pessimism, Age, and Cancer Mortality. *Psychology and Aging, II*, 304–309. Adapted by permission.

Younger patients who had survived with recurrent or metastasized cancer had significantly lower pessimism scores than those in that age group who did not survive.

Negative Mood and Heart Health   In general, the immune system is not as strongly implicated in heart health as it is in infection or cancer. As we saw earlier in our discussion of research on negative mood, it is often the case that mood is studied as an *outcome* rather than a *cause*. In this vein, researchers have suggested that depression, as an outcome, deserves more attention as an underdiagnosed problem for people with heart problems such as myocardial infarction or cardiovascular disease (e.g., Musselman, Evans, & Nemeroff, 1998). Still, there are some prospective studies indicating that negative mood, and depression in particular, is a risk factor for heart disease and related mortality.

One such study following people for 13 years concluded that people with major depression had a 4.5 times greater risk of heart attack than those without depression (Pratt et al., 1996). Other studies measuring depressive symptoms as opposed to major depression estimate risk of first heart attack for those with higher depression scores to be 1.5 to 2 times higher (Glassman & Shapiro, 1998).

Another prospective study followed over 3700 adults who were over the age of 70 at the start of the study. The researchers made a distinction between what they called new depression and chronic depression. Newly depressed participants were those who were depressed at the outset of the study but had not been either three or six years before. Chronically depressed participants were depressed at the outset *and* at either three or six years before. It was discovered that for men, new depression (but not chronic depression) increased the risk of contracting heart disease and dying from it. In fact, it was concluded that newly depressed older men were twice as likely to have a cardiovascular disease event than were men who were either chronically depressed or not depressed at all (Penninx et al., 1998). Because these studies statistically controlled correlated risk factors (including age), we can conclude that depression increases risk of heart disease, *independent of these other factors*. However, further studies will need to be done before we can implicate the immune system as a way of explaining this risk.

Negative Mood and HIV Infection   Given what we know about the general effects of mood on the immune system, and that AIDS is an immune-system disease we might expect significant effects of negative mood on HIV infection and AIDS. There have been several fairly large studies in this area, which have provided quite contradictory results.

Burack and colleagues (1993) measured depression in a group of 277 HIV-positive men. They then tracked T-helper cell activity in these men for five years (T-helper cell activity is an important predictor of prognosis for people who are HIV positive). The depressed men showed a significantly greater decline in this cell activity than the non-depressed men did. There was no relationship between depression and the onset of HIV or mortality, however. Lyketsos et al. (1993) studied over 1700 men and found that depression was *not* linked to T-helper cell decline over an eight-year period. In a review of these two studies (Kiecolt-Glaser and Glaser, 1995), it was pointed out that the men in the Lyketsos study started with a lower baseline T-helper level than did the men in the Burack study. This suggests the possibility that depression affects only those who have a relatively high T-helper cell count.

To test this possibility, the Burack data were reanalyzed by dividing the men into high and low T-helper baseline cell counts. When this was done, it was discovered that depression affected the men whose cell counts were initially high but not those whose counts were initially low. So it may well be that depression affects HIV-positive individuals more when their T-helper cell counts are relatively high.

Stress and Immune Function for Persons Living with AIDS

Researchers at an Ottawa Hospital have investigated the link between emotional states such as stress and depression on immune functioning among people living with AIDS (Balfour, et al., 2003). Sixty-one people took part in the study, in which they were asked to complete the Perceived Stress Scale and a measure of depression. Outcome measures included HIV disease progression, in particular CD4 counts. Remember that CD4 refers to helper T cells, and that these are believed to be particularly important in the progression of HIV.

It was found that stress and depression together accounted for 17 percent of the variance in CD4 counts, thus supporting a growing body of literature linking psychological state with symptoms associated with AIDS.

CASE 3-1

Two Different Reactions to a Diagnosis of Cancer

Jack and Stephen had never met. They were sitting across from one another, leafing through magazines in a waiting-room at the cancer clinic. Both had recently found out that they had prostate cancer. The news had been upsetting for both men. However, from the moment when their respective family physicians told them the news, each had reacted quite differently. In this case study, we will describe these different reactions and speculate on the effect they might have on the progression of the disease for each man. We will base our speculation on what we know from PNI research with cancer patients.

Both men were in their early 60s. Both were happily married. Jack kept in close contact with his two children, who were both married and had children of their own. Stephen didn't hear from his children much since they had started lives of their own. He saw them at major holidays and that was about it.

The most significant difference between the two men was in the way they had taken the news that they had cancer. Jack was upset, of course, but he considered himself to be relatively young and determined. He went to the library and took out books on prostate cancer to learn more about the disease and what his options were. He also checked out the Internet for information. He felt thankful that he wasn't in very much pain at this point and was confident that he could handle the treatment and that it would work.

Stephen responded differently. When he was told he had prostate cancer, he suddenly felt very old. He had heard of others who had the disease and they were all in their 70s and 80s. He felt bitter that he had contracted a dis-

(continued on next page)

ease that put him in such an infirmed category. He decided that this would be the way his life would end—prematurely and terribly. Sure, he would go through with the treatments, but he had no confidence that they would work. He was convinced that his quality of life was about to fall apart permanently and that there was nothing that could be done about it. Soon, he began to feel depressed much of the time.

Other aspects of these men's lives were different as well. When Jack came home from the doctor and told his wife his diagnosis, she had said that the two of them were going to grow old together and that was that. She maintained an upbeat attitude and helped Jack through the times when he got discouraged or was in discomfort. Jack's friends and neighbours responded the same way.

Stephen had a different experience. His wife had been devastated by the news that her husband had cancer. They had both just retired and they had plans to travel and enjoy life. Now, in her mind, all of those plans would come to nothing. When Stephen would get depressed, he was difficult to be around. At these times, his wife would leave him alone. Stephen didn't have many friends, and those he had felt awkward around now because he felt that he had a horrible disease that made him different from them.

If it were the case that Jack and Stephen were at the same stage of illness when they were diagnosed, and that they we were similar in all other aspects of their health, PNI research findings would suggest a more favourable prognosis for Jack. He has an optimistic attitude and he believes in the efficacy of the treatment. These cognitions help him avoid getting

depressed, and depression has been shown to accelerate cancer progression. Jack also has a strong support system in the form of family, friends, and neighbours. This support is associated with better survival rates for cancer patients.

Stephen is on a much less encouraging course. His depression has the potential to suppress his immune system to the extent that his cancer could worsen over time. This, of course, would only depress him more. Somehow, this cycle needs to be broken and Stephen needs to get help for his depression. His social support network isn't strong, which is another disadvantage for Stephen. He needs to change his thinking in this regard as well. Perhaps if he gave his friends more of a chance, they could be more supportive of him and this would help him feel less depressed. Also, as hard as it may seem for him, Stephen needs to be a more positive companion for his wife. For her part, she needs to persevere through the difficult times brought on by Stephen's depression and try to maintain an optimistic and positive approach to his treatment and their future together.

Although Stephen's response and that of his wife are understandable, they are not going to help Stephen. They must try to make changes in the way they are reacting to Stephen's illness. All of this is easier said than done. Fortunately, there are counsellors who specialize in helping families cope with illness. We emphasize the need for such counselling here, because an improvement in Stephen's mood and thinking will likely increase the competence of his immune system and thus better the chances of his survival, not to mention his overall quality of life.

Personality and Cancer

You can imagine how compelling it would be to explore the possibility that certain types of people are more likely than others to get cancer. A number of people have taken on this exploration; most notably, Eysenck and Grossarth-Maticek. They studied over 1000 Jewish concentration camp survivors, comparing their mortality data to 367 Jewish people who had no connection with concentration camps (Grossarth-Maticek, Eysenck, & Boyle, 1994). They discovered that mortality rates for cancer and coronary heart disease were more than twice as high for concentration camp survivors. The authors argued that the concentration camp experience changed those people in permanent ways and that these changes, independent of general life stress, age, or sex, accounted for the increased mortality rates.

From this and other studies like it, Grossarth-Maticek and Eysenck formulated what has been called the **diathesis-stress model** of illness. A *diathesis* is a factor that predisposes someone to illness. The illness will result when people with this predisposition are exposed to conditions that combine with the diathesis to compromise health. In this case, the researchers argued that the experience of being in a concentration camp engendered certain personality characteristics that, when combined with stress, put a person at greater risk for cancer. The personality characteristics constituted the diathesis.

Just what are these personality characteristics? They include such things as consistent feelings of helplessness or hopelessness as well as suppression of emotional expression. This combination was identified as Type 1 by Grossarth-Maticek, who also identified five other personality types in his research. Each of these types was associated with a different health outcome. In longitudinal studies, Type 1 was predictive of contracting cancer. These types were based on a number of fairly complex criteria, including feelings regarding valued people and objects (Grossarth-Maticek, Eysenck, & Vetter, 1988).

Grossarth-Maticek's research has come under considerable criticism, however (Amelang, 1997). Methods of data collection have been reported inconsistently in a variety of papers, so that it is unclear just how questionnaires were administered to such large groups of people (over 5000) or what specific criteria were used to place people in one of the six personality types. In spite of this criticism, the search for the "cancer-prone" personality continued.

After the work of Grossarth-Maticek and colleagues, Eysenck presented what he called the **Type C personality**. This cancer-prone personality was analogous to the Type 1 category. Consistent with the diathesis model, Eysenck asserted that the Type C personality doesn't cause cancer in and of itself. Rather, it *interacts* with other factors, such as smoking, to yield a risk factor that is much more toxic than smoking alone. More recently, Eysenck hypothesized that the immune system was involved in these personality-cancer links. In particular, he has cited evidence to suggest that cortisol is the biological link between repressed emotion and immunocompromise relevant to cancer (Eysenck, 1996).

Social Support and Immune Functioning

Our exploration of psychological factors has thus far focused on the individual. We don't exist in isolation, however. What role does our social network play in our ability to maintain effective immune functioning? Are some people healthier than others because of the nature of their social world? There is a mound of evidence indicating that one's social network can have a profound impact on one's health, both in terms of staying healthy and recovering from illness or surgery. In the late 1970s, Berkman and Syme (1979) presented data showing that "all-cause mortality rates" are twice as high for people who are socially isolated. This risk ratio was similar to that for cigarette smokers. A number of studies show that the immune system is involved when it comes to the beneficial effects of social contact. Cohen and Herbert (1996) review research demonstrating these effects as well as the detrimental effects of being alone.

Some of these studies measure **social support** rather than social isolation. Social support, defined as the interpersonal resources we have at our disposal to help us avoid or cope with difficult times in our lives, is a very important concept in health psychology. Social support includes emotional support, informational support, and tangible or practical support (also called instrumental support).

One study investigating the role of social support (Kang, et al., 1998) measured social support and stress among 133 high school students, some of whom had asthma. They found no main effect for social support on immune functioning. However, they did find an *interaction* between stress and social support suggesting that support *buffered the effects* of stress on the students' immune systems during exam time. We must also remember that social support can come in the form of organized *support groups*. Participants in these groups might gain a number of benefits beyond emotional support. For example, information, relaxation training, and stress management techniques are often part of such programs. It can be difficult, therefore, to isolate which factor, or combination of factors, is having an effect on the immune system in these cases.

Social Support and Cancer   Research has generally shown that social support is beneficial for cancer patients (see, for example, Holland & Holahan, 2003), Fewer studies, however, have been able to link these benefits to immune function. Levy and colleagues (1990) found that female cancer patients who reported higher levels of emotional support had higher levels of NK cell activity. Other research suggests that this immunological advantage translates into better survival rates. Goodwin and fellow researchers (1987) found that married cancer patients had better survival rates than did patients who were not married. Similarly, Hislop and colleagues (1987) and Waxler-Morrison and co-investigators (1991) found that longer survival with breast cancer was associated with being married and having support from friends, relatives, and neighbours. Maunsell, Jacques, and Deschenes (1995) also found that married women and women with confidants lived longer after being diagnosed with breast cancer. On the other side of the equation, Reynolds and Kaplan (1990) found that women who were socially isolated had twice the risk of contracting hormone-related cancer.

Social Support and HIV   The effects of social support on immune-system status in HIV-positive men have been investigated in at least two studies. In one, Goodkin and colleagues (1992) studied 62 symptom-free HIV-positive gay men. They found that NK cell activity was greater for men who were low in stress and who reported higher levels of social support. This suggests that social support helps people low in stress but not those experiencing high levels of stress. This might seem to contradict the notion that social support is most useful as a buffer against high stress, but because this is an interactional design, we can't simply conclude that only people low in stress have good social support.

In another study, Theorell and colleagues (1995) looked at changes in T-helper cell counts in 48 HIV-positive men over a five-year period. They found that social support did have a significant effect on these counts but that it took time for that effect to be realized. Figure 3-5 shows that there was little difference between the high- and low-support men in the first two years of the study. However, after that, the men with low support showed a much more dramatic decline in T-helper cell counts. Remember that these cells are considered to be important in the prognosis of people who are HIV positive.

What can we conclude from these studies on social support and immune function? While the effects on immunity aren't as striking as those for stress, social support is clearly beneficial to health. This is especially true for people who are low in stress to begin with. It is also worth investigating further the possibility that the effects of social support are more significant over longer time periods than in short bursts.

PROPOSED BIOLOGICAL MECHANISMS TO EXPLAIN WHY PSYCHOLOGICAL STATES AFFECT THE IMMUNE SYSTEM

We have reviewed many studies indicating that psychological states and traits can influence our immune system in a variety of ways. This influence increases or decreases our susceptibility to a range of medical conditions and helps or hinders our ability to cope with these conditions once we have them. An important question remains to be answered, however. Just

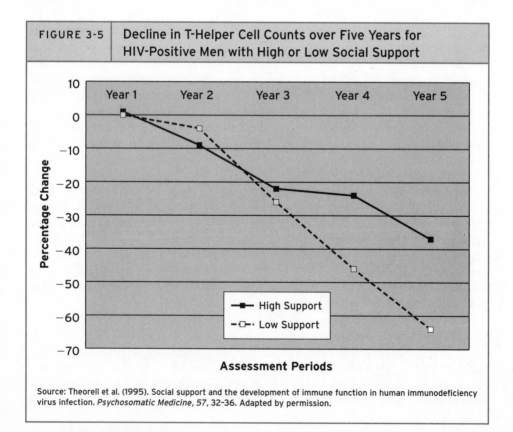

FIGURE 3-5 | **Decline in T-Helper Cell Counts over Five Years for HIV-Positive Men with High or Low Social Support**

Source: Theorell et al. (1995). Social support and the development of immune function in human immunodeficiency virus infection. *Psychosomatic Medicine, 57,* 32-36. Adapted by permission.

how does our biological makeup allow for this influence? When looking for mechanisms that link psychological factors to health, researchers tend to cite four possible sources—the endocrine system, which controls hormones; the sympathetic nervous system; the immune system; and behaviour (see Kiecolt-Glaser et al., 2002a for a concise review).

Our immune (or endocrine) system, and thus our health, is controlled, in part by hormonal secretions. Catecholamines and cortisol are good examples of hormones that are affected by psychological states such as stress, thus providing one mechanism linking stress and health.

The sympathetic nervous system is also activated during times of stress, stimulating our "fight-or-flight" response. The immune system is affected by **glucocorticoids**, which are substances released by the adrenal glands upon stimulation from the sympathetic division when we are under stress. We also know that lesions to the hypothalamus affect immune functioning (see Maier et al., 1994 for a review of this research). Following this reasoning, it has been hypothesized that people whose sympathetic divisions are more reactive would be more likely to experience immunosuppression when under stress. This has been called the **reactivity hypothesis** (Cacioppo et al., 1998). In support of this hypothesis, it has been shown that people who show higher levels of cardiovascular reactivity also show the greatest immune changes when in stressful situations (Kiecolt-Glaser et al., 1992; Manuck et al., 1991; Sgoutas-Emch et al., 1994). We are talking here about people whose heart rate and other autonomic functions require less stimulation to kick into "fight-or-flight" mode. This explains immunologic changes in the face of acute stressors. Kiecolt-Glaser and Glaser (1995) speculate further that chronic stressors have lasting effects on cardiovascular reactivity that bring about the same susceptibility to stress-related immune changes. They suggest that people whose sympathetic division is particularly reactive might be at greater risk for infectious disease. In times of stress, the body must make a priority decision. Does energy go into combating the stressor or fighting off antigens? The answer is that we give priority to the stressor. For those who react more markedly to those stressors, their immune functioning may be further compromised, on both a short-term and long-term basis.

Psychological states also affect behaviour, which can directly and indirectly affect immunity. For example, stress and depression can disrupt sleep. It is during sleep that some important immunity-regulating hormones are produced. Stress is also associated with increased alcohol and drug use, which also affects our health.

At least one more question remains. What is the adaptive advantage of a biological system that places greater priority on fight-or-flight responses than on fighting off disease? Our ancestors required biological resources to deal with immediate concerns in the form of fight-or-flight responses. It did them little good to be free of upper respiratory infection if their very survival was in jeopardy. Disease control wasn't a priority. Further, when under attack it is advantageous to inhibit inflammation due to injury, so the immune system has to be temporarily suppressed. Today, we might argue otherwise, but we are living with the vestiges of our ancestors' biological priorities.

FUTURE DIRECTIONS FOR PSYCHONEUROIMMUNOLOGICAL RESEARCH

Given the importance and complexity of PNI research, there is much to do in the future. At least three directions have been suggested for this future research (Maier et al., 1994):

1. We need to know more about which psychological factors affect which specific aspects of immune functioning. We must be careful not to jump to generalizations such as, "Stress compromises immune function." We need to know more about the relative timing of stressor, immunosuppression, and antigen introduction. Exactly when are we most susceptible to disease?

2. We must continue to promote research that includes disease as an endpoint while concurrently measuring immune functioning.

3. Because psychological factors affect other aspects of biological functioning that can, in turn, affect health (e.g., fatigue), we need to learn more about the interaction between these factors and immune functioning. And because the immune systems of older adults are particularly susceptible to compromise, this population deserves particular attention in future research (Kiecolt-Glaser & Glaser, 2001).

KEY TERMS

acquired immunity (p. 58)

acute stressor (p. 62)

antigens (p. 57)

antimicrobial substances (p. 59)

B lymphocytes (p. 58)

diathesis-stress model (p. 80)

enumerative assay (p. 60)

focal infection (p. 57)

functional tests of immunity (p. 60)

glucocorticoids (p. 83)

helper T cells (p. 59)

immune-system memory (p. 58)

immunocompetence (p. 56)

interleukins (p. 59)

localized infection (p. 57)

memory B cells (p. 58)

microorganisms (p. 57)

mitogen (p. 61)

natural-killer (NK) cells (p. 59)

NK cell cytotoxic activity assay (p. 61)

NK cell lysis (p. 61)

non-specific immunity (p. 59)

pathogens (p. 57)

psychoneuroimmunology (PNI) (p. 56)

reactivity hypothesis (p. 83)

resistance (p. 63)

seroconversion (p. 58)

social support (p. 81)

specific immunity (p. 58)

specificity (p. 58)

states and traits (p. 72)

stress intrusion scores (p. 67)

suppressor T cells (p. 59)

systemic infection (p. 57)

tolerance (p. 58)

type C personality (p. 80)

upper respiratory infection (URI) (p. 66)

viral challenge studies (p. 68)

chapter four

Communication in Medical Settings

CHAPTER OUTLINE

Perceiving and Interpreting Symptoms

Seeking Medical Care

   Delaying Medical Care

Physician-Patient Interaction

   Basic Models of Physician-Patient Interaction

   Physician-Patient Communication

Adhering to Medical Advice

   Assessing Adherence

   Frequency and Cost of Non-Adherence

   What Factors Predict Adherence?

   Improving Patient Adherence

Health Outcomes

KEY QUESTIONS

1. What factors influence our perception and interpretation of symptoms?
2. Why do people delay in seeking medical care?
3. How have researchers conceptualized physician–patient relationships?
4. What patient and physician characteristics lead to poor communication?
5. How widespread is patient non-adherence?
6. How can we improve patient adherence to medical advice?
7. Does patient adherence lead to better health outcomes?

Lynn is visiting her physician, primarily because she has recently been experiencing a lot of stomach discomfort. However, this isn't Lynn's only complaint. In addition to her stomach problems, Lynn hasn't been sleeping, she has more blemishes on her face than usual, and her mother has recently been diagnosed with adult-onset diabetes. Lynn is quite concerned about her. Upon visiting her physician, Lynn decides she will present her symptoms, in order of ease of describing them. Lynn says "My face has been worse than usual lately, I haven't been getting enough sleep, and I've had a lot of butterflies in my stomach these last few weeks." Lynn doesn't bother to mention her concern about her mother to the physician because she already has a lot of issues to discuss and knows the physician can't possibly help her mother during this visit. Lynn's physician dismisses the "butterflies" because Lynn has downplayed this symptom and hasn't reported any pain in her stomach. He also assumes Lynn hasn't been getting enough sleep simply because she has been busy lately. The doctor therefore decides that Lynn is primarily there to seek help for her "worse than usual" face. He provides her with a prescription for a topical ointment and sends her on her way. The main reason for Lynn visiting her physician, her upset stomach, is never discussed.

Compare Lynn's visit with her physician to the more positive visit experienced by Alexander and his parents to the emergency ward.

Alexander is an 18-month-old toddler who just loves to run. However, running is a relatively new talent and he sometimes forgets a few required details, such as looking where he's going! After a head-on collision with the corner of a kitchen cupboard and a resulting gash on his forehead, his parents take him to Emergency to get his cut sutured. As expected, there is a wait before Alexander can see a doctor. Once Alexander sees the doctor, the stitchwork begins. The physician seems to realize it is a very stressful situation for the young family. The physician quietly reassures Alexander that everything is going to be okay. Then Mom and Dad are told how to care for the laceration and all their questions are answered. They are allowed to stay in the room to lessen Alexander's anxiety, and when the suturing is complete Alexander is given a "rubber glove balloon" and a popsicle.

Most people have had both positive and negative experiences with physicians. Lynn's experience exemplifies a situation in which a patient isn't completely satisfied with the outcome of a visit with a physician. In this case, Lynn didn't have all of her concerns addressed during the physician–patient interview. Indeed, her primary concern, stomach problems, wasn't even mentioned by her physician. In contrast, it is obvious that Alexander, or at least his parents, were very satisfied with their interaction with the emergency room physician. From the moment Alexander arrived at Emergency, it was obvious why he was seeking treatment. Treatment was provided for Alexander and his parents had all of their questions answered.

Effective communication was a major contributing factor to the satisfaction Alexander's parents felt with the treatment they received from their physicians, whereas the lack of communication between Lynn and her physician resulted in a negative experience for her.

Communication is central to the physician–patient relationship. In this chapter, we will discuss how both physician and patient behaviours contribute to faulty communication. As well, we will outline the impact communication has on physician–patient relationships, adherence to medical advice, and health outcomes. However, before we begin our discussion of communication in the medical setting, we must consider the factors that lead one to seek medical advice in the first place.

PERCEIVING AND INTERPRETING SYMPTOMS

How do we decide when to seek medical advice? Clearly, Alexander's parents knew they should seek medical care for their son. The cut on his forehead and the dripping blood were fairly obvious clues. But what led Lynn to seek medical advice? Many of her symptoms are sensations that people experience every day; people often have blemishes on their skin and stomachaches from time to time. But they don't seek medical advice each and every time one of these "symptoms" arises. How do we decide when to seek medical advice?

Perceiving symptoms is not as easy as it may seem. People have difficulty deciphering and even noticing some symptoms. For instance, people often don't notice even highly visible external symptoms such as a mole-like lesion that may be melanoma (Miles & Meehan, 1995). It is therefore not surprising to learn that people also have difficulties accurately assessing their internal states. For example, people's estimates of their own heart rate are not well correlated with physiological indices (Pennebaker, 1983). These differences account partly for the considerable variability regarding when an individual will seek medical advice.

Certainly, there are individual differences in the perception of symptoms. Have you ever noticed how some people seem to keep going no matter what, whereas others seem to adopt the sick role the instant they are faced with a minor impediment. Some of these individual differences are constant over time. That is, individuals who pay a lot of attention to their internal states are consistently more likely to notice a symptom than others are (Pennebaker, 1983; Pennebaker, 1994). This does not necessarily mean that these people are more accurate in their interpretation of sensations; in fact, they may overestimate changes in their physiological functions, such as heart rate and nasal congestion.

Stressful periods in people's lives can precipitate or aggravate the experience of symptoms. People who have experienced a great deal of stress are more vulnerable to illness (see chapter 3). People who believe they are more likely to contract an illness will also attend more closely to their bodies. This inward focus of attention may lead them to interpret stress-related physiological changes, such as accelerated heart rate or breathing, as symptoms of illness (Cameron, Leventhal, & Leventhal, 1995).

Our current mood also affects our perception of our health (Salovey et al., 1991). People in a good mood view their own health more positively than do those in a bad mood. We have all experienced being in such a good mood that we didn't notice our normally aggravating aches and pains, as well as being in such a bad mood that we notice every discomfort, no matter how minor. Research backs up these experiential observations. People in a good mood report fewer symptoms and fewer illness-related thoughts. In contrast, people in a bad mood report more symptoms, are less likely to believe that any behaviours they engage in will relieve symptoms, and assume they are more vulnerable to future illness (Salovey et al., 1991; Leventhal et al., 1996; Stegen et al., 1998). One study (Croyle & Uretsky, 1987) found that inducing a temporary bad mood in participants led them to judge their health more negatively and to report more symptoms than those participants who had been put into a good mood.

Situational factors also influence whether we will recognize a symptom. When the environment is exciting or demands a great deal of attention or concentration, people are less likely to notice internal symptoms (Pennebaker, 1994). Internal symptoms are also likely to go unnoticed when an individual is engaged in physical activity. Pennebaker (1983) relates many findings that are consistent with this view. He has observed, for example, that "individuals are more likely to notice itching or tickling sensations in their throats and emit coughs during boring parts of movies than during interesting portions" (p. 191).

There are also age differences in the reporting of symptoms. Elderly people frequently complain of physical symptoms that prompt them to seek medical intervention. There is evidence to suggest that normal age-related bodily changes are perceived by older people as illness (Gott et al., 1999; Haug, Musil, Warner, & Morris, 1997). Other researchers have suggested that the tendency for symptoms to increase as one ages may be partially due to the decreased cognitive performance that some adults experience as they age (Frisoni, Fedi, Geroldi, & Trabucchi, 1999). In other words, mild cognitive impairment is associated with the perception of poorer body functioning. These studies suggest that older adults may over-report their symptoms. However, a study of cancer patients discovered that older adults were less likely than younger adults to notice cancer symptoms (Mor et al., 1990). Other studies report that older men delay seeking help for symptoms that might be viewed as embarrassing, such as those indicative of sexually transmitted disease (Gott et al., 2003; Pitts et al., 2000). Thus, the issue of age differences in the recognition of symptoms is quite complex.

In summary, symptom recognition depends on several factors. Individual differences in attention to one's body as well as transitory situational factors that alter the direction of one's attention influence the perception of symptoms. When attention is directed inward, symptoms are more likely to be recognized. On the other hand, when attention is directed outward, by physical activity or a distracting environment, symptoms are less likely to be noticed. Age differences as well as our current mood also influence symptom recognition.

Once a symptom is perceived, it must then be interpreted. How a symptom is interpreted is influenced by a number of factors, including prior experience with the symptom. If, for example, your mother and your siblings have had their appendixes removed, you are more likely to consider appendicitis whenever you experience pain in your lower abdomen. Other people, who do not share this family history, would likely consider other causes for the pain before considering appendicitis.

A symptom's meaning is also influenced by how common it is within one's family, friends, acquaintances, and culture (Croyle & Hunt, 1991). Symptoms that are perceived as commonplace are generally considered to be less serious than more rare or unusual ones (Croyle & Ditto, 1990; Peay & Peay, 1998, 2000). As strange as it may seem, the simple fact that a symptom or condition is widespread may lead people to attach little significance to it, sometimes unwisely.

Cultural factors can affect how quickly and what kind of symptoms are recognized and reported (Klonoff & Landrine, 1994). For example, one study compared the symptom recognition reported by Anglos and Mexicans (Burnum, Timbers, & Hough, 1984). The researchers reported that Mexicans were more likely than Anglos to report symptoms that occurred frequently. In contrast, Anglos were more likely than Mexicans to report only those symptoms which they experienced infrequently. Another study (Alonso et al., 1998) noted that there are cross-cultural differences in the reporting of vision problems. Specifically, cataract patients in Canada and Spain were less likely to report trouble with their vision than were Danish or American patients. These reports could not be accounted for by either clinical or socio-demographic factors.

A very important consideration in assessing the symptoms that people report is the role of learning. In a very real sense, we learn how to experience symptoms. It is therefore likely that people in different cultures receive different "lessons" about the experience of symptoms. For example, in Western culture, men have traditionally been socialized not to complain about emotional and physical symptoms of discomfort as this is seen to be a sign of weakness. Not surprisingly, men are less likely than women to report such symptoms (Nicholas, 2000). At a very young age, children are taught both directly and by example which symptoms are important and which are trivial. A parent's concern over a fever and seeming lack of concern over a superficial cut provide a child with powerful cues about which symptoms to attend to and which to ignore. Our families contribute to our interpretation of symptoms in other ways, as well. We often consult our family and friends for help in interpreting the meaning of a symptom. These advisers form a **lay referral system**, an informal network of non-practitioners who offer their own interpretations long before any medical treatment is sought (Suls, Martin & Leventhal, 1997). People in the lay referral system provide advice when someone mentions the symptoms, requests an opinion, or even if he or she simply looks sick. The friend or relative responds with personal views of what the symptom is likely to mean: "Connor and Liam both had rashes like that. It turned out it was a reaction to the new brand of bubble bath their Mom had bought" (c.f. Croyle & Hunt, 1991). The friend or relative provides advice about seeking medical attention: "Parker's temperature was getting quite high and he ended up having convulsions. You'd better call your doctor." He or she may also recommend various home remedies, such as "soak a wool sock in boiling water and vinegar and then wrap it around your neck, your sore throat will be gone in no time" (e.g., Stoller, 1984).

| CASE 4-1 | **Delay in Seeking Treatment** |

One day after Dean returned from a four-hour bike ride, he noticed that one of his testicles was quite sore. He thought the sensation was odd, but he quickly rationalized that he had just spent a considerable amount of time in the "saddle" and that this was likely responsible for his discomfort. The dis-

(continued on next page)

comfort did not completely go away but Dean, an aspiring professional cyclist, continued to spend a large amount of time on his bike. About a month later he was thinking about his testicular soreness again. He realized that the discomfort wasn't subsiding. He vowed to visit a physician the next chance he got. Unfortunately, he was off to Dijon, France in two days to try out for a professional cycling team and would likely have to wait until he returned to Canada before he could visit the physician. Three weeks later Dean returned to Canada. He hadn't experienced much discomfort when he was in France because he had been caught up in the excitement of fulfilling his dream of getting paid for doing what he loved. Back home, in his own environment, he became aware that his discomfort was becoming more intense. Obviously, there was more wrong with him than simply spending too many hours training. He was extremely anxious as he made an appointment to see his family physician. The next day he visited his physician. This visit led to a number of medical tests to aid the physician in making a diagnosis. The physician felt it was likely that Dean had testicular cancer. Subsequently, this diagnosis was confirmed and the prognosis was not good. Dean was told that he had only a 50–50 chance of surviving because the cancer was at such an advanced stage.

The advice provided by the lay referral network varies in its usefulness. Sometimes, it is very helpful. For example, a study conducted at the Children's Hospital in Montreal determined that mothers who consulted their lay referral system about their child's symptoms were less likely to take their children to the emergency department unnecessarily. Although much of the advice provided by the lay referral network is helpful, lay persons are far more likely than health professionals to recommend actions that worsen the condition or delay seeking appropriate and needed treatment.

SEEKING MEDICAL CARE

When do people seek medical care? The answer to this question is more complex than simply stating that people visit their physician when they have experienced one or more symptoms. In spite of the fact that 75 to 90 percent of the general population at any given time experience symptoms that could be considered clinically relevant, only about one-third of them seek medical care (DiMatteo, 1991). Studies of illness behaviour indicate that *when* a person seeks help is a function of the specific nature of the symptoms experienced as well as of their social and personal needs.

Perhaps the most obvious determinant of when a person seeks help is the type of symptoms experienced. Symptoms that are new, unexpected, painful, disruptive, highly visible, or that affect highly valued parts of the body are interpreted as more serious and are more likely to lead someone to seek medical care (Eifert et al., 1996; Meechan, Collins, & Petrie, 2003; Turk & Melzack, 2001). If one's symptoms are recognizable from past experiences and are believed to be unimportant or explainable, such as muscle aches after an athletic competition, they will probably be ignored. However, if the symptom interferes with daily activities such as job performance or participation in athletic events, medical care is usually sought. Symptoms also gain a person's attention if they attack a highly visible part of the body such as the face or eyes, or if they are important to one's self-identity (such as a lump in a woman's breast; Meechan, et al., 2003). Above all, the symptom that leads a person to seek medical care most quickly is the experience of pain. Few of us enjoy pain and as a result we will attempt to eliminate the painful experience as fast as possible (Turk et al., 1985).

Delaying Medical Care

Dean was lucky. He won his battle against testicular cancer. However, his odds of survival would likely have been better if he had not delayed so long in seeking medical advice. Delay in seeking diagnosis and treatment is clearly linked to increases in morbidity and mortality of cancer patients (Ramirez et al., 1999; Richards et al., 1999). Perhaps Dean would have sought medical care sooner if it was more obvious that his symptoms required medical treatment. In medical emergencies, such as when someone sustains a severe injury, people often seek help in a matter of minutes or hours. Referring back to Alexander, the little boy with the cut on his forehead, we can assume that his parents wasted no time in getting him to the hospital as quickly as possible.

Other emergency situations are more ambiguous. Most heart attack victims initially attribute their symptoms to such conditions as gas pains, ulcers, gallbladder diseases, or even the common cold (Gentry, 1979). Patients suffering from a myocardial infarction (more commonly referred to as a heart attack) typically arrive at the hospital or into the care of paramedical staff at some point between one hour and several days after the onset of their symptoms. Most often the time from onset of symptoms to the initiation of medical help is between two-and-a-half and four hours. Studies show that heart attack victims spend about 65 percent of that time trying to decide whether their symptoms require medical treatment. Even after they have correctly attributed the symptoms to a serious condition, such as a heart attack, people will waste a substantial amount of time before taking direct action to receive treatment.

What is responsible for such delay? Researchers have attempted to answer this question. In doing so, they have developed a model to outline different stages of delay. Researchers refer to **patient delay** as the period between an individual's first awareness of a symptom and treatment of that symptom. Total patient delay occurs in a sequence of stages (Andersen, Cacioppo, & Roberts, 1995). As the diagram in Figure 4.1 illustrates, the stages are 1) **appraisal delay**, the time it takes for a person to decide that a symptom is a sign of illness; 2) **illness delay**, the time between recognizing one is ill and deciding to seek medical care; 3) **behavioural delay**, the time that elapses between the decision to seek medical care and acting on this decision by making an appointment; and 4) **medical delay** (scheduling and treatment), the interval between making an appointment and first receiving medical care.

Safer, Tharps, Jackson, and Leventhal (1979) conducted an early study identifying stages of delay in seeking medical care. These researchers interviewed 93 patients who were waiting to see a physician at a hospital clinic or emergency room. They assessed patients' reactions to their symptoms and determined at what point these patients first interpreted their symptoms as illness, when they decided to seek medical care, and when they actually took steps to bring the problem to a medical professional. Not surprisingly, those who demonstrated the least delay were those in the greatest pain. The total delay in

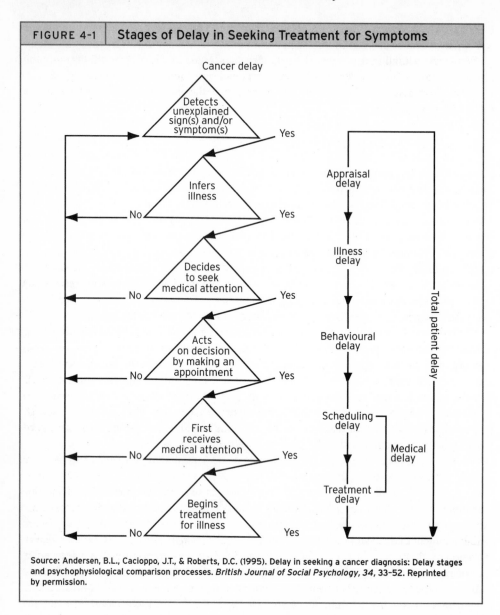

FIGURE 4-1 | Stages of Delay in Seeking Treatment for Symptoms

Source: Andersen, B.L., Cacioppo, J.T., & Roberts, D.C. (1995). Delay in seeking a cancer diagnosis: Delay stages and psychophysiological comparison processes. *British Journal of Social Psychology, 34,* 33–52. Reprinted by permission.

seeking care was significantly longer for patients who currently had other problems in their lives (such as a troubled marriage), who had read about their symptoms, who were older, and who had waited for the symptoms to go away. The best predictor of illness delay was whether the person had a new symptom. Patients were more likely to see an old symptom as normal and to tolerate it for a long period of time before deciding to seek medical care. Understandably, patients who imagined they were severely ill and imagined negative consequences of being ill had lengthy illness delays. And, not surprisingly, people who believed they could not be cured also delayed treatment.

The findings of the previous study (Safer et al., 1979) should be interpreted somewhat cautiously because of its methodological limitations. First, because the study included only persons who actually sought medical care there is no way to generalize conclusions concerning delay to those persons who had a symptom but did not seek treatment. Second, the study uses retrospective data. This is particularly important, because the patients were asked to recall and specify the point at which they first noticed the symptom, when they first felt they were ill, and when they decided to seek treatment. Because the patients are asked to remember this information rather than report it as it was happening, there may be inaccuracies in the information. A prospective study, in which the participants maintain a diary of their symptoms and their appraisals of those symptoms, would be a more effective way of studying delay behaviours.

Recent research investigating delay behaviours has focused almost exclusively on cancer patients. Studying this population's delay behaviour is most appropriate because, as previously mentioned, delays in treatment for cancer have a significant influence on survival rates (Ramirez et al., 1999; Richards et al.,1999). A meta-analysis of 12 studies estimated that 34 percent of women with breast cancer symptoms delay seeking medical advice for three months or more (Facione, 1993). Both prospective (e.g., Andersen et al., 1995) and retrospective research reveals that appraisal delay accounts for the majority of the total delay time.

In her review of the literature, Facione (1993) reports that both high and low levels of fear are associated with longer delays in reporting breast cancer symptoms. Fear, for these women, may include fear of doctors and hospitals, cancer, embarrassment, chemotherapy, disfigurement, pain, loss of femininity, and loss of control, to name but a few. Women with a tremendous fear of a diagnosis of cancer because of all these associated repercussions will delay having to deal with these issues (Facione & Giancarlo, 1998; Lauver, Coyle, & Panchmatia, 1995; Timko, 1987). On the other hand, those with very little fear are likely to delay seeking medical advice because they feel it is unnecessary.

Social influences may also affect delay behaviour. Many women believe that if they are diagnosed with breast cancer their male partner will abandon them (Facione & Giancarlo, 1998). And while a number of studies reveal that marital status is unrelated to delays by patients (e.g., Ramirez et al., 1999), there is support for the hypothesis that the role responsibilities of married women with children influence delay behaviour (Facione, 1993; Facione, Giancarlo, & Ingram, 1999; Lauver, Coyle, & Panchmatia, 1995). Women report that devoting time and attention to the needs of others, making domestic arrangements prior to the biopsy, arranging for childcare during the summer and school holidays, and dealing with work-related demands all receive priority over discovered breast cancer symptoms.

Another factor that has been considered in delay behaviour is the age of the patient. Age is often reported as having an effect on patient delay. However, findings haven't always been consistent (e.g., Mor et al., 1990). Ramirez and colleagues (1999); Richards and colleagues (1999); and Sainsbury, Johnston, and Haward (1999) all report that older age is associated with longer symptom-reporting delay by breast cancer patients. Unfortunately, these investigators have not utilized the stages of delay model provided by Andersen and colleagues (1995), outlined in Figure 4-1. However, these studies do divide the time between onset of symptoms and start of treatment (total delay) into two main phases: delay by patients, defined as time between onset of symptoms and time of first medical consultation; and delay by providers, which is any delay between first medical consultation and start of treatment. Analysis based on this definition of delay reveals that older women are more likely to engage in patient delay than are younger women. However, younger women experience more delay by their health care providers (Ramirez et al., 1999). Based on the results of the study conducted by Richards and colleagues (1999), we can conclude that the health care providers were less likely to delay treatment of the older women because the older women were at a more advanced stage of cancer (likely resulting from their delay in seeking medical advice). Fortunately, delays by providers "do not seem to be associated with decreased survival in patients presenting with breast cancer" (Sainsbury et al., 1999, p. 1132).

| CASE 4-2 | **One Surgeon's Story: Invincible or In Denial?** |

What accounts for the delay behaviour of a 37-year-old male surgeon diagnosed as having a malignant, non-Hodgkins lymphoma (cancer of the lymph nodes)? Jorge delayed identifying his symptoms as those of a possible serious illness even though he was trained to recognize the importance of such symptoms in his patients.

One morning, Jorge noticed a small lump on his jaw while shaving. He found the lump curious, but he certainly wasn't going to worry about it. As a general rule, physicians have a unique ability to think of themselves as invul-nerable to the ailments and misery that they are exposed to each day. Jorge was in complete denial and he ignored the lump. As time went by, the lump slowly enlarged and he casually showed it to his physician friends. He thinks they said not to worry but he really can't remember. Finally, at a dinner party one night, a woman with no medical training asked, "What is that thing under your jaw?" Jorge, still believing all was well, set up an appointment with a surgeon. He underwent surgery, five months of radiation treatment, and has lived to tell his story (Shlain, 1979).

In summary, there are a number of factors that contribute to patient delay, including characteristics of the symptom, age, gender, societal role obligations, and psychological attributes such as fear. Even physicians who are familiar with illness symptoms and know the importance of treating these symptoms promptly are not exempt from patient delay; consider the behaviour of Jorge, described in Case 4-2. A final, extremely important, factor contributing to people's decisions to use medical services is the quality of the relationship they have with their physicians. This important relationship is the topic of the next section.

PHYSICIAN-PATIENT INTERACTION

Onions (1986) defines a patient as "a sufferer, one who is under medical treatment, or a person to whom something is done" and a client as "one who is under the protection or patronage of another, a dependent." There is some controversy about whether *patient* or *client* is the most appropriate term for referring to someone who is receiving health care. A review of the literature reveals a plethora of opinion but little research on the issue.

A single North American study on this topic was conducted in Vancouver, British Columbia (Wing, 1997). This study includes the responses of 101 people who were attending a back-pain clinic. Each person was given a short letter saying "There is an interesting discussion in hospitals at this time about the term that we use for people we try to help" (p. 288). Respondents were then asked to indicate if they prefer the term *client* or *patient*. To avoid selection bias for the first option, the letters with *patient* first and those with *client* first were alternated. The overwhelming majority of respondents (74) stated a preference for the term *patient*. Nineteen respondents preferred *client*, and the remaining eight had no preference.

The results obtained by Wing are similar to those reported in overseas studies. A New Zealand study found that 87 percent of visitors to a hospital on an outpatient basis preferred to be called patients (Elliot & White, 1990). Similarly, a study conducted in Australia discovered that 84 percent of patients and their companions attending outpatient departments preferred the term *patient* (Nair, 1998). There appear to be no sex differences in this preference; however, a slight trend was noted in the preference for *patient* in older age groups (Nair, 1998). Clearly, the preference, at least in these settings, is to be called *patient*.

An issue that has been, and should be, of concern to health care professionals is whether their attitudes and behaviours are shaped (especially adversely) by the use of a particular term for the people they help. Imrie (1994) suggests that using the term *patient* serves as a useful reminder to health care professionals that those being helped do suffer and should be treated with compassion. Moreover, Atkinson (1993) implied that the term "sufferer" has a passive connotation. Certainly, the implication of passiveness is what may make someone dislike being referred to as a "patient."

Although there are concerns related to the use of the term *patient*, there are also concerns about the implications of the term *client*. Raphael and Emmerson (1991) identify a number of points to consider before adopting the term *client*. These include 1) denial that the person has an illness or that certain treatments may be necessary (e.g., insulin for diabetics); 2) implication of effective choice of treatment and responsibility for remuneration, two conditions that cannot be met in all disease states and economic situations (e.g., a man with paranoid schizophrenia, dangerous to himself and society, has no insight or ability to make decisions about treatment that, although associated with risks, may control the condition); and 3) lack of the special elements of care and compassion implicit in the term *patient*.

Undoubtedly there are arguments in favour of each term. In this text we choose to use the word *patient*, but hope there can be a shift in the passive connotation of the term. We may best heed the logic of a participant in Nair's (1998) study, who remarked "there is nothing in a name, provided there is care" (p. 593).

Basic Models of Physician–Patient Interaction

A crucial element in the typical interaction between a patient and a health care practitioner is the nature of their relationship. A classic article in the field of health psychology, written by Thomas Szasz and Marc Hollender in 1956, outlines three basic models they believed characterized the nature of the physician–patient relationship.

The **active–passive model** describes a relationship in which the patient is unable to participate in his or her own care and to make decisions for his or her own welfare because of the severity of the medical condition. For example, when a patient has a severe injury or is in a coma the physician is responsible for providing care and making decisions on behalf of the patient; obviously, the patient is not in a position to provide any input. Consider the following situation:

> Dennis gashed himself with a knife while camping in the bush. He cut an artery and the blood was spurting out. His buddies placed him in the back of their pickup truck and sped down the highway toward the nearest town. By the time they reached the hospital, Dennis was unconscious. A few seconds after they arrived at the hospital emergency ward, Dennis was placed on a gurney and wheeled to the operating room. Then Dennis' clothing was ripped off and the severed artery was found and tied. At the same time, others were working to find a vein that had not collapsed in order to put in an intravenous line. The entire emergency room staff worked with skill and speed. Dennis, who was unconscious, could neither participate nor fight their efforts.

The **guidance–cooperation model** applies when the patient seeks advice from the physician. The patient answers the questions that are asked about his or her symptoms but the physician is responsible for determining diagnosis and treatment. In essence, the physician is responsible for the thinking and decision making. This model would likely be followed if a person had an infection or a sprain. Consider the following example:

> Henry was told by his physician to "take one of these little pills three times a day. If you do what I tell you to, you will be just fine." Henry was convinced that asking the physician questions would be challenging physician authority, so he simply nodded in agreement. Henry was to take the medication to control his hypertension. However, he couldn't seem to remember to take the pills. This may have been due to the fact that he didn't feel sick (hypertension is often referred to as "the silent killer") or because he had never been told exactly what the medication would do.

In the **mutual-participation model**, the patient has more responsibility than in the other models. In this model, the physician and patient make joint decisions about every aspect of care, from deciding what diagnostic tests the patient should undergo to the choice and implementation of treatment. Input and responsibility are shared equally by physician and patient. The two work together in a partnership. Here's an example:

> Patient: I don't know how I'll be able to eliminate caffeine from my diet. That will be quite a challenge, especially if there needs to be an immediate reduction in my caffeine consumption.

> Physician: What do you think you'll be able to manage? Can you try to reduce your caffeine intake a little bit every day?

> Patient: I can try but it won't be easy. And, you don't just mean reducing coffee drinking, do you? You also mean reducing the amount of chocolate I consume. I think I'm going to be pretty grumpy over the next while, perhaps you should warn my partner.

> Physician: Is there anything you can think of that I might be able to do to help you?

> Patient: Tell me again exactly why this is necessary. Also, is there anything else I should be doing to help my medical condition?

Do you think this scenario characterizes a typical interaction between a physician and patient? Or, does the patient in this scenario seem unusually assertive? According to some researchers, assertiveness and active involvement on the part of the patient are the precursors of an effective partnership with the physician. The mutual–participation model is seen as the ideal relationship between physician and patient. However, the typical physician–patient relationship is one in which the physician possesses a greater degree of power than the patient.

Power is an issue that we will return to later in the chapter. For now, let's continue with our discussion of physician–patient relationship models. Szasz and Hollender (1956) were the first to provide a theoretical model of the physician–patient relationship, but they were not the last. Other models have been put forth over the years (e.g., Emanuel & Emanuel, 1992), but until recently none have used empirical techniques to determine whether patterns of interaction style in the physician–patient relationship correspond to the theoretical approaches found in the literature.

Roter and colleagues (1997) used audiotape analysis to describe communication patterns in 537 patients seen at 11 outpatient, private, and group primary care settings in the United States and Canada. Their analysis revealed five distinct communication patterns. The first, **narrowly biomedical** communication patterns, were characterized mainly by biomedical talk (e.g., "The medication may make you sleepy"), closed-ended medical questions (e.g., "Are you in pain when you walk?"), and very little discussion of psychosocial topics (such as problems of daily living, emotions, and issues regarding social relations.) The narrowly biomedical pattern occurred in 32 percent of the visits. The second pattern was described as **expanded biomedical**. This pattern also includes numerous closed-ended medical questions but has more moderate levels of biomedical and psychosocial exchange for both physicians and patients. This pattern was common to 33 percent of the visits. The third pattern, **biopsychosocial**, reflects a balance of psychosocial and biomedical communication. The biopsychosocial pattern occurred in 20 percent of visits. The **psychosocial** pattern was the fourth pattern identified by Roter and her colleagues. This pattern includes substantially more psychosocial exchanges than the previous patterns. An example of such an exchange is "It is important to get out and do something on a regular basis. The recreation centre is a great place to find the company of other seniors." Eight percent of visits are considered psychosocial. The final pattern was coined **consumerist**. This pattern of communication also represented eight percent of visits. The consumerist pattern suggests the use of the physician as a consultant who answers questions rather than one who asks them.

It is somewhat difficult to compare the model proposed by Roter and colleagues (1997) with that proposed by Szasz and Hollender (1956) because of the different terminology used in describing the models. However, it is clear that both models place the interactions on a continuum where at one end the patient has little involvement in the decision-making process or in contributions to the interaction and at the other end is at least on par with the physician in guiding the interaction. Szasz and Hollender stated that the mutual–participation model was "essentially foreign to medicine." Now, more than 40 years have elapsed and this statement no longer seems to be true. Roter and colleagues' study suggests that while collaborative models do not predominate, they are certainly evident in primary care practice.

Is the collaborative model the preferred model of physician–patient interaction? According to patients (Fraley & Altmaier, 2002; Roter et al., 1997), the collaborative model, or in Roter's terminology, the psychosocial pattern, is preferred. Somewhat surprisingly, physicians were especially satisfied with the consumerist pattern, reporting that these visits made good use of their time. Patients were moderately pleased with these interactions, though they didn't receive the highest patient satisfaction ratings. Inasmuch as the patients who engaged in this pattern of communication were younger than others, there may be a cohort effect, suggesting that younger generations of patients will be consumerist in their relationships with physicians. In Roter and colleagues' study, the consumerist pattern only occurred in a small proportion of visits. We might speculate that this pattern will increase as younger cohorts get older and develop more chronic conditions and therefore become more frequent users of health services. The patterns least preferred by both patients and physicians were the biomedical patterns. Biomedical patterns of communication were used most often by younger, male physicians and by those physicians interacting with patients who were more sick, were older, and had a lower income.

Focus on Canadian Research 4-1

Patient-Centred Care

Researchers at the University of Western Ontario (McWilliam et al., 2000; Stewart et al., 1995; Stewart, et al., 2000) have refined and tested a patient-centred model of physician–patient interaction that was first proposed by Levenstein (1984). This model highlights the need to integrate the conventional understanding of disease with each patient's unique experience of illness. The model is viewed as a total-person approach to patient problems. Six interconnected components are included in the model (Weston & Brown, 1995).

1. *Exploring both the disease and the illness experience*. Identification of disease, or problems in terms of abnormalities of structure and/or function of body organs and systems, takes place just as it would if a physician subscribed to the biomedical model. However, the patient-centred model focuses on four key dimensions of patients' illness experience: i) what the patients believe is wrong with them; ii) what their feelings (e.g., fears) are about being ill; iii) the impact of the illness on their daily functioning, and iv) how they believe the physician should proceed.

2. *Understanding the whole person*. The physician should come to understand both the patient's disease and experience of illness in the context of the patient's life (e.g., the patient's cultural beliefs, the patient's stage of life, the patient's family situation, etc.).

3. *Finding common ground*. Physicians and patients must reach agreement in three principal areas if they hope to develop an effective management plan: a) the specific problems and priorities; b) the goals of treatment, and c) the role of both the physician and the patient.

4. *Incorporating prevention and health promotion*. The physician and patient must work together to enable the patient to take the steps required to control and improve his or her own health.

(continued on next page)

5. *Enhancing the patient–physician relationship.* Every patient–physician interaction provides the opportunity to build rapport. The establishment of an effective relationship will aid the physician in recognizing the specific approach that should be taken with the patient in order to meet the patient's needs (e.g., recognizing vulnerability and offering support).

6. *Being realistic.* Physicians must recognize their own limits. They must manage their time and emotional energy in a way that provides the most benefit to their patients.

Physician–Patient Communication

Information-Giving   The collaborative model of physician–patient communication preferred by most patients requires their involvement in making decisions about their treatment. But in order to participate in these decisions, patients need information. Physicians provide information to their patients about a number of things, including the patient's diagnosis, possible causes of the problem, and methods of treatment. Information-giving is a very important element of the physician–patient interview, and yet researchers have found that "patients tend to be more dissatisfied about the information they receive from their physicians than about any other aspect of medical care" (Waitzkin, 1985, p. 83). For their part, when questioned about the amount of time they believed they spent giving information to their patients, physicians drastically overestimated the amount of time they were engaged in this task. Specifically, in an average 20-minute interview physicians estimated that they spent approximately nine minutes giving information to their patients. In reality, the physicians spent an average of one minute giving information to their patients.

In related research, Waitzkin (1984, 1985) asked physicians to rate patients' desire for information and their belief in the helpfulness of giving information. Completing a questionnaire based on the same scale, patients rated their desire for information and the benefits of this information to them. Patients reported wanting to know almost everything about their condition and feeling that this information would be extremely beneficial. Physicians, on the other hand, underestimated the patients' desire for information 65 percent of the time, and only 6 percent of the time did they overestimate a particular patient's desire for information. Physicians also reported a much lower belief in the benefits that this information would have for patients.

A number of studies have demonstrated that physicians sometimes choose to withhold information from their patients in an attempt to protect their patients from worry. For example, family doctors who had made a diagnosis of Parkinson's disease, a degenerative nerve disorder, were very concerned about protecting their patients (Pinder, 1990). Specifically, the physicians had difficulty deciding how, when, and whom to tell and deciding just how much information to share about the patient's diagnosis and prognosis. The physicians tended to be positive and overly optimistic. For instance, they avoided detail about medications, were low-key about side effects, and did not explore the problems of long-term use of anti-Parkinson's medication. Most patients, on the other hand, wanted to be given as much information as possible, including information about their medication and its side effects.

Participation   Although the vast majority of patients would like to be informed about what their illnesses are and how to treat them, some want more details about the illnesses, self-administration of treatment, and involvement in decisions than others do (Krantz, Baum, & Wideman, 1980). Thus while many patients are dissatisfied with the amount of information they receive from health professionals and are concerned that information is being withheld from them (Phillips, 1996), many elderly patients prefer that the health professional make health-related decisions for them (e.g., Woodward & Wallston, 1987). Knowing patient preferences is invaluable. Research shows that providing the amount and type of participation patients want in their health care enhances patients' adjustment to and satisfaction with medical treatment (Bennenbroek et al., 2002; Martelli, Auerbach, Alexander, & Mercuri, 1987). Moreover, patients who report a preference for assuming an active role in their treatment tend to recover faster than those who prefer an inactive role (Brody et al., 1989; Mahler & Kulik, 1991).

Just as patients differ in the amount of participation they want regarding their health, health professionals differ in the amount of involvement they are likely to encourage. As we might predict, some physicians are more inclined than others to share their authority and decision making, even among their colleagues (Eisenberg, Kitz, & Webber, 1983). A mismatch between the patient's and the physician's desire for participation can be detrimental to their relationship. Further, as we will discuss in more detail in the next chapter, mismatches of this type will frequently result in an increase in stress experienced by patients during medical procedures. When determining how much information and involvement to provide each patient, health professionals clearly need to consider the needs of the patient.

When physicians interact with patients in a warm, friendly, confident manner, they are viewed as both competent and nice.

General Patient Satisfaction   Considering the needs of the patient is certainly an important component of a physician's role. Most people can recall both positive and negative experiences they have had with physicians. When people talk about their negative experiences, they often mention the physician's hurried manner, insensitivity, lack of responsiveness, apparently faulty diagnoses, or useless treatment. However, most people can also provide details of an interaction with a physician that was exemplary. Patients praise physicians who take their time and answer all their questions. Many of the positive attributes patients recount include personal factors about the physician. Patients show a strong preference for practitioners who have a warm and expressive emotional style as opposed to those who are emotionally neutral (e.g., Clowers, 2002; Coulter, 2002; Thomas, 1987; & Zachariae et al., 2003).

Patient satisfaction with medical care is primarily a function of the quality of the physician–patient relationship. A particularly important consequence of this is that patients often judge the competence of a physician by their emotional satisfaction with care as well as by the degree of confidence their physician demonstrates (Ben-Sira, 1980; Johnson, Levenkron, Suchman, & Manchester, 1988). For example, a warm, friendly, confident practitioner will likely be judged to be more competent than a cool, aloof practitioner regardless of actual skills possessed (Buller & Buller, 1987; DiMatteo, 1979; DiMatteo, Linn, Chang, & Cope, 1985). The important implication of this finding is that patients who are satisfied with the emotional aspects of their care are more likely to want to return to that physician and are more likely to keep future appointments (DiMatteo, Hays, & Prince, 1986; Ross & Duff, 1982). In reality, the technical quality of care and the manner in which it is delivered are unrelated. In Canada, most complaints by the public about physicians deal not with clinical competency problems but with communication problems (Simpson et al., 1991; Richards, 1990).

Patient Satisfaction, Communication, and Malpractice Claims   Patient dissatisfaction and poor communication between patients and physicians may lead patients to file malpractice suits against their physicians (Levinson, 1994). In the year 2001, 1308 malpractice suits were launched, and 96 trials took place, in Canada (The Canadian Medical Protective Association, 2001). The connection between poor communication and complaints is evident in the Complaints Committee's reports of the College of Physicians and Surgeons of Ontario (CPSO). The Committee states that "inadequate communications between MDs and patients or patients' families is still the underlying cause for most of the problems that the CPSO is asked to investigate" (cited in Stewart et al., 1999, p. 25).

As we have already mentioned, patients have preferences and expectations about their interactions with physicians. The physician's awareness of the patient's expectations during a visit is critical in achieving effective communication. And only with effective communication are patients likely to be satisfied with their medical care (Williams, Weinman, Dale, & Newman, 1995; Stewart et al., 1999; Stewart et al., 2000). A number of studies have revealed an association between poor communication and malpractice claims (Hickson et al., 1992; Hickson et al., 1994; Vincent, Young, & Phillips, 1994). The most frequently identified communication problems were inadequate explanation of diagnosis or treatment and patients feeling ignored. However, physicians misleading patients, not understanding patient and family perspectives, devaluing patient and family views, as well as rushing or neglecting patients were also linked to malpractice claims. Whereas the combination of a bad outcome and patient dissatisfaction is said to be "a recipe for litigation," when patients and their families feel the physician was caring and compassionate malpractice suits happen less frequently (Levinson, 1994).

A study conducted by Levinson and colleagues (1997) took a somewhat different approach than previous research to identify specific communication behaviours associated with malpractice claims. Physicians and surgeons were randomly selected from the databases of companies providing malpractice insurance in Oregon and Colorado. Ten routine office visits were audiotaped for each of the 124 participants. Analysis of the conversations revealed significant differences in communication behaviours between physicians who had and those who had not been subjected to malpractice claims. "No-claims" primary care physicians gave more orienting statements about the flow of a visit (e.g., "First I will examine you, and then we will talk about your condition"), laughed and used more humour, facilitated communication (e.g., asking opinion and checking understanding), encouraged their patients to talk, and spent more time with their patients (18.3 vs. 15 minutes). Roughly half of the physicians were primary care physicians and the other half surgeons. Levinson and his colleagues found no behaviours that distinguished between claims and no-claims surgeons.

Undoubtedly, there is a link between communication, patient satisfaction, and malpractice claims. Although researchers have documented a number of components of poor communication possibly responsible for this link, further research is required to explain some of the anomalies (e.g., between physicians and surgeons). While studies investigating the link between communication problems and malpractice claims began relatively recently, research exploring more general communication problems during the physician–patient consultation began decades ago. We now turn our attention to some of this more general research.

Physician Behaviours Contributing to Faulty Communication Having exchanged introductions and established initial rapport, the next step for a physician is to determine what issues the patient wishes to discuss. What is his or her agenda for the consultation? Why has the patient come today? These are questions that cannot be addressed unless the practitioner listens to the patient. In a landmark study (Beckman & Frankel, 1984), physicians were found to interrupt their patients after only 18 seconds! In recent years, this behaviour has improved only slightly; now patients are given 23 seconds to speak before they are interrupted (Marvel, Epstein, Flowers, & Beckman, 1999).

Research (Marvel et al., 1999) clearly demonstrates that even minimal interruptions to patients' initial statements can prevent other concerns from being mentioned at all or can make important complaints arise late in the consultation. By asking patients to provide further comment on any one problem, patients' options are restricted and they are prevented from expanding on other information. For example, a patient may have mentioned headaches but is interrupted before he or she can mention having experienced recent palpitations and marital problems. "Tell me more about your headaches" or worse, "Where do you get the pain?" restricts the discussion to the headaches and limits both the patient's options and the effectiveness of the interview as a whole.

Allowing patients to complete their opening statement without interruption should not be a difficult task for practitioners, as patients usually take less than 60 seconds to do this. In Beckman and Frankel's (1984) research, not a single patient took longer than 150 seconds to complete an opening statement, even when encouraged to continue. Yet, in only 28 percent of the cases are patients given the opportunity to finish their explanations of concerns (Marvel, Epstein, Flowers, & Beckman, 1999). When patients are interrupted, they are given the opportunity to return to, and complete, their opening statement only two percent of the time (Frankel & Beckman, 1989).

Physicians seem to assume that the first complaint the patient mentions is the only one the patient has. However, patients come to an office visit with an average of three concerns they wish to express (Kaplan et al., 1995; Stewart et al., 1986). Further, the order in which patients present their problems is not related to their clinical importance; the first concern presented is no more likely than the second or third to be the most important, as judged by either the patient or the physician (Beckman & Frankel, 1984).

To make matters worse, patients and physicians do not always agree on the nature of the patient's chief complaint (Starfield et al., 1981; Burack & Carpenter, 1983). If you remember Lynn from the beginning of this chapter, you will recall that her major complaint was not addressed by her physician. Lynn's primary reason for visiting her physician was to determine what was causing her stomach problems. However, this was not the first symptom Lynn described to her physician, because she also had some other concerns. Lynn left the physician's office still wondering what was responsible for her stomachache. Stewart, McWhinney, and Buck (1979) discovered that 54 percent of patients' complaints were not elicited during the medical interview. These shocking findings have led researchers to devise interview methods that improve communication during the physician–patient interview (e.g., Maguire & Pitceathly, 2002; Silverman, Kurtz, & Draper, 1998).

Medical Jargon   Another contributing factor to poor communication in the physician–patient interview is the physician's use of **medical jargon** and technical language. For example, the term *splenomegaly* conveys a considerable amount of information to health professionals, but very little to patients. Splenomegaly describes an enlargement of the spleen (a large gland-like organ situated in the upper left side of the abdomen that breaks down red corpuscles) often related to progressive anemia (reduction below normal in the hemoglobin, the volume of packed red blood cells) with no evidence of leukemia or disease of the lymph glands (DiMatteo, 1991). Even if the patient asks the physician for the meaning of splenomegaly, he or she is likely to need the physician to explain the explanation! Test your knowledge of common medical terms by attempting the quiz in Box 4.1.

A classic study (Korsch, Gozzi, & Francis, 1968) revealed that more than half of mothers interviewed reported being confused by the terms pediatricians used during a consultation that had just taken place. Why do physicians use medical jargon when talking to patients? There are a number of reasons.

One reason physicians use medical jargon is because they tend to overestimate the amount their patients can understand (Guttman, 1993). A number of studies have tested patient knowledge of medical terminology. In a typical study, physicians and nurses make lists of medical words that they believe patients understand. When these same words are presented to patients, surprisingly few can define the terms accurately. For example, in the study conducted by Thompson and Pledger (1993) less than half of the patients could define the words *abscess*, *tumour*, *diuretic*, or *cyst* adequately. Moreover, even simple everyday words can be ambiguous when used in a medical context (Hadlow & Pitts, 1991). For example, Mazzullo, Lasagna, and Griner (1974) showed that 52 percent of those interviewed thought that a medication prescribed "for fluid retention" would cause fluid retention.

BOX 4-1	Do You Know What These Medical Terms Mean?

The following 10 medical terms were used in Thompson and Pledger's (1993) study of patients' understanding of medical jargon. Match the terms with the definitions given below:

Do You Know What these Medical Terms Mean?

1. _____ malignant   6. _____ benign

2. _____ incubation   7. _____ chronic

3. _____ acute   8. _____ cyst

4. _____ abscess   9. _____ suture

5. _____ diuretic   10. _____ edema

A. A localized collection of pus in a cavity formed by the disintegration of tissue.

B. The accumulation of excess fluid in a fluid compartment.

C. Persisting for a long time.

D. The provision of proper conditions for growth and development.

E. Having severe symptoms and a short course.

F. Not recurrent: favourable for recovery with appropriate treatment.

G. An agent that promotes urine secretion.

H. A closed sac or capsule containing liquid or a semisolid substance.

I. A joining together of separated tissue or bone, or material used to achieve this joining.

J. Any condition that, if uncorrected, tends to worsen so as to cause serious illness or death, e.g., cancer.

The answers are provided below. Did you obtain a perfect score? If you had been asked to define each of the terms rather than simply fill in the blanks with the provided answers, do you think you would have scored as well?

1-J, 2-D, 3-E, 4-A, 5-G, 6-F, 7-C, 8-H, 9-I, 10-B

Another reason practitioners use medical jargon when speaking to patients is because patients often believe that the sophisticated vocabulary of the physician represents intelligence. Perhaps they feel that they will be better taken care of by a physician who is obviously intelligent.

A more cynical view of the reason for using medical jargon was provided by the famous heart surgeon Dr. Michael DeBakey, who said "Most doctors don't want their patients to understand them! They prefer to keep their work a mystery. If patients don't understand what a doctor is talking about, they won't ask him questions. Then the doctor won't have to be bothered answering them" (Robinson, 1973). Another famous physician, Howard Waitzkin (1985), explained jokingly that if you wanted to forestall any additional questions from the patient you could simply connect the term *itis* (meaning "inflammation of") to whatever organ was troubled (for example, "stomachitis").

More commonly, however, health professionals may use medical jargon with their patients because they simply forget that their patients do not share the same medical vocabulary. Practitioners have spent a number of years in medical school learning this vocabulary, they use it when speaking with their colleagues, and they just naturally use the same vocabulary with their patients.

Unfortunately, when health providers are aware that patients may not understand medical jargon they sometimes go to the opposite extreme and engage in baby talk and simplistic explanations. One example comes from a surgeon who said to an elderly man "We're just going to pop you into the operating theatre to have a little peek into your tummy." Toynbee noticed that the term "pop" was used quite frequently in the hospital by many of the hospital staff. Another physician said, "Nurse, would you just pop off her things for me? I want to examine her." Nurses also "popped" patients in and out of washrooms and wheelchairs, into and out of hospital gowns, beds, and bandages (Toynbee, 1977).

The ideal alternative to the use of medical jargon and baby talk is for practitioners to provide **non-discrepant responses** and **multilevel explanations** when speaking to their patients (Waitzkin, 1985). A non-discrepant response is one that uses the same level of vocabulary that the patient uses when asking the question. For example, if a patient asks about her "lump," the physician might reply by saying we have to remove part of the lump to determine if there is cancer in it. A multilevel explanation is one that initially uses medical jargon but then explains the jargon using everyday language. The use of multilevel explanations educates the patient in medical terminology, as seen in this example: "We'll have to conduct a biopsy to determine if the tumour is malignant. In other words, we'll have to remove the lump to determine if there is cancer in it." The use of medical jargon by health professionals is therefore appropriate if it is explained to the patient or if the patient is already familiar with the terminology.

Time Factors   Another factor thought to limit a physician's ability to communicate effectively is the time available for the consultation. In our discussion of communication issues linked to malpractice claims, we mentioned that if patients felt rushed they were more likely to file a suit. Stewart and her colleagues (1999) reviewed the literature pertaining to communication and time and maintained that "the literature is not clear on this subject perhaps because communication is defined and measured in many different ways" (p. 26).

A number of studies indicate that a long consultation is not required to communicate effectively with patients. Arborelius and Bremberg (1992) reported that positive consultations took less time than negative consultations. In this study, a positive consultation was defined as one where both physician and patient had a positive impression of the consultation; whereas a negative consultation was one where both parties had a negative impression of the consultation. Further, during positive consultations, more time was devoted to patient ideas and concerns. Henbest and Fehrsen (1992) reported that consultations that were **patient-centred** did not take longer than those that were less patient-centred. Patient-centred approaches tend to include more open-ended questions by the physician, such as, "Can you describe when the pain is most severe?" compared to **doctor-centred** approaches in which physicians tend to ask questions that require only very brief answers. Referring back to Roter's (1997) classification of physician–patient relationships, we would say that patient-centred approaches most closely resemble psychosocial patterns of communication, whereas doctor-centred approaches are more similar to biomedical patterns. You may remember that patients tended to prefer the psychosocial pattern and that both patients and physicians liked the biomedical pattern the least. Another study (Clark et al., 1998) found that physicians who were educated about communication issues were rated more favourably by their patients than physicians who did not take part in the education program. This occurred even though, on average, the physicians who had received communication training reported spending less time with them than the physicians who had not received such training. A trend toward lower patient satisfaction with longer visits has also been shown in other studies (e.g., Hornberger, Thorn, & MacCurdy, 1997).

In contrast, the results of some studies indicate a more thorough communication requires longer consultations. For example, studies by Hornberger et al., (1997) and Marvel (1993) concluded that there is a tradeoff between increasing the length of the consultation, the goals of the physician, the goals of the patient, and the many and varied issues professional organizations counselling physicians deem as important. Howie, Porter, Heaney, and Hopton (1999) surveyed patients at the end of a consultation with their physician and reported that patients were more satisfied on a number of dimensions after a long consultation than a short one.

Patient volume has also been related to the length of consultation and patient satisfaction (Zyzanski, Strange, Langa, & Flocke, 1998). Patients visiting high-volume physicians were less satisfied with their interaction than those patients visiting moderate- or low-volume physicians. The patients of high-volume physicians reported less follow-up on patient problems, less attention to patient responses, and less adequate explanations.

Other factors may lead to difficulty in physician–patient communication. The literature reveals that certain topics are described by physicians as being more difficult to discuss, such as alcohol use (Arborelius & Thakker, 1995), stress (Russell & Roter, 1993), and conditions related to particular parts of the anatomy (Larsson, Johanson, & Svardsudd, 1994). Also, some patient characteristics were reported as causing communication difficulties. These characteristics include the socioeconomic status and age of the patient (Bain, 1979). In particular, physicians had more problems communicating with teenagers (Jacobson, Wilkinson, & Owen, 1994) and the elderly (Pereles & Russell, 1996). These communication difficulties may affect the length of the consultation.

Patient Behaviours Contributing to Faulty Communication

PATIENT DECEPTION   Not surprisingly, patients also find some topics difficult to discuss with physicians. Both younger and older patients may experience difficulty and embarrassment discussing topics related to sexually transmitted diseases or sexual behaviours (Gott et al., 2003; Pitts, 2000). Patients may avoid the topic altogether or, if asked directly, they may give false information. Researchers at the University of Victoria (Lewis, Brimacombe, & Matheson, 2003) asked female patients attending a birth control clinic whether they had falsified information during the preceding physician–patient consultation. Approximately one half (46.4 percent) of female respondents admitted withholding or lying about their sexual histories to the physician during the consultation.

The list of topics that patients admit to lying about is long. Burgoon, Callister and Hunsaker (1994) noted that 50 percent or more of the participants in their study admitted to lying "often" or "always" about adherence to medical regimens, exercise behaviours, amount of stress they were under, and financial status. Information about other topics was lied about with less frequency.

LACK OF INFORMATION-SEEKING BEHAVIOURS   Given patients' desire for information from their physicians, we would expect that they would request additional information during the medical interview. However, patients do not engage in many information-seeking behaviours when communicating with their physicians (Beisecker & Beisecker, 1990). In a study conducted by Tuckett, Boulton, and Olson (1985, cited in Silverman, Kurtz, & Draper, 1998), 76 percent of patients said that they had specific doubts or questions during the interview that they did not mention to the physician. When asked why they did not ask the physician questions, patients gave the following reasons: 1) it was not up to them to ask questions, express doubts, or behave as if their view was important (36 percent); 2) they were afraid of being less well thought of by the doctor (22 percent); 3) they were frightened of a negative reaction from the doctor (14 percent); 4) they were too flustered or hurried to ask coherently (27 percent); 5) they doubted that the doctor could tell them any more at the moment (22 percent); 6) they forgot or were waiting until next time to ask, when they would be more certain of what they thought was reasonable to ask (36 percent); and 6) they feared the truth (9 percent).

REMEMBERING   Even if a patient understands all the terminology used, he or she may not remember everything the health care practitioner said. In a review of the literature, Ley (1988) notes that in the hospital setting patients remember approximately 60 percent of the information they are told. When Tucket and colleagues (1985) looked more closely at the information patients recalled, they found that only 10 percent of patients couldn't remember the key points they had been told. That is, most patients could remember the gist of what they heard even if they could not remember all the details.

Anxiety contributes to patients' inability to remember information from a medical interview. Specifically, when people are anxious (as they often are in medical situations) they find it difficult to concentrate and to process incoming information. Again, this is true even when patients understand the information they are being told. A physician describes her experience when told she had cancer in just these terms. She said that even though she knew exactly what her physician was telling her, as soon as she got the "news," she zoned out. She began thinking about what this would mean in terms of all the adjustments she would have to make in her life, whether she would survive, etc., and in doing so she didn't hear another word her physician said to her.

Poor communication between physicians and patients is negatively correlated with patient adherence to treatment regimens. In the words of Moira Stewart and her colleagues at the University of Western Ontario, "Patient–doctor communication and patient adherence are inexorably linked because the interaction provides the context within which the recommendations to be complied with are delivered" (1999, p. 27). Next we will take a closer look at the topic of adhering to medical advice.

ADHERING TO MEDICAL ADVICE

Traditionally, medical professionals have used the term **compliance** to refer to the degree to which patients carry out the behaviours and treatments that physicians and other health professionals recommend. But because the term *compliance* can be interpreted as implying reluctant obedience, many health professionals prefer the term **adherence** (although some use the terms interchangeably). What does it mean to adhere to medical advice? Although we may immediately respond to this question by saying that being adherent means we take medication as a physician has prescribed, adherence is much more than that. Adhering to the advice of a health professional, may mean maintaining healthy lifestyle practices, such as eating properly, avoiding stressful situations, getting enough sleep and exercise, abstaining from smoking, limiting our intake of alcohol; as well as carrying out other behaviours that promote good health. If we do not follow the advice of our health professional, we are said to be **non-adherent**.

How prevalent is the problem of non-adherence? This question is actually more difficult to answer than one might first assume (Turk & Meichenbaum, 1991). Patients may fail to adhere to any of the different types of medical advice just outlined, and they can violate each of these types of advice in many different ways. Thus, failing to take one's medication as prescribed could mean taking medication in the wrong amount or at the wrong time, or discontinuing the medication before the prescribed time has elapsed.

Creative non-adherence is a particularly interesting form of non-adherence This kind of non-adherence is intentional and involves modifying or supplementing the recommended treatment regimen. These alterations are often based on private theories about a health problem and its treatment. For example, the patient may decide that particular symptoms meriting treatment were ignored by the health professional; he or she may then augment the treatment regimen, perhaps including over-the-counter medications or home remedies that interact with prescribed medication in unpredictable, even dangerous ways (Kaplan, 1990). Sometimes, however, these modifications are useful. For example, some patients are thought to have a better idea of how to control their blood glucose level than their health care provider does. Similarly, parents who adjust their child's asthma regimen can control asthma better than if they precisely follow a prescribed regimen. The reason for this is that there are often fluctuations in the severity of asthma (e.g., seasonal variability) and the parents can adjust the treatment in response to their child's needs at the time.

Assessing Adherence

To determine how prevalent the problem of non-adherence is, we must be able to assess it. There are at least seven methods researchers can use to measure patient adherence. They can 1) ask the health professional; 2) ask the patient; 3) ask other people; 4) watch for appointment non-attendance; 5) count pills; 6) watch for treatment non-response, and 7) examine biochemical evidence (Haynes, McDonald, & Garg, 2002; Turk & Meichenbaum, 1991). One of the easiest methods of measuring adherence is to ask the health professional who works with the patient to estimate it. Generally, though, health professionals' estimates of their patients' adherence are inaccurate, often only slightly better than chance (e.g., Blackwell, 1997; Gross et al., 2002; Metry & Meyer, 1999). Typically, health professionals overestimate patient adherence. Another simple approach to measuring adherence is to ask the patient. However, patients also tend to overestimate their adherence, perhaps because they know they should follow "doctor's orders." Health professionals' and patients' reports of adherence are very subjective and may be biased by lying and wishful thinking. The same bias may result when family members are asked to assess the patient's adherence.

More objective measures of patient adherence include pill counting and biochemical tests. In pill counting the medication remaining in the dispenser is compared to the amount that should remain at this point in the treatment regimen to determine if the patient has been following directions. However, even if the right quantity of medication is found, the patient may not have been compliant. We would not know if the patient took the medication at the right times, in the correct amount, or if, wanting to please the health professional, simply discarded some of the medication. Some researchers (e.g., Cramer et al., 1989) have installed microprocessors in the lids of pill containers to record when the pill bottle is opened. Biochemical tests can be conducted, for example, on the patient's blood or urine to determine if the patient has ingested recently. This method of assessment is both time-consuming and expensive. In addition, there are problems with this technique resulting from individual differences in absorption and metabolism of drugs. We should also point out that biochemical tests do not measure the degree of adherence; the presence of a drug simply identifies that the patient ingested some amount of the drug at some time. It does not indicate that the patient took the proper amount at the proper time.

Frequency and Cost of Non-Adherence

Despite the difficulties in assessing adherence, researchers have been able to estimate the prevalence of non-adherence. In general, the rate of non-compliance with medical or health advice is approximately 50 percent. However, the actual range of adherence to prescribed medications, for example, varies from 0 to 100 percent (e.g., Haynes, McKibbon, & Kanani, 1996; McDonald, Garg, & Haynes, 2002). DiMatteo (1994) reported that at least 38 percent of patients do not follow short-term treatment plans (e.g., completing a prescription for medication), and as many as 43 percent do not adhere to recommendations for long-term treatment (e.g., taking hypertensive medication). Moreover, over 75 percent of patients are unwilling or unable to follow suggested lifestyle changes such as exercising regularly or eating a low-fat diet.

The cost of non-adherence is considerable. It is estimated that non-adherence costs Canadians several billion dollars annually (Coambs et al., 1995; MacLeod, 2002). Both direct and indirect costs are incurred when patients fail to adhere. Direct costs result from excessive hospital expenditures (e.g., for people admitted to hospital due to non-adherence of prescription medications), excessive nursing home expenditures (medication non-adherence is the primary reason for elderly patients having to reside in nursing homes), and excessive treatment costs of ambulatory care (e.g., additional visits to a physician). Indirect costs result from reduction in worker productivity due to sick days taken, less efficient work due to illness, and costs associated with premature death.

As you can see, the monetary costs of non-adherence are enormous. But more important, the personal costs due to non-adherence are also immense. Non-adherence often results in people becoming sicker or dying. Why, then, do people fail to adhere to medical recommendations? Although researchers are not completely sure how to answer this question, they have discovered a number of factors that are linked to non-adherence. These factors are outlined in the next section.

What Factors Predict Adherence?

Characteristics of the Treatment Regimen   Some medical recommendations require patients to change *longstanding habits*. For example, a physician may suggest that a patient go on a restricted diet, stop smoking cigarettes, begin a program of regular exercise, or avoid stressful situations. These changes can be thought of as lifestyle changes. Although some patients will adhere to these recommendations, particularly if they are at a high risk for serious illness (Pederson, 1982) it is more likely that people will not make these lifestyle changes (e.g., Turk & Meichenbaum, 1991). Patients presumably do not make these changes because the effort involved in making them seems greater than the health risks of not making them.

Both *complexity* and *duration* of the regimen prescribed also play a role in non-adherence. If you are told to "take one of these pills after meals, one of these other pills every eight hours, two of these pills at bedtime, and these pills as needed" you will likely have some difficulty following the "doctor's orders." As you might predict, the greater the variety of medications one must take and the more complex the schedule, the more likely people are to make an error, thereby failing to adhere to the medical regimen (Cramer et al., 1989; Haynes et al., 2002; McDonald et al., 2002).

Surprisingly, little evidence exists that unpleasant *side effects* lead to non-adherence. Although intuitively we would assume if someone didn't like a treatment he or she would discontinue it, this does not appear to be the case. Instead, it appears that most people who engage in non-adherence do not consider side effects to be a very important factor (Masur, 1981).

As mentioned before, the longer the *duration* of the treatment the less likely people are to adhere to it. Researchers at McMaster University (Haynes et al., 2002; McDonald et al., 2002) reviewed numerous studies comparing adherence rates to the length of treatment and concluded that in most cases, non-adherence increases as duration of therapy increases. Often, long-term treatment programs are for illnesses that have no visible symptoms, such as hypertension. Understandably, people are less motivated to adhere to a treatment if there are no apparent symptoms to indicate they are unwell.

Because people are less likely to adhere to medical recommendations if they do not perceive symptoms of illness, it follows that *severity of an illness* will not lead to adherence unless symptoms are perceived by the patient. The more obvious a symptom is, the more likely people are to adhere to treatment. Perhaps this is one of the reasons why a person's experience with pain is correlated with adherence (Becker, 1979).

Personal Characteristics of the Patient   Adherence is also linked to personal attributes of patients, such as their age, gender, and cultural background. The association between adherence and age is very complex. Adherence can either increase or decrease with age, depending on the specific illness, the timeframe, and the treatment regimen prescribed. Some research has revealed a curvilinear relationship between age and adherence. In a large-scale, longitudinal study (Thomas et al., 1995) investigating colorectal cancer screening, those who adhered best were approximately 70 years old; the worst adherers were younger than 50 years of age or older than 80. Another study (Park et al., 1999) found a surprising pattern of medication adherence in arthritis patients. This study found an age-related cognitive decline among participants. Yet, the older participants actually adhered to their treatment regimen better than middle-aged patients. A busy lifestyle associated with middle age was found to be more of a determinant of non-adherence than was cognitive functioning.

Adherence rates are also related to age in children. Both cancer patients and diabetic children are more likely to adhere to treatment regimens at younger ages (e.g., until about 9 years of age) (Jonasson et al., 1999; Manne et al., 1993). These results may be explained by the decreasing responsibility parents have for their children's treatment as they get older (LaGreca & Stone, 1985).

Researchers have found very few gender differences in overall adherence rates (McDonald et al., 2002). Some differences do emerge, however, when we look at adherence to specific medical recommendations. For instance, women seem to be better than men at adhering to dietary restrictions (Laforge, Greene, & Prochaska, 1994) and at taking medication for mental disorders (Sellwood & Tarrier, 1994). There are, however, very few gender differences in such things as taking antihypertensive or diabetic medication (e.g., Monane et al., 1996), or establishing and maintaining an exercise program (Emergy, Hauck, & Blumenthal, 1992).

Cultural differences in adherence rates are rare, but have also been noted (McDonald et al., 2002). Most often when cultural differences appear, they occur when the patient is from a culture that does not believe in modern medical recommendations, preferring their own traditional healers (DiNicola & DiMatteo, 1984). One study (Sanderson et al., 1998) documented ethnic differences in adherence to cardiac procedures. Fewer African-Americans adhered to the treatment regimen compared to Caucasians. Interestingly, these researchers noted that compared to Caucasians, fewer African-American patients recalled physicians recommending the cardiac procedures. When procedure recommendations were recalled, no ethnic differences were found in adherence rates. This finding emphasizes the need for effective communication in the physician–patient consultation.

Physician Characteristics   As we might predict, patients' adherence improves as confidence in their physician's competence increases (Gilbar, 1989). However, you may remember that the physician who is perceived with positive attributes such as kindness is more likely to be perceived as competent than one who is seen as unfriendly. It follows that people are more likely to adhere to medical recommendations if their physician is viewed as warm, caring, friendly, and interested in the welfare of patients (DiNicola & DiMatteo, 1984). When physicians exhibit a good bedside manner by making eye contact, smiling, and even joking and laughing, patient adherence improves.

Physician-Patient Interaction   Earlier in the chapter, we outlined a number of elements inherent in physician-patient communication and physician-patient relationships that influence patient adherence. For instance, if the patient does not understand instructions (e.g., due to the use of medical jargon), does not ask questions to clarify the instructions the physician provides, or does not remember those instructions, adherence is not possible. If a physician's expectations and a patient's expectations about what role each party should play in the interaction differ, patients are less likely to follow the physician's medical recommendations. In the next section, we will see how the element of social influence in the physician–patient relationship can be used to increase a patient's medical adherence.

Improving Patient Adherence

Social Influence in the Physician–Patient Relationship
In any interaction, people influence one another. This is certainly true in the physician–patient interaction. During the physician–patient interview, the physician attempts to influence the patient to adhere to a regimen, and to a lesser extent, the patient attempts to influence the physician. The ability to influence people or shape their beliefs, attitudes, or behaviours is called "social power" (Raven, 1974; French & Raven, 1959). Social psychologist Bertram Raven (1974) has described six forms of social power: informational power, reward power, coercive power, expert power, legitimate power, and referent power. Each of these forms of social power is illustrated below with examples in which a physician, Dr. Code, attempts to influence a patient, Mr. Watson. Mr. Watson is 48 years old, overweight, and is suffering from hypertension. His treatment regimen involves adherence to a low-sodium diet, weight loss, moderate exercise, and antihypertensive medication twice a day. Currently, Mr. Watson is not following the treatment regimen proposed by Dr. Code. That is, Mr Watson has not altered his diet, he rarely exercises, and he takes his medication when he "remembers."

Informational power is based exclusively on the content of the communication. Physicians have a large amount of knowledge that they can provide in an attempt to influence the patient. In this form of social power, it is the information or the facts presented that may lead to social influence. "Mr. Watson, your cholesterol level, 235, puts you at risk for a heart attack. With your uncontrolled blood pressure, that risk is increased 500 percent," said Dr. Code. The facts Dr. Code has presented to Mr. Watson should persuade Mr. Watson to change his beliefs and his behaviour. Mr. Watson will follow the physician's advice because he is trying to avoid a heart attack, and the facts suggest that he needs to alter his behaviour to avoid one. Thus, there is nothing about the *physician* that leads the patient to change his behaviour; any behaviour change is solely the result of the *information* that the patient has been presented with. Informational power is independent of any social factors related to the physician. The remaining forms of social power are socially dependent. That is, social influence results from something about the health care practitioner or about his or her relationship with the patient.

Reward power stems from the health care practitioner's ability to provide rewards. Rewards can be either tangible (e.g., money, free drug samples) or intangible (e.g., approval, praise, time, availability). "Mr. Watson, I would be very pleased if you could make a commitment to take your medication as I've prescribed and to, at least, reduce the salt in your diet." In this instance, if Mr. Watson changes his behaviour and does what the physician has advised he has done so because he wants his physician to think highly of him. The patient is attempting to attain a reward, in this case praise. Although the patient may also report other factors he believes are responsible for his behaviour change, a primary factor responsible for the behaviour change is the reward.

Coercive power stems from the health care practitioner's ability to mete out punishment for failure to comply. In the practitioner–patient relationship the punishment is limited to the practitioner withholding praise or services. "Mr. Watson, if you can't follow the treatment plan I've suggested, I'm afraid I won't be able to treat you anymore."

Expert power stems from the patient's belief that the health care practitioner has knowledge and skill pertaining to health matters. "That's right Mr. Watson, there is a lot of research looking at how one can reduce the risk of heart attacks by lowering blood pressure. The researchers all agree that the best course of action is for the patient to lose weight if overweight, and to take medication to reduce high blood pressure. That is what you need to do. If you can fit exercise into your schedule you should do that as well. I'm very familiar with this research, you really need to trust me on this one."

Legitimate power stems from the patient's belief that a health care practitioner can make medical demands of him or her. Obviously, we expect those demands to be in the best interest of the patient. While such power is ultimately backed up by coercive power, if the patient has respect for the physician no coercion is necessary. "Mr. Watson, as your physician, I suggest you follow the treatment plan I have outlined for you."

Referent power stems from the patient's desire to identify with a particular person or group. The person or group the patient desires to identify with does not need to be the influencing agent, the health care practitioner. "Mr. Watson, I know you are aware that your friend, Mr. Gilbert, also has problems with his blood pressure. Mr. Gilbert has been able to stick with the treatment plan we devised." In this example, Mr. Watson may be motivated to be as compliant as his good friend, Mr. Gilbert. More commonly, however, the health professional acts as referent. "I find it very hard to find time to exercise too. My schedule seems so hectic. Yet, I do exercise at least three times a week and I certainly feel better as a result." Of course, the health care practitioner can only use him or herself as a referent if the patient has a desire to be like him or her in some way. To have referent power, the target of influence must perceive the practitioner to be likable, benevolent, admirable, and accepting. The referent power is derived from the patient's own desire to model his or her behaviour after the practitioner. The motivation to adhere comes from the social–emotional aspect of the physician–patient relationship.

Usually, the health professional will use a number of kinds of social power, in combination, at any given time. Rarely would the health professional use only one form of power in any single communication with the patient. As we discuss in other chapters, it is important that people perceive themselves as having personal responsibility or control over their own health behaviours. When health professionals use expert, legitimate, coercive, or reward powers to influence their patients, the patients will likely attribute their compliance to external incentives. Consequently, the patients will be less likely to perceive themselves as having personal control over their behaviours. According to Brehm (1966), if people feel that they lack personal control they experience **reactance**, a psychological state that motivates them to regain a sense of control and restore their lost freedom. This reactance may help to explain why patients sometimes act against what appears to be in their own best interests by quitting treatments before they are completed. For example, cancer patients have been known to quit their chemotherapy treatments before they have been completed out of frustration about their lack of control over their own health. Rodin and Janis (1982) suggest that the use of expert, legitimate, coercive, and reward powers might be beneficial for patient compliance in the short-term, but in the long-term the use of these forms of power might be detrimental.

In addition, Rodin and Janis (1982) suggest that the use of referent and informational power will promote internalization. **Internalization** involves the patient changing his or her existing pattern of beliefs to accommodate the beliefs advocated by the health care practitioner. Thus, internalization leads a patient to perform a behaviour even when the patient no longer feels under the scrutiny of a health care practitioner. It is expected that the same circumstances that promote internalization also increase patients' feelings of personal control because the patients perceive themselves to be acting on the basis of internal, self-motivated norms and goals. Therefore, referent and informational power may be the best forms of power for health care practitioners to use.

Over the last couple of decades, the patient has asserted more power in the physician–patient relationship. One reason for this may be the increased level of education attained by people in Western society. The average person is better informed now than ever before about health. It is interesting to note that models of physician–patient relationships did not include a profile wherein the patient dominates until relatively recently. Roter and colleagues (1997) note that young patients often choose to interact with their physicians by controlling the consultation (e.g., asking the majority of questions). Whatever the cause of this change, it may necessitate health professionals to alter their style of social influence to maintain patient adherence. Moreover, there are additional strategies available to improve patient adherence.

Educational Strategies   Educational strategies to improve adherence are abundant. Health education is aimed at filling in the gaps in patient understanding about the need to follow medical recommendations (Coambs et al., 1995). Types of patient education vary considerably and include package inserts, written information sheets to reinforce verbal instructions, one-on-one counselling, small group sessions, lectures, demonstrations, and mailed information. In Canada, health education is provided by hospital, clinic, community, worksite, and private programs. As well, pamphlets and brochures are readily available to supplement and reinforce verbal instructions (Coambs et al., 1995).

Behavioural Strategies   Behavioural strategies can also be effective in increasing patients' motivation to adhere to their treatment regimens (DiMatteo & DiNicola, 1982; Miller & Stark, 1994). Providing *prompts and reminders* as cues may encourage patients to perform recommended activities. These cues may include notes posted at home, reminder phone calls from a clinic, or even certain forms of drug packaging (e.g., dispensers with dated compartments or other built-in reminders). *Tailoring the regimen* so that activities in the treatment are fitted to habits and routines in the patient's daily life may also help. For example, taking medication is easiest to do if it is tied in with another activity such as brushing one's teeth in the morning. *Self-monitoring* is another way to encourage patient adherence; the patient keeps a written record of regimen activities, such as monitoring his or her resting heart rate or documenting foods eaten during the day. *Contingency contracting*, whereby the patient and health professional (or parent, if the patient is a child) negotiate a series of treatment activities and goals as well as rewards based on the patient's fulfillment of these activities, can also help. For example, "a diabetic child and his or her parents may enact a contract that specifies a particular reward for each day the child does his or her insulin injection without argument" (Miller & Stark, 1994, p. 81). These techniques have a clear advantage in that the patient must actively participate in their design and execution (Turk & Meichenbaum, 1991). Further, the patient can usually carry out these strategies without assistance.

Social Support   Social and emotional support can provide much needed motivation for patient adherence, particularly when the regimen is long-term or requires lifestyle changes (e.g., Peck & King, 1985). Family and friends can provide positive encouragement about the treatment activities and help to ensure they occur. Social support can also be provided by self-help groups, patient groups, and organizations established to help with specific health conditions. Patients who receive encouragement, inspiration, reminders, and aid in carrying out the regimen are believed to be more likely to comply than those who do not.

Unfortunately, research evaluating these strategies is not encouraging (Haynes, McKibbon, & Kanani, 1996; Roter et al., 1998). The strategies appear to have a fairly weak effect on patient adherence. However, the more comprehensive the program of intervention, the more effective the outcome. Roter and colleagues contend that the most powerful interventions include combinations of all three strategies—educational, behavioural, and social or affective. Haynes and his colleagues have outlined which of these strategies is most effective for short-term (less than two weeks) and long-term treatment regimens (see Box 4-2).

| BOX 4-2 | **Methods of Increasing Adherence** |

Short-term treatments

Counselling about the importance of adherence

Written instructions about taking medicines

Reminder packaging (e.g., calendar packs, dosettes)

Long-term treatments

Combinations of:

Instruction and instructional materials

Simplifying the regimen (e.g., less frequent dosing, controlled release dosage forms)

Counselling about the regimen

Support group sessions

Reminders for medications and appointments

Cuing medications to daily events

Reinforcement and rewards (e.g., explicitly acknowledging the patient's efforts to adhere)

Self-monitoring with regular physician review and reinforcement

Involving family members and significant others.

Source: Haynes, R. B., McDonald, H. P., & Garg, A. X. (2002). Helping patients follow prescribed treatment. *Journal of the American Medical Association, 288*, 2880-2883.

HEALTH OUTCOMES

How important is it to adhere to medical recommendations provided by health care professionals? This is another question that is not easy to answer. By not adhering to treatment regimens, people increase their risk of developing health problems or of prolonging or worsening their current illnesses. Approximately 20 percent of hospital admissions are thought to result from patient non-adherence to medical recommendations (Ley, 1982). One study documented that both male and female heart patients who did not adhere well to medication recommendations were almost three times more likely to die in the next year than those who adhered fairly closely (Gallagher, Viscoli, & Horwitz, 1993; Horwitz et al., 1990).

Other studies have not shown a strong relationship between loyal adherence and improved health. Haynes and colleagues (1996) reviewed more than 1500 studies on adherence to medication and concluded that it does not generally lead to better patient health. Other researchers have conducted longitudinal research and found that after four years compliant patients were not much more improved on a variety of disorders than were non-adherent patients. A few things may help to explain this discrepancy. First, this study relied on self-reports of adherence, and, as we saw earlier there are a number of problems inherent in this form of data collection. Second, it may be that four years is not enough time to observe the results of non-adherence. Finally, other factors, including heredity and environmental conditions, may have had an influence on the course of the illnesses.

Perhaps another possibility to be explored in determining the importance of adherence is that complete adherence may not be necessary. Perhaps there are only certain levels of adherence that are required to obtain health benefits. If this is the case, it may explain why there are few differences between those who adhere completely and those who do not adhere. For example, consuming 80 percent of the medication prescribed has been described as the minimum rate of adherence necessary to treat hypertension effectively (Epstein & Cluss, 1982). Unhealthful non-adherence might then be defined as "the point below which the desired preventive or therapeutic result is unlikely to be achieved with the medication prescribed" (Parrish, 1986, p. 456).

In summary, non-adherence appears to be a fairly common phenomenon. There are a number of factors associated with non-adherence, including poor physician–patient communication; complexity and duration of the regimen; age, gender, and cultural background of the patient; and affective characteristics of the physician. Several strategies have been devised to increase adherence to medical regimens (e.g., educational and behavioural strategies) but researchers question their effectiveness. Furthermore, researchers have been unable to find a significant benefit to high levels of adherence. However, it may be that more moderate levels of adherence contribute to health benefits thereby explaining the lack of differences between high- and low-level adherers.

KEY TERMS

active-passive model (p. 96)

adherence (p. 108)

appraisal delay (p. 91)

behavioural delay (p. 91)

biopsychosocial communication pattern (p. 97)

coercive power (p. 112)

compliance (p. 108)

consumerist communication pattern (p. 97)

creative non-adherence (p. 108)

doctor-centred (p. 105)

expanded biomedical communication pattern (p. 97)

expert power (p. 113)

guidance-cooperation model (p. 96)

illness delay (p. 91)

informational power (p. 112)

internalization (p. 113)

lay referral system (p. 89)

legitimate power (p. 113)

medical delay (p. 91)

medical jargon (p. 103)

multilevel explanations (p. 105)

mutual-participation model (p. 96)

narrowly biomedical communication pattern (p. 97)

non-adherence (p. 108)

non-discrepant responses (p. 105)

patient-centred (p. 105)

patient delay (p. 91)

psychosocial communication pattern (p. 97)

reactance (p. 113)

referent power (p. 113)

reward power (p. 112)

chapter five

Hospital Stays and Medical Procedures

CHAPTER OUTLINE

The Hospital As a Distinct Culture
A Hospital Patient's Loss of Control
How Patients Cope with the Hospital Culture
The Role of Nurses in Hospital Culture
Patient-Centred Care: An Ideal in the Hospital

The Psychological Impact of Medical Procedures
The Psychology of Mammography
The Psychology of Magnetic Resonance Imaging

Day Surgery

In the Hospital
The Emergency Department
Recovering from Surgery
The Intensive-Care Unit
Discharge
Palliative Care

KEY QUESTIONS

1. What are the psychological effects of high-tech medical procedures?
2. What is it like to be a patient in a hospital?
3. How does the experience of being a patient in a hospital differ from one department to another?
4. What are the factors affecting a person's ability to cope with a hospital stay and what roles do staff play in that coping process?
5. In what ways does a person attempt to regain a sense of control when in the hospital?

As soon as Hanna walked into the hospital, she was reminded of all the hospital dramas she had watched on television. Staff were scurrying through the halls with a sense of purpose and urgency. Families sat in waiting areas, talking quietly among themselves, some looking composed, others worried and anxious.

Today Hanna was part of the drama. Her doctor had made an appointment for her to have a mammogram. She had never had one before, though she believed that early detection was very important. But early detection of what? Hanna hoped that the mammogram would detect nothing.

Hanna finally found the radiology department after following a blue line on the floor that wound through the halls of the hospital. She was shown to a small changing room where she was asked to take off her upper garments and put on a gown that looked more like a discarded bed sheet. Where else would she be asked to put on something like this and then sit in a waiting room with a bunch of other people wearing discarded bed sheets? And there were so many people. The nurses and technologists were obviously used to the crowds, though. They were moving people in and out very efficiently.

When Hanna's name was called, she jumped to her feet. She could feel the butterflies in her stomach as she went into the examination room. The procedure went smoothly, though Hanna would never have called it comfortable. Fortunately, she had a technologist who seemed to know just how to empathize with her and make her feel at ease. Before she knew it, she was in her own clothes and out in the hall, following the blue line back to the main entrance.

Most of us have been inside a hospital. However, unless you work in a hospital or have spent a considerable amount of time in one, you probably feel a bit out of place when you walk through the doors. People in unique garb might be wheeling unfamiliar machines through the halls, sometimes connected to other people! The place has its own collection of peculiar smells, and it's full of sick people, some of them dying. Indeed, a hospital is its own world. It is this world that we will be investigating in this chapter. If you have ever walked through the halls of a hospital and wondered about the psychological impact of the place, then you have thought like a health psychologist.

Hanna's example reminds us that, not only is a hospital an unfamiliar and somewhat dramatic place, we usually encounter it when we are not at our best. We might be worried or anxious, or just plain unwell. In this state, we are put through procedures that can feel quite intimidating and that are designed to look for things we don't want to have in the first place.

In this chapter, we will start by looking at a hospital the way an anthropologist might look at a different culture. We will explore and attempt to understand the psychological impact of each department as we move through the world of a hospital.

THE HOSPITAL AS A DISTINCT CULTURE

Imagine being asked to spend a week in a place you have never been before. In this place, most of the people dress quite differently from you. They speak your language, but they also speak another language to one another. It is a language that you cannot comprehend. They will speak this language even when you are with them and they are talking about you. In fact, these people have very different rules of social interaction. They will ask you very personal questions and expect detailed answers, even though they have just met you. They will wake you in the middle of the night. They will prevent you from getting out of your bed when you want to and will make you get up when you want to stay in bed.

And there are rituals. Many visitors to this place must first provide a small amount of their blood to the inhabitants before they are allowed to stay. These people take some of their visitors and make large incisions in their bodies, often removing body parts. They may discard these body parts or keep them and study them. When it is time to leave, the visitors may be made to exit in a chair with wheels, even though they would rather walk.

Does this sound like the sort of place you would like to visit? Does it sound somewhat alien? The place we are describing is, of course, a hospital. When viewed as a distinct culture, with its own set of interaction patterns, rules, and rituals, it is easy to see why hospital stays can be quite disorienting and stressful.

The average length of a hospital stay is getting shorter as medical technology advances and budgets shrink. The Canadian Institute for Health Information reports that the average length of an acute care hospital stay dropped by 4 percent between 1995 and 2000 (*Hospital days and average length of stay for Canada, Provinces and Territories, 1994/95 to 1999/00*, 2001). Nevertheless, a stay in hospital is still a very significant event in most people's lives. In Canada, the average length of a hospital stay in 1999 and 2000 was 7.1 days. This average does not include newborns, emergency visits, or people receiving chronic care.

While some hospital stays can be difficult and lengthy, others are very brief, like that experienced by Hanna from our opening vignette. She is an **outpatient**, which means that she will not be staying overnight. Her particular procedure, a mammogram, is quite brief and fairly **non-invasive**. This means that she did not have an incision or have anything inserted into her. Nor did she have to ingest substances to aid in the radiographic procedure. Even so, as we will see in a moment, a mammogram can bring on its share of anxiety.

Other patients will be **day care patients**. This means they will be having a procedure that is more involved than Hanna's mammogram but still will not be staying overnight. They might be having laser surgery to remove cataracts from their eyes. Or they might be having tubes inserted in their ears to treat recurring infections. Day care patients might be put under general anesthetic, and so they tend to be admitted early in the day and discharged by late afternoon. These patients usually need to be accompanied by someone who can be sure they get home safely and comfortably after the procedure. These patients will also get one of those identification wrist bands that are so often associated with hospital stays.

Still other patients enter the hospital under emergency circumstances. They may enter by way of the emergency room and be treated and released from there in the same day. Others may be admitted through emergency and end up staying overnight or longer. Indeed, some may be unconscious when admitted and need to have their circumstances explained to them when they regain consciousness in some other part of the hospital. Clearly, this is a very different experience from those of day care patients or others who have had their procedure booked for a long period of time and have gone through the anticipation. Some will have gone through this waiting period only to be told just before their scheduled admission day that their procedure has been postponed. Sometimes the consequences of waiting are minor, amounting to frustration and inconvenience. Sometimes they are dire. In Canada in 2002, 237 people died while waiting for organ transplants. In that year, 4001 people received transplants.

The admission procedure can have important effects on a patient's psychological response to being in hospital. Some patients see it a sign that something traumatic and frightening is going on. For others, there is a sense of relief that the waiting is over and something constructive is going to be done. Whatever the pattern of admission, it must be emphasized that the admission procedure often constitutes a patient's first encounter with the hospital. As such, it carries all the weight we would expect of a first impression in shaping the patient's perceptions of the hospital experience.

Studies conducted in the 1990s captured well the loss of control that often accompanies a hospital stay. Spencer and colleagues (1995) document the case of a 30-year-old man who suffered a spinal cord injury and had to spend 116 days rehabilitating in hospital. You can well imagine the challenges associated with learning to adapt to the disability incurred by a spinal cord injury. Interestingly, the investigators discovered through daily interviews with the patient that adaptation to his long-term hospital stay was almost as challenging. In fact, the injury and the hospital had a similar effect on the patient. Each took away some of the control he once had over his life. Adaptation to both hospital and injury meant regaining as much of that control as possible.

A study conducted in the Netherlands clearly showed that patients feel they relinquish control to others during hospital stays (Halfens, 1995). Seventy-two people were asked to complete the Health Locus of Control Scale, which measures their sense of internal control, external control (luck, fate, and circumstance), and control by powerful others. Participants completed the scale three times; nine days before admission, during their stay, and seven days after being discharged from the hospital. Figure 5-1 shows the significant increase in people's scores on the powerful-other subscale during their hospital stay. Their scores on the internal and external subscales did not change over time, suggesting perhaps that, in the face of all this control by powerful others, we still try to maintain the belief that we are in as much control as we were before being admitted to hospital.

More recently, a survey of women's hospital experiences identified three factors that were closely connected to their satisfaction with the experience (Polimeni & Moore, 2002). These were respect through communication, maintenance of dignity, and day-to-day control. The more these elements were compromised, the greater the level of dissatisfaction experienced. While most women reported being satisfied with their hospital experience, many still made reference to their perceived powerlessness. For surgical patients, hospital stays are improved when adequate information is provided about their surgery and their recovery, as well as general information about their upcoming stay and the sensations that

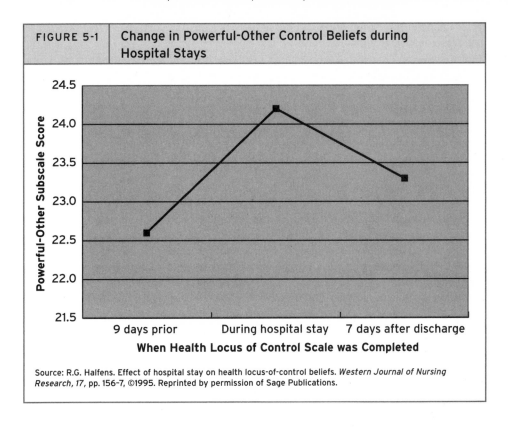

| FIGURE 5-1 | Change in Powerful-Other Control Beliefs during Hospital Stays |

Source: R.G. Halfens. Effect of hospital stay on health locus-of-control beliefs. *Western Journal of Nursing Research, 17*, pp. 156-7, ©1995. Reprinted by permission of Sage Publications.

will be part of it (Krupat, Fancey, & Cleary, 2000). This need for information is closely related to the patient's sense of control in that it affects perceptions of the value of the information received.In other words, the stronger a patient's need for control, the more he or she will value the information received.

For children entering a hospital, the feeling of loss of control can be even greater. This is especially true when the hospital stay involves medical trauma (Rennick, 2002). Researchers at McGill University have discovered that children whose hospitalization involved more invasive procedures felt they had less control over their health.

A Hospital Patient's Loss of Control

Upon entering the hospital, the new patient finds it to be what Erving Goffman (1961) describes as a **total institution**. In other words, the hospital takes control of virtually every aspect of a patient's life. Patients are expected to adapt to the hospital's schedule, to eat and sleep at specified times, to receive visitors only during designated hours, to conform to hospital procedures, and to make their bodies available for examination when requested.

How patients react to this loss of control in the hospital environment varies greatly from person to person. Yet, some general patterns have been noted in patients' reactions to the hospital environment. As one example of a particularly traumatic kind of hospital experience, people faced with end-of-life decisions can be placed along a continuum in terms of the control they would like to maintain. At one end is the "activist" (Kelner, 1995) who wants total control. At the other end of the continuum is the "delegator" (Kelner, 1995), who wants to relinquish that control.

Practitioners' impressions of patients can also be affected by the patients' behavioural responses to a loss of control. Attempts to regain control can be misunderstood as attempts to be "difficult." One example of such a patient was a 74-year-old man who had had his gallbladder removed and had postoperative psychological and medical complications. He "was labelled a problem patient by the surgeon, resident, intern, and day staff nurse. In the questionnaire, the resident said the patient's uncooperativeness made it difficult to perform routine procedures on him. The surgeon wrote that the patient was 'lachrymose, combative, and generally impossible'...the surgeon added that the patient had called him names, lied, and generally carried on" (Lorber, 1975, p. 218).

The behaviours of the "bad patient" are viewed as a form of **reactance** (Brehm, 1966). For these patients, loss of control is perceived as an unacceptable challenge to their freedom, which may arouse anger and must be resisted. Thus, the so-called problem patient's complaints and demands for additional attention may be angry attempts by the patient to reestablish at least a small measure of personal freedom. Patients who are younger, better educated, or accustomed to being able to control their environment are more likely to respond with reactance (Taylor, 1979). Seligman (1975) investigated the idea that constant frustration can produce **learned helplessness**. Seligman's research with animals demonstrated that some learn to do *nothing* when put into stressful situations in which they have no control. Because these animals learned that there was no solution to their predicament, they simply gave up. They also failed to make adaptive responses when put into similar situations where they could have gained some control; that is, they generalized their learned helplessness. The concept of learned helplessness has been applied to hospital settings as well, to explain why **empowering care** yields independence and **disempowering care** yields dependence (Faulkner, 2001). It is Faulkner's contention that disempowering care results in learned helplessness; whereas, empowering care results in learned mastery. He has demonstrated this in a study with hospitalized older adults (mean age 79 years). At mealtimes, patients were either given considerable aid (i.e., over-assisted) or told they were in control. This simple difference improved independence at mealtimes. As a follow-up, Faulkner placed half of the patients in the learned helplessness condition and the other half in the self-control condition and found that the latter group became more independent.

We have discussed how loss of control may cause reactance or helplessness in hospitalized patients. Neither behaviour is likely to be adaptive for the patient. Although good patients may be well liked by the hospital staff, they are suffering from learned helplessness, they are at risk for norepinephrine depletion, general erosion of health, and the possibility of sudden death. Patients who respond with reactance, by contrast, are likely to experience anger, heightened secretion of stress hormones, and the possible aggravation of cardiovascular problems (Taylor, 1979).

We have already mentioned the link between the provision of information and control, but this crucial link deserves a closer look. Krupat and colleagues make the point that, about 20 years ago, many people facing surgery were poorly informed about their upcoming procedure. Some did not even know which organ was going to be the focus of the surgery. In response to this problem, a number of programs have been developed to train practitioners in the skills of information giving. A comprehensive study of patients from over 60 hospitals assessed the extent to which this provision of information affected patients' perceptions of the hospital stays. It was found that the provision of general information was the single best predictor of patients' satisfaction. This was also significantly correlated with patients' sense of control. These relationships were unaffected by other patient factors such as age or desire for information (Krupat et al., 2000).

Numerous studies have reported the benefits of providing information to patients in preparation for surgery. However, unlike those in the Krupat et al. study, not all people have been shown to respond well to the provision of information. For example, some people, known as **monitors**, welcome information and seek it out, whereas others, called **blunters**, avoid it. These concepts are well-demonstrated in a classic study by Suzanne Miller and Charles Mangan (1983), which showed how individual differences may affect responses to information about medical procedures. In this study, women about to undergo a diagnostic procedure for cervical cancer were divided into monitors and blunters based on their preference for information in a variety of naturalistic stress situations. Half the monitors and half the blunters were randomly assigned to either a high- or low-information condition. Patients in the high information group were given a 20-minute verbal and visual preparatory communication detailing the procedure they were about to undergo. The other half of the monitors and blunters also spent 20 minutes with the research assistant but were given only minimal information about the upcoming procedure; the rest of the time was spent providing information on general nutrition. Measures of the patients' distress were taken in the form of pulse rates at three times: before receiving the information, after receiving the information but before the examination, and after the examination. Patients who showed the least physiological stress in response to the exam were those who were given the amount of information that fit their preferences. In other words, monitors given a large amount of information showed low physiological stress and, blunters given little information showed low physiological stress. Monitors who were given little information and blunters given a large amount predictably showed much greater stress.

We would expect that, in preparation for potentially stressful events, such as hospital procedures, monitors and blunters would adopt different approaches. In terms of advice for practioners, though, there is more to this story. Some practitioners and researchers argue that an informed patient simply copes better, and so all patients should receive information in their preparation for a hospital stay. Others have called this homogeneous approach to hospital preparation the **uniformity myth** (Kiesler, 1966; Miró, Turk, & Rudy, 1991).

Whereas the Miller and Mangan study (1983) reminds us that we should match the amount of information provided with an individual's coping style, recent research has shown that *all* patients, regardless of their coping style, benefit from relaxation training prior to surgery (Miró & Rosa, 1999). Perhaps this is because monitors tend to experience greater stress and anxiety generally, as they scan for information and, ruminate over the problem at hand (Ben-Zur, 2002; Miller, 1996). Thus, monitors benefit from the relaxation itself and blunters from the distraction it provides.

What can we conclude from all this regarding preparation for surgery? All patients appear to benefit from relaxation training. This training appears to be most effective when the patients are encouraged to focus on distraction (e.g., "think of a very relaxing place") rather than physiology (e.g., "feel your muscles relaxing") (Miró & Rosa, 1999). Of course, all patients need a certain amount of information as well, or else they will risk being confused and disoriented by their hospital stay. Ideally, the exact amount of information provided would be matched with coping style, provided a practitioner was privy to that knowledge.

There are other ways of improving psychological control in patients. For example, researchers in Hamilton, Ontario, increased patients' perceptions of control by giving them the option of walking to the operating room rather than being transported on a stretcher (Porteous & Tyndall, 1994). During the study, 111 of 160 patients chose to walk to the operating room. Only two of these patients were not satisfied with their choice. The reasons given by these patients included becoming uncomfortable waiting and believing that he or she "would have felt more pampered on a stretcher" (Porteous & Tyndall, 1994, p. 23). However, the majority of patients were satisfied with their decision, stating that as a result they "felt better, less like a sick person...more in control" (Porteous & Tyndall, 1994, p. 23). These examples suggest ways that hospitals can increase patients' perceptions of control with solutions that are fairly easy to implement.

Depersonalization   A feeling of lack of control is only one of the complaints patients have about hospitals. They also report experiencing **depersonalization** or **dehumanization**. Depersonalizing environments take away people's sense of individuality, making them feel more like objects than people (you may have felt a bit like this when asked for your student number rather than your name).

Depersonalization can result from many things one encounters in the hospital setting. For example, if you need to undergo even a fairly simple medical procedure it is likely that you will be required to follow a set procedure or routine and that the medical staff will also follow a routine. For instance, a pregnant woman may be required to undergo a glucose tolerance test to ensure that she has not developed gestational diabetes. Before this test begins, it will be explained to the woman that she must drink a very sweet "cocktail" and then remain in the hospital or lab for a number of hours so that her blood sugar can be monitored at various points. To aid the technologist and ensure all pertinent information is shared with the patient, it is likely that the technologist will begin a spiel (which obviously has been repeated many times) in which he or she "runs on" for a period of time, never seeming to pause for a breath, before finishing what he or she has to say. Although all the facts may be relayed to the patient during this interaction, it is unlikely that he or she will be able to retain all this information. The routine of the technician is an example of a very impersonal interaction.

Depersonalization can also result from providing little information to the patient regarding the state of his or her health or the nature of his or her treatment, or by nonpersonal treatment by medical staff (Taylor, 1979). Phillip Zimbardo, a psychologist, has described the following example of depersonalization from his own experience as a patient:

> Recently when I was being given emergency treatment for an eye laceration, the resident surgeon abruptly terminated his conversation with me as soon as I lay down on the operating table. Although I had no sedative, or anesthesia, he acted as if I were no longer conscious, directing all his questions to a friend of mine-questions such as, "What's his name? What occupation is he in?" As I lay there, these two men were speaking about me as if I were not there at all. The moment I got off the table and was no longer a cut to be stitched, the surgeon resumed his conversation with me, and existence was conferred upon me again (Zimbardo, 1970, p. 298).

Depersonalization may also be experienced when one is required to wear a hospital gown, when one is referred to by ailment rather than by name, and when one's privacy is not respected; all of which do occur. However, hospitals are improving. Today, many hospitals encourage their patients to bring their own pajamas and other personal effects. As well, patients are made as comfortable as possible in their environment.

How Patients Cope with the Hospital Culture

There appear to be two main ways that patients cope with loss of control and exposure to surroundings that are strange to them. One is by relying on other patients; the other is by adopting either a passive or active approach to the stay. In her book, *Life on the Ward*, Coser (1962) analyzes how patients help each other cope, by pointing out that the social support patients provide each other is based on their shared submission to what we now call "powerful others" (Wallston, Wallston, & DeVellis, 1978). This support is also based on shared disability and inconvenience. Even though these might be temporary conditions, patients are brought together like motorists in a snow storm. They provide support by joking together about their conditions and generally by building solidarity. Interestingly, this probably helps patients cope with the hospital culture, but it may make it harder to adapt to life outside the hospital if the stay is a long one.

Coser's book was published in the 1960s, during a time when patients' experiences in hospitals were being studied extensively. By the 1970s, however, this level of study had diminished considerably. Zussman (1993) suggests that this was due, in part, to the nature of the modern hospital. In it, stays are short and technology dominates the medical landscape. To make his point, he refers to intensive care units (ICU). In these facilities, which are taking up more and more of a hospital's floor space, "technical virtuosity" (p. 176) and frequent deaths prevent patients from forming bonds with each other, and these factors discourage staff from forming therapeutic bonds with patients.

Indeed, the ICU, with its strong orientation to physiology, can create the sense of depersonalization we discussed earlier. At the same time, it must be emphasized that lives are saved in ICU. Those who work in these units may argue that there is no point in forsaking technical intervention for personal care if it means the person is more likely to die. Clearly, the ideal is a balance between technology and a human touch.

For outpatient procedures and consultations, patients today often take advantage of social support by bringing a companion (Schilling et al., 2002). A study of 1300 patients ranging in age from 18 to over 65 found that companions were brought into examination rooms 16 percent of the time. The vast majority of these companions were family members. Both patients and practitioners saw advantages in having this third person involved. Specifically, the companion can help communicate the patient's concerns and help remember instructions and advice (Schilling et al., 2002). Patients said that their companions were helpful 83 percent of the time when they accompanied them in the examination room.

The Role of Nurses in Hospital Culture

The hospital is populated by physicians, orderlies, administrators, technologists, and other staff. Arguably, though, a hospital's culture is affected most by its nurses—they are usually the largest group in the hospital, and nurses have the most person-to-person contact with patients. Indeed, nurses are called "patient advocates," in large part because they get to know the patients better than do other hospital staff and they are most responsible for the day-to-day care of the patient. We will be talking about the profession of nursing in more detail in chapter 6. For now, let's look at the ways nurses affect hospital culture and patients' ability to cope with it.

Cultures have their rituals, or shared activities that take on meaning in terms of defining those cultures. Hospitals are no exception, and because of the importance of nurses to the hospital culture, nursing practice has been analyzed regarding the rituals common to it. Two general types of nursing rituals have been identified—**therapeutic rituals** and **occupational rituals**. Therapeutic rituals deal mostly with patient–nurse interactions. Occupational rituals concern the socialization of nurses into the profession. As such, they focus on interactions among nurses (Wolf, 1993).

People studying hospital culture (medical ethnographers) have identified administering medication and bathing patients as two important therapeutic rituals (Holland, 1993). Physicians prescribe the medication patients must take, but it is the nurse's job to see that this is done. Often, patients are very cooperative and nurses reward this with a show of appreciation. Sometimes, however, patients resist taking their medication, and the ritual changes to one that some nurse educators have called "assertive empathy." In these cases the nurse is effectively saying, "I know you don't like this, and I can understand why, but you must take it."

Patient bathing connotes a level of helplessness on the part of the patient and caring on the part of the nurse. Some patients are more comfortable with this relationship than others. Having the process ritualized makes it easier for the nurse to complete the task, maintaining a controlled and appropriate level of intimacy and, when necessary, a firm resolve that the job must be done.

Holland (1993) identifies at least four important components of occupational rituals. First, there is the uniform. Nursing uniforms vary from hospital to hospital, though they have a long history of meaning in relation to hospital culture and its association with religious institutions. Whatever the uniform may look like, the function is the same. It identifies the person as a member of the profession, subject to the codes of conduct and ethics that go with it.

The second component is the hierarchy of authority, both within the nursing profession, and between professions; that is between physicians and nurses. Ritual in this context extends to the nature and direction of criticism allowed; namely, it rarely flows *up* the hierarchy. In fact, it has been discovered that violations in hospital-infection prevention practices are less likely to be acted upon if someone lower in the hierarchy finds someone higher violating the practice (Raven, Freeman, & Haley, 1982).

Authority, and the power that accompanies it, are key issues in the hospital culture. Some have argued that, for nursing care to be effective, there must be a sharing of power with patients (Kettunen, 2002). Nurses derive their power from their knowledge. Patients derive theirs from their disclosure of information and opportunities to interrupt and direct the flow of conversation. Others have stressed that the achievement of this power balance is essential to a patient's satisfaction with the hospital experience and the reduction of interpersonal conflict that can result when roles are not clearly delineated (Kools, 2002). This power balance might be particularly important for patients who prefer taking an active role in their care (Harrison, Kushner, Benzies, Rempel, & Kimak, 2003).

The third component of occupational ritual is language. For language to define a culture, it must be unique to that culture. For example, nurses will describe a patient who is not allowed to eat or drink as being "nil by mouth" (Holland, 1993, p. 1466). This isn't the sort of phrase you would hear anywhere else but in a hospital. Language is also used to ritualize the delicate decisions surrounding death by employing euphemism. A decision may have been made not to resuscitate a patient if heart or respiration stops. Nurses may call this situation a "no code." Much of this language is used when nurses communicate their change-of-shift reports (Wolf, 1993). This clearly ritualized activity for nurses helps to maintain the norms of the profession.

All patients have needs and expectations regarding the care they receive from nurses when they are in this strange world called a hospital. What are these needs and expectations and how well do the rituals of nursing meet them? In answering these questions, the two types of care nurses provide should be taken into consideration. These are **technical care** and **socioemotional care**. The former refers to the handling of prescribed medical procedures; the latter to the interpersonal skills required to help patients maintain a sense of optimism and psychological well-being.

Generally, patients aren't great judges of technical care. Most are lay people when it comes to medicine and don't have much experience with medical procedures. Asking them to assess the technical aspects of their care would be like asking them to judge a figure skating competition when they don't know a Lutz from a triple toe loop. On the other hand, patients are good judges of socioemotional care. They know what a pleasant disposition looks like. They know what kindness and patience look like. They know when they have been treated with respect. For these reasons, patients often articulate their needs and expectations in terms of socioemotional care (Leiter, Harvie, & Frizzel, 1998).

There is an exception to this, however. Patients' satisfaction is determined by nurses' technical expertise when the patients' physical comfort and pain levels are involved. In one study, when nurses were asked what constituted the most important aspects of good nursing care, they cited listening to the patient. This answer acknowledges the value of socioemotional care. In that same study, however, when patients were asked, they said the most important aspect of good nursing care was knowing how to give shots and IVs and managing equipment (Larson & Ferketich, 1993).

Whether patients' expectations focus on the technical or socioemotional care they receive from nurses, there is little doubt that their overall satisfaction with their hospital stay is determined, in large part, by the care the nurses provide. This relationship between patient satisfaction and nursing care is highlighted in a fascinating study conducted by researchers at Acadia University in Nova Scotia (Leiter, Harvie, & Frizzel, 1998) (see Focus on Canadian Research). In this study, Leiter and colleagues correlated patient dissatisfaction with nurses' self-reports of professional burnout. **Burnout** is a state that results from excessive patient loads, or as Leiter and colleagues put it, from nurses experiencing a "gap between expectations to fulfill their professional roles and the structure of the organization" (p. 1613). The most common symptoms of burnout include exhaustion, cynicism, a lack of belief in one's professional competence, and a low sense of accomplishment. Burnout is an all-too-common problem in health care that we will address further in chapter 6.

If patients' satisfaction is determined primarily by socioemotional care, then their satisfaction should be affected by the degree of burnout existing in the hospital unit in which they are treated. The question is, does nurse burnout show itself enough to be correlated with patient satisfaction? It is this question that Leiter and colleagues addressed. Focus on Canadian Research describes a study in which a number of strong correlations were found between elements of burnout and patients' ratings of nurses. This study provides convincing evidence that patients' ratings of nursing care are based primarily on socioemotional aspects of that care and that when nurses are overtaxed, their ability to provide that care is seriously compromised.

Patient-Centred Care: An Ideal in the Hospital

In Zussman's words, hospital patients are more than just "the human backdrop for dramatic enactments of professional socialization" (Zussman, 1993, p. 173). Yet, in the traditional biomedical approach, the needs of health care professionals are paramount (Ponte et al., 2003). Contrast this with a **patient-centred approach**, in which patients and families become active members of the treatment team (Ponte et al., 2003).

There are of course limits in how far we can go in dedicating resources to patients' psychosocial needs. In a San Francisco-area hospital, model units were created that featured home-like environments, art, and music. The nurses were specially trained to promote greater patient involvement in decision making, to provide more personalized care, and to increase the health education provided to patients. Not surprisingly, patients who were randomly assigned to these patient-centred units reported greater satisfaction with their stays (Martin et al., 1998). Administrators of Canadian hospitals must strike a balance between dedicating such extensive resources to patients' psychosocial needs and providing environments that address patients' fundamental biomedical needs.

Focus on Canadian Research 5-1	Burnout and the Capacity to Care

Title: The correspondence of patient satisfaction and nurse burnout.

Researchers: Micheal Leiter, Phyllis Harvie, and Cindy Frizzel.

Purpose: To determine whether there is a relationship between nurses' self-reports of burnout and patients' ratings of nursing care.

Method: More than 700 nurses completed the Maslach Burnout Inventory. This measured the extent to which they felt exhausted, cynical, and critical of their professional ability. Burnout is related to high demands created by such things as patient overloads. Nine hundred and thirty-one patients completed the Patient Judgments of Hospital Quality Questionnaire. This is a measure of their satisfaction with various aspects of their hospital stay. Of special interest was the subscale in which patients rate nursing care. Average scores for nurses working within a hospital unit were correlated with average nursing care ratings given by patients in that unit. A wide range of hospital units was used in the analysis.

Results: Strong correlations were found between nurses' reports of various aspects of burnout and patients' ratings of nursing care.

(continued on next page)

Nurse Self-Report	Correlation with Patient Rating of Nursing Care
Exhaustion	−.73
Cynicism	−.53
Intention to quit	−.53
Work meaningfulness	.79

Conclusion: Patients' impressions of the care they receive from nurses is related to the nurses' feelings about their work as expressed in their self-reports of burnout. This is a correlational study, so we cannot draw conclusions regarding cause and effect. Having said this, it is worth exploring the very real possibility that burnout seriously affects nurses' capacity to provide socioemotional care for their patients. This study suggests that patients are sensitive to nurse burnout. This is a particularly important topic, given the vital role nurses play in helping patients cope with their hospital stays.

THE PSYCHOLOGICAL IMPACT OF MEDICAL PROCEDURES

In our opening vignette, Hanna came to the hospital as an outpatient to undergo a medical procedure. Because so many people's experiences of hospitals come from having had an outpatient procedure, we will investigate the psychological impact of some of these procedures. In this analysis, we will make the point that there is always more to a medical procedure than what meets the practitioner's eye. Patients attach considerable meaning to the process that may go well beyond the biomedical purpose of the procedure. To illustrate this, let's return to Hanna, who is having a mammogram, and explore the psychological impact of this procedure.

The Psychology of Mammography

One valuable way to understand the potential negative psychological impact of a medical procedure is to consider its **invasiveness**. The term is self-explanatory, though it is worth noting that invasiveness has both physical and psychological components. In a physical sense, health practitioners determine the invasiveness of a procedure by the extent to which it involves piercing the skin or entering the body with instruments—physically "invading" the body. In a psychological sense, a procedure is invasive if it has the potential to cause embarrassment, shame, or discomfort. This is often the result of procedures that intrude into intimate parts of the body (Weller & Hener, 1993). Not surprisingly, a patient's ability to adapt to a procedure is predicted, in large part, by the invasiveness of that procedure (Campbell-Heider & Knapp, 1993), though a procedure's potential results probably outweigh its invasiveness as a predictor of stressfulness (Kowalcek, Muhlhoff, Bachmann, & Gembruch, 2002).

Invasiveness isn't an all-or-nothing thing. Rather, procedures can be placed on a *continuum* of invasiveness based on the definitions we have just introduced. If you have experi-

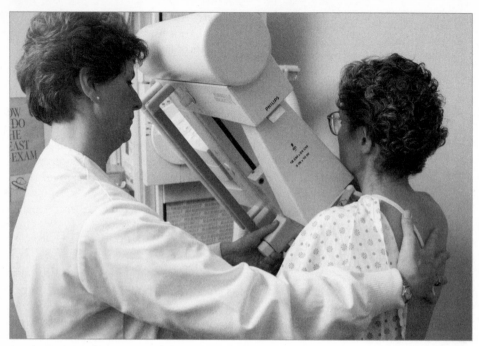

A woman undergoing mammography.

enced a range of medical procedures in your life, you could probably rank them in terms of their invasiveness; even the different parts of a general physical examination vary in this way.

Mammography is, at most, moderately invasive. Nonetheless, there is considerably anxiety surrounding the procedure, not so much because of what is done but because of what might be found. Abnormal mammogram results can bring on fear, anxiety, and depression. This is also true for other screening tests, such as Pap tests for cervical cancer (Pasket & Rimer, 1995).

It could be argued that psychological distress is a necessary element of cancer screening, and a relatively small price to pay for the lives that are saved by early detection. However, estimates vary considerably regarding just how many lives are saved with cancer screening, especially mammography. Evidence is far greater for the benefits of screening for other forms of cancer such as cancer of the cervix (Sasieni, Adams, & Cuzick, 2003). Clearly, in these cases, the benefits of reduced mortality outweigh the psychological costs.

When calculating the cost–benefit ratio of mammography or any other screening procedure, we must take **false-positive** results into consideration. These are results that indicate abnormality when none actually exists. A perfectly reliable test has no false positives, but mammograms are not perfectly reliable. The rate of false positives for mammograms is generally considered to be quite high. A study in Europe estimated the rate of false positives to vary between 1 and 14 percent, depending upon the call-back procedures of the clinic (Lynge, Olsen, Fracheboud, & Patnick, 2003). This high rate of false positives creates a dilemma regarding mammography screening, since it can put women through unnecessary anxiety.

A study of the psychological impact of mammography found that women who feel susceptible to breast cancer do not have their anxiety reduced by a normal mammograpm (Absetz, Aro, & Sutton, 2003). That same study found that women who experienced false positives developed a greater sense of risk for breast cancer. These women increased their frequency of breast self-examination, but lost confidence in their ability to perform the examinations well.

One form of false positive is a **benign breast biopsy**. In this case, women with abnormal mammograms are called back for a biopsy procedure, and the results show no evidence of malignancy. Positive results from biopsies occur between 10 and 40 percent of the time (McCreery, Frankl, & Frost, 1991), so the majority fit into the benign category. A study of women who experienced a benign breast biopsy showed greater short-term psychological distress than did those in a healthy control group (Andrykowski et al., 2002). If Hanna learns that her test has yielded abnormal results and that she is to return for follow-up testing, she will likely see herself as a cancer patient until proven otherwise. And even if follow-up tests prove negative, she may well think it is just a matter of time before the cancer appears for real (Wardle & Pope, 1992).

Regardless of how distressing a call-back or negative biopsy might be, women who experience these false positives are not more likely to stop regular screening. In fact, they may be *more* likely to attended regular screening appointments, because they feel more susceptible to breast cancer. A study of over 2400 women in the state of Vermont found that women experiencing false positives were 1.4 times as likely as women with true-negative results to return for a mammogram within 18 months (Pinckney, Geller, Burman, & Littenberg, 2003).

The vast majority of mammograms are performed on women. This does not mean, however, that the anxiety accompanying positive and false-positive results is a female phenomenon. We turn now to a slightly more invasive procedure that is commonly used for both men and women, to develop an understanding of how the nature of the machine can affect patients' psychological response to the procedure.

The Psychology of Magnetic Resonance Imaging

Magnetic resonance imaging (MRI) has become a very popular diagnostic tool. This is because the images produced are superior to those obtained through radiography and the patient is not exposed to radiation (x-rays). The procedure is moderately invasive for at least two reasons. First, it is not uncommon for patients to require an injection of a contrast solution prior to their scan. Second, the patient must enter a confined space, in some cases for 30 minutes at a time, for tests that can last over two hours in total, if the patient is having a complete head and neck scan.

How confining is the space? Patients must enter a long cylinder, called a bore, that is either 55 or 70 centimetres in diameter. People with wide shoulders must pull them in to enter the bore. Once inside, the patient must remain very still. To achieve this, his or her head may be held in place with Velcro straps. The temperature in the bore often reaches 27 degrees Celsius, and the machine makes a loud banging sound during the scan.

Claustrophobia is the greatest psychological concern for those undergoing MRI procedures. This is most prevalent for people who are having scans that require them to enter the bore head first. Before their scan, these patients are asked, often repeatedly, if they have problems with enclosed spaces. The newest design of MRI scanner features an open side so the patient isn't completely enclosed, thereby reducing claustrophobic reactions. At present, though, most hospitals use closed-bore models.

It is important to acknowledge that the psychological effects of MRI can be either short-term or long-term. Short-term effects include anxiety and claustrophobia during the exam as well as something called **motion artifacts**. These are distortions to the MRI image caused by a patient's movement, sometimes referred to as "ghosts" because of the nature of the images produced (Constable, 2003). In some cases, these artifacts can make diagnosis difficult; in others, they can render the scan useless, thus requiring a re-scan. It has been estimated that up to 40 percent of all scans have motion artifacts to varying degrees, impairing the quality of the diagnosis 8 to 17 percent of the time. Some motion artifacts are caused simply by the patient's breathing. Long-term psychological effects might include a newly formed apprehension of enclosed spaces that surfaces weeks or months after the MRI experience.

To assess short-term effects, researchers measured pre-exam worry in 297 patients over the age of 16 years who were about to undergo a head-first MRI. They also asked them after the exam to indicate how anxious they had been during the exam (this was measured by way of the State Anxiety Inventory.) In addition, motion artifacts were noted, to determine whether they were related to patient anxiety (Dantendorfer et al., 1997). Only 1.2 percent of the participants found the MRI "hardly bearable." On average, anxiety levels dropped from pre-exam to post-exam, and females experienced significantly more anxiety than males. The size of the bore (55 or 70 cm) had no effect on anxiety. When asked what was most unpleasant about the experience, participants cited the fact they had to stay still, the banging sound, and the narrowness of the bore. Motion artifacts occurred in 17 cases. Twelve of these cases had expressed pre-exam worry. It should be noted, however, that over 100 patients expressed pre-exam worry and the majority of these (88.5 percent) did *not* have motion artifacts.

Other studies have discovered that claustrophobic reactions are not uncommon during MRI procedures. Some researchers report such reactions in up to 20 percent of cases (Lukins, Davan, & Drummand, 1997). Others estimate that claustrophobia occurs about 5 to 10 percent of the time, though moderate to severe anxiety has been reported in 37 percent of cases (Katz, Wilson, & Fraser, 1994).

Long-term psychological effects have also been found. In one study, 10 percent of patients reported feeling nervous in enclosed spaces one month after their scan (Kilborn & Labbe, 1990). In another, it was discovered that a small percentage of people had their first claustrophobic experience *after* having their MRI (Melendez & McCrank, 1993). McIsaac and her colleagues found that 30 percent of their participants' feelings of claustrophobia had increased one month after their MRI, and 33 percent said they were reluctant to have another scan (McIsaac et al., 1998).

Anxiety and claustrophobia are obviously linked in MRI procedures. For this reason, studies have attempted to apply what is known about claustrophobia to better understand the aversiveness of these procedures. One widely accepted view of claustrophobia is that it is composed of two fears—**fear of suffocation** and **fear of restriction** (Rachman & Taylor, 1993). Studies have measured these fears in MRI patients to determine the extent to which they predict adverse reactions to the procedure (McIsaac et al., 1998). Of 80 participants, 11 reported that they felt panic during the exam. Not surprisingly, these people did score higher on measures of claustrophobia. In fact, McIsaac and her colleagues found a correlation of .51 between anxiety experienced during the exam and their measure of claustrophobia. More specifically, they found a .41 correlation between fear of restriction and exam anxiety, and a .57 correlation between fear of suffocation and anxiety. These researchers suggest that fewer problems would occur during the MRI exam if, prior to an exam, hospital staff administered a short version of the questionnaire that assesses these fears rather than simply asking patients if they are claustrophobic. It is interesting to note that, while other studies have found that claustrophobia worsens one month after an MRI, one study found that fear of restriction and suffocation improved when the MRI had been completed without anxiety (Harris, Robinson, & Menzies, 1999).

The general conclusion from this work is that most adults can get through an MRI, though many are made uncomfortable or anxious by the experience. If an MRI exam has these effects on adults, how does it affect children? One study of pediatric oncology patients (children with cancer) found that 30 percent reported moderate to extreme distress during an MRI. The worst part for them, though, was not claustrophobia; rather, it was the insertion of an intravenous line (Tyc et al., 1995). This same study found that parents' estimates of their children's distress were higher than that actually reported by the children.

Just under 4 percent of the 491 children in another study were unable to complete the exam, though it should be noted that children under the age of eight years were routinely sedated for their MRI. In that study, children said that, apart from injections, the banging sound was the worst part of the MRI experience (Marshall, Smith, & Weinberger, 1995).

Sedation is one way to help children get through an MRI exam, although it is not an ideal technique. Other interventions have been introduced that reduce the need for sedation. For example, in a hospital in which children under the age of six were routinely sedated for MRI, 10 children averaging under five years of age were given audio tapes containing music and a story that invited the children to create mental pictures. It was discovered that only three of these ten children required sedation, compared to eight of ten in a matched control group (Smart, 1997).

For adults, the intervention of choice is sedation. However, it is not always effective. In fact, one study found that 13 percent of patients had taken medication to reduce their anxiety (called anxiolytic medication), yet they were the very patients who reported the most pre-MRI anxiety, in spite of having taken the anxiolytic medication (Katz, Wilson, & Fraser, 1994). Of course, this doesn't mean that the medication did not reduce their anxiety levels, since we don't know what those levels were prior to their taking the sedative. Still, we do know that sedation did not bring their anxiety levels down to the average. In an analysis of sedative usage for MRI patients, Murphy and Brunberg (1997) found that over 14 percent of 939 patients over the age of 18 years required sedation (of these, 36 percent were male and 64 percent were female). Murphy and Brunberg also discovered that sedation was more common for patients having MRI brain scans.

Non-pharmaceutical interventions include techniques such as hypnosis (Simon, 1999), relaxation, and distraction from the aversive properties of the MRI experience (Quirk & Wagner, 1995). The effect of anxiety-reducing audio tapes was assessed in a study that divided adult patients into three groups. The first acted as a control group, with no tapes. The second listened to anxiety-reducing tapes before their scans. The third listened to the tapes before and during their scans. All participants completed the State Anxiety Inventory as well as the Fear Survey Schedule (a measure of phobias) before and after their scans. Compared to the control group, anxiety decreased for both groups listening to the tapes; however, there was no added benefit from listening to the tape during the scan. Interestingly, all groups reported increased MRI fears at a one-month follow-up, regardless of which group they had been in. This indicates that the tapes helped relieve short-term but not long-term effects. These long-term, or return, effects are not uncommon for fear responses (Wood, 2000).

In summary, the clear images produced by MRI scans come with certain psychological costs, especially for people who enter the bore head first. Generally, about 70 percent of all people cope with the procedure reasonably well, though some may find that their general discomfort with enclosed spaces has worsened as a result of their MRI experience. Between 10 and 20 percent of patients find the MRI experience to be very difficult, and 3 to 5 percent cannot complete the exam. The open-sided design of new machines should make for a significant improvement in people's ability to cope with the procedure.

DAY SURGERY

The procedures we have described so far have varied in their invasiveness, but none have involved surgery. However, **day surgery**, also called *day care surgery*, is another common way in which people experience hospital settings. As the term suggests, this is surgery in which patients do not stay in the hospital overnight. They may have cataracts removed from their eyes through laser surgery, they may have urological procedures like cystocopies to investigate urinary infections or widen the urethra, or they may have surgery to implant tubes in the ears to treat recurring ear infections. In fact, there are many procedures that are now conducted in which the patient does not have to stay in the hospital overnight. When this is handled well, there are considerable advantages, both in terms of hospital costs and patient welfare.

Research in Europe indicates that parents have very positive attitudes toward day surgery as an option, at least when the surgery is tonsillectomy. When called the day after the surgery, every parent stated that they were happy that their child had spent the night at home. In the two weeks following the tonsillectomy, 13 percent of patients visited a physician and 17 percent of the families called for information (Kanerva, Tarkkila, & Pitkaranta, 2003).

A British study identified the key elements to successful day surgery in pediatrics, and then assessed the extent to which these elements were in place (While & Wilcox, 1994). The three key elements were 1) adequate preparation, in the form of information for parents and children; 2) timely, as opposed to premature, discharge; and 3) adequate home support. Data collected in British hospitals in 1992 indicated that there was room for improvement in these areas. Some of the information presented was inappropriate for pediatric day surgery patients, for example, "The patient must not operate heavy machinery for 24 hours." Often, there was no information given regarding post-discharge care. One of the results was that children experienced considerable emotional upset when they returned home. We can only speculate on the extent to which these findings apply to modern Canadian pediatric units. Regardless, they provide a valuable template for successful pediatric day surgery experiences.

IN THE HOSPITAL

We now shift our focus to those people who spend at least one night in hospital. In the language of health statistics, this is called a **hospital separation**. In 1997 and 1998, there were over 10 200 days spent in hospital per 100 000 Canadians.

The Emergency Department

The emergency department of a hospital deserves the attention of health psychologists for a number of reasons. First, it is a common point of entry for many patients. Second, patients often come to emergency in a state of distress or even disorientation, depending on the nature of their problem. Their treatment needs are pressing, and they are in a setting where it is likely that many other people have equally pressing treatment needs. The way hospital staff interact with these people from their first encounter in admission is very important.

In psychological terms, admission procedures are important because they constitute the patient's first impression of the hospital. Have you ever noticed that hotels spend a disproportionate amount of money on the architecture and furniture in the lobby, and that the reception staff is trained to be extremely pleasant? Clearly, hotel owners have read the literature on first impressions. But Canadian hospitals are not hotels. The admissions area of emergency departments can get very hectic, and the questions that need to be asked are far more personal than those asked at the reception desk of a hotel. Still, patients' impressions of the care they receive in a hospital will be affected by the demeanor and efficiency of the admissions staff. This "personal touch" might be easier to implement for patients who are coming into the hospital for a planned procedure in which there is little sense of urgency and the patient is prepared to provide the information required. However, many hospital admissions are not planned. They occur through the emergency department, which is arguably the toughest test of a hospital's admission procedures and the one that can have the greatest impact on the patient, if he or she is conscious.

In order to meet the various psychological needs of emergency patients there must, at the very least, be an emergency department that has sufficient staff and organization to provide expert attention as soon as possible after the patient has entered the hospital. An important early step in emergency medicine is **triage** (Concheiro, Diaz, Luaces, Pou, & Garcia, 2001), which is the sorting and classifying of patients to determine priority of need and proper location and means of treatment. The admission and other staff must also have the interpersonal skills needed to communicate a sense of caring. Asking questions while fixing one's gaze on a computer screen doesn't establish real communication. Neither does stoicism. Often all that is required is someone who will pay immediate attention to the patient-to-be, by indicating that a doctor or nurse will be with him or her as soon as possible. Patients and their families appreciate knowing if there is going to be a wait and why.

In practice, most people visiting an emergency department are not admitted to the hospital. In fact, one study found that 29 percent of patients presenting at emergency were discharged without a specific treatment or investigative procedure (Cooke, Arora, & Mason, 2003). Surprisingly, of these discharged patients, 15 percent had arrived by ambulance.

It could be argued that the realities of emergency room work clash with the expectations of patient-centred care, and that, in general, emergency departments are simply not the places where psychological issues can be given any priority.

There are, however, things that can be done to improve patients' psychological experiences in emergency. These improvements could start with the admission procedure, which some researchers have suggested should be taken away from the emergency area and be staffed by physicians and nurse practitioners who can send patients directly to the appropriate part of the hospital (Mayled, 1998). In addition, health practitioners could be better trained in the skills required to provide clear yet brief explanations of diagnosis and treatment options (see chapter 4 on communication in medical settings.) Patients in emergency departments also benefit from **continuity of care** in which one named staff person (usually a nurse) takes primary responsibility for a patient for the duration of his or her stay in emergency. The most expensive improvements required may well be architectural ones. Crowding in emergency departments reduces privacy and increases distress. Well-designed departments can reduce crowding and provide adequate spaces for consultation with patients while at the same time minimizing staff movement between treatment stations.

Recovering from Surgery

We have looked at people who enter the hospital for just one day to have some surgical procedure performed. Of course, there are also many people whose surgical procedures are major enough to require hospital-based recovery. For a number of reasons, postoperative recovery can be a difficult time psychologically. In addition to having to cope with the unfamiliar surroundings of the hospital, postoperative patients must manage varying degrees of incapacitation, unfamiliar bodily sensations, actions that may be painful or uncomfortable (like forced deep breathing and coughing), and uncertainty about the expected rate of recovery.

One way to help many patients through the postoperative period is by providing good preoperative education. This is designed to make clear to the patient just what to expect in terms of sensations, recovery rates, instructions, etc. Indeed, we have known for some time that good preoperative instructions can reduce postoperative pain and length of stay (Egbert, Battet, Welch, & Partlet, 1964). This preparation is called **psychoeducational care** (Devine, 2003; Lenz & Perkins, 2000). When applied to the postoperative period, psychoeducational care refers to the provision of information regarding self-care practices, further procedures, and typical patterns of recovery.

Pain Management Following Surgery

One of the most important factors determining a patient's satisfactory recovery from surgery (and consequently the length of his or her hospital stay) is pain management. Pain affects mood, and mood (depression, in particular) affects length of stay for certain patients (Schubert, Burns, Paras, & Sioson, 1992; Zalewski et al., 1994). We will be discussing pain and pain management more generally in chapter 10. At this point, we will look specifically at patients recovering from surgery. Of course, pain levels vary, though moderate to intense pain is not uncommon following some surgical procedures. In these instances, the pain is most often treated through pharmacological analgesics such as morphine, though relaxation and other non-pharmacological techniques are also used.

A number of challenges arise when providing pain medication for postoperative patients. One challenge is to ascertain correct dosage. Undermedication will discourage the patient and be ineffective. Overmedication may be harmful when strong drugs such as opioids are used. Another challenge is the psychological issue of control we discussed earlier in the chapter. Patients may not like being dependent upon other people to relieve their pain. In asking for pain medication, patients might feel that they are being weak or "whiny." Finally, they might not want to give the impression that their recovery is not going well and thereby risk lengthening their stay in hospital (Taylor, Hall, & Salmon, 1996).

To deal with these challenges, in the 1980s, hospitals introduced **patient-controlled analgesia (PCA).** As the term suggests, PCA puts the control of analgesic administration in the hands of the patient (Alon, Jaquenod, & Schaeppi, 2003). This can be done a number of ways, from intravenous administration to oral tablet. One common way is to give the patient a devise that, when pressed, releases a certain dosage of the prescribed analgesic intravenously. The devise allows practitioners to set the dosage as well as the **lock-out interval**, which is the time period between allowable dosages.

What happens when the responsibility for analgesic administration is passed to the patient? In general, studies have had encouraging outcomes. For example, women who had undergone gynecological tumour surgery required lower dosages of analgesics postoperataively when using PCA (Standl et al., 2003). Colon surgery patients who were in the PCA group used less sedation and analgesia and enjoyed faster recovery times than did the group whose medication was administered by staff (Roseveare et al., 1998). Similarly, bone marrow transplant patients reported lower pain intensity and used less medication when in the PCA group (Zucker et al., 1998). A study of cardiac surgery patients found that the PCA group reported less pain postoperatively, but that they used more medication than the nurse-administered group did (Boldt et al., 1998). All of these studies were prospective in design, with randomized assignment to group.

Another study included a third group of patients who were in a patient-controlled condition but received a placebo rather than an analgesic (Stainer, Grond, & Maier, 1999). A placebo is a substance that does not contain active medication but might bring about desired effects for psychological reasons, such as the patient's belief that it will work. Patients in this "patient-controlled placebo" group administered twice the amount of medication as patients receiving opioid analgesic.

While results using PCA are generally positive, studies that have used different surgical procedures have produced varying results. For example, a study of patients undergoing gynecological surgery (laparoscopy) showed no difference between PCA and intermittent injection regarding pain, sedation, nausea and vomiting, hospitalization, or patient satisfaction with postoperative analgesia. The authors of that study do not recommend PCA for this surgery (Rosen et al., 1998). One study of children found that the PCA group used more morphine than the staff-administered group following appendectomy (Villareal, Brown, & Lawson, 1998).

It has been suggested by some researchers that PCA would be more successful if patients received training in the procedure before their surgery (Owen & Plummer, 1997). As a test of this, a group of patients was shown an educational videotape on PCA prior to surgery. This group had more positive attitudes toward PCA and greater pain control and satisfaction four and eight hours after surgery than did the group not shown the tape (Knoerl, Faut-Callihan, Paice, & Shott, 1999). Another study placed half of the PCA patients in a preoperative tutorial group and half in a control group (Griffin, Brennan, & McShane, 1998). It turned out that both groups used the same amount of morphine and reported similar pain levels, but the tutorial group experienced less nausea between 6 and 24 hours after surgery.

The effectiveness of PCA might also be affected by staff attitudes toward it. For example, nurse–patient relationships can be strained if nurses feel that they should have the responsibility for analgesic administration (Taylor, Hall, & Salmon, 1996). This may be one reason why Fulton (1996) found that nurses' attitudes toward PCA ranged from being very in favour of it to rejecting it absolutely. Some nurses may very well believe that they are accountable for their patients' pain levels, and this belief may run counter to PCA. Other nurses may believe that they are being accountable by introducing PCA properly and providing good patient teaching regarding its use.

The research on PCA shows that it restores some sense of control for the patient and results in effective pain management in the majority of cases. It is not surprising, therefore, to find that it is commonly used in Canadian hospitals. The research is inconsistent, however, about whether the PCA approach results in more analgesic use than do staff-administered approaches. The differences between studies may be due to differences in the nature of the surgery featured in each. Also, it is possible that there are some patients who are not well suited to PCA. Certainly, education regarding its use is advised for all patients who opt for it.

The Intensive-Care Unit

Nowhere in the hospital is modern technology more prominent than in the intensive-care unit (ICU). It is the unit in which life-support machinery is employed and where patients are closely monitored by a staff whose nurse-to-patient ratio is the lowest in the hospital. We made the point earlier in this chapter that the intensive-care units of hospitals are growing rapidly in terms of the number of beds dedicated to them. For these reasons, and because it is a place where health practitioners often have to make life-or-death decisions, the ICU is an important area of study for health psychologists.

Interviews with patients after they have been in ICU have yielded some very interesting data regarding their experiences. Pallavicini-Gonzalez and colleagues (1995) discovered that patients in ICU go through three distinct stages. First, there is what the authors call the **incommunication stage**. In this stage, patients are either unconscious or barely conscious. Their memories of the experience are poor, but the memories they do have are somewhat strange. The equipment is imposing and the passage of time is unclear. The second stage is called the **readaptation stage**. At this point, the patient becomes aware of his or her struggle to recover. It is during this stage that the patient recognizes his or her dependence on the machines, especially the ventilator, which helps patients breathe. The equipment provides some reassurance and the staff is seen as helpful. The final stage is the **reflexion stage**. In this stage, the patient tries to piece together the details of the experience, wanting to know what happened to him or her.

Not all patients experience these stages, and some are moved out of ICU before they get through all three stages, which might explain why some patients have no recollection at all of their time in the unit. In fact, Russell (1999) discovered that 34 percent of the 298 patients he interviewed had no memory of being in ICU, 42 percent had some memory of it, and 24 percent reported having clear memories of their ICU experience.

Russell's interviews of patients six months after they had been in ICU in Melbourne, Australia, represent some of the most comprehensive data currently available on the psychological aspects of the ICU experience. Some of the people interviewed said it was like

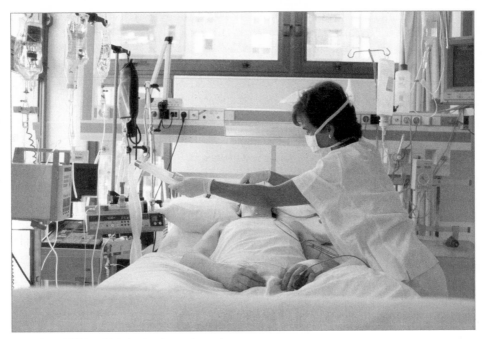

A modern ICU in which technology abounds.

being in a science fiction movie. Others likened the experience to being in a factory, and still others said it was like being in a war zone.

Consistent with the readaptive stage identified by Pallavicini-Gonzalez, Russell's participants remembered the close surveillance of technology and staff providing them with a sense of safety. Interestingly, though, they reported that the staff provided a feeling of safety more than the machines did. In fact, 76 percent of the participants had either a vague memory of the technology or no memory of it at all. Of those who did remember it, some found it reassuring, while others were frightened by it because of a lack of knowledge regarding what the machines were for. Many of these machines monitor vital physiological processes and can be set to sound an alarm if levels drop below or rise above a set level. Not surprisingly, patients found these alarm sounds to be quite frightening when they did not know what they signalled. Much of this fear can be alleviated if nursing staff provide basic explanations of the functions of the machines.

Indeed, the data from Russell's interviews suggest strongly that *communication* is a key factor in determining a patient's psychological reaction to ICU. However, there are a number of reasons why communication is sometimes poor in ICU. For instance, it has been found that nurses sometimes deliberately minimize communication with the patient in order to minimize their own anxiety (Leathart, 1994). Not talking to patients makes it easier to *dehumanize* them. This concept, taken from social psychology, refers to seeing people as objects rather than as human beings. Health practitioners may do this, not because they are uncaring, but because it is easier emotionally to think of an ICU patient as "the acute MI in bed three" rather than as Mr. Chen who has six grandchildren, and may die.

Communication is also inhibited by the fact that patients in ICU tend to be unresponsive (Turncock, 1991). Some, of course, are unconscious. If they are conscious, they may have tubes inserted in their throats. Nevertheless, communication is still important. Just because a patient can't respond does not mean he or she can't *hear*. This is illustrated most graphically by the recollection of one of Russell's interviewees:

> I remember hearing a voice saying "His blood pressure's dropping, it's 60, 57, 55." Another voice saying, "Tell me when it is 50 and we can all knock off." I still think of that sometimes (p. 789).

Overheard remarks like these carry a great deal of psychological weight for patients. Russell discovered that these remarks were remembered six months later and, as the quote suggests, may be remembered forever. These remarks were cited by Russell's participants as a major source of upset. Another patient recalled hearing one staff person telling another that they might as well pull the plug. It is doubtful that the staff member would have made that remark had he or she known the patient could hear.

When staff do talk to patients, they tend to focus on procedure—what is going to be done—rather than on the patient's condition and progress (Baker & Melby, 1996). Information regarding progress may be very important for patients who have entered the readaptation stage and are aware of the struggle that faces them.

Russell also asked participants if they would want to go in ICU again if they were seriously ill or injured. Eighty percent said they would, 10 percent said they would leave that decision to the doctor, and 10 percent said they would not want to be a patient in ICU again, even if their condition warranted it. Finally, Russell discovered that some patients need to revisit the ICU after their recovery to put the experience behind them. These revisits can be good for staff morale, too. Unfortunately, they can be difficult to schedule in a unit in which trauma is an everyday experience.

From the work of Russell and others, we can conclude that the psychological impact of ICU can be strong and lasting. Many patients credit the technology and staff with saving their lives, though recurring thoughts or dreams about the experience are not uncommon. As is the case throughout the hospital, communication is central to reducing the distress of being in ICU. Staff must assume that patients can hear them, and they must provide feedback regarding the patient's condition and progress.

This feedback must also be provided for the families of the patients, who, in the spirit of family-centred care, are essential to the patient's treatment. Family members experience the enormous stress of seeing the patient critically ill and in an unpredictable condition. They also see other patients who may be dying, and they hear alarms sounding on a regular basis (Lower, Bonsack, & Guion, 2003).

Communication with family and visitors is often a low priority for ICU staff who are busy with critically ill patients (Greenwood, 1998). However, this communication is extremely important because the decisions made in ICU and NICU (neonatal intensive care unit) can involve end-of-life issues. These decisions are often fraught with ethical dilemmas. Who should make these decisions? Two prevalent, yet somewhat contradictory, models are called upon when answering this question (Leuthner, 2001). The **Expertise Model** implies that the physician and the intensive care team are best equipped to make end-of-life decisions. They are best informed and most objective. The **Negotiated Model** implies a sharing of the decision between the practitioners, patient, and family. Of course, in ICU, the patient is not always able to provide input, and so family and loved ones are left to represent the patient.

For ethical reasons, Leuthner and others argue in favour of the Negotiated Model because it reduces paternalism on the part of the practitioner and includes the family in one of the most important decisions they will ever face (Carter & Leuthner, 2002; Leuthner, 2001). A study of parents' wishes regarding end-of-life decisions in NICU has suggested that parents want the final call to be with the health care professionals because the burden of the decision is just too great for most parents to bear (Brinchmann, Forde, & Nortvedt, 2002). Having said this, the same authors advocate for keeping the family well informed and as involved as possible in this extremely difficult process.

Discharge

For some patients, leaving the hospital involves more than simply gathering up one's belongings and walking out the front door. It is often the case that further treatment is required, or at the very least, rest and general convalescence. This means that there must be some form of support provided for patients after discharge. All of these considerations require **discharge planning**, a process in which post-hospital care is organized and risk is assessed (Tennier, 1997). By risk, we are referring to such things as social problems, a lack of support, and medical conditions that result in a high degree of dependency (Evans & Hendricks, 1993).

It is interesting to compare the impressions of practitioners and patients when it comes to discharge planning. A study in Switzerland found considerable discrepancies in this regard (Rentsch, Luthy, Perneger, & Allaz, 2003). When asked if the discharge was planned or being planned, 41 percent of patients reported that no discharge plan had been made. In only 27 percent of the cases did health care team members feel this way. Also, the health care teams felt the discharge plans had already been discussed in 51 percent of the cases compared to patients' impressions that such plans had been discussed in only 41 percent of them.

Caring for a family member who has just returned home from the hospital can put a strain on family resources. Someone might have to take time off work, and expectations stemming from traditional roles within the family may provide challenges (Lemos, Suls, Jenson, Lounsbury, & Gordon, 2003). These authors discovered that male and female cardiac patients returning home tried to persevere with their traditional gender-typed roles. In other cases, special equipment may be required. There may be added expenses for such things as in-home nursing care.

BOX 5-1	The Neonatal Intensive-Care Unit

We have looked at what it is like for adults to be in ICU with its collection of machines, tubes, and IV drips. But can you imagine a patient who weighs less than one kilogram (under two pounds) being hooked up to all this, caught in a battle for life? These are some of the patients in the neonatal intensive care unit (NICU). Some have been born prematurely, and then taken quickly away from the delivery room to NICU. Other newborns (neonates) may be full-term births but may have suffered from a prenatal (before birth) or perinatal (during

(continued on next page)

birth) condition that requires intensive care. It could be argued that the NICU is the most emotionally intense unit in the hospital, for both parents and staff.

This emotional intensity is captured well by Ellen Morris (1999), a nurse in NICU:

> The daily span of emotions in the NICU is long and varied: unspeakable sadness when parents have to make the soul-destroying decision to take their baby off life support—a decision that deserves respect—and the inescapable feeling of having little control over the unexpected death of an infant thought to be doing well. But balancing the sadness is the elation we all feel when a baby no longer needs to be intubated, when a mother and father hold their baby for the first time, or when an infant finally breastfeeds months after birth. My greatest satisfaction, though, comes from seeing a child born with the odds against him, discharged home at last to a loving family (p. 23).

This mother's description reminds us that parents might not know just what emotions to feel when their baby is taken to NICU:

> The delivery was bittersweet: my husband caught a glimpse of Alyssa as they whisked her away. We didn't know if we should be thrilled to be parents of a tiny girl who weighed little more than a loaf of bread or brace ourselves for the real potential for tragedy. Our friends and relatives didn't know whether to offer congratulations or condolences (Jed, 1999, p. 22).

Parents' stress levels are often extremely high in NICU. One factor that predicts parents' stress is when and where they first see their baby (Shields-Poe & Pinelli, 1997). Even parents of full-term infants are shocked when they first see the wiring, tubing, and blinking lights, combined with the noises the machines make in NICU (Jamsa & Jamsa, 1998). With this in mind, staff and psychologists can help prepare the parents by giving them a sense of what to expect and what is common in NICU. Family-centred care is obviously very important in NICU, as is *primary care*, which means that the same nurse cares for a given baby throughout the stay (Morris, 1999). Parent involvement is encouraged. They must learn to care for their new baby and may be able to notice subtle but important changes that the busy nursing staff could miss.

In working with the parents, an approach has been advocated that goes by the acronym TEAM (Ward, 1999). In the TEAM approach, the practitioner will *T*each, by preparing the parents for the NICU and explaining the equipment, *E*mpower the parents by giving them tools to be involved in the care as soon as possible, *A*ssess the family's needs and develop a discharge plan, and *M*onitor how well the program is meeting the parents' needs and how well the parents are coping. Health psychologists can play an important role in the TEAM approach, especially given that NICU can be a hectic place for nursing staff.

In addition, there will be instructions to follow regarding such things as medication, diet, and activity levels. These can be complicated, and they can be made worse by a patient who stubbornly refuses to follow the regimen. All of these potential strains are magnified in a home where relationships are not strong to begin with. Good discharge planning tries to take as many of these factors into account as possible.

Imagine the possible sources of anxiety at discharge time for those parents whose babies spent the first weeks of their lives in NICU. Research in this area has discovered that parents' anxiety is related not only to the baby's condition (such things as weight and central nervous system complications), but also the perceived personal and social resources of the parents (Auslander, Netzer, & Arad, 2003).

What about the other end of the age spectrum? It has been estimated that the average hospital stay for people under the age of 65 in Canada is 7.7 days (Wells, 1997). Compare that to the average for people 65 years and over, which is 35.3 days. Elderly patients, then, are likely to have a more difficult time at discharge because they have grown accustomed to hospital support and routine. Problems with discharge planning for elderly patients are compounded by the fact that the planning is time-consuming, and so it must be started early. This means that discharge planning is taking place before the patient's medical condition has been clearly ascertained and effectively treated. One study that analyzed the discharge-planning process for 31 elderly patients discovered that, for 27 of the patients, their planning started before their medical status was clearly determined. As a result, discharge plans had to be altered in 26 of these 27 cases (Wells, 1997). As you can imagine, patients find these changes upsetting, especially when they lengthen the hospital stay. In fact, even the communication of early discharge decisions can be stressful because, at that point, the patient might have trouble imagining being capable of managing at home. One attempt to reduce the stress associated with discharge plans involves conducting an accurate assessment of the patient's cognitive functioning upon admission to hospital (Sands et al., 2003). It has been found that this level of functioning helps predict a patient's ability to cope upon discharge.

There are other challenges involved with discharge planning for elderly patients. They may have other functional problems secondary to the medical condition being treated but still very important to consider regarding discharge. Can they walk unaided? Can they see and hear well? Also, what are the physical capabilities of the principal caregiver? This question is especially important if the caregiver is an elderly spouse. One way to take these functional limitations into account is to involve family members in the discharge-planning process. In the study of the 31 patients mentioned above, it was found that this involvement was sporadic (Wells, 1977), even though the staff regularly discussed discharge, or at least they thought they had (Rentsch et al., 2003).

The major dilemma in working with elderly patients is how to balance adequate care with the patient's desire for autonomy. Patients may have realistic worries about "never being the same again" after their hospital stay (Keefler, Duder, & Lechman, 2001). To cope with these worries, they may shun assistance or attempt to veto discharge plans that create an impression of dependence rather than independence. Social workers, psychologists, health care workers, and family members must help the patient make discharge plans that achieve this balance between safety and autonomy, and they must do so without being patronizing or dictatorial. The key is to involve the patient in the discharge-planning process as much as possible. This requires a sensitive understanding of the patient, the options available, and his or her health. This understanding can only be achieved if all involved adopt a team approach.

Palliative Care

Most patients are discharged from the hospital because their condition is improving and their prognosis is good. This does not apply to all patients, though. Some have illnesses that are **progressive**, meaning they will continue to worsen in spite of treatment; and when a progressive illness is **advanced**, it is at a stage where death is imminent. For these patients, care shifts from an attempt to cure the illness to a regimen intended to control pain and other symptoms. A primary goal becomes the pursuit of as good a quality of life as is possible for the remaining time the patient is expected to live. Other goals include control of symptoms, family support and satisfaction, and maintaining a focus on patients' perceptions of purpose and meaning in their lives (Kaasa & Loge, 2003). These are the goals and focus of **palliative care**. This care involves compassionate communication; an understanding of patient and family values and goals of care; the relief of suffering; management of pain, depression, delirium, and other symptoms; an awareness of the processes of grief; and sensitivity for the soon-to-be bereaved survivors (Abrahm, 2003).

In Victoria, Deanna Hutchings has proposed a model for palliative care based on the Theory of Human Becoming that dovetails nicely with the fundamentals of palliative care. The model contains a number of important elements, including caring for the whole person and maintaining a necessary presence and dialogue with the dying person (Hutchings, 2002).

Once the decision has been made to move to palliative care goals, another important decision to be made is where the palliative care will be administered. There are three common choices—the hospital, the home, or a hospice. Hospice facilities represent a compromise between the comfort of home and the medical support of a hospital. At this point, we will focus more on palliative care as provided by hospitals. Having said this, it is important to note that hospital palliative care may also involve discharge planning and all the issues we discussed earlier in relation to that process, if the patient and family express a desire to move the site of care to the home or elsewhere. Because of this, palliative care is most successfully provided by multidisciplinary teams that include such people as physicians, nurses, social workers, chaplains, and psychologists. A review of studies assessing the effectiveness of such teams discovered that they yielded as good or better outcomes than individual planners concerning patient and family satisfaction, patients being cared for as they wished, a reduction of family anxiety, and patient pain and symptom control (Hearn & Higginson, 1998).

We have said that one of the goals of palliative care is pain management. And yet, in many cases pain is undertreated in palliative settings. A study of over 2800 seriously ill patients revealed that 23 percent were living with moderately severe or extremely severe pain. No wonder that 49 percent preferred a course of treatment aimed at relieving that pain, and that 51 percent said they would rather die than permanently live with their pain. Half of the patients who are able to communicate during the last few days of their lives report moderate to severe pain (Ng & von Gunten, 1998).

It is difficult to know why pain is undertreated in palliative care. It is possible that patients, trying to appear stoic or brave, do not communicate their pain very well (Poole & Craig, 1992). Other factors that contribute to poor management of pain include insufficient knowledge of pain assessment and therapy on the part of clinicians, inappropriate concerns about the side-effects and addictive properties of opiods, a tendency to focus more on disease management than symptom control, and patients' lack of cooperation with therapy (Portenoy & Lesage, 1999). Whatever the reason, it is clear that pain assessment is yet another problem that is best approached with clear communication. Family and friends can help give practitioners a clear sense of the patient's discomfort, and practitioners can learn to read non-verbal cues that indicate pain.

Staff working in palliative care face death on a daily basis. To cope with this, they must shed the prevailing belief in acute care that death is tantamount to failure (Payne & Kalus,

1998). They must adjust their goals to make them consistent with those of palliative care. Moreover, they must come to grips with their own anxieties and fears about death. Perhaps this is why one study found that hospice nurses were less death avoidant and less concerned about their own death than emergency room nurses were (Payne, Dean, & Kalus, 1998).

While practitioners in acute care do everything they can to keep patients alive, practitioners working in palliative care must make difficult decisions that will actually result in a patient's death. Technology exists to keep patients alive virtually indefinitely—long after there is any hope that the patient will regain consciousness. Independent of debates about **euthanasia** (the deliberate ending of a patient's life to relieve suffering), palliative care practitioners must decide when it has become futile to keep a patient artificially alive. It is a physician's responsibility to give a **do not resuscitate order**, stating that CPR or other interventions will not be used if the patient stops breathing.

As we discussed in the section on the ICU, the ethics of this decision are complex. Most practitioners believe that seriously ill patients deserve the right to be involved in resuscitation decisions. However, how does the physician decide which patients are sufficiently "seriously ill" to warrant that discussion? When this decision is made, the patient moves from the world of the living to that of the dying (Teno & Coppola, 1999). In some palliative care units, these discussions are initiated with patients who are expected to live less than six months. At this point, palliative care units provide what has been called a **mixed management model of care**. They prepare the patient for eventual death while at the same time providing life-sustaining treatments (Teno & Coppola, 1999).

KEY TERMS

advanced illness (p. 144)

benign breast biopsy (p. 131)

blunters (p. 123)

burnout (p. 127)

claustrophobia (p. 131)

continuity of care (p. 136)

day care patients (p. 119)

day surgery (p. 134)

dehumanization (p. 124)

depersonalization (p. 124)

discharge planning (p. 141)

disempowering care (p. 122)

do not resuscitate order (p. 145)

empowering care (p. 122)

euthanasia (p. 145)

expertise model (p. 140)

false positive (p. 130)

fear of restriction (p. 132)

fear of suffocation (p. 132)

hospital separation (p. 135)

incommunication stage (p. 138)

invasiveness (p. 129)

learned helplessness (p. 122)

lock-out interval (p. 137)

mixed management model of care (p. 145)

monitors (p. 123)

motion artifacts (p. 132)

negotiated model (p. 140)

non-invasive procedures (p. 119)

occupational rituals (p. 126)

outpatient (p. 119)

palliative care (p. 144)

patient-centred approach (p. 128)

patient-controlled analgesia (PCA) (p. 137)

progressive illness (p. 143)

psychoeducational care (p. 136)

reactance (p. 122)

readaptation stage (p. 138)

reflexion stage (p. 138)

socioemotional care (p. 127)

technical care (p. 127)

therapeutic rituals (p. 126)

total institution (p. 121)

triage (p. 135)

uniformity myth (p. 123)

chapter six

The Health Care Provider

CHAPTER OUTLINE

Physicians

Why People Choose a Career in Medicine

Medical School

Physicians' Emotional Involvement in Their Work

Physicians and Stress

Gender Issues in Medical Practice

The "Feminization" of Medicine

Male and Female Physicians' Perceptions of Themselves, Their Work, and Their Careers

Gender Differences in the Provision of Patient Care

Nursing

The Nature of Modern Nursing

Stress in Nursing

Other Health Care Professionals

  Physical Rehabilitation and Physiotherapists

  Technologists

A Final Word

KEY QUESTIONS

1. What is medical school like?
2. What are the common challenges and stressors in medical practice?
3. What are the possible consequences of excessive stress for a physician?
4. What do nurses do?
5. How stressful is nursing and what are the factors affecting that stress?
6. What are the main gender-related issues in health care?
7. What are the psychological factors relevant to physical rehabilitation, and what role do physical therapists play in addressing those factors?
8. How do technologists help people cope with potentially stressful high-tech diagnostic and treatment procedures?

Jason's older sister was a doctor. He remembered how she had studied for an entire summer for her MCAT exams, a requirement for entrance to many medical schools. Then came the interviews and the anxious waiting to see if she had been accepted. Jason also remembered very clearly the day his sister learned that she had been accepted into medical school. She was thrilled; her parents were thrilled. Even Jason was thrilled even though he was only 10 years old at the time.

Jason remembered all this because he was now studying for his MCAT exams. Like his sister, he had given up an entire summer to study, putting in 40 or 50 hours a week. There were times, though, when he doubted whether it was all going to be worth it. When he talked to his sister recently, she made it clear that the practice of day-to-day medicine, and the rigours of medical school, weren't always as thrilling as that day when she found out she had been accepted into medicine. The workload at medical school was staggering. And when she became a physician, she discovered that her ability to actually cure people was more limited than she had expected.

On her more discouraging days, she felt as though her job was to help people cope with conditions that either never went away or went away only to come back. Certainly, medical science had no magical power to heal. And there was the pager. At first, it had seemed like a symbol of her success. Now it felt more like a ball and chain. It beeped at the most inconvenient of times, and she had to answer it. But despite all these negatives, Jason's sister said that she ultimately felt proud to be a physician and that she really did feel that she was helping people in important ways, but that being a doctor wasn't as glamorous as it might appear to people outside the profession.

Very little of my work was glamorous in the TV drama sense, but much of it was intense.

A family physician (Coombs, 1998, p. 175).

In chapter 1, we made the point that health psychologists receive different training from most other people working in health care. The main difference, of course, is the emphasis placed on biomedical knowledge in the training of physicians, nurses, technologists, physiotherapists, and so on. These differences in background make for understandable differences in perspective when it comes to health and health care. While understandable, these differences still must be overcome if health psychologists are to make contributions to people's health.

It is important for health psychologists to have an appreciation for the training health care providers receive and the stresses they deal with on a daily basis. For example, it is of little use to simply tell a family physician that he or she must spend more time listening to patients and explaining things to them if we have no appreciation for the number of patients that physician must see in a given day. Similarly, a nurse may appear less compassionate than a patient would like simply because that nurse has a large patient load that includes some seriously ill people. In short, health psychology must be practised within the realities of the health care system.

In this chapter, we will look closely at what it is like to be a health care provider. Our main objective is to provide some understanding of the realities of their work. The hope is that the interventions we suggest as health psychologists will be better received and more feasible if we have this understanding.

PHYSICIANS

Few professions match medicine for responsibility and status. The ability to alleviate suffering, and the responsibility for life itself can make a career in medicine both intensely satisfying and extremely stressful. In Canada, we have gone from a surplus to a shortage of physicians in the last 10 years (Chan, 2002). Between 1993 and 2001, there was a 5.1 percent decline in the number of physicians practising in this country, and a corresponding 7 percent increase in the workloads of general and family practitioners. While these trends might not translate into major changes to the way health care is delivered, it still raises concern (Watson, Roos, Katz, & Bogdanovic, 2003). In this section, we will explore reasons why people want to become physicians, then we will look closely at the medical school experience. We will then discuss some of the realities of day-to-day practice.

BOX 6-1	Are There Enough General and Family Practitioners in Canada?

The overall number of physicians in Canada is on the decline and the workloads of general and family practitioners are increasing. These facts combine to predict that we will soon face a crisis regarding the number of general and family practitioners in the country.

In their final year of medical school, students have to make their preferred residency choice. These choices provide

(continued on next page)

indications of the distribution of the kinds of physicians we can expect in Canada. In recent years, fewer and fewer students have been choosing family and general practice. In 2003, 29 percent of the residency positions available in family medicine were unfilled (Sullivan, 2003). This occurred in spite of the fact that 115 students did not get their first choice in a residency position. At present, it is estimated that Canada is approximately 3000 general practitioners short of the population's needs (Gutkin, 2003).

What are the consequences of this shortage? For one thing, Canadians are having a harder time finding a family doctor. Thirty percent of our population has no family doctor, and 4.5 million people in the country tried unsuccessfully to find one between 2002 and 2003 (Gutkin, 2003). Because the health of the population has been shown to improve with access to primary care physicians (Starfield, 1994), attempts are made to keep the ratio of general practitioners to specialists at 50:50 in Canada (Gutkin, 2003). Current statistics, however, indicate that we are in danger of falling below this ratio.

What can be done? Some advocates have called upon medical schools to emphasize the value of and satisfaction to be found in family practice (Gutkin, 2003). Others have said that the teaching of family medicine must be given higher priority (Malkin, 2003). But others argue that medical students cannot be cajoled into a form of practice that has lower perceived status and career opportunities (Whatley, 2003). One solution stemming from this position is to allow practising specialists who have grown dissatisfied with their practice to re-certify as family practitioners. In addition, the reputation of family practice as featuring overwork and underpay must change (MacKean & Gutkin, 2003).

Why People Choose a Career in Medicine

The reasons people choose a career in medicine are not particularly surprising. A study in Britain found that students were drawn to medicine because of career opportunities, a desire to work with people and help patients, and the chance it provided to use their personal skills and pursue their interests in science (Crossley & Mubarik, 2002).

Considerable research has looked at personality factors in medical students and practitioners. One personality test, the Myers-Briggs Type Indicator, was designed specifically to be applied to career choice. Based on the work of Carl Jung, the Myers-Briggs measures personality attributes along continuums of introversion–extraversion and thinking–feeling (objective, impersonal decision making versus subjective decision making), and judging–perceiving (decisive and orderly versus flexible and adaptive). A study of 12 medical schools in the United States using the Myers-Briggs found that those scoring higher on introversion and feeling were more likely to choose family medicine; whereas, extraverted, thinking types were more likely to choose surgical specialties (Stilwell, Wallick, Thal, & Burleson, 2000).

Gender differences also surfaced in the Stilwell et al. study. Males were more likely than females to choose surgery. We will explore gender differences among physicians in more detail in a moment.

Generally, medical students score higher on measures of perfectionism than first-year arts students do (Enns, Cox, Sareen, & Freeman, 2001). Perfectionism, though, can be either adaptive or maladaptive. It is adaptive when it is associated with striving for achievement. It is maladaptive when it is associated with excessive concerns about being evaluated. Medical students who score higher on adaptive perfectionism had higher expectations for their academic success and were more conscientious. Other research has found that, among personality traits, conscientiousness is the best single predictor of success in medical school (Ferguson, James, O'Hehir, & Sanders, 2003), though nothing predicts this success better than past academic performance, which explains about 23 percent of the variance in medical school grades (Ferguson, James, & Madeley, 2002). Students scoring higher on the measure of maladaptive perfectionism were more prone to distress in the form of depression and hopelessness (Enns et al., 2001).

Medical School

Because health psychologists need to understand what it is like to be a health care professional, and because the intense training a physician receives is biomedical rather than psychosocial, it is helpful for people studying health psychology to have an appreciation for the nature of medical school training. Such an appreciation may allow us to understand the comments of one medical student who said of his sociology class, "I waited for half an hour for a *fact* to write down" (Sinclair, 1997, p. 166; author's emphasis). Or another student who said of his psychology class, "Psychology's interesting when she (the lecturer) is talking about (doctor–patient) interaction, but nothing much else" (Sinclair, 1997, p. 166).

There have been a number of good books written about medical school, some for premed students who want to know how to survive medical school, others by anthropologists and other social scientists trying to understand the culture of medical school. One book that actually does both is *Surviving Medical School*, by Robert Coombs (1998). In his book, Coombs takes the reader through medical school, year by year.

The Pre-Med Syndrome   If there is such a thing as a medical school mentality, and Coombs presents a convincing case that there is, it may well start before students even enter medical school. Pre-med students are often considered to be highly competitive and non-cooperative. In fact, cases have been documented of students sabotaging other students' labs to gain a competitive edge. Students exhibiting the pre-med syndrome are more likely to take classes solely to meet requirements and improve their GPA. They cannot afford to try a course that might expose an academic weakness. Finally, these students tend to have romanticized expectations of medical school. Of course, not all pre-med students fit this syndrome, but enough do to make this sense of extreme competitiveness and glorified expectations a problem for those who are accepted into medical school.

First Year   No matter how much warning an incoming student may have had, he or she is always surprised by the workload in first-year medicine. The volume of work and the time pressures are overwhelming. One student said, "It's like trying to drink from a fire hose" (Coombs, 1998, p. 19). In fact, it is virtually impossible to learn everything that is presented. This causes first-year students to wonder if they should have gone to medical school in the first place. Their self-confidence might plummet. Yet, they don't complain to their peers because that would make them look weak, and there is a social taboo against weakness. Despite the onslaught of material, few students fail first year. Somehow, they survive.

Second Year The second year is often considered the most stressful academically. Having said that, students come to accept the fact that they can never know everything there is to know. They tell first-year students not to be upset that they can't possibly learn everything, but first-year students don't usually listen.

For second-year students, a transformation begins to take place. They tend to become more assertive and confident. They ask questions that show they are now focusing on what needs to be known for the patient's sake, rather than for the exam. Concurrent with this, second-year students begin to really feel the financial strain of medical school. Most don't feel they can continue to rely on their families for financial support, and costs continue to mount.

The social relationships of many second-year students begin to take on a unique quality. A differentiation emerges between those on the "inside" and those on the "outside" of medical school. Second-year students report enjoying an elevated status among those on the "outside," yet, loneliness is common. This is due in part to the fact that many people on the "outside" don't understand medical school and are generally unsympathetic to students' complaints about it. They reason, "How hard can school be? You don't have to work for a living. And besides, you're going to be a doctor and make lots of money."

Third Year In most medical programs, third-year students begin to receive their clinical experience. They interact directly with patients in a hospital setting. This yields a whole new set of insecurities, for, in spite of the fact that they have learned a great deal in their first two years, they still do not know enough to take on the duties of a physician. A third-year student is not yet a physician but is expected to act like one. This becomes especially evident when third-year students must perform physical examinations. Students say that their lack of confidence was blatant when they were drawing blood or starting IVs, for example. Third-year students in clinical training are struck by the large gap between their textbooks and the real patients they are treating. Patients almost never lay out their symptoms as neatly as in a textbook. This leaves the student feeling uncertain and inadequate. Interestingly, Coombs reports that patients are usually quite accepting of these students.

In these clinical settings, it is imperative that students learn as much as they can. However, the teaching in these situations can be sporadic, given the demands of clinical work on the physicians. Students report that they are sometimes taught, but often just feel like they are getting in the way.

A number of challenging issues emerge for third-year students—issues that they must either come to grips with or be plagued by throughout their careers. For example, they must accept that they will make mistakes. They must strike a balance between clinical competence and unrealistic expectations of perfection. There is also the challenge of contagion. Few of us have to worry that we will get seriously ill from contact with people in our jobs. The physician, however, must deal with this all the time. There are many contagious diseases physicians are exposed to, such as SARS. One student admitted to spending less time than he should have with a typhoid fever patient because of fear of contagion. That student is not alone.

Closely related to this danger is the susceptibility to accidents that may compromise a student's health. In a study of medical students at the University of Washington School of Medicine, almost half of one graduating class reported having had a needle-stick injury or being splashed with fluids that were infectious (Turk, 1993). A study in France revealed that 38 surgeons per 100 per year had experienced a percutaneous (through the skin) injury (Denis et al., 2003). This study found no differences between practitioners and students in the incidence of blood-related accidents. A study conducted in England, Wales, and Northern Ireland found that there had been 588 of these injuries between July 1997 and June 2000. Of these, 200 had been to doctors and 210 to nurses and midwives (Evans, Duggan, Baker, Ramsay, & Abiteboul, 2001).

It is in the clinical training of third year that most students have their first encounter with critically ill patients. Students are taught to cope by immersing themselves in the work, using humour, and coming to realize that death is not always tantamount to failure. Dealing with death is in itself another major challenge. Students learn to dehumanize their patients in order to cope with death. They may refer to patients in parts and pieces, talking about "the pancreas in 371." The practice of medicine can become a battle between death and medical science—a battle in which the patient becomes an object or "playing field." When personal feelings about death do arise, they are rarely discussed, again for fear of appearing weak or unsuited to the profession.

It is important to note that, while our discussion focuses on physicians, many of these challenges also apply to other health professionals. Nurses are an excellent example. In one case, a nurse was reported to have organized a service for a patient who had died after a long hospital stay. No other nurses attended the service. When asked why, one nurse said that if she started to cry for this patient, she would cry for all the patients she had seen die and would never stop crying (Coombs, 1998).

Fourth Year   By senior year, a student's socialization into the medical community is virtually complete. He or she will likely have developed a manageable level of emotional distancing from patients. This is to say that the student is not so distant as to appear uncaring, but not so close as to suffer from the exhaustion of limitless caring, sometimes called **compassion fatigue**. Also, by this point most students have lost their sense of idealism regarding medicine, beginning to accept that there are limits to a physician's powers to heal and always be correct.

Internship and Residency   In the first year post-graduation, a physician does a year of **internship**. Rather than marking the end of the labour-intensive training period, internship, if anything, appears more demanding still. Work schedules of 90 to 120 hours per week are not uncommon in some hospitals. After internship comes **residency**. Residents, or house officers, as they are sometimes called, are susceptible to burnout. They encounter a rather sudden increase in accountability, and a decrease in sleep. A study of on-call residents found that the length of uninterrupted periods of sleep ranged from 40 to 86 minutes (Lurie et al., 1989). The Accreditation Council for Graduate Medical Education has since passed new regulations for medical residents in the United States (*Resident Duty Hours Language: Final Requirements*, 2003). According to these regulations, residents will have to work a maximum of 80 hours per week, with no shift longer than 24 hours, and with 10 hours of rest between shifts. Even with these new rules, residents maintain a gruelling schedule.

To help residents cope with the demands of on-call nights, they are advised to prioritize their sickest patients, respond to their beepers quickly, and always try to prevent rather than treat (Peterkin, 1998). To make matters even more challenging, residents who work in urban hospitals, especially late at night, must be aware of danger signs signalling potentially violent patients.

Physicians' Emotional Involvement in Their Work

At the beginning of this chapter, we quoted a family physician who said that his work wasn't as dramatic as television but that it was still intense. It is important for health psychologists to learn to appreciate the emotional intensity of physicians' day-to-day experiences. One of the best ways to do this is to talk with physicians and get first-hand accounts. This requires a close enough relationship for the physician to feel comfortable disclosing some personal feelings and accounts, however. We must remember, also, that physicians themselves report a reluctance to discuss emotional aspects of their work. Another way to gain insights into what physicians face on an emotional level is to read sections of medical journals in which physicians write candidly about dilemmas they have faced. For example, try reading the section entitled "Heart and Soul" in the *Canadian Medical Association Journal,* "A Piece of My Mind" in past issues of the *Journal of the American Medical Association,* or "Personal Views" in the *British Medical Journal.*

In an issue of the *British Medical Journal,* a physician describes clearly and concisely the dilemma presented by uncertainty in medical diagnosis:

> In a burst of honesty her doctor had the temerity to admit that variations in practice exist. Instead she wants a cut-and-dried answer because that is her expectation. Behind her are years of conditioning to believe that as medicine is a science it must produce hard facts and straightforward answers (Harrison, 1999, p. 793).

In these sections of medical journals, you may read articles like "No Pretending Not to Know," in which a physician recounts a case involving an ultrasound exam confirming that a woman's fetus had no skull or brain. At first, he grappled with the question of who should inform the woman who has just undergone the exam. In this case, as the radiologist, he could have let her own doctor tell her, or perhaps the resident obstetrician. However, the woman could sense something was wrong. There was no avoiding the truth, as the physician's description makes abundantly clear:

> "Did you see the baby's head?" Her question couldn't have been more to the point. My internal debate about who should tell her the results becomes academic. I pull up a chair next to her. "We've found something wrong with your baby, Mrs. J. Your baby's brain didn't develop." She is stunned, and for what seems like several minutes she says nothing. From her facial expression I can tell that she doesn't really understand. I try again to explain what is wrong with her baby. "What will happen when the baby is born?" she asks. I tell her that her baby will live a very short time and then die. She wants to know if there is any way her baby can live and even be somewhat normal: I have to tell her no (Brown, 1988, p. 2720).

Few professions require their practitioners to have such emotionally draining conversations. Of course, not all conversations between patients and physicians involve negative emotions. There is the elation of normal childbirth and the relief patients feel when they are informed they are not seriously ill. The point is that such extreme emotional experiences are potentially exhausting and distracting. For this reason, most physicians find that they must learn to control their emotions, avoiding the peaks and valleys their patients may encounter. To do this requires the ability to distance oneself from one's patient. It is difficult, however, to do this and still make it clear that the physician truly cares for his or her patient's well-being.

As we saw in our discussion of medical school, medical students often dehumanize their patients by referring to them as body parts rather than as people. This is another way to maintain emotional control. Another is to use humour, which can neutralize situations that would otherwise be very sad. For example, some physicians will use the initials CTD to describe a patient who is about to die; CTD stands for "circling the drain" (DiMatteo, 1991, p. 267).

Physicians and Stress

The responsibility inherent in being a physician has the potential to be very stressful. A study of over 2000 Canadian physicians discovered that 38 percent described their practice as being very or extremely stressful (Burke & Richardsen, 1990). In addition to the basic responsibilities that come with caring for patients, there are other aspects of a physician's work that can add to the problem. For example, physicians often work under time pressure (Richardsen & Burke, 1991). If you have ever sat in your doctor's waiting room for any length of time, you will probably have noticed how often the phone rings as people try to make appointments. Many of these people want to see the doctor as soon as possible and so they are "fit in." While we appreciate this consideration as patients, it makes for a hectic day for the physician, who must try to somehow strike a balance between giving people ample time and moving patients through in a timely fashion. And all of this is thrown into chaos if an emergency occurs. It is not surprising that work overload is cited by physicians as a significant source of stress (Burke & Richardsen, 1990). A large 1998 study in Canada found that 62 percent of physicians considered their workload to be too heavy (Sullivan & Buske, 1998). This situation persists today (Bergman, Ahmad, & Stewart, 2003).

Overload leads to **burnout**, a condition that was first identified among nurses, but is now recognized in numerous health professionals. The symptoms of burnout have been well-documented. They include emotional exhaustion, perceived ineffectiveness, cynicism, and dissatisfaction with relations with co-workers (Spickard, Gabbe, & Christensen, 2002). There is a lack of correspondence between what practitioners think they should be doing and what they actually are doing (Maslach & Leiter, 1997). The best way to prevent burnout is to focus on one's own well-being throughout one's career. This can be done by spending more time with friends and family, focusing on spiritual and personal needs, finding meaning in work, setting limits at work, and maintaining a positive outlook (Weiner, Swain, Wolf, & Gottleib, 2001).

Of course, despite physicians' best efforts, some patients will die, and physicians must face the stress of communicating bad news to patients and their families. This stressor is more common in some specialties than others, such as oncology. In a study of this source of stress, 38 physicians were asked to recall a time when they had given a patient bad news. The physicians were then asked some questions based on their memory of the encounter. Most physicians followed published guidelines when giving bad news, though this did not eliminate the stress they felt when doing so. They felt that they had done an effective job of reducing their patients' distress but that their own discomfort and stress had started prior to the encounter and lasted beyond the end of the encounter. The conclusion of this research was that published guidelines on the giving of bad news are helpful in reducing patient distress, but more attention has to be paid to the distress felt by the physician (Ptacek, Fries, Eberhartd, & Ptacek, 1999).

Considerable research indicates that male and female physicians experience stress differently. For example, one study showed that workload, *per se*, was not a predictor of psychological distress for women (Gareis & Barnett, 2002). Instead, manageability of hours, or schedule fit, was. This points to the fact that women physicians face a somewhat different set of stressors from men. They face greater discrimination in the workplace, and in a larger context, experience strain between their work and family roles (Robinson, 2003). It is worth noting that, despite these challenges, female physicians report a high degree of job satisfaction (Robinson, 2003). This may be due to the fact that female physicians seem to do a better job at placing limits on their work-related demands than male physicians do (Arouni & Rich, 2003).

There has been considerable research aimed at discovering the extent to which these stress levels put physicians at greater risk for suicide than the general public. One study in Britain reported that female physicians were more likely than females in the general public to commit suicide; whereas, male physicians were *less* likely than males in the general population (Hawton, 2001). Based on this, Hawton concluded that female physicians were at greater risk for suicide. However, another author pointed out that because rates of suicide are lower for females generally, in fact, the rates for male and female physicians were not significantly different from one another (Verberne, 2002).

Uncertainty as a Source of Stress   Another significant source of stress that is not always obvious to the general public is **uncertainty**. We like to think that medicine is a precise science, but it is not. In an article by Lurie and Sox (1999), the authors make two important points regarding uncertainty. First, "Clinical examinations and other diagnostic tests are imperfect" (p. 493); and second, "The consequences of medical decisions are inherently uncertain at the decisive moment" (p. 493). This means that a given diagnosis is often accompanied by a degree of uncertainty, and **prognosis**, a prediction of how a medical condition will change in the future, is even more uncertain. Physicians work for the most part with probabilities rather than absolute certainties.

Indeed, Lurie and Sox (1999) advocate the use of probability statistics varying from 0 to 1 when talking about prognosis and health outcomes, rather than imprecise language such as "possible" or "unlikely." This assumes that patients can understand the meaning of something like a .7 probability and that physicians can determine probabilities, based not only on what research and experience tell them regarding the frequency of a given medical outcome, but also on the unique characteristics of the patient being treated.

Imagine a dialogue between a neurosurgeon and a patient who is trying to decide whether or not to have back surgery.

Patient: I don't mind going through the surgery if I know it will work. Will it take my pain away?

Physician: For people with your condition, the probability that the surgery will relieve your pain is .7.

Patient: Point seven? That would be great a batting average in baseball, but I'm not sure what it means for me.

Physician: It means that for every ten times I performed this operation on someone like you, I would expect it to be successful seven times.

Patient: Yeah, but you're only going to perform it once on me.

It is likely that the majority of patients don't have a good understanding of the meaning of probability statistics (Kahneman & Tversky, 1973). It is also likely that they do not have a good idea of how much uncertainty exists in medical decision making. In a study of this, patients were asked to estimate the accuracy with which diagnosis would be made for six different conditions presented to them as written descriptions (Hamm & Smith, 1998). Interestingly, the patients' estimates did not differ across conditions. This suggests that people have a general belief about how correct medical science is and apply that belief regardless of the condition in question. The medical truth is that some conditions are considerably easier to diagnose than others and so certainty varies from one situation to the next.

Further, the patients' estimates of accuracy were quite unrealistic. In particular, they underestimated the likelihood of a false-positive diagnosis. Taken collectively, then, this means that patients believe that diagnostic certainty is greater than it really is, regardless of the condition being diagnosed. It should be noted, though, that patients who have direct experience with a given condition were slightly better at estimating the diagnostic accuracy associated with it.

This level of faith in medical science only adds to the potential stressfulness of uncertainty for the physician. A patient thinks a physician should know and does know exactly what the diagnosis is and what the treatment should be; while, on the other side of the consultation, the physician is very aware of the level of uncertainty that exists. The physician's response to this situation ranges from communicating that uncertainty with a probability statistic to denying the uncertainty altogether (Hamm & Smith, 1998).

All of this takes place in a context in which each party may be concerned with some possibility of which the other isn't even aware (Bergh, 1998). In addition, physicians commonly identify a treatment plan and then name the illness to fit the plan (for example, bronchitis; see Bergh, 1998). Patients are also often more interested in the physical explanation than in the treatment anyway. Taken together, these phenomena mean that these parties aren't really interacting in a way that makes it any easier for the physician to deal with the stress of uncertainty (Bergh, 1998).

Of course, one way for the physician to cope with uncertainty is to deny it. When a group of physicians was presented with an identical video depicting an atypical breast case, half of them diagnosed benign breast disease, one-third identified breast cancer as the most probable initial diagnosis, 6 percent called it normal, and 9 percent gave a diagnosis unrelated to breast disease (McKinlay et al., 1998). Generally, physicians' reports of certainty were high in this study. Now, before you give up on medical decision making altogether, remember that the decision making simulated in this study is *preliminary* in nature. Further tests would likely be ordered to yield a more definitive diagnosis. However, diagnostic uncertainty may result in excessive testing, which is another source of stress for physicians and patients.

As we have already mentioned, medical tests don't completely eliminate uncertainty either. Tests differ in their **sensitivity** and **specificity**. Sensitivity refers to a test's ability to pick up true positives—actual cases of the disease. Specificity refers to its ability to pick up true negatives—cases where disease is definitely *not* present (see Lurie & Sox, 1999).

A final point to make about uncertainty in medical decision making is that it is more common among primary-care physicians than it is among specialists. **Primary-care physicians** include those in general and family practice. Differences between primary-care physicians and specialists regarding certainty are not due to differences in skill levels. They exist because physicians of all types tend to solve problems through pattern recognition. Primary-care physicians see a wider range of symptoms; therefore, they have far too many patterns to remember and often too few of any particular symptom to even form a pattern in the physician's experience. Also, more problems are presented early in their history to primary-care physicians, before patterns have been well established. In contrast, the specialist sees a much narrower range of problems and symptoms, usually when they have reached a stage where the diagnosis has become more clear.

In spite of these differences between primary-care physicians and specialists, patients usually report greater satisfaction with their primary-care physician than with their specialist, because the former provides continuous, person-focused care. By contrast, the specialist tends to provide low-continuity, disease-focused care (Rosser, 1996). This may mean that patients are less concerned about specialized diagnostic certainty than they are about the nature of the relationship they have with the physician. Or, it may simply be because patients generally believe that levels of certainty are high and similar across diagnostic settings (Hamm & Smith, 1998).

Regardless of these patient perceptions, the most important points to remember here are that decision-related uncertainty is a significant source of stress for physicians, and that there is no easy solution to the problem. Perhaps this is why physicians sometimes cope by using rather dark humour. For example, DiMatteo (1991) describes physicians telling one another that a patient has GOK (p. 267), which stands for "God Only Knows."

Physician Impairment   The conditions accompanying stress are doubly problematic for a physician. Not only do they compromise the physician's own quality of life, they compromise the physician's ability to provide care to others. For these reasons, researchers looking at physician stress have coined the term **physician impairment**. It refers to a state in which stress-related symptoms interfere with the physician's ability to perform his or her job.

One of the most troubling causes of physician impairment is substance abuse. While alcoholism and drug addiction are no more prevalent among physicians, use of prescription drugs, especially those used to treat psychological distress, is more prevalent among physicians, due in part to their access to these drugs (O'Connor & Spickard, 1997). Issues of dependency have prompted a call to make alcohol and drug problems a health promotion issue for physicians (Brewster, 2001). Weir points out that it can be difficult for physicians to seek treatment because the admission of a drug or alcohol dependency can have implications for their licensing. As a result, they are more likely to deny their problem or suffer alone. By the time the problem surfaces in the workplace, it is probably well advanced. This reticence to seek treatment is unfortunate for many reasons, not the least of which being that recovery rates are around 80 percent when treatment is sought. This treatment is most effective when it is uninterrupted and residential, featuring family involvement and prudent return to practice with adequate follow-up and support (Weir, 2000).

GENDER ISSUES IN MEDICAL PRACTICE

No analysis of health care practitioners would be complete without a discussion of gender issues. Among physicians, men and women bring different attributes to their work, they make somewhat different career choices, they perceive their work differently, and they communicate with their patients differently. Further, patients' own gender influences preferences for the gender of their physicians.

The "Feminization" of Medicine

In Canada in 1991, 26 percent of all physicians were female. By 1996, the figure had jumped to 30 percent (Statistics Canada). Furthermore, in most Canadian medical schools today, females constitute 50 percent or more of the students (Sullivan, 1990). In the United States, the percentage of women in first-year medical school jumped from virtually zero in 1960 to 46 percent in 2000 (Robinson, 2000).

The trend toward increased proportions of female physicians has led some theorists to speculate on the changes this will bring to the profession. The **feminization of medicine**, as this trend has been called, may bring about changes to the balance between cure and care we talk about later in the chapter in our discussion of nursing. It may also affect the nature of interactions between patients and physicians (De Koninck, Bergeron, & Bourbonnais, 1997). To get a clearer sense of how this might happen, let's look at some specific ways in which male and female physicians differ in their practice of medicine.

Male and Female Physicians' Perceptions of Themselves, Their Work, and Their Careers

Male and female medical school graduates present somewhat different assessments of their personal attributes (Clack & Head, 1999). A study in Britain found that men were more likely to cite leadership potential, spirit of curiosity, and tolerance of ambiguity and uncertainty as personal attributes. Women were more likely to identify their ability to inspire confidence in others and their ability to listen as well as their caring and compassionate nature (Clack & Head, 1999). As we will see, these differences in the way medical graduates see themselves are manifested as differences in the way men and women carry out the work of medicine as well. In the Clack and Head study, men and women were equally likely to make reference to their excitement with the subject of medicine, their perseverance, and their open-mindedness.

A study in Finland assessed physicians' self-reported values. These were defined as desirable goals that serve to guide the physicians through their lives (Neittaanmäki et al., 1999). It was found that female physicians were more likely to value close friends and what the authors called "universalism," which referred to world peace and an unpolluted environment. Women were also more likely to say they valued doing a good job and gaining the respect of others. These values manifest themselves in some of the differences in the career choices and interaction styles of male and female physicians. This also applies to a study conducted in North America in which male medical students said the quality they most valued in their own physician was competence, whereas for female medical students this quality was compassion (McFarland & Rhoades, 1998).

Regarding career choices, a study by researchers at Université de Laval in Québec City discovered that female physicians place more importance on their private lives when making professional life decisions than do their male counterparts (De Koninck, Bergeron & Bourbonnais, 1997). Interviews with female physicians yielded some clear statements about the way values affected their career choices:

"What is important for women is not the size of their practice, the income, or publications, but the type of practice, personal satisfaction, fulfilling needs..." (a female physician interviewed, De Koninck, Bergeron, & Bourbonnais, 1997). Another woman put it this way: "I didn't want to be just a doctor...I wanted a family, children...I wanted a life that I would call normal...I said to myself, if I go into neurosurgery, I'll never be able to" (a female physician interviewed, De Koninck, Bergeron, & Bourbonnais, 1997).

In a study of medical students at the University of Toronto, 27 percent of the men said they would choose surgery compared to only 10 percent of the women (Baxter, Cohen, & McLeod, 1996). These differences were based, in part, on perceptions regarding the lifestyle demands of the work and the amount of interaction (or lack thereof) surgeons have with patients. Other research with medical students has found that men say they wanted to work longer hours than women did and that women are more likely to want to spend leisure time with their family and friends (McFarland & Rhoades, 1998). Consistent with this, only four percent of orthopedic surgeons in the United States are women (Rowley, Baldwin, & McGuire, 1991).

Once they have made their career choice, female and male physicians have different perceptions of their work. Females are more likely to feel what is called **role strain**. This means that they feel torn by the demands of multiple roles, never being able to handle any of them to their satisfaction. These roles may include physician, mother, and wife, to name a few. This is compounded by the fact that women report feeling a greater sense of responsibility to others (Gross, 1998).

Given that medicine has historically been male dominated, it is not surprising that women physicians are more likely to perceive discrimination than men are (VanIneveld et al., 1996). A study of internal medicine housestaff in Canada found that 70 percent of female residents said they had experienced discrimination by attending physicians, whereas only 23 percent of male residents reported such discrimination. Similarly, 88 percent of female residents reported discrimination from patients (38 percent of male residents reported this) and 71 percent of female physicians reported discrimination from nurses, compared to 35 percent for male residents (VanIneveld et al., 1996). Female physicians were also much more likely to state that they had experienced sexual harassment from attending physicians, peers, and patients than male residents were. In a study of over 450 female physicians in Ontario, 76 percent said that they had experienced sexual harassment from patients (Phillips, 1996). Perhaps one of the most upsetting findings from the VanIneveld study was that 40 percent of all residents reported having experienced physical assault.

Joyce Tinsley (1998) makes the point that discrimination can work both ways. Tinsley presents examples of males in an otherwise all-female medical team who report that their opinions are devalued and that they are excluded from the group's conversations.

Gender Differences in the Provision of Patient Care

Clear differences emerge when the communication styles of male and female physicians are studied. For example, females tend to be more in favour of collaboration with their patients in treatment, they spend more time with their patients, and they are more likely to discuss psychosocial issues and deal with patients' emotions (Roter & Hall, 1998). Women have been found to be more egalitarian than authoritarian in their use of language with patients, often using words such as "let's" (West, 1993).

In terms of making medical decisions, some research suggests that female and male physicians differ while other research does not. For example, a study in Finland (Mattila-Lindy et al., 1998) looking at medical decisions regarding women's reproductive health, including such things as obstetric practices and hormone therapy during and after menopause, found very few differences between male and female physicians. In contrast, a study of physicians across Canada found that female doctors were more liberal regarding their patients' access to amniocentesis than male physicians were. Female physicians also favoured broader access to prenatal diagnostic tools such as ultrasound (Bouchard & Renaud, 1997). In the United States, it was found that women were more likely to get mammograms if they had a female physician (Lurie et al., 1993). Consistent with this, a study in Washington State showed that female patients of male physicians were twice as likely not to have had a mammogram in the last two years (Anderson & Urban, 1997). The interesting thing about the Washington State study is that it controlled for patient characteristics. For example, women with female physicians tended to be younger than those with male physicians.

The differences among these studies could be attributed to differences in physicians' attitudes toward women's health issues in the countries involved. It is also possible that differences between men and women regarding their clinical decision making could be explained by differences in their training. Consistent with this, an analysis of over 70 000 patients seen at the Queen's University Family Medical Centre over a five-year period between 1988 and 1993 found that female residents in family medicine saw 68.4 percent of the female patients. This means that, in the final stages of their training, female physicians see significantly more female patients than male physicians do, at least in family medicine (Sabir, Godwin, & Birtwistle, 1997).

Given these differences, what do we know about patients' preferences for female or male physicians? You might hypothesize that patients generally favour a physician whose gender is the same as their own. Indeed, a study in the 1960s found that urban women preferred female physicians, even at a time when there were significantly fewer of them than there are today (Hopkins et al., 1967). However, more recent research indicates that this preference exists in some cases but it is not universal. A study in the United States found that, of those patients who chose their physician, the least satisfied were females who chose female physicians (Schmittdiel, J.V., Grumbach, & Quesenberry, 2000). The most satisfied were male patients who chose female physicians.

It might stand to reason that patients' preferences regarding the gender of the physician would depend on the nature of the examination being conducted, given that some exams are more personally intrusive than others. With this possibility in mind, researchers looked at patients' perceptions of male and female physicians giving anal and vaginal exams (Van Elderen, Maes, Rouneau, & Seegers, 1998). Both male and female patients rated female physicians higher than males on a curing dimension for giving anal examinations. For vaginal exams, which were of course rated only by female patients, females were rated more highly on the curing dimension, the caring dimension, and a consulting dimension (see "Nursing" section below for more on curing and caring). Patient preferences are certainly more complex than simply having men wanting male physicians and women wanting female ones.

NURSING

Modern nursing in Canada is a profession facing many challenges. The constant changes in medical science demand that nurses stay absolutely current in their knowledge. The roles that nurses play in modern hospitals are expanding to include many advanced areas such as transplant specialization and cardiac care. In fact, the area of advanced practice nursing is a rapidly expanding one in Canada.

The Nature of Modern Nursing

When most lay people think of nurses, they think of people who are involved in **caring** for patients in hospital. This is distinct from the role of the physician, which focuses on the **curing** of people (Watson, 1988). In providing care, nurses make sure that medication is properly administered, that hygienic and dietary needs of the patients are taken care of, and that the emotional needs of the patient are considered as well. In general, they are patient advocates in the hospital setting. Of course, nurses work in settings other than hospitals. They also work in community settings, as public health nurses, as home care nurses, and so on. All of these roles that we commonly associate with nursing have existed for many years.

There are those who believe that the caring side of health care is being eroded somewhat as modern medicine becomes more technical and specialized (Krebs et al., 1996). They feel that this change shifts health care to a cure orientation. Cure is of course very important; however, when the cure–care balance is disrupted, a health care system is created in which cure is given higher status. This can result in a devaluing of the nurse's role, which is a problem because the reality in health care is that care is more prevalent than cure. There are two ways that nurses are attempting to make the importance of their role clear. First, they are emphasizing the importance of a care orientation. Second, they are engaging in training and job re-definition so that they can become more actively involved in cure-related practice.

This advanced training and re-definition of roles in modern nursing has given rise to **advanced practice nursing**. The Canadian Nurses Association (CNA) defines advanced practice as "the role of a nurse working within a specialty area where superior clinical skills and judgement are acquired through a combination of experience and education" (CNA, 1997a, p. 2). In advanced practice, nurses' roles expand to include teaching, consultation, and research. While advanced practice expands the role that nurses play in health care, concerns have been expressed that this might come at the expense of their caring role (Donnelly, 2003) and that the challenges brought on by multiple roles within the practice will increase nurses' stress levels (Cummings, Fraser, & Tarlier, 2003; Musclow, Sawhney, & Watt-Watson, 2002). However, if these concerns can be dealt with, they need not outweigh the benefits of providing nurses with the opportunity to contribute more fully to the care of patients.

There are a number of general categories of advanced nursing practice. One is the **clinical nurse specialist**. Nurses with this specialty hold a master's or doctoral degree in nursing and have extensive experience in a given clinical specialty. Another category is the

nurse practitioner. The nurse practitioner often works in rural, remote settings. In these settings, where physicians are often in short supply, the nurse practitioner performs functions that might otherwise be performed by a physician. Thus, the Canadian Nurses Association points out that, for the nurse practitioner, "caring and curing overlap" (CNA, 1997a, p. 4). This category is formally recognized in Ontario, where university-level programs exist for the training of nurse practitioners, and health legislation is now reflecting this expanded role for nurses in Alberta and Ontario. As is often the case when roles change and expand, there is debate in health care regarding the most appropriate scope and boundaries for positions such as the nurse practitioner.

Nursing, then, is a profession in which ongoing education has become essential in order to keep up with advances in technology and nursing research. Many people entering the profession come in with a four-year bachelor's degree in nursing rather than a registered nursing degree that may take two to three years to attain. It is clearly a field with exciting challenges. At the same time, nursing can be a very stressful profession, as we will see later in this section, and funding cutbacks in health care affect nursing significantly. Thus nursing is a profession in which the demands are high and the resources often inadequate.

Add to this the prediction by the Canadian Nurses Association that, according to an independent study, we will have a shortage of nurses in the order of 59 000 to 113 000 by the year 2001, and there is cause for concern (CNA, 1997b). This projected shortage will result from an aging workforce in nursing and a lack of young people entering the profession. In addition, the population in general is aging, putting increasing demands on the health care system. The Canadian Nurses Association predicted that the demand for registered nurses would climb by 46 percent between 1993 and 2001 (CNA, 1997b).

Why should all this matter to health psychologists? There are a number of reasons. First, increased demands combined with a shortage of resources is a recipe for stress. As we will see in this section, stress is a problem in nursing, for both nurses and patients. You may remember from our discussion of hospital stays in chapter 5 that we cited Canadian research indicating patient satisfaction was correlated with nurses' self-reports of burnout (Leiter, Harvie, & Frizzel, 1998) (see Focus on Canadian Research 5-1, p. 128). Burnout and stress are closely related. Second, people in health care are not immune to lifestyle-related illnesses—illnesses they spend so much time treating. Third, a considerable amount of hospital research in health psychology involves nurses. Nurses may be asked to administer research protocols in addition to their regular duties. When conducting this research, it is essential to have some understanding of the demands such involvement places on the nurses' already hectic schedules and the implications that our conclusions and recommendations will have for nurses' work.

Stress in Nursing

People who work in professions in which suffering is common are susceptible to something called **compassion fatigue** (Schwan, 1998). Even for the most caring of people, there are limits to the amount of energy one can dedicate to other people's welfare. When those limits are exceeded, the nurse with compassion fatigue must either become less compassionate or reduce the number of patients he or she treats. For nurses who work in trauma-related settings, the symptoms of compassion fatigue mimic those of post-traumatic stress disorder, including such things as anxiety, exhaustion, and sleep disruption. Closely related to compassion fatigue is burnout, which we have already discussed in this chapter.

The consequences of stress and its related conditions, compassion fatigue and burnout, are significant. One study found a significant relationship between patient incidents, such as falling and medication errors, and nurses' scores on a stress index (Dugan et al., 1996). Not only do patients notice burnout when being cared for (Leiter, Harvie, & Frizzel, 1998), nurses with burnout miss more shifts, so patients may miss the nurses entirely (Parker & Kulik, 1995). Worse still, nurses who suffer prolonged burnout tend to leave the profession altogether (Parker & Kulik, 1995).

The causes of stress are numerous and begin as soon as the nurse enters nursing from training. In fact, the transition from student nurse to practitioner can be the first major source of stress. This has been called **reality shock** (Kramer, 1974) and is defined as the reaction to the discrepancy between a training environment and an actual work environment. Newly hired nurses will report that they thought they had been adequately trained but have quickly realized that they still have much to learn, and that it must be learned quickly (Charnley, 1999). The sudden role shift from student to practising nurse can be frightening, since nurses now feel that they should know everything. They find it hard to cope with the volume of work and feel guilty when things don't get done in a timely way. New nurses sense a gap between the high standards of care they were taught and the lower standards that are the reality of nursing due to heavy demands and limited resources. One conflict many nurses must resolve is the one that exists between the humanistic, nurturing nature of nursing on one hand, and the high-tech, high-traffic demands of modern medicine on the other. Finally, there is the stress of "learning the system," which entails a wide range of things, from finding out where supplies are kept to developing relationships with colleagues (Charnley, 1999).

For experienced nurses, stress appears to come from a number of sources, from the work environment to job responsibilities (Santos et al., 2003). Work environment appears to be particularly important; a study of 270 nurses in Australia reported that their main source of distress was abuse from colleagues. This took the form of abusive language, rudeness, and humiliation (Farrell, 1999). The sheer volume of a nurse's work responsibilities and the need for multitasking in modern nursing are also often-cited causes of stress. At any given moment, a nurse may be required to take numerous tests, manage supplies, complete paperwork, administer medications, and reassure worried family members (Flakus, 1998). Long hours can also be a problem as a number of hospitals have moved to 12-hour shifts. Stress has been shown to be higher for nurses in these shifts compared to their eight-hour counterparts (Hoffman & Scott, 2003).

It would stand to reason that some nursing specialties are more stressful than others. For example, oncology (pediatric oncology, in particular) features higher degrees of turnover than some other specialty areas (Hinds et al., 1998). Booth (1998) has studied the intense stress that accompanies unexpected patient death during surgery. This is particularly stressful because the surgical staff may feel that the death was caused by the intervention (and they may be correct). Even if the surgery was the only hope for the patient, staff are often left with the feeling that unexpected death during surgery was due to human error, whether it was or not. Few other professions feature doubts over one's own sense of competence combined with confrontations with mortality.

Stress is a significant problem in nursing but is not an insurmountable one. There are ways in which nurses can cope effectively with the stressors of their job, and there are ways institutions can improve the work environment to reduce those stressors. For the nurses themselves, coping ability depends on personal factors and social factors (Boey, 1999).

Personal factors include personality characteristics and coping strategies. For example, nurses with high self-esteem and a clear sense of control are less prone to stress. In terms of coping strategies, those who are more stress resistant tend to avoid negative emotion-focused coping. Instead, they use problem-focused coping, trying to find ways to make their job more manageable rather than dwelling upon the frustration and anxiety they may feel. **Social factors**, as the term implies, refer to those elements of the nurse's social network, such as family, friends, and coworkers.

One of the grand ironies of work in the helping professions is that many people working in them spend most of their energy looking after other people and very little looking after themselves. After all, most people who are drawn to professions like nursing want to help others. The problem, of course, is that if nurses don't look after themselves they become more vulnerable to stress and burnout, and ultimately less effective at helping others.

In this vein, we are reminded of what airline flight attendants say to passengers before takeoff. It goes something like this: "In the unlikely event of cabin depressurization, a yellow mask will drop from the overhead compartment. Place the mask over your nose and mouth and begin breathing normally. *If you are travelling with young children or others who need assistance, put your mask on first, before assisting others*." At the heart of this instruction is the reality that we can't help others if we pass out ourselves. This works as an excellent metaphor when teaching nurses the importance of maintaining their own health. It is particularly relevant in light of research that has shown that nurses do often neglect their own health needs—nurses tend to be more overweight than the general population (Pratt, Overfield, & Hilton, 1994), student nurses smoke more than those in other professions, have irregular eating habits, and report some binge drinking (Diltmar, Haughey, O'Shea, & Brasure, 1989). On a more positive note, research in Ireland has shown that practising nurses engage in more health-related behaviours than student nurses do (Hope, Kelleher, & O'Connor, 1998).

The feeling of being in control that is so helpful in reducing stress can be greatly influenced by hospital management. According to the **Job Strain Model**, a job with high strain is one that features both high demands and low control (Karasek, 1979). Policies intended to enhance nurses' sense of control have indeed been shown to reduce stress and burnout. Such policies include group meetings, better communication up and down the hierarchy, more say in job design, and so on. (Felton, 1998). When these are in place, it is also likely that nurses will feel more committed to their institutions, which is another antidote to burnout (Hinds et al., 1998).

BOX 6-2	**Problem-Based Learning: Training Students to Think Like Practitioners**

Problem solving is perhaps the most important and common mental task performed by physicians. A patient presents one or more symptoms and it is the physician's job to ask the right questions to determine the cause of the symptoms and what to do about them. What brings the symptoms on? What relieves them? What further information is needed? What tests need to be done? When these questions have been answered, a diagnosis must be made and a course of action determined.

(continued on next page)

Studies have shown that expert physicians and novices don't tend to think the same way (Thomas, 1997). Experts begin rapidly generating hypotheses from the beginning of a consultation with a patient. They are able to test a number of these hypotheses simultaneously as the consultation progresses. In general, they generate better hypotheses because they have a better knowledge base.

Other health care professionals must also be problem solvers, though they may focus more on becoming skilled at carrying out certain procedures. Incoming students have little or no experience with diagnostic problem solving or the procedures involved in health care. How can they best be trained, in a relatively short period of time, to be practitioners?

One of the most popular approaches to this training challenge is called **problem-based learning (PBL)**. The curricula employed in PBL use actual cases in an attempt to simulate practice settings (Doucet, Purdy, Kaufman, & Langille, 1998). Students are given a case and must work in groups to solve the problems presented in it. With PBL, students spend more time working autonomously, using resources such as the library to learn what they need to know to solve the problems presented in the case. It is believed that by so doing they will retain the knowledge longer and develop better clinical skills (Antepohl & Herzig, 1999). Three hallmarks of PBL are the stimulation of prior knowledge (what do I already know that will help me with this case?), learning in context to improve retention, and the elaboration of knowledge through discussion with other group members (Saarinen-Rahiika & Binkley, 1998).

Problem-based learning was first developed in Canada. It was introduced into the curriculum at McMaster University in Hamilton, Ontario in 1965 (Saarinen-Rahiika & Binkley, 1998). Since then, it has been adopted in a number of Canadian universities and in institutions around the world, including Harvard. In some schools, the entire curriculum is taught this way; in others, PBL is introduced after one or two years of lecture-based presentation. In still others, individual courses are taught using PBL.

Some of the most extensive research on the effectiveness of PBL has been conducted by David Kaufman and his colleagues when he worked at Dalhousie University in Halifax. Problem-based learning was implemented by Dalhousie's Faculty of Medicine in 1992. The first PBL graduating class in 1996 was compared to previous lecture-based classes in their performance on Canadian national licensing exams. It was discovered that the PBL class performed better than previous classes on the psychiatric, preventative medicine, and community health components of the exam. There were no differences between the PBL class and other classes on clinical reasoning scores (Kaufman & Mann, 1998). Problem-based learning has also been used in **continuing medical education (CME)** and has been shown in this context to be superior to lecture-based approaches (Doucet, Purdy, Kaufman, & Langille, 1998). This might be expected, given that CME is intended for practitioners who are returning for further education and have a greater wealth of experience to draw on.

Problem-based learning may well alter the way students think during their training, but it doesn't necessarily affect *what* they think. Susan Philips (1997) from Queen's University in Kingston,

(continued on next page)

Ontario, has analyzed the content of a number of cases used in PBL curricula. She concluded that the biomedical, body-as-machine focus of medical training is not altered or reduced by a PBL approach.

Hospital Cleaners: Invisible Yet Vital Members of a Hospital's Staff

In this chapter, our discussion of health practitioners has focused on physicians and nurses. This is because these are the most prevalent people in health care. However, they are certainly not the only people who play important roles in health care and, in particular, in the hospital. Other essential members of the health-care team are dieticians and cooks, orderlies, administrators, psychologists, and lab technologists, to name a few.

One group who are essential to the provision of health care in a hospital are the hospital cleaners. However, they are often placed at the bottom of the hospital's hierarchy. In an in-depth study of cleaners in Québec hospitals, Messing (1998) explored both the reasons for this problem and its consequences.

In Messing's study, hospital cleaners told her that there was a common misconception that their job was easy. In fact, this was reflected in their pay scales, which were divided such that "heavy" cleaners were paid more than "light" cleaners. The irony was that "heavy" cleaners used machines to do their work and "light" cleaners did their work by hand, often on their knees. Also, like so many jobs, the cleaners were only noticed when there was a problem. No one seemed to notice the pride they took in their work; to improve the cleanliness of the sections they were responsible for, many cleaners found ways to combine their cleaning agents to improve their effectiveness, while others brought some of their own supplies to do the work.

There are also broader, sociological reasons for the devaluing of cleaners. The majority are women, who historically have been expected to clean things up without getting recognition for the importance of the job. The cleaners' work becomes associated with housework, which is considered unimportant by a society that values the money-making potential of a job. Also, many of the cleaners are members of cultural minorities and are of lower socioeconomic status than other hospital workers, and so a lack of respect for their work carries overtones of cultural, racial, and social prejudice.

These realities are important to health psychologists for a number of reasons. First, cleaners actually interact with the patients quite a bit while doing their work, yet, because the cleaners are an "invisible" component of the system, they rarely receive any training on how to do so. For example, cleaners must regularly decide whether or not to disturb a patient without having any clear sense of the patient's current condition.

In other cases, patients ask cleaners to do things for them that might be contraindicated. In Messing's study, she

(continued on next page)

was told of a cleaner who got in trouble for getting a glass of water for a preoperative patient who was to have no fluids. Better communication between cleaners and other staff would have avoided that problem. Cleaners also worry about contagion. One cleaner reported that, after cleaning a patient's room for a number of days, she arrived to find a quarantine sign on the door. No one had told her just how serious the problem was. Finally, because there is so little communication with hospital cleaners, spaces are sometimes poorly designed and equipment poorly placed making it hard to clean. This physical strain can result in absenteeism as cleaners deal with musculoskeletal and cardiovascular problems, which are common to their job. Hygiene is clearly essential to the effective running of a hospital. However, for reasons relevant to psychology, namely communication problems and stereotyping, this vital aspect is often compromised in the ways we've discussed.

OTHER HEALTH CARE PROFESSIONALS

Focus on Canadian Research serves as a reminder that physicians and nurses are not the only health care professionals deserving of a health psychologist's attention. In this section, we will look at two other health care professions in which psychology can play a central role. Certainly, our list of professions discussed in this chapter is far from exhaustive. You are invited to think of ways in which psychology can make constructive contributions to the work of others providing health care.

CASE 6-1	The Long Road Back

One of the most disturbing things for May was that she has no memory whatsoever for the event that has left her feeling so debilitated. One minute she felt fine, and the next she woke up in a hospital, having no idea how she got there. She did know, however, that something terrible had happened. This was because she could feel nothing in her right arm or right leg and she couldn't talk.

May, who was 61 years old, had suffered a stroke, or cerebrovascular accident (CVA), as it is known medically. During the stroke, the blood supply to the left side of her brain had been cut off due to a blockage in the artery. May's family had been told that no one could say for sure just how profound her disability would be. It would depend on biology, medicine, some luck, and May's willingness to go through rehabilitation.

The first few days in the hospital, May did show some improvement. Some of her speaking ability returned, much to the relief of her family, but she still found verbal communication enormously frustrating. And she was experiencing great difficulty with movement; getting up to go to the bathroom was a major undertaking. She wondered how she and her husband would ever manage outside the hospital. These thoughts were so discouraging for May that there were times when she wished the stroke had just killed her and put an end to everything.

(continued on next page)

That cloud began to lift, however, when May met Joyce. Joyce was the physical therapist assigned to help May on her long road to rehabilitation. Joyce's skill and encouragement became vital to May, who found herself working harder than she had at any time in her life. Soon May started to feel like a professional athlete, training for the biggest game of her career.

The psychology of rehabilitation is as important as sports psychology is for elite athletics.

Physical Rehabilitation and Physiotherapists

In Case 6-1, you met May, a woman who had suffered a stroke that affected every aspect of her life. Many of the challenges faced by May and her physical therapist as they work on May's rehabilitation are psychological in nature. In addition to knowing what May is capable of and what exercises to give her each day, Joyce must be sensitive to issues of motivation, adherence, mood, and social support.

Somewhat surprisingly, there is not a large literature investigating these issues in physical rehabilitation. This is unfortunate, because much could be learned by studying the way physical therapists work with their patients. Ideally, such an understanding would allow health psychology to contribute to the effectiveness of that work.

Goal Setting It is clear that physiotherapists must enter into a partnership with their patients if they hope to be successful. In other words, the relationship cannot be one in which the patient is passive and dependent upon the therapist. Nowhere is this more evident than in the area of goal setting (Taylor & Taylor, 1997). We know from sports psychology that people are much more likely to work toward a goal if they have had a say in *choosing* that goal. This is not usually done by the athlete alone, nor should it be done by the patient alone. This is because the athlete and patient cannot be entirely objective regarding what is possible. In some cases, patients might let discouragement get the better of them, and set goals that are not ambitious enough. In other cases, they may become impatient and set goals that cannot be reached in the short-term, setting themselves up for frustration.

An interesting observational study looked at goal-setting behaviour in male stroke patients who had physical therapy in the hospital and in their own homes (von Koch, Wottrich, & Holmqvist, 1998). It was observed that the patients seemed to take on different roles when at home. They were more likely to express their goals and take initiative when working with their therapist.

Adherence Closely related to goal setting is adherence (Sluijs, Kerssens, van der Zee, & Myers, 1998). The physiotherapist cannot oversee all the work a patient must do. For improvement to occur, a patient like May must work diligently on rehabilitation on her own. She must adhere to the rehab regimen that she and the physiotherapist have agreed upon. All these factors are interrelated; for example, if May feels that she was part of the goal-setting process, she will feel more committed to achieving these goals and will be more likely to adhere to the regimen. Education, cognitive interventions, and behavioural interventions also affect adherence.

Behavioural Interventions Most rehabilitation patients need some form of **external reinforcement**. That is to say, the physiotherapist, friends, family, and other practitioners must encourage and praise the patient's successes. For May, improvement will not be measured on a minute-to-minute basis. She will need to be reminded of what she can do today that she could not do during the early weeks of her rehabilitation. Also, May will need to find ways to **self-reinforce**. She must pat herself on the back and maybe even give herself tangible rewards for achieving certain goals. One of the best things about physical rehabilitation is that at least some of the success can be *measured objectively*. May can measure how much further she has walked, and how much more clearly she can speak as she progresses through the regimen. Objective criteria for success are the bread and butter of behavioural interventions. They allow for reinforcement to be directly contingent upon desired behaviour and allow the patient and physiotherapist to *shape* the program by gradually increasing observable standards.

Cognitive Interventions The power of effective behavioural interventions is clear in physical therapy. However, May's program cannot rely solely on behavioural strategies. It must also focus on her thinking, and that is the stuff of cognitive interventions. There are at least two areas in which this is crucial. First, May must believe that she can reach an identified goal. You may remember from chapter 1 that we call these **efficacy beliefs**. These beliefs can be tricky to instill. It isn't usually enough to simply *tell* someone that he or she is capable of doing something. Those messages must be based on some *evidence* that the patient will accept as being reasonable. Efficacy beliefs, then, are often built on past successes. A classic example is an attained goal that the patient initially thought was unattainable. Also, it is possible that experienced physical therapists alter their patients' efficacy beliefs simply by the way they interact with them. In other words, they assume that the patient is capable, and the patient lives up to that assumption. More research needs to be done on the efficacy-enhancing strategies employed by physical therapists, however, to confirm this.

The second crucial target for cognitive interventions is the patient's **attributions**. These are the explanations a person gives for his or her successes and failures. In May's case, as with all patients, it will be essential that she attribute her success *internally* (Wiegmann & Berven, 1998). In other words, she must take credit for her improvement, citing things like her hard work and fighting spirit. If she tries to attribute her success to Joyce, her physiotherapist, Joyce must politely deflect that back to May. So, if May says, "You're a saint, Joyce. I could never do this without you", Joyce, should reply with something like "Thanks for the compliment, May, but you're the one who's the great worker here."

Positive efficacy beliefs and internal attributions of success greatly increase the likelihood that May will adhere to her regimen when Joyce is not around. Most of all, these ways of thinking move May toward *independence*, which is an important goal of physical rehabilitation.

Pain Management In our discussion of physical rehabilitation, we must address the issue of pain management, since pain is a common problem for many patients in rehabilitation. Chapter 10 addresses pain in detail, so we will not repeat the concepts presented there. At this point, it is important to remember the obvious—pain makes rehabilitation harder. This means that all of the pain management strategies discussed in chapter 10, such as relaxation, distraction, and interpretation of pain, are major topics for people working in physical therapy. Also, pain is a very good indicator of a patient's progress.

In our discussion of physical rehabilitation, we have not included a separate section for motivation. This is because motivation is involved in each of the sections we did include. Partnerships improve motivation, as do reinforcers and effective cognitive interventions. In fact, rehabilitation parallels athletics in terms of the importance of motivation. This makes sense, because there is considerable overlap between health psychology and sport psychology in the area of rehabilitation. You will note this overlap again when you read about recovery from athletic injuries in chapter 8 on health and physical activity.

The literature that does exist in the area of motivation and rehabilitation makes clear reference to sport contexts when it introduces topics such as goal setting, relaxation, mental imagery, and positive thinking (Taylor & Taylor, 1997). Of course, May does not have to be an ex-professional athlete to do well in her rehabilitation (though she reports feeling like one at times). This point is made very well in a discussion of motivation factors associated with the physical rehabilitation of five women between the ages of 80 and 94 (Resnick, 1996). In this discussion, Resnick makes reference to goal setting, the use of humour, communicating a sense of caring, and engaging in a partnership with the patient that acknowledges the power of each partner to effect successful rehabilitation.

Technologists

Much of the high-tech equipment found in hospitals and clinics is operated by technologists who go through two or more years of training. They learn how to operate the equipment and about the biomedical assessments the equipment performs. Technologists, then, combine a desire to help others with an interest in technology. They often represent the human side of what has become a highly mechanized world of diagnostic and treatment procedures.

In diagnosis, experienced technologists can often tell a normal test result from an abnormal one, yet they are not allowed to pass these impressions on to the patient. This can be particularly difficult, because the patient might desperately want to know the technologist's opinion. Because many patients know that the technologist cannot provide a diagnosis, the patients may subtly probe the technologist with questions like "Well, what do you think?" or "How does it look?" The technologist, in reply, must say "The radiologist will go over your test results with you" or "We'll be sending the results to your doctor." The patient may interpret this evasion as an attempt on the technologist's part to avoid giving bad news, which can make the patient anxious.

| CASE 6-2 | **Can High-Tech Be Human?** |

Chen consulted his doctor about a recurring pain on the right side of his abdomen. His apprehension level went up measurably when he heard the words "barium enema." He had never had one before, so he wasn't exactly sure what it was. All the same, it sounded embarrassing and awful. To make matters worse, the enema was only part of the examination he was to go through to discover the source of the pain. A machine was going to be pushed into his abdomen like it was some sort of balloon. And what was this pain anyway? The very imposing machinery and embarrassing procedures made him feel as though he had something seriously wrong with him.

Thankfully, Chen met an experienced technologist who had a pretty good idea of what he was feeling. She told him just what the enema would involve. It didn't sound too pleasant, but at least he knew how long it would take and what it would feel like. She explained just what she was doing each step of the way. Just as important, she talked with Chen about things that had nothing to do with the test, giving him the sense that he was, indeed, a normal person going through a common experience.

As Case 6-2 portrays, experienced technologists are very good at helping patients through procedures that may be physically or psychologically difficult. These include everything from nuclear medicine tests to radiation therapy for cancer. Technologists may help their patients by presenting **procedure-based information**, which addresses *what* will be done and why. They may present **sensation-based information**, concerning what a procedure will feel or sound like and how long it will last. Or they might engage in **interpersonal small talk**, which has nothing to do with the procedure but helps distract patients from their anxiety (Poole & Kallhood, 1996).

A FINAL WORD

In this chapter, we have presented a series of profiles of health practitioners and the work they do. Since we are not physicians, nurses, physiotherapists, or technologists (or other practitioners), we had to rely on published research and first-hand interaction with practitioners to create these profiles. Given the consistency with which such phenomena as stress, training, and other issues are discussed, it is clear that these profiles apply widely across the professions we have discussed. By the same token, we must never lose sight of the fact that there is considerable variation among practitioners. Some never experience stress or gender-related discrimination. Some find medical school to be quite straightforward and manageable. Others have been virtually paralyzed by these things. In order to truly understand what these professionals experience, we urge you to talk to people who work in health care to get first-hand accounts of their work. The main objective in this chapter has been to convince you that it is vital for people in health psychology to make the effort to get to know what it is really like to work in health-related professions.

KEY TERMS

advanced practice
  nursing (p. 161)
attributions (p. 170)
burnout (p. 154)
caring (p. 161)
clinical nurse specialist
  (p. 161)
compassion fatigue (p. 152)
continuing medical
  education (CME)
  (p. 165)
curing (p. 161)
efficacy beliefs (p. 170)
external reinforcement
  (p. 169)

feminization of medicine
  (p. 158)
internship (p. 152)
interpersonal small talk
  (p. 172)
job strain model (p. 164)
nurse practitioner (p. 162)
personal factors in stress
  (p. 164)
physician impairment
  (p. 157)
primary-care physicians
  (p. 157)
problem-based learning
  (PBL) (p. 165)

procedure-based
  information (p. 172)
prognosis (p. 155)
reality shock (p. 163)
residency (p. 152)
role strain (p. 159)
self-reinforcement (p. 169)
sensation-based
  information (p. 172)
sensitivity (p. 156)
social factors in stress
  (p. 164)
specificity (p. 156)
uncertainty (p. 155)

chapter seven

Health Promotion

CHAPTER OUTLINE

The Development of Health Promotion in Canada

    The Goals of Health Promotion in Canada

    Health Promotion Mechanisms

Improving Health Promotion by Applying Principles of Psychology

    Prominent Theories in Health Psychology Applied to Health Promotion

    The Social Psychology of Health Promotion

    The Elaboration Likelihood Model of Persuasion

    Fear Appeals: An Example of Health Promotion by the Peripheral Route

    The Application of Other Social-Psychological Principles to Health Promotion

The Precede-Proceed Model

Assessing the Effectiveness of Health Promotion Programs

KEY QUESTIONS

1. What are the goals of health promotion?
2. How has health promotion developed in Canada?
3. How can the principles of psychology be applied to improve health promotion efforts?
4. How can we best evaluate the effectiveness of health promotion programs?

A group of twelve teenagers is sitting around a table. They are watching a 60-second videotape. On the tape, another group of teenagers is standing around in a playground. A few are smoking cigarettes. Gradually, one of the teens on the tape begins to turn into a cigarette, much to the shock and horror of her friends. Fortunately, though, this terrible transformation helps them see the error of their ways. They throw away their cigarettes and start playing basketball. When they do, their friend morphs back to her old self.

After watching this tape, the group sitting around the table is asked to comment on it. They have been brought together as a focus group to provide insight into the impact of video campaigns such as this one. The teens say that they are insulted by the video. They find it demeaning and ineffective. They highly doubt if this approach would make them or their friends quit smoking

This is discouraging. Millions of dollars have been invested in the production and airing of this 60-second piece. Yet, if the focus group is to be believed, it will do nothing to reduce the number of teenagers who smoke.

The feedback provided by that focus group reminds us that health promotion is no easy task. While many definitions have been forwarded, most refer to *health promotion* in terms of strategies intended to maintain or improve the health of large populations. The World Health Organization defines **health promotion** simply as "the process of enabling people to increase control over, and to improve, their health" (Ottawa Charter for Health Promotion, 1986). Yet, even with this seemingly straightforward definition, the fact that health promotion takes so many forms—from smoking-cessation programs to patient education, public awareness campaigns, and political activism—makes it difficult to state in concrete terms just what health promotion is. It is important to note that the WHO definition and the examples we provide in this chapter view health promotion as a process rather than an outcome in and of itself (Rootman, et al., 2001).

Health promotion strategies, like the quit-smoking campaign in our opening example, are often undertaken at a federal level of government. They are therefore usually very large, and often experimental, making their effectiveness difficult to measure directly. Further, the challenges inherent in attempting to change attitudes and behaviour on such a large scale are daunting. Yet governments must persevere despite these difficulties, because effective health promotion is essential to our well-being.

Health promotion is also practised at an international level. The World Health Organization (WHO) has a Health Promotion Department using political and sociological approaches to try to improve the health of the world's citizens. A good example of one of their initiatives is the *Mega Country Network*. This network attempts to affect health worldwide by involving the world's most populous countries. The program includes countries with populations of 100 million or more, accounting for over 60 percent of the world's population (WHO web site, 2003, www.WHO.org). It includes such goals as the promotion of healthy diets, physical activity, and elimination of tobacco use.

Canada has played an active role in the WHO health promotion initiatives and has developed its own health promotion strategy. Let's look at the development of this work in Canada, and then describe the Canadian strategy in some detail. This should provide you with a general sense of what health promotion entails.

THE DEVELOPMENT OF HEALTH PROMOTION IN CANADA

Canadian governments have actually been in the business of health promotion since the 1700s. Back then, the main task was regulatory in nature, coming up with rules of operation for hospitals and regulations regarding sanitation. In the early 1900s, once this regulation was firmly in place, the focus could be shifted to educating the general public about the value of proper sanitation (Badgley, 1994).

In the first half of the 1900s, provincial health promotion programs were started in Ontario (1921), Manitoba (1929), Québec (1943), and Newfoundland (1949). National programs followed, for example, *ParticipAction*, aimed at increasing Canadians' activity levels (started in 1971), the *Hole in the Fence* program, to curtail drug use (started in 1973), and *Dialogue on Drinking* (started in 1976).

Other examples of health promotion programs in Canada include the Prince Edward Island Heart Health Program, the Sun Smart campaign in Alberta, and Healthy Communities in British Columbia. Later in this chapter, we will take a more detailed look at some of the more prominent programs in Canada.

In Canada, successful health promotion as we now know it has been a clearly stated goal of federal governments since at least the mid-1970s. The kick-start came in 1974 from then Minister of Health and Welfare Marc Lalonde's paper, *A New Perspective on the Health of Canadians*. In it, he identified lifestyle as an important factor in health and well-being and, as such, an important target for health promotion and education.

In 1986, then Minister of Health and Welfare Jake Epp published *Achieving Health for All: A Framework for Health Promotion* (Epp, 1986). In it, Epp referred to the World Health Organization's definition of health promotion and applied it to Canada. Most important, in that paper Epp presented a framework that has guided health promotion and related research in Canada ever since.

We present this framework in Figure 7-1. Its categories sum up what health promotion is all about. Notice the scope of the goals; everyone in the country should find some relevance in the framework. Notice also the implications regarding locus of responsibility. All health promotion programs place the primary responsibility for good health on the individual rather than on medical staff or medical facilities.

Consistent with this emphasis on personal responsibility is the World Health Organization's reference to control in its definition of health promotion. Also note that self-care and mutual aid are cited as health promotion mechanisms in the Canadian framework. In other words, one goal of health promotion is to encourage people to look after themselves. Another is to encourage them to look after each other. A cynical view of these goals might suggest that they represent ways in which the government is shirking its responsibility to look after us. The reply to that cynicism is that there are limits to how much a government can do to look after its citizens.

In fact, some authors have argued that if health promotion is to be truly effective, it must be based on a social movement rather than a government edict (Labonte, 1990; O'Neill, Rootman, & Pederson, 1994). In other words, the real promoters of healthy choices must be the general public. For example, we know we are getting somewhere in terms of health promotion when parents won't start the car until every child's seatbelt is fastened. Another example of success can be found in the number of community-initiated programs that have been started independent of federal or provincial mandates.

FIGURE 7-1	Canada's Framework for Health Promotion		
Aim	Achieving health for all		
Health challenges	Reducing inequities	Increasing prevention	Enhancing coping
Health promotion mechanisms	Self-care	Mutual aid	Healthy environments
Implementation strategies	Fostering public participation	Strengthening community health services	Co-ordinating healthy public policy

Source: Epp (1986). Achieving health for all: A framework for health promotion. *Canadian Journal of Public Health, 77,* 393-430.

Labonte (1987) provides a three-level framework for successful community-oriented health promotion. His analysis provides a useful taxonomy of health promotion and is very reminiscent of the biopsychosocial approach introduced in chapter 1.

The first level identified by Labonte is **medical**. This level of health promotion is disease-based and the goal is disease treatment. For example, a community might develop a program to help people recover from heart attacks or devote funding to finding a cure for cancer. The second level deals with **public health**. This level is behaviour-based and the goal is disease prevention. A good example of a behaviour-based intervention would be the promotion of safe sex, or drinking-and-driving counterattack programs. The third level is **socioenvironmental**. At this level, the orientation is toward social change and public health policy. Examples include such things as legislation to reduce poverty or school board policies to provide lunches for school children.

Of course, one of the goals of health promotion at the governmental level is to save those governments money on health expenditures. In Canada, where health care is socialized, total health expenditures topped $112 billion in 2002. In 2001, we spent about $3300 per person on health (Canadian Institute for Health Information, 2002). The public sector's share of expenditures in 2002 was more than $79 billion per year (Canadian Institute for Health Information, 2003, National Health Expenditures Database). When we consider that a great deal of that money is spent on treating conditions that are preventable, we can see why health promotion is important from a fiscal as well as a medical perspective.

Because serious illness is tragic and traumatic, as well as expensive, it is not surprising to find an emphasis on health promotion in Canada today. People who study health at the sociological level of the biopsychosocial approach will argue that saving money and saving lives often amount to the same thing in that they are accomplished by the same strategies.

These strategies focus on prevention more than cure, and they feature messages that are intended to affect self-care behaviour, usually through attitude change. We now take a closer look at Canada's health promotion framework to develop an understanding of what forms these strategies can take.

The Goals of Health Promotion in Canada

In chapter 1, we traced the major topics of health psychology as they have developed over the years. As we work through Canada's framework for health promotion, you will see that a number of these same topics receive attention. Look for potential applications of research on coping, social support, and stress reduction as examples. You will also see that the level of emphasis is far broader than the purely biological. In keeping with the biopsychosocial approach, you will find elements in the framework related to individual psychology (e.g., self-care), sociology (e.g., strengthening community health services), and geography (e.g., healthy environments).

Health Challenges   When Canadians think of their health care system, they are more likely to think of its equity rather than its inequity. It is, after all, a system designed to promote and provide equal access for all. The truth, however, is that inequities do exist in the Canadian health care system. These inequities may be based on differences in geography, culture, age, education, income, or labour-force status. For example, less than 6 percent of people in the highest income bracket in Canada rate their health as only fair or poor compared to 27 percent in the lowest income group (Tremblay, Ross & Berthelot, 2002). These income-related disparities also apply to infant mortality rates and life expectancy (Wilkins, Berthelot & Ng, 2002). Significant inequities also exist between the Aboriginal and non-Aboriginal communities. A study of Aboriginal people living off reserves showed their self-reported health to be poorer than that of a non-Aboriginal population matched for socioeconomic level and health behaviours (Tjepkema, 2002).

It is obvious that our health changes as we age. We need to know about the specific nature of those changes and also about the ways in which our health needs change as well (Chen & Wilkins, 1998). This is a particularly important health-promotion challenge given the growing percentage of people in Canada who are over the age of 65. Age-related health concerns are not restricted to our seniors, however. We know that our adolescent population has its own set of health promotion issues as well. Central among these are risk-related behaviours such as cigarette smoking (Chen & Millar, 1998). As we saw in the example that opened this chapter, it is the job of health promotion to influence these behaviours.

The nature of people's occupations can be another source of health-related inequity. This is due, in part, to the differences in stress levels associated with various jobs (Wilkins & Beaudet, 1998). We also know that certain risk-related behaviours are more common among people in particular occupations. For example, in 1994 and 1995, 43 percent of people working in construction, transportation, or mining smoked cigarettes daily. By comparison, only 18 percent of people in so-called "white collar" occupations smoked every day (Gaudette, Richardson, & Huang, 1998).

These inequities are prime targets for health promotion programs. The question is, what sorts of behaviours must be promoted to foster constructive change in people's health? The framework presented in Figure 7-1 represents an attempt to answer this question, as does the following section on **health promotion mechanisms**.

| Focus on Canadian Research 7-1 | Do People with Higher Incomes Live Longer? |

When it comes to health promotion research, Canada is a world leader. Such units as the University of Toronto's Centre for Health Promotion and UBC's Institute for Health Promotion Research are very active research centres. Much research is also conducted through Statistics Canada. The primary source of data for this research are the National Population Health Surveys. Other large national databases are also used, such as the Canadian Mortality Data Base and the Canadian Community Health Survey.

Researchers using the Canadian Mortality Data Base and census data from 1971 to 1996 have been able to assess income-based differences in mortality across the country. Causes of death were analyzed using international coding standards, though residents of long-term care facilities were excluded because census data that would indicate household income level does not apply well to institutions.

Income was divided into five equal categories, called *quintiles*, from richest to poorest. In these categories, total number of deaths and deaths by various causes were calculated.

Using this methodology, it is possible to track changes in mortality rates for various groups over time. For example, researchers discovered that income-related disparities in life expectancy have diminished by well over one year for both men and women between 1971 and 1996. Also, infant mortality rates for Canada's highest income bracket have dropped from 10.2 infants per 1000 births in 1971 to 4.0 in 1996. In the poorest quintile, infant morality has dropped over the same period from 20 to 6.4 per 1000 births. You can see some important trends here. First, there has been a significant drop in infant mortality rates overall. Second, that drop has been greater among those in the lowest quintile (Wilkins, Berthelot & Ng, 2002).

These trends hold up for many health statistics. For example, mortality rate tables for a wide range of causes of death show that 1) mortality rates have dropped since 1971; 2) mortality rates are higher for poorer members of the population; 3) the gap in mortality rates between rich and poor is narrowing.

There are, of course, some exceptions. For example, mortality rates for lung cancer have increased since 1971 for females (from 8.8 per 10 000 people to 30.7 for all income levels combined).

Health Promotion Mechanisms

How can we best meet the health challenges laid out in the framework in Figure 7-1? This is the central question for people working in health promotion. The framework provides three answers: 1) we must be encouraged to look after ourselves; 2) we must be encouraged to look after each other; and 3) we must make our environments healthier by reducing pollution, improving safety, etc.

As we review these health promotion mechanisms, notice again where the *locus of responsibility* is placed—squarely on the shoulders of the citizen. Remember that this is a key assumption of the health promotion process. Spending money encouraging people to look after themselves costs considerably less and results in better quality of life than having the government look after them. It has been estimated that obesity alone costs the Canadian health care system over $1.8 billion a year in the treatment of obesity-related medical problems. The most prevalent of these are high blood pressure, Type II diabetes, and coronary artery disease (Birmingham et al., 1999). About one-third of all Canadians are obese, as defined by having a body mass index of 27 or greater. Moreover, the problem of obesity is getting worse among children and youth. Between 1981 and 1996, the prevalence of obesity has more than doubled in both boys and girls (Canadian Health Network, 2003, http://www.canadian-health-network.ca/) so you can imagine the saving in money and reduction of health problems if at least some of those people could be convinced to manage their diets in a healthier way.

Hence the rationale for an emphasis on **self-care**. Self-care refers to such things as exercise, diet, risk behaviours, voluntary screening, and regular medical checkups. Effective health promotion programs have measurable effects on these behaviours and, consequently, the general health of Canadians.

In the late 1940s, the province of British Columbia became one of the first places in the world to introduce regular screening for cervical cancer (Wardle & Pope, 1992). The test used in this screening is called a **Pap test** or **Pap smear**. When compared to screening tests for other kinds of cancer, the Pap is considered to be among the most effective. By *effective*, we mean that it is an accurate early detection strategy that has significantly helped reduce cervical cancer mortality rates. The death rate from cervical cancer has declined by almost 50 percent since the Pap test was introduced over 25 years ago. The current survival rate is estimated to be 74 percent over five years (Health Canada, 2003, http://www.hc-sc.gc.ca). In spite of this fact, older women, who are more at risk for cervical cancer than are their younger counterparts, do not receive Pap tests as often as they should (Lee, Parsons, & Gentleman, 1998).

The Canadian Pap test data illustrate a truism in health promotion—the work never ends. To be sure, there is tangible success. For example, the majority of women in Canada do have Pap tests; in 1998 and 1999, 82 percent of women between the ages of 40 and 49 had received a Pap test in the last three years (Cervical Screening in Canada: 1998 Surveillance Report).

The very important topic of smoking cessation also fits in the self-care category. According to the 2002 Canadian Tobacco Use Monitoring Survey (CTUMS) there were 5.4 million smokers over the age of 15 in Canada, representing 21 percent of that age group. Quit-smoking campaigns, therefore, are a major concern for people working in health promotion. It was estimated that, in the year 2000, close to 47 000 people in Canada would die from tobacco-related diseases (Ellison, Mao, & Gibbons, 1995). This number can be lowered substantially in future years if current smokers can find a way to quit smoking, but that is easier said than done.

In spite of what we know about the dangers of cigarette smoking, health promotion in this particular area of self-care runs into problems brought on by the social pressure and addiction that accompany smoking. Attempts to simply frighten people away from cigarettes have been discouragingly unsuccessful (Becker & Janz, 1987; Sutton & Eiser, 1984). The relative ineffectiveness of this approach obviously makes health promotion more difficult. It isn't enough to parade grim statistics or blackened lung tissue in front of people to make them avoid smoking. The good news is that smoking is on the decline in Canada, even among youth aged 15 to 19. In 1999, 28 percent of this age group smoked. By 2002, that number had dropped to 22 percent (CTUMS, 2002). Even with this trend, though, we have a long way to go with health promotion in this area, especially when one considers that most smokers start when they are young. Programs must involve much more than simple appeals to fear. Later in this chapter, we will look more closely at the use of fear appeals and what must be added to make them effective.

Improving self-care among citizens is a fundamental objective of any health promotion program. But because people do not live in isolation from one another, in addition to looking after ourselves, we must also look after each other. We have a responsibility to family, friends, loved ones and, for that matter, society as a whole when it comes to health and safety. This responsibility is highlighted in the Canadian framework by the promotion mechanism called **mutual aid**.

A large body of literature in health psychology supports the framework's inclusion of mutual aid as an important promotion mechanism. The general conclusion of this literature is that it is healthy to have other people around (for a review, see House, Landis, & Umberson, 1988). Mortality rates are lower in communities featuring a high level of social integration; close-knit communities are healthier.

Health psychologists are very interested in **social support**—that collection of interpersonal resources we have at our disposal to help us avoid or cope with difficult times in our lives. Social support is remarkably beneficial. Research indicates that strong support systems affect a number of health indicators, including how long a person can expect to live (Ross & Mirowsky, 2002).

Specifically, social support has been shown to affect survival rates among cancer patients. In a well-known study by David Spiegel and colleagues, breast cancer patients were randomly assigned to either a year of weekly support group meetings or routine medical care (Spiegel, Bloom, Kraemer, & Gottheil, 1989). Patients in the support groups survived an average of 36.6 months, compared to control group patients who survived an average of 18.9 months. A number of other studies have also documented the beneficial effects of social support on people's ability to cope with cancer and survive it (for a review, see Blanchard et al., 1995).

We will be referring to social support often in this book. It is a very important resource when coping with stress, which we discussed in detail in chapter 2. Also, as we have mentioned, social support is a critical factor in people's ability to cope with serious illness, a topic we will return to in chapter 11.

It is important to know that social support doesn't always "just happen." Also, some people benefit from it more than others do. And social support comes in a number of different forms, some of which are easier to promote than others. We turn now to factors that affect the amount of support a person might receive, in an attempt to determine specific goals of health promotion strategies in the area of mutual aid.

Perhaps the most important point to make at the outset of this exploration is that social support is related to other elements of Canada's health promotion framework—most notably "Reducing Inequities." For example, seniors living on low incomes have less support than their more affluent counterparts. We also know that as people get older, their number of unmet needs in terms of health-related social assistance goes up (Chen & Wilkins, 1998).

To understand how health promotion can be used to help reduce these inequities, we must divide social support into two general types, based on the source of the support. First, there is **naturally occurring support**. This is the support we get from friends, relatives, coworkers, and others in our own social networks. If you have just had triplets, you might have friends or family over to help out with meals or household chores or to look after the babies so you can get some sleep. This would be an example of naturally occurring support.

The other kind of support is called **agency-provided support**. This is support that is provided by agencies and organizations formed to fill the void when naturally occurring support is either lacking or unavailable. Imagine that you had those triplets just after moving to a new city where you didn't know a soul. You might be relieved to find that there was a support group for parents of multiple births in that city. This would be a group made up of people like you who help each other and find community resources to provide further help.

When we study social support in the context of serious illness, we find that many people who are seriously ill don't have many people "like them" who share their illness. For example, wives of prostate cancer patients can be loving and extremely supportive, but they can't have had prostate cancer. For this reason, prostate cancer support groups are popular among men who want information and empathy that can only come from other patients. This is another important reason for agency-provided support.

Now let's get back to the role of health promotion. What is its main job here? In terms of mutual aid, health promotion campaigns must encourage the creation of support groups and attendance at them. This is especially true for segments of our population in which support is less available, as well as for people whose ability to cope can be improved by spending time with others who have similar illnesses or other health problems.

We have just seen that social support can be categorized in terms of its source. Social support can also be categorized by its type (House, 1981). For example, we can receive **practical support**, sometimes called *tangible support*, which includes help with the demands of daily living—getting meals, going to doctor's appointments, mowing the lawn, and so on. Also, there is **informational support**, which could include such things as being told about treatment options, typical recovery times from treatment or injury, or what to do to speed recovery. Finally, there is **emotional support**. This is provided by people who take the time to understand our fears and frustrations, who help calm us during anxious times, who help bring our moods up, or who distract us from our worries.

When we know the types of support that people need, we can do a better job of providing that support. Imagine how you would respond if you found out that a close friend had just been diagnosed with cancer. You might know exactly what to do. On the other hand, because this is a thankfully rare thing to have to contend with, you might feel awkward. Do you call your friend right away or do you wait? If you call, what do you say? What should you do? What can you do to help? These are difficult questions that can paralyze us.

If you knew that people who have been diagnosed with cancer need practical, informational, and emotional support, you might be better able to answer those difficult questions and provide support. Perhaps your friend needs a ride to an appointment. Maybe kids need rides to school. Or perhaps there is something your friend needs to know and you might be in a position to find out. In terms of emotional support, maybe you just need to be there to listen. The point is that we can use health promotion to educate people about these ways of providing support. Further, we can promote the clear benefits of providing this support. In chapter 11, you will find further data from studies proving that mutual aid—social support—is of tremendous benefit to people with serious illnesses. For now, it is important to know that good health promotion programs can increase the likelihood that such support is forthcoming and that it will be effective by ensuring that it matches people's needs (Reynolds, 2001).

In examining Canada's health promotion framework, you will see that mutual aid isn't the only element for which social support is relevant. Consider also the two implementation strategies of *fostering public participation* and *strengthening community health services*. While these strategies clearly require the involvement of professionals from a variety of segments of the health care system, they also require the participation of the general public. Support groups obviously grow out of public participation and they are commonly offered through community health service facilities.

In this section, we have used Canada's health promotion framework to provide some examples of the challenges faced by people working in health promotion. The number of health promotion programs that could be mounted in a country as vast and varied as Canada is virtually infinite. However, by using the framework, we can consolidate this number to a very manageable set of goals. We must find ways to promote self-care and mutual aid and we must reduce health-related inequities. These goals are not unique to Canada. Indeed, they are common to health promotion programs worldwide.

IMPROVING HEALTH PROMOTION BY APPLYING PRINCIPLES OF PSYCHOLOGY

Now that we know what the main goals and challenges are for health promotion in Canada, we will now look at the ways psychology can be used to help achieve these goals. In this section, we will draw on the major theories of health psychology that we introduced in chapter 1. We will also look closely at theories taken from social psychology.

Prominent Theories in Health Psychology Applied to Health Promotion

Much of health promotion is targeted at people's thinking. The assumption here is that one way to change behaviour is to change the beliefs relating to that behaviour. This line of reasoning is very consistent with the **health belief model**, the **theory of reasoned action**, and the **theory of planned behaviour**, all of which were introduced in chapter 1.

Recalling those theories, you will remember two important elements: 1) the importance of people's beliefs regarding their vulnerability to a threat and 2) the effectiveness of a given course of action to reduce that threat. In addition, it is important that people place a high value on their health. Because of their importance to health-related behaviour, many health promotion programs are designed specifically to affect these beliefs and values.

Health promotion programs, then, must provide information regarding the likelihood that someone will suffer a health problem (vulnerability information) and advice on how one can reduce that likelihood (information regarding efficacy of preventative behaviours). Prominent theories in health psychology can inform decisions regarding content for health promotion. For example, the theory of reasoned action and the theory of planned behaviour both acknowledge that people weigh the potential *costs* and *gains* of a given behaviour before adopting it. With this knowledge in mind, health promotion programs geared toward physical activity, such as Canada's Healthy Living (Vitality) program, which grew from the well-known ParticipAction Program, focus on the gains rather than the costs of exercise. They emphasize the fun of exercise, not the fatigue that may result. These programs make the point that physical activity can be convenient, uplifting, and healthy. In so doing, they target people's beliefs regarding cost and gain. For some examples of these programs and messages, visit the Health Canada Web site and click on Healthy Living (http://www.hc-sc.gc.ca/). As you can see, the theories of health psychology are called upon to form the foundation of health promotion programs. These programs also rely on research findings from the field of *social psychology*. This is because health promotion involves **persuasion**, which is a social phenomenon.

The Social Psychology of Health Promotion

Persuasion is the attempt to change people's attitudes and beliefs. An **attitude** is a cognition in which a person *evaluates* some target. Attitudes involve words like *good* or *bad*, and verbs such as *like* or *dislike*. Health promotion programs thus attempt to change attitudes when they try to persuade people that low-fat diets are *good*, and that people should *like* them. We might call this *health advertising*.

In chapter 1, we defined a "health belief" as something we think to be true concerning our health. More generally, beliefs are our personal encyclopedias of the world. They are the things we consider to be true. Beliefs are different from attitudes in that they are not evaluative in nature. For example, we might hold the *belief* that yogurt contains less fat than ice cream and this belief might support the attitude that yogurt is *good* for us.

Health promotion programs try to affect what people believe to be true and what they *like* and consider *good*. Over the years, social psychologists have conducted extensive research on persuasion (for a detailed review, see Olson & Maio, 2003). Well-proven principles have emerged from this research that can be applied to health promotion. Several examples follow.

The Elaboration Likelihood Model of Persuasion

Research investigating people's attitudes toward political candidates has discovered that there are basically two routes through which these attitudes are influenced (Petty & Cacioppo, 1981). The first, called the **central route**, refers to the use of logic, facts, and reason. Political campaigns using the central route present statistics and logical arguments in favour of a given candidate or perhaps in opposition to a candidate. Health promotion programs using this route will present statistics and medical facts.

The second way is called the **peripheral route**. This involves an appeal to emotion and general impression. Political campaigns using this route will focus on the looks and charisma of the candidate. Health promotion campaigns using the peripheral route feature healthy-looking people or show graphic depictions of the potential horrors resulting from risk behaviour.

Research in social psychology shows that some people are influenced more by central routes and others more by peripheral routes. This means that health promotion campaigns must cover both bases. Statistical presentations, which make use of a central route, must be packaged well to appeal to people who are more influenced by peripheral routes.

A number of studies have applied the elaboration likelihood model to health promotion. In the area of AIDS prevention, for example, it has been suggested that there might be problems with programs focused exclusively on providing facts. People may become overloaded with information; if it is not packaged in ways that arouse constructive emotional responses (Mulvihill, 1996; Helweg-Larsen & Collins, 1997). A study of the influence of a mammography promotion message found that women who reported a low level of involvement with mammography were more influenced by favourable peripheral cues such as colour film (rather than black and white) and popular music (Kirby & Ureda 1998).

Fear Appeals: An Example of Health Promotion by the Peripheral Route

One fairly obvious application of the peripheral route is the use of what are called **fear appeals**. The term is self-explanatory. The assumption, of course, is that we can change people's behaviour by presenting frightening accounts of what will happen to them if they continue a given behaviour (for example, smoking) or if they don't adopt a behaviour (for example, dental hygiene).

There is considerable theoretical support for this assumption. For example, main components of the theory of planned behaviour include *perceived threat* and *personal vulnerability*. Fear appeals are designed to intensify people's beliefs regarding this threat and the extent to which they are vulnerable. In other words, **threat perception**, the belief that a threat is real and that we are vulnerable to it, is more important than simple fear arousal.

Long before the introduction of the theory of planned behaviour, Hovland and colleagues' **drive-reduction theory** was used to explain fear appeals. Drive-reduction theory argues that we are driven to reduce the tension brought about by deprivation or other states to which we have an aversion (Hovland, Janis, & Kelley, 1953). According to this theory, fear appeals should work because we are driven to reduce fear, and when we are successful, the behaviour that we use to reduce the fear is reinforced.

However, if the fear arousal is *too high*, the person will respond in ways other than the recommended behaviour. There are a number of reasons for this, but the main one is that very frightening messages present situations and outcomes that appear to be so awful that we don't think we can deal with them effectively no matter what we do. As a result, the recommended behaviour looks ineffective in comparison to the potentially catastrophic nature of the threat. For example, can I prevent the devastating effects of cancer by eating broccoli? In answering this question, many people would see a mismatch in strength between the threat and the behaviour and so remain uninfluenced. They carry on with their old behaviour because the high-fear message makes the situation look too hopeless to do anything about anyway. In this case, we don't believe in the *efficacy* of the behaviour to

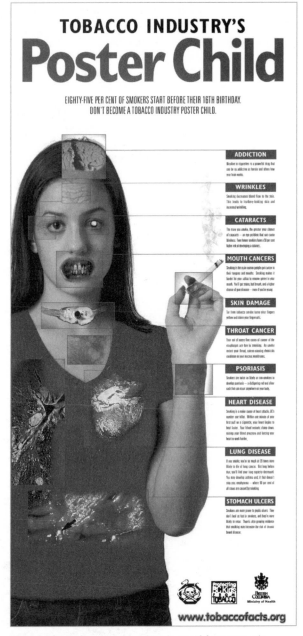

Posters like this one take advantage of fear appeals.

deal with the threat. Modern analysis of the mechanisms behind fear appeals indicates that the *efficacy beliefs* we talked about in chapter 1 might be more important than the amount of fear aroused by the message (Ruiter, Abraham & Kok, 2001).

These efficacy beliefs take two forms—**response efficacy** (the belief that the behaviour will reduce the threat), and **self-efficacy** (the belief that one can carry out the behaviour). Another problem with high-fear messages is that our self-efficacy suffers when we are afraid. To illustrate this, ask yourself how reassuring are instructions on how to employ a backup parachute in the event that the main chute doesn't open? Imagine yourself listening to these instructions. In the event that you were plummeting to earth under the full force of gravity, are you confident that you would be able to carry out those backup

Supermodel Christy Turlington represents a peripheral approach to health promotion.

instructions? Or would you be too afraid to remember the instructions and carry them out correctly? Confidence levels vary from person to person under such circumstances. Concerning health promotion, we might undermine people's confidence in their ability to perform self-examinations for cancer if we portray cancer in particularly frightening ways. This may be why 54 percent of women who were sent a reassuring letter listing "encouraging facts" about breast cancer made an appointment for a mammogram, whereas only 42 percent made an appointment after receiving an anxiety-arousing letter listing "worrisome facts." Interestingly, only 38 percent made an appointment when they received a standard letter listing no facts at all (Kendall & Hailley, 1993).

The point is that the effectiveness of fear appeals depends very much on people's *responses* while frightened. This makes the fear-appeal approach very tricky. Perhaps the best analysis of the various types of responses to fear appeals comes from what is called the **parallel response model** (Leventhal, 1970). According to this model, recipients of fear-arousing messages focus on either *fear control* or *danger control* or some combination of the two. Put simply, people who focus on **fear control** are not likely to change their behaviour in constructive ways. Instead, they will engage in what more recently has been called **emotion-focused coping** (Folkman & Lazarus, 1985; Folkman et al., 1986; Lazarus & Folkman, 1984) in which they attempt to reduce the discomfort of a situation without trying to change the situation itself.

There are a number of possible responses for those with a fear-control motive. People who respond to fear appeals in this way are more likely to *deny* their personal vulnerability to a threat by saying something like "This is a really awful thing, but it won't happen to me." They are also more likely to *minimize* the threat by thinking "This really can't be as bad as people say it is." They tend to be *inattentive* when the message is presented and they will avoid thinking about it afterward. Finally, they might engage in *source derogation*, in which they discredit the source ("They don't know what they're talking about") or dislike the source ("My school counsellor is always such a downer—nothing but doom and gloom messages"). For a more detailed review of these responses, see Eagly and Chaiken (1993).

None of these responses leads to constructive change, which is the goal of health promotion. On the other hand, **danger control** does. This is a form of **problem-focused coping**, in which the person attempts to alter the situation or create conditions in which stress and danger are reduced (Lazarus & Folkman, 1984). There are two important things to note about danger control. First, it usually leads to constructive change when the danger is health related. Second, danger control can proceed *without fear*. In fact, as we saw earlier, fear might inhibit danger control if it is too strong.

In terms of health promotion, danger control usually takes the form of *risk reduction*. From this perspective, you can imagine the wide range of behaviours that fit in the category of danger control. Wearing a seatbelt, exercising, and practising safe sex are all examples of danger control behaviours. The key, then, in fear appeals, is to encourage danger control instead of fear control.

When can we expect a person to respond with fear control and when can we expect danger control? Leventhal's parallel response model doesn't answer this important question; Kim Witte's **extended parallel process model** does (Witte, 1992). Witte's model extends the work of Leventhal by postulating a relationship between the amount of fear presented in a message and the nature of the person's response. Witte argues that low-fear messages stimulate neither fear control nor danger control, since neither fear nor danger appears to be an issue. In contrast, high fear messages will stimulate fear control. They will also stimulate danger control if the message is accompanied by an effective *behavioural recommendation*.

Even when presented with these workable suggestions, some people will focus primarily on fear control. This is largely due to the habitual coping strategies of the person receiving the message. We looked closely at coping styles in chapter 2 in our discussion of stress and coping. The important point here is that fear appeals differ in their effectiveness, partially because of the different coping approaches adopted by the receivers of the appeals. It is also true, though, that some of the effectiveness of a fear appeal is determined by the strength of the fear message. If the fear is too high, then fear control often becomes the person's first priority, which doesn't lead to constructive change, especially if the high fear is not accompanied by a clear suggestion for reducing the threat. Moreover, high fear reduces people's concentration and processing ability, so they might not be particularly receptive to the suggestion anyway (Christianson, 1992).

As you might expect, there are quite a few published studies that test the effects of fear appeals in health promotion programs. By looking at some of them we can draw some final conclusions about the use of fear appeals.

One study in Holland presented Dutch adolescents with anti-smoking messages that varied in a number of ways, one being the severity of the fear component. How did adolescent smokers respond to the more severe messages? As predicted by the parallel response model, almost half were defensive rather than receptive. In other words, they engaged in fear control (van Wel & Knobbout, 1998). Just over half the adolescents in that study, though, expressed a desire to quit smoking. The question is whether that desire would be translated into action, or danger control.

In a study of AIDS-related public service announcements, it was discovered that fear-arousing announcements were more effective than humorous, erotic, or fact-based messages in increasing the intention to use condoms. This effect was greater for women than for men (Struckman-Johnson, Struckman-Johnson, Gilliland, & Ausman, 1994). Another study using AIDS-prevention messages concluded that people must have a strong sense of self-efficacy regarding the recommended behaviour for the fear appeal to work (Witte, 1994). If people believe they are capable of carrying out the recommended behaviour, they will focus on danger control rather than fear control. This also means that the message must enhance self-efficacy at least as much as it arouses fear. In the case of AIDS prevention, we can present messages that emphasize the terrible consequences of being HIV positive (i.e., fear appeal), but we would be better off to put more emphasis on how people are very capable of greatly reducing the risk (i.e., self-efficacy).

What can we conclude from our analysis of fear appeals as a health promotion strategy? Clearly, messages that do nothing more than frighten people without providing suggestions of ways to reduce the fear are likely to be counterproductive. On the other hand, if we arouse fear and accompany that with recommendations on ways to reduce the threat as well as a convincing argument that these ways are within the capabilities of the people receiving the message, then we increase our chances of success. "Success" in terms of health promotion means that people will pay attention to our message, remember it, and behave in ways that are consistent with it by reducing health risks and increasing well-being. (For a detailed theoretical analysis of fear appeals, see Ruiter, Abraham and Gerjo, 2001).

The Application of Other Social-Psychological Principles to Health Promotion

We know that people are more likely to be influenced by messages the more often they are repeated (Zajonc, 1968). Advertisers have known this for decades, as evidenced by the number of times we will see the same commercial in a 30-minute television program. Slogans take advantage of the repetition effect by being repeated in every different ad that appears in a given campaign. Health promotion campaigns could take greater advantage of slogans, as advertisers do. Imagine the effect if a health promotion campaign had come up with the phrase "Just do it."

Of course, advertising campaigns are far more than just repeated words and phrases. We must also consider who is saying those words. When we adopt a central route, we want to use people who are very credible, which is to say that they are seen as being knowledgeable and believable. Not surprisingly, research has shown that sources perceived to be credible tend to be more persuasive than non-credible ones (Birnbaum, Wong, & Wong, 1976). If we are mounting an anti-smoking campaign, for example, we might want to put a physician on camera. If it is a drinking and driving counterattack program, we could use a police officer who is often first on the scene of motor vehicle accidents.

If, on the other hand, we are using a peripheral approach, we will focus on the *attractiveness* of our speaker, or we might want to pick someone who is famous. This is why anti-drug abuse campaigns use professional athletes as speakers.

Good health promotion campaigns use both credible and popular speakers. As an example, imagine that you had been asked to design a program to reduce the incidence of drinking and driving at high school graduations. Sixteen percent of teenage males and seven percent of teenage females report that they drink and drive (Health Canada, 1995), and that number may well go up at graduation celebrations. Your counterattack programs for high schools, aimed at affecting the drinking and driving behaviour, would be most effective if they combined messages from first-response police officers (because they are highly *credible*) and school presidents (because they are *popular*).

Social psychologists have learned that the nature of the *audience* must also be taken into account when planning persuasive pitches. For one thing, it is important to know whether the audience is initially in favour of your position or against it. If the audience is in favour of your position, then it is best to present only one side of an argument or message. For example, if you are trying to increase the exercise rates of a group of ex-athletes, you would only have to talk about the virtues of staying active. Presumably, this audience would be in favour of the idea of exercise at the outset but might need some encouragement to adopt a plan that would get them back to their old activity levels.

If, on the other hand, you were talking to people who had never been very active, it is more likely that they would have considered and adopted some beliefs about the downside of exercise, making them initially less in favour of your pro-exercise position. In this case, your pitch must address both sides of the argument—specifically, the pros and cons of exercise. Of course, when addressing the cons you must refute them or, at least, minimize them. For example, you could acknowledge that exercising takes time, but not an inordinate amount of time, to realize tangible benefits.

Why must we present these two-sided programs to this type of audience? Again, the answer comes from social-psychological research in persuasion. It turns out that, if you fail to acknowledge the cons when presenting a message to an audience that is not initially on your side, they tend to generate counterarguments to your one-sided pitch on their own (Greenwald, 1968; Osterhouse & Brock, 1970). In fact, they will be doing this instead of paying attention to your pitch! Can you remember ever being presented with a one-sided argument by someone you disagreed with, all the while thinking of rebuttals that started with "Yes, but..."?

Following this principle, health promotion campaigns must acknowledge that quitting smoking isn't easy, that the first few days of an exercise program may seem too tiring, that such a program must be planned out to accommodate busy schedules, and so on. If these sorts of realities are not dealt with, many people will simply bring them up on their own as justification for resisting the program.

In addition to the audience's initial position, a health promotion program must consider that audience's *knowledge level*. When talking to small audiences, people in health promotion can make educated guesses about an audience's knowledge level. However, this is much more challenging when planning national campaigns. How much do people know about heart anatomy, for example? Early research found that people's knowledge of medical terminology was poor (Samora, Saunders, & Larson, 1961). A more recent update of that study showed that knowledge had improved somewhat, but not impressively so. When people were presented with 50 medical terms to define, only two of 224 adult participants were able to define all 50; this for a sample in which 71 percent had postsecondary education (Thompson & Pledger, 1993).

Obviously, Canadians vary tremendously in their knowledge of medical language and procedures. For this reason, good health promotion campaigns must be basic enough to include as many people as possible without insulting anyone's intelligence. This can be a tricky balance to achieve.

Complicating the issue of knowledge is *literacy*. In Canada in 1994, 62 percent of Canadians could meet everyday reading needs, but 2.9 million adults could not deal with most everyday written material because of inadequate reading skills (Canadian Survey of Literacy Skills, 1994). More recently, it has been discovered that there are regional differences in literacy. Using a five-level scale and testing people in the official language of their choice, a large study of literacy in Canada discovered that 18 percent of people in Ontario and the western provinces were reading at the lowest level, Level One. This compares with 25 to 28 percent in Quebec and the Atlantic provinces. In this case, "Level One" means that a person can probably read the instructions on a medicine bottle well enough to determine dosages, but more intricate instructions would not be understood (Jones, 1996). (See also http://www.literacy.ca/litand/1.htm).

In addition, there are people in Canada who are not fluent in English or French. According to Statistics Canada census figures, over 450 000 people in Canada cannot understand spoken English or French. That figure represents 1.6 percent of our population. In British Columbia, 2.6 percent of the population cannot understand spoken English or French. Effective health promotion campaigns for these segments of our population must be either highly visual or multilingual.

Poole and Ting (1995) discovered that Indo-Canadian maternity patients scored lower on tests of knowledge of hospital procedures, baby care, and self-care than did Euro-Canadian patients. Language barriers are cited as a significant reason for these differences.

It is clear, from studies such as this, that patient education and health promotion will be more effective when presented in a person's native language and, preferably, by people of the same cultural background.

In summary, we have seen that theories of psychology can and must be applied to the design and implementation of health promotion campaigns. When we consider these theories, we develop a greater appreciation for the complexities of health promotion. Changing the minds and behaviour of large groups of people is no easy task. The good news is that people who can be convinced to change their behaviour often come to endorse that behaviour and go on to carry out health promotion for others.

THE PRECEDE-PROCEED MODEL

People working in health promotion would benefit greatly from a theoretical framework that would guide them in the planning of their programs. Not only would this provide structure and direction for the planning process, it would also provide a set of criteria by which an existing program could be assessed. This is exactly what the precede–proceed model (Green & Kreuter, 1991) does. The model was designed as a way to facilitate and analyze health promotion programs from the planning stages through to their implementation and impact.

There are two key attributes to the model. One is the identification of stages involved in the planning, implementation, and evaluation of health promotion programs. The other is the identification of causal pathways among the components that are the concern of health promotion. Table 7-1 presents the model. The "precede" phases of the model relate to the

TABLE 7-1	The Precede-Proceed Model of Health Promotion Planning, Implementation, and Evaluation			
				← PRECEDE
Phase 5	Phase 4	Phase 3	Phase 2	Phase 1
Administrative and policy diagnosis	Educational and organizational diagnosis	Behavioural and environmental diagnosis	Epidemiological diagnosis	Social diagnosis
Health promotion	Predisposing factors			
Health education	Reinforcing factors	Behaviour and lifestyle	Health	Quality of life
Policy regulation organization	Enabling factors	Environment		
Phase 6	Phase 7	Phase 8	Phase 9	
Implementation	Process evaluation	Impact evaluation	Outcome evaluation	

PROCEED →

Source: Green & Kreuter (1991). *Health promotion planning: An educational and environmental approach.* Mountain View, CA: Mayfield publishing. Adapted by permission.

planning of health promotion programs. The "proceed" phases relate to the implementation and evaluation of that program. By examining table 7-1, you can see that the model has an element of symmetry that helps clarify it conceptually. We begin by moving from right to left across the top of the model then proceed by moving from left to right across the bottom. In so doing, we end up where we started, with a focus on health and quality of life. We can walk through the phases of the model to develop an appreciation for its logic.

We begin in phase 1 by diagnosing quality of life. If there were no problems here, there would be no need to continue with our health promotion plan. However, there are always problems because there is never a case in which an entire population is disease, disability, or accident free. In phase 2, we would conduct an epidemiological diagnosis. This means that we would identify patterns of health and illness in our population. In terms of causation, the model assumes that these health patterns affect quality of life. Phase 3 requires a diagnosis of behavioural and environmental factors that explain our epidemiological data. We are now beginning to create a causal pathway from behaviour and environment, to health, to quality of life. In phase 4, we assess factors affecting behaviour and environment. What biological, psychological, or social factors influence behaviour? (This should remind you of the biopsychosocial model.) What factors affect environment? In the final phase of planning, phase 5, we would devise programs and policies meant to create optimal environments that are physically healthy and that reinforce healthy behaviours.

Now we are ready to "proceed," which is to say implement our plan and evaluate its effects. In phase 6, we would implement our education programs, new health policies, environmental regulations, and so on. These may take advantage of some of the psychological theories we discussed earlier in the chapter. To assess the effectiveness of these programs, we would first enter the Process Evaluation phase (phase 7). At this point, we would evaluate the extent to which our programs were affecting the factors that predispose people to healthy behaviour and reinforce that behaviour. In addition, we may also be trying to bring about conditions that foster improvements in people's physical environments. In phase 8, we assess impact by measuring changes in behaviour, lifestyle, and environment since the program began. These changes should, in turn, bring about better health and, ultimately, better quality of life. This brings us back to where we started.

A good example of the implementation of the precede–proceed model would be a program that was designed to increase the physical activity levels of senior citizens (Frankish, Milligan, & Reid, 1998). This program would stem from the belief that health-related quality of life is influenced by active rather than sedentary behaviours and lifestyles. The next step (phase 4) is to identify factors that would predispose a person to activity and other factors that would reinforce it. Now we are ready to design a health promotion program that takes advantage of psychological theory to positively affect these factors. When we move in the "proceed" direction, we would implement our program and evaluate the extent to which it brings about predisposing and reinforcing factors that favoured active living (phase 7). Next we would evaluate the extent to which these events actually had an impact on the seniors' behaviour and, more generally, their lifestyles—were people being more active? (phase 8). Finally, we would need to determine whether the seniors' health had improved and, along with it, their quality of life.

The Precede-Proceed Model has been tested in over 600 published studies, addressing everything from the use of bicycle helmets (Stanken, 2000) to HIV transmission among university students in South Africa (Petersen, Bhagwanjee, & Makhaba, 2001), making it the most widely tested model of its kind. One of the advantages of the model is that it works in conjunction with any other model or theory of health promotion design. For example, in phase 5, planners could use the health belief model as their guide, trying to educate people about their vulnerability beliefs and beliefs regarding the efficacy of the behaviour in question. The model has been criticized for being too individually oriented, with its emphasis on behaviour and lifestyle (Luschen, Cockerham, & Kunz, 1996). An expanded model might take the social and cultural context of that behaviour into consideration.

ASSESSING THE EFFECTIVENESS OF HEALTH PROMOTION PROGRAMS

Health promotion programs are labour-intensive initiatives that can be expensive. It is important, therefore, to find ways to assess their effectiveness. In health promotion, the magnitude of the interventions and the desired effects can make evaluation of impact difficult. Fawcett et al. (2001) identify no fewer than 12 challenges inherent in evaluating health promotion programs that are pitched at the community level. These authors point out that it can be difficult identifying just what is determining the health of the community, much less evaluating programs designed to affect those determinants. Furthermore, some of the endpoints of health promotion, such as "community capacity" or "quality of life," while important, are abstract in nature. Getting definitive measures of changes in rates of child abuse and domestic violence on a population level can be difficult. For one thing, under-reporting is often a problem. And then there is the lag time between the implementation of a promotion program and the benefit that is realized. Some health promotion benefits, such as reduced cardiovascular disease, can take years to realize. These are just some of the challenges identified by Fawcett and his colleagues.

When we evaluate health promotion outcomes, we can begin to reduce the complexity by identifying a finite number of levels for these outcomes (Anderson, et al., 2000). At the top level, we could put **health and social outcomes**. Here, we would measure quality of life, ability to function independently, and reduced morbidity and morality. At the next level down, we could identify **intermediate health outcomes**. We would measure such things as lifestyle, provision of health services, and environmental factors. At the next level, we could identify **health promotion outcomes**. These would include many of the examples we have talked about in this chapter, such as changes in literacy, community capacity, and health policy. Finally, we could identify **health promotion actions**. Here, we would measure *processes*, such as health education programs and political lobbying. These levels are intended to be causally linked from bottom to top. Health promotion actions should affect health promotion outcomes, which should in turn affect intermediate health outcomes and finally overall health and social outcomes. Our evaluation plan would need to target one or more of these levels to assess the effectiveness of the health promotion program. Once we had targeted a level for our evaluation, there are well-defined steps that we could follow (Rootman, et al., 2001). Table 7-2 lists these.

TABLE 7-2	Steps involved in the evaluation of health promotion initiatives	
STEPS	**CONSIDERATIONS**	
Step 1: Describing the program	Develop a familiarity with the program you are evaluating in terms of its context, goals, and constituents.	
Step 2: Identifying the issues and questions	What needs to be known about the program? What do the program's constituents mean when they ask "Is the program working?"	
Step 3: Designing the data-collection process	Will qualitative and/or quantitative methods be used? What will your sources be?	
Step 4: Collecting the data	Careful and systematic data collection is required	
Step 5: Analysing and interpreting the data	Will you be looking for themes? Is your analysis theory driven?	
Step 6: Making recommendation	What can you confidently conclude from your analysis and what will you tell the constituents?	
Step 7: Dissemination	Who should be made aware of your evaluation?	
Step 8: Taking action	What should be done as a result of your evaluation?	

Source: Based on Rootman recommendations, referenced from: Rootman, I., Godstadt, M., Potvin., and Springett, J. (2001). A framework for health promotion evaluation. In Rootman, I., et al, (eds.). *Evaluation in health promotion: Principles and perspectives*. Copenhagen, WHO Regional Office for Europe, 2001 (WHO Regional Publications, European Series, NO. 92, pp. 7-38).

KEY TERMS

agency-provided support (p. 181)

attitude (p. 183)

central route to persuasion (p. 183)

danger control (p. 187)

drive-reduction theory (p. 184)

emotion-focused coping (p. 187)

emotional support (p. 181)

extended parallel process model (p. 187)

fear appeals (p. 184)

fear control (p. 187)

health and social outcomes (p. 193)

health brief model (p. 182)

health promotion (p. 174)

health promotion actions (p. 193)

health promotion mechanisms (p. 178)

health promotion outcomes (p. 193)

informational support (p. 181)

intermediate health outcomes (p. 193)

medical level (p. 176)

mutual aid (p. 180)

naturally occurring support (p. 181)

pap test (p. 179)

pap smear (p. 179)

parallel response model (p. 187)

peripheral route to persuasion (p. 184)

persuasion (p. 183)

practical support (p. 181)

problem-focused coping (p. 187)

public health level (p. 176)

response efficacy (p. 185)

self-care (p. 179)

self-efficacy (p. 185)

social support (p. 180)

socioenvironmental level (p. 176)

threat of planned behaviour (p. 182)

theory of reasoned action (p. 182)

threat perception (p. 184)

chapter eight

Health and Physical Activity

CHAPTER OUTLINE

The Nature of Physical Activity

Physical Activity and the Five Components of Health
  Rates of Physical Activity

The Five Forms of Physical Activity

Psychological Benefits of Physical Activity
  Physical Activity and Sense of Self
  Physical Activity and Cognitive Functioning
  Physical Activity and Mood

Physical Benefits of Physical Activity

Adherence to Physical Activity

Psychological Factors Affecting Performance in Exercise and Sport
  Relaxation
  Self-Talk

Imagery

Goal-Setting

Physical Activity and Injury

KEY QUESTIONS

1. How would you evaluate the balance in your life with regard to the mental, physical, social, motivational, and spiritual well-being dimensions discussed in this chapter?

2. Have you ever had an injury in sport, exercise, or another physical activity? How did it affect you psychologically?

3. Have you ever been concussed? If yes, what grade was it?

4. How would you describe your own adherence to health-enhancing activities? What factors affect people's adherence?

Donna had been a fitness instructor for three years. She was an active person, and she couldn't imagine another job that would allow her to stay as fit and physically active as this one did. She was an upbeat person, and people who attended her classes seemed to appreciate that.

There were times, however, when the job was quite frustrating. Although some of Donna's clients were very dedicated and never missed an aerobics class, most were very hit and miss. When she got frustrated, Donna would think about the dozens of people who would come to one or two of the first classes of a season and then never come back. They had invested money in the class and had seemed very committed at the beginning. But then they would disappear, never to be seen again.

Donna wondered if it was something about her. But all of her fitness instructor colleagues had the same problem. Whenever Donna went to a garage sale, there always seemed to be relatively new pieces of exercise equipment for sale—a stair-climber, a rowing machine. Donna couldn't figure out why so many people become physically active through exercise programs but don't stay with them.

One of the most significant issues in health care and well-being are the personal choices people make. This chapter is about choices and the decisions individuals make with regard to physical activity. Many of us will admit that the first commitment in our daily schedule that we will sacrifice when the demands for time begin to overwhelm us often relates to physical activity. We say things like "I won't be able to go for a walk today as I have too much work to do" or "I won't be able to attend exercise class this evening as I need to spend time with my family." The implication, of course, is that we have no choice in the matter. In the examples given, it is the fault of our job and our family that we do not exercise today. We are not even prepared to take responsibility for the decision. When it comes to priorities in our lives, physical activity is often low on the list. For many of us, exercising does not occupy a space in our day-timer; we tend to think "I'll do it if time allows and, if it doesn't, I can always do it tomorrow."

THE NATURE OF PHYSICAL ACTIVITY

In this chapter we focus on health issues relevant to physical activity, exercise, and sport. The literature indicates that one can attach quite different meanings to each of these terms. Biddle and Mutrie (2001) have promoted physical activity "in the belief that many forms of physical activity are healthy." (p. 3). They identify both exercise and sport as elements or sub-components of physical activity while recognizing that distinctions between these constructs are not always obvious and often overlap. Dubbert (2002) points out that, although psychologists continue to be involved in the promotion of physical activity and exercise for disease prevention and rehabilitation, the research and interventions skills learned in these situations are now being applied to athletic performance. Hays (1999) suggests that, although exercise and sport may have different implications, the two fields are clearly related and the effects of exercise are usually considered within the field of sport psychology. **Sport psychology** focuses on the influence of psychological factors on sport behaviour, whereas **exercise psychology** is concerned with the influence that sport and exercise have on psychological behaviour. Hays states that, "Exercise psychology attends to the body-to-mind relationship, whereas sport psychology is directed toward the mind-to-body relationship" (Hays p. 240). Gauvin and Spence (1995) define exercise as "leisure activity (as opposed to occupational physical activity) undertaken with a specific external objective, such as the improvement of fitness, physical performance, or health, in which the participant is advised to conform to recommended mode, intensity, frequency, and duration of such activity" (p. 435). The purpose of the activity is important in this definition. If we go to the gym to ride a stationary bike or play basketball to improve our fitness, this is considered exercise; whereas, if walking is part of our work (e.g., a postal worker), it is not considered exercise as it is not being done to improve our fitness. Understanding the intention of the activity appears important in determining whether or not it is exercise. We can push a hand-mower, shovel snow, or chop wood to either get some exercise or to cut the grass, clear the driveway, or get some wood for the fire. The intention is different, but the outcome is the same. Alternatively, Casperson, Powell and Christenson, 1985) have suggested that **physical activity** can be a part of either leisure or work activities, as it is a function of bodily movements produced by skeletal muscles. Whether it is purposeful or without intention, it involves the expenditure of energy. Gauvin, Levesque, & Richard (2001) have described four parameters of physical activity: type, frequency, intensity, and duration. Type identifies the physiological systems that are used in a particular activity such as aerobic, strength, endurance, and flexibility. Frequency is concerned with how much the activity is engaged in over a time period. Intensity describes the load imposed on physiological systems by an activity (e.g. strenuous). Duration indicates the temporal length of a particular activity. **Physical fitness** refers to physiological functioning and describes attributes we have that influence the ability to perform physical activity (Casperson et al.). Different forms of physical fitness have been identified (Kaplan, Sallis, & Patterson, 1993). These include cardiorespiratory endurance, muscular endurance, muscular strength, body composition, and flexibility.

Typical definitions of **sport** are often too inclusive, and it is difficult to distinguish between activities such as games, recreation, play, leisure activity, and sport. Wann (1997) suggests that most definitions of sport are too narrow and exclude that individual often described as the "weekend athlete." He defines sports as "activities involving powers and skills, competition and strategy, and/or chance, and engaged in for the enjoyment, satisfaction, and/or personal gain (such as income) of the participant and/or others (e.g., spectators), including organized and recreational sports, as well as sport as entertainment" (p.3). The importance of including sports activities that fall outside of the traditional realm of competition is supported more recently by Biddle and Murtrie (2001). It is our sense that a definition that includes the youngster playing recreational sport for the first time and motivated only by intrinsic enjoyment and the professional athlete who entertains others and makes his or her living in sport is most appropriate.

We now will consider a personal journey that one individual, Peter, made when confronted with ill health. His story, in a slightly edited version, is presented here.

CASE 8-1	Peter's Story

March 4, 1995, is a memorable day in my life. It had been a busy Saturday for me. In the morning I exercised at a local gym and in the afternoon I did some yard work. In the evening I worked on some files in my home office. That night I was feeling tired and experiencing some pain in my back. I was also short of breath. At approximately 9:30 p.m., I decided to have a hot bath to see if that would ease the discomfort in my back. My wife Brenda commented that I looked peaked and pale. As I got into the bathtub, the pain, rather than dissipating, became more intense. I had also developed a severe headache to go along with the now excruciating pain in my back. I got out of the bath and spoke with my wife, who said I was a shade of gray-green. I remember feeling faint to the point that I thought I might lose consciousness.

At this point, Brenda suggested that she take me to the hospital. I do not remember much of the trip. The hospital admissions staff asked a few questions upon my arrival and seemed to know what was happening to me. At about midnight, the resident physician

informed me that I had had a heart attack. The words "heart attack" scared the living hell out of me. I was moved up to the critical care unit early on Sunday morning. I was given morphine intravenously and my blood pressure was constantly monitored. When my family arrived at the hospital, it must have been a shock for them to see me in such a state. My eight-year-old son was very disturbed, and I could see the tears welling up in his eyes. A person beside me had passed away and was being removed from the ward. My son asked, "Does this mean you are going to die too?" The question hit me hard and I too began to cry. I told my son, "I will be here for a long time, so don't you worry."

I left the hospital on March 10, 1995. It was my daughter's tenth birthday and I wanted to be home for it. In order to be discharged, I had to prove to the hospital staff that I could walk up a flight of stairs and around the ward. This may seem a mundane physical task; however, I can assure you that it was very tiring for an individual in my condition. I was able to spend the evening with my

(continued on next page)

daughter, although not as an active participant. It just felt great to be home.

The next year was an emotional roller coaster. I was not sure if I was going to live or die. A full year passed and my emotions were so torn that I descended into a depression. *Depression* was an unfamiliar word for me and caused me great anguish. My family physician suggested I get physically fit again. I had always been a physical person; however, in the last year I had abandoned exercise for fear I would have another heart attack. After talking with my physician, I started going back to the gym.

The exercise certainly helped. After about a year, my weight had dropped, but I still didn't *feel* any better. My diet included more of the good foods I was supposed to eat. I ate more vegetables and fruit and less meat, but I also continued to eat high-fat and high-calorie foods. In mid-1998, we bought a Sheltie pup. He provided me with the incentive to walk twice a day. But, just as important, his energy and companionship completely changed my mood. I was finally starting to *feel* better.

In late 1998, I saw an advertisement in the *Vancouver Sun*. St. Paul's Hospital was looking for volunteers to participate in an atherosclerosis-reversal program. I immediately replied to the advertisement and, when I did not hear back, called insistently. There was no way I was not going to be a participant in a program that could reduce my risk of atherosclerosis. I was accepted into the program and started in January 1999.

The first step was to be interviewed by the coordinator, who described the objectives of the program. I then met the nurse clinician. She further described the program and directed me to the first of my tests. The stress test measured my overall level of fitness and the blood tests measured choles-

terol, triglycerides, and homocystein. These initial tests served as a baseline for subsequent tests.

I next met the dietician, who weighed me and measured the circumference of my hips and waist. I learned that these are very critical measurements. The waist-to-hip ratio should be less than 0.9 to 1.0. I weighed 217 pounds on my first visit and today am 198 pounds. My waist-to-hip ratio is between 0.85 and 1.0. These are solid improvements over a short period of time. I consume about 30 grams of fat per day, whereas before I entered the program I probably consumed approximately 100 grams of fat per day. Do I feel better now? You bet!

My next contact was the exercise specialist, who developed a program to fit my needs. I review the progress I am making on my monthly visits and she suggests alternatives or new exercises to help me achieve the results I want. She also uses calipers to measure my body fat. Each time I have improved. I feel extremely fortunate to have been chosen to be a part of this program and to have the benefits of experts who advise me on lifestyle, diet, exercise, and mental well-being.

Through trial and error, I have arrived at the following recommendations for living a healthy lifestyle: 1) choose positive friends and discard the negative ones; 2) read as much as you can about health, and share information with those who need and want it; 3) take time for yourself; 4) relax, 5) thank your family and others who make a difference in your life; and 6) be open to new experiences and new friends. In summary, I believe we can change if we want to. Sometimes it takes negative situations to force us into changing our lifestyle, and rediscovering what it means to be alive.

PHYSICAL ACTIVITY AND THE FIVE COMPONENTS OF HEALTH

Peter's story demonstrates the reality of lifestyle change. For him, the alternative to making such a change was unacceptable. The choices he faced and the decisions he made touch upon many of the issues relating health psychology to physical activity. Greenberg and Pargman (1989) describe a health–illness continuum anchored by four points: death, illness, health, and perfect health. Peter has moved close to the extremes of the continuum. To have been faced with the real possibility of death and to now be moving between health and perfect health demonstrates the power of personal change processes. For Greenberg and Pargman, each point on the continuum between death and perfect health is made up of five components: mental, physical, emotional, social, and spiritual health. Regardless of the position an individual occupies on the continuum, wellness is a function of balance between the five components. The goal is to be well rounded in all areas.

Pargman (1998) believes that those involved in sport and exercise need to appreciate how physical activity can contribute to wellness. It is important not to invest in any area disproportionately, as wellness is achieved through balance. Each of these areas influences and is influenced by the others. This principle of reciprocity is clearly indicated in Peter's story, in which growth in all five areas is evident. Not only has he moved a significant distance on the continuum of health and illness, he has achieved a greater sense of balance in his life. Clearly, his physical health has improved dramatically. This is a matter of objective record, and improvements in this regard are evident whenever he visits the clinic for another round of tests.

Conversations with Peter reveal that in the other four areas he feels that his life has improved in positive ways. Mentally, he is more focused and self-confident. Emotionally, he describes himself as being more stable and less reactive. He exudes a sense of optimism that is infectious and wonderful to observe. Socially, he is active and fun to be around. He seeks out rather than avoids social experiences. Although he may not describe spiritual changes in his life, it is obvious that things have happened. By his own admission he has in a sense been "reborn." Although these four components of health (mental, social, emotional, and spiritual) are subjective and therefore difficult to quantify, they are perhaps the most important elements of change for him as they have the greatest impact on the quality of his life. He has discovered the joy of what Csikszentmihalyi (1997) has described as **active** compared to **passive leisure**. Active leisure is an extremely positive experience associated with activities such as hobbies, playing a musical instrument, and exercise. He states that when people engage in activities such as these, they "tend to be more happy, motivated, concentrated, and more often in flow than in any other part of the day. It is in these contexts that all the various dimensions of experience are most intensely focused and in harmony with one another" (p. 39).

Rates of Physical Activity

It has been recommended that we should have at least 30 minutes of moderate exercise every day (Pate, 1995). Dubbert (2002) has summarized recent advances in physical activity and exercise research by concluding that "moderate-level activity has significant health benefits but that vigorous activity should also be encouraged for those who are able and willing to increase the intensity of their effort" (p. 527). Although an appropriate program of exercise is recognized as part of a prescription for physical and psychological health, it is clear that many individuals do not get sufficient exercise and that for those who initiate a program of exercise the levels of adherence are low. A frequently cited statistic in this regard is based on early research by Dishman (1988). He found that 50 percent of those who began a structured exercise program discontinued it within the first six months. There appears to be consistency to these findings as Eastabrooks (2000) reported that while 30 percent of North Americans exercise on a regular basis, 50 percent of those who begin an exercise program stop within six months. We will return to the issue of adherence later; now we will focus on the incidence of exercise behaviour.

Based on data collected in 1996–97, Statistics Canada (1999) reports that 57 percent of Canadians over the age of 15 years exercise three or more times a week, with the highest percentage being for those in the 15 to 19 years of age group and the lowest in the 65 years of age and over group. Exercise in this instance includes activities that are considered to be vigorous (e.g., calisthenics, jogging, racquet sports, brisk walking, dance) and that continue for a period of at least 15 minutes. Some would suggest this is a somewhat generous definition; however, it does allow us to examine exercise involvement according to age and gender in Canada. The percentage of Canadians who exercise three or more times per week is slightly higher for women, at 58 percent, compared to 56 percent for men. The highest percentage, at 73 percent, is seen in men 15 to 19 years old, whereas the lowest, at 47 percent, is for women over 65 years old. Twenty-two percent of the sample indicated that they exercised less than once a week or never. With regard to specific forms of exercise, data obtained by Statistics Canada in the National Population Health Survey in 1994–95 indicate that when Canadians are asked to list the physical activities they have engaged in during the past three months, walking (61.1 percent) is the most frequently chosen of the 19 activities listed. This is followed by home exercise (25.2 percent), bicycling (25.2 percent), swimming (23 percent), running or jogging (13.6 percent), weight training (11.2 percent), fishing (10.7 percent), and baseball or softball (10.1 percent).

The inclusion of fishing as a physical activity indicates how far the definition can extend. Some of the uniquely Canadian activities on the list are influenced by seasonal restrictions. Winter activities such as skating (8.5 percent), ice hockey (4.8 percent), downhill skiing (4.4 percent), and cross-country skiing (2.9 percent) obtained relatively low scores compared to some other activities. Obviously the point in the year at which Canadians are asked about their physical activity in the previous three months will greatly affect their responses. This same seasonal variation may also result in regional variations in exercise activity. The 1994–95 data indicated that those living in British Columbia were more likely to engage in regular exercise (30 percent) than those in rest of the Canadian provinces, for which the figure was 20 percent or lower. It is interesting to note that in 1997 Canadians indicated they watched television almost 23 hours per week (Statistics Canada, 1999).

A report by King, Boyce, and King (1999) summarizes information obtained on three occasions (1989–90, 1993–94, and 1997–98) comparing the health of Canadian adolescents to that of those in 10 European countries. Over this period, there was a decline in the percentage of Canadian adolescents who exercised two or more times outside school hours. However, this was balanced by an increase in those involved in intensive exercise more than four hours per week. It is suggested that this may be due to a movement toward more structured activities such as team or club activities which, although they may occur less frequently, involve more organization and participation time. Across all three data points, boys were more likely to exercise than girls. Of the 11 countries involved, Canadian youth were ranked at the mid-range with regard to their physical activity level. The increasingly sedentary lifestyle of Canadian adolescents is further reflected by the fact that 20 to 30 percent of those surveyed indicated that they watched television four or more hours per day. It was also noted that there were marked increases in playing computer games over this time period. This was particularly the case for boys.

THE FIVE FORMS OF PHYSICAL ACTIVITY

It is obvious that there are many different types of exercise and physical activity; however, physiologically there are five forms of exercise. Three of them—*isometric, isotonic,* and *isokinetic*—are based on the principle of resistance, which involves placing demands on, or overloading, the muscles to affect both muscle strength and endurance. **Isometric** exercise involves contraction of a muscle group against an immovable object without movement in the body. This may seem counterintuitive, as there is no noticeable body movement; however, the contraction of the muscles improves muscle strength, although it does little for endurance. **Isotonic** exercise is the form of exercise most of us associate with weightlifting or "bodybuilding." This involves using weights or calisthenics to place tension on the muscle by shortening or lengthening the muscle group. Most of the exertion occurs in one direction. Over time it can be expected that such a program will improve both muscle strength and endurance. **Isokinetic** exercise is the most efficient method of developing muscle strength and endurance as it involves placing tension on a muscle group through a complete range of motion. The difficulty is that training in this area requires specialized, often expensive equipment designed to vary the load placed on the muscle group according to muscle strength and position.

The two other forms of exercise are *aerobic* and *anaerobic*. Given that the word *aerobic* means "with oxygen," these can be defined in terms of the relationship between exercise and oxygen use. In **anaerobic exercise**, intense effort is expended over a short period of time. The oxygen taken in is less than the oxygen required, so that a deficit needs to be made up. A sprint to first base in a softball game, an all-out effort to catch a thrown football, or even an attempt to demonstrate how fast we can still run the 100-yard dash can leave us "gasping for air." Conversely, **aerobic exercise** involves an increased consumption of oxygen over an extended period of time. The oxygen being taken in is sufficient to replace that being used. Therefore, although the exercise may be strenuous it does not result in an oxygen deficit. It is the sustained nature of aerobic exercise that produces the health benefits associated with it, as the intensity and duration of the exercise stimulates the cardiovascular, pulmonary, and muscular systems, improving the efficiency with which the body uses oxygen. Common forms of aerobic exercise include jogging, swimming, cycling, cross-country skiing, paced walking, and activities done in a fitness facility— "aerobics" classes or working out on equipment like an exercise bike, a treadmill, a rowing machine, or a stair-master. Sports associated with high levels of aerobic fitness include soccer, ice hockey, basketball, marathon running, and triathlons.

PSYCHOLOGICAL BENEFITS OF PHYSICAL ACTIVITY

The psychological and physical benefits of physical activity have been widely documented in both the empirical and lay literature. At this point in our examination of these phenomena, it seems appropriate that we look at some of the claims that have been made in support of involvement in these activities. Central to this discussion is the integration of mind and body. As Mahoney (1996) points out in a text on exercise and sport psychology, "The body is back and so is the mind. They are not separate realms. They never were" (p. xv). He suggests that psychology is in the midst of a "phase transition," in which new paradigms are being established that recognize the complexity of the mind–body integration. He states, "One of the areas where such integrations and elaborations are particularly evident is that of exercise and sport psychology" (p. xv). Individuals who exercise frequently often make statements that indicate they believe their commitment to such activities has an impact on their psychological well being. We hear positive comments such as, "I exercise because it helps me cope with the stress of my work"; "When I run I leave the world behind and go into the zone"; or "Exercise makes me feel good about myself." On the downside, comments such as, "If I don't get my workout in, I get depressed"; or "I need to exercise every day" are not uncommon. Pargman (1998) also suggests that "People feel better about themselves when they believe they look better" (p. 116).

Although anecdotal evidence of the psychological benefits of exercise exists, concerns have been raised about methodological issues in the empirical evaluation of this relationship (Landers & Arent, 2001; Kircaldy & Shephard, 1990; Morgan, 1997; Pargman, 1989). One issue concerns the choice of experimental and control groups. The initial health status of the experimental group (i.e., whether they are depressed, anxious, or recovering from a physical illness) will affect the impact of an exercise program and therefore the degree to which the results can be generalized. How an exercise program affects one mentally would be expected to be somewhat dependent on an individual's psychological starting point. A control group that is excluded from participation in an exercise program may not provide the appropriate comparison for a group that is assigned to an exercise condition and receives ongoing support to continue participation. Adherence to exercise programs has already been mentioned as a problem and may result in difficulties in evaluating those who remain in compared to those who drop out of an exercise program. Among those who continue with an exercise program will be individuals like Peter who are committed to a lifestyle change that is independent of a particular form of exercise.

Evaluation of change may be difficult using standard clinical measures, particularly those originally designed to assess psychopathology rather than the more subtle changes one might expect through becoming involved in an exercise program. In this regard, the work of Ostrow (1996), who has developed an extensive directory of psychological tests appropriate to the sport and exercise field, is important.

Physical Activity and Sense of Self

Despite concerns such as these, there is an increasing body of evidence to support a correlation between involvement in physical activity and improvements in psychological health. For example, it has been postulated that participation in physical activity improves one's *self-concept*. In 1981, Folkins and Syme reviewed the existing research regarding physical fitness training and improvements on psychological variables related to perceptions of the self. They concluded that only about 15 percent of the studies reviewed were of an acceptable standard; however, those that were indicated that physical fitness training results in improved mood, work behaviour, and self-concept. They stated that the "personality research with the highest payoff has been that which focuses on self-concept" (p. 380). What may be most important is the *perception* of change, which may occur quite independently of changes in physical fitness.

Reviewing the literature on self-esteem and exercise 16 years later, Sonstroem (1997) came to essentially the same conclusion. More recently, Fox (2000) reviewed 36 studies published since 1972 and concluded that 78 percent of these indicated positive changes in physical self-esteem or self-concept in response to physical activity; although it is not clear what it is that makes people feel better about themselves. However, as Brannon and Feist (2000) have summarized, "It may not be necessary to know the exact variables responsible for improved self-esteem as long as increased feelings of self-worth and self-confidence are associated with an exercise program" (p. 491). Exercise may indirectly influence one's self-esteem. Brannon and Feist conclude that "participation in an exercise program is strongly associated with feeling good about oneself" (p. 491). Numerous tests have been constructed to measure concepts related to perceptions of the self. Many of those who work in the exercise and sport field believe that not only does a relationship exist between involvement in these activities and the participant's psychological state, but that it can be objectively measured in a manner that demonstrates acceptable levels of validity and reliability. Some examples are provided here to give a sense of the different ways in which this relationship is viewed.

The Exercise Identity Scale (Anderson & Cychosz, 1994) was designed to "assess the extent to which exercise is descriptive of one's concept of self" (Ostrow, 1996, p. 245). *The Physical Self-Description Questionnaire* (Marsh et al., 1994) assesses an individual's sense of physical self-concept. *The Self-Acceptance Scale for Athletes* (Waite, Gansneder, & Rotella, 1990) is designed to be a sport-specific measure of individual differences in the perception of self-acceptance, defined as "valuing and feeling good about oneself regardless of one's shortcomings or failures as an athlete" (p. 266). *The Physical Estimation and Attraction Scales* (Sonestroem, 1978) proposes to assess "(a) self-perception of physical fitness and athletic ability, hypothesized to be a component of global self-esteem (estimation) and (b) interest in vigorous physical activity (attraction)" (Ostrow, 1996, p. 255). Finally, the *Elite Athlete Self Description Questionnaire* (Marsh, Hey, Johnson & Perry, 1997) was constructed to assess components of self-concept in elite athletes. The model proposes that self-concept in an elite athlete is made up of six components—skill level, body suitability, aerobic competence, anaerobic competence, mental competence, and performance.

One of the most widely cited psychological variables thought to affect performance in the realm of physical activity is **self-efficacy**, a construct that has been carefully articulated in the work of Bandura (1977, 1986, 1990, 1998). He defines perceived self-efficacy as "people's judgement of their capabilities to organize and execute courses of action required to attain designated types of performances. It is concerned not with the skills one has but with judgements of what one can do with whatever skills one possesses" (Bandura, 1986, p. 391). It is important to distinguish self-efficacy, a situation-specific belief that reflects an individual's perception of his or her ability to succeed at a particular task at a specific time, from self-confidence, which reflects a global trait associated with overall performance expectations. As Bandura (1990) points out, "confidence" as a colloquial term is an idea that permeates physical activity; however, it does not indicate direction. An individual can be quite confident that they will be unsuccessful, whereas self-efficacy involves the affirmation of performance capabilities. The implication of the theory is that, provided an individual has the required skills and the appropriate incentives are in place, self-efficacy will predict actual performance. Performers in all fields are frequently told that all they need is a "little more confidence" in their ability and they will realize their goals. So persuasive is this belief in the importance of confidence that it is often held out as the deciding factor in determining the outcome of one's actions. Individuals who have highly developed technical and physical skills often fall short of their goals simply because they are unable to use these skills in the relevant context, whereas those with limited technical and physical abilities often achieve well beyond their, and others', expectations because they believe in themselves.

Every one of us can relate to those times when we thought we were well prepared for an event only to find our performance deteriorating due to what we often describe as a "loss of confidence." As Jackson and Csikszentmihalyi (1999) have observed in discussing the challenge–skills (CS) balance, "It is not the objective skills that become critical in the CS balance, but rather how one perceives one's skills in relation to the relevant challenges. It is important to realize that what you *believe* you can do will determine your actual experience more than your actual abilities" (p. 17).

There is almost a mystical quality attributed to experiencing the upper reaches of performance achievements, or what Bandura (1989) has described as "transcendent accomplishments". Bruce Jenner, the decathlon champion at the 1976 Olympic games held in Montreal, described the transformation he underwent during the competition: "A strange feeling began to come over me...I started to feel that there was nothing I couldn't do if I had to. It was a feeling of awesome power, except that I was in awe of myself, knocking off these p.r.'s (personal records) just like that. I was rising above myself, doing things I had no right to be doing" (Jenner, 1976, p. 77).

This sense of transcendence is often expressed in terms of overcoming physical barriers that had seemed insurmountable. The most famous of these is the four-minute mile. Considered a physical impossibility, it became commonplace following the remarkable performances by Roger Bannister and John Landy at the Commonwealth Games in Vancouver in 1954 when they became the first individuals to run the mile in under four minutes in competition. It is reported that, prior to 1954, over 50 medical journals contained articles indicating that it would not be possible for a human to run a mile in under four minutes. The next year, four more runners broke the four-minute barrier. Obviously, the athletes who followed so quickly in breaking the same barrier did not change physically or technically in this short time frame. What was now different was their belief that it could be done. What had been overcome was a mental limitation, not a physical one. Bannister, in describing the experience of breaking the four-minute mile states, "The moment of a lifetime had come. There was no pain, only a great unity of movement and aim. The world seemed to stand still, or did not exist. The only reality was the next two hundred yards of track under my feet. The tape meant finality—perhaps extinction" (Bannister, 1955, p. 213–14). Bannister has predicted that humans will run the mile in 3.5 minutes. The current world record for the mile is 3 minutes and 43.13 seconds, held by Hicham El Guerrouj who set the record in 1999.

What is being described here is not self-confidence in the true sense, as this is a global trait that reflects on expectations of overall performance. What is being described is the situation-specific set of beliefs identified in Bandura's theory of self-efficacy. Successful performers are well aware of this difference. They honestly acknowledge that the skills they have developed in a particular activity do not generalize to other activities in any significant way. Despite this recognition of the specificity of their skills, they still identify themselves as having "confidence" rather than "self-efficacy" because this is the language they know. To say that an individual "oozed self-confidence" is clearly more meaningful than saying he "oozed self-efficacy."

Researchers in the area (e.g., Bandura, 1998; Feltz, 1988; Hardy, Jones, & Gould, 1996) have described the exercise and sport field as an excellent arena in which to study self-efficacy. It provides a microcosm of relevance and immediacy in which to examine the phenomena. Bandura (1990; 1998) speaks specifically to the role of self-efficacy in the context of athletic performance. He points out that athletes develop their skills to a high level of expertise and are often asked to execute these skills under situations of extreme stress against individuals who are also highly skilled. Skills performed with remarkable ease in practice often become fragile under the pressure of competition due to self-doubt. Minimal differences in skill execution will be reflected in significant differences in outcome. Successful athletes believe in their ability to focus on the task, ignore distractions, deal with mistakes and failures, cope with fatigue and pain, and ultimately to perform to the best of their ability in the circumstances in which they find themselves. They have succeeded in what Bandura (1990) has termed the "development of resilient self-efficacy."

Bandura (1998) has identified four sources of efficacy expectations: *performance accomplishments, vicarious experience, verbal persuasion,* and *emotional arousal.* **Performance accomplishments** or enactive attainments are the most influential source of self-efficacy, as they are based on actual experiences of mastery. Success increases self-efficacy and failure decreases it, although factors such as the perceived difficulty of the task, the effort expended, adverse external circumstances, and the temporal sequencing of events affect the strength of the relationship. For example, although early failure experiences may decrease self-efficacy, initial setbacks, if eventually mastered as the result of commitment and effort, can strengthen one's belief that even the most difficult of obstacles can be mastered. Improved self-efficacy will incorporate occasional failures with ease and will generalize to other situations, although the degree of similarity to the original task will determine the extent of the generalization process.

Vicarious experience, which is gained through observing or visualizing others perform a skill, can alert one to one's own capabilities and raise the observer's sense of self-efficacy. How many times have we said to ourselves, "If they can do it, so can I." We follow the ski instructor down the hill, observing every move, or we watch the tennis instructor's serve and then try to duplicate it. These models increase our sense of our own capabilities and teach us better ways to do things. Observing an individual whom we feel competent fail in a task may serve to decrease our own sense of capability. Although important in determining self-efficacy expectations, vicarious experiences are weaker than actual performance experiences. They may, however, confirm a sense of inability or, conversely, cause one to persist despite performance failures, to ultimately achieve success. We can all identify those moments when we persisted at a task despite repeated failure simply because we observed success in someone else and believed that eventually we would be able to do it. Our sense of determination is derived from our belief that, like the model, we will ultimately be successful.

Verbal persuasion refers to the commonly used strategy of attempting to persuade others or ourselves that the capability exists to achieve a desired outcome. Although considered a weaker strategy than performance accomplishments and vicarious experience, verbal persuasion can result in sustained and increased effort. However, the utility of this strategy is predicated on a sense of realism. To promote an unrealistic sense of competence in an individual who does not possess the necessary skills will likely result in a perform-ance failure that serves to decrease self-efficacy and faith in verbal persuasion. Those involved in teaching others have to be cautious as to how they use persuasion to improve performance. If it serves to remove self-doubts and allows existing skills to emerge, then it has served its purpose. However, if the results of an individual's actions serve to discon-firm your persuasive abilities, your credibility will be undermined.

The least powerful source of efficacy expectations is **emotional arousal** or physiolog-ical state. Individuals evaluate their capabilities, to a certain extent, according to their assessment of their physiological state. For example, high levels of arousal may be per-ceived as debilitating and predictive of failure and therefore result in a decrease in self-efficacy. The optimal level of arousal to perform a particular task will depend not only on the nature of the task but on the causal inferences made about the arousal itself. Arousal may be interpreted positively or negatively according to the attributions we make about our physiological state. Strategies such as relaxation techniques will allow an individual to modify arousal levels in the desired direction. The high level of arousal we experience prior to engaging in a particular task might be interpreted either with anxiety and fore-boding or with excitement and anticipation, depending on the attributions we make about our physiological state.

There is a substantial research literature supporting the framework provided by self-efficacy theory in relation to performance in both exercise and sport. Research that demonstrates improved self-efficacy as a function of participation in exercise includes that of Bozoian, Rejeski, & McAuley (1994); Michalko, McAuley, & Bane (1996); McAuley & Corneya (1992); McAuley, Schaffer, & Rudolph (1995); and Rudolph & Butki (1998). In the sport domain, self-efficacy has been demonstrated to be an important discriminating fac-tor in research by Feltz & Lirgg (2001); George (1994); Mahoney, Gabriel, & Perkins (1987); and Weiss, Wiese, & Klint (1989).

Examples of tests that are specifically related to the measurement of self-efficacy include the *Exercise-Specific Self-Efficacy Scale* (McAuley, 1991), designed to "examine individuals' perceived capabilities to exercise in the face of barriers to participation" (Ostrow, 1996, p. 246). The *Physical Fitness Self-Efficacy Scale* (Bezjak & Lee, 1990) assesses "participants' perceived competence and confidence in performing tasks involv-ing components of health-related physical fitness" (p. 501).

Physical Activity and Cognitive Functioning

Physical activity and exercise have also been examined in terms of their impact on infor-mation processing and cognitive functioning (Biddle & Mutrie, 2001; Etnier et al., 1997; Landers & Arent, 2001; Pargman, 1998; Tomporowski & Ellis, 1986). Does involvement in exercise have the facilitative effect on mental abilities that those who engage in exercise and sport frequently report? Does the ability to remember or discriminate improve? Based on their initial review of the existing literature, Tomporowski & Ellis (1986) concluded that the results to that point were inconsistent, mainly due to a lack of a coherent methodology for examining the issue. They suggested that exercise, due to its effect on the central nervous system, will initially improve attentional processes; however, as the intensity or duration of the exercise increases, this will be negated by the effects of increasing muscular fatigue. The implications for the assessment process are obvious. They concluded that "the dominant state determines the ability of subjects to perform tests of cognition. Thus, it may be possible for exercise to either facilitate or impair performance on the same cognitive test depending on the level of physical fitness of the subject and the point at which the subject is tested" (p. 344).

The recent meta-analysis by Etnier and colleagues (1997) further explores this relationship. They reviewed 134 relevant studies and concluded that exercise and fitness have a small yet positive impact on cognitive functioning. However, they also suggest that this may be true for chronic, but not for acute, exercise. The indication is that exercise administered in an acute manner will have little impact on cognition, whereas chronic exercise that produces gains in fitness will improve cognition. This conclusion "would support the physiological mechanisms as explanations for the beneficial effects of exercise or fitness upon cognition" and "would suggest that the adoption of a chronic exercise program may be a useful intervention for enhancing cognitive functioning" (p. 267).

This improvement in cognitive functioning through exercise is further supported in a recent review by Dubbert (2002). She also draws attention to the recent work of Kramer *et al* (1999) which describes improvements in cognitive functioning in the elderly associated with regular aerobic exercise. With Canada's aging population, the positive effects of exercise in this area may have particular significance.

Physical Activity and Mood

An extensive body of literature has looked at the impact of exercise and physical activity on mood states, with the primary focus being on anxiety and depression. This research does have some methodological problems, such as the use of anecdotal versus empirical evidence, the assessment of mood state, the actual effect-size found, the representativeness of the data, and the mechanisms used to explain the findings. Despite these concerns, there is evidence that exercise is effective in reducing anxiety in some people (Hackfort & Spielberger, 1989; Landers & Petruzzello, 1994; Landers & Arendt, 2001; McAuley, Mihalko, & Bane, 1996; Raglin & Morgan, 1987; Salmon, 2000). This effect applies in particular to state, as compared to trait, anxiety. The mechanism by which physical activity produces an anxiolytic effect is not clear. Morgan, who has been concerned with the effect of exercise on mood states for many years, has suggested that exercise provides a distraction or "time out" from the pressures and anxieties of daily living (Bahrke & Morgan, 1978). For many of us, this model will have considerable intuitive appeal. Our exercise time is a period of the day when we can leave the world behind. We are removed from our obligations or are at least less aware of them, are often inaccessible to others, and are completely focused on the task before us.

Exercise can serve as an effective distraction; however, many activities can fulfill this function if this is all that is required. Is there a moderating effect that is unique to exercise? Tate and Petruzzello (1995) have demonstrated a differential pattern of anxiety responses for those engaged in exercise compared to those in a resting control condition. Research by McAuley, Mihalko, & Bane (1996) indicates that anxiety levels increase during exercise and then decrease significantly following exercise. These authors are concerned that anxiety and arousal are confounded in the measurement of state anxiety. Research by Rejeski, Hardy, & Shaw (1991) indicates that anxiety decreases in a linear fashion during exercise, whereas arousal increases during exercise and decreases noticeably following exercise. This seems a reasonable position and helps explain what appear to be confusing results. Biddle and Mutrie (2001) summarize the research by concluding that exercise results in small to moderate reductions in anxiety; that the effect is there for both acute and chronic exercise, and both state and trait anxiety; that anxiety is reduced both during and following exercise; and that individuals who are high in aerobic fitness display a reduced physiological response to psychosocial stressors. It should be noted that in the directory of tests for exercise and sport there are 31 tests described to assess anxiety in a wide variety of exercise and sport situations.

The impact of exercise on depression has been the subject of research for a considerable length of time. As in research discussed previously, methodological problems limit the conclusions that can be drawn. However, there is evidence that physical activity can decrease *non-clinical* depression (e.g., Biddle & Murtrie, 2001; Jasnowski, Holmes, & Banks, 1988; Stein & Motta, 1992). With regard to clinically depressed individuals, initial research by Griest and his colleagues examined the effect of running as a treatment and reported decreased levels of depression in those involved in a running program, suggesting that exercise is an effective treatment (1984). Reviews by Martinson (1990, 1993, 1994), Martinson & Morgan (1997) and North, McCullagh, & Tran (1990) conclude that both aerobic and anaerobic exercise are effective treatments for depression; that exercise has *not* been shown to be effective with severe depression; that fitness levels are lower for clinically depressed individuals; and that there is no evidence that exercise can prevent relapse. Biddle and Mutrie (2001) provide an excellent summary of research in this area, again making the distinction between non-clinical and clinical depression. With regard to non-clinical depression, the conclusion is that there is an antidepressant effect associated with exercise that results in moderate decreases in depression, that this effect is present for both acute and chronic exercise and for groups different in age and gender, and that lower levels of depression are related to a physically active lifestyle. With clinical depression the results are more equivocal; however, the conclusion is that the benefits are much greater than the risks, the physical health benefits are important and ultimately that "physical activity and exercise should be advocated as part of the treatment for clinically defined depression" (p. 219).

Another area in which the psychological impact of exercise and physical activity has been evaluated is in regard to stress, where it has been indicated that physical activity may buffer the effects of stress (this topic was considered in more detail in chapter 2, on stress and coping). In their recent review of the impact of physical activity on mental health, Landers and Arendt (2001) conclude that "exercise is related to, but does not cause, desirable changes to occur in anxiety, depression, stress reactivity, positive mood, self-esteem, and cognitive functioning. The overall magnitude of the effect on these variables ranges from small to moderate, but in all cases, these effects are statistically significant" (p. 759).

PHYSICAL BENEFITS OF PHYSICAL ACTIVITY

The physical benefits of physical activity can be expressed in different ways. For some, they may be manifested in a high level of fitness and the physical appearance that goes with it. For others, it may mean the absence of disease and the promotion of health and longevity. For still others, it may simply be the expression of an optimistic, positive lifestyle. Kavussanu and McAuley (1996) found that highly active individuals are significantly more optimistic and less pessimistic than inactive individuals. Numerous studies, some of which have been enormous undertakings, have demonstrated the positive benefits of exercise. For example, the longitudinal research of Blair and colleagues (1989) examined the role of physical fitness on mortality rates in over 10 000 men and 3000 women over an average of eight years. Exercise appeared to reduce the risk of mortality from all causes, particularly cardiovascular disease and cancer. Some of the benefits attributed to physical activity include improved cardiovascular functioning and a reduced risk of cardiovascular disease; improved muscle strength and endurance; increased cardiorespiratory fitness; improved flexibility; improved weight control and fat metabolism; improved sleep; prevention of bone density loss; a reduction in poor health habits such as cigarette smoking and alcohol consumption; reduced risk of injury; and increased energy. If involvement in exercise and sport can decrease mortality and increase longevity, they assume a most important status in our culture.

We will now focus our attention on the important role of physical activity in the prevention of cardiovascular disease. Since the 1950s, considerable evidence has accumulated to demonstrate that those who are physically active are less likely to develop and die from coronary heart disease (CHD). Miller, Balady, & Fletcher (1997) have stated that "a sedentary lifestyle carries approximately the same risk for the development of coronary artery disease as the more traditional risk factors of cigarette smoking, hypertension, and hypercholesterolemia" (p. 220). Early research examined the presence of CHD in individuals according to their occupation and the level of physical activity required in their work (Kahn, 1963). Individuals whose work involved a high level of physical activity appeared to be at a decreased risk for CHD (Brand, Paffenbarger, Scholtz, & Kampert, 1979). The next level of evaluation involved the comparison of physically active and inactive individuals according to measures of energy expenditure. The most influential of these evaluative studies is the Harvard Alumni Study carried out by Paffenbarger and his colleagues. They assessed men who had graduated from Harvard University over a 50-year period according to their weekly expenditure of energy and divided them into two groups, high and low activity. They reported that men who were physically active had a 25 percent lower mortality rate from any cause and were 36 percent less likely to die from CHD (Paffenbarger, Wing, & Hyde, 1978). The Framingham Heart Study evaluated CHD in both men and women and found that when the very active were compared to the very inactive groups with regard to CHD, the risk for the latter group was approximately three times greater (Dawber, 1980). Also, exercise rehabilitation has been found to significantly decrease mortality in survivors of myocardial infarction (Haskell et al., 1994). Miller, Balady, & Fletcher (1997), after an extensive review of the literature, provide a series of summary statements that suggest a very positive role for exercise in the prevention and rehabilitation of cardiovascular disease. Biddle and Murtrie (2001) more recently conclude their research review by stating "that both physical fitness (at least cardiovascular fitness) and habitual physical activity are both inversely related to CHD risk in adults" (p.16).

It should be noted that the possible protective role played by physical activity with regard to illnesses such as stroke and cancer is still emerging. For example, with stroke, there is evidence that physical activity provides protection, particularly for those who are middle-aged and older (Abbot, Rodriguez, Burchfiel, & Curb, 1994). The impact of physical activity in protecting against cancer appears positive, particularly for men. For example, Lee, Paffenberger, & Hsieh (1992) reported that participants in the Harvard Alumni Study who were physically active were much less likely to develop prostate cancer than those who were inactive. An international forum on physical activity and health held in Quebec in 1995 (*Research Quarterly for Exercise and Sport, 1995*) resulted in statements of consensus including the following: whereas a sedentary lifestyle increases the risk of atherosclerosis, hypertension and diabetes, regular exercise decreases it; physical activity benefits the musculo-skeletal system, and decreases in functional capacity with age are due, in part, to insufficient physical activity; the risk of colon cancer and perhaps breast cancer is decreased through physical activity; and physical activity for all ages is a very effective strategy for improving health. Despite these statements, Biddle & Murtrie (2001) conclude that the relationship between the benefits derived from physical activity and disease prevention and health promotion is still not well understood.

ADHERENCE TO PHYSICAL ACTIVITY

Despite the many psychological and physical benefits attributed to physical activity, a disturbingly small percent of individuals exercise on a regular basis. For those who do exercise, a significant issue is **non-adherence**, an inability to stay with an exercise program. The most frequently cited statistic in this regard is based on the initial work of Dishman (1988), and more recently that of Estabrooks (2000), which indicates that approximately 50 percent of those involved in a physical activity program drop out within the first six months. This may seem counterintuitive, as we think of ourselves as being in the midst of an exercise and sports boom. Fitness centres are everywhere, fitness equipment is easily available, and sports participation seems to be increasing, particularly through the recreational and master's sports movements.

Taylor (1994) believes that the avoidance of exercise and sport is not difficult to understand, as exercise can be initially somewhat aversive and offers few immediate rewards. The environment can be unappealing, the activities monotonous, progress is often slow, a lack of expertise may be obvious, and social comparison with experienced exercisers can be unpleasant. The first experience in an aerobics course or an exercise room can be most threatening. With regard to sports involvement, a lack of skills development and knowledge of rules combined with an often highly competitive environment can be a threat to self-esteem.

To a large extent, the positive benefits of exercise and sport emerge with time and will ultimately outweigh the initial impediments. Zifferblatt (1975) suggested some time ago that the likelihood of compliance is directly related to the visibility of the cues or reasons as to why the individual should comply. When the reasons are vague or ambiguous the likelihood of compliance is low, whereas if they are specific, relevant, or salient the likelihood of compliance is high. The implication is that initial experiences in exercise and sport often do not provide enough reasons as to why one should continue. They may become obvious, but it will take time.

To better understand the factors affecting adherence to physical activity, numerous theoretical models have been used. Many of these were introduced in chapter 1 and include the health belief model (Becker & Maiman, 1975); the theory of reasoned action (Ajzen &

Fishbein, 1980); the theory of planned behaviour (Ajzen, 1985); self-efficacy theory (Bandura (1977); the transtheoretical model (Prochaska & DiClemente, 1983); and the relapse prevention model (Marlatt & Gordon, 1980). These models were developed in the context of other behaviours and it is still not clear how relevant they are to physical activity. Important predictors of adherence include physical proximity to the exercise area, availability of time, spousal support, group size and constitution, socioeconomic status, choice of exercise, and injury (LeUnes and Nation, 2002). It seems that the issue of salience is most important here. We need to know what rewards await us as a consequence of our sustained commitment to physical activity.

Kirschenbaum (1998) has proposed that involvement in sport and the models that sport psychology has developed provide a strategy for increasing adherence to physical activity. This idea may be important given the indications that health psychologists have achieved only modest success in this regard (Dishman and Buckworth, 1997). He uses a self-regulatory model to identify seven steps designed to improve athletic performance. He believes that this model is similar to that used by health psychologists to increase adherence, and that sport can be used as a target for exercise adherence. By focusing on the commitment many individuals have to sport, psychologists can design strategies to increase adherence to exercise. The energy expended in sport can be considerable, and the modification of existing patterns could result in even greater expenditures. Kirschenbaum suggests that "not only could we target extant interest in sport as a goal in health psychology, but we could use sport psychology interventions to maximize involvement in such sports. These interventions could help participants enjoy their sports more fully, thereby sustaining their involvement in them" (p. 17). The extraordinary commitment that many individuals display to their sport can be used to indirectly increase their levels of physical activity and produce physical and psychological health benefits.

PSYCHOLOGICAL FACTORS AFFECTING PERFORMANCE IN EXERCISE AND SPORT

We will now examine in more detail some of the developments in the sport psychology field that have implications for health psychology in general, and the choices individuals make regarding their health behaviour, in particular. There are two principal areas of concern in sport psychology. One is performance enhancement as it relates to the development of psychological skills that can be used to optimize athletic performance. The second has to do with clinical issues, such as injury, depression, or eating disorders; any of which may compromise an athlete's performance.

We will focus initially on psychological skills as they can be applied to sport and life. This is important, for it recognizes that these are not only sport skills, they are life skills, and their utility extends beyond the domain of sport. This position is often recognized anecdotally by coaches who are aware of their impact on others, particularly young athletes, and view themselves as teachers of life skills. Danish, Pettipas, and Hale (1993) have developed a psychoeducational model for sport psychology that focuses specifically on the teaching of life skills, which they describe as "life development intervention." They suggest that sport is an effective and accessible analogy for the teaching of life skills. It is obvious that most young athletes will not go on to a career in sports; for these people, "growing up means further defining their identity, discovering other skills and interests, and, it is hoped, applying some of the valuable principles learned during sport participation to their adult pursuits. These transferable behaviours and attitudes are called *life skills"* (Danish, Nellen, & Owens, 1996). An area of specific concern in this life-skills program is helping young people make appropriate decisions with regard to health-enhancing, as opposed to health-compromising, behaviours. Smith (1999) has addressed the assumption that sports skills will generalize beyond the athletic environment.

In describing psychological skills training in sport, a distinction is sometimes made between **psychological skills** and **psychological methods** (Vealey, 1988). Concerns such as arousal or attentional control relate to psychological skills, and issues such as relaxation, goal setting, or imagery are psychological methods; the latter serve to develop the former. Others have suggested that the distinction should be made between "basic psychological skills," which can be used on their own and "advanced psychological skills," of which the basic skills can be a component (Hardy, Jones, & Gould, 1997). In this discussion, we will focus on the basic skills, as they can be used in a psychological skills training program that can be applied both within and outside the sport and exercise domain. A recent edition of the *Journal of Applied Sport Psychology* concerned with the topic of excellence investigates the relationship between sport and business (Jones, 2002; Weinberg & McDermott, 2002), sport and the performing arts (Hays, 2002; Poczwarsdowski & Conroy, 2002), sport and acting (Martin & Cutler, 2002) and sport and police work (Le Scanff & Taugis, 2002). These skills have application in models of stress management that have been adapted for sport. Examples would be Kirschenbaum's (1997) self-regulatory model, Meichenbaum's (1975) stress-inoculation training, Smith's (1980) cognitive-affective stress management training, and Suinn's (1972) visuomotor behaviour-rehearsal program. However, it has been suggested that rather than using specific programs such as these, the component skills of a psychological training program should be taught and used according to individual needs (Hardy, Jones, & Gould 1997).

Relaxation

The ability to relax is an essential skill in coping with the pressure of athletic performance (Cox, 2002). Most individuals will acknowledge some degree of performance anxiety in anticipation of the demands of a task. **Relaxation skills** enhance one's ability to reduce anxiety to manageable levels, so that energy can be used to positively influence performance. Many of us experience "butterflies" prior to a performance, which is not a problem if we can teach them to "fly in formation." Relaxation skills assist in this process. It is also recognized that an effective performance, which is effortless and automatic, is more likely to occur in a relaxed state (Taylor, 1996; Kirschenbaum, 1997). Many successful athletes have developed relaxation skills on their own through a process of trial and error. However, there may be limitations to their ability to relax under pressure. Relaxation is viewed as a learned skill that needs to be applicable to the performance circumstances. For example, watching television or reading a book is relaxing; however, these activities, which are external to the individual, are not applicable to a performance situation. In this context we are describing an internal response usually described in either physical or mental terms.

The most widely practised form of relaxation in sport is the technique of progressive muscular relaxation (PMR) pioneered by Jacobson (1938) (see chapter 2, p. 58). It involves focusing attention on different muscle groups within the body (e.g., the biceps, shoulders, or stomach) and progressing systematically through the entire body. Initially in the training of PMR, the individual is encouraged to tense the muscle briefly before relaxing it on command. Jacobson felt that this was necessary to allow one to learn the distinction between tension and relaxation. With training, the tensing is eliminated and muscle groups are combined so that what previously took 30 minutes to accomplish can be achieved in a period as short as 30 seconds. The individual has learned what Benson (1976) has termed the "relaxation response." It is important that as familiarity with the technique increases, the ability to relax is generalized to the relevant performance domain. It seems that PMR is most effective in coping with the somatic or physiological components of anxiety, whereas strategies such as mental rehearsal and the management of self-talk may be more appropriate to coping with cognitive anxiety. It is also recognized that proper breathing is an effective strategy for increasing levels of relaxation and successfully coping with anxiety. The deep, rhythmical breathing associated with relaxation can quickly replace the shallow, staccato breathing associated with tension and anxiety. Training in breath control can be most helpful in inducing and maintaining states of relaxation (Cox, 2002).

Self-Talk

Self-talk is a term used in sport psychology to describe one of the ways that people think (Cox, 2002). What do athletes say to themselves? It is a frequent observation that athletes talk to themselves a great deal, sometimes very negatively. Monitoring an athlete's self-talk gives us an opportunity to evaluate his or her perceptions and beliefs. We can identify cognitive distortions and irrational ways of thinking that might disrupt performance. It has been reported that patterns of self-talk can distinguish successful from unsuccessful performers (e.g., Orlick & Partington, 1988; Weinberg & Gould, 2003).

Williams and Leffingwell (1996) have identified different functions that self-talk can serve in sport, including correcting bad habits, focusing attention, modifying activation, increasing self-confidence, increasing efficacy, and maintaining exercise behaviour. With regard to correcting bad habits, self-talk can be used to correct faulty technique. To focus attention, an athlete might say "watch the ball" or "execute." In modifying activation, the athlete might want to increase or decrease arousal levels. The self-talk might take the form of "relax" or "let go," as opposed to "push" or "work." Self-confidence may involve changing the tendency to call oneself a "loser" to saying "yes" to oneself.

With regard to exercise behaviour, it has been suggested by Gauvin (1990) that those who maintain exercise have positive and motivating self-talk in comparison to the negative self-talk of non-exercisers. Once inappropriate patterns of self-talk have been identified, the concern is to modify this behaviour in the appropriate direction. This involves a restructuring process that replaces maladaptive cognitions with more adaptive ones.

The ongoing work of the eminent psychologist Albert Ellis (1975) in developing Rational Emotive Behavior Therapy (REBT) is most relevant here. REBT involves the modification of irrational thoughts by identifying patterns of faulty reasoning. In *absolute thinking* events are viewed in all-or-none terms such as "I must always do well." *Overgeneralization* involves drawing global conclusions on the basis of single events; for example, "I am never going to win a match." *Catastrophization* involves viewing minor concerns as disasters, for example, "Losing that match is the end of my career." In REBT, irrational beliefs are actively disputed and individuals learn to substitute more rational ways of thinking. Ellis (1994) gave an invited address to Division 47, Exercise and Sport Psychology, at the 1993 American Psychological Association convention. His presentation was concerned with "The Sport of Avoiding Sports and Exercise." He believes that those who avoid exercise and sport have a low frustration tolerance that may be combined with a fear of failing. He states that "REBT helps them to discover and dispute their grandiose demands and absolutist musts" (p. 258). Ellis describes an intensive REBT program designed to help avoiders transform their inhibitions into healthy choices. In sport psychology, athletes are encouraged to restructure their self-talk and focus their attention on the task or process in a positive manner (e.g., Kirschenbaum, 1997; Rushall, 1984).

Imagery

The role of imagery in sport and exercise has been well documented for some time (Hall, 2001; Weinberg & Gould, 2003). For instance, 99 percent of Canadian athletes who participated in the 1984 Olympic Games indicated that they used imagery techniques to improve their performance (Orlick and Partington, 1988). Some of these athletes indicated that they used imagery techniques for up to three hours in preparation for competition. There is a difference between *imagery* and *mental rehearsal* (Hall, 2001; Jones, Hardy, & Gould, 1997). The former is a sensory experience that is performed in the absence of external stimuli, whereas mental rehearsal is a technique that involves the use of imagery to mentally practise a skill.

A distinction is made between **internal** and **external imagery** (Hall, 2002). In external imagery, the individual is a third-person, passive, external observer of his or her actions. Internal imagery is a much more active experience, in which the individual imagines being inside his or her own body experiencing a situation as close to reality as possible. Several explanations have been given for the mechanisms underlying the relationship between imagery and performance (Gould & Damarjian, 1996; Hall, 2002). The psychoneuromuscular theory suggests that imagery causes the actual motor pattern to be rehearsed and therefore practised. According to symbolic learning, imagery provides the opportunity to symbolically practise an event. As one athlete said, "It felt like *déjà vu*, like I had done it before."

With regard to an imagery training program, Gould and Damarjian (1996) make several recommendations, including the following. "Practice imagery on a regular basis, use all senses to enhance image vividness, use both internal and external perspectives, facilitate imagery through relaxation, use videotapes or audiotapes to enhance imagery skills, develop coping strategies through imagery, emphasize dynamic kinesthetic imagery, imagine in real time, use imagery in practice and competition" (p. 48). Driskell, Copper, and Moran (1994) carried out a meta-analysis of the literature and concluded that mental practice has a "positive and significant effect on performance" (p. 481). They acknowledge, however, that although it is an effective strategy for improving performance, it is less effective than physical practice. They suggest that this makes it most appropriate for difficult or dangerous training situations, for situations in which opportunities for physical practice are minimized, and simply as a strategy for supplementing normal training routines. However, as Hall (2001) has indicated, we are still progressing in our understanding of imagery and how it can be used most effectively.

Goal-Setting

The final psychological skill we will discuss in this section is goal setting, a motivational strategy for improving performance (Barton, Naylor & Holiday, 2001; Duda & Hall, 2001; Weinberg & Gould, 2003). Goal-setting represents one of the most widely researched areas in the field, as considerable research in goal-setting in industrial and organizational fields has been applied to sports. The research on goal setting provided by Locke and his colleagues, beginning with his important paper in 1968, has been highly influential. Several important consistencies have emerged from this work. The indications are that higher levels of performance are achieved through difficult goals, specific goals, and a combination of both short-term and long-term goals (Locke, 1968; Locke and Latham, 1985; Locke and Latham, 1990).

Two different goal perspectives have been identified (Duda, 1992); **ego orientation** and **task orientation**. The former is focused on success and failure, with success often coming at the expense of others. Individuals subscribing to the former like to win. The latter describes individuals who derive their satisfaction from the sense of competence they experience as they improve. Their focus is on effort and their *own* performance rather than that of others. These are not independent positions, and successful performers often make use of both of them (Duda & Hall, 2001).

Three different types of goals have been described in the literature (Hardy, Jones, & Gould, 1996). **Outcome goals** are concerned with the results or outcomes of events and usually involve comparisons to others. These goals might be expressed as a need to finish first in a race, with even finishing second being equated with losing. **Performance goals** describe an outcome that can be achieved independently of others' performance; a novice marathoner may describe a desire to run her next race in less than four hours. **Process goals** focus on specific processes that a performer will be concerned with during a performance. A tennis player may indicate that during a match he plans to manage his self-talk.

Weinberg (1996) provides a number of goal-setting principles based on his review of the relevant literature. They are as follows: "Set specific goals, set realistic but challenging goals, set both long- and short-term goals, set goals for practice and competition, 'ink it, don't think it,' develop goal-achievement strategies, set performance goals, set individual and team goals, provide support for goals, provide for goal evaluation" (p. 11).

This review of psychological skills training has focused on the four basic skills that are fundamental to understanding the more complex skills such as attentional control, emotional control, confidence and self-efficacy, motivation, and coping with stress. A particular skill may have more relevance at a particular time than at another and what works for one individual may not work as well for another. As we discussed earlier, these are not skills unique to exercise and sport; however, in the sport and exercise context, they can be useful in helping us to improve our performance and to enjoy ourselves. All indications are that we are more likely to continue to engage in exercise and sport if we enjoy it.

PHYSICAL ACTIVITY AND INJURY

The final issue we will consider in this chapter is of a more clinical nature—the psychological consequences of injury during physical activity, specifically sport and exercise. Clearly, injury is an event that occurs with an extremely high frequency in this context. Most

| Focus on Canadian Research 8-1 | **Health and Physical Activity** |

Although the history of research in the field of physical activity, exercise, and sport psychology is relatively recent, Canada has played an important role in its development. In a publication by Salmela, (1992) Canada was third only to the United States and Germany in the number of individuals who worked in the area of sport and exercise psychology.

If you are interested in pursuing educational opportunities that exist in Canada in the field of exercise and sport psychology, you might want to look at the web site of the Canadian Society for Psychomotor Learning and Sport Psychology (www.scapps.org) which provides information on the society, membership, conferences, employment opportunities and links to other relevant organizations. This organization was organized in 1969 and formally recognized as a society in 1977. The recently published *Handbook of Sport Psychology* (Singer, Hasenblas, & Janelle, 2001) contains eight chapters contributed by Canadian researchers.

One example is an excellent chapter by Vallerand and Rousseau of the University of Quebec at Montreal. They use a hierarchical model of intrinsic and extrinsic motivation to help better understand motivation in the context of exercise and sport. Another is a review of expert performance in dance and sport in which Starkes and Jack of McMaster University in Hamilton are co-authors with Helson of Belgium. They identify behaviours that differentiate experts from those who are less skilled. Recent issues of major international journals in the field all feature research by Canadians.

In the *Journal of Sport and Exercise Psychology* the work of Dunn, Dunn, and Syrotuik (2002) of the University of Alberta on the relationship between perfectionism and goal orientation is reported. They examine athletes to identify both adaptive and maladaptive perfectionist orientations.

An excellent review article by Botterill and Brown (2002) in the *International Journal of Sport Psychology* suggests that sport is an excellent place in which to study emotion. In athletics, emotions can be both facilitative and debilitative to performance.

The *Journal of Applied Sport Psychology* reports on the research by Bloom, Stevens, and Wickwire (2003), of McGill and Brock Universities, which examines coaches' perceptions of team building and the development of strategies designed to improve cohesion and ultimately performance. This is only a sample of Canadian researchers working in physical activity, exercise, and sport; however, it provides an introduction to the vast literature that exists.

of us will remember an injury we experienced while engaged in sport or exercise and could identify some of the psychological consequences of this event. We are also made very aware through the media of the injuries that regularly sideline our athletic heroes. Sometimes these are acute and sometimes they are chronic. The physical and psychological impact of these injuries is usually minimal; however, at times the impact be very serious, extremely costly, and even career threatening (Weinberg & Gould, 2003; Williams, 2001).

A particular individual's reaction to a sports injury is a complex issue and will depend on numerous factors. These include the nature and severity of the injury, the role and importance of sport in the individual's life, and the response of the individual's support network. For example, athletes often state that the attention they receive from coaches and other support staff decreases dramatically when they are injured. Attention is given to those who can compete rather than those who cannot. An injured individual can also be a vicarious reminder of what can happen to others; and for this reason the uninjured may not want the injured athlete around. The injured are also made painfully aware of what they are missing. One injury that has received considerable attention recently is concussion (see Box 8-1).

| BOX 8-1 | **Concussion** |

Athletes often describe it as "having your bell rung," while to the health professional it is known as a **closed head injury** or **concussion**. With disturbing frequency we read in our newspapers of the athlete whose career has been threatened by a blow to the head. After suffering a concussion during an NBA basketball game, an athlete stated, "The last thing I remember is checking into the game, then the next thing I remember is lying on the table and them asking me if I remember things. A long time elapsed between them. That's the scary part about it...that your mind can be altered like that" (Kingston, 1999).

Concussion is a bruising of the brain, and represents a serious sports injury. It can result in severe neurocognitive deficits, permanent disability, and even death. There is evidence that even mild concussion can result in neuropsychological impairments (Macciocchi et al., 1996). Concussions are commonly described according to two types. An **acceleration-deceleration injury** occurs when an immobile head is hit by a moving object or a moving head hits an immobile object. A **rotational injury** usually results from a blow to the side

of the head. A related concern in concussion is **second-impact syndrome**. This results when an athlete who has suffered a concussion returns to activity too soon and receives another blow to the head, which can result in much greater trauma to the brain than that initially experienced. **Post-concussion syndrome** is a term frequently seen in the press today. This describes a set of symptoms including memory problems, difficulties in concentration, and complaints such as headaches, dizziness, and irritability.

It is important to remember that concussions can be experienced without losing consciousness, and there is no visible physical evidence of concussion. The usual signs and symptoms of concussion include any period of loss of consciousness; confusion and inability to focus attention; disorientation; slurred or incoherent speech; delayed verbal and motor responses; inappropriate emotional behaviour; memory deficits; and lack of coordination. Other signs include complaints such as headaches, dizziness, ringing in the ears, nausea/vomiting, impaired vision, seeing stars, and sensitivity to light.

(continued on next page)

Three grades of concussion have been identified. A **grade-one** concussion does not involve a loss of consciousness, although the individual may display transient confusion and should be taken out of the activity and examined for post-concussive symptoms. Someone with a grade one concussion can return to the activity if any abnormalities or symptoms have cleared within 15 minutes. A **grade-two** concussion also does not involve a loss of consciousness; however, the concussion symptoms persist beyond 15 minutes. The individual should be taken out of the activity and not allowed to return. He or she should be seen the same day by a medical professional and should only return to their sport after one asymptomatic week and neurologic clearance by a physician. A **grade-three** concussion involves any loss of consciousness, brief or prolonged. The athlete may need to be taken to hospital by ambulance if still unconscious or if there are other concerns such as neck pain. A neurologic evaluation is required initially and further assessment will be necessary to determine when the athlete can return to the sport. Multiple concussions of any grade will further complicate the recovery process. The decision to return to activity should always be based on a physician's evaluation.

Concussion represents a serious problem in the sport and exercise field. With increasing public awareness of this problem, we have become more interested in understanding the nature of concussion and, most importantly, to focus on the prevention of brain injury.

When individuals experience a sports injury, a wide range of emotions may be experienced, such as anger, disbelief, frustration, fear, anxiety, guilt, panic, loneliness, and depression. A number of models have been proposed to help us better understand the psychological processes associated with an athletic injury. There are essentially two different kinds of approaches; those that focus on the stages of reaction and those that take a cognitive appraisal position. Stages-of-reaction approaches assume that individuals will pass through a series of stages in a set order. These approaches derive from the model developed by Kübler-Ross (1969) to explain the experience of death and dying. She described five stages an individual who is dying goes through—denial and isolation, anger, bargaining, depression, and acceptance. In this context, the injury is considered to be similar to death and, indeed, many who suffer a debilitating injury view it this way. This model has been adapted to sport by Astle (1986) and Lynch (1988), who provide strategies for assisting those involved in the psychological rehabilitation of the injured person. The cognitive appraisal approach views an injury in the context of a stress and coping model (Brewer, 1994: Williams, 2001). An individual's emotional and behavioural responses to an injury will be determined by their personal appraisal of the event and their choice of coping strategies.

Brewer, Raalte, and Linder (1991) describe what they consider to be the primary responsibilities of a psychologist working with an injured athlete within a sports medicine context. The first involves an initial assessment of the individual's psychological status. The second is to facilitate, where necessary, communication between the physician and the athlete. The third is to provide the athlete with psychological skills to assist in the coping and rehabilitation process. These skills might include several we have discussed previously, such as relaxation training, goal setting, imagery and mental rehearsal, and cognitive restructuring. The fourth responsibility of the psychologist is to facilitate and provide social support for the injured athlete. The psychologist may be involved in actively seeking the assistance of others to develop a support network. The role of the psychologist is being increasingly recognized as a crucial component in the intervention and management of injuries that occur in the context of sport and exercise (Brewer, 2001).

We have come a long way in our discussion of physical activity, exercise, and sport and, as we bring this chapter to a close, we return to our friend Peter. It has been five years since he began his rehabilitation program.

| CASE 8-2 | **Peter's Story: An Update** |

It has now been several years since I outlined my journey from having a heart attack in March of 1995 toward recovery. I provided some statistical evidence of my improvement in terms of my diet, my exercise, and my frame of mind. The goal that I was trying to attain was that of an elevated level of fitness. To this extent, I exceeded my objective, although there were costs involved. I had forgotten about the real goal, which was to attain a healthy level of fitness. Instead I had pushed myself to limits of fitness attained by individuals who are significantly younger than me. My ego beat out the reality of the situation. When you have a significant blow to your health, such as a heart attack, you make room for improvement, or you stay *status quo*. The second alternative never appealed to me so consequently I endeavoured to be the healthiest that I could be. Having a heart attack is generally considered to be a negative situation; however, my family have viewed it as a positive

health situation for me. They have noticed a psychological change in me. I am more friendly and I do not lose my temper as much as I once did. I have always been quite competitive, anxious, and what some might describe as a Type A personality. Since my heart attack my family has noticed that I spend more time with them and focus more on the "what nows" than on the "what ifs." I focus now on what is important—family, health, lifestyle, and friends. This involved developing processes that worked for me. I tried not to focus on what the results would be but rather to let the process take care of itself. The results came; I lost weight, I gained muscular strength, and along with this I improved my psychological outlook on life. Today I am in the best physical condition of my life. I enjoy an excellent family life and I have interesting, positive, and loyal friends. I have maintained the fitness levels I desire and I derive joy from my time with my family and friends. What else is there?

KEY TERMS

acceleration-deceleration injury (p. 218)

active leisure (p. 200)

aerobic exercise (p. 202)

anaerobic exercise (p. 202)

closed head injury (p. 218)

concussion (p. 218)

ego orientation (p. 216)

emotional arousal (p. 207)

exercise psychology (p. 197)

external imagery (p. 215)

grade-one concussion (p. 219)

grade-three concussion (p. 219)

grade-two concussion (p. 219)

internal imagery (p. 215)

isokinetic exercise (p. 202)

isometric exercise (p. 202)

isotonic exercise (p. 202)

non-adherence (p. 211)

outcome goals (p. 216)

passive leisure (p. 200)

performance accomplishments (p. 206)

performance goals (p. 216)

physical activity (p. 197)

physical fitness (p. 197)

post-concussion syndrome (p. 218)

process goals (p. 216)

psychological methods (p. 213)

psychological skills (p. 213)

relaxation skills (p. 213)

rotational injury (p. 218)

second-impact syndrome (p. 218)

self-efficacy (p. 204)

self-talk (p. 214)

sport (p. 198)

sport psychology (p. 197)

task orientation (p. 216)

verbal persuasion (p. 206)

vicarious experience (p. 206)

chapter nine

Health-Compromising Behaviours

CHAPTER OUTLINE

Substance Abuse

   Smoking

   Alcohol Use

   Illicit Drug Use

Unsafe Sexual Behaviours

Obesity

   Biological Factors That Contribute to Obesity

   Psychosocial Factors That Contribute to Obesity

   Sociocultural Factors That Contribute to Obesity

   Prevention and Treatment of Obesity

   Pharmacological Treatment of Obesity

   Behavioural Treatment of Obesity

   Surgical Treatment of Obesity

Eating Disorders

    Biological, Cultural, and Psychological Contributors to Eating Disorders

    Treatment for Eating Disorders

KEY QUESTIONS

1. What factors prompt adolescents to begin smoking?
2. How can we help people addicted to smoking, alcohol, or illicit drugs quit these habits?
3. Why do people engage in unsafe sexual behaviours?
4. What factors contribute to obesity in our society?
5. Why does the incidence of eating disorders differ for men and women?
6. How can the stages of change model be applied to the prevention and treatment of health-compromising behaviours?

Jennifer began to smoke in high school. She was a bright girl who enjoyed the academic side of school but didn't always find the social side of school easy. When she began junior high school, also known as middle school, she noticed a radical shift in how her friends spent their time. Instead of playing sports and watching movies, her friends were now more interested in smoking, partying, and meeting guys. For a time, Jennifer resisted her friends' suggestions that she not be so uptight, that she learn to relax and start socializing at parties. However, Jennifer found that she was spending more and more time by herself and grew lonely. It seemed to her that the easiest way to fit in and regain friendships was to begin smoking. Both of Jennifer's parents smoked, so if she began it wouldn't cause much upset in the family. So she did begin. and continued to smoke even after graduating from high school.

After high school, Jennifer went in search of a job. She wanted to work as a journalist or perhaps behind the scenes at a radio or television station. She was told that the best experience she could gain would be at a small-town radio or television station, where she would be expected to complete all the tasks of producing a story by herself; she'd have to find a story, write the story, take pictures, and deliver the story on air. Jennifer followed this advice. She found a job in a small town working for a local television station. In this new environment, Jennifer was able to give up smoking. Very few of the other people who worked at the television station smoked and, of course, she no longer saw her high school friends, at least not on a regular basis. Jennifer was lucky. Unlike so many people who have a difficult time quitting, Jennifer was able to quit smoking on her own relatively easily.

Many years later, when Jennifer was going through the turmoil of a "messy" divorce, she began to smoke again. It all started when after a lengthy meeting with her lawyer she found herself craving a cigarette. After a couple of days she gave in to this craving and bought a package of cigarettes. She smoked a single cigarette and found that this did alleviate some of her stress—she welcomed the relief. Yet, she knew smoking was unhealthy. She didn't want her children to model her behaviour and didn't want their health endangered as a result of her behaviour, so she never smoked indoors or let her children see her smoke. Fortunately, once the divorce was settled and she had obtained custody of her children, she was again able to kick the habit.

In this chapter, we will focus on specific health-compromising behaviours and the health hazards that are a product of these behaviours. Most of the behaviours we have chosen to focus on are behaviours that are voluntary in nature, at least initially. For example, we will examine the leading cause of premature death in Canada, which is smoking. We will also examine what is referred to as the obesity epidemic. And, in our discussion of disordered eating we will introduce you to a disorder that has only recently been identified, muscle dysmorphia. To begin, we will turn our attention to the most prevalent health-compromising behaviour in our society—smoking.

SUBSTANCE ABUSE

Smoking

Age and Gender Differences in Smoking   There are few habits as potentially deadly as smoking cigarettes. Smoking is the number one preventable cause of death and disease in Canada. In 1996, smoking accounted for approximately 45 000 deaths. It has been estimated that at least one-quarter of all deaths among persons aged 35 to 84 years in Canada are attributable to tobacco use (Ellison, Morrison, de Groh, & Villeneuve, 1999). The Canadian Tobacco Use Monitoring Survey documents that more than 21 percent of Canadians 15 years of age and older smoke (Health Canada, 2003). The good news is that smoking rates have been declining and have decreased four percent since 1997. Traditionally, more males than females have smoked cigarettes. However, more and more females are smoking. In this most recent survey, 24 percent of female teens aged 15 to 19 smoked compared to 20 percent of teen boys. It is also worth mentioning that although more adolescent girls than boys smoke, adolescent boys who do smoke, smoke more than do adolescent girls.

Sociocultural Differences in Smoking   Rates of smoking vary substantially by socioeconomic status (National Population Health Survey, 1996–97). The percentage of people who smoke tends to decline with increases in income as well as in education and job prestige. Those in the lowest income bracket report the highest rates of smoking (40 percent of men and 36 percent of women). Smoking rates decrease with an increase in income, to lows of 16 and 13 percent among men and women, respectively, in the highest income bracket. The highest rates of smoking in Canada occur among Aboriginal people, about double the overall rate in the Canadian population as a whole (Reading, 1997). In 1997, adult smoking rates within the Aboriginal population were highest in the youngest age groups surveyed, those between the ages of 20 and 24 years (72 percent) and 25 to 29 years (71 percent). There is a steady decline in smoking with increasing age—those 75 years of age and older report the lowest rate of smoking, at 23 percent. Prevalence of smoking has also been documented by immigrant status (Chen, Ng, &

Wilkins, 1996). Recent non-European immigrants are significantly less likely than the Canadian-born population to smoke. In fact, for all immigrants, the number who smoke generally increased with the length of time in Canada. This leads us to conclude that there is something about our Canadian culture that promotes smoking. Unlike for the Canadian-born population, there is no clear relationship between smoking and income status for immigrants.

Why Do People Smoke?   Considering that most people are aware that smoking is bad for them, that is, that smoking is linked to a wide variety of negative health consequences, it is puzzling that so many people smoke. This behaviour is even more puzzling when we realize that the first few times people smoke, they likely cough, find the taste unpleasant, and may even experience dizziness and nausea. Why would someone voluntarily engage in this behaviour? Why after their first experience would they want to smoke again?

Beginning to Smoke   Smoking often begins during adolescence, when peer influence is strong. Numerous studies have found that adolescents are more likely to smoke if their friends smoke (Biglan, Duncan, Ary, & Smolkowski, 1995; Conrad, Flay, & Hill, 1992; Stanton, Mahalski, McGee, & Silva, 1993). When adolescents first try smoking, they usually do so in the company of their peers and with their peers' encouragement (Leventhal, Prochaska, & Hirschman, 1985). Then once adolescents begin to smoke, this behaviour is reinforced by their peers. Not surprisingly, it is estimated that more than 70 percent of all cigarettes smoked by adolescents are smoked in the presence of a peer (Biglan et al., 1984). Interestingly, girls are repeatedly offered cigarettes more than are boys (Charlton, Minagawa, & While, 1999).

Do you remember Jennifer who we introduced you to at the beginning of this chapter? Jennifer was greatly influenced by peer pressure in her decision to begin smoking. Both her parents and many of her friends smoked. In a sense, the cards were stacked against her, as she was surrounded by many situational factors associated with smoking. Researchers have documented that adolescents are more likely to smoke if they have parents or older siblings who also smoke (e.g., Biglan et al., 1995). These findings suggest that both modelling and peer pressure are likely to be important causative factors of smoking.

The image of the smoker also seems to be important. One study (Stanton et al., 1993) showed that "image" was a major reason for smoking among 11-year-olds. Other studies have found that boys and girls between the ages of 11 and 15 years often associate smoking with being attractive to the opposite sex, being "glamorous" and "exciting." The image of the smoker is also that he or she is rebellious, tough, and mature (Dinh, Sarason, Peterson, & Onstad, 1995). The media certainly plays a role in formulating an image associated with smoking. Witnessing cigarette smoking in popular films leads college students to view smoking as more commonplace than it actually is, and it also increases their current desire to smoke (Hines, Saris, & Throckmorton-Belzer, 2000; McCool, Cameron, & Petrie, 2001). Youngsters dealing with the insecurities of adolescence may find that cigarettes enable them to convey the image they would like to (Aloise-Young, Hennigan, & Graham, 1996). Researchers estimate that advertising is responsible for 34 percent of experimentation with cigarettes (Pierce et al., 1998).

Although situational factors (e.g., peer pressure) are thought to be the most important determinants in the initiation of smoking, personal characteristics also seem to be related to smoking behaviour. Characteristics such as low self-esteem, dependency, powerlessness, and social isolation all increase the tendency to imitate others' behaviour (Ennett & Bauman, 1993). People who are rebellious and engage in risk-taking behaviours such as having multiple sex partners, using marijuana, and binge drinking are more likely to smoke than are people who do not engage in such behaviours (Emmons, Wechsler, Dowdall, & Abraham, 1998; Lipkus, Barefoot, Williams, & Siegler, 1994). Sometimes teenage girls choose to smoke in an effort to control their weight (Crisp, Sedgwick, Halek, Joughin & Humphrey, 1999). To summarize, adolescents tend to begin smoking because of four factors—parental modelling, peer influence, cigarette advertising, and personal characteristics. But what factors are responsible for people becoming regular smokers?

BOX 9-1 | **Health Warning Labels on Cigarette Packaging**

Most smokers do not view themselves as being at increased risk for experiencing a heart attack or developing cancer because of their habit (Ayanian & Cleary, 1999). Our federal government plans to change that. Since December 2000, Canadian smokers have been exposed to the world's largest and most graphic warning labels. The warning labels must cover the top 50 percent of the front and back of the principal display surface (Canadian Cancer Society, 2003). There are 16 different images on these labels, many of them depicting what happens to organs after their owner has spent a lifetime smoking (e.g., a diseased mouth, a lung tumour, a brain after a stroke). The cigarette packaging also contains additional messages including tips on quitting smoking.

Will these warning labels achieve their goal? Research investigating whether health warnings have an impact on behaviour provide mixed results. While adults in a bar who were prompted to read a health warning about alcohol consumed less alcohol than those

not prompted to notice the warning, a small study found evidence that watching cigarette advertisements with mandatory health warnings actually increased viewers' desire to smoke compared to those who watched the same advertisements with the warning removed (Hyland & Birrell, 1979; Malouff, Schutte, Winer, Brancazio & Fish, 1993). A sample of adolescents who took part in a longitudinal study also demonstrated this boomerang effect in response to knowledge of warning labels on magazines and billboard advertisements (Robinson & Killen, 1997). That is, greater knowledge of warning labels was related to a subsequent increase in smoking.

Recent studies have specifically investigated the effectiveness of new large warning labels on tobacco products. In Poland 30 percent of the front and back of package surfacing must read "Tobacco smoking causes heart disease" and "Tobacco smoking causes lung cancer" (Thompson, 1999). Australian health warnings covered

(continued on next page)

more than 15 percent of the packages with a large warning on the front of the package and an elaboration of the warning on the back (Borland, 1997). These studies have consistently shown significant changes in smoking behaviour and knowledge of health hazards in response to the introduction of the labels.

Canada's warning labels are the most graphic and the largest in the world. Australia, Thailand, and the United States are enhancing their warning labels. Most of these new labels will be modelled directly on the Canadian warning labels. Warning labels with illustrations are thought to be up to 60 times more effective than those with text alone. Geoffrey Fong, of the Department of Psychology at the University of Waterloo, has received funding from both Canadian and American granting agencies to determine whether the warning labels are noticeable, effective, and lead to smokers thinking about the consequences of smoking; whether smoking behaviour changes; and whether boomerang effects occur. Only time will tell.

WARNING

TOBACCO USE CAN MAKE YOU IMPOTENT

Cigarettes may cause sexual impotence due to decreased blood flow to the penis. This can prevent you from having an erection.

Health Canada

WARNING

CIGARETTES CAUSE MOUTH DISEASES

Cigarette smoke causes oral cancer, gum diseases and tooth loss.

Health Canada

These graphic images and warnings are among 16 the Canadian government has required tobacco companies to include on all cigarette packaging.

Becoming a Regular Smoker Although the majority of people try smoking at least once in their lives, most people do not become regular smokers. For those who do become habitual smokers the habit generally develops slowly, often taking years (Chassin, Presson, Pitts & Sherman, 2000). Researchers have not discovered why some people become regular smokers and others do not. There does not seem to be a single reason why people smoke. Rather, it appears that different people smoke for different reasons.

Much of the research investigating this topic has stemmed from the theoretical position of Silvan Tomkins (1966, 1968). Tomkins put forth four explanations as to why people who begin to smoke continue to smoke on a regular basis. Some people smoke to achieve a positive affect. In other words, a **positive-affect smoker** smokes to increase stimulation, to relax, or to gratify sensorimotor needs. In contrast, **negative-affect smokers** are people who smoke to reduce negative affect such as anxiety, distress, fear, or guilt. You may recall that Jennifer from our opening vignette first began to smoke to reduce loneliness. Later, she began to smoke again to deal with the stress in her life resulting from divorce proceedings; Jennifer would be considered a negative-affect smoker. Other people smoke simply out of habit. **Habitual smokers** probably initiated smoking to achieve a positive affect or reduce a negative affect but continue to smoke without awareness of why they are doing so. These people do not derive any benefits from smoking. Finally, **addictive smokers**, those who develop a psychological dependence on smoking, are keenly aware of when they are not smoking. That is, they feel something is amiss when they are not smoking. Addictive smokers can tell you exactly how long it has been since their last cigarette and how long it will likely be before their next one. These people have cigarettes with them at all times and usually keep at least one extra package on hand for "emergencies."

Because different people have different reasons for smoking, strategies to quit smoking vary in their effectiveness. For example, one study found that people who smoke for pleasure show a sharp drop in the number of cigarettes they smoke when their cigarettes have been dipped in vinegar, whereas those who smoke for other reasons (e.g., addiction) do not. In contrast, people who smoke primarily from habit show a marked reduction in the amount they smoke when asked to keep a record of cigarettes smoked, whereas this is not the case for those who smoke for pleasure (Ikard & Tomkins, 1973; Leventhal & Cleary, 1980).

The psychological reasons people continue to smoke are certainly important, but heredity may also play a role. Researchers have not definitively determined the link between heredity and smoking, but three possible explanations have been put forth. First, genetic factors may underlie certain personality traits associated with smoking (e.g., rebelliousness). Second, heredity may determine the extent to which people find tobacco pleasant or unpleasant. Third, genetically based differences in reaction to nicotine influence the degree to which people exposed to nicotine become dependent on it (Pomerleau, Collins, Shiffman, & Pomerleau, 1993).

Once people begin smoking regularly, they become physiologically dependent on the nicotine in cigarettes. However, before discussing the theories that attempt to explain the addictive quality of nicotine, we should first describe how nicotine initially affects us. When a person inhales smoke from a cigarette, nicotine passes through cell membranes in the mouth and nose en route to the lungs, where alveoli absorb it and carry it to the blood (e.g., Henningfield, Cohen, & Pickworth, 1993). In a very short time, the blood has carried the nicotine to the brain. In the brain, nicotine triggers the release of various chemicals that activate both the central and sympathetic nervous systems, resulting in increases in heart rate and blood pressure. This entire process takes approximately seven seconds. Now, let's return to our discussion of nicotine addiction.

The exact nature of nicotine addiction is not clear. However, a number of theories have been put forth in an attempt to explain it. The **nicotine fixed-effect model** maintains that nicotine produces addiction by stimulating specific reward centres in the central nervous system (Hall, Rappaport, Hopkins, & Griffin, 1973). According to this model, nicotine has the paradoxical capacity to produce feelings of mental alertness and relaxation simultaneously. In contrast, the **nicotine regulation model** proposes that smokers develop an optimal level of nicotine in their bodies and then smoke in order to maintain this level and avoid withdrawal symptoms (Jarvik, 1973). These models both have limitations and have also been criticized because they focus entirely on the physiological aspects of addiction (e.g., Shiffman et al., 1995).

The **multiple regulation model** of smoking is a more comprehensive model of smoking than either the nicotine fixed-effect model or the nicotine regulation model (Leventhal & Cleary, 1980). The multiple regulation model maintains that the physiological effects of nicotine interact with the psychological functions of smoking to produce addiction. According to this model, emotional regulation is central to smoking, with nicotine levels being regulated because these levels have become conditioned to various emotional states. Let's demonstrate this by way of example. Consider Kelly, who is a 15-year-old shy, socially anxious teenager. To reduce her social anxiety, Kelly tends to smoke at parties and in other social situations. Once Kelly finishes a cigarette, however, the anxiety reappears and the level of nicotine in her blood begins to drop. As this is repeated over time, an increase in anxiety becomes conditioned to the decline in nicotine levels. This reinforces smoking behaviour because smoking increases nicotine levels and also reduces anxiety. Although this model seems to account for the addictive nature of smoking better than theories that focus exclusively on either psychological or physiological aspects, it too does not account for all that is known about smoking.

The **biobehavioural model** developed by Pomerleau and Pomerleau (1989) maintains that people use and come to depend on the effects of nicotine to regulate cognitive performance and emotional affect. More specifically, when nicotine reaches the brain it triggers the release of such chemicals as acetylcholine, norepinephrine, dopamine, endogenous opioids, and vasopressin. These chemicals improve memory, enhance pleasure, and facilitate task performance. Further, these chemicals decrease symptoms of nicotine withdrawal and feelings of anxiety, tension, and pain (McGehee et al., 1995). According to the biobehavioural model, regular smokers have trouble quitting because when they decrease their nicotine level they notice a reduction in concentration, attention, and memory; and an increase in anxiety, irritability, and moodiness.

Health Consequences of Smoking   As previously mentioned, smoking is the number one preventable cause of death and disease in Canada. Research conclusively shows that smoking reduces life expectancy by several years. Ellison and his colleagues (1999) at Health Canada determined that the rate of premature deaths (before age 70) was twice that among lifelong smokers than among those who had never smoked for both males and females. Smoking also increases the risk of many illnesses, including cancer and cardiovascular disease (Thun et al., 1995). And the more you smoke, the worse your odds become.

In an effort to protect its citizens from the health hazards and economic burden of tobacco consumption and exposure to tobacco smoke, Canadian Minister of Health, the Honourable

Anne McLellan, signed the Framework Convention on Tobacco Control (FCTC) on July 15, 2003. Member countries of the World Health Organization prepared the FCTC. Their goal is to aid in the prevention, cessation, and harm reduction of tobacco (Health Canada, 2003).

SMOKING AND CARDIOVASCULAR AND CEREBROVASCULAR DISEASE   Together, cardiovascular and cerebrovascular diseases were responsible for 73 000 deaths (34.7 percent) in Canada in 1997 (Statistics Canada, 2003). In general, the risk of dying of cardiovascular disease is about twice as high for smokers as for non-smokers (CDC, 1993).

Smoking is thought to contribute to cardiovascular disease in a number of ways. There is some evidence that cigarette smoking increases the level of serum cholesterol, and the size of plaque, within the arteries. Amazingly, the progression of atherosclerosis in smokers is estimated to increase by as much as 50 percent during a three-year period (Tell et al., 1994; Howard et al., 1998). Nicotine itself may also contribute to heart disease. Nicotine has a stimulant effect on the nervous system, resulting in increases in heart rate, blood pressure, and cardiac output, combined with constriction of blood vessels. Fortunately, the risk of heart attack and stroke, like that of cancer, declines when people quit smoking (Critchley & Capewell, 2003; Kawachi et al., 1993).

SMOKING AND CANCER   Cancer is one of the leading causes of death in Canada. In 1997, 27.2 percent of deaths in Canada were attributed to various forms of cancer (Statistics Canada, 2003). Although almost 80 percent of smoking-related deaths in Canada result from lung cancer, smoking is also responsible for deaths from cancer of the lip, oral cavity, pharynx, esophagus, pancreas, larynx, urinary bladder, and kidney (Ellison et al., 1999). Researchers in the United States have documented the correspondence between the rise in lung cancer deaths and the prevalence of smoking since the 1930s. These researchers (e.g., McGinnis, Shopland, & Brown, 1987; Shopland & Burns, 1993) state that the rate of mortality from lung cancer began to rise approximately 15 to 20 years after the rate of smoking started to rise. These rates have paralleled each other since that time.

SMOKING AND CHRONIC OBSTRUCTIVE PULMONARY DISEASES   Chronic obstructive pulmonary diseases (COPD) include a number of respiratory and lung diseases, such as chronic bronchitis and emphysema. They accounted for 9618 deaths (or 4.5 percent of all deaths) in Canada in 1997 (Statistics Canada, 2003). Virtually all COPDs are experienced by smokers. In other words, these conditions are relatively rare in non-smokers (Whitemore, Perlin, & DiCiccio, 1995). In general terms, smoking irritates and damages respiratory organs. This damage leads to reduced airflow when breathing and is particularly noticeable when trying to exhale with force.

Environmental Tobacco Smoke

We have looked at what happens to the health of people who smoke. What we have not considered is the number of people who are affected by **environmental tobacco smoke (ETS)**, also known as secondhand smoke. Most Canadians spend more time indoors than outdoors, and tobacco smoke is a key contaminant in indoor air quality. Breathing ETS is called **passive smoking**. Health Canada estimates that more than 300 Canadian non-smokers die each year from lung cancer caused by exposure to ETS (Health Canada, 1999). The number of non-smokers who die from cardiovascular disease as a result of ETS is likely much higher, given that researchers have estimated that at least 10 times the number of non-smokers die from ETS-related cardiovascular disease than do from ETS-related lung cancer. Pregnant women, fetuses, and young children are especially susceptible to the effects of ETS. Resulting health consequences include complications of pregnancy and low birthweight, increased risk of sudden infant death syndrome and ear infections, reduced lung development, and increased severity of asthma and other respiratory illnesses. In an effort to protect people many municipalities now have restrictions on smoking in public settings. For example, all but 10 percent of the workforce report working in an environment where there are smoking restrictions. In addition, more and more people agree that smoking should be banned from public places like bars and restaurants (Health Canada, 2003).

Quitting Smoking   As previously mentioned, smoking is an **addiction**. That is, once people begin to smoke regularly most become physically or psychologically dependent on it. Therefore, if someone wanted to quit smoking he or she would have to go through a period of **withdrawal**. Withdrawal refers to the unpleasant symptoms that people experience when they stop using a substance they have become dependent on. When a person reduces or eliminates nicotine intake he or she will experience short-term symptoms such as a reduction in concentration, attention, and memory, combined with an increase in anxiety, irritability, and moodiness (Shadel et al., 2000). The good news is that if you do quit smoking, your odds steadily improve. After 15 or 20 years as a non-smoker, your odds are similar to those of people who have never smoked (Critchley & Capewell, 2003; LaCroix et al., 1991; Ockene, Kuller, Svendsen, & Meilahn, 1990). Although the benefits of quitting smoking are the same for everyone the reasons people choose to quit vary (see figure 9-1).

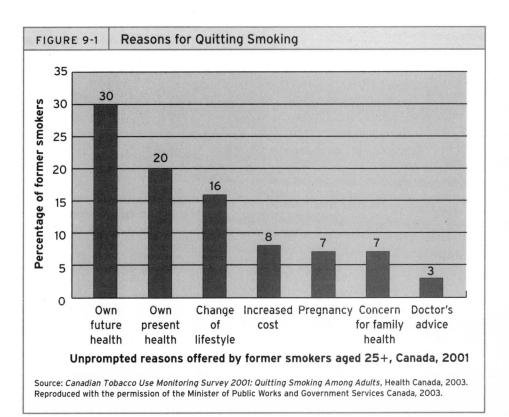

| FIGURE 9-1 | **Reasons for Quitting Smoking** |

Unprompted reasons offered by former smokers aged 25+, Canada, 2001

Source: *Canadian Tobacco Use Monitoring Survey 2001: Quitting Smoking Among Adults*, Health Canada, 2003.
Reproduced with the permission of the Minister of Public Works and Government Services Canada, 2003.

QUITTING ON ONE'S OWN   The vast majority of individuals who quit smoking will quit on their own, without any professional help (Schacter, 1982; Cunningham, 1999). Though heavy smokers report finding it more difficult to quit and experience more unpleasant effects from quitting than do light smokers, there is no difference in success rates between the two groups. However, there are age differences in success rates. Younger light smokers are more likely than heavy smokers to give up smoking. In contrast, among older smokers, heavy smokers were more successful at quitting. This difference may result from older smokers having experienced health problems due to their smoking habits that necessitate quitting smoking (Cohen et al., 1989; Coambs, Li, & Kozlowski, 1992). We should point out that although most people can stop smoking on their own, most do not succeed in their first attempt (Rose, Chassin, Presson, & Sherman, 1996). The majority of individuals who quit smoking will relapse within a year, and most relapses occur in the first three months (Ockene et al., 2000).

QUITTING WITH THERAPY   If people cannot quit smoking on their own, they often seek help from others. Most therapies include nicotine-replacement therapy, psychological interventions, or both. Therapies that combine both nicotine replacement and psychological interventions, known as multidimensional approaches, are considered most effective (Cinciripini et al., 1996; Niaura & Abrams, 2002).

Nicotine-replacement therapy provides some form of nicotine replacement for the nicotine former smokers previously obtained through smoking. Typically, nicotine gum or the nicotine patch are used. *Nicotine gum* provides small amounts of nicotine when chewed. The *nicotine patch*, on the other hand, resembles a large bandage and releases a small continuous dose of nicotine into the body's system. Patches with smaller and smaller doses of nicotine are worn until the person is no longer addicted to the nicotine. A 17 to 18 percent cessation rate is achieved by people who use nicotine gum versus 9 percent for placebo gum, whereas a 22 percent cessation rate is achieved by those who use the nicotine patch compared to about 9 percent for a placebo patch (Tsoh et al., 1997). If the drug bupropion is combined with the patch, a 35 percent cessation rate is obtained (Jorenby et al., 1999). Nicotine inhalers and nicotine nasal sprays are also available. No matter what form of nicotine replacement is used, it will be more effective if various psychological approaches to treatment are used as well (Cinciripini et al., 1996; Niaura & Abrams, 2002).

The psychological approaches to smoking cessation generally take one of two different forms—aversion therapies or self-management strategies. **Aversion therapies** involve pairing the behaviour to be eliminated, in this case smoking, with some unpleasant stimulus so that smoking will elicit negative sensations. The three most common forms of aversion therapies are electric shock, imagined aversive scenes, and rapid smoking. *Electric shock* can be paired with smoking situations so that when a person smokes he or she is shocked and made uncomfortable. When *aversive scenes* are employed, people are directed to think of an aversive scene that includes beginning to smoke, followed by something disgusting (e.g., you take the cigarette out of the pack and are about to light it when you suddenly vomit all over your cigarette, your hands, and the lighter. The smell is so foul you can hardly stand it. You drop the cigarette and the lighter and as you turn away and head toward the bathroom to clean yourself up you begin to feel much less nauseous). The third technique, *rapid smoking*, is very seldom used. Rapid smoking involves placing the smoker in a small, enclosed room where he or she inhales from a cigarette rapidly every few seconds while concentrating on the smoke, the stinging burn in the throat, and other unpleasant elements. Aversion strategies may help in the initial stages of quitting smoking but the effects are seldom long-term.

Self-management strategies are designed to help people overcome the environmental conditions that perpetuate smoking. *Self-monitoring* requires that people record each cigarette smoked, the time of day, where they were, who they were with, and their mood. Self-monitoring in itself reduces smoking, but the information obtained also aids in formulating other approaches to smoking cessation. *Stimulus control* strategies focus on removing the cues that lead a person to smoke. For example, if a person always smokes during a coffee break when sitting in the staff room, that person may want to go for a walk or have their coffee break in a different location. *Behavioural contracting* involves establishing a contract according to which a person will be rewarded for fulfilling the contract or punished for failing to do so. These contracts often involve the person depositing a large sum of money that they will lose if they do not adhere to the contract.

These are only a few of the strategies that can be used to help people quit smoking. Box 9-2 outlines a large-scale attempt to encourage people to quit smoking.

BOX 9-2	**COMMIT: The Community Intervention Trial for Smoking Cessation**

The National Cancer Institute's Community Intervention Trial for Smoking Cessation (COMMIT) was a seven-year, multicentre, cooperative research project involving eleven pairs of matched communities (ten in the United States and one in Canada) representing over 20 000 smokers. It was the most extensive tobacco-control study ever undertaken in North America. Branford, Ontario served as the intervention community in Canada and Peterborough, Ontario as its comparison. The goal of COMMIT was to increase the priority of smoking cessation as a public health issue and to increase social norms and values supporting non-smoking. Initially, surveys were conducted at each site to determine the prevalence of smoking and attitudes towards smoking (see Taylor, Goldsmith, & Best, 1996). Anti-smoking intervention strategies were then implemented and the effects of these interventions measured.

Researchers worked with each intervention community to determine and implement the most suitable intervention strategies for their population. Some of the intervention strategies used in Brantford were smoking policy workshops and consultations at the worksite; between-worksite challenges and competitions; publicizing smoking-control activities and awareness campaigns through the media; development and maintenance of a cessation resources guide; and preparation and distribution of a semiannual newsletter. In addition, heavy smokers were recruited and became part of the "Smokers' Network." These individuals were provided with "survival kits" (with both humorous and useful contents for stopping smoking) and were encouraged to participate in a "Quit and Win" contest. Contest participants were asked to commit to remaining smoke-free for 30 days in exchange for the chance to

(continued on next page)

win a substantial prize. This strategy proved quite popular and was repeated numerous times. There were between 50 and 200 participants each time. A final strategy worth mentioning were the "sting" operations. These involved young people under legal age attempting to purchase cigarettes. The results of these attempts were then made public to inform the community about the ease of access to tobacco for underage smokers. The smoking cessation interventions took place for four years, from 1989 to 1993 (Lindsay et al., 1996).

Results of these interventions were somewhat disappointing. For example, the number of heavy smokers in the intervention communities who quit smoking was not significantly different from the number who quit in the comparison communities. However, light-to-moderate smokers in the intervention communities were more likely to quit than those in the comparison communities (COMMIT Research Group, 1995a, 1995b). There were also substantial changes in favour of stronger anti-smoking policies over the course of the trial. However, this attitude change occurred in both intervention and comparison communities and was consistent with findings across North America (Taylor et al., 1998). It may be that global attitude changes need more time to develop in response to the intervention, or that concurrent global campaigns diluted the effects of this more local campaign. Certainly, a change in public attitude was witnessed in response to the sting operations in Brantford from one year to the next (Lindsay et al., 1996). As well, positive changes resulted when a representative from Alcoholics Anonymous spontaneously initiated the establishment of a non-smoking chapter of AA (Zanna et al., 1996).

Alcohol Use

Alcohol Consumption   About 53 percent of Canadians (63 percent of men and 43 percent of women) drink alcohol at least once per month (Health Canada, 1999). Women are more likely than men to be non-drinkers. Men are more likely than women to report being "heavy" or "binge" drinkers, that is, to have consumed five or more drinks on at least one occasion in the past year. The proportion of men and women who drink at least one drink per month rises steadily with increases in income. This is a pattern that is in direct contrast to that found for smoking. You may remember that smoking rates decrease steadily with income level. If we look at episodes of binge drinking, we see that 24 percent of men in the two lowest income levels who were drinkers reported at least one episode of binge drinking, compared to 43 percent of men in the highest income bracket. A J-shaped curve is produced when the rate of binge drinking among women according to income level is plotted. The rate of binge drinking among women drinkers in the lowest income level was 13 percent in the Health Canada study. This dropped to 10 percent at the next income level, then slowly climbed to 19 percent at the highest income level.

Age is another factor associated with drinking. Although rates of drinking for adults have been decreasing over the last couple of decades, there are disturbing indications that the proportion of adolescents who drink is increasing (Canadian Centre on Substance Abuse, 1999). For example, the Nova Scotia Student Drug Use Survey reported that 57 percent of students drank alcohol in 1998; a 12-percent increase from 1991. Similar rates of drinking are reported by students in the other Atlantic provinces (Prince Edward Island, 53 percent; New Brunswick, 56 percent; Newfoundland, 58 percent) and in Ontario (60 percent) (cited in Health Canada, 1999). Not surprisingly, the percentage of adolescents who have tried alcohol increases with age. In British Columbia, 47 percent of boys and 41 percent of girls have tried alcohol by age 13 (McCreary Centre Society, 1999). This figure increases to 80 percent for both males and females aged 17 years. Other provinces have also noted an increase in drinking with age (Health Canada, 1999). In Nova Scotia, 21 percent of Grade 7 students and 58 percent of Grade 9 students reported drinking alcohol in the previous year. The rates are similar in Newfoundland and Labrador (20 percent of Grade 7 students and 59 percent of Grade 9 students) and in Ontario (32 percent of Grade 7 students and 56 percent of Grade 9 students). Previously, we discussed the prevalence of binge drinking in adults. Unfortunately, this rate seems to be even higher in adolescents. In British Columbia, for example, more than 40 percent of the 12- to 18-year-olds who reported ever having a drink had engaged in a binge at least once during the past month! This figure had increased 7 percent from 1992 to 1998 for both males and females (McCreary Centre Society, 1999). And, Aboriginal Canadian adolescents are reported as having a risk as much as six times greater than other Canadians for developing alcohol problems (Canadian Centre on Substance Abuse, 1999).

American studies indicate that the use of alcohol is lowest among older adults (U.S. Department of Health and Human Services, 1998). However, this may be due more to heavy drinkers dying younger than to older people modifying their drinking habits as they age. Prospective studies have found only a small decline in alcohol use as people become older (National Institute on Alcohol Abuse and Alcoholism, 1988).

The Effects of Alcohol The alcohol used in beverages is called **ethanol** or **ethyl alcohol**. This alcohol is a depressant drug and, like other depressant drugs (e.g., tranquilizers and painkillers), it slows down the nervous system, which may cause drowsiness, induce sleep, or relieve pain. Even the initial apparent stimulant effect actually results from depression of centres in the brain that inhibit our actions and control our behaviour. After one drink, the majority of people report feeling more relaxed. With more than one drink, a person may feel more outgoing and self-confident, but some people will become aggressive, depressed, or withdrawn. At higher doses—even below a blood-alcohol concentration of 0.08, the legal limit for driving a car in Canada—thinking, judgment, and ability to estimate distance can be impaired and reaction times increased (Alberta Alcohol and Drug Abuse Commission, 1999).

Excessive use of alcohol can have adverse effects on almost every system of the body. For example, chronic alcohol abuse causes liver disease and damage to the stomach, pancreas, and intestines. Moreover, chronic drinking causes high blood pressure, depression of the immune system, and is associated with coronary artery disease, and cancer of the throat, larynx, mouth, esophagus, and liver (Alberta Alcohol and Drug Abuse Commission, 1999). Other consequences of drinking include blackouts, hangovers, and even death. Blackouts are periods of memory loss that occur while a person is drinking heavily. Hangovers, on the other hand, occur after drinking has stopped. Hangovers are caused by mild alcohol withdrawal and may be experienced eight to twelve hours after a bout of heavy drinking. The symptoms of a hangover include fatigue, headache, nausea, and sometimes vomiting and shakiness. Death may occur following moderate doses of alcohol taken together with other depressant drugs, such as sleeping pills and tranquillizers, or from an overdose of alcohol as a result of excessive consumption. This kind of consumption has been associated with events such as college fraternity initiations. For example, some college students have been known to participate in the dangerous behaviour of "funnelling," putting a funnel in someone's mouth and pouring liquor into the funnel. This method of drinking can be lethal because it easily provides too much alcohol.

Although, as noted above, there are many dire negative consequences to excessive drinking, there are, in fact, health benefits for light to moderate drinkers. Numerous studies (Berkman, Breslow, & Wingard, 1983; Friedman & Kimball, 1986; Kitamura et al., 1998) have reported that moderate drinking has survival advantages for men. Specifically, this research has shown that light to moderate drinkers are at less risk of developing coronary heart disease and possibly stroke (Maclure, 1993; Sacco et al., 1999). Although the relationship between drinking and survival is less clear for women, one study found that women who drank from three to eighteen drinks per week had a reduced risk of death, particularly from cardiovascular disease (Fuchs et al., 1995). However, women who drank more than 18 drinks per week had an increased risk of death from other causes (e.g., breast cancer and cirrhosis). We should point out that early studies indicated that red wine was the kind of alcohol that resulted in survival advantages. More recent research has found no particular advantage of one kind of alcohol over another. Wine, beer, and liquor are all thought to produce the same advantages (Parker et al., 1996; Rehm et al., 1997). Researchers believe that consuming alcohol increases levels of high-density lipoprotein (HDL), which is responsible for a decreased risk of heart attacks (Gaziano et al., 1993; Linn et al., 1993).

Explaining Drinking Behaviour   It has been suggested that drinking is commonplace in North America because it is so widely accepted. But perhaps drinking is well accepted because it is so commonplace. Regardless, drunkenness or problem drinking is not acceptable, and it is therefore important to explain why this behaviour occurs (McMurran, 1994). The **disease model** of problem drinking maintains that alcoholism is a disease brought about by the physical properties of alcohol (Jellinek, 1960). The **alcohol dependency syndrome model** states that at certain times and for a variety of reasons people do not exercise control over their drinking and this leads to problem drinking (Edwards & Gross, 1976). A number of elements are said to be essential for alcohol dependency syndrome to develop, including a salience of drink-seeking behaviour (meaning that drinking begins to take priority over all other aspects of life) and an increased tolerance for alcohol. Someone with an increased tolerance for alcohol may gradually become accustomed to going about their daily routine "at blood alcohol levels would incapacitate the non-tolerant drinker" (Edwards & Gross, 1976, p. 1059). Although this model remains popular in certain circles it has been criticized because of its emphasis on the physical properties of alcohol and its neglect of the cognitive and social learning aspects of drinking (McMurran, 1994)

Cognitive–physiological models propose that people drink because alcohol influences cognitive functioning, allowing people to escape tension and negative self-evaluations. One of these models, the **tension reduction hypothesis**, maintains that people drink alcohol because of its tension-reducing properties. Although there is little empirical support for this theory, some research suggests that alcohol may lead people to avoid tension-producing behaviours or situations (Rutledge & Sher, 2001). The **self-awareness model** suggests that drinking inhibits the use of normal, complex information-processing strategies such as memory and information acquisition, making people less self-aware (Hull, 1981, 1987; Hull & Bond, 1986). Decreased self-awareness leads to decreased monitoring of behaviour, resulting in the disinhibition and decrease in self-criticism that often occurs when people are drinking. Simply stated, some people may consume alcohol to avoid self-awareness. A third cognitive–physiological theory developed to explain drinking behaviour is called **alcohol myopia** (Steele & Josephs, 1990). Alcohol myopia refers to a drinker's decreased ability to process information outside a narrow range (myopia). This effect also helps to lower inhibition of impulsive responses. Alcohol myopia is characterized by people behaving more excessively (more friendly, more aggressive, etc.), having a tendency to inflate self-evaluations, and experiencing *drunken relief* or a tendency to worry less and pay less attention to their worries.

The **social learning model** proposes that people drink because they experience positive reinforcement for doing so (e.g., the taste or the effects of alcohol are pleasant) or because they observe others drinking and model this behaviour. For example, you may try drinking because your friends drink and you may continue to drink in the company of your friends. Or, once you have tried drinking you may like the taste of the beverage or you may notice a change in your behaviour that you like (e.g., you feel less shy after having a drink). Social learning theory can explain why people begin to drink, why they continue to drink in moderation, and why some people drink to excess. Excessive drinking may occur because of modelling (your friends are also drinking to excess) or because once you stop drinking you experience negative reinforcement in the form of a hangover or withdrawal symptoms. According to the social learning model, drinking behaviour is learned and can therefore also be unlearned. A number of treatment techniques to help people overcome excessive drinking habits rely on social learning principles.

Preventing and Treating Alcohol Abuse   Attempts to prevent alcohol abuse have taken a number of forms. Public policy and legal approaches include implementing age restrictions for individuals buying or consuming alcohol. Health promotion and education strategies incorporating social influence approaches are found to be useful in helping adolescents avoid drinking heavily. These may include discussions and films regarding how peers, family members, and the media influence drinking, or modelling and role-playing specific refusal skills (e.g., saying "No thank you, I don't drink") and how to deal with high-risk situations (Donaldson, Graham, Piccinin, & Hansen, 1995; Kivlahen et al., 1990; Klepp, Kelder, & Perry, 1995).

Like those who quit smoking, the majority of people stop drinking without treatment (Cunningham, 1999). Authorities in the field of problem drinking prefer to use the term *unassisted change* (McMurran, 1994). This term may be somewhat misleading, because support is likely provided to the individual by many people in an informal manner (Sobel, Sobel, Toneatto, & Leo, 1993). However, many individuals who cannot quit drinking on their own seek formal treatment. Twelve-step programs such as Alcoholics Anonymous (AA) have become increasingly popular. Yet, this kind of program doesn't seem to be more effective than other formal treatments. One controlled study (Brandsma, Maultsby, & Walsh, 1980) found that participants who were seeking treatment through AA had a higher dropout rate (68 percent) than those in any of the other treatment groups in the study (57 percent). Psychotherapy, drug therapy (e.g., disulfiram, commonly known as Antabuse) and aversion therapy (e.g., electric shock) have all been used with limited success (Miller & Hester, 1980; Schuckit, 1996). Relapse is a persistent problem with all alcohol treatment approaches. Most often, a relapse will occur within three months after the end of treatment. After a year, only about one-third of those who complete the program are still abstinent (Baker, Cooney, & Pomerleau, 1987).

Canada's Drug Strategy (Health Canada, 2000b) adopts the "stages of change" model for guiding both treatment processes and prevention goals. You may remember this model from chapter 1. If we apply the model to drug use, we note the stages an individual goes through in deciding to use a particular substance (Health Canada, 2000b, p. 34):

Pre-contemplation	Not considering use
Contemplation	Thinking about initiating use
Preparation	Intending to use
Action	Initiating use
Maintenance	Continuing to use
Relapse	

For anyone who is not considering alcohol use or anyone who is thinking about initiating use, primary prevention is the key. If an individual is currently using or continuing to use, a harm reduction strategy is appropriate. Whatever an individual's current state there are specific activities and messages that can be adopted (e.g., implementation of more intensive approaches for those in the preparation, action, or maintenance stages).

Drinking and Driving   We mentioned previously that drinking influences our thought processes. Unfortunately, alcohol causes people to think less negatively about drinking and driving (MacDonald, Zanna, & Fong, 1995, 1998). The result is disastrous—people drink and drive and are often involved in motor vehicle accidents. According to the 1996/97 National Population Health Survey, 10 percent of Canadians who have a driver's license and consume alcohol admitted to driving after consuming "too much" alcohol. Men (13 percent) are more likely than women (5 percent) to report drinking and driving, and young drivers aged 18 and 19 years report drinking and driving more than do other age groups (Health Canada, 1999). Because judgment and decision making are impaired it is not surprising that intoxicated individuals are often involved in traffic accidents. Among fatally injured drivers in 1996, 35 percent were legally impaired. Statistics are not available for the number of innocent victims injured or killed (Health Canada, 1999).

Illicit Drug Use

Compared with those who succumb to the effects of smoking cigarettes and drinking alcohol, relatively few people die from the effects of illegal drugs. For example, cocaine, the most lethal of the illicit drugs, kills only one person for every 1000 killed by tobacco products (Rouse, 1998). Of course, even one death from illicit drugs is too many. Illicit drugs present certain risks not found with legal drugs, regardless of pharmacological effects. A person purchasing illicit drugs may be told he or she is buying one drug and then receive another; illegally manufactured drugs may be contaminated with other very toxic chemicals; and users never really know what drug or how much of a particular drug they are taking.

How prevalent is the use of illicit drugs? Health Canada (2000) reports that the use of illicit drugs is as great now as at any time in history. The most commonly used illicit drug in North America is marijuana. Seven percent of Canadians reported using marijuana in the 1994–95 National Public Health Survey. However, the rate of young people using marijuana (young people are the most frequent users of illicit drugs) has been increasing (Health Canada, 2000). In 1998, 40 percent of students in British Columbia reported using marijuana, up from 25 percent in 1992 (McCreary Centre Society, 1999). Similar increases have been found in Nova Scotia (from 17 percent in 1991 to 38 percent in 1998) and in Ontario (from 12 percent in 1991 to 25 percent in 1997) (Health Canada, 1999). About half of those who have used marijuana report having done so in the past month.

Adolescents are also most likely to use other illicit drugs. Surveys of the general population indicate that fewer than one percent of Canadians use crack cocaine, LSD, or speed. However, 11 percent of adolescents in British Columbia report using hallucinogens (e.g., LSD and ecstasy) 7 percent report using cocaine, and 2 percent report using heroin. Studies conducted in other provinces have shown significant increases in the use of a number of drugs by students. For example, LSD, non-prescription and prescription stimulants, mescaline, cocaine or crack, PCP, heroin, and inhalants have all been reported as being used more in 1998 than in 1991 (Health Canada, 1999). We now turn our attention to the health problems associated with some of the more common illicit drugs.

Cannabis Adolescents use cannabis more than do any other age group in Canada. In fact, recent surveys indicate that youth are as likely to use cannabis as they are tobacco (Health Canada, 2000). Cannabis, or marijuana, is composed of the leaves, flowers, and small branches of *Cannabis sativa*, a plant that grows in almost every climate. Delta-9-tetrahydrocannabinol (THC) is the intoxicating ingredient of marijuana. Is smoking marijuana a potential health hazard? Marijuana leads to disturbances in short-term memory, judgment, and time perception (Ferraro, 1980). When large doses are consumed, heart rate is increased. A rapid heart rate may lead to health hazards for people who have coronary problems. However, few authorities regard marijuana as a major health risk.

Marijuana has been used in medical situations because of its physiological effects. It has been used as an appetite stimulant for AIDS patients and has been used medically to treat glaucoma, relieve pain, and prevent the vomiting and nausea associated with chemotherapy (Grinspoon & Bakalar, 1995; Ware, Doyle, Woods, Lynch & Clark, 2003).

Why do people use marijuana in spite of the aforementioned side effects? They do so to experience euphoria, a sense of well-being, relaxation, and heightened sexual responsiveness. The desired psychological effects of marijuana seem to depend, in part, on setting and personal expectation. It's not surprising that those who attain these psychological effects are usually experienced marijuana smokers who expect to attain them. Marijuana use does not lead to physiological dependence and withdrawal symptoms do not occur with cessation of marijuana use.

LSD, PCP, and MDMA LSD (lysergic acid diethylamide, commonly referred to as "acid"), PCP (phycyclidine) and MDMA (3,4-methylenedioxymethylamphetamine, most often referred to as "ecstasy") are drugs that are classified as **hallucinogens**. These drugs dramatically affect perception, emotions, and mental processes. As their name suggests, they can cause hallucinations. Hallucinations can elicit feelings of euphoria but can also cause one to feel threatened; and this fear, anxiety, or panic can cause the user to behave quite violently. More often, however, users report a sense of well-being and heightened tactile sensations and emotions. The effects of MDMA usually last up to eight hours and those of LSD up to twelve hours, while the effects of PCP may last as long as several days when taken in a single dose. However, the effects of high doses of PCP have been known in some cases to last from 10 days to 2 weeks (Alberta Alcohol and Drug Abuse Commission, 2002).

Short-term physiological reactions to hallucinogens include increased blood pressure, heart rate, and temperature; dilated pupils; impaired motor skills and coordination; dizziness; and nausea. Larger doses can cause convulsions, coma, and death. Persistent speech problems, memory loss, severe depression and anxiety, and social withdrawal have also been noted following prolonged use.

Cocaine   Cocaine is a **stimulant** drug, extracted from the coca plant indigenous to the Andes Mountains in South America. Cocaine is most often snorted through the nasal passages but is also smoked and "freebased," that is, injected intravenously. Cocaine provides a sense of well-being, heightened attention, and a powerful euphoria. This effect lasts approximately 15 to 30 minutes. When the effects wear off, the user is often left with a feeling of fatigue, sluggishness, and a strong desire to "use" again. Increased doses do not make the euphoria last longer and can endanger the cardiovascular system.

Studies exploring long-term cocaine use among young adults have found mixed results regarding the relationship between heavy use of cocaine and various cardiovascular risk factors (Braun, Murray, & Signey, 1997; Rowbotham & Lowenstein, 1990). Using cocaine causes blood vessels to constrict, heart rate to increase, and blood pressure to speed up suddenly. It can also trigger cardiac arrhythmia. These factors may cause a stroke or myocardial infarction. Physiological withdrawal symptoms do not accompany cessation of cocaine use but psychological dependence does seem to occur.

Preventing and Treating Illicit Drug Use   Programs aimed at preventing teenage drug abuse are similar to those aimed at preventing smoking. Children and adolescents can be educated through the schools and mass media about the deleterious effects of drug abuse. These educational programs are based on social influence and life skills training methods that teach children and adolescents how to resist starting to use drugs (Botvin et al., 1990; Botvin & Willis, 1985). A second preventative technique that is common in all Western countries is the use of laws to limit the legal access to drugs. Unfortunately, this approach may produce other social problems (e.g., a large criminal enterprise) (Robins, 1995). Finally, encouraging parental monitoring of their children has been found to reduce the likelihood that children will try drugs (Chilcoat, Dishion, & Anthony, 1995).

Treatment programs for drug abuse are similar to those for alcohol abuse. In fact, it's not uncommon for formal treatment centres to treat both forms of abuse. The most promising treatment approaches include both behavioural and cognitive methods, such as self-management techniques (NIAAA, 2000). Unfortunately, as with the treatment of alcohol and smoking, there is a high rate of relapse, and the first six months after treatment are critical. Many drug treatment programs now include follow-up or "booster" sessions to help people remain abstinent.

The use of drugs and alcohol directly results in numerous health consequences. Their use also leads to indirect health consequences. For instance, individuals who are intoxicated are more likely to engage in risky behaviours such as unsafe sexual practices (MacDonald, MacDonald, Zanna, & Fong, in press; MacDonald, Zanna, & Fong, 1996, 1998). We will now look further at the practice of unsafe sexual behaviours.

UNSAFE SEXUAL BEHAVIOURS

The negative effects of unsafe sexual behaviours are numerous. In addition to unplanned pregnancies, unsafe sexual behaviours can lead to serious health consequences, such as sexually transmitted diseases (STDs), infertility, and HIV infection. Results from the 1994/95 National Public Health Survey indicated that 51 percent of female and 29 percent of male sexually active 15 to 19-year-olds (excluding those with a single sex partner and those who were married, in a common-law relationship, divorced, or widowed) had had sex without a condom in the past year. Among those aged 20 to 24 years, 53 percent of sexually active females and 44 percent of sexually active males reported having had sex without a condom during the previous year.

Few studies have investigated the sexual behaviour of Canadian Aboriginal populations (Calzavara et al., 1999). However, Canadian Aboriginals have rates of sexually transmitted disease as much as four times higher than the rate in the general population. This may indicate that Aboriginals may be more likely than the general population to engage in unsafe sexual behaviours (Jolly, Orr, Hammond, & Young, 1995). A recent survey (Calzavara et al., 1999) of 11 reserve communities in Ontario found that only 9 percent of those who had engaged in vaginal intercourse in the previous year reported always using condoms. Moreover, only 11.2 percent of those who engaged in anal intercourse reported always using condoms. These statistics were derived from a sample of individuals who were 15 years old or older and single (32 percent), married or common-law (45 percent), and separated, divorced, or widowed (29.4 percent).

Why do people not use condoms when engaging in intercourse? Researchers (MacDonald et al., 1990) attempted to gain insight into this question by conducting a national survey of 5500 first-year Canadian college and university students between the ages of 16 and 24. The students reported not using condoms because they were embarrassed about purchasing them, they had difficulty discussing condom use with their partner, they believed that condoms interfered with sexual pleasure, and because they already used oral contraceptives. Another factor associated with not using condoms was insufficient knowledge of HIV/STDs. Amazingly, in the study with Aboriginals mentioned previously, nine percent of those who reported being sexually active over the previous year had not heard of AIDS (Calzavara et al., 1999). A number of factors were not significant in influencing condom among the students surveyed, including grade point average, fear of acquiring an STD or AIDS, history of STDs, and trust in partner's information about previous experiences. While almost half of the students believed that carrying a condom makes others think that one is willing to have sex, this belief was not related to condom use. The reasons provided by the general population for participating in unsafe sexual behaviours are similar to those provided by the students surveyed in the study by MacDonald et al. (e.g., Boroditsky, Fisher, & Sand, 1995).

A variety of theoretical approaches have been used in an attempt to understand sexual and reproductive health behaviours (see Fisher & Fisher, 1998, for a review of these theories). Some of these theories have been developed outside the domain of sexual and reproductive health and applied within it; for example, the health belief model (Rosenstock, Stretcher, & Becker, 1994), the theory of reasoned action (Fishbein & Ajzen, 1975), the theory of planned behaviour (Ajzen, 1991), and the stages of change model (Prochaska & Velicer, 1997). You may remember reading about these theories in chapter 1. Other theories have been developed and applied specifically within the area of sexuality and reproductive health, including the sexual behaviour sequence model (Byrne, 1977), the AIDS risk reduction model (Catania, Kegeles, & Coates, 1990) and the information–motivation–behavioural skills model (Fisher & Fisher, 1992, 1999). We now turn to a discussion of the information-motivation-behavioural skills model.

The **information–motivation–behavioural skills model** (Fisher & Fisher, 1992; Fisher & Fisher, 1999) maintains there are a number of steps one must go through before one will engage in safe sex practices. First, a person must recognize and accept that he or she is sexually active. Second, the person must create a "sexual and reproductive health agenda." In other words, the individual must be motivated to engage in safe sex practices to prevent pregnancy and infection. Third, the individual must be capable of engaging in behaviours that fulfill this agenda. For example, he or she must be able to negotiate cooperation in contraceptive and condom use with a partner. If cooperation is not forthcoming, the individual must be able to exit the situation. This model also acknowledges that it is frequently necessary to engage in public sexual and reproductive health behaviour acts (e.g., condom purchasing, HIV testing). To maintain safe sexual practices over time, an individual must have this behaviour reinforced. Finally, the individual must be able to adjust sexual and reproductive health behaviour scripts appropriately as his or her needs change over time. For example, it may be appropriate to shift from condom use to non-use in a monogamous relationship after a window period, mutual STD and HIV antibody testing, and discussion of how to continue mutual monogamy and how violations of this agreement will be handled. Of course, this change in practice can only take place if the individuals in the relationship are mature enough to accept the responsibilities and risks associated with this agreement. We cannot emphasize strongly enough that it is inappropriate to shift from condom use to monogamy as a strategy for safe sex behaviour after a brief period of "getting to know" one's partner or for younger couples, whose relationships tend to be less stable and long lasting (Misovich, Fisher, & Fisher, 1996).

OBESITY

Obesity has been recognized by the World Health Organization as one of the top 10 global health problems. It is predicted that obesity could have as great an impact on health as smoking (Kelner & Helmuth, 2003; Statistics Canada, 2002). The Canadian Community Health Survey 2000–01 indicates that more than 15 percent of our adult population, or one out of every seven people, is obese. The number of obese Canadians is increasing rapidly. For example, between 1994–5 and 2000–01 the number of obese Canadians grew from approximately 2.2 million to almost 2.8 million. Perhaps not surprisingly, obesity levels increase with age, particularly for men. The lowest levels of obesity occur in urban areas of the country, most notably in Vancouver, Toronto, and Montreal (Statistics Canada, 2002).

What exactly is obesity? **Obesity** refers to an excess of body fat, which normally accounts for about 25 percent of weight in women and 18 percent in men (Bray, 1998). The most commonly used measure of obesity is the **body-mass index (BMI)**. Both Health Canada and the World Health Organization define obesity as a BMI of 30.0 or greater (Health Canada, 2003; WHO, 1998). To calculate your BMI divide your weight in kilograms by your height in metres squared:

$$BMI = (kg)/(m)^2 \text{ or } BMI = (lb. \times 700)/in./in.$$

(Or, if you are more familiar with imperial measurement, multiply your weight in pounds by 700. Divide this product by your height in inches. Then divide it again by your height). Alternatively, you might prefer to use the BMI calculator at the National Institute for Health (NIH) Web Site (www.nhlbisupport.com/bmi/), where you simply enter into the computer your height and weight, using either metric or imperial measurement, and your BMI will be calculated for you. Keep in mind that although the BMI estimates total body fat, it may not be accurate for selected populations (e.g., the elderly, certain ethnic groups, and persons with large muscle mass). For example, Arnold Schwarzenegger's BMI index might suggest that he is obese. However, we know better and we would suggest that he is fit rather than fat. More complex methods (e.g., densitometry) are available to professionals who require a more accurate measurement of body fat (Sheperd, 2003).

Generally speaking, as one's BMI increases so does one's risk of early mortality. A large prospective study following more than one million adults in the United States for 14 years documented that participants with a BMI of 40 or above had a relative risk of death two to six times that of their thinner counterparts with a BMI of 24 (Calle et al., 1999). Other studies report similar findings. For example, Bender and colleagues (1998) study found that a BMI under 32 was not linked to premature death, a BMI of 36 was related to a slight increase in mortality rates, and a BMI greater than 40 more than doubled the risk of premature death. However, we must point out that the relationship between body weight (BMI) and increased risk of death is actually J- or U-shaped. That is, those who are underweight have a slightly increased risk of mortality compared to those classified as normal weight (e.g., Lindsted & Singh, 1997; Fontaine, Redden, Wang, Westfall & Allison, 2003). In essence, the relative risk of death is highest among the thinnest and the heaviest individuals in our society.

TABLE 9-1	Health Risk Classification According to Body Mass Index (BMI)	
BMI	Classification	Risk of Developing Health Problems
<18.5	Underweight	Increased
18.5–24.9	Normal weight	Least
25.0–29.9	Overweight	Increased
30.0–34.9	Obese class I	High
35.0–39.9	Obese class II	Very high
>=40.0	Obese class III(Morbid obesity)	Extremely high

Source: *Canadian Guidelines for Body Weight Classification in Adults*, Health Canada, 2003. Reproduced with the permission of the Minister of Public Works and Government Services Canada, 2003.

Obesity contributes to an immense burden of not just physical, but also economic and emotional, suffering. The physical ailments that contribute most to premature death associated with obesity are hypertension, type 2 (adult onset) diabetes, and coronary heart disease (Birmingham, Muller, Palepu, Spinelli, & Anis, 1999). Obesity also predisposes one to arthritis, gout, gallbladder disease, sleep apnea, complications following surgery, and possibly also to various forms of cancer (Pi-Sunyer, 2003). The economic burden of obesity was estimated to exceed $1.8 billion in Canada for the year 1997. This was approximately 2.4 percent of total health care expenditures for that year (Birminham et al., 1999). In the United States, these costs were estimated to be $99 billion in 1995 (Wolf & Colditz, 1998). Personal costs are also prevalent. One prospective study documented that overweight adolescents were less likely to marry, had lower household incomes, and completed significantly fewer months of high school (despite equal grades) than their non-overweight counterparts (Gortmaker, Must, Perrin, Sobol & Dietz, 1993). Prejudice and discrimination when seeking college admissions, employment, or a place to live are also consequences experienced by those who are overweight (Wadden, Womble, Stunkard & Anderson, 2002). Despite these obstacles, some studies report that there is no evidence of an effect of being overweight on self-esteem in the general population (Gortmaker et al., 1993; Wadden et al., 2002). However, other studies report that overweight women are more likely to report being depressed or suicidal than are non-overweight women (e.g., Carpenter, Hasin, Allison & Faith, 2000). Certainly, depression, anxiety, and binge eating are more common in those who are overweight and are currently seeking weight reduction (Wadden, Brownell & Foster, 2002).

The statement "Genes load the gun, the environment pulls the trigger" (Bray, as cited in Wadden, et al., 2002, p. 512) fairly accurately summarizes the contributions of genetics and the environment to obesity. Genes are partly responsible for variance in BMI (Allison et al., 1996; Bouchard, 1994; Price, 2002). Genes also contribute to individual differences in basal metabolic rate (people with naturally lower basal metabolic rates burn fewer calories); in amount of weight gained after overeating; and in body fat distribution (Wadden et al., 2002). Some individuals are simply born with a genetic predisposition to obesity and our current cultural environment contributes to its exhibition.

Biological Factors That Contribute to Obesity

Heredity   Twin studies, adoption studies, and family studies indicate that genes contribute to the development of obesity. The strength of the heritability of obesity is akin to the strength of heritability of height (Friedman, 2003; Meyer & Stunkard, 1994). Maes, Neale, and Eaves (1996) reviewed the literature on the familial resemblance of BMI. Based on data from more than 25 000 twin pairs and 50 000 biological and adoptive family members, the following correlations were computed: 0.74 for monozygotic twins, 0.32 for dizygotic twins, 0.25 for siblings, 0.19 for parent-offspring pairs, and 0.06 for adoptive relatives. These figures provide convincing evidence that there is substantial heritability for obesity. Maes and colleagues conclude that genes account for approximately 67 percent of individual differences in BMI. The results of other studies corroborate these conclusions (e.g., Bulik, Sullivan & Kendler, 2003, Meyer & Stunkard, 1994).

Hormones and the Brain   The biological system that regulates our food intake and energy expenditure is extraordinarily complex and not well understood. Consider that over the period of ten years, an average individual consumes approximately ten million calories. Typically, the person will experience only a slight change of weight in that ten years. In order for such a slight weight variation, food consumption must be within 0.17 percent of energy expenditure over the entire decade (Friedman, 2003). Achieving this balance is quite an accomplishment; it is highly unlikely that a nutritionist counting calories could be so precise in matching food consumption with energy expenditure.

How does our body maintain such a constant weight? The **set-point theory** proposes that the body contains a set-point that works like a thermostat regulating heat in a home. When one gains weight, powerful biological control mechanisms diminish caloric intake. When one loses weight, similar mechanisms respond by increasing hunger levels until the person's weight returns to its ideal or target level. In 1994, a key element of this homeostatic system was discovered—the hormone **leptin** (Zhang et al., 1994). Leptin reports to the neurons of the hypothalamus (a key regulatory centre in the brain) whether there are sufficient fat stores in the body or whether additional energy is needed. Leptin is produced by fat cells, therefore when fat stores increase, the body's level of leptin increases. This, in turn, suppresses the neurons that stimulate hunger and activates those that reduce food intake. When there is a decrease in body fat the reverse occurs—leptin levels decrease, resulting in stimulation of appetite and a reduction of energy expenditure (Friedman, 2000; Friedman, 2003).

If this homeostatic system can maintain weight within a relatively narrow range, why are some individuals obese and others are not? There appear to be individual differences in sensitivity to leptin. It may be that obese individuals are simply less sensitive to leptin or that they are leptin-resistant (Considine & Caro, 1996; Friedman, 2003). This would explain why obese people tend to have more leptin in their bodies. They must produce more of the hormone to compensate for their lack of sensitivity (Nakamura et al., 2000). In very rare conditions, individuals may lack the hormone leptin completely (See Case 9-1).

CASE 9-1	**Hormones Contribute to Regulation of Body Weight**

Two young English girls have become famous as a result of their obesity. The older, nine-year-old, cousin had legs so large she could barely walk. The younger cousin could consume more than 1100 calories at a single meal. That's half of what the average adult will eat in a day! The girls were found to lack the weight-regulating hormone leptin. In order to treat their obesity the girls were given leptin injections. After only a few such injections their calorie consumption decreased by a dramatic 84 percent. Their new appetites were now similar to those of other children their age. The outcome is amazing. Both girls are now at body weights considered normal for their size and are enjoying normal lives (Farooqui, et al., 2002; Friedman, 2003).

Psychosocial Factors That Contribute to Obesity

Hunger and eating behaviour are not controlled solely by biological factors. In fact, our biology is now almost maladaptive in our environment of food abundance and sedentariness. Currently, social norms and values serve to reinforce behaviours that promote obesity. We associate food with celebrations, rewards, and social occasions. Therefore, it is not surprising that we turn to food when anxious or depressed (e.g., Arnow et al., 1992; Polivy & Herman, 1987.)

Stress and Eating   Stress affects people differently, and consequently it also affects people's eating behaviours differently. Approximately half the population will eat more when feeling stress and the other half will eat less. (Willenbring, Levine, & Morley, 1986). People of average weight who are not preoccupied with food often ignore or misinterpret physiological cues to hunger and therefore eat less. In contrast, stress can cause dieters to lose control, causing disinhibition or counterregulation, and consequently, overeating (e.g., Heatherton, Herman, & Polivy, 1992; Polivy, 1996).

Stress may also influence the food choices people make. In one study (Grunberg & Straub, 1992), participants watched either a stressful video about eye surgery or an enjoyable travelogue. Snack foods consisting of salty peanuts, bland rice cakes, and sweet M & M candies were placed within arm's reach. The sweet M & M's were consumed less often by those watching the stressful video. There was an exception, however; women who were frequent dieters chose the sweets in the stressful situation. Other research has shown that salty foods are often chosen in response to stress (Willenbring et al., 1986).

Sociocultural Factors That Contribute to Obesity

There is clear evidence that our eating and activity habits are influenced by the people around us. When people move from a less developed country to a more modern country where food, particularly rich food, is plentiful, they tend to gain weight. For example, Bhatnager and colleagues (1995) tracked individuals who migrated to West London from Punjab, India. Compared to their siblings who remained in Punjab, those who took up residence in London gained body weight. Similarly, the dietary fat intake of Pima Indian women living in Arizona was almost double that compared to their relatives remaining in Mexico (Ravussin, Valencia, Esparza, Bennett, & Schulz, 1994).

On a more immediate level, we are influenced by our parents' eating behaviours (e.g., diet, portion size; Klesges, Eck, Hanson, Haddock, & Klesges, 1990). Parents may influence their children's eating behaivours by encouraging them to overeat. The result, not suprisingly, is that these children are more likely to become obese adults (Berkowitz, Agras, Korner, Kraemer, & Zeanah, 1985) Even our pets are influenced by the family environment. One study found that 44 percent of the dogs owned by obese people were obese, compared with only 25 percent of the dogs owned by people of normal weight (Mason, 1970).

Environmental and Hunger Cues   Most of us live a lifestyle that is laden with time pressures. We are exposed to an environment bursting with highly advertised, highly accessible foods (e.g., fast food restaurants, buffet restaurants, food franchises in school cafeterias; Hill et al., 2003). Is it any wonder that we respond to these cues by eating more prepackaged and fast foods? The way we respond to cues in our environment led Schachter (1971) to propose the **internality–externality hypothesis**. This hypothesis asserts that in people of normal weight, feelings of hunger and satiety come from within, in the form of internal stimuli (e.g., hunger pangs or feelings of fullness). In contrast, obese people are more in tune with external stimuli (e.g., time of day, smell or sight of food) for determining their level of hunger. Although highly influential, there has not been consistent support for this hypothesis. For example, Rodin (1981) discovered that internal sensitivity is not a characteristic unique to normal weight persons. Likewise, externality can lead to overeating in everyone, regardless of weight category. To further understand the relationship between external stimuli and eating behaviour, Herman and Polivy have focused their research on this topic (see Focus on Canadian Research 9-1).

Focus on Canadian Research 9-1	Eating Behaviour: Can You Restrain Yourself?

Peter Herman and Janet Polivy, both of the University of Toronto, have spent nearly 30 years studying eating behaviour. In 1975, Herman and Polivy (as cited in Straub, 2001) proposed the **restraint theory** of eating behaviour. According to their theory, external sensitivity is linked to *restrained eating* (or strict dieting), rather than to body weight. When one is preoccupied with body-weight norms food consumption will swing between restrained eating and overindulging.

In a typical study (e.g., Herman & Polivy, 1980), participants are classified as either high or low on restraint based on their responses to questions such as "How often are you dieting?" and "Do you give too much time and thought to food?" Initially, the participants are given food to consume, for example a milkshake Subsequently, participants take part in a "taste test," and they are allowed to "taste" as much food (e.g., ice cream) as they like from the selection that is offered. The researchers are only interested in the amount of food

consumed and each plate of cookies or dish of ice cream is measured after the participant is finished "tasting." The restrained eaters, who frequently think about food and are more likely to be dieting, consume more food than do the *unrestrained eaters* (those who are not trying to limit their food intake).

Subsequent studies have determined that restrained eaters are more sensitive and reactive to food cues than are unrestrained eaters. Consequently, their appetites increase in response to these cues and they will consume more food than if not exposed to such cues. Both cognitive and olfactory cues produce increased intake of food by restrained eaters compared to unrestrained eaters. The specific food does not seem to alter results (Fedoroff, Polivy, & Herman, 1997). However, restrained eaters eat more only when the food presented to them to eat is the same as the prior food cues (Fedoroff, Polivy, & Herman, 2003).

Variations on this research have discovered that restrained participants'

(continued on next page)

own hunger ratings can be affected by fictitious hunger reports, but their actual food consumption remains unaltered (Herman, Fitzgerald & Polivy, 2003). Another variation determined that restrained eaters who were led to believe that they weighed five pounds more than they actually did consumed more food during a subsequent "taste test" than did those who were provided with their true weight or a weight that was five pounds lighter than their actual weight. The authors contend that lowered self-worth and a worsening of mood experienced by those who were led to believe they were heavier than they really were led them to abandon their dietary control and overindulge (McFarlane, Polivy, & Herman, 1998).

Herman and Polivy's research also highlights the dynamic connection between dieting and overeating. One of their studies investigated the effect of anticipated food deprivation on food consumption in restrained and unrestrained eaters. Participants completed a taste test immediately after being assigned to either a diet condition (in which they expected to diet for a week) or a control condition (no diet). Unrestrained eaters consumed the same amount of food no matter what condition they had been assigned to. In contrast, restrained eaters had greater food intake when assigned to the diet condition than when assigned to the control condition. These and similar findings indicate that restricting one's eating or dieting to lose weight may have unanticipated deleterious effects (e.g., eating binges and preoccupation with food and eating). Polivy (1996) recommends that a healthful, balanced diet is the best approach to "dieting."

Prevention and Treatment of Obesity

Clearly, prevention is the best way to attack the current obesity epidemic. Pi-Sunyer (2003) reports that education at two levels is essential. On one level, we must educate the public. Campaigns like those for smoking should be launched. As well, because we know that people consume more energy than they expend, Hill et al. (2003) advocate that only a small reduction in net energy input will prevent further increases in obesity rates. Based on the average weight gain in the U.S. population of 1.8 to 2.0 pounds per year, Hill determined that on average people have an energy gap of 100 kcal a day. To reduce this energy gap, we should either reduce our caloric intake by 100 or find a way to expend more energy. Walking a mile by adding 2000 to 2500 extra steps throughout the day would burn 100 calories for most people. Alternatively, eating 15 percent less a day by reducing portion sizes should accomplish the same goal. Childhood obesity has become increasingly prevalent over the last 20 years; therefore, we should take extra steps to encourage children to make healthy food choices and to exert energy (Ball & McCargar, 2003). On another level, Pi-Sunyer states that more health care professionals should become equipped to educate and treat obese people. These health care professionals must be provided the nutritional knowledge and counselling skills that will equip them to facilitate lifestyle changes in their patients (Pi-Sunyer, 2003).

For many, education about prevention of obesity comes too late and treatment is required. Historically, dieting has been the most common approach to losing weight. At any given time, nearly 44 percent of women and 29 percent of men in the United States are trying to lose weight (Serdula, et al., 1999). Some individuals are motivated to lose weight because it reduces health risks, whereas others are motivated to lose weight to improve their appearance. The majority of people who try to lose weight do so on their own rather than following preset guidelines. Approximately 20 percent of people follow healthy guidelines that restrict their caloric intake and supplement their balanced diet with exercise (Serdula et al., 1999). Weight loss is usually successful following this approach or when structured meal plans and grocery lists are provided (e.g., Wing, et al., 1996).

Generally when people do lose weight by dieting they are not able to keep the weight off. Paradoxically, the more people try to control their weight, the more their weight increases in the long run (Stice, Cameron, Killen, Hayward & Taylor, 1999). Frequently people will lose the same ten pounds over and over again. This repeated cycle of weight loss and gain is referred to as yo-yo dieting (Brownell, 1988). Unfortunately, frequent dieting has a negative impact on psychological well-being and is often accompanied by compromised psychological functioning in the form of impaired concentration, food preoccupation, and binge eating (McFarlane, Polivy, & McCabe, 1999). Although dieting is a requisite to losing weight, the best approach is to lose weight gradually and to make permanent lifestyle changes that can be maintained.

Pharmacological Treatment of Obesity

Both prescription and over-the-counter drugs are often used to reduce appetite and restrict food consumption (Bray & Tartaglia, 2000). Stimulants, such as amphetamines, have provided short-term weight loss. Stimulants result in weight loss because they increase metabolism and reduce appetite. However, to remain effective, ever-increasing doses must be consumed. This may result in physical dependence, a health hazard worse than obesity. Most currently available obesity drugs are not very effective and have negative side effects. Leptin, a hormone discussed earlier, is currently being tested in both animal and clinical trials, however initial trials have been disappointing (Gura, 2003; Wadden et al., 2002). Investigators expect that additional research on the genetics of body weight regulation will provide new drug targets (Gura, 2003). However, the physiology of weight control is complex and "most researchers doubt that a pharmaceutical 'silver bullet' will be found that will allow us all to achieve healthy weights" (Komaroff, 2003).

Behavioural Treatment of Obesity

Behavioural treatments described previously in the context of smoking cessation have also been applied to reducing obesity. Behavioural treatment of obesity is at least as effective as pharmacological treatment (Wadden et al., 2002). Typically, individuals will take part in a program that lasts approximately 20 weeks. The program will likely include one or more of the following strategies:

- Stimulus control procedures that identify and modify external cues to eating (e.g., confining food intake to a particular place and time such as in the dining room at meal time).
- Self-monitoring and record keeping of the type and quantity of food eaten each day. This provides awareness of the foods that are eaten and the situations in which one eats.

- Self-control techniques to control the amount eaten or to slow the act of eating (e.g., dieters can be instructed to place the proper proportion of food on their plate at one time and once all of the food is on the plate to eat by replacing their fork after each bite).
- Social support to help control stress that may arise (e.g., having a dieting "buddy," joining a program such as Weight Watchers, or enlisting the help of a friend or family member).
- Contingency contracts, also known as behavioural contracts, that consist of rewards for achieving goals (or punishments for not reaching a goal). The contracts may be self-monitored or another person may be enlisted to monitor the behaviour and reward or punish accordingly.

A behavioural treatment program usually leads to a loss of 8.5 to 9.0 kg, or approximately 9 percent of initial body weight (e.g. Wing, 2002). Regrettably, without further treatment, those who lost weight using behaviour therapies are likely to regain approximately one third of the weight lost in the subsequent year.

Surgical Treatment of Obesity

Surgical interventions are a radical way to control extreme obesity (BMI > 40). In 1969, Mason and Ito developed a procedure called a **gastric bypass** that is still widely used today. In this procedure a small pouch is created at the bottom of the esophagus to limit food intake. Food that enters the pouch bypasses the stomach and part of the intestine. Those who undergo this procedure can expect to lose approximately 30 percent of their initial weight during the first 18 months. Approximately 25 percent of the weight loss will be maintained (Albrecht & Pories, 1999; Wadden et al., 2002).

| CASE 9-2 | **Bulimia Nervosa in Teenagers** |

Julia is an attractive girl of normal weight who has always been concerned with her appearance. If you ever want to know what clothes are trendy, take a look at what Julia is wearing. She can even tell you what colours of lipstick and fingernail polish are "in" this month. How does she know this? She reads magazines like *Elle* and *Cosmopolitan* religiously. Her friends are also very "up to date," and in junior high school they jointly began to engage in a behaviour they felt was "fashion-able." As a group, the girls would go into the washroom and throw up. Julia says she was not all that concerned with losing weight but she didn't want to gain any either. In fact, the purging began more because it seemed to be a "cool" thing to do rather than because of concerns Julia might have had about her own weight. Unfortunately, the purging changed from a group activity to something she did frequently on her own. It soon became a habit for Julia to vomit after eating—a very unhealthy habit.

EATING DISORDERS

In Case 9-2, Julia's behaviour is indicative of an eating disorder known as **bulimia nervosa**. Bulimia nervosa involves recurrent episodes of binge eating followed by purging. The purging strategies used most frequently are vomiting and laxative use. This disorder can result in numerous medical problems, such as anemia, inflammation of the digestive tract, heart arrhythmias resulting from electrolyte imbalances (which may cause sudden death), and irreversible erosion of dental enamel (British Columbia Eating Disorder Association [BCEDA], 1998). Although some bulimics are overweight, most, like Julia, are of normal weight. Despite the fact that the behaviour may begin as a group activity, in general, bulimics are aware that their behaviour is not normal, and they are ashamed of it. Because of this, they usually try to hide their behaviour from others. In addition to reporting negative aspects of the disorder such as shame and preoccupation with weight or shape, patients with bulimia nervosa also describe positive aspects of the disorder. These positive aspects include being able to eat and not get fat and as a way to combat boredom. (Serpell & Treasure, 2002).

The binge portion of the bulimic episode is often impulsive, and bulimics are likely to engage in other impulsive and reckless behaviours as well (Fischer, Smith, & Anderson, 2003). For example, kleptomania is more common among bulimics than among the general population. Although the items stolen are usually associated with the bulimic's binging and purging (such as food or laxatives), it isn't uncommon for a bulimic to steal clothing, cosmetics, alcohol, or other unneeded items. Bulimics are also more likely than the general population to engage in spending sprees or sexual promiscuity because of their impulsive nature (e.g., Matsunaga et al., 2000).

The number of patients being diagnosed with eating disorders is increasing (Polivy & Herman, 2002; Walsh & Devlin, 1998). A survey of adolescents across British Columbia found that in the seven days preceding the survey, unhealthy weight control practices (e.g., purging after meals or using diet pills) were admitted to by 6 percent of the male students and 7 percent of the female students (McCreary Centre Society, 1993). Although eating disorders are most common among adolescents and adults, even children suffer from eating disorders. Seventy percent of children with eating disorders are female. In the adolescent and adult eating disorder population, 90 to 95 percent of those with eating disorders are female. How prevalent are eating disorders? Although there are no Canadian statistics available, in the United States bulimia has been found to occur in 1 to 20 percent of individuals, depending on the population under study (BCEDA, 1998). The University of Toronto Program for Eating Disorders (Kruger, McVey, & Kennedy, 1998) has noticed an increasing proportion of patients who suffer from bulimia nervosa, and reports that the number of patients with bulimia nervosa outnumbers those with anorexia nervosa by at least two to one (Polivy & Herman, 2002).

Anorexia nervosa is an eating disorder characterized by a dramatic reduction in food intake and extreme weight loss. According to the DSM-IV (American Psychiatric Association, 1997), the diagnostic criteria for anorexia nervosa are maintaining a body weight at less than 85 percent of normal weight for one's age and height, an intense fear of fatness, disturbance in the way one's body weight or shape is experienced, and amenorrhea for at least three consecutive months. Anorexics are very fearful of gaining weight and consequently will refuse food and may engage in excessive exercise. Yet, anorexics are very preoccupied with food and may spend a lot of their time cooking for others or engaging in other pursuits that revolve around food. The self-starvation in anorexia will lead to low blood pressure, heart damage or cardiac arrhythmias, and eventually death. At the point of near starvation, the person will lose the hair on his or her head and fine hair growth (lanugo) will appear on the face and body. Anorexics are also at increased risk of osteoporosis (e.g., Mehler, 2003).

Anorexia is less prevalent in the general population than bulimia (ranging from 0.5 percent to 4 percent). Anorexia occurs most often in Caucasian adolescent females from the upper social classes and those who practise ballet, model, or are competitive in sports (Steinhausen et al., 1997; Thompson & Sherman, 1993). Yet, anorexia is increasingly being seen in patients who are very young, male, less affluent, and people of colour (Gard & Freeman, 1996; Story et al., 1995; Thompson & Sherman, 1993). There is some indication that gay men are slightly over-represented among anorexics (Carlat, Camargo, & Herzog, 1997). However, researchers state that both male and female anorexics are more likely than the general population to identify themselves as asexual.

Biological, Cultural, and Psychological Contributors to Eating Disorders

Biological, cultural, and psychological factors may all be possible contributors to eating disorders. Twin studies have documented that both twins are more likely to suffer from eating disorders if the twins are identical rather than fraternal (Klump, McGue & Iacono, 2000; Walters & Kendler, 1995). Other researchers have also reported an increased risk of eating disorders among relatives (Agras, Hammer, & McNicholas, 1999; Whelan & Cooper, 2000). Neuroendocrine factors, which might or might not be genetic in origin may contribute to eating disorders (Polivy & Herman, 2002)

In North American society, there is pressure on individuals to be thin and stay youthful. This expectation is learned at a very young age. When children reach puberty and naturally gain weight, many become distressed. Often adolescents will try to control their weight by dieting. Unfortunately, this strategy is sometimes carried too far, and this is when many eating disorders begin. In fact, dieting is the most important predictor of new eating disorders (Patton et al., 1999). Eating disorders are more likely to occur in individuals from families in which eating disorders, psychopathology, alcoholism, or sexual abuse exist or have taken place (Polivy & Herman, 2002). The media is also partly to blame for this pressure. Researchers (e.g., Stice, 1994) have documented that females who have greater exposure to media containing a high concentration of body images show more characteristics of eating disorders than do females with less exposure to this media.

Psychological factors associated with eating disorders include issues of control, low self-esteem, extreme sensitivity to other's feelings, perfectionism, maturity fears, and distorted body image (BCEDA, 1998). Hilde Bruch (1973, 1978, 1982), who spent more than 40 years studying eating disorders, reported that anorexics typically are troubled female adolescents who feel incapable of changing their lives. These young women are from families that do not encourage autonomy and are perceived by the adolescent as overdemanding. More recent research corroborates this view and implies that insecure attachment is common in eating disordered populations (Ward et al., 2000a, b). To exert some control in their lives, they exert control over the thing closest to them, their bodies.

Many individuals who suffer from eating disorders do not perceive their bodies accurately, a condition referred to as **body dysmorphic disorder** (Chung, 2001). Women, in general, see themselves as one-fourth larger than they really are (Thompson, 1986). Men may also see themselves as larger than they really are but they do so to a lesser degree and, unlike women, many of these men may want to be larger (Geist et al., 1999; see Box 9-3). Both anorexics and bulimics tend to overestimate their body size to a greater extent than does the general population.

BOX 9-3	Muscle dysmorphia: The body dysmorphic disorder especially for men.

For men, the fear of being and looking like a "97-pound weakling" is not new, as a look through the ads in old comic books will attest. Yet, today more than ever, many men fear that they are too small and skinny. In the words of Roberto Olivardia, "They feel like Clark Kent and long to be Superman" (2001, p. 254).

While conducting research on anabolic steroids, Olivardia and his supervisor, Harrison Pope, met several large and muscular bodybuilders who confided that they felt small and frail (Pope, 2001). Sometimes these people were referred to as experiencing "reverse anorexia" or "bigorexia," but the term most often used today is **muscle dysmorphia** (Olivardia, 2001). There is some debate as to whether muscle dysmorphia should be classified in the American Psychiatric Association's Diagnostic and Statistical Manual as a subcategory of body dysmorphic disorder, a subcategory of obsessive compulsive disorder; or whether it and anorexia nervosa should be in a category on their own (Chung, 2001). However, most people agree on the criteria for making a diagnosis of muscle dysmorphia (Olivardia, 2001, p. 255): 1) a preoccupation with the idea that one's body is not sufficiently lean and muscular; 2) clinically significant

distress or impairment in social, occupational, or other areas of functioning; 3) a primary focus on being too small or inadequately muscular.

Due to their preoccupation with their body, individuals with muscle dysmorphia look at their bodies in the mirror many times a day. The need to look in the mirror becomes so strong that "one young man got into several car accidents because he compulsively checked a large hand-held mirror while driving to ensure that he wasn't getting smaller" (Olivardia, 2001, p. 255). Obviously, a preoccupation such as this can be detrimental. Many men with muscle dysmorphia are so obsessed with working out that they lose their jobs. Lawyers, doctors, and businessmen relinquish their careers so they can spend more time working out (Olivardia et al., 2000; Pope, 2001). A few specific examples include a lawyer who was fired because he often took three-to-four-hour lunch breaks to fit in his workout, a student who missed a final exam because the time conflicted with his workout, and a man who missed the birth of his child so he could lift weights (Olivardia, 2001). Another behaviour characteristic of individuals with muscle dysmorphia is hiding one's body. These individuals are so ashamed

(continued on next page)

of their bodies that they avoid situations where their bodies will be exposed to others. Many even refuse to take their shirts off at the beach (Pope, 2001).

What causes muscle dysmorphia? Biological, psychological, and sociocultural explanations have all been put forth (Olivardia, 2001). There may be an underlying biological or genetic predisposition to experience muscle dysmorphia. Also, low self-esteem and masculinity issues are typical in men with muscle dysmorphia. Achieving a body that is respected and admired by others may be a response to these psychological issues. The explanation that has received the most attention, however, is sociocultural in nature. That is, boys and

men are now experiencing appearance-related societal pressures similar to those that women have experienced for decades. The ideal male body in our culture is becoming increasingly more muscular. A look at either centrefold models in Playgirl magazine (Leit, Pope, & Gray, 2000) or male action toys such as G.I. Joe (Pope et al., 1999) confirm this. We also know that when exposed to muscular images, like those presented in advertisements, men will show a greater discrepancy between their own perceived muscularity and the level of muscularity that they consider ideal (Leit, Gray & Pope, 2002). Thus, it is likely that there are a number of factors contributing to muscle dysmorphia.

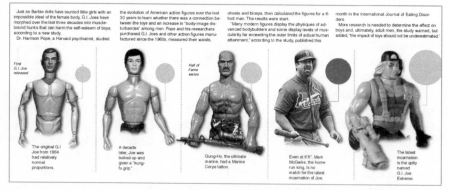

Just as Barbie dolls have taunted little girls with an impossible ideal of the female body, G.I. Joes have morphed over the last three decades into muscle-bound hunks that can harm the self-esteem of boys, according to a new study. Dr. Harrison Pope, a Harvard psychiatrist, studied the evolution of American action figures over the last 30 years to learn whether there was a connection between the toys and an increase in "body-image disturbances" among men. Pope and his researchers purchased G.I. Joes and other action figures manufactured since the 1960s, measured their waists, chests and biceps, then calculated the figures for a 6-foot man. The results were stark. "Many modern figures display the physiques of advanced bodybuilders and some display levels of muscularity far exceeding the outer limits of actual human attainment," according to the study, published this month in the International Journal of Eating Disorders. More research is needed to determine the effect on boys and, ultimately, adult men, the study warned, but added, "the impact of toys should not be underestimated."

First G.I. Joe released

The original G.I. Joe from 1964 had relatively normal proportions.

A decade later, Joe was bulked up and given a "kung-fu grip."

Hall of Fame series

Gung-Ho, the ultimate marine, had a Marine Corps tattoo.

Even at 6'5", Mark McGwire, the home run king, is no match for the latest incarnation of Joe.

The latest incarnation is the aptly named G.I. Joe Extreme.

G.I. Joe has become more muscle-bound over the last three decades. The latest G.I. Joe, G.I. Joe Extreme, has a body that is unattainable by even the largest bodybuilders. Is the current North American cultural ideal of the male body so large and muscular that it represents an unattainable standard?

Treatment for Eating Disorders

Successful treatment for eating disorders is literally a matter of life or death. This is particularly true for anorexics, because nearly 6 percent of all anorexics die from their disorder (Neumarker, 1997). Not surprisingly, anorexics are very difficult to treat because they believe that the one aspect of their environment they can control is their own body. As long as they refuse to eat they maintain control. As starvation continues, anorexics eventually reach the point of exhaustion and possible physical collapse. At this point, treatment is usually forced on them. The first goal of treatment is to medically stabilize the patient and increase his or her weight (Goldner & Brimingham, 1994). Weight restoration is a step in the treatment process but is not a cure. Anorexics need to change both their body image *and* their eating habits. Cognitive behaviour therapy attempts to eradicate the irrational beliefs of patients while maintaining a warm and accepting attitude. For example, anorexics are to avoid absolutist thoughts like, "If I put on one pound, I'll go on to gain one hundred." Similarly, they are educated about nutritional facts. Superstitious beliefs like "Laxatives prevent the absorption of calories" are dispelled. Patients are also encouraged to recognize that others do not have the same high standards for their behaviour that they do (Thompson & Sherman, 1993). Family therapy is often included in the treatment process. It has been found that family participation positively influences the results of therapy (Eisler et al., 1999).

Bulimia is much easier to treat than anorexia, because bulimics are aware that their eating habits are not normal. As a result, they are motivated to change these behaviours. Treatment for bulimia usually includes cognitive-behavioural therapy. This is often combined with drug therapy. Typically therapy begins by patients being instructed to monitor their eating habits. An individualized treatment program is then developed to help break down patterns of behaviour that maintain disordered eating and will include such things as reinforcement, relaxation training, and cognitive restructuring (Thackwray, Smith, Bodfish, & Meyers, 1993). Specific techniques might include increasing the regularity of meals, eating a greater variety of foods, delaying the impulse to purge as long as possible, and eating foods in new settings not previously associated with binges (Agras et al., 1989; Kirkley, Schneider, Agras, & Bachman, 1985). The cognitive-behavioural techniques implemented should address the pathological concerns bulimics have about their weight and eating in addition to increasing perceptions of self-esteem. Drugs, especially antidepressants, are used in managing bulimia. It has been determined that they decrease the frequency of binges (Mitchell & de Zwaan, 1993). However, drugs do not treat the cause of the problem and as such, they should only be used to treat bulimia in conjunction with other forms of therapy (Compas et al., 1998).

Unfortunately, as many as half of previously treated eating-disorder sufferers will continue to have eating problems. The difficulty in treating eating disorders effectively, coupled with their increasing prevalence, suggests that researchers should focus more on ways to prevent eating disorders rather than focusing almost exclusively on treating them after they have developed (Battle & Brownell, 1996; Mann et al., 1997).

KEY TERMS

addiction (p. 231)

addictive smokers (p. 228)

alcohol dependency syndrome model (p. 236)

alcohol myopia (p. 237)

anorexia nervosa (p. 251)

aversion therapies (p. 232)

biobehavioural model (p. 229)

body dysmorphic disorder (p. 253)

body-mass index (BMI) (p. 243)

bulimia nervosa (p. 251)

disease model (p. 236)

environmental tobacco smoke (p. 230)

ethanol (p. 235)

ethyl alcohol (p. 235)

gastric bypass (p. 250)

habitual smoker (p. 228)

hallucinogens (p. 239)

information–motivation–
behavioural skills model
(p. 242)

internality-externality
hypothesis (p. 247)

leptin (p. 245)

multiple regulation model
(p. 229)

muscle dysmorphia
(p. 253)

negative-affect smoker
(p. 228)

nicotine fixed-effect
model (p. 229)

nicotine regulation model
(p. 229)

nicotine-replacement
therapy (p. 232)

obesity (p. 243)

passive smoking (p. 230)

positive-affect smoker
(p. 228)

restraint theory (p. 247)

self-awareness model
(p. 236)

self-management
strategies (p. 233)

set-point theory (p. 245)

social learning model
(p. 237)

stimulant (p. 240)

tension reduction
hypothesis (p. 236)

withdrawal (p. 231)

chapter ten

Pain

CHAPTER OUTLINE

The Significance of Pain

Pain Perception

Theories of Pain

   Gate Control Theory

   Neuromatrix Theory

Neurochemical Basis of Pain and Pain Inhibition

Acute versus Chronic Pain

Psychosocial Factors and Pain

   Gender Differences

   Cultural Differences

The Measurement of Pain

   Psychophysiological Measures

   Behavioural Assessment

Self-Reports of Pain

Assessing Pain in Infants and Children

Assessing Pain in Older Adults

Pain Control Techniques

Pharmacological Control of Pain

Surgical Control of Pain

Transcutaneous Electrical Nerve Stimulation

Acupuncture

Physical Therapy

Massage

Relaxation

Distraction

Biofeedback

Hypnosis

Multidisciplinary Pain Management Programs

KEY QUESTIONS

1. What are the benefits to experiencing pain?

2. How do early theories of pain differ from more contemporary theories?

3. How does acute pain differ from chronic pain?

4. How does the culture people belong to influence their experience of and response to pain?

5. What are the different methods used to measure pain?

6. How does pain measurement differ in children and adults?

7. What are some of the pain control techniques available to the pain sufferer?

8. Why are multidisciplinary pain management programs so successful?

At 22 years of age, Jake was a happy-go-lucky, athletic apprentice chef in an exclusive restaurant. He loved his job and took it very seriously. One day, when the master chef was away, two boxes of chickens were delivered. Jake cut up the chickens and packaged them for the freezer. Not long after, he became very ill. Jake was finally diagnosed as having been infected with Salmonella, caused by a bacterium that is usually present on raw chicken meat. Jake was quarantined in the hospital where he spent 10 days and lost 30 pounds.

Upon his discharge from the hospital, Jake rapidly resumed his old activities—he went back to work and immediately returned to playing soccer. However, six weeks later, a host of new symptoms appeared: joint pain, urethritis (inflammation of the urethra), and conjunctivitis (inflammation of the eye). This triad of symptoms is indicative of Reiter's syndrome. Reiter's syndrome occurs in two to three percent of patients exposed to bacteria known to promote it (including that which produces Salmonella). In North America, 30 in every 100 000 individuals will experience this syndrome at some point in their lives. The incidence rate is five times higher for males than for females. Although most people recover from this illness in six months, in some it "grumbles on" for 12 or more months, and a small minority develop unremitting and potentially disabling arthritis. Unfortunately, Jake was one of the unlucky ones. His physician told him his pain would increase over time and that he would eventually lose mobility—not an easy prognosis for anyone to accept and especially not for an active person at such a young age.

With his eternal optimism, Jake continued to embrace life. He made a career change and found a job where he would be interacting with others all day—he became a bus driver. This job was the perfect fit for Jake, because he loved people and almost everyone he came in contact with became an instant friend. At the beginning Jake rarely exhibited any pain. He married and had two children. As the years passed, his pain increased and, as a result, he took more and more painkillers. As the pain became more and more excruciating, it got to the point where he was consuming 14 Tylenol Threes a day (far exceeding the recommended dosage). Then, 13 years after the initial diagnosis, he just couldn't keep it "together" any longer.

Jake became extremely depressed and began to experience anxiety attacks. He was off work for a few months but he then returned to his jovial self. Once back at work, he drove a bus for only three weeks before he had to go on leave again. Emotionally, he was sinking deeper and deeper. He became suicidal and began abusing his medication, taking far more than the physician had prescribed. Secretly, he also began abusing alcohol. Jake was checked into a hospital where he would receive psychiatric help. After a number of weeks in the hospital, Jake was discharged and seemed to be in better spirits. Unfortunately, Jake will have to live with physical pain for the rest of his life. He has tried, in his words, "every pain management technique available." In addition to pharmacological treatment, he has tried acupuncture, guided imagery, meditation, physical exercises, and massage therapy. He recently returned from a 10-day stay at a pain clinic. Jake said that the pain management techniques at the clinic ranged from group hugs to a few very painful procedures where he screamed louder than he had ever screamed before. Jake states that the most beneficial aspect of this visit was that he learned that he really wasn't "so bad off." Many of the other patients were currently experiencing more pain than he was, and the ordeals that they had gone through were heartrending. Currently, Jake continues to be in good spirits, he participates in aqua therapy, and visits a massage therapist.

He knows that he will be taking medication for the rest of his life, and very recently his physician told him he may have to give up the idea of ever driving a bus again.

Jake's pain is considered chronic or long-term. The pain that Jake experiences as a result of Reiter's syndrome has affected him in many ways. It has affected him emotionally. Jake can no longer work in the job he loves and is currently living on disability payments; a situation that is hard on his self-esteem. It is not surprising that depression and anxiety are often experienced by people with chronic pain. His social life has changed considerably and for more than a year he didn't want to see even his closest friends. Obviously, the pain has affected him physically as well. Jake can no longer play soccer with his teammates. He only hopes that he will still be able to kick the soccer ball around with his children when they are old enough. It is true that pain of any kind usually leads people to change their activity level. As this chapter explains, such pain behaviours are an important component of the pain experience.

THE SIGNIFICANCE OF PAIN

After reading about Jake, the idea of a life without pain might sound rather appealing. You would feel no pain when falling down, when stubbing your toe, or when slamming your finger in the car door. Headaches would not exist. You would feel no pain while exercising, and giving birth might even be considered a pleasant experience. But before you conclude that life would be wonderful with no pain, consider the case of Miss C., a young Canadian girl who was a student at McGill University (Melzack & Wall, 1996). Miss C.'s father, a physician, suggested to his colleagues in Montreal that they should examine her. Miss C. was highly intelligent and seemed normal in every way except that she had never felt pain. As a child, she had bitten off the tip of her tongue while chewing food and had suffered third-degree burns on her legs after kneeling on a hot radiator to look out a window. In fact, Miss C. could not remember ever sneezing or coughing, and she had neither the gag reflex nor the corneal reflex that protects the eyes.

The physicians who examined Miss C. subjected her to tests that would have felt like forms of torture in a normal person. They administered electric shocks to different parts of her body and immersed her limbs in hot water at temperatures that usually produce reports of burning pain. They immersed her limbs in cold water for prolonged periods and pinched tendons. She felt no pain. In addition, her heart rate, blood pressure, and respiration remained normal throughout the tests.

As a result of her inability to experience pain, Miss C. had severe medical problems, including pathological changes in her knees, hip, and spine. Melzack and Wall (1996) explain that insensitivity to pain can lead people to remain in one position too long, causing inflammation of the joints. Even worse, the failure to feel pain leads one to neglect injuries; as a result, healing is impeded. Injured tissue can easily become infected. These infections are very difficult to treat, particularly if they extend to the bone.

Miss C. died when she was only 29 years old of massive infections that could not be brought under control. Miss C.'s insensitivity to pain directly contributed to the infections that killed her.

Thus, there are benefits to experiencing pain. Pain is known to serve at least three functions. First, the pain that occurs before serious injury, such as when we step on or pick up hot, sharp, or otherwise potentially damaging objects, has real survival value. It produces immediate withdrawal that prevents further injury. Second, the pains that prevent further injury serve as the basis of learning to avoid injurious objects or situations that may occur at a later time. Third, pains due to damaged joints, abdominal infections, diseases, or serious injuries set limits on activity and enforce inactivity and rest, which are often essential for the body's natural recuperative and disease-fighting mechanisms to ensure recovery and survival.

An individual's experience of pain is often obvious to others.

PAIN PERCEPTION

When a person comes in contact with injurious stimuli, signals of tissue damage follow a particular route from **afferent (sensory) neurons** of the peripheral nervous system to the spinal cord and then to the brain. The afferent nerve endings that respond to pain stimuli are called **nociceptors**. When activated, these nerve endings generate impulses that travel to the central nervous system. The afferent peripheral fibres that transmit pain impulses are

A-delta fibres and **C-fibres**. A-delta fibres are associated with sharp, distinct pain. The A-delta fibres are small, myelinated fibres that transmit impulses very quickly. In contrast, C-fibres transmit impulses more slowly because they are unmyelinated. The C-fibres, which comprise over 60 percent of all sensory afferents, are involved when pain is diffuse, dull, or aching (Melzack & Wall, 1996). The afferent fibres group together after leaving the periphery, and this grouping forms a nerve. The nerves then enter the dorsal horns of the spinal cord; these contain several layers, or laminae, each of which receives incoming messages from afferent neurons. The cells in the first two layers form the substantia gelatinosa, and it is here where sensory input information is thought to be modulated. Sensory aspects of pain are strongly influenced by activity in A-delta fibres, which send messages through the thalamus on their way to the brain's cerebral cortex. Here the A-delta fibres signal sharp pain. The motivational and affective elements of pain appear to be more heavily determined by the C-fibres, which send pain messages to the brain stem and lower portions of the forebrain.

THEORIES OF PAIN

Gate Control Theory

In 1965, Melzack and Wall proposed the **gate control theory** of pain. This theory improved on earlier theories of pain by recognizing the contribution that psychological factors have on our perception of pain (Melzack, 1999). According to the gate control theory, pain is not a sensation that is transmitted directly from the peripheral nerve endings to the brain. Instead, the theory emphasizes that sensations are modified as they are conducted to the brain by way of the spinal cord. They are also influenced by downward pathways from the brain that interpret the experience. Melzack and Wall propose that there is a structure in the dorsal horns of the spinal column, a gate-like mechanism, that is able to control the flow of pain stimulation to the brain.

According to the gate control theory, information enters the dorsal horns of the spinal cord by way of primary afferent neurons. This information passes through the substantia gelatinosa, where the information is modulated by stimulation from the periphery as well as by feedback from the fibres descending from the brain. This then affects the activity of the transmission cells, causing them to either conduct (excitatory influence) or not conduct (inhibitory influence) pain sensations to the brain.

Melzack and Wall (1965) proposed that the experience of pain is affected by the balance of activity in the small and large nerve fibres. This activity determines the patterning and intensity of stimulation. Activity in the small A-delta and C-fibres causes prolonged stimulation in the spinal cord. This type of activity promotes sensitivity and opens the gate, which produces pain. In contrast, activity in the large A-beta fibres tends to close the gate.

The gate may be closed by activity in the spinal cord and also by messages descending from the brain. A specialized system of large-diameter, rapidly conducting fibres, called the **central control trigger**, activates selective cognitive processes that then influence, by way of descending fibres, the opening and closing of the gate. The experience of pain is thus influenced by past experience, attention, and other cognitive activities through the central control trigger. Consequently, affective reactions such as anxiety, depression, fear, or focusing on an injury can exacerbate the experience of pain by affecting the central control trigger, thus opening the gate. Intense involvement in other activities, or relaxation, or positive experiences can mute the pain experience by causing the gate to close.

Consider observations made by Beecher (1959) during World War II. An injury or wound sustained by a civilian produces pain (the gate is open). However, a soldier with the equivalent injury does not experience the same amount of pain, because the soldier is distracted by the environment (the gate is closed). Suppressing the pain of injuries allows individuals to defend themselves during attack and to escape from further harm. Evidence in support of this observation can be seen in the amount of analgesic requested by patients from each group. A civilian patient will ask for significantly more analgesic than will a soldier who sustained the same injury (Watkins & Maier, 2000).

This theory also explains how injuries can go virtually unnoticed. If sensory input is sent into a heavily activated nervous system, the stimulation may not be perceived as pain. A hockey player may fracture a rib during a game but not notice the acute pain because of excitement and concentration on the game. It isn't until after the game is over that the player notices the pain. At this time, the nervous system is functioning at a different level of activation, and the gate is more easily opened.

The gate control theory was arguably the leading theory of pain for over 25 years. The theory continues to spur research and generate interest in the psychological and perceptual factors involved in pain. However, the gate control theory is not able to explain several chronic pain problems, such as **phantom limb pain** (see Box 10-1).

BOX 10-1	**Phantom Limb Pain**

In 1866, the first account of phantom limbs was published. It appeared not in a scientific journal as one might expect but in the *Atlantic Monthly*, as an anonymously written short story. In "The Case of George Dedlow," the main character loses an arm to amputation during the Civil War. At one point, he awakens in the hospital after, unbeknownst to him, both his legs have also been amputated.

> [I was] suddenly aware of a sharp cramp in my left leg. I tried to get at it...with my single arm, but, finding myself too weak, hailed an attendant. "Just rub my left calf...if you please."
>
> "Calf?...You ain't got non, pardner. It's took off" (cited in Melzack, 1992, p. 120).

The author happened to be Wier Mitchell, the foremost American neu-

rologist at the time. Historians have proposed that Mitchell chose to publish this account in the *Atlantic Monthly* anonymously because he was unsure how his colleagues would respond to the concept of phantom limb pain. He feared that they would not believe that amputated arms and legs could be felt by their previous owners.

In fact, the phenomenon of phantom limbs is common to those who have undergone amputation. The limb is very vivid to the amputee, who can usually tell you the precise position of the phantom. A phantom limb behaves very much like a normal limb. Usually, a phantom arm hangs straight down at the side when the person sits or stands but moves in perfect coordination with other limbs during walking. Similarly, a phantom leg bends like a normal leg

(continued on next page)

would when its owner sits; it stretches out when the individual lies down; and it becomes upright during standing (Melzack, 1992).

Occasionally, the amputee becomes convinced the limb is stuck in an unusual position. Melzack (1992) noted that one man believed his phantom arm extended straight out from the shoulder, at a right angle to the body. Consequently, whenever the man walked through a doorway he would turn sideways so that his arm would not hit the wall. Another man slept only on his front or side because his phantom arm was bent behind him and got in the way when he tried to rest on his back.

Particularly initially, the phantom limb may seem so real to the amputee that the amputee might try standing up on a phantom foot or answering a phone with a phantom hand. The most extraordinary feature of phantom limbs is their reality to the amputee. A phantom limb can experience many sensations including warmth, cold, and pressure. A phantom limb can feel wet (as when an artificial arm is seen entering into a lake during a swan dive). It can also feel itchy, which can be very annoying. Fortunately, scratching the apparent site

of discomfort can sometimes actually relieve the distress. It may sometimes seem that the phantom limb is sweaty, prickly, or even being tickled (Melzack, 1992).

Of course, the sensation in phantom limbs that causes the most distress to the sufferer is pain. Researchers (Jensen, Krebs, Nielsen, & Rasmussen, 1985; Krebs et al., 1984) have found that 72 percent of amputees had phantom limb pain one week after amputation, and that 60 percent had pain six months to seven years later. Although the pain usually starts soon after amputation, sometimes it does not appear for weeks, months, or even years. The pain is often characterized as burning, cramping, or shooting and can vary from being occasional and mild to continuous and severe (Melzack, 1992).

Originally, it was believed that one must first possess and then lose a limb and the corresponding nerves to experience phantom pain. However, there is now considerable evidence of phantoms in people born without limbs and in those who experienced limb amputation in very early childhood (e.g., Melzack, Israel, Lacroix, & Schultz, 1997; Ramachandran, 1993).

Neuromatrix Theory

In response to recent findings, Melzack (1993, 2001) has proposed an extension to the gate control theory entitled the **neuromatrix theory**. This theory places a greater emphasis on the brain's role in pain perception. According to this theory, a genetically determined neuromatrix or network of brain neurons, "distributed throughout many areas of the brain, comprises a widespread network of neurons which generates patterns, processes information that flows through it, and ultimately produces the pattern that is felt as a whole body" (Melzack, 1993, p. 623). The neuromatrix-generated patterns are called *neurosignature patterns*. These patterns may be generated from sensory inputs, however they may also be innately produced, such as in the case of phantom limb pain. The neurosignature patterns are responsible for producing a multidimensional experience of pain. Like the gate control theory, the neuromatrix theory maintains that pain perception is part of a complex process that is affected by sensory input, activity of the nervous system, and past experiences and expectations.

NEUROCHEMICAL BASIS OF PAIN AND PAIN INHIBITION

The gate control theory of pain asserts that the brain can control the amount of pain an individual experiences by transmitting messages down the spinal cord to block the transmission of pain signals (Melzack & Wall, 1965, 1996). There is evidence that supports this view. David Reynolds (1969) conducted a now classic study in which he implanted an electrode in the midbrain portion of a number of rats' brain stems. The exact location of the electrode varied from one rat to the next. Then, he made sure that the rats could feel pain by applying a clamp to their tails. Not surprisingly, each rat responded by demonstrating pain. Several days later, Reynolds tested whether stimulation through the electrode would block pain. At the same time as the rats were electrically stimulated he again applied the clamp. Those rats with electrodes in the area of the midbrain known as the **periaqueductal gray area** did not exhibit pain. Those rats that did not experience pain in response to having their tails clamped later had abdominal surgery performed on them while the periaqueductal gray area of their brains was being electrically stimulated. Again, the rats did not feel any pain. This phenomenon has been termed **stimulation-produced analgesia (SPA)**. Reynolds' findings encouraged researchers to look for the neurochemical basis of pain. Subsequently, *endogenous opioids* were identified.

Endogenous opioids are opiate-like substances produced within the body that regulate pain. They are naturally occurring substances in the brain, spinal cord, and glands. They appear to act as an internal pain relief system by slowing or blocking the transmission of nerve impulses, in much the same way as do exogenous opioids such as the drugs heroin and morphine (Watkins & Maier, 2000). Researchers have identified three main groups of these endogenous opioids—beta-endorphin, proenkephalin, and prodynorphin (Akil et al., 1984).

The system of endogenous opioids and their function in the body is very complex. Researchers do not have a full understanding of the mechanisms by which they work. However, it is apparent that having internal pain-relieving chemicals serves an adaptive function. It may be that because pain and emotions are closely linked, studies have found that psychological stress can trigger endogenous opioid activity (Bloom, Lazerson, & Hofstadter, 1985; Winters, 1985). There is also evidence that intense physical exercise can trigger the release of beta-endorphin, resulting in natural, short-term pain suppression and subjective feelings of physical well-being (Akil et al., 1984). The release of endogenous opioids may help to explain how injured athletes in competition and soldiers on the battlefield continue to function after being injured with little or no perception of pain.

CASE 10-1	**Acute versus Chronic Pain**

Riley is 28 years old and is just finishing his residency in anesthesiology. Today, Riley received an invitation to his high school reunion. Riley had enjoyed high school and, in particular his participation in school sports. He played volleyball and basketball, but the sport he enjoyed most was football. He decided that returning to his hometown for his high school reunion would

(continued on next page)

be just the break he needed from life at the hospital.

The first night of the reunion weekend Riley met up with many of his former buddies and they reminisced about their football success. They really had been one of the greatest teams in the high school's history. In fact, six of the team members had gone on to play football in university, and four others had turned professional. The guys decided to get together for a scrimmage before the weekend was out.

On Sunday morning, 16 members of the former team gathered for a scrimmage. The guys played hard and even the spectators were impressed with the quick moves the players exhibited. After the game, the guys vowed to get together every year on the last weekend of August for a scrimmage.

Riley flew home on Sunday night. When he tried to rise from his seat at the conclusion of the flight, he experienced a sharp pain in his back. Slowly and carefully, he eased himself into a standing position. He had obviously overdone it at the scrimmage earlier that day. Riley knew he was going to be extremely stiff the next day. He decided

that a walk before bed might help ward off some of the stiffness.

Compare Riley's experience of pain to that experienced by Michelle.

Michelle has been a professional pairs figure skater for almost 20 years. She and her partner have decided they will call it quits at the end of the current season. One factor that played a part in this decision is Michelle's pain. For the last few years, Michelle has found it increasingly difficult to land the jumps and throws that she and her partner practise over and over on a daily basis. After landing each throw and after landing each jump, Michelle experiences a sharp searing pain in her knees. After each practice session, Michelle must ice her knees to help alleviate the pain, swelling, and tenderness. Not only does Michelle have a hard time landing her jumps, she has also noticed that she is having some difficulty simply walking. It is likely that Michelle will be diagnosed with osteoarthritis. Although Michelle is going to miss skating, she hopes that a less physically demanding schedule will ease some of the pain she has been experiencing.

ACUTE VERSUS CHRONIC PAIN

Medical professionals make an important distinction between two main kinds of clinical pain—acute and chronic. Case 10.1 presents these two different types of pain in the examples of Riley and Michelle's individual experiences. Riley is suffering from **acute pain**. Acute pain seems to serve to warn of impending tissue damage or the need for convalescent rest. A toothache, the discomforts of childbirth, a broken limb, and postoperative pain are all forms of acute pain. Acute pain is by definition temporary, lasting less than six months (Turk, Meichenbaum, & Genest, 1983; Turk & Melzack, 2001). The physiological responses to acute pain seem partly proportional to the stimulus intensity. It can cause considerable anxiety and distress. Fortunately, painkillers can often ease the discomfort, and as the injury begins to heal, the anxiety subsides.

But sometimes the pain lingers on. When it lasts longer than six months, pain is considered **chronic**. Any condition that is expected to bring only acute pain but continues for six months without resolution is considered to be chronic pain (Moulin et al., 2002). Michelle, like Jake in the chapter-opening vignette, is experiencing chronic pain. A recent Canadian study revealed that 27 percent of men and 31 percent of women currently experience chronic pain (Moulin et al., 2002). Chronic pain can be intermittent or constant, mild or severe. It varies a great deal depending upon its type (Turk et al., 1983). **Chronic recurrent pain** does not become progressively worse. It is characterized by intense episodes of acute pain followed by relief. For example, a person who suffers from migraine headaches may have excruciating headaches lasting from hours to days, but then may have several pain-free weeks or months. By comparison, the person who has **chronic intractable benign pain** has pain all the time, with varying intensity. People who suffer from lower back pain generally experience their pain continually and find that they can do little to reduce it. Finally, **chronic progressive pain** involves continuous discomfort that gradually intensifies as the condition worsens. It is typically associated with malignancies or degenerative disorders such as cancer and advancing arthritis.

In many types of chronic pain, the disease process is primarily responsible for the pain experienced. However, psychosocial factors may also play a role. Although tissue damage may result in the initial acute pain that the person experiences; subsequently, psychosocial factors may play a more prominent role. To clarify this process, we must distinguish between respondent and operant pain (Fordyce, 1976, 1978). **Respondent pain** refers to pain that occurs in response to noxious stimulation or tissue damage. In contrast, **operant pain** is pain that is reinforced by the person's environment. Typically, people in pain will alter their behaviour in an attempt to reduce the pain. For example, a person may limp, guard a painful arm, avoid exercise, or even stay in bed to avoid pain. When such **pain behaviours** either reduce the pain or prevent it from getting worse, the tendency to continue the behaviour is reinforced. As the pain behaviours appear successful at preventing or reducing the pain, the person will continue to engage in these behaviours for fear that the pain will return if they are discontinued. Consequently, these behaviours are particularly resistant to change.

The verbal and behavioural expressions of pain also have a powerful effect on other people. When an individual complains of pain, displays pain on his or her face, or exhibits an abnormal gait or posture, he or she may receive attention, concern, and even assistance from those witnessing these behaviours—this can further reinforce pain behaviour (von Baeyer, Johnson, & McMillan, 1984). Researchers have discovered that chronic pain sufferers who report higher levels of satisfaction with social support also exhibit higher levels of pain-related behaviours. Positive attention provided by supportive spouses in response to the expression of pain may inadvertently maintain or increase an individual's expression of pain and the experience of disability (Turk, Kerns, & Rosenberg, 1992). In one study, the best predictor of pain and activity level was the individual's perception of his or her spouse's solicitousness in response to the expression of pain. Chronic pain sufferers whose spouses showed higher levels of concern reported greater levels of pain and lower activity levels compared to those whose spouses exhibited less concern (Flor, Kerns, & Turk, 1987).

One of the most common complaints described by those with chronic pain is the resulting sleep disturbance (American Pain Society, 1999). A large majority (79 percent) of those experiencing moderate or severe chronic pain complain about the difficulties they have in falling to sleep. As well, these individuals are frequently awakened as a result of the pain. In the morning, they wake up exhausted. They are tired and drained of energy, not merely from lack of sleep but also because the continuous pain wears them down (Sternbach, 1986). It is not surprising that these chronic pain sufferers also find themselves irritated by little things and trivial comments of those around them. These people recognize that they are snapping at their friends and family for insufficient reasons, yet they cannot seem to stop. This often leads those with chronic pain to withdraw from their families and friends.

The chronic pain sufferer who withdraws from family and friends experiences little social or recreational life. In addition, 59 percent of those with moderate or severe chronic pain have had to leave their jobs (American Pain Society, 1999). As a result, people's standard of living is reduced and an added strain is put on the family. Ironically, if compensation is received for the pain experience because it resulted from an injury on the job or perhaps in an automobile accident, this may exacerbate the perceived severity of pain and distress (Turk & Okifuji, 1996; see Focus on Canadian Research 10-1). In addition, both personal and career goals may be set aside because the sufferer's life is beginning to revolve around pain (Karoly & Ruehlman, 1996).

All of the previously mentioned behaviours resulting from the experience of pain have an impact on one's emotional state. Many chronic pain sufferers are irritable, and many report being listless, unable to cope, and depressed (American Pain Society, 1999). Chronic pain and depression sufferers share many of the same symptoms. Merskey (1986) reports that almost all published studies of psychiatric and psychological test findings of chronic pain patients report mild but significant depression. Further, approximately 50 percent of hospitalized depressed patients report pain as a major symptom. These are daunting statistics, especially when one considers that depression is known to exacerbate pain and pain-related behaviours (Kessler, Kronstorfer, & Traue, 1996; Kroner-Herwig et al., 1996). Fortunately, once pain is controlled there is a significant improvement in individuals' abilities and moods. For example, a national study in the United States found that 84 percent of chronic pain sufferers whose pain is now under control feel happy and upbeat, compared to 41 percent who provided this response before their pain was controlled (American Pain Society, 1999).

Focus on Canadian Research 10-1

Chronic Pain on Trial

In an article entitled "Chronic pain on trial: The influence of litigation and compensation on chronic pain syndromes," Thomas Hadjistavropoulos (1999), from the University of Regina, describes a current controversy surrounding chronic pain. According to Hadjistavropoulos, the litigious nature of North American society influences the pain symptoms reported by patients (see also Merskey & Teasell, 2000, 2002).

Cross-cultural research suggests there may be some truth to this argument. For example, Bella (1982) compared the proportion of patients in Australia who reported "late-whiplash syndrome" resulting from car accidents

(continued on next page)

with patients in Singapore. In contrast to its frequency in Australia, the late-whiplash syndrome was extremely rare in Singapore, and when it occurred it often involved patients of European background. Another study compared American patients to patients from New Zealand (Carron, DeGood, & Tait, 1985). New Zealand's nonadversarial legal system compensates all victims regardless of fault and without the need to prove injury at work. The results of this study determined that 49 percent of the American sample received pain-related compensation compared to 17 percent of the New Zealand sample. Further, the American patients reported greater emotional and behavioural disruption as a result of chronic low back pain. This occurred even though the two samples of patients initially described experiencing similar degrees of pain. Carron et al. concluded that the absence of an adversarial system in New Zealand contributed to the difference.

The results of this cross-cultural research may have lead, in part, to the conclusions drawn in a report by the *Task Force on Pain in the Workplace* of the International Association for the Study of Pain (IASP) (Fordyce, 1995). The task force implied in their report that extended pain and disability following certain kinds of low back pain are primarily the result of operant and societal factors. Specifically, assigning an individual disability status was said to expose that individual to "potentially debilitating circumstances that include excessive rest, well-intentioned but harmful treatments, and overprotection by family members" (Hadjistavropoulos, 1999, p. 62). The report outlines that disability claims resulting from low back pain have shown enormous increases. Yet, there is no evidence that back injuries are becoming more frequent or severe. The report characterized individuals with non-specific low back pain as "activity intolerant" and suggested that wage replacement benefits should not exceed six weeks unless there was evidence to indicate a disabling condition other than non-specific low back pain.

The IASP report has led to considerable controversy (e.g., Block, 1997; Craig, 1996; Fordyce, 1996; Loeser, 1996; Merskey, 1996a, 1996b). The Canadian chapter of IASP, for example, characterized the report as incomplete and as representing the opinion of a limited number of individuals. Hadjistavropoulos (1999) states that despite good intentions, the report could have disastrous consequences for some injured persons. In an attempt to remedy this situation, Hadjistavropoulos has developed a number of strategies that may reduce compensation costs for chronic pain while also reducing patient suffering.

1. Health care practitioners should do more to encourage patients to return to work. Rather than prescribe rest for musculoskeletal pain patients, these patients should be encouraged to return to work. Catchclove and Cohen (1982) show that this encouragement has a significant impact on the number of individuals that will return to work.

2. Employers should attempt to reduce job dissatisfaction in the workplace. Studies have shown that improvements in work conditions and the work environment facilitate the recovery of many injured workers (see Turk, 1997).

3. Physicians should strive to enhance diagnostic accuracy. Research sug-

(continued on next page)

gests that pain patients are frequently inaccurately or incompletely diagnosed. For example, Hendler and Kozikowski (1993) found that 66.7 percent of patients referred to a pain diagnostic centre had been misdiagnosed.

4. Researchers should continue research on malingering. Health care practitioners need to be able to determine when someone is pretending to be in pain or exaggerating the severity of his or her symptoms. At present, there is not a method to confidently assess when someone is malingering (Main & Spanswick, 1995).

5. Researchers should identify types of patients who may be particularly susceptible to the effects of compensation and litigation.

6. Law-makers must modify the adversarial nature of the North American litigation/compensation system. Countries (e.g., New Zealand) that have removed the adversarial relationship between employer, claimant, and the insurer allow income compensation for accidental injury without the need to prove the injury at work and by allowing rapid rehabilitation intervention (Walsh & Dumitru, 1988).

PSYCHOSOCIAL FACTORS AND PAIN

Gender Differences

Clinical research has documented that women are more likely than men to experience a variety of recurrent pain. Recurrent pain can result from many ailments, including migraine and other headaches as well as musculoskeletal, back, and abdominal injury (Berkely, 1997; LeResche, 2000). In most studies, women report more severe levels of pain, more frequent pain, and pain of longer duration than men (Unruh, 1996; Unruh, Ritchie, & Merskey, 1999).

Researchers agree that there are gender differences in the perception and response to pain (see Giles & Walker, 2000 or Unruh, 1996 for reviews). The extent of these differences is under debate. Anita Unruh (1996), from Dalhousie University, has identified three key issues surrounding gender differences and pain: 1) the manner in which women and men perceive and respond to pain; 2) the psychosocial and biological factors that may influence gender variations in pain experience; and 3) the response of the health care system to the pain presented by women and men.

Laboratory research has documented how men and women differ in their pain responses (Riley et al., 1998; Koltyn & Vaughn, 1999; Sullivan, Tripp & Santor, 2000). For example, Lowery, Fillingim and Wright (2003) reported that women have a lower pain threshold and lower pain tolerance than men have. To determine a participant's pain threshold, researchers will inflict pain on the participant by one of a number of methods. A commonly used method is known as a "cold-pressor task." This entails participants submerging their hand in cold water until they experience pain. They indicate to the researcher, usually by pushing a button, when this point is reached. At this time participants are said to have reached their **pain threshold**.

Researchers are sometimes interested in identifying participants' *pain tolerance* levels rather than their pain threshold. The **pain tolerance** level is either the duration of time a person is willing to endure a stimulus beyond the point where it began to hurt, or the intensity of the stimulus a person will endure beyond that point. When the participants "can't stand it" any longer, they have reached their level of pain tolerance. Once the participants have indicated that they have reached their limit, they can remove their hand from the noxious stimuli. Laboratory studies investigating gender differences in pain threshold and pain tolerance have not yielded consistent results (e.g., Giles & Walker, 2000). Some researchers (e.g., Berkley, 1997; Lautenbacher & Rollman, 1993) argue that these inconsistent results are due to the variety of noxious stimuli used by investigators to determine pain threshold and pain tolerance. For example, Koltyn and Vaughn (1999) documented that men and women differed in heat and pressure pain ratings but not in cold pain ratings or pain thresholds.

Other critics argue that apparent gender differences in response to pain are actually due to differences in reporting pain. Some researchers (Robinson et al., 1999) believe that female participants in lab studies give a more unbiased report of their pain than do male participants. Men feel there is a social cost to admitting publicly that something hurts. Men are taught to "tough out" pain and so in the lab they endure more discomfort. In contrast, women feel little pressure to endure unnecessary pain and therefore have no trouble admitting when something hurts. It is plausible that societal beliefs about gender differences in response to pain are a product of different societal gender-role expectations. Unruh (1996) points out that when we experience pain, we engage in a process of cognitive appraisal. That is, we determine what this experience means to us. To determine the meaning of an event we ask ourselves the following questions: "What does it mean?" "In what way does it affect me?" "Should I be concerned?" and "Is any action required on my part?"

The meaning given to an event is an important consideration in determining one's response to the event. Women with multiple roles and responsibilities resulting from childcare, care for elderly parents, household management, and paid employment have more than one reason to appraise pain as threatening. They may therefore attend to pain sooner in an effort to minimize its intrusiveness (Johnson, 1991; Crook, 1993).

Although psychosocial factors may influence pain perception, underlying biological differences in pain mechanisms may also predispose women to have more pain. For example, there are known gender differences in brain chemistry, metabolism, physical structures, and hormonal variations that may influence the biological mechanisms of pain transmission, pain sensitivity, and pain perception (Giles & Walker, 2000; Unruh, 1996).

Both biological and psychosocial factors related to the experience and reporting of pain by men and women may lead to differences in the way men and women are treated by the health care system. For example, psychosocial factors may be responsible for women describing their pain in more detail and with more expressive and social language than do men (Crook, 1982). As a result of these descriptions, women are more likely to receive a psychogenic interpretation of their pain by their physicians, particularly when the pain is not directly related to tissue damage. Unruh (1996) claims that these interpretations may "cause women to receive more attention for psychological aspects of pain but inadequate pain relief" (p. 159).

Women are also perceived by physicians and nurses to dramatize or exaggerate their pain. As a result, they are provided less analgesia than are men (e.g., Calderone,1990: McDonald, 1994). Men, on the other hand, are thought to minimize their pain and its consequences. This attitude may lead men to seek medical attention only when the pain characteristics have become more extreme, which may result in the pain being more difficult to treat. It is also true that men seem to implement fewer coping strategies than women in response to pain. Unruh, Ritchie, & Merskey (1999) documented that men have less social support and are less likely to engage in problem-solving and palliative behaviours to deal with their pain than women. Until there is conclusive evidence to explain pain-related gender differences, health professionals should be attentive to possible biases in expectations about pain response and pain behaviour in men and women.

Cultural Differences

Pain is something that people all around the world experience. However, cultural background and social context will affect each person's experience, expression, and treatment of pain (Edwards & Fillingim, 2003; Edwards, Fillingim & Keefe, 2001; Riley et al., 2002; Zatzick & Dimsdale, 1990). These differences result from the meaning each culture attaches to pain and from stereotypes associated with various cultural experiences. Consider, for example, members of certain African cultural groups who walk on burning coals and pierce their bodies with spikes, yet show no outward appearance of pain. Similarly, in North America, body piercing and tattooing are commonplace in certain age and social groups. In both instances, stoicism is expected, while expressions of pain might be ridiculed. In comparison, some Mediterranean peoples encourage the open expression of pain (Straub, 2002).

If we focus on pain derived from one specific cause, such as cancer, we see that cultural differences still exist. For example, Europeans and North Americans consider pain to be a common experience for cancer patients, and pain experts state that pain is undertreated (Calvillo & Flaskerud, 1991; Streltzer, 1997). In contrast, experts from Asian countries do not consider cancer pain to be as much of a problem. These different attitudes lead to differences in treatment—approximately 70 percent of patients in Europe receive opiates for cancer pain. In contrast, only about four percent of Asian cancer patients receive this medication. It is possible that these variations may be due more to physicians' beliefs than to patients' pain. Support for this idea is provided by an American study that reported that the culture of the nurse influenced the interpretation of patients' pain (Calvillo & Flaskerud, 1991).

THE MEASUREMENT OF PAIN

Pain is a challenge to assess because people have difficulty describing pain objectively. If you have cut your arm, you can point to the wound. Or, if you are concerned that you might have broken a bone, this can be determined by radiography. Pain lacks these objective referents. Yet, assessing pain is very important in determining treatment for patients and evaluating the effectiveness of different pain-reducing methods. As a result, clinicians and researchers have developed many techniques for measuring the pain felt by an individual. These generally fall into three major categories: 1) psychophysiological measures; 2) behavioural assessment; and 3) self-reports. Each technique has certain advantages and certain limitations.

Psychophysiological Measures

Pain has both sensory and emotional components that can produce changes in the auto-nomic nervous system as well as other physiological conditions. The physiological changes resulting from the pain experience can be assessed using psychophysiological measures (Lykken, 1987).

One psychophysiological measure researchers use for assessing pain is an **elect-romyograph**, or EMG, which measures the electrical activity in muscles which reflects the level of muscle tension. Because muscle tension is associated with certain pain states, such as headaches and low back pain, we would expect that EMG recordings would be differ-ent for people experiencing pain and those not experiencing it (Blanchard and Andrasik, 1985). Measures of **autonomic activity**, such as heart rate, respiration rate, blood pressure, hand surface temperature, and skin conductance assess generalized arousal, which may provide an emotional indicator of pain. Another instrument that measures pain is the **elect-roencephalograph**, or EEG. The EEG measures electrical activity in the brain. When a person's sensory system detects a stimulus, such as pressure on one's heel, the signal to the brain produces **evoked potentials** or a change in EEG voltage. The evoked potentials increase with the intensity of stimuli and decrease when people take analgesics (Chapman et al., 1985).

Even though psychophysiological measures objectively assess bodily changes that occur in response to pain, these bodily changes may also occur in response to other factors (e.g., attention, diet, and stress). Therefore, whenever possible, psychophysiological meas-ures should be used in conjunction with other approaches in assessing pain.

Behavioural Assessment

Other measures of pain have focused on *pain behaviours*. Pain behaviours are behaviours exhibited when a person is in discomfort. They include non-verbal expressions (e.g., facial and vocal cues), distortions in movement and posture, irritability, and restrictions or avoid-ance of activity (Turk, Wack, & Kerns, 1985). Analyses of pain behaviours provide a basis for assessing how pain has disrupted the life of patients. Procedures have been developed for assessing specific pain behaviours in both daily activities and structured clinical settings.

Assessment of Pain Behaviour in Day-to-Day Activities In assessing day-to-day activities, researchers and clinicians might be interested in the amount of time the suf-ferer spends in bed, for example, or how many complaints he or she expresses. Does he or she bend over very carefully or not at all? Does he or she seek help in moving, walking, or climbing stairs? Does he or she walk with a limp? Family members or significant others in the patient's life are often the best people to make these assessments. If these people are willing to help, they can be trained to make careful observations and keep accurate records. A procedure documented by William Fordyce (1976) recommends that the assessor com-pile a list of from five to ten behaviours that generally signal when the patient is in pain. This list might include such behaviours as requesting medication, moaning, or verbalizing pain. The assessor is then trained to watch for these behaviours in the patient and to keep track of their frequency and duration. The assessor is also trained to monitor how people, including the assessor, react to the client's pain behaviour. This procedure is useful for assessing the patient's pain experiences, the impact they have on the patient's life, and the social context that may maintain these behaviours.

This system has been refined (Turk et al., 1983) and includes the addition of a spouse diary and a significant-other pain questionnaire. The supplemental spouse diary requires the spouse to record the time, date, and location (e.g., in the car or at home in bed) of severe pain episodes. The spouse records his or her own actions and feelings in response to these pain episodes. In addition, the spouse estimates the effectiveness of such actions along a six-point scale from "did not help at all" to "seemed to stop the pain completely." The second supplement, the significant-other pain questionnaire, is made up of 30 items inquiring about the patient's severity of pain and its effect on work, recreation, and family relations. A number of the questions pertain to the significant other's feeling and responses toward the patient and the pain situation. These supplemental assessment devices can be compared with the patient's own diary and pain questionnaire over the same period.

Assessment of Pain Behaviour in Clinical Settings   In clinical settings, procedures are available for health care practitioners to assess the pain behaviour of patients. For example, in hospitals nurses may use the UAB Pain Behavior Scale (Richards, Nepomuceno, Riles, & Suer, 1982) during routine care of patients. The nurse has the patient perform several activities and rates ten pain behaviours (e.g., mobility, medication use) on a three-point scale: "none," "occasional," and "frequent." These ratings are assigned numerical values and summed for a total score.

A number of studies have focused on assessing discomfort in patients suffering from low back pain (Keefe, Williams, & Smith, 2001; Polatin & Mayer, 2001). In the typical study, patients performed a standard set of activities. For example, Chris Kleinke and Arthur Spangler (1988) asked patients to walk, pick up an object on the floor, remove their shoes while sitting, and perform several exercises such as trunk rotations, toe touching, and sit-ups. In each study, the patients were videotaped, and trained assessors rated their performance for several pain behaviours, including sighing, grimacing, rubbing, bracing, and engaging in guarded movement. Patients are also asked to rate the intensity of their pain, thus allowing a validity check of the observers' ratings. For each behaviour except grimacing, the observers' and patients' ratings were highly correlated. These studies suggest that behavioural assessments of pain can be made relatively easily and reliably.

Self-Reports of Pain

The third and most obvious approach to pain measurement is to ask people to describe their pain, either in their own words or by filling out a rating scale or questionnaire. These are the most common types of pain assessment. In treating a patient's pain, health care practitioners ask where the pain is, what it feels like, how strong it is, and when it tends to occur.

Interviews   Interviews about pain can provide valuable information. In addition to a description of pain, such interviews can determine the history of the pain problem. The history would include when the pain was first experienced, how it developed, and the techniques used for controlling it. Factors seeming to trigger or exacerbate the pain can be discussed. The patient's emotional adjustment and whether or how the patient's lifestyle has been altered can also be explored. The information obtained in these interviews can be supplemented with information provided by significant others in the patient's life.

Rating Scales Rating scales are one of the simplest and most direct measures of pain. Therefore, it is not surprising that rating scales are the most frequently used measures of pain (Reading, 1989, Jensen & Karoly, 2001). These scales are usually used to measure pain intensity. Sometimes, patients are simply asked to respond verbally to the statement, "On a scale from 1 to 10, with 10 being the most excruciating pain possible, and 1 being the lowest level of pain detectable, how much pain are you currently experiencing?" Or, the health care practitioner may ask the patient to respond to this statement on a scale of 1 to 100. In either of these cases, the basic question is really the same. However, the form of the scale can vary (see Figure 10-1).

| FIGURE 10-1 | **Rating Scales for Pain Measurement** |

Visual Analog Scale:
Mark a point on the line to show how strong your pain is

————————————————————————————————————

no pain   worst pain imaginable

Box Scale:
Rate the level of your pain by circling one number on the scale, where 0 means "no pain" and 10 means "worst pain imaginable"

| 1 | 2 | 3 | 4 | 5 | 6 | 7 | 8 | 9 | 10 |

Verbal Rating Scale:
Circle the phrase that best describes your pain

Not Painful   Slightly Painful   Moderately Painful   Very Painful   Extremely Painful

---

The **visual analog scale** is simply a line anchored on the left by the phrase "no pain" and on the right by a phrase such as "worst pain imaginable." People rate their pain by marking a point on the line. The **box scale** is similar to the visual analog scale in that the scale is labelled at the ends with the phrases "no pain" and "worst pain imaginable." However, rather than simply marking a point on a line, patients are provided a series of numbers in boxes and must choose the number that best indicates the degree of pain they are experiencing. A third rating scale is the **verbal rating scale**, in which patients are asked to describe their pain by choosing the phrase that most closely resembles the pain they are experiencing.

Rating scales are quick and easy to use, allowing people to rate their pain frequently. Averaging ratings across time gives a more accurate picture of the amount of pain a person generally experiences than does a single rating (Jensen & McFarland, 1993). Turk, Meichenbaum, and Genest (1983) describe how this method can be used to identify patterns of pain in chronic pain patients. Multiple ratings provide a record to determine if the patient's pain is generally improving or getting worse. In addition, they allow patterns in the timing of severe pain to be recognized. For example, it may be that severe pain occurs most often first thing in the morning or later in the day. Or, it may be that on certain days the patient's pain is more severe. If these patterns can be identified, the patient may be able to alter his or her schedule or environment to accommodate or eradicate at least the most severe pain.

Pain Questionnaires Pain questionnaires were developed to address the realization that pain is not unidimensional. That is, the experience of pain is much more than a feeling of discomfort that can be described in terms of its intensity. Melzack asserts that describing pain on a single dimension is like "specifying the visual world only in terms of light flux without regard to pattern, color, texture, and the many other dimensions of visual experience" (1975, p. 278). In an effort to measure the multidimensional nature of pain, Melzack (1975) developed the McGill Pain Questionnaire (MPQ).

The McGill Pain Questionnaire (see Figure 10-2) offers patients the opportunity to describe their pain on three broad dimensions—sensory, affective, and evaluative. *Sensory* qualities of pain include its temporal, spatial, pressure, and thermal properties; *affective* qualities include fear, tension, and autonomic properties; *evaluative* qualities are the subjective overall intensity of the pain experience.

The MPQ has four parts. Part 1 consists of front and back drawings of the human body. Patients are asked to indicate on these drawings the areas where they feel pain. Part 2 consists of a list of 78 descriptive words, separated into a total of 20 subclasses. Patients are instructed to select a word from each subclass that most accurately characterizes their pain. The words are ordered in increasing intensity (e.g., hot, burning, scalding, and searing). Each word in each class has an assigned value based on the degree of pain it represents. In the previous example, "searing" would contribute the largest number of points and "hot" would contribute the lowest number. These points are summed across the 20 subclasses and the total score is called the "pain-rating index." This index is the most commonly used part of the questionnaire. Part 3 of the MPQ asks how patients' pain has changed with time. Part 4 contains a series of verbal rating scales. One of these scales inquires about the amount of pain the patient is experiencing at the present time. This scale provides a separate score called the Present Pain Intensity (PPI) score.

There are many advantages to the MPQ over previous instruments for measuring pain. The MPQ's largest contribution is its measurement of more than one dimension of pain. Also, patients suffering from similar pain syndromes often identify the same patterns of words from the MPQ to characterize their pain, just as those with different pain syndromes (e.g., cancer, arthritis, headaches, or phantom limb pain) identify different words to characterize their pain (Melzack & Wall, 1996). Yet, there are drawbacks to the MPQ. For instance, because a fairly strong vocabulary is required to complete the questionnaire, the MPQ is not useful for assessing pain in young children or in people who do not have a strong grasp of the English language.

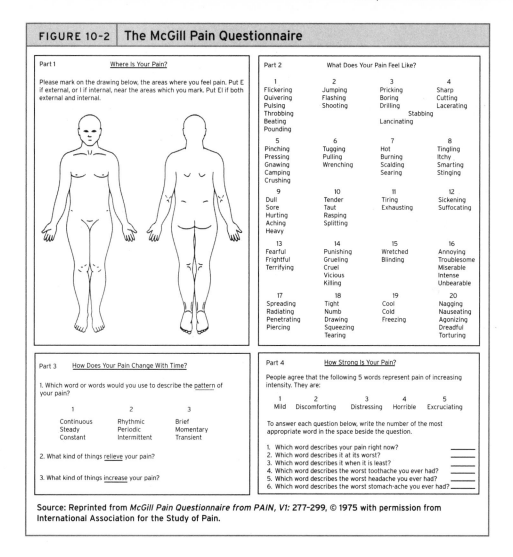

FIGURE 10-2 | The McGill Pain Questionnaire

Part 1   Where Is Your Pain?

Please mark on the drawing below, the areas where you feel pain. Put E if external, or I if internal, near the areas which you mark. Put EI if both external and internal.

Part 2   What Does Your Pain Feel Like?

1	2	3	4
Flickering	Jumping	Pricking	Sharp
Quivering	Flashing	Boring	Cutting
Pulsing	Shooting	Drilling	Lacerating
Throbbing		Stabbing	
Beating		Lancinating	
Pounding			

5	6	7	8
Pinching	Tugging	Hot	Tingling
Pressing	Pulling	Burning	Itchy
Gnawing	Wrenching	Scalding	Smarting
Camping		Searing	Stinging
Crushing			

9	10	11	12
Dull	Tender	Tiring	Sickening
Sore	Taut	Exhausting	Suffocating
Hurting	Rasping		
Aching	Splitting		
Heavy			

13	14	15	16
Fearful	Punishing	Wretched	Annoying
Frightful	Grueling	Blinding	Troublesome
Terrifying	Cruel		Miserable
	Vicious		Intense
	Killing		Unbearable

17	18	19	20
Spreading	Tight	Cool	Nagging
Radiating	Numb	Cold	Nauseating
Penetrating	Drawing	Freezing	Agonizing
Piercing	Squeezing		Dreadful
	Tearing		Torturing

Part 3   How Does Your Pain Change With Time?

1. Which word or words would you use to describe the pattern of your pain?

1	2	3
Continuous	Rhythmic	Brief
Steady	Periodic	Momentary
Constant	Intermittent	Transient

2. What kind of things relieve your pain?

3. What kind of things increase your pain?

Part 4   How Strong Is Your Pain?

People agree that the following 5 words represent pain of increasing intensity. They are:

1	2	3	4	5
Mild	Discomforting	Distressing	Horrible	Excruciating

To answer each question below, write the number of the most appropriate word in the space beside the question.

1. Which word describes your pain right now? _____
2. Which word describes it at its worst? _____
3. Which word describes it when it is least? _____
4. Which word describes the worst toothache you ever had? _____
5. Which word describes the worst headache you ever had? _____
6. Which word describes the worst stomach-ache you ever had? _____

Source: Reprinted from *McGill Pain Questionnaire from PAIN, V1: 277–299*, © 1975 with permission from International Association for the Study of Pain.

The MPQ is the most commonly used pain questionnaire (Piotrowski, 1998). It has been used to assess chronic pain in both clinical populations (e.g., patients with cancer pain and headache pain) and in laboratory research (e.g., Chapman & Syrjala, 1990; Dudgeon, Raubertas, & Rosenthal, 1993; Gagliese & Katz, 2003; Hunter & Lynch, Clark & Sawynok, 2003). A short form of the MPQ is now available (Melzack, 1987). The short form also includes multidimensional assessment and correlates highly with scores on the standard MPQ.

However, the MPQ is not the only pain questionnaire available. The West Haven–Yale Multidimensional Pain Inventory (MPI) assesses many aspects of psychological and physical functioning and can provide a comprehensive assessment of the lives of pain patients (Kerns, Turk, & Rudy, 1985). The MPI comprises 52 items divided into three sections. The first section measures 1) pain severity; 2) pain's interference with patients' lives; 3) patients' dissatisfaction with their present functioning; 4) patients' view of the support they receive from others; 5) patients' perceived life control; and 6) patients' negative mood states. The second section measures patients' perceptions of the responses of significant others. The final section identifies how frequently patients engage in each of 30 different daily activities.

Many pain questionnaires have been developed for both general and specific uses, for example, the Pain Anxiety Symptoms Scale (McCracken, Zayfert, & Gross, 1993). Some of these questionnaires have been developed for use with particular populations. For instance, the Dalhousie Everyday Pain Scale (von Baeyer, Baskerville, & McGrath, 1998) was developed for use with children; the Parents' Postoperative Pain Measure was designed to assist parents in the at-home assessment of their children's pain (Finley, Chambers, McGrath, & Walsh, 1999). Other questionnaires have been developed for use with specific pain syndromes, for example, the Chronic Pain Coping Inventory (Jensen, Turner, Romano, & Strom, 1995). However, the McGill Pain Questionnaire is by far the most common instrument used by clinical practitioners and researchers (Piotrowski, 1998). In fact, it has been translated and adapted for use in 20 languages including Arabic, Chinese, Japanese, German, Italian, and Spanish (Melzack & Katz, 2001)

Assessing Pain in Infants and Children

Assessing pain in infants and children is often more challenging than assessing pain in adults. Obviously, infants can not complete self-report questionnaires. Similarly, young children have difficulty expressing their experience of pain because of their limited language abilities and their level of cognitive development. Therefore, pain assessments conducted on these populations cannot follow the standard questionnaire format used with adults (McGrath & Gillespie, 2001; Stevens, 1997).

At one time, it was believed that very young infants were insensitive to pain (Fletcher, 1988; Merskey, 1970; Sheridan, 1992). Currently, experts believe that infants feel pain with the same intensity that adults do (McCain & Morwessel, 1995). If we cannot ask newborns whether they are in pain, or how much pain they are in, what should we do? A sample of 72 neonatal intensive care unit (NICU) nurses were asked which indicators they used to interpret the experience of pain in the infants entrusted to their care (Howard & Thurber, 1998). The 10 pain indicators used by the NICU nurses, listed in decreasing order of frequency, were fussiness, restlessness, grimacing, crying, increasing heart rate, increasing respirations, wiggling, rapid state changes, wrinkling of forehead, and clenching of fist.

Canadian researchers (e.g., Hadjistavropoulos, Craig, Grunau, & Johnston, 1994; Hadjistavropoulos, Craig, Grunau, & Whitfield, 1997) have documented the relative importance of each of the cues available when judging infant pain. They have discovered that while cry characteristics seem to command attention, cues provided through infant facial activity are weighted more heavily in adults' judgments of newborn pain. These facial characteristics include a brow bulge, eyes squeezed shut, a taut tongue and a deepened nasolabial furrow (the line or wrinkle that runs down from either side of the nose to the outer corners of the mouth). Facial characteristics also appear to convey more information to judges than does the infant's bodily activity.

Measurement of facial characteristics has been incorporated in the Neonatal Facial Coding System (NFCS). The NFCS was developed by Grunau and Craig (1987) to provide a detailed, anatomically based, and objective description of newborns' reactions to potentially painful stimuli. This instrument was developed primarily for use by researchers. It requires the researcher to assign a value of "1" or "0" to each facial action (brow bulge, eye squeeze, nasolabial furrow, open lips, vertical stretch mouth, horizontal stretch mouth, lip purse, taut tongue, and chin quiver). The scoring is completed by microanalyzing videotaped recordings of the infant.

As children get older, more instruments are available to assess their pain (Beyer & Wells, 1989; Stevens, 2001). Children's behaviour can be observed and their pain rated by using scales such as the Dalhousie Everyday Pain Scale (von Baeyer, Baskerville, & McGrath, 1998). Self-report measures may also be used with children. However, these measures provide considerably less detail to the health professional than do self-report measures used with adults, in part, because of the descriptors young children use to describe their pain. Elizabeth Job, a graduate student at the University of British Columbia, recently interviewed 106 children between the ages of three and six years. She discovered that the word "pain" didn't appear in the children's vocabularies until they were old enough to attend kindergarten. Instead, children tend to use words like "ouch," "ow," and "hurt" to describe their pain (Job, 2003). Preschool children may be asked to indicate the degree of their "hurt" by choosing a photograph from a scale of facial expressions (e.g., Faces Pain Scale Revised, Hicks et al., 2001). The Oucher scale displays six photographs of a child's face, showing increasing levels of discomfort. Colour scales, ladder scales, or line drawings of faces are measures available for health professionals to use when assessing young children's pain. One visual analogue scale developed for children includes a straight, horizontal line with a happy, smiling face at one end and a sad, crying face at the other. Pain questionnaires have also been developed for use with children. Examples of pain questionnaires for children include the Pediatric Pain Questionnaire (Varni, Thompson, & Hanson, 1987) and the Children's Comprehensive Pain Questionnaire (McGrath, 1987).

Assessing Pain in Older Adults

Interest in and research on pain in older adults is relatively recent (Gagliese, 2001). Questions have been raised about the appropriateness of using certain pain assessment tools with this population. These questions are justified when one acknowledges that the failure rate of older adults on VASs is as high as 30 percent. That is, older adults often provide incomplete or unscorable responses on VASs (Gagliese & Melzack, 1997). A better option to assess pain in older adults is the VRS. Older adults state that they prefer using verbal descriptors and these scales also seem to provide a more accurate measure for this age group (Bensesh, 1997). Preliminary evidence suggests that the MPQ, with its emphasis on adjectival descriptors of pain, is a useful measurement tool for this age group (Gagliese & Melzack, 1997).

Attempts to measure pain behaviours in this population have met with limited success (Gagliese, 2001). For example, a protocol was developed to simulate the movements of older adults' activities of daily living. However, many of the individuals were not able to complete the protocol because it triggered severe pain (Weiner et al., 1996). Using a different approach, a study was conducted to identify the accuracy of judgments of older adults' facial expressions of pain. Although this study resulted in higher pain ratings ascribed to older than to younger patients it was unclear if the higher pain ratings were due to objective changes in facial expression, to preconceived notions held by the judges that older adults experience more pain, or if a combination of these factors was responsible for the results (Matheson, 1997). Obviously, pain assessment with cognitively intact older adults is difficult with the measurment tools currently available. Pain assessment in cognitively impaired persons and those with communication disabilities presents additional challenges. Research in this area is still in its infancy (Gagliese, 2001; Hadjistavropolous, von Baeyer, & Craig, 2001).

PAIN CONTROL TECHNIQUES

Pharmacological Control of Pain

The traditional and most common method of controlling pain is through pain-relieving medications. **Peripherally acting analgesics**, also known as non-narcotic analgesics, are probably the most frequently used analgesics (Melzack & Wall, 1996; Sunshine & Olson, 1989). Included in this group are such common pain relievers as acetylsalicylic acid (e.g., Aspirin), acetaminophen (e.g., Tylenol), and ibuprofen (e.g., Advil). These drugs work by reducing inflammation at the site of tissue damage and inhibiting the synthesis of neurochemicals in the peripheral nervous system that facilitate the transmission of pain impulses. Peripherally acting analgesics provide substantial pain relief for a wide variety of pain conditions, especially arthritis and other conditions involving inflammation (Anderson et al., 1985; Kanner, 1986). Although peripherally acting analgesics are generally available over the counter, they do have side effects and may interact with other drugs. Used in recommended amounts, however, they are generally safe and are effective when dealing with mild to moderate pain.

Centrally acting analgesics are pain-killing medications called **narcotics**. Narcotics work by binding to opiate receptors in the central nervous system (Aronoff, Wagner, & Spangler, 1986; Twycross & McQuay, 1989). These drugs are either derived directly from the opium poppy, as are codeine and morphine, or they are synthetically reproduced but based on opium molecules, as are heroin, methadone, and the brand-name drugs Percodan and Demerol. These drugs operate on the central nervous system by imitating the effects of the body's endogenous pain relief system. Specifically, the molecules in these drugs bind to receptors for endorphins and enkephalins in the brain and spinal cord, blocking the transmission of pain signals. They are considered the most potent pain relievers available. They are frequently used to alleviate labour pain, postoperative pain, and chronic progressive pain experienced by some terminal cancer patients.

Although narcotics are extremely useful for relieving pain, they also have disadvantages. For example, narcotics are known to be psychoactive; they depress respiration; they have tremendous potential to produce tolerance, so that higher and higher doses are needed to achieve the same effect; and they can be addictive (Aronoff et al., 1986, 2000).

There is considerable controversy about the likelihood of a patient becoming addicted to narcotics. Some researchers argue that this is a very real possibility whereas others believe that this issue has been blown out of proportion (Aronoff, 2000; Melzack & Wall, 1996; Passik & Weinreb, 2000). Studies of both acute and chronic pain patients have found that few patients actually become addicted (e.g., Twycross & McQuay, 1989). Research suggests that when allowed to self-administer narcotics, patients recovering from surgery use less medication than would have been given by hospital staff. For further discussion of this topic, refer to the section on patient controlled analgesia in chapter 5.

Local anesthetics, such as novocaine and lidocaine, make up a third category of chemicals for relieving pain (Winters, 1985). These medications can be applied topically but are much more effective when injected at the site where the pain originates. You would likely have received a local anesthetic from your dentist before he or she began drilling or pulling a tooth. Likewise, you may have received a local anesthetic before receiving sutures. Local anesthetics work by blocking nerve cells from generating pain impulses (Winters, 1985). Although they work well to block impulses in pain fibres, they also block impulses in motor neurons. Consequently, you will have little or no control over your mouth, tongue, lips, and cheeks for several hours after a dental procedure if you received a local anesthetic prior to it.

Other drugs affect pain indirectly. For example, **sedatives**, such as barbiturates, and **tranquillizers**, such as diazepam (Valium), are depressants; that is, they depress bodily functions by decreasing the transmission of impulses throughout the central nervous system (Aronoff et al., 1986). These drugs probably do not directly affect pain but rather reduce patient anxiety and help the patient to sleep (thereby escaping the pain for a while and resting so as to better tolerate the pain when awake). Antidepressants also help patients who are in pain by reducing the depression that may accompany pain. In addition, it is believed that they affect pain-related neurotransmitters.

There has been a dramatic increase recently in research on drug combinations that enhance pain reduction (Dalal & Melzack, 1998). This research involves 1) drugs that have not traditionally been viewed as analgesics, such as antidepressants and sedatives; 2) drugs that have been viewed as effective analgesics in their own right, such as opioids and some antiinflammatory drugs; and 3) combinations of both types, such as opioids and antidepressants. Combining drugs in the treatment of pain increases analgesia resulting from their interaction or due to additive effects. For instance, opioid analgesia is enhanced when combined with the administration of amphetamines. Further, a combination of drugs may reduce the side effects of the drugs because the amount of each drug administered is reduced, or because of the way the two drugs interact. For example, the general cognitive decline and drowsiness experienced from the administration of opioids can be counteracted by introducing amphetamines.

Surgical Control of Pain

Surgical treatment of pain is the most extreme form of treatment available to pain patients. Surgery is considered only as a last resort, after all other treatment options have been exhausted (Cullinane, Chu & Mamelak, 2002). Surgical techniques include those that attempt to interrupt the transmission of pain from the periphery to the spinal cord, as well as those that disrupt the flow of pain sensations from the spinal cord to the brain. However, not all patients experience relief from their pain following surgery and for those who do, relief may be temporary. We now know that the nervous system has regenerative abilities that enable pain impulses to reach the brain via different neural pathways. As a result, surgical techniques that were once relatively common are rarely performed today.

Transcutaneous Electrical Nerve Stimulation

More effective than surgery is **transcutaneous electrical nerve stimulation (TENS).** **TENS** involves placing an electrode on the surface of the skin, close to where the patient feels pain, and applying electrical stimulation. This stimulation affects all nerves within approximately four centimetres of the skin's surface. Although stimulation is usually applied for approximately 20 minutes, the duration of pain relief usually lasts several hours, and occasionally lasts for days or weeks. There is considerable individual variation in the amount of pain relief experienced. Generally, the more frequent the stimulation the longer

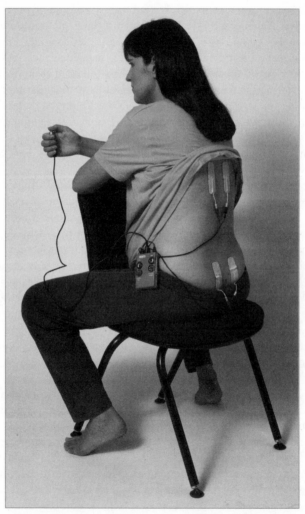

Transcutaneous electrical nerve stimulation (TENS) machines are easy to use and can help to relieve pain. Portable TENS machines allow individuals to engage in daily activities while their nerves are being stimulated.

the pain relief persists. For example, daily stimulation may provide gradually increasing relief over periods of weeks, months, and even years (Kim & Dellon, 2001; Melzack, 1989).

The advantage of TENS is that it is non-invasive and does not need to be performed by a licenced practitioner. Once the appropriate points are located, the treatment can be self-administered by the patient under the physician's supervision. The electronic units that supply the electrical stimulation are often portable and can be equipped with rechargeable batteries making it relatively easy to administer TENS at home (Melzack, 1989).

The effectiveness of TENS in reducing acute muscular and postoperative pain in the majority of patients is well documented (Hare & Milano, 1985). In a moving example, Chapman (1984) describes a nine-year-old boy who began receiving TENS while still unconscious after kidney surgery. After he regained consciousness, the hospital staff asked repeatedly if he felt pain in his belly. The boy continually replied, "No, it doesn't hurt." What is completely astonishing is that the boy did not realize he had already undergone surgery. When the surgeon left the room the boy spoke casually with the others in the room. When asked whether there was anything he feared, he began to cry and confessed his terror of the expected operation that would remove his kidney. His surprised nurse tried to reassure him that the surgery had already been done, and that there was nothing to worry about. He refused to believe her. "But don't you remember?" she contended, "that's why they put you to sleep this morning—so they could do the operation." The little boy looked very threatened. "It's not true!" he shouted, "It's not true!" When asked why it couldn't be true, he asserted confidently, "Because I haven't got any bandages." He was asked to feel his belly. When he did, an expression of astonishment came over his face. At that moment, he declared he felt pain, and he began to cry.

Although TENS is useful in treating acute pain, its effectiveness in treating chronic pain is less clear (Finsen et al., 1988). Some patients with arthritis have achieved substantial and long-lasting relief from pain using TENS (Bradley, 1983; Hare & Milano, 1985), and studies comparing the effectiveness of TENS to acupuncture in treating low back pain report that the two techniques are equal in terms of reducing pain (Andersson & Holmgren, 1975, Fox & Melzack, 1976; Laitininen, 1976). However, TENS produces short-lived relief to patients experiencing other chronic conditions, including phantom limb pain (Johnson, 1984; Minor & Sanford, 1993).

Acupuncture

Acupuncture is an ancient Chinese pain control technique that has been in continuous practice for at least 2000 years (Melzack, 1989). Basically, the procedure involves the insertion of fine needles (made of steel, gold, or other metals) through specific points in the skin then twirling or electrically charging them to create stimulation to the peripheral nerves. The effects of acupuncture are not immediate and the needles must be stimulated for approximately 20 minutes to produce analgesia. In addition, the stimulation must be fairly intense and continuous. However, the analgesia can last for hours after the stimulation has ended.

The practice of acupuncture is part of a complex theory of medicine in which all diseases and pains are believed to be due to disharmony between *yin* (spirit) and *yang* (blood). In China, where this philosophy is more widely accepted, five to ten percent of surgical operations are conducted with the use of acupuncture as the only form of analgesia. The patients must volunteer for the procedure and the surgeries using acupuncture analgesia are

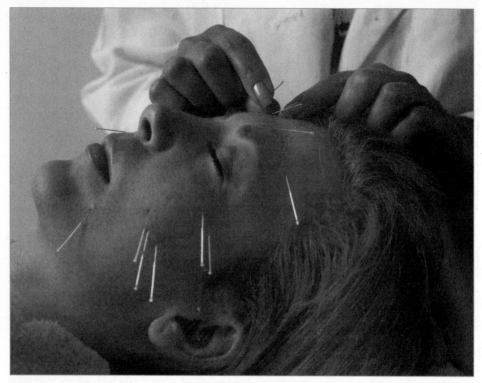

Stimulation of the peripheral nerves by acupuncture needles provides varying degrees of pain relief.

relatively straightforward, with little likelihood of complications. In Western countries, acupuncture is rarely used for surgery; it is seen instead as a treatment for less intense pain.

Laboratory studies have shown that acupuncture produces only mild analgesia in most people. Further, the degree of pain relief experienced is now known to be dependent on the intensity of the stimulation, rather than the exact point of stimulation. Traditionally, it was believed that exact points on the body, outlined on acupuncture charts, must be stimulated to have the desired effect. For example, certain points on the nose and ear were associated with the small intestine, whereas other points were associated with the kidneys, heart, or abdomen. Interestingly, individuals who derive the most benefits from acupuncture are the same individuals who benefit most from hypnotism.

Acupuncture is becoming more widely practised in North America, and its popularity may continue to grow. A survey of health care professionals at two Cancer Care Ontario centres revealed that acupuncture was the nonpharmacologic strategy for the management of cancer pain that participants were most interested in learning more about (Sellick & Zaza, 1998).The National Institute of Health (NIH) acknowledges that acupuncture has been somewhat successful for pain conditions involving tissue damage or tenderness, such as that experienced in postoperative dental pain. In addition, the NIH asserts that there are many situations in which acupuncture may be useful as an adjunct treatment or possibly an acceptable alternative to traditional treatments (e.g., headache, myofascial pain, osteoarthritis, low back pain, carpal tunnel syndrome, and tennis elbow) (Carlsson & Sjölund, 1994, 2001; JAMA, 1998; Lu, Lu, & Kleinman, 2001; Zeltzer, 2002).

Physical Therapy

Physical therapy involves a variety of treatment approaches to help patients who suffer from both acute and chronic pain. Patients usually work with a physical therapist to prepare an individualized treatment program. The program should provide daily or weekly goals that allow for gradual but steady progress. The program should progress rapidly enough to ensure the patient experiences a feeling of accomplishment but slow enough to prevent overexertion or re-injury. In order to restore their range of motion, patients who have undergone surgery or experienced injury should exercise regularly. Exercise also benefits arthritis patients because it helps maintain joint flexibility and prevents joints from deteriorating (Minor & Sanford, 1993). In addition, exercising is extremely beneficial for low back pain patients who need to maintain flexibility and develop strength in key muscles to provide support for their spines (Alaranta et al., 1994; Moffett et al., 1999). As part of an exercise program, patients are typically also taught body mechanics and proper posture to prevent further injuries.

Massage

Several years ago, a massage was considered a luxury. Today, massage therapy is one of the pain management techniques that Canadian physicians are keen to learn more about (Sellick & Zaza, 1998). Massage therapy is used to ease muscle pain and other pains, including that resulting from cancer. The procedure consists of systematic stroking and kneading of the body. The two main types of massage therapy are Swedish massage and Shiatsu massage. **Swedish massage** is a set routine of basic strokes to work the body and includes slow, gentle stroking movements, known as *effleurage*, to warm and relax tissue and to stimulate blood circulation. A deeper massage is also conducted with movements such as friction, percussion, and *pettrisage* (massage in which the muscles are kneaded and pressed). **Shiatsu massage** is based on the belief that there is a flow of energy through the body and that at times energy blockages develop. Consistent with this belief, energy blockages are released through the strong and sustained pressure of the massage at specific points on the body.

Research conducted with 32 hospital staff at a large teaching hospital investigated the usefulness of Swedish massage (Katz, Wowk, Culp, & Wakeling, 1999). Participants received either a series of eight 15-minute, on-site massage treatments or eight sessions of seated rest. Those in the massage group experienced significant reductions in pain and tension levels compared to the control group that received seated rest. This pain and tension relief persisted for up to a day or longer following the massage. An added benefit experienced by those who received the massage treatments was an increase in overall mood.

Relaxation

Many of the same relaxation strategies that are used to cope with stress (see chapter 2) are effective treatment for both acute and chronic pain. Relaxation is often used in conjunction with other pain management strategies and is thought to be an essential part of both biofeedback and hypnotic treatment. The rationale for relaxation training is straightforward—continual muscle contraction is considered both a cause and an effect of pain (Dolce & Raczynski, 1985). Researchers have found that muscle tension results in lactic acid build-up in muscles and also decreases blood flow to muscles. Both of these factors result in significant increases in people's experience of pain.

As discussed in chapter 2, relaxation can be accomplished by many different techniques, including **progressive muscle relaxation** and meditation. How successful has progressive relaxation been in the management of pain? In a meta-analysis of studies, Carlson and Hoyle (1993) reported that progressive muscle relaxation was generally helpful in coping with stress-related disorders such as migraine and tension headache, depression, hypertension, and low back pain. However, the actual effect size varied substantially from study to study, in part because of variation in the experimental procedures. Relaxation training was most effective when patients had participated in a sufficient number of training sessions, when they had been trained individually rather than in a group, when the patients used audiotapes to supplement their training, and when the patients had enough time to master the technique.

But how long do the effects of relaxation treatment for pain last? Edward Blanchard and colleagues have addressed this issue by conducting a five-year follow-up investigation of chronic headache patients (Blanchard, Andrasik et al., 1987; Blanchard, Appelbaum et al., 1987). These patients had all experienced an average of 18 years of headache resulting either from muscle-contraction (tension-type) or "vascular" headache, which includes both migraine and combined (migraine plus tension-type) headache. These patients completed training for progressive muscle relaxation in ten sessions over eight weeks. Those patients whose headache pain had not improved by at least 60 percent were offered additional treatment in the form of biofeedback. The treatment effects endured over time. That is, five years after the initial treatment patients reported headache pain at levels similar to those reported immediately after taking part in the treatment. The headache pain did not return to pretreatment levels. Other research has supported this conclusion, with patients experiencing durable relief from both relaxation and biofeedback for at least two years (Blanchard, 1987).

Meditation is another form of relaxation. *Meditative relaxation*, developed by Herbert Benson and colleagues (e.g., Benson, Beary, & Carol, 1974) is derived from various religious meditative practices but has no religious connotations. With Bensonian relaxation, the patient attempts to focus attention fully on a single thought or image. Often a very simple syllable such as "ohm" or "one" is repeated slowly over and over again with each breath. This process usually takes place in a quiet environment where the participant sits with eyes closed and muscles relaxed for a period of approximately 20 minutes.

Mindfulness meditation is a related strategy for achieving relaxation. This type of meditation has its roots in Buddhist practice. Participants engaged in mindfulness meditation do not try to ignore unpleasant thoughts or sensations. Instead, they are instructed to focus on any thought or sensation as it occurs but to view these thoughts in a non-judgmental manner. As Kabat-Zinn (1993) explains, "Observing without judging, moment by moment, helps you see what is on your mind without editing or censoring it, without intellectualizing it or getting lost in your own incessant thinking" (p. 263).

There are very few controlled studies evaluating the effectiveness of meditation. Those studies that have been published report mixed results. Some studies suggest that meditation is not successful as a pain control technique (Holmes, 1981), whereas others report that meditation is more effective than relaxation, biofeedback, or cognitive-behavioural strategies (Murphy, 1996). More studies are required to accurately determine whether meditation is a useful technique for managing pain.

Guided imagery can be considered a form of relaxation and can also be classified as a technique that relies on distraction. With guided imagery, the participant is told to imagine a calm, peaceful, and pleasant image. The image should be relatively unchanging, and the participant is told to focus all of his or her attention on the image.

Guided imagery is a technique suggested to pregnant mothers for use in childbirth. Women in labour are told to choose a focal point, either real or imagined, that they can concentrate on when giving birth. The focal point may be the image of waves washing onto the beach, for example, or a picture of a loved one.

Children are also encouraged to use guided imagery when undergoing cancer treatment. One child described skiing down a mountain as fast as he could. He commented on the warmth of the sunshine but insisted that focusing on the speed with which he skied in and out of the gates was how he became most "absorbed" in his image.

The effectiveness of guided imagery has not been established (see Eller, 1999 for a review). When used to manage pain, guided imagery is most often used in conjunction with other pain control techniques. Thus the unique contribution of guided imagery is difficult to establish. Studies conducted on guided imagery suggest it is superior to biofeedback in treating headaches (Ilacqua, 1994), aids burn victims in coping with pain (Achterberg, Kenner, & Lawlis, 1988), and reduces postoperative pain and length of hospital stays for child surgical patients (Lambert, 1996).

Distraction

Like guided imagery, **distraction** involves focusing one's attention on something other than the sensation of pain. As we mentioned earlier, athletes, soldiers, and others who are "caught up" in what they are doing may not immediately notice when they have injured themselves. Although we sometimes engage in distraction unknowingly, it is also possible to consciously apply the technique of distraction to help control the experience of pain. We can distract ourselves by focusing on a completely different activity, such as listening to music, singing a song, playing a video game, doing arithmetic problems, or reading a book. Researchers at Dalhousie University note that when five-year-olds are watching a program on television during immunization they experience lower levels of pain than when faced with a blank TV screen (Cassidy et al., 2002).

Distraction can also involve reinterpreting the event that is resulting in pain. Bandura (1991) provides a description from an eight-year-old boy who is re-interpreting a painful event: "As soon as I get in the dentist's chair, I pretend he's the enemy and I'm a secret agent, and he's torturing me to get secrets, and if I make one sound, I'm telling him secret information, so I never do." The boy goes on to say that this is good practice because he is going to be a secret agent when he grows up. There may be times when this technique works too well. On one occasion, the boy got quite absorbed in his role; when the dentist asked the boy to rinse his mouth, the boy snarled and said "I won't tell you a damned thing." The dentist and apparently even the boy were surprised by this outburst.

Distraction techniques are particularly useful for reducing acute pain, such as that experienced during some medical and dental procedures. However, that doesn't mean that individuals experiencing chronic pain don't use distraction to cope with their discomfort (Santavirta et al., 2001). An individual who experiences chronic pain is likely to use distraction most often when he or she anticipates a sharp rise in pain. For example, distraction would be particularly useful when a person suffering from chronic lower back pain must endure a bumpy car ride to the physician's office or when an arthritic patient needs to climb a flight of stairs.

Biofeedback

Biofeedback is a procedure used to teach patients to exert voluntary control over a bodily process that they are usually unaware of, such as heart rate. This technique is described in detail in chapter 2 as it pertains to coping with stress. However, biofeedback is also used to control pain. For example, biofeedback has been applied to the treatment of migraine headaches, temporomandibular joint pain, arthritis, low back pain, pelvic pain, pain associated with cerebral palsy, and Reynaud's syndrome (a condition in which the blood supply to the extremities is interrupted, resulting in pain, numbness, and tingling) (Sarafino & Goehring, 2001; Turk, Zacki, & Rudy, 1993; Ye et al., 2003).

Hypnosis

Hypnosis is one of the oldest techniques used to control pain (Hilgard & Hilgard, 1975; Fredericks, 2001). In the early nineteenth century, sensational tales appeared of physicians performing major surgery on patients who had been hypnotized. In 1829, it was reported that a French surgeon, Dr. Cloquet, removed a malignant tumour and several enlarged glands from a 64-year-old woman who had been hypnotized. In order to accomplish this feat, an incision was made from the woman's armpit to the inner side of her breast, in other words, the incision went half way across her chest. Yet the woman, who had not received any drugs, conversed with the physician during the surgery and showed no signs of experiencing pain (Kroger, 1957; cited in Chaves & Barber, 1976).

Hypnosis is often considered an altered state of consciousness that involves several components. First, a state of *relaxation* is necessary so that a hypnotic trance can be induced. Second, *distraction* or diversion of attention from the pain experience is established (this step is also referred to as "narrowing of attention"). Next, the practitioner *suggests* to the patient that the pain is diminishing. In this step, the practitioner may suggest that the pain is being replaced by a more pleasant sensation, such as warmth (Barber, 1986; Orne & Dinges, 1989).

The hypnotic procedure can take a number of forms. Consider Dylan, a 26-year-old who is currently experiencing extreme pain in his left arm resulting from a fall he experienced while snowboarding.

Scenario One:
Dylan's practitioner first induces hypnosis and then suggests, "The arm is going to begin to feel numb, with a pins-and-needles sensation as though it has received novocaine, and it will go

entirely to sleep." After a period of giving such suggestions, the practitioner adds, "This numbness is now so complete that there will be no pain sensation whatsoever, though you just might be able to feel my touch."

These suggestions rely upon Dylan imagining sensations he has had in the past—numbness, pins and needles, and the feeling that novocaine has been injected and that the arm has gone to sleep. If Dylan can imagine these sensations well enough to actually experience them, he will also gain control over the pain sensation in his arm.

Scenario Two:
Dylan's practitioner first induces hypnosis and then suggests, "Your arm will begin to float up, bending at the elbow." After this is repeated a few times, the practitioner grasps Dylan's arm and adds, "You now see your arm floating down, slowly, and gently your arm is cradled in your lap."

This procedure, first described by Erickson (1967), is an indirect way of suggesting away pain. Dylan's arm no longer seems to belong to him. Consequently, he no longer feels pain in his arm.

Scenario Three:
Dylan's practitioner first induces hypnosis and then suggests, "Collect your pain in your left hand. As you do so slowly make a fist. Squeeze your fist tighter as you continue to capture the pain." After a number of these suggestions, the practitioner adds, "You have gathered all of the pain in your hand, now throw it away."

This technique relies on the experience of focusing on the left hand and providing the sensation of muscular tension and pressure to facilitate the response to suggestion. This tension and pressure leads Dylan to believe he is in fact holding something (i.e., the pain) and therefore there can no longer be any pain left in his body. The practitioner might also have Dylan relive an experience he had before experiencing pain in his arm, thereby indirectly eliminating the pain.

Unfortunately, hypnosis does not work for everyone. For people who are highly responsive to suggestion, hypnosis can be very helpful in pain relief. However, researchers are not entirely sure whether hypnosis actually blocks pain or simply interferes with the reporting of it. Under hypnotic suggestion, people tend not to show behavioural signs of pain, such as grimacing or tensing their muscles. As well, hypnotized people report verbally that they feel no discomfort (Hilgard & Hilgard, 1975). They may recognize that they are in pain, but they indicate that the pain is not affecting them or does not matter to them. However, under hypnosis, people still show the classic physiological reactions of pain, such as changes in respiration and increased heart rate and blood pressure (Orne, 1989).

Researchers have yet to achieve a complete understanding of the mechanism responsible for the success of hypnosis. Consequently, modern physicians have been reluctant to adopt it in their clinical practice. However, there is now considerable documentation demonstrating the effectiveness of hypnosis for patients undergoing surgery, childbirth, and dental procedures as well as for those receiving treatment for burns, low back pain, cancer pain, and headaches (Barber, 1986; Iserson, 1999; Linden, 1994; Orne & Dinges, 1989; Sellick & Zaza, 1998). For example, in a classic study, Spiegel and Bloom (1983) randomly assigned 54 women with metastatic breast cancer to three groups. Group one members met weekly for 90 minutes and comprised a support group. During the session, the women underwent hypnosis for approximately five to ten minutes. The women assigned to group two also had a 90-minute weekly support group meeting but did not undergo hypnosis. The third group received only the usual medical treatment. One year later, the women in groups one and two reported significantly less pain compared to group three, with group one reporting the least pain. In fact, group three, the control group, actually reported an increase in pain and suffering a year after the experiment commenced. Many studies have reported an added benefit of using hypnosis in the treatment of pain—patients who receive hypnosis report less anxiety than do patients who receive other forms of pain treatment (Liossi & Hatira, 1999, 2003; Mauer et al., 1999).

Multidisciplinary Pain Management Programs

Pain clinics and pain management programs have been developed to aid the chronic pain patient. Our review of existing pain treatments illustrates that no single method of treatment is completely effective. Further, the success of each method of treatment varies considerably from one patient to the next. Therefore, a treatment approach that combines several treatment methods is likely to succeed for the largest percentage of patients and provide the greatest pain relief for each individual. The good news is that a recent Canadian study revealed that almost all patients are currently receiving several forms of treatment for their pain. Typically, the treatment involves a nonpharmacological treatment in addition to medication (Moulin et al., 2002).

The concept of having special institutions to provide multidisciplinary treatment for pain originated with John Bonica. He founded the first pain clinic at the University of Washington Medical School in 1960. There are now thousands of pain clinics across North America. The structure, methods, and quality of pain clinics vary widely. Many pain clinics are private institutions, whereas others are affiliated with medical schools, universities, or hospitals. Some clinics provide inpatient care, while others provide treatment on an outpatient basis. Often the program will include the interdisciplinary efforts of physicians, psychologists or psychiatrists, physical therapists, and occupational therapists (Rains, Penzien & Jamison, 1992). However, there are countless experts who can be included or consulted in any particular program (e.g., neurologists, rheumatologists, orthopedic surgeons, acupuncturists, massage therapists, etc.).

Initially, patients are assessed to determine the qualitative nature of their pain. This assessment typically involves documenting the location, sensory qualities, severity, and duration of the patient's pain as well as its onset and history. Determining the patient's current emotional and mental state, the degree to which family and work lives have been interrupted, and how the patient has coped with the pain in the past is also part of the initial assessment. This assessment allows for the program to be customized to match the needs of the patient (Chapman, 1991; Rains et al., 1992; Turk & Stacey, 2000). Goals for each patient are established, and the program is constructed to help the patient attain those goals.

The goals and objectives of different pain management programs may vary. However, they typically include reducing the patient's experience of pain, improving physical and lifestyle functioning, improving social support and family life, decreasing reliance on medications, and reducing the patient's need to use health care services (Follick, Ahern, Attansio, & Riley, 1985; Rains et al., 1992). The programs generally include specific treatment components for attaining each goal. For example, most programs include patient education to provide patients with a more complete understanding of the nature of their condition. Patients may take part in discussions about nutrition, medications, depression resulting from pain, how to combat sleep disturbances, and assertiveness or social skills. Usually patients are also educated about various methods of pain control. For instance, relaxation training and exercise are regular components of pain clinic programs. Guided imagery, acupuncture, massage, and other pain-reducing strategies may also be included. Familial and vocational counselling are also incorporated in many pain management programs.

How effective are multidisciplinary pain management programs? Numerous studies have documented that chronic pain sufferers who receive treatment at multidisciplinary pain centres report much less subsequent pain and are far more likely to return to work than individuals who receive standard pain treatment (Cutler et al., 1994; Flor, Fydrich, & Turk, 1992). Consider the evaluation of the pain management program at the Miller-Dwan Hospital Pain Control Center in Minnesota (Cinciripini & Floreen, 1982). Participants taking part in the program at the time of evaluation were men and women who had suffered intractable pain from known injuries or diseases (e.g., arthritis) for at least one year. At the time, all of the participants were unable to work because of the disabling pain they were experiencing. The participants took part in the program on an inpatient basis for four weeks, with weekends off. In this program, patients participate as part of a group. All patients took part in the full program, which included a medication-reduction procedure, physical therapy, relaxation and biofeedback training, self-monitoring, behavioural contracting, cognitive-behavioural group therapy, and family involvement and training. The patients' behaviour and functioning was assessed at the start of the program, at the end of the program, and at six and twelve months following program completion. Upon completing the program, patients' activity levels had increased and their pain experiences, pain behaviours, and medication use had sharply decreased. Amazingly, 90 percent of the patients were no longer taking analgesic medication. Follow-up assessments revealed that participants continued to be physically active and that approximately half of them were employed. The participants' pain continued to decrease. The average pain rating reported by participants before treatment was 4.6 on a 10-point scale, at the time of program completion it was 2.2, and after 1 year it was 1.2. This program can certainly be regarded as successful.

What makes a multidisciplinary pain management program so effective? Many would argue that it is the combination of pain treatments that make a multidisciplinary program effective. However, a recent study has documented patients' assessments of how helpful they believe each component of a multidisciplinary program has been for them. Perna, Durgin, and Geller (1999) randomly selected sixteen female and nine male chronic pain patients' files. All of the patients had completed a comprehensive multidisciplinary 20-day pain management program. At the conclusion of the program, patients completed a form that asked them to rate on a scale from 1 to 10 "the helpfulness" of each of the treatment modalities they had participated in; a score of "1" indicated not at all helpful whereas a score of "10" indicated the most helpful. Mean scores and the order of patient-rated helpfulness for each modality were as follows: group therapy (8.64), individual therapy (8.29), mind-body (7.95), physical therapy (7.75), biofeedback (7.68), medical office visits (6.80), occupational therapy (6.56), aqua therapy (6.33), vocational therapy (6.00), osteopathic manipulation (4.40), and trigger point injection (2.40). It is interesting that interventions aimed at mental activity were chosen as most helpful, particularly when, as the authors point out, all the patients in the study were on workers' compensation and likely stood to benefit from de-emphasizing psychological issues.

Not all chronic pain patients benefit from the treatment provided at a pain clinic, but most do. You may recall that Jake, who we introduced you to at the beginning of this chapter, had recently returned from a 10-day stay at a pain clinic. Jake was a prime candidate for this kind of treatment because his pain had not been relieved even after trying "every pain management technique available." Jake was skeptical about the benefits he might receive at the clinic and certainly some of the pain management techniques worked better for him than others. For example, he felt that the acupuncturist caused more pain than he relieved. Fortunately, not all of the treatments were perceived in this way. Jake thought that many of the exercises he learned from the physiotherapist were quite helpful. Jake derived other benefits from his stay as well. He now possesses more coping skills and social support than he did when he entered the program. In addition, over the course of his stay he dramatically reduced the amount of medication he was taking.

Multidisciplinary pain management programs represent a truly biopsychosocial approach to pain management. They can provide medical, psychological, physical, and occupational therapy. They can also improve chronic pain sufferers' psychological and physical functioning and reduce their pain, pain behaviour, and drug use.

KEY TERMS

A-delta fibres (p. 262)

acupuncture (p. 283)

acute pain (p. 266)

afferent (sensory) neurons (p. 261)

autonomic activity (p. 273)

box scale (p. 275)

C-fibres (p. 262)

central control trigger (p. 262)

centrally acting analgesics (p. 280)

chronic intractable benign pain (p. 267)

chronic pain (p. 266)

chronic progressive pain (p. 267)

chronic recurrent pain (p. 267)

distraction (p. 287)

electroencephalograph (EEG) (p. 273)

electromyograph (EMG) (p. 273)

endogenous opioids (p. 265)

evoked potentials (p. 273)

gate control theory (p. 262)

guided imagery (p. 287)

hypnosis (p. 288)

local anesthetics (p. 280)

meditation (p. 286)

multidisciplinary pain management programs (p. 290)

narcotics (p. 280)

neuromatrix theory (p. 264)

nociceptors (p. 261)

operant pain (p. 267)

pain behaviours (p. 267)

pain threshold (p. 270)

pain tolerance (p. 271)

periaqueductal gray area (p. 265)

peripherally acting analgesics (p. 280)

phantom limb pain (p. 263)

physical therapy (p. 285)

progressive muscle relaxation (p. 286)

respondent pain (p. 267)

sedatives (p. 280)

shiatsu massage (p. 285)

stimulation-produced analgesia (SPA) (p. 265)

Swedish massage (p. 285)

tranquillizers (p. 280)

transcutaneous electrical nerve stimulation (TENS) (p. 282)

verbal rating scale (VRS) (p. 275)

visual analog scale (VAS) (p. 275)

chapter eleven

Chronic and Life-Threatening Illnesses

CHAPTER OUTLINE

Cancer
  Physical Problems
  Psychological Distress
  Cancer Treatment
  Helping People Cope with Cancer

Diabetes
  Diabetes and Psychological Distress
  Helping People Cope with Diabetes

Diseases of the Cardiovascular System
  Psychological Distress in Cardiovascular Disease
  Helping People Cope with Cardiovascular Disease

HIV and AIDS
  Psychological Distress and HIV/AIDS
  Helping People Cope with HIV and AIDS

Other Chronic Conditions

Quality of Life

The Tradeoff between Duration and Quality of Life

Quality of Life As a Subjective Phenomenon

Death and Dying

Patients' Reactions to Death

Bereavement and Grief

KEY QUESTIONS

1. What are the most common examples of chronic and life-threatening illnesses?
2. What are the physical challenges posed by common chronic and life-threatening illnesses?
3. What are the psychological issues and sources of distress for people with chronic and life-threatening illnesses?
4. How can health psychologists and others help people cope with various chronic and life-threatening illnesses?
5. What do we mean by quality of life in this context and why is it important when treating people with chronic and life-threatening illnesses?
6. What psychological reactions are common to people who face the real possibility of premature death?
7. How can we help people cope with the possibility of premature death, and how can we help family and friends when they lose a loved one to serious illness?

At first, Mario attributed his fatigue to a lack of sleep. However, his fatigue persisted, even on days when he had slept well the night before. And then there was the light-headedness, especially when he hadn't eaten for a while. Once it got so bad that Mario actually felt disoriented.

After a trip to his doctor and some blood tests, Mario found out that he had Type II diabetes. He was discouraged by the diagnosis. It sounded so serious. He had heard of people dying or going blind from diabetes. Just as discouraging was the fact that he was going to have to make significant changes to his life that would be permanent. This was because diabetes is a **chronic condition**. It doesn't go away or get better. Instead, people with chronic conditions must learn to cope with them on a daily basis.

Mario was going to have to change his diet and closely monitor it. He was going to have to lose weight, too. These major changes were going to be particularly difficult for Mario to make because, for the first time in his life, he was feeling very depressed and fearful. Fortunately, his wife and friends were supportive, and there were some excellent information sessions put on by the hospital, so Mario did not have to feel alone in facing the daily challenges brought on by diabetes.

In this chapter, we will look at the psychology of *chronic conditions*—those that people live with for life; and *serious conditions*; which are life threatening and often accompanied by severe symptoms. For most of us, illness is **acute**, which means it is episodic in nature, having a defined beginning and end. But chronically ill people might not view their illness in episodic terms, however, and this can make their condition especially hard to cope with (Gathcel & Oordt, 2003). It is not surprising that health psychology has dedicated a great deal of research effort to understanding these conditions, which are often accompanied by emotional distress. Mario's reaction to his diagnosis of diabetes is not uncommon. Many people feel anger, depression, and fear when they learn they must cope with serious or chronic illnesses. However, in most cases these emotional reactions are not conducive to successful coping. Table 11-1 presents four different ways in which physical symptoms may be responded to psychologically by the chronically ill. A chronically ill person may well experience each symptom pattern resulting in a confusing mix of psychological responses.

TABLE 11-1	The Range of Symptom-Related Experience for People with Chronic Illness
Symptoms that are:	**Produce:**
constant	discouragement and fear
lessened or in remission	hope
unpredictably erratic	anger and frustration
relentlessly progressive	exhaustion and a sense of being overwhelmed

Source: Goodheart, C.D., and Lansing, M.H. (1997). *Treating people with chronic disease: A psychological guide.* Washington, DC: American Psychological Association.

We'll look closely at a number of conditions that are either chronic, serious, or both. We'll also look at the factors affecting people's ability to cope with these conditions and how people can be helped to cope better. You may remember that, in chapter 1, we made the point that major causes of death have changed since the beginning of the twentieth century. While viruses and bacteria were the main killers in 1900, diseases of lifestyle and environment—cancer and cardiovascular diseases—are now the main culprits. In this chapter, we are going to look closely at what it is like to have these and other diseases.

CANCER

In 2001, it was estimated that there would be over 134 000 new cases of cancer diagnosed in Canada (*Canadian cancer statistics: Current incidence and mortality*, 2001). The four most common types are lung (21 200 cases in 2001), breast (19 500), prostate (17 800), and colorectal (17 200). For every 100 000 men in Canada, 227 died of cancer in 2001. For women, that figure is 151. These mortality figures peaked in 1989 and have since dropped back to rates that are very similar to those in 1972.

The probability that a man will develop cancer at some time in his life is 40 percent. For women, the probability is 35.5 percent. Remember that these are lifetime statistics.

One's likelihood of getting cancer differs considerably according to one's age. For example, someone between the ages of 30 and 39 has less than a one percent chance of getting cancer; whereas someone between 70 and 79 has about a 16 percent chance (*Canadian Cancer Statistics: Current Incidence and Mortality*, 2001). In our lifetime, we will all either know people who have cancer or we will have to cope with it ourselves.

| CASE 11-1 | **An Unwelcome Diagnosis** |

Anna's life changed the day her physician discovered a lump in her breast during a routine examination. Then came the mammogram, the biopsy, and the result she had feared. She had a malignant tumour in her breast. Just the day before, she had been most concerned about her workload, her children's over-enthusiastic soccer coach, and her husband's reluctance to paint the kitchen. Suddenly, all of that seemed to pale in comparison to the questions that now had to be answered. Had the cancer spread? Could all the cancer be removed with a lumpectomy or would she require a mastectomy? How could she cope with that? What would her husband think? There would be more tests and more procedures. She remembered a colleague at work who had died from breast cancer. Was Anna going to die? She could not answer any of these questions. All she knew for sure was that she had never been so afraid in her life.

Cancer is not one disease, but many. The experience of a patient with one form of cancer can differ radically from that of another patient with a different form. The study of and treatment of cancer is called **oncology**. Oncologists often specialize in a particular *site* where cancer occurs in the body. This specialization is further indication of the differences between types of cancers, or **sites of cancer**, as oncologists would refer to them. For example, one group of oncologists might specialize in cancers of the genitourinary system. These oncologists would treat prostate cancer. Others may focus on the central nervous system. The site at which the cancer occurs, and the symptoms associated with it, is a significant factor in determining a person's psychological reactions to a diagnosis of cancer.

What all forms of cancer share is the uncontrolled growth of abnormal cells. General cell growth is, of course, common throughout the body. This growth is controlled as cells wear out and are replaced. Cancer cells are different. They grow in an uncontrolled manner and destroy normal cells in the process. When these abnormal cells form a mass, it is called a tumour. This tumour may be localized, or cells may spread to other parts of the body. When this happens, the cancer is said to have **metastasized**, or spread. Metastasized cancer is considerably harder to treat, since the treatment cannot be localized. Early detection of tumours reduces the likelihood that the cancer will have metastasized and thus increases chances of survival. In Case 11-1, Anna hoped that her physician had detected the lump early, so that the cancer would not have had time to spread. The Canadian Cancer Society has an informative web site for those seeking more information on cancer. It can be found at www.cancer.ca.

Whatever the site of the tumour, a diagnosis of cancer can have a profound effect on a person. Some will view it as a death sentence, others as the ultimate challenge of their lives. Many will go through strong denial in the early stages in an attempt to cope with trauma that is unprecedented in their lives. Even after receiving her diagnosis, Anna may deny that she has cancer. Patients must cope with aggressive treatments that bring on side effects that are worse than the symptoms of many other diseases. They must face the real possibility that their lives will be shortened, and they must also face the possible stigma associated with serious illness. Friends and colleagues aren't always adept at providing support for the cancer patient. Their own fear and lack of familiarity with cancer can get in the way. There is evidence, though, that the stigma of cancer is diminishing and that people are becoming more adept at lending support to friends and family members with the disease (Bloom & Kessler, 1994).

The nature of cancer patients' suffering has been categorized into three general areas—physical, psychological, and social (Kuuppeloäki & Lauri, 1998). According to research in which cancer patients were asked to complete questionnaires about their suffering, approximately 60 percent of cancer suffering is related to physical factors (Kuuppeloäki & Lauri, 1998). These factors break down further into two subcategories—illness-caused and treatment-caused. The most common physical complaints are fatigue, pain (Ferrell, Smith, Cullinane, & Melancon, 2003), and side effects of chemotherapy, which we will discuss in a moment. About 44 percent of suffering relates to psychological factors. The two most prevalent reactions are depression and fear. Depression is a particularly great risk at the initial diagnosis (Ferrell et al., 2003), when or if the cancer metastasizes, and when the patients are in poor physical condition. About 13 percent of suffering relates to the patients' social lives. The primary problem here is withdrawal. While the stigma of having cancer appears to be lifting (Bloom & Kessler, 1994), it is still the case that many patients experience significant disruptions in their social lives.

Adolescents with cancer report cancer-related limitations as long as two years after they have been treated. These include such things as being unable to play contact sports or, for one teen who had suffered a brain tumour 14 years earlier, experiencing fear every time he had a headache.

Physical Problems

As we have said, fatigue and pain have been identified as two of the most common physical problems faced by cancer patients (Ferrell et al., 2003). Pain management, then, is a major challenge for patients and for those providing treatment. One source of frustration in this regard is the fact that cancer pain tends to be undertreated. It has been estimated that more than 90 percent of cancer pain can be controlled by current treatments; however, these treatments are underused (Paice, Toy, & Shott, 1998). Why is this? It is not because practitioners are not inclined to do everything they can to reduce patients' suffering. Rather, the patients' attitudes and behaviour appear to explain why more people are in pain than need be.

For example, patients' fears about building up a tolerance to analgesic medication and, to a lesser extent, an addiction to it, keep them from seeking adequate pain-relieving treatment (Paice, Toy, & Shott, 1998). Yet most of these fears are unfounded. Thomason and colleagues (1998) identified patient-related barriers to taking analgesics for their cancer pain. The first was forgetfulness, followed by the belief that the pain should be tolerated. Patients also reported concerns regarding side effects. For these and a host of other reasons, patients may be unwilling to report mild or moderate pain, making it difficult for practitioners to prescribe adequate medication (Thomason et al., 1998). (See chapter 10 for more on pain management.)

Psychological Distress

As you can well imagine, there are many different psychological reactions involved in the cancer experience. Two of the most common and most distressing for patients and their families are fear and depression. Breast cancer patients' most common concerns during the early stages of their illness include issues of body integrity; and fear of radiation therapy, cancer relapse, and death (Wu, 2001).

For some patients, fear and depression become chronic, even if cancer treatment is proceeding successfully. They may fear recurrence or that the cancer will metastasize (Bishop & Warr, 2003). They may fear the side effects of the treatment and the changes to their self-image (Steginga, Occhipinti, Wilson & Dunn, 1998).

Depression is a common form of psychological distress for cancer patients (e.g., Payne et al., 1999; Thompson & Shear, 1998), although it is more prevalent with some forms of cancer than others. For example, depression is diagnosed at a higher rate for pancreatic cancer, a disease that tends to have a poor prognosis (Zabora, 2001). A study of 52 consecutive patients undergoing radiation therapy for various forms of cancer found that 16 of them (31 percent) were depressed (Jenkins, Carmody, & Rush, 1998). Depression results in poorer quality of life, less compliance with medical treatment, longer hospital stays, and higher mortality rates (Newport & Nemeroff, 1998). Depressed patients also report greater pain intensity (Sist et al., 1998). To compound the problem, a patient's depression is positively correlated with family caregivers' depression (Kurtz, Kurtz, Given, & Given, 1995).

Analysis of cancer-related depression has shown that it is linked to **intrusive memories**. These are unwanted thoughts, often visual in nature, that are related to memories the patient has about cancer. They usually involve illness and death, often that of a friend, relative, or someone in a movie. These intrusive memories result in poor coping because they produce an anxious preoccupation with cancer, as well as a sense of helplessness and hopelessness (Brewin et al., 1998).

Brewin and colleagues studied 65 cancer patients who were either severely or mildly depressed, comparing them to a group of 65 non-depressed cancer patients. Thirty-two percent of mildly depressed patients and 43 percent of severely depressed patients reported intrusive memories, even though most of the participants had received their diagnoses years before. Only 11 percent of the non-depressed patients reported such memories. Also, the number of intrusive memories was greater for the depressed patients (Brewin et al., 1998).

The extent to which a person with cancer experiences depression and anxiety may be related to the person's coping style. For example, he or she may cope by focusing on ways to reduce the emotional impact of the disease. This is called **emotion-focused coping**. Alternatively, the person might engage in **problem-focused coping**. In this case, the person might seek information about the disease, closely follow treatment recommendations, and actively address the stressors associated with cancer and its treatment. In emotion-focused coping, the tendency is to avoid thinking about possible stressors because to address them would be upsetting. Patients who had been diagnosed 10 weeks prior to taking part in a study of coping styles showed less depression and anxiety if they adopted a problem-focused approach. This was particularly true of participants who believed they could control the progression of their cancer (Osowiecki & Compas, 1998). However, coping style *did not* predict depression and anxiety four months later. Interestingly, the same study found that people using emotion-focused coping did not experience significantly less emotional distress, suggesting that the approach wasn't serving its purpose. See Table 11-2.

TABLE 11-2	A comparison of emotion-focused and problem-focused coping	
	Emotion-focused coping	Problem-focused coping
Main objective	To reduce the experience of unpleasant emotions associated with the situation	To learn about the situation in order to affect factors that are causing the problem
Coping style	Avoidant	Active
Typical Behaviours	Avoid thinking about the situation	Seeking information, following recommendations, and analyzing factors involved

Another way to think about coping styles is to divide them into **active** and **passive coping**. These terms are fairly self-explanatory. Active coping is more likely to be problem-focused. Passive coping places the responsibility for coping in the hands of others. Generally, active coping is associated with better psychological outcomes and less distress (Bishop & Warr, 2003).

There is disagreement regarding the extent to which coping style affects the physical progress of the disease. In addition to the active/passive distinction, coping approaches have also been categorized according to fighting spirit, helplessness/hopelessness, denial, and avoidance (Petticrew, Bell, & Hunter, 2002). For example, prostate cancer patients who were attending a support group were more likely than non-attenders to have adopted a coping style that was low in hopelessness and high in fighting spirit (McGovern, Heyman, & Resnick, 2002). Also, patients in another study who were considered to have adapted poorly to their cancer diagnosis showed low fighting spirit and high helplessness/hopelessness (Montgomery, Pocock, Titley, & Lloyd, 2003).

However, after conducting a review of the literature that investigated the relationship between these coping strategies and patients' survival and recurrence rates, Petticrew and colleagues came to the conclusion that coping strategy did not affect survival or recurrence. Their review has been criticized for grouping studies that used different definitions and measures of coping styles (Watson, Davidson-Homewood, Haviland, & Bliss, 2003), and for ignoring relevant research (Mitchell & Kumar, 2003). Petticrew et al., have responded to these criticisms and held to their conclusions. All agree that more research is needed. This is particularly important because, when interpreting coping styles, it is easy to fall into the trap of inadvertently and unfairly blaming the cancer patient for lack of progress because he or she hasn't adopted the "right" coping style or "isn't trying hard enough." Also, it has been suggested that clinicians who encourage a fighting spirit and generally positive attitude might inadvertently be discouraging patients from expressing important emotions (Byrne, Ellershaw, Holcombe, & Salmon, 2002).

Cancer Treatment

Cancer is most often treated through surgery, radiation therapy, chemotherapy, or hormone therapy, or some combination of these. Hormone therapy is used for cancers such as prostate and some breast cancers when tumour growth is stimulated by the presence of certain hormones. The therapy is designed to reduce the existence of these tumour-stimulating hormones. Anna, from our chapter-opening vignette, will probably have surgery to remove her tumour and, possibly, part or all of her breast. She may also have radiation therapy before surgery to shrink the tumour and chemotherapy after surgery to treat any cancer that may have spread.

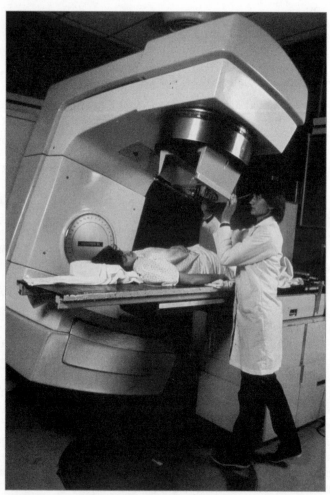

A radiation therapy machine. Machines like this one deliver precise dosages of radiation designed to shrink tumours.

Some cancer patients fear the treatment more than the disease itself. For example, prostate cancer patients on hormone therapy usually experience persistent fatigue. Moreover, their sex drive is severely diminished and they may start developing female secondary sex characteristics such as breast enlargement. Other forms of treatment also come with common side effects that can make coping difficult.

We have already talked about recovery from surgery in chapter 5, on hospital stays and medical procedures. In that chapter, we made the point that pain management was an important component of the recovery process. This is particularly true for cancer patients recovering from their surgery. Other psychological issues exist for cancer patients who undergo surgery. One is the anxiety associated with the outcome of the surgery. Were all the cancerous cells removed? Was there evidence that the cancer had metastasized? How much normal tissue had to be removed? Will this affect normal functioning when I recover from the surgery?

Another very important issue in cancer surgery is **disfigurement**. Cancer surgery that requires the removal of a considerable amount of normal tissue is called **radical**. Radical surgery has the potential to change not only a person's normal functioning but their appearance and autonomy as well. Cancers of the head and neck may require surgery that changes facial shape. Throat cancer surgery may require the removal of the larynx that is responsible for making speech sounds. As a result of this surgery, patients often require the use of a prosthetic speech device that dramatically changes the sound of their voice. Colorectal cancer is one of the four most common cancers in Canada, afflicting 59 men and 38 women per 100 000 in 2001 in Canada (*Canadian cancer statistics: Current incidence and mortality*, 2001). If surgery is required to remove part of the colon, a patient may require a prosthetic replacement of the lower colon. This requires that the patient wear a colostomy bag to collect waste materials; the person may also lose control of the bowel.

One of the better known surgical procedures for breast cancer patients is mastectomy. Patients can experience depression and disruptions in sexual activity as a result of radical mastectomy, in which part or all of a breast is removed. Not surprisingly, patients tend to cope better with the much less radical lumpectomy surgery (Moyer, 1997). Surgery, then, comes with considerable psychological and physical costs. Opting against surgery, however, runs the real risk of having the tumour grow and spread. For young patients, decisions regarding surgery are usually easier to make than for elderly patients, who might suffer more from the surgery than the cancer and who wouldn't have as many years left to lose to cancer as a younger person would.

Radiation therapy is used to shrink tumours. It can be used prior to or following surgery or may be used on its own. Radiation therapy is usually administered on an outpatient basis, though patients' experiences with radiation therapy will differ significantly depending on the site of their cancer. A person may have just a few treatments or as many as 30 or more over the course of several weeks, as is the case with many prostate cancer patients.

Patients with head and neck tumours may have to undergo preliminary dental work before their radiation treatments can begin. They must be fitted with a mask that will hold their heads in precisely the same position each time they come in for a treatment. Patients with tumours in abdominal regions may be fitted with a body mould that they are placed in before treatments to ensure accuracy. They may also be "tattooed" with small cross-hair target marks to help the radiation technologists line up the beams that position the treatment. These radiation tattoos are reminders of their radiation experience and their cancer.

Some patients will display them proudly; others will do their best to ignore them. Side effects from radiation therapy depend on the extent to which the radiation hits neighbouring cells and organs.

Surgery and radiation therapy are treatments intended to deal with specific sites as precisely as possible. In cases in which it is suspected that the cancer has metastasized, or to help prevent it from doing so, **chemotherapy** is used in addition to surgery and/or radiation therapy. It is called an **adjuvant therapy** when used in conjunction with other therapies in this way. Rather than attacking specific sites, the powerful drugs used in chemotherapy are distributed throughout the body, with the exception of the brain in some circumstances.

As is the case with radiation therapy, the side effects of chemotherapy are caused by unavoidable harm being done to healthy cells. These side effects include fatigue, nausea, hair loss, erosion of oral and gastrointestinal mucosa that can result in pain and diarrhea, and increased susceptibility to infection (Stuber, 1995). The number of side effects and their intensity vary depending upon the drug and the dosage. Fatigue is reported in up to 70 percent of chemotherapy and radiation patients (Dimeo et al., 1999). In some cases, fatigue is severe enough that the dosages have to be limited. It has been found, however, that exercise in the form of pedalling a stationary bike (in the supine position) can significantly reduce fatigue in high-dose chemotherapy treatment (Dimeo, 2002; Dimeo, 2001).

Interestingly, of all the side effects associated with chemotherapy, 35 of 60 breast cancer patients identified hair loss as being the most difficult to deal with (Tierney, Taylor, & Closs, 1992). There are a number of understandable psychological reasons for this, many of which relate to one's sense of identity. We look very different without our hair. It is a distinctive, defining characteristic for us. When Phil Zimbardo wanted to simulate a loss of identity for "prisoners" in his famous prison simulation study, he had them wear nylon stockings on their heads to simulate baldness (Haney, Banks, & Zimbardo, 1973) because people look remarkably similar without their hair. At the same time, her hair loss signals a new identity—that of a cancer patient. People will differ in how comfortable they are with this new identity. They may find distinctive hats, scarves, and wigs to help them reestablish a sense of uniqueness and normality. One of our students who had gone through chemotherapy chose not to cut his hair for years after it grew back.

The nausea and vomiting many patients experience as a side effect of chemotherapy have received considerable study. Most chemotherapy treatments are administered in clinics on an outpatient basis or in physicians' offices. The patient then returns home to cope with the side effects. It is not uncommon for patients to begin feeling nauseated *before* they receive their treatment. This is called **anticipatory nausea**, and it is explained in terms of classical conditioning (Jacobson et al., 1995). The setting in which the treatment is administered, the medical staff involved, and the smells of the room all become potential conditioned stimuli that bring on nausea in anticipation of the treatment. And to make matters worse, it is possible that immune suppression may be another conditioned response that accompanies anticipatory nausea.

When patients are given chemotherapy, they are also often given medication intended to reduce nausea and vomiting, called **antiemetic medication**. This can be administered before and after chemotherapy and radiation treatments. Studies have shown it to be effective for some patients (e.g., Abbott et al., 1999; Barbounis et al., 1999; Sohara et al., 1999), but certainly not all (Hickok et al., 2003). Whether antiemetic medication is used may depend on the nature of the cancer and whether or not it could interfere with the effectiveness of the treatment (Muustedt et al., 1999).

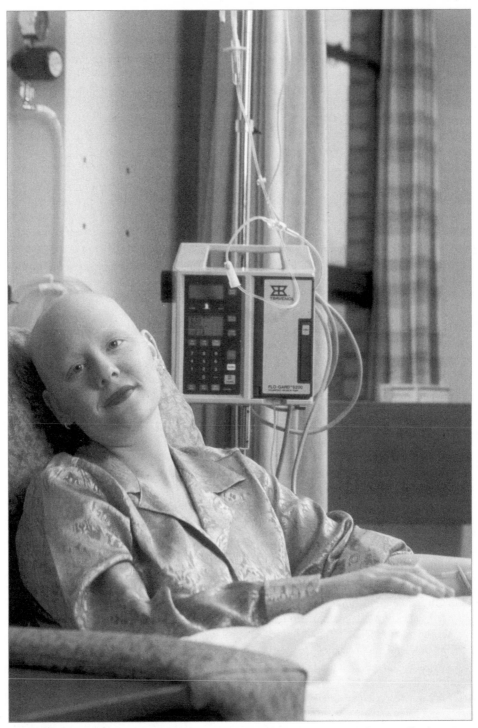

Hair loss can change the identity of patients undergoing chemotherapy. Some patients cover up with distinctive scarves and hats. Others display their new-found baldness comfortably.

Helping People Cope with Cancer

Social Support   It is clear that cancer provides many challenges to a person's capacity to cope. It is important to realize also that for virtually every cancer patient there is a family and a collection of close friends who are also affected by the disease. With this in mind, comprehensive cancer care adopts a **family orientation**. In essence, the family becomes the patient. The lives of spouses and children can be changed dramatically when a family member is diagnosed with cancer. At the same time, family and friends will be called upon to provide much needed support for that person. The strain on the family can be overwhelming (Baider, Cooper, & Kaplan De Nour, 1996). The family's ability to cope with cancer will be directly related to the extent to which they have learned in the past to be flexible in stressful situations (Goodheart & Lansing, 1997). A family that has never communicated well in stressful situations will have to learn to do so if a family member gets cancer.

Modern medicine has sophisticated treatments for malignancies. It can even provide medication for depression and anxiety. However, when it comes to coping with cancer on a long-term basis, there is no substitute for a strong social support network (e.g., Hoskins et al., 1996). We discussed social support in chapter 7, on health promotion. We return to it here because of its importance as a mechanism for helping cancer patients and their families cope with serious illness. We know that social support is beneficial, but just how does it work? Those attempting to answer this question have taken a close look at the *social* nature of social support. What is it about some interactions that are so helpful and supportive?

We all know that sometimes it is enough to just "be there" as a sounding board for someone's concerns or to alleviate loneliness, which can be a serious problem for cancer patients. Also, support can be provided by helping with practical problems, like giving a lift to an appointment, doing some cooking, or taking out the garbage. Some forms of support, especially some forms of emotional support, require that people *communicate* with one another. This has been called **help-intended communication** (Goodman & Dooley, 1976) and is defined as communication that attempts to alleviate emotional distress. The interesting thing about help-intended communication is that, despite its good intentions, it doesn't always work. In fact, sometimes it can be perceived by the person with cancer as being *un*helpful (Dunkel-Schetter, 1984).

To identify some of the differences between helpful and unhelpful communication, Pistrang, Barker, and Rutter (1997) analyzed conversations between recently diagnosed breast cancer patients and their husbands. They audiotaped conversations and then played them back for the participants to get their impressions of what had been helpful and what had been unhelpful. Many women felt that a husband's attempts to lighten the conversation were unhelpful because they suggested that he didn't empathize with what she was going through. Similarly, attempts to "look on the bright side" may be seen as unhelpful because they fail to acknowledge legitimate fears and concerns.

While microanalyses such as these can provide valuable insights into the interactive aspects of social support, they can also be somewhat daunting for those trying to provide this support. When we become preoccupied with "saying the right thing," we may become paralyzed and thus entirely unhelpful. The general conclusion to draw from work like that of Pistrang and colleagues is that support providers should acknowledge the person's concerns and fears as being legitimate while trying to help the person find effective ways of dealing with them. We can do this without dwelling on the intricacies of every word we say.

The fact that a patient's husband might think he is being helpful while she thinks he is being unhelpful indicates that perceptions are very important when it comes to social support. In fact, it may well be that our beliefs about the *availability* of our support are as important as the actual support we receive (Komproe et al., 1997). The reassurance we get from knowing that support is out there if we need it has been shown to reduce depression and encourage cancer patients to actually seek support. This, in turn, reduces feelings of helplessness. This is reminiscent of what Vancouver residents say when asked how they can appreciate the city's mountains that are so often obscured by cloud. They say, "It's important just knowing that they are there." When it comes to our social support networks, just knowing that they are there is very important.

Many patients also benefit from having a **navigator**. This person, often a nurse, community health worker, or social worker, can help Anna find her way through the sometimes complicated world of cancer treatment (Carter, 2003). The navigator can also help Anna prepare for her appointments in terms of knowledge and expectations.

Empathy is an important element of support. Family and friends can provide some, but to truly empathize, two people must have experienced the same situation. For cancer patients, this means interacting with other patients in more formally organized support groups or being paired with volunteers who have had similar cancer experiences. Research has shown that a well-timed visit from a volunteer can help breast cancer patients feel less isolated and more optimistic about the future (Dunn, Steginga, Occhipinti, & Wilson, 1999).

Community agencies and cancer centres coordinate such groups. In addition to providing empathy, these support groups can be good sources of information as new patients meet with others who have learned through experience how best to cope with various aspects of the disease. Studies have shown that support groups are of considerable benefit for prostate cancer patients. They help men feel more informed about the illness and more involved in the treatment (Gregoire, Kalogeropoulos & Corcos, 1997; Kaps, 1994), and they provide opportunities to talk with other patients about difficult issues (Poole et al., 2001). In short, support groups provide good opportunities for problem-focused coping.

Having said this, it isn't necessarily true that support groups are good for all patients. Support groups often emphasize education, and so they suit people who cope best by being informed. You may remember from chapter 5, on hospital stays and medical procedures, that these people are called *monitors*. Remember also that some patients cope best by blocking out information. These people are called *blunters* (Miller, 1980). It is very possible that blunters would have to change their coping style to benefit from support groups.

Social comparison processes may help explain why some people benefit from support groups while others do not (Bogart & Helgeson, 2000). When we engage in **social comparison**, we look to the opinions and experiences of others to determine what is right and wrong, normal or abnormal. We use this information to help guide us in our decision making (Festinger, 1954). This process is akin to the subjective norm component of the theory of reasoned action (Fishbein & Ajzen, 1975), which we discussed in chapter 1. When we engage in social comparison, we can compare *upward*, by looking at people who are better off than us, or we can compare *downward*, by looking at people who are worse off.

In support groups, upward comparisons are made with group members who are seen to be coping better than the person doing the comparing, and downward comparisons are made with those seen to be doing worse. Patients who view upward comparisons as evidence that they can get better or downward comparisons as reminders that they should be thankful because they could be worse off, would be more likely to attend a support group. On the other hand, people who find upward comparisons discouraging because they feel worse off by comparison and downward comparisons depressing because they see themselves eventually declining to that state, would not be likely to attend. For example, a person recently diagnosed with a brain tumour may attend a support group and meet people whose cancer has advanced to the point where they are terminally ill. The person could be thankful that her disease isn't that bad, or she could be frightened by the prospect that her disease will progress the same way. The majority of people attending support groups make downward comparisons and feel better for having done so (Bogart & Helgeson, 2000). For Anna, then, a support group would be as beneficial as her thinking and coping styles would allow it to be.

While cancer is undeniably distressing, it is not uncommon for cancer survivors to report positive outcomes from their cancer experience (Cordova, Cunningham, Carlson, & Andrykowski, 2001). These positive experiences fit in the category of **posttraumatic growth** (Tedeschi & Calhoun, 1995). This growth is often attributed to **benefit finding** (Katz, Flasher, Cacciapaglia, & Nelson, 2001) a term that refers to what might be called finding the "silver lining in the cloud." Growth can also stem from changing or affirming one's sense of spirituality (Gall & Cornblat, 2002), developing a greater appreciation of life, seeing new possibilities, and recognizing personal strength (Tedeschi & Calhoun, 1995).

Psychotropic Medication and Psychotherapy For many cancer patients, the depression and fear they experience can be adequately managed with the help of social support, whether from family, friends, or a support group. Support networks may be readily available for the patient or may be created with the help of the hospital, community, or social worker. For some patients, however, more intensive intervention is needed. These people may need to work with a clinical psychologist, counselling psychologist, or psychiatrist.

Psychiatrists might prescribe antidepressant medication such as fluoxetine (Prozac), which has been shown to be effective in treating depression in people with advanced cancer (Fisch et al., 2003). However, it is possible that complications may arise from taking antidepressant medication in conjunction with other cancer-related treatments, and so drug interactions have to be taken into consideration when antidepressants are prescribed (Franco-Bronson, 1996). There has also been some debate concerning the possibility that some antidepressants may stimulate tumour growth, since this outcome was reported in a study using rodents. A study of humans, however, found no evidence of increased risk of recurrence or further tumour growth in patients taking antidepressants (Weiss, McFarland, Burkhart, & Ho, 1998).

Because of the concerns associated with the use of medication, and because psychotherapy has been shown to be effective as a means of helping cancer patients, psychotherapeutic interventions are not uncommon. One goal of psychotherapy might be to help patients adopt a problem-focused approach to their cancer (Greer & Moorey, 1997; Nezu et al., 1998). Goodheart and Lansing (1997) have outlined a series of steps to follow when developing a psychotherapeutic treatment strategy for working with people who are chronically ill. These steps apply very well to cancer patients and their families.

The first step is to *obtain sufficient medical information*. Some of this can be obtained from the patient. This may be difficult or burdensome for the patient, however, so the therapist must be able to communicate well with medical staff. Second, the therapist must *assess the person's psychological status and response to the illness*. In so doing, the therapist must weigh the demands of the illness against the coping resources of the patient. Also, the therapist must develop a sense of the person's psychological state before the illness. Third, the therapist must *integrate a theoretical orientation*. To probe the person's feelings and unstated anxieties, the therapist might adopt a psychodynamic orientation. To address functional quality-of-life issues, a behavioural orientation might be adopted. The key is to offer a range of interventions and then to match the intervention with the patient's most pressing needs.

Clinical psychologists, psychiatrists, and counsellors often work with people in groups. These therapeutic groups differ from support groups in that they are guided by a professional trained in psychotherapy, with the emphasis shifting somewhat from the provision of information to strategies to alleviate depression and anxiety. Therapy of this nature has been shown to reduce the physical and emotional distress associated with radiation therapy (Forester et al., 1993). Indeed, research reviews on the outcomes of group psychotherapy for cancer patients have identified considerable evidence that such therapy is effective (Fawzy & Fawzy, 1998; Rieger, Touyz, & Wain, 1998).

Earlier in the book, we mentioned the research of David Spiegel and colleagues (1989), in which women with metastasized breast cancer who were randomly assigned to a support group lived almost twice as long as those in the control condition. What makes these sessions so effective? Spiegel and colleagues identify a number of aspects. First, the members are encouraged to express emotions and confront their concerns about death. Second, a sense of group cohesion is built, increasing the sense of social support. Third, participants are taught to improve their communication skills, given that talking about one's cancer can be quite difficult. Fourth, they are given relaxation training.

Consistent with the notion of family-oriented care, psychotherapy is also often provided for families of the person with cancer. It has been estimated that 29 percent of family caregivers experience psychological distress severe enough to warrant clinical intervention (Rodrigue & Hoffmann, 1994). The roles of family members change when one of them is diagnosed with cancer. Household responsibilities must be shared as one or more members become the principal caregiver. There can also be financial difficulties if the person with cancer must take an extended leave from work. Family members may need help managing the psychological burdens associated with taking on various caregiving roles and, in some cases, being a "midwife to death" (Brown & Stetz, 1999). In these cases, grief counselling may also focus on the entire family.

Psychological interventions are also used to help patients cope with cancer-related pain. For example, hypnotherapy has shown promising results (Sachs, 1992), as has visual imagery and relaxation training with children (Kuttner, 1997). For example, Dr. Leora Kuttner has worked with children undergoing painful procedures at the British Columbia Children's Hospital. She has children focus their attention on bubble blowing as a form of distraction. She has also used hypnosis as well as relaxation through biofeedback. Using the latter technique, Dr. Kuttner teaches children how to use cues in order to relax.

Given the prevalence of cancer and the myriad of coping challenges associated with the disease, it is clear that health psychologists can make significant contributions to the quality of life of cancer patients and to the coping abilities of the patients' families.

DIABETES

Over 1.1 million people in Canada have diabetes, with the disease being more common among males. About 17 people per 100 000 die from diabetes in a given year (*Diabetes in*

Canada, 2nd Edition, 2003). Diabetes occurs when the pancreas produces too little insulin, which is needed to help the body use sugar for energy. People with Type I diabetes produce very little or no insulin. As a result, they are called **insulin dependent**. According to Health Canada, about 10 percent of all diabetics are Type I. People with **Type II diabetes** do produce insulin, but they either don't produce enough or they can't use their insulin effectively. About 90 percent of all diabetics are Type II. There is a third type, called **gestational diabetes**, which is a temporary condition affecting two to four percent of all pregnant women.

Type I diabetes is more prevalent among people of Aboriginal, African, and Latin-American decent, and among people who have a history of diabetes in their family (Health Canada web site). Type II diabetes is more common among people over the age of 45, especially if they are obese. In fact, nearly 50 percent of Type II patients are over the age of 60 (Morley, 1998). For people with Type I diabetes, symptoms usually come on quite quickly and are severe. They include such things as frequent urination, unusual thirst, extreme hunger, unusual weight loss, and extreme fatigue. People with Type II diabetes might also experience frequent infections, and cuts and bruises that take a long time to heal.

People with Type I diabetes must monitor their blood sugar levels very carefully and take insulin, usually by self-administered injection, on a daily basis. While the vast majority of Type I patients monitor their blood glucose levels, a large study in Germany found that only 41 percent do so as often as they should (Haupt et al., 1996). People with Type II diabetes do not have to take insulin; however, they must also monitor their blood sugar and maintain a well-controlled diet. It is not uncommon for people diagnosed with Type II diabetes to become depressed and discouraged. These psychological states can have a serious effect on their willingness to follow the regimens necessary to control their disease.

Diabetes and Psychological Distress

As is the case with most chronic illnesses, fear and depression are two of the most common psychological problems for people with diabetes.

Fear and Diabetes   Diabetic patients' fears tend to focus on the possible long-term consequences of the disease. These include amputation, cardiovascular disease, kidney failure (nephropathy), neurological problems, blindness (retinopathy), and stroke (Hendricks & Hendricks, 1998). These fears cause problems because they tend to get in the way of disease management for the patient (Straus, 1996). Consistent with the health belief model, diabetic patients who become fearful may doubt the efficacy of the management program in the face of these potentially terrible consequences.

People with Type I diabetes have other fears as well. They might fear self-injection or self-testing (Mollema, Snoek, Ader, Heine, & van der Ploeg, 2001). They might also have concerns when their blood sugar levels get out of balance. This condition, called **hypoglycemia**, brings on adverse physical symptoms such as fatigue. It can also be accompanied by disorientation, confusion, and negative mood. In extreme cases, hypoglycemia can lead to seizure or loss of consciousness. Disorientation and negative mood states that can accompany hypoglycemia can have upsetting social consequences. For example, a spouse, partner, or friend will often notice that a person is becoming hypoglycemic before the person notices it themselves. When the other person points this out, the suggestion might be met with anger and confusion (Ritholz & Jacobson, 1998). After the person gets his or her blood sugar stabilized, there is the discouragement of realizing that he or she can't always take quick action to remedy the condition, and guilt about blowing up at someone else who was only trying to help.

BOX 11-1	Diabetes among Canada's Aboriginal Population

Fifty years ago, diabetes was virtually unheard of among Canada's Aboriginal peoples. Today, its prevalence in this population is three times the national average. Diabetes is more prevalent for First Nations people living on reserve than off, pointing to risk factors such as diet. The diets of Canada's First Nations people have been influenced significantly by non-Aboriginal trends. Fast foods and high-sugar products such as pop and candy bars are replacing more traditional foods in First Nations' diets. The result has been this high rate, and earlier onset, of diabetes. This is compounded by later detection, such that by the time the disease is diagnosed it is more severe than it would be in other populations (*Diabetes among aboriginal (First Nations, Inuit and Metis) people in Canada: The evidence*, 2002). All of this has resulted in the conclusion that diabetes has reached epidemic proportions among our Aboriginal peoples.

What can be done to address this problem? To help answer this question, Grams and colleagues (1996) held focus-group sessions with the Haida Gwaii in the Queen Charlotte Islands, where 17 percent of the adults in one village suffered from diabetes. Through these discussions, it was discovered that the Haida found diabetes to be a very upsetting condition. They feared death and suffered grief from the loss of the things they loved to do and the things they loved to eat. They had a strong desire to regain personal control. The researchers concluded that attempts to help the Haida manage diabetes must not be dictatorial or prescriptive in nature. Rather, they must respect the way the Haida's feelings about the disease are manifest and work to give them a sense of control over their symptoms and valued aspects of their lives that suffer because of diabetes.

Type I diabetes often occurs in childhood. When it does, parents become very involved in disease management. Because of this, the parents' fears are just as relevant as those of the child. These include long-term complications, early death, and severe insulin reactions (Drozda et al., 1997). For example, parents of children who have had a diabetes-related seizure or loss of consciousness are significantly more afraid of hypoglycemia than are parents of diabetic children who have not suffered in this way (Marrero, Guare, Vandagriff, & Finebert, 1997). Parents must also find ways to help their children cope with daily routines that are usually much more structured than those of other children. These structures, and the symptoms of diabetes, can make diabetic children feel different from their healthy peers (Drozda et al., 1997).

Depression and Diabetes   Depression and discouragement are frequent psychological consequences of diabetes. Depression is twice as prevalent among diabetics as among non-diabetics, and it is estimated to affect 10 to 14 percent of people with diabetes (Anderson, Freedland, Clouse, & Lustman, 2001) Diabetics often have trouble talking to others about hypoglycemia and the emotions associated with it. As a result, they may feel isolated or unsupported. Moreover, as we have already mentioned, they may have a difficult time accepting help when it comes during a hypoglycemic episode. It is not surprising, then, that depression is significantly related to a diabetic's quality of life (Kohen, Burgess, Catalán, & Lant, 1998).

To complicate matters, depression and blood sugar are linked bidirectionally. Low blood sugar worsens depression and, in turn, depression reduces the likelihood that people with diabetes will monitor their blood glucose levels regularly. Not surprisingly, depression is also worse for people who suffer diabetes-related complications such as cardiovascular problems, and it also increases the risk for such complications (Lustman et al., 1998; Lloyd, Mathews, Wing, & Orchard, 1992). For these reasons, it is very important to treat depression to break the cycle of depression and worsening symptomology.

Helping People Cope with Diabetes

There are at least two major goals of programs designed to help diabetics. The first is to ensure cooperation with the disease-management regimen. The second is to treat psychological distress. As you can probably tell, these two goals are closely related. We have already seen that psychological distress decreases cooperation with the disease-management regimen. Also, poor management results in worse symptoms and complications, which in turn bring on more distress.

One way to break this cycle is cognitive behaviour therapy (CBT). It is important to explore this option, since antidepressant medication can have unwanted side effects for diabetics. Fortunately, research indicates that CBT can be just as effective as medication (Jacobson & Weinger, 1998). Lustman and colleagues randomly assigned diabetic patients to either a CBT group or a control condition. They discovered that 85 percent of the CBT group showed relief from depression compared to only 27 percent of the control patients. It was also encouraging to note that at follow-up, 70 percent were still not depressed, compared to 34 percent of the controls.

Educational and support groups are also provided for people with diabetes. These are usually offered as part of a hospital education program that patients attend on a regular basis to learn more about the disease and its management, as well as to have their blood glucose and other indicators measured. At these sessions, patients can do much more than learn about nutrition and exercise. They also meet other patients, many of whom are coping well with their diabetes. This provides them with important information regarding efficacy; namely, that diabetes can be controlled. They also get "inside information" on disease control and emotional coping that can only come from other patients.

Family and friends of people with diabetes can help by being aware of the emotional side of the disease. The fears regarding long-term consequences are real. And when someone is experiencing hypoglycemia, it is important to remember that mood changes and disorientation might make him or her appear unreceptive to help. This does not mean that help shouldn't be offered.

DISEASES OF THE CARDIOVASCULAR SYSTEM

The most recent figures available indicate that almost 79 000 Canadians died in one year (1999) from cardiovascular disease. In that year, 35 percent of all male deaths and 37 percent of all female deaths in Canada were attributed to cardiovascular disease. As far back as 1994, cardiovascular disease was costing the Canadian economy over $18 billion per year (*Heart disease information: Incidence of cardiovascular disease*, 2003).

When health psychologists work with and study people with heart and cardiovascular disease, they typically focus on three types of conditions. There are people who have suffered a heart attack, or myocardial infarction (MI), as it is known medically. Of particular interest are people who have had their *first* MI. The medical and psychological challenge for these people is to reduce the likelihood that they will have a second MI, which far fewer people survive. A second group consists of people who have had a **coronary artery bypass graft (CABG)**. This is commonly called bypass surgery, a procedure in which healthy arteries from other parts of the body, often the legs, are grafted into the coronary artery system to, as the term implies, bypass blocked arteries. The third group consists of people who have had **angioplasty**. In this procedure, a bubble-like device is inserted into the artery at the point of the blockage, thus expanding the artery and allowing for better blood flow. In a similar procedure, a cylindrical piece of metal called a stent is inserted to support the walls of the vessel. Other procedures, such as excimer laser coronary angioplasty, make use of laser technology (Karaca, Ilkay, Akbulut, & Yavuzkir, 2003; Topaz et al., 2003). Bypass surgery and angioplasty are used to treat a condition called **myocardial ischemia**, in which there is a lack of blood flow to the heart muscle.

Psychological Distress in Cardiovascular Disease

Patients with cardiovascular disease often suffer accompanying psychological distress. Not only does this affect their quality of life, it puts them at greater risk for further morbidity (more disease or complications) and mortality. Lorne's reaction to being hospitalized in CCU, which we describe in Case 11-2, is a common one. When reality sets in and he comes to accept that he really has had a heart attack, Lorne's protests will subside (Krantz & Deckel, 1983).

One common form of psychological distress accompanying cardiovascular disease is anxiety. Trait anxiety results in poorer quality of life for cardiac patients (Engebretson et al., 1999). A heart attack can be a frightening experience, so it is not surprising to find that some patients live in fear of having another one. As a result, these patients become crippled by their cardiac history. This means that they curtail their activity levels far more than their disease status requires. This phenomenon, called **cardiac invalidism** (Riegel, Dracup, & Glaser, 1998), creates two major problems for the patient. First, the patient stops engaging in some of the things that defined his or her quality of life, such as tennis, golf, or sexual activity. Second, the patient lapses into a sedentary lifestyle that is not conducive to good cardiovascular health.

Anxiety is particularly strong for people who experience cardiac arrest, in which their heart actually stops beating and they must be resuscitated. In the first few weeks after cardiac arrest, phobic anxiety and panic symptoms are not uncommon (Ladwig, 1997). An additional problem with these reactions is that panic symptoms often mimic heart prob-

CASE 11-2	**Short-Term Reactions to First Myocardial Infarction**

One day when Lorne was mowing his lawn, he felt a strong pain in his chest that radiated to his shoulder and down his left arm. He began to sweat profusely and feel nauseated, and, had he not knelt down on the grass, he would surely have fainted. It was in this position that his wife found him as she came out to do some gardening. She quickly got him to the car and to the hospital, where he was diagnosed as having had a heart attack.

When Lorne was settled in the cardiac care unit (CCU) of the hospital, he began to feel better. It struck him as ridiculous that he had actually had a heart attack and he told the nurses so. Surely they had made a mistake. He told them that he should not be made to stay in the hospital, especially hooked up to a heart monitor. He was a busy man. He had a big meeting the next day and there were things he had to prepare. In fact, Lorne became a bit obnoxious as he lay in the hospital bed. The nursing staff did their best to calm him and tell him that he really needed to be right where he was.

lems or heart attack. This, in turn, fuels the sense of panic, and a vicious cycle is started that compromises the person's cardiac health. Fortunately, this anxiety stabilizes for most patients in time, though many experience intrusive thoughts about the event and try to avoid anything that might remind them of their resuscitation (Ladwig et al., 1999).

Perhaps the most common form of psychological distress associated with cardiovascular and heart disease is depression. In fact, the incidence of major depression is three times greater for coronary artery disease patients than it is for the general population (Rozanski, Blumenthal, & Kaplan, 1999). In addition, depression is a risk factor for the development of cardiovascular disease (Ward, Tueth, & Sheps, 2003). This is especially true for clinical depression, rather than depressive mood, which is more transient in nature (Rugulies, 2002).

Researchers have also investigated the long-term effects of depression on the outcomes of cardiovascular patients. Five-year follow-up studies have shown that people with major depression are more likely to be hospitalized for cardiac problems than are patients with minor depression (Sullivan, LaCroix, Spertus, Hecht, & Russo, 2003). As well, depression is a better predictor of mortality in the five years post-diagnosis than other forms of psychological distress, such as anxiety or anger (Frasure-Smith & Lesperance, 2003).

There is evidence to suggest that this depression might be more problematic for women, especially those who are older. It has been estimated that women are twice as likely to suffer post-MI depression than men are (Frasure-Smith et al., 1993). One study found that 23 percent of female cardiac patients, including those with problems other than heart attack, were depressed. Yet, women are not generally encouraged as emphatically to attend rehabilitation programs that would help with this depression (Lavie, Milani, Cassidy, & Gilliland, 1999).

Depression is particularly problematic for older cardiac patients. Patients over the age of 65 who are depressed are more than twice as likely to report difficulties with activities of daily living (ADL) (Steffens et al., 1999). Also, the consequences of depression appear to be somewhat more severe for women. In a study that monitored women for one year after their heart attack, 8.3 percent of depressed women died of cardiac causes compared to 2.4 percent of non-depressed women (Frasure-Smith et al., 1999).

The physiological mechanisms by which depression increases risk of mortality for cardiac patients are not entirely clear (Grippo & Johnson, 2002). However, it is known that depressed coronary heart disease patients have higher heart rates than do non-depressed patients (Carney et al., 1999). Also, regarding autonomic control, depressed patients do not adjust their heart rate well in response to blood pressure changes (Watkins & Grossman, 1999). Given the finding that people with depression are at greater risk for heart attack, it appears that there is a bidirectional relationship between depression and cardiovascular disease. It becomes imperative, therefore, to treat the depression and break this dangerous cycle.

Helping People Cope with Cardiovascular Disease

In addition to the support of family and friends, cardiac patients can benefit from rehabilitation programs and, where appropriate, psychotherapy. Modern rehabilitation programs for people recovering from heart attack, bypass surgery, or angioplasty are holistic in nature. That is to say, they address all aspects of the participant's life, from diet to exercise to psychological well-being. Rehabilitation programs for people who have had one myocardial infarction have been shown to reduce mortality by 20 to 25 percent and improve psychological status in terms of reduced negative affect and state anxiety (Engebretson et al., 1999).

Rehabilitation programs may differ somewhat from location to location, but most share certain elements in common. Participants have their physical condition monitored. They are provided with education regarding their medication and the reduction of risk factors. They are also put on programs intended to reduce those risk factors, focusing on diet, exercise, and stress reduction. One such program, which featured three 75-minute sessions a week over 12 weeks, reduced levels of anxiety, depression, and confusion while increasing the participants' sense of vigour. This was particularly true for participants with high trait anxiety, which is a risk factor for further morbidity and poor quality of life (Engebretson et al., 1999). Another program tailored specifically for women yielded lower depression, anxiety, and hostility and increased exercise capacity and quality of life for the participants (Lavie, Milani, Cassidy, & Gilliland, 1999).

Another important psychological factor to address in therapy with cardiac patients is anger. Anger is a risk factor for coronary heart disease (CHD), especially when expressed as hostility. Moreover, one episode of intensely expressed anger can trigger a fatal heart attack for people with severe CHD. Therapy intended to reduce anger features a number of components. Participants are taught to monitor their emotions so they can identify times when anger is a problem (Mayne & Ambrose, 1999). They are also taught relaxation skills. In terms of their thinking, participants go through what is called **cognitive reappraisal and restructuring**. In this, they learn to think differently about the things

<table>
<tr><td>Focus on
Canadian
Research 11-1</td><td>**Is Feeling Down Bad for the Heart?**</td></tr>
</table>

Since the mid-1990s, Nancy Frasure-Smith and her colleagues at McGill University have been leaders in the investigation of the relationship between cardiovascular disease and depression. One of their recent studies (Frasure-Smith & Lesperance, 2003) followed patients for five years after they had a myocardial infarction. Frasure-Smith and her team administered a collection of self-report measures to assess such things as depression, anxiety, anger, and perceived social support soon after the participants had their heart attack. The researchers then kept track of mortality statistics over the five-year period. The participants were 896 patients taken from 10 hospitals in the Montreal area. The purpose of the study was to determine the extent to which each of those psychological states helped predict mortality after heart attack.

They found that 155 people died during the five-year period. Of those deaths, 121 were cardiac-related. After taking factors such as sex and age into account, Frasure-Smith et al. then used correlation methods to determine which psychological factors best predicted mortality.

A number of psychological measures correlated significantly with mortality. These included depression and anxiety, as well as a more general measure of psychological distress (the General Health Questionnaire). Neither anger, stress, nor social support was a significant predictor of mortality, however. Of all the measures, depression was the best single predictor of mortality.

that tend to make them angry. For example, they may have been blaming other drivers for traffic jams or may mistakenly assume that people who frustrate them do so intentionally. Participants also spend time on behavioural change, in which they learn to control their voice tone, breathing, etc.

With all the proven benefits, you might think that cardiac rehabilitation programs are well attended, but they are not. In the United States, only 15 to 30 percent of MI, CABG, and angioplasty patients complete a rehabilitation program, and dropout rates are quite high (King & Teo, 1998). Researchers at the University of Alberta have suggested that psychological factors affect these attendance rates. Such factors as self-efficacy, motivation, and social support may all be predictive of program completion (King & Teo, 1998). Again, this suggestion is consistent with the health belief model and theory of reasoned action discussed in chapter 1. These theories predict that attendance would be higher for people who thought the program would work and who knew others who had either attended successfully or who encouraged them to do so.

For some patients, rehabilitation programs are not enough to help them overcome depression and medications are prescribed. For example, sertraline has shown promise for safe use as an anti-depressant soon after acute MI (Carney & Jaffe, 2002).

HIV AND AIDS

Acquired immune deficiency syndrome (AIDS) was first reported in Canada in 1982. By 2002, over 18 300 cases had been reported in the country (Health Canada, 2002). The number of people who die from AIDS continues to drop each year. However, the number of people who are HIV positive continues to climb. In 1996, there were an estimated 40 000 people in Canada living with HIV **(human immunodeficiency virus)**. By 1999, that number had jumped to 50 000 (*AIDS*, 2003).

There are some groups that are at greater risk than others for contracting AIDS. These include men who have sex with men (MSM), injection drug users (IDU), those who receive blood and blood products, and our Aboriginal population (see Box 11-2.).

The proportion of newly diagnosed cases of AIDS has dropped significantly among men who have sex with men; from 75 percent between 1985 and 1994 to 37 percent from 1997 to 1999. However, among injection drug users, the rate has increased from 9 percent to 30 percent (*AIDS: The AIDS/ HIV Files*, 2002).

The symptoms of **AIDS** include persistent fever; swelling of the lymph glands on the neck and under the arms; frequent fatigue; diarrhea; sweating during sleep; and yeast infections in the vagina, ears, and tongue. Since these symptoms aren't unique to HIV, a person with concerns should see his or her physician.

| BOX 11-2 | AIDS and Canada's Aboriginal Population |

In 1993, two percent of all AIDS cases were known to be Aboriginal persons. By 1999, that proportion had grown to ten percent (*HIV/AIDS among Aboriginal persons in Canada: A continuing concern*, 2003). The proportion dropped during 2000 and 2001, but it then climbed in 2002 to reach over 14 percent.

AIDS develops at an earlier age within Canada's Aboriginal population. Twenty-five percent of the Aboriginal people living with AIDS (PLWA) population is under the age of 30, compared to 17 percent for non-Aboriginal PLWA.

Twenty-three percent of Aboriginal (PLWA) are female, compared to just eight percent of the non-Aboriginal PLWA population. Females represented almost half of HIV diagnoses between 1998 and 2002, compared to 20 percent in the non-Aboriginal population. AIDS and HIV, therefore, are growing problems for Aboriginal peoples. Among these growing numbers, young people and women are disproportionately represented (*HIV/AIDS among Aboriginal persons in Canada: A continuing concern*, 2003).

Human immunodeficiency virus gradually breaks down the body's immune system, making it susceptible to a host of other infections, including neoplasms such as non-Hodgkins' lymphoma and Kaposi's sarcoma. Prolonged HIV infection results in AIDS. Human immunodeficiency virus can be transmitted through unprotected vaginal or anal sex, the sharing of needles, or during pregnancy or childbirth, when a mother can transmit HIV to her child.

Psychological Distress and HIV/AIDS

HIV and AIDS are different from most other chronic and serious illnesses in a number of ways. First, though modern medicine has made encouraging strides in prolonging the lives of persons living with HIV and AIDS, there is still no cure for AIDS, and the person living with it knows it will eventually be fatal. In addition to a set of symptoms that can be very difficult to endure, there is the fact that people living with AIDS often suffer from stigmatization (Joachim & Acorn, 2000). Their self-esteem and well-being suffer as they internalize this stigma (Lee, Kochman, & Sikkema, 2002). Unlike many other serious illnesses, AIDS has the problem of contagion and the related problem of myths about contagion. Compared to sufferers of other serious illnesses, AIDS patients tend to be younger. Also, AIDS patients may feel personal responsibility or guilt regarding their illness. Finally, many people with AIDS have lost people from their social network to the very disease they are trying to cope with. For all these reasons, people with HIV and AIDS must deal with a host of unique psychological challenges (Kelly, 1998). Generally, psychological distress is worsened if there is a lack of acceptance by family members, and isolation is exacerbated by not attending a support group or knowing other people with HIV (Lee et al., 2002; Schmitz & Crystal, 2000)

Anxiety is a virtually universal problem for persons living with AIDS (Phillips & Morrow, 1998). This anxiety stems from uncertainty about the future, the losses that are experienced, the social stigma, the prejudice that a PLWA's offspring endure, and the disease process itself (Phillips & Morrow, 1998). An HIV-positive diagnosis can be traumatic enough to elicit symptoms of post-traumatic stress disorder (PTSD), which is often related to major depression. One study discovered that 30 percent of HIV-positive gay and bisexual men showed symptoms of PTSD, and one-third of those showing such symptoms had onset that came six months or more after their HIV-positive diagnosis (Kelly et al., 1998). PTSD symptoms were more prevalent for men who had a history of PTSD prior to their HIV diagnosis.

Helping People Cope with HIV and AIDS

Providing psychotherapeutic interventions for people with HIV and AIDS can be challenging, not only for the reasons that make the illnesses themselves difficult to cope with, but because psychotropic medication may actually make other symptoms worse. For example, some antidepressants, such as selective serotonin reuptake inhibitors (SSRIs) can worsen sleep disturbances, weight loss, sexual dysfunction, and fatigue. Other medication may have fewer of these effects but still cause headache or dizziness and interact poorly with other medication (Elliott et al., 1999). It has also been suggested that the beneficial effects of medication may be only short-term (Evans et al., 1999).

When providing psychotherapy for people who are HIV-positive or who have AIDS, a number of clinical issues must be considered (Kelly, 1998). Unlike other diseases, it can be difficult for HIV/AIDS patients to disclose their disease status to others. Telling someone you have a blocked artery just isn't the same as telling that person you are HIV-positive. To compound things, persons living with AIDS have higher rates of bereavement and may have been caregivers themselves, especially if they are gay men or intravenous drug users (IDU). For these reasons, persons living with AIDS must often reestablish their social support systems. They must also make and maintain major changes in terms of risk-related behaviour and adhere to medical regimens that can be complex and extensive.

Psychotherapy issues for persons living with AIDS have changed somewhat over the past few years due to advances in medicine that prolong life expectancies (Fox & Gourlay, 2000; Gushue & Brazaitis, 2003). **Highly active antiretroviral treatment (HAART)** (Gray, Chretien, Vallat-Decouvelaere, & Scaravilli, 2003) and **protease inhibitor** drug combinations are significantly prolonging the lives of persons living with AIDS. People living with HIV now live an average of 10 years before developing AIDS (*AIDS*, 2003). The psychotherapeutic issues are changing accordingly. Not surprisingly, psychological status is often related to disease-related milestones such as the first notification of seropositive status, first symptoms, and first sign of AIDS-defining illness (Kelly, 1998). Therapy for people dealing with these and other factors is often conducted in groups. The therapist must take into account the makeup of the group, given that AIDS affects many different types of people. For example, a group consisting exclusively of gay men is quite different from one in which there are gay men, intravenous drug users, and heterosexual women.

Groups may adopt a cognitive focus in which they help participants stop being plagued by intrusive thoughts, or when they address irrational beliefs that lead to depression and anxiety. Group therapy has been proven effective (Lee, 1999). In addition, the groups can take on a behavioural focus, looking at ways to cope with problems at home and at work, strategies for regaining social support, and ways to relax and manage stress. In general, it has been found that psychological interventions for persons living with AIDS are effective in improving psychological status, but do not affect medical status (Lamping et al., 1993).

Those providing care to people living with AIDS are in need of considerable support. When the person living with AIDS is from the gay community, it is not uncommon for their caregivers to be from that same community. They may well have seen many of their friends and loved ones die. They may fear HIV infection themselves or know that they are, in fact, seropositive.

Finally, we must hearken back to chapter 7, on health promotion, to remind ourselves that *prevention* is a very important issue when it comes to HIV and AIDS. All the psychological principles discussed in chapter 7 apply well here. We cannot rely too heavily on fear appeals. Rather we must convince people of the efficacy of safe sex and careful needle use while at the same time making salient the potential threat of AIDS.

OTHER CHRONIC CONDITIONS

Cancer, cardiovascular disease, diabetes, and AIDS are four of the most commonly studied chronic conditions in health psychology. There are, of course, other chronic conditions that are equally pressing for the patients experiencing them. Included in this list would be Parkinson's disease and arthritis. More generally, there are many people who live with physical and mental disabilities. Each of these conditions carries its own set of coping challenges.

For example, major depression occurs in 40 to 50 percent of all people with Parkinson's disease (Gotham, Brown, & Marsden, 1986, cited in Evans, 1999). This causes further problems in terms of memory, language, and motor performance. Not surprisingly, depression can also be a problem for people coping with the chronic pain of arthritis (Mangelli, Gribbin, Buchi, Allard, & Sensky, 2002), a disease that affects about one percent of the population and between five and seven percent of those over the age of 65. One study found that 36 percent of patients with arthritis (average age = 57 years) had scores indicative of clinical depression, which is above the norm for the general population (Walsh, Blanchard, Kremer, & Blanchard, 1999). As is the case with depression and most chronic conditions, the depression and disease symptoms tend to worsen together. Also, depression is related to feelings of isolation and self-blame and is worse for people who feel a lack of control over their illness (Murphy, Dickens, Creed, & Bernstein, 1999).

Additionally, there are many people who cope with permanent physical disabilities that may impair their movement or sensory capacities. One of the main obstacles for people with disabilities is presented by the attitudes of people without disabilities. These attitudes, which may range from pity to understanding to impatience, are often formed in childhood and might be based on stereotypes rather than first-hand experience (Bracegirdle, 1995; Harper, 1999).

The quality of life of people living with disabilities depends on their belief that they are engaged in meaningful activities. Another important factor is their sense of social integration, which is, of course, related to the extent to which they are accepted by others (Viemeroe & Krause, 1998). When trying to understand the psychological factors associated with coping with a disability, it is important to consider when the person became disabled. People who have recently become disabled may still be struggling with changes in their sense of self and a reevaluation of their identity (Iwai, 1996; Mpofu & Houston, 1998).

Psychotherapy for people with physical disabilities has yielded encouraging results, although many psychotherapists do not see clients from this population nor do they specialize in the unique needs of people with physical disabilities (Hurley, Tomasulo, & Pfadt, 1998). These unique needs include such things as an accurate assessment of the person's physical capabilities and an understanding of the person's beliefs regarding his or her disability. Also, as is the case with many chronic conditions, there are the caregivers to consider, who may be very burdened by their responsibilities (Dumont, St. Onge, Fougeyrollas, & Renaud, 1998).

QUALITY OF LIFE

In this chapter on chronic and serious illness, we have made repeated reference to a patient's "quality of life." Just what does this mean? When we refer to **quality of life** in the context of serious and chronic illness, we are talking about the extent to which symptoms and treatment affect a person's physical, social, cognitive, and emotional functioning. Further, we are interested in how the person *prioritizes* and *values* these functions, so that we can develop a more complete understanding of the impact the condition and treatment are having on the person's life.

It may seem obvious that quality of life would be a primary concern in the treatment of people with serious and/or chronic illness. However, this has not always been the case. This is because treatments that might alleviate some of the medical symptoms of the disease can have very negative effects on other aspects of a patient's life. If the treatment plan is focused solely on biological factors, such as tumour size, it is easy to lose sight of the price the patient is paying for that treatment in a more holistic sense. This is especially true for cancer patients, remembering that they can often be subjected to treatments producing side effects that are worse than the symptoms of the disease.

Two issues become important when quality of life is made a priority as a treatment outcome. First, those providing treatment must be sensitive to the *tradeoff* between duration of life and quality of life. Second, the patient must be an integral member of the decision-making team, because quality of life is primarily a *subjective* phenomenon (Gathchel & Oordt, 2003).

The Tradeoff between Duration and Quality of Life

Regarding serious illness, treatment efficacy is often defined by the extent to which the treatment prolongs the life of the patient. For example, a person with throat cancer may have surgery that will prolong his or her life by five years. Without the surgery, he or she might live one year. Thus, the treatment is deemed reasonably efficacious because it has the potential to prolong the person's life by four years. Of course, after the surgery, which will very possibly involve the removal of his or her larynx, a prosthetic device will be needed in order to talk. The patient's voice will not resemble his or her own and will sound somewhat mechanical. Also, there will be high levels of postoperative pain. In this case, the tradeoff is clear—five years with an artificial voice and pain versus one year with his or her own voice and much less pain. The fact that the two options are clear does not make the decision an easy one, however.

The point of the example, of course, is that this decision must be based primarily on quality of life. If the person is an opera singer who cannot stand the thought of having a mechanized voice, then his or her quality of life would be compromised so severely by the surgery that it ceases to be a viable option. On the other hand, if the patient has a granddaughter who is getting married in 18 months and the patient dearly wants to be at the wedding, surgery is a good option because his or her quality of life is defined in terms of the wedding rather than his or her voice.

Figure 11-1 presents a graphic representation of what practitioners and patients must consider (Albertsen, 1998). In Figure 11-1a, the decision is quite straightforward. The therapeutic gain from the treatment is realized immediately from the time of treatment, as indi-

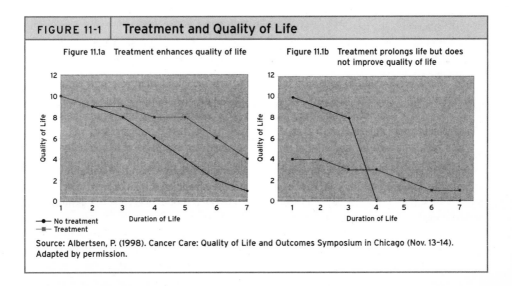

FIGURE 11-1 | **Treatment and Quality of Life**

Figure 11.1a Treatment enhances quality of life

Figure 11.1b Treatment prolongs life but does not improve quality of life

(y-axis: Quality of Life; x-axis: Duration of Life)

—●— No treatment
—■— Treatment

Source: Albertsen, P. (1998). Cancer Care: Quality of Life and Outcomes Symposium in Chicago (Nov. 13-14). Adapted by permission.

cated by the distance between the treatment and no treatment lines at the start of the graph. Also, this gain is maintained for seven years, and the duration of life is equivalent with or without treatment. This would be analogous to the types of treatment gains typically found in coronary bypass surgery or angioplasty for older patients. The decision in figure 11-1b is more difficult. Without treatment, the patient could live a high quality life for approximately three years. With treatment, she would live at least twice as long but at a much lower quality of life. It is not until those lines cross, at about 3.5 years, that any therapeutic gain is realized by the treatment. This graph is representative of the kinds of decisions some cancer patients must make.

Quality of Life As a Subjective Phenomenon

Quality of life must be measured **phenomenologically**, that is, by asking the person directly to report on the phenomenon. In this respect, quality of life is like freedom. If someone says she is free, then she has freedom, regardless of whether she lives in an oppressive regime or on a deserted island. To illustrate this, consider the following conversation between a physician and her patient:

Patient: If I have this operation, will I be able to play competitive tennis again?

Physician: No. It will give you at least five more years of life, but your mobility will be restricted so that tennis would be very difficult.

Patient: Then I don't want the operation.

Physician: Because of tennis?

Patient: Yes.

Physician: But it's only a game!

For the physician, the notion that someone would rather not live than live without tennis is unthinkable, as it may be for you. However, what the physician thinks or what you and I think is irrelevant, because this is a quality of life decision, which is by definition subjective.

Most of the quality of life questionnaires in use today acknowledge the subjectivity of the phenomenon when they ask respondents to indicate not only if they are able to perform a given function, but also how *important* the function is to the person. A good example is the Functional Assessment of Cancer Therapy (FACT) scales (Cella et al., 1993). After completing each subscale that assesses such things as emotional well-being, the respondent is asked how important emotional well-being is to him or her. Research measuring the effects of psychotherapy and exercise use scales like the FACT to assess impact (Courneya et al., 2003).

There are others who have argued that the use of these scales, even when they do ask questions about importance, do not account for the subjectivity of quality of life (Clark, 1998). This is because the person designing the scale chooses the aspects to be included and also the language with which these aspects are described. This is like putting words in the patient's mouth. To remedy this, some researchers are conducting focus groups with cancer patients to learn how these patients talk about their disease (e.g., Clark, 1998). When this is done, patients bring up things that are not featured in most scales, which tend to be quite biomedical in their focus. For example, 30 to 40 percent of a group of prostate cancer patients said they regretted their treatment choice (Clark, 1998), which is something that isn't explored in quality-of-life questionnaires as a rule. Another consideration when measuring quality of life is whether the assessment is **multidimensional** or **global**. The scales we have been discussing have been multidimensional in that they assess different aspects of quality of life, such as physical, emotional, and social functioning. A global approach would require just one question, for example, "How would you rate your quality of life today?" (Gough, Furnval, Schilder, & Grove, 1983). Generally, multidimensional approaches are favoured because they allow for an assessment of how an illness is affecting specific areas of a person's life.

DEATH AND DYING

Obviously, one of the most traumatic aspects of serious illnesses is that people die from them. For this reason, any attempt to help people cope with chronic and serious illnesses must address the prospect of premature death; in some cases, this prospect is very real.

Patients' Reactions to Death

Our thinking about death and the process of dying has been influenced greatly by the foundational work of psychiatrist Elizabeth Kübler-Ross (Kübler-Ross, 1969). Through her work, we moved from the belief that dying people did not want to know or talk about their death to the realization that they *did* want to talk about their impending death. Another important contribution was her theory identifying a series of reactions a person might experience when facing his or her own death. When her theory was first published, it was presented as a stage theory, which is to say that the reactions were postulated to occur in a particular sequence (Kübler-Ross, 1969). Now, it is believed that the reactions she identified may be common to many patients but that not all patients experience all reactions, nor do they in a particular order.

The first reaction identified by Kübler-Ross is **denial**. Denial is a defence mechanism we call upon when we are confronted with novel and severe trauma. The news that one is about to die certainly fits in that category. When people receive this news, they may think the physician is not being serious, or that some mistake has been made. They may make long-range commitments, ignoring the fact that their prognosis indicates they will not be alive to keep them.

Anger is a reaction that often follows denial. The patient might get angry at the medical system for being "incompetent" and for "all its fancy equipment and pills" being unable to prevent the patient from dying. He or she might get mad at the unfairness of it all. The anger may spread to family and friends. The dying person may become angry with them for not being helpful enough or trying to be too helpful, regardless of what they are actually doing. This can be difficult for family and friends to understand. A person may also respond by **bargaining**, trying to do things that will buy more time. Perhaps the person will volunteer for research or make strong commitments in terms of religiosity or spirituality.

We have discussed depression quite extensively in this chapter, so it will come as no surprise to learn that Kübler-Ross identifies it as a common reaction to dying. Depression is common and understandable, but it is still problematic because it often means the person gives up, thus unduly hastening death.

Finally, there is **acceptance**. If and when a person reaches this point, he or she is likely to be at peace. Perhaps death is viewed as a relief. In fact, the patient might be considerably more peaceful than the family members and friends who are preparing for bereavement. Acceptance is emotionally very different from depression. Acceptance tends to come later than depression in the dying process and is not accompanied by a sense of despondency.

TABLE 11-3	Reactions to impending death
Reaction	**Description**
Denial	Refusing to acknowledge the potential seriousness of a diagnosis or condition, perhaps to the point of making long-range plans in spite of a poor prognosis.
Anger	Often in response to feelings of unfairness, anger can be directed at health care professionals, family, or others.
Bargaining	"Buying more time" by taking on altruistic projects or striving to make self-improvements.
Depression	Can be associated with giving up, or feelings of helplessness and hopelessness.
Acceptance	Being at peace with one's situation and possibly viewing death as a relief.

Source: Kübler-Ross, (1969). On death and dying. New York: MacMillian.

Group therapy for people with serious illnesses must confront participants' feelings regarding death. If not, some of these people may die without the very important sense of reassurance that allows them to die peacefully (or, as people who work in palliative care might say, successfully). When patients do talk about death, a number of issues emerge (Block & Billings, 1995). They are often concerned about physical and psychological suffering and fear losing their decision-making capacity at a time when they feel they must make important decisions. Seriously ill patients are also concerned about the possible suffering of their friends and family. These patients may also worry about the relationship they have with their primary-care physician and other medical staff. In addition, existential and spiritual issues can be very important.

Given these issues and concerns, what are the most important assurances therapists can give to seriously ill group members? Certainly, global assurances like "Everything will be just fine" won't be very helpful. Molyn Leszcz and Pamela Goodwin, from the University of Toronto and Mount Sinai Hospital, respectively, have identified some key assurances that can be offered (Leszcz & Goodwin, 1998). These include assurance that the person will not die lonely or alone, that the person's wishes will be respected, and that every effort will be made to minimize physical suffering. Of course, for wishes to be respected they must be clearly communicated, which can only be done if the group doesn't collude to avoid discussions about death, fearing that discussing death will somehow bring it on (Leszcz & Goodwin, 1998).

Bereavement and Grief

It is also important to consider the family, friends, and loved ones who are left to cope with the patient's death. They are coping with **bereavement**, which is the loss of someone close to them. **Grief** is a common psychological response to bereavement. The bereaved are clearly an at-risk population (Walsh-Burke, 2000). They suffer higher death rates and suicide rates than the rest of the population. They have a higher incidence of depression and substance abuse, and they have more medical problems. For these reasons, many grieving people either seek grief counselling or are sent for it. If they seek it themselves, the success of the intervention is significantly greater (Allumbaugh & Hoyt, 1999).

There are a number of possible approaches that can be taken in grief therapy (Allumbaugh & Hoyt, 1999). The therapist may pick one or a combination of them, depending on the needs of the participants and the preferences of the therapist. For example, there is the psychodynamic approach, in which the therapist becomes a temporary substitute for the deceased as the bereaved person addresses unfinished issues related to mourning. There is the client-centred approach, in which the therapist offers nurturance and empathic understanding, paraphrasing the feelings of the person rather than prescribing solutions to him or her. With the cognitive approach, the therapist tries to expose dysfunctional or irrational beliefs. For example, the bereaved person might think that his life is effectively over now that his wife has died. By thinking this way, he is ignoring the support offered by his friends and family and is discounting all the things he can still do in his life. Another approach is behavioural, in which the therapist and bereaved person focus on problem solving, using goal setting and skill learning to help the person cope with his or her loss. Research indicates that grief counselling does help people cope with loss, although, as we mentioned, it is more effective when the clients choose to go rather than when they are sent.

KEY TERMS

acceptance (p. 322)

acquired immune deficiency syndrome (AIDS) (p. 315)

active coping (p. 299)

acute illness (p. 295)

adjuvant therapy (p. 302)

anger (p. 321)

angioplasty (p. 311)

anticipatory nausea (p. 302)

antiemetic medication (p. 302)

bargaining (p. 321)

benefit finding (p. 306)

bereavement (p. 322)

cardiac invalidism (p. 311)

chemotherapy (p. 362)

chronic condition (p. 294)

cognitive reappraisal and restructuring (p. 313)

coronary artery bypass graft (CABG) (p. 311)

denial (p. 321)

disfigurement (p. 301)

emotion-focused coping (p. 298)

family-oriented care (p. 304)

gestational diabetes (p. 308)

global measures of quality of life (p. 321)

grief (p. 323)

help-intended communication (p. 304)

highly active antiretroviral treatment (HAART) (p. 317)

human immunodeficiency virus (HIV) (p. 315)

hypoglycemia (p. 308)

insulin-dependent diabetes (Type I) (p. 308)

intrusive memories (p. 298)

metastasized (p. 296)

multidimensional measures of quality of life (p. 321)

myocardial ischemia (p. 311)

navigator (p. 305)

non-insulin dependent diabetes (Type II) (p. 308)

oncology (p. 296)

passive coping (p. 299)

phenomenological (p. 320)

posttraumatic growth (p. 306)

problem-focused coping (p. 298)

protease inhibitor (p. 317)

quality of life (p. 318)

radiation therapy (p. 301)

radical surgery (p. 301)

sites of cancer (p. 296)

social comparison (p. 305)

social support (p. 304)

chapter twelve

Health and the Internet

CHAPTER OUTLINE

What Is the Internet?
   Search Engines

Patterns of Internet Use

Examples of Health-Related Resources Available on the Internet
   Medical Articles and Reports
   Services
   Health Initiatives and Health Promotion
   Surveys
   Support

Assessing the Quality of Health Information on the Internet
   Usability
   Accessibility

How People Process Information from the Internet

Implications of Internet Use for Individual and Public Health

Patient-Physician Relationships

Practitioners' Use of the Internet

Hospital Web Sites

Equality of Access

The Challenges of Using the Internet Effectively

Health-Related Uses of the Internet in the Future

KEY QUESTIONS

1. What is the Internet?
2. What sorts of health-related information are available on the Internet?
3. How do people use the Internet to find health-related information?
4. What impact is the Internet having on the health of individuals and populations?

When George's doctor told him he had Type II diabetes, a lot of things started to make sense. This was why he had been thirsty all the time, why he had been making so many trips to the bathroom, and why he was feeling tired. Still, after George left his doctor's office, many questions started to surface for him. Would he need to monitor his blood sugar? Could he manage the new diet? Would diabetes shorten his life?

When George told his daughter about his diagnosis, she suggested that he go on the Internet to learn more about diabetes. George had certainly heard of the Internet, but he was a self-proclaimed "techno-peasant" who had only used a computer once to input a golf score at a tournament. He didn't even own a computer.

All the same, he wanted to learn more about his condition, so he went to the local library and was shown how to access the Internet. When he typed the word "diabetes" into the search engine, he was astounded by the number of sites that came up. There were literally millions of them. He decided to click on the first one listed, which happened to be the site of the American Diabetes Association. George learned many things as he worked his way through this site. The first thing he learned was that his symptoms were very typical of the disease. He also learned that his doctor had been right all these years about having George lose weight. He decided to make a list of questions for his doctor and to work with him to make a plan that would help him control his diabetes.

George has now joined the ranks of those who use the Internet as a health information provider. As you will see in this chapter, Internet use is becoming increasingly common, and it is having a significant impact on the way people think about their health and consume health services. In 2003, when we typed the word "diabetes" into a search engine called Google, the Internet found 6 350 000 sites in 0.08 seconds! When we typed in "breast cancer" we received 2 590 000 hits; prostate cancer 842 000; cystic fibrosis, 291 000; multiple sclerosis, 645 000. These numbers are going up daily. Try typing some health-related terms into the search field of an engine like Google and see what you get.

In terms of the percentage of the population using the Internet, Canada ranks second in the world. Only Sweden has a higher percentage of Internet users (*How Canadians find health information on the Internet*, 2003). What do these countries have in common? Both are relatively affluent, and both must deal with geographic challenges, either in terms of distance or terrain. These challenges are very relevant to health, given what we know in Canada about disparities in health associated with distances people must travel to access a physician (Ng, 1997).

The Internet is particularly relevant to health in Canada. Geography provides challenges for health care access, computer technology is relatively more available than in many other countries (though disparities still exist within Canada in this regard), and a wealth of information is available on the Internet. Thus, the Internet has the potential to have a positive impact on the health of Canadians.

In this chapter, we make reference to a number of health-related web sites. Where appropriate, we also indicate the date when we last accessed that site; however, web sites and their addresses are subject to change. In fact, a recent study of web site attrition found that, of 184 web sites studied, 59 percent of those that existed in 1999 could not be found using the same web addresses in 2002 (Veronin, 2002).

While it is likely that some of the sites mentioned in this chapter will be active for a long time, it is still possible that some will be eliminated, or perhaps their addresses will change. Even if this is the case, we hope they will stand as good examples of the phenomena we discuss in this chapter.

WHAT IS THE INTERNET?

Almost everyone has heard of the Internet, though not everyone knows exactly what it is. While some might think of it as the world's largest storehouse of information, in fact the Internet doesn't actually store anything. Instead, it provides connections between computers that store information. A University of California, Berkeley site refers to the Internet as "a giant international plumbing system" (*What is the Internet, the World Wide Web, and Netscape?* 2002).

Browsers, such as Netscape and Internet Explore, and search engines, such as Google and Lycos, allow for convenient use of the Internet. They use the connections provided by the Internet to find locations where desired information is stored. These locations are called **URLs** (uniform resource locators). The Internet allows for a very rapid and comprehensive search of information stored on countless computers around the world, provided these computers can connect to the Internet and the custodians of that information want it shared.

Another very useful aspect of the Internet is the way information is presented on screen. In addition to being able to present text, graphics, motion, and sound, an Internet-based site typically contains **links**. These use hypertext to allow the user to click on the link, often a piece of text or graphic, and be taken quickly to another related site, or another portion of the site being explored. For example, an **e-journal** (a journal that is accessible through the Internet) can create a link for every reference cited in the article. If you click on the reference you can be taken directly to that article (or at least its bibliographic information). The site of the American Diabetes Association, for example, includes a home page with numerous links to everything from basic information about diabetes to ways one can donate to fundraising campaigns.

The URL for most web sites begin with the letters "www," which stands for the world wide web. There is more to the Internet than the web, however, and the other components also figure prominently in people's health-related usage of the Internet. One widely used component is e-mail. Messages can be sent to individuals or to groups, and users can belong to groups, via mailing lists, newsgroups, or Listservs, so that they can take part in group conversations or receive messages automatically from an information provider. Messages can also be stored or tracked according to their theme or source. E-mail is convenient and inexpensive, though it is not particularly secure (Grohol, 1999) and, as many of us have come to learn, it can become almost tyrannical in its demand for our attention.

The Internet also allows for the sharing of complex files that might contain large data sets, graphics, or other media. These are often shared via an **FTP**, or file transfer protocol.

Search Engines

We have already introduced the idea of a **search engine**. This is an Internet service that scans the web with remarkable speed and thoroughness. Given the overwhelming amount of information available on the Internet, search engines are essential to effective use. When George typed in "diabetes" he was given a list of over 6 million sites. The first one in the list was the American Diabetes Association. If you have done searches like this, have you ever wondered how it is determined which sites appear in that first-page listing of ten sites? As you can imagine, this is a very important question for people who want their sites to be prominent.

One answer, of course, is relevance. But how does a search engine determine relevance? The search engine looks for key words in the site and matches them with the word or words you have put in the search field. Thus, designers of sites might try to present key words that mirror the kinds of language people use when doing their searches. There is more to it than that, though. In fact, there are companies that offer consultation in "search engine positioning" or "search engine optimization."

PATTERNS OF INTERNET USE

It is virtually impossible to determine just how many people use the Internet. Usage is far too widespread. Also, we must define what we mean by "use." Our best estimates, taken from research in Canada, Britain, the United States, and Australia, are that between 40 and 60 percent of people use the Internet at least once per week (Emmanouilides & Hammond, 2000; *GVU's WWW user surveys: Frequency of use*, 1997; StatsCan, 2002). In Canada, 49 percent of all households have at least one person who regularly uses the Internet at home, and over 70 percent of those households went online at least once a day in 2001 (StatsCan, 2002). Surveys have also been conducted looking specifically at health-related Internet use in Canada (see Focus on Canadian Research 12-1).

EXAMPLES OF HEALTH-RELATED RESOURCES AVAILABLE ON THE INTERNET

Not only is there a great deal of health information on the Internet, it covers a wide range of topics. What follows is a description of some of the more commonly accessed resources.

Focus on Canadian Research 12-1	Canadians' Use of the Internet for Health-Related Information

Between 1997 and 2000, Statistics Canada conduced a large survey called the Household Internet Use Survey (HUIS). More than 34 000 people over the age of 15 living in private households were surveyed about such things as their use of the Internet to acquire health-related information. Some of the results of this and other Statistics Canada surveys are reported in a publication entitled *Canadian Social Trends* (Stevenson, 2002).

The survey revealed that nearly 6 million people in Canada sought health-related information on the Internet in the year 2000, making it the third most popular topic (behind online shopping and news). The number of people seeking health-related information more than doubled between 1997 and 2000.

What are the characteristics of these searchers? They tend to be regular Internet users. Fifty-two percent of women surveyed said they had used the Internet for health purposes compared to 41 percent of men. Households with children are more likely to do health-related searches on the Internet.

Just what are they looking for? The most commonly accessed health web sites present details about a specific disease. Specifically, they are looking for new research, and diagnosis and treatment possibilities. Also popular were web sites about lifestyle topics (diet and exercise, for example), sites that matched symptoms to conditions, and web sites about medications. Web site visits do not appear to be dictated by the nature of the custodian of the site. Canadians are as likely to visit sites maintained by drug companies as they are ones looked after by government or non-profit organizations.

Stevenson also points out that, while searching the Net is more convenient and potentially more comprehensive than looking through medical books, there are some reasons for caution. For example, unlike most books, web sites often do not make clear where the information has come from, a point stressed also by the World Health Organization (WHO, 1999). In addition to providing information, the site might also have the purpose of selling products. This might result in bias when it comes to advice about treatment alternatives.

Medical Articles and Reports

Health Canada is a rich source of health information. Try their URL, http://www.hc-sc.gc.ca/ and have a look around. If you did this in July of 2003, as we did, you would see reports on Severe Acute Respiratory Syndrome (SARS), Bovine Spongiform Encephalopathy (BSE) (commonly known as mad cow disease), and West Nile virus. Some of these articles are written for the general public, others are targeted to health care professionals. Good articles are not only well written, they are also well referenced. Claims and statistics are linked to sources that the reader can find and assess. Of course, this is no

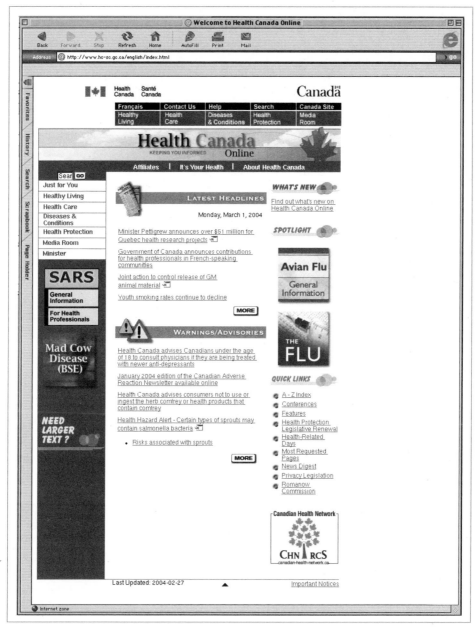

The home page of Health Canada (or the Health on the Net foundation) features a wealth of information.

different from good articles in any medium. It becomes more of an issue with the Internet, though, because of its widespread use and potential misuse.

Let's return for a moment to George, who is searching the Internet for information about diabetes. You might remember that the first site listed by the search engine was the American Diabetes Association. It is likely that this site will provide a great deal of useful information for George. However, George also wanted to find a Canadian site. The librarian advised him to use the Health Canada site we were just talking about. From their home page, he chose Diseases and Conditions. When he clicked on this link, he found seven specific conditions that were given headings of their own; one being diabetes. Here George found a wealth of information in a form that was readable and thorough.

Another example of an informative Canadian site is the Centre for Health Evidence, affiliated with the University of Alberta and University of Manitoba (http://www.cche.net/ CHE/home.asp, accessed June 30, 2003). The purpose of this site is to support evidence-based practice, thus supporting medical decision making that relies on research findings and not just on intuition. As such, it is geared primarily for practitioners and practitioners-in-training. Publications found on this site include such things as a newsletter on evidence-based practice produced at McMaster University.

Yet another good Canadian site is run by the Canadian Institute for Health Information (CIHI) (http://secure.cihi.ca/cihiweb/dispPage.jsp?cw_page=home_e, accessed June 30, 2003). The information found here is particularly helpful for researchers, policy makers, and practitioners. A number of the reports, however, provide useful information for the general public.

Services

Imagine the following story: Shortly after moving to Halifax, Maureen and her husband had triplets. Needless to say, this changed everything for them. At times, they found it difficult to cope, especially since they knew very few people in town. One day, while working on her computer, Maureen typed the following into her search engine: "multiple births Halifax." This yielded 10 300 hits! The very first one was a URL for The Parents of Multiple Births Association–Halifax Region.

Other organizations, like the Alzheimer Society of Canada, provide valuable information and services across the country. For example, if you live in Manitoba, you could use the Society's web site to discover that there were offices in Winnipeg, Brandon, Winkler, Portage La Prairie, and Whitemouth. Each comes with contact information, including an e-mail address. The Society's URL is http://www.alzheimer.ca (accessed July 1, 2003).

Still other Internet-based services help people make treatment-related decisions. Using the tools provided by these sites, people can view interviews with practitioners and other consumers and obtain information pertaining to the specific decision they face (Schwitzer, 2002). These tools have considerable potential to provide help with difficult decisions, when used in concert with one's own physician.

Health Initiatives and Health Promotion

You won't be surprised to learn that the Internet is a widely used vehicle for health promotion (see chapter 7). The Health Canada home page in July of 2003 featured something called "SummerActive 2003," a name that sounds very much like the now defunct

ParticipAction program. SummerActive ran during May and June of 2003 and was "designed to increase awareness about the importance of physical activity, healthy eating, and tobacco-free lifestyles to health" (http://www.hc-sc.gc.ca/english/lifestyles/summer-active.html, accessed June 30, 2003).

The World Health Organization web site features health initiatives on a global scale (http://www.who.int/en/, accessed July 4, 2003). Good examples from June 2003 include World No Tobacco Day 2003, the WHO Global Conference on SARS, and the Global Alliance for Improved Nutrition (GAIN).

If you have ever tried to quit smoking or know someone who has, you might know that you would come up with no fewer than 810 000 hits from a Google search using the words "quit smoking." Some of these sites promote tobacco-free living, some provide free quit-smoking support, some sell smoking cessation products, and still others get you into chat rooms and newsgroups.

Surveys

Canada does a very good job of surveying its population on issues relating to health. More importantly, a considerable amount of the data from these surveys is available on the web for free. Just one of hundreds of examples can be found at http://www.hc-sc.gc.ca/pphb-dgspsp/publicat/lcd-pcd97/ (accessed July 2, 2003). This site contains charts describing the leading causes of death in Canada. Of course, we have accessed many sites like this one in writing this book.

On a provincial level, web sites like the one for The McCreary Centre Society, which addresses the health of young people in British Columbia, describes numerous health initiatives for that population. You can read about the McCreary Centre Society in Focused Module A where we discuss survey methodology and the Adolescent Health Survey. This initiative is documented on their web site (http://www.mcs.bc.ca/, accessed July 3, 2003).

Support

While there are numerous services providing support on the web, there are also groups of individuals engaged in e-mail conversations that take place outside the purview of any formal support service. It is quite possible that someone caring for a person with Alzheimer's disease could "meet" someone halfway around the world engaged in the same challenges. These relationships can be extremely important to the individuals involved (Wright & Bell, 2003).

ASSESSING THE QUALITY OF HEALTH INFORMATION ON THE INTERNET

The quantity of information available on the Internet is unparalleled. The *quality* of that information can vary considerably, however. How, then, can we assess quality? One way is to rely on others to provide that assessment. Organizations such as the Internet Trade Bureau provide what might be called seals of approval for business-related Internet sites. Services like this one monitor complaints against sites and provide a list of these upon request.

Services also exist that provide accreditation or "seals of approval" for health-related web sites. One such example is Health on the Net (HON) http://www.hon.ch/ (accessed

TABLE 12-1	Health on the Net Foundation principles used to assess quality in health-related web sites
Principle	**Description**
1. Authority	Advice is given by those who are medically trained and qualified, unless it is made clear that other forms of qualification apply.
2. Complementarity	The purpose of the site is to support relationships with health practitioners, not replace them.
3. Confidentiality	Any health data presented or information provided by visitors to the site is kept strictly confidential.
4. Attribution	Sources of data and claims are clearly provided.
5. Justifiability	Claims are supported by appropriate and balanced evidence.
6. Transparency of authorship	Contact addresses, including that of the Webmaster, are provided so that further information can be sought.
7. Transparency of sponsorship	Any organizations, public or private, contributing funding are identified.
8. Honesty in advertising and editorial policy	The advertising policy of the site is described. Advertising will be presented so that it is clearly distinguishable from other site content.

Source: Health on the Net Foundation http://www.hon.ch/, accessed July 1, 2003.

Health on the
Net Foundation   medCIRCLE

These symbols indicate that a health web site has been reviewed and approved by the Health on the Net Foundation or medCIRCLE.

June 30, 2003). The HON code of conduct allows for the display of the HONcode icon by web sites meeting HON quality criteria, which are based on principles outlined in table 12.1 (*HON Code of Conduct for medical and health Web sites*, 2003). These criteria are consistent with those recommended by other bodies, such as the World Health Organization, the Canadian Health Network (which is maintained by the federal government), and the American Accreditation HealthCare Commission.

Regardless of the source, the advice to consumers of health-related Internet information tends to make a number of common points. First, Internet-based information should not and cannot replace the information one receives from one's own health care professionals. Information taken from the Internet may well help inform a patient and allow him or her to get more out of a visit with a physician, but it is not a substitute for that visit.

Second, we must put in the work to find out everything we can about the source of the information provided on the Internet. The Canadian Health Network provides a very helpful set of questions to ask when assessing sources in terms of credibility, currency, disclosure, and claims. Regarding the nature of claims made on a site, the World Health Organization provides some "red flags" to look for. Phrases such as "scientific breakthrough" or "miraculous cure" should be met with skepticism, as should long lists of diseases and symptoms that supposedly can be cured by a given treatment. As a case in point, in June of 2003, Health Canada advised Canadians not to use a product called Empowerplus, which has been sold over the Internet as a treatment for bipolar disorder, anxiety disorder, panic attacks, attention deficit disorder, schizophrenia, autism, Tourette's syndrome, fibromyalgia, and obsessive compulsive disorder (http://www.hc-sc.gc.ca/english/protection/warnings/2003/2003_41.htm, accessed July 1, 2003).

Third, when buying health products via the Internet, consumers should demand the same quality assurances they would find in a trusted pharmacy. These include such things as information about safety of use, instructions regarding proper use, indications that regulatory procedures have been followed, and assurance that your personal information will be kept confidential. WHO also points out that products with the same name may actually be different depending upon the country they come from (WHO, 1999).

Usability

The quality of an Internet site is determined in large part by the quality of information it provides. But there is more to consider. The site must also be easily *usable*. The National Cancer Institute defines **usability** in terms of "the quality of a user's experience when interacting with a product or system" (*Usability basics*, 2002). Using their criteria, we could assess the usability of a given site by answering the following questions. How easy is it to learn how to use the site? Once you have learned how to use the site, how efficiently can you navigate through it and get the information you need? When the site is revisited, is it easy to remember the navigation rules? How often are errors made when accessing the site? How much did you like using the site?

How can web designers improve the usability of their sites? According to the National Cancer Institute (*Research-based web design & usability guidelines*, 2002), two important considerations are the design of the site, including its layout and use of graphics and links, and the nature and organization of the content provided.

Regarding the design, a usable web site establishes the level of importance of its components and communicates those levels clearly. A web site is confusing if a link to a short newspaper article on SARS is given the same prominence as a link to a one-screen explanation of the condition, which is given the same prominence as a description of the organization providing the information. Web designers must answer the question: What should the user see first on the screen in order to best facilitate navigation and comprehension?

Also, usable web sites must adopt a consistent layout from page to page. It is confusing to have a menu listed down the left side of the screen for one section of a web site, only to have it disappear when one moves to another section. Consistency not only increases ease of use, it can also be used to indicate to the user just where he or she is on the site. A consistent menu bar can be highlighted to indicate location in relation to other locations. This is very important because it is easy to get lost in the maze of pages that some web sites feature. All of these features are intended to reduce the user's workload.

In terms of content, the most obvious consideration is to make it useful. Designers must avoid content for its own sake, drawing the erroneous conclusion that bigger is always better where web sites are concerned. Because of the way we process information from a screen, short sentences and paragraphs are preferable. Newspapers have been using this style for a long time. Similarly, attention must be paid to the length of the pages as they appear on the screen. Also, it is important to provide good printing options. The user should be able to print text without the intrusion of extensive graphics, and the printed pages should fit on standard-sized paper.

Accessibility

When we consider usability of a web site, we must consider usability for all who want to use it. This is especially true for health-related web sites, where people with disabilities or challenging conditions may well be the most interested users. Given the increasing prominence of web-based information in our lives, web designers and governments are taking a great interest in the accessibility of web sites, as we are doing for buildings, public transit, and any facility intended for equitable use. Later in this chapter, we will look at demographic and socioeconomic factors that affect equal access to web-based information. Here, we will look at making the Internet accessible for people with varying physical and cognitive challenges.

Accessibility has been taken on as a major issue by the World Wide Web Consortium (W3C). They provide excellent web-based resources on the topic (Brewer, 2001) included as part of their Web Access Initiative (WAI). Of particular value to those without an extensive background in such things as assistive software is a set of hypothetical scenarios describing web use by people with various disabilities (Brewer, 2001).

Many people would endorse the use of colour coding to help simplify web site navigation. While this is a good idea for many users, it is a problem for those who are colour blind. Similarly, graphics that make use of colour to show symptoms or prescription use are not well suited for colour-blind users. To make the site more accessible for these individuals, text-based descriptions should complement the use of colour.

People with learning disabilities such as dyslexia can face real challenges when reading material off a screen or, for that matter, a page. For these people, text-to-speech software now exists that can turn problematic text into understandable language. Text that is broken up by numerous graphics or other displays might make it difficult for this software to function efficiently. Also, while graphics can be helpful for some people with learning disabilities, animated graphics can be confusing to follow. Web sites can be designed, however, in ways that allow the user to freeze the graphic. This increases accessibility for people with certain learning disabilities.

People with colour blindness or dyslexia have a real set of challenges. These are multiplied for people who are legally blind. For these users, assistive software takes the form of screen readers. These readers can bog down, however, when trying to read complicated tables, especially those that do not have clear headings for columns and rows. They also run into trouble with sites that rely heavily on abbreviations (a habit that seems to be a particular affliction of those in health care!). Reducing this reliance and providing tables that are well labelled and accompanied by good captions will help make web sites more accessible for users who are blind.

Hard-of-hearing or deaf users can read things off the screen, but they are excluded from information that takes the form of streamed audio. In such cases, for lectures, radio programs, or other material, these users need transcripts. If they are taking part in a real-time discussion on the web, these transcripts must keep up with the audio material.

This list of examples is by no means exhaustive. Indeed, it barely scratches the surface in its description of challenges faced by many people using the web. Brewer provides a more extensive list of examples as well as a good list of assistive software as of 2001. Like everything relating to information technology, that list is surely growing.

The Treasury Board of Canada is one organization in this country that has taken on the challenge of helping make web sites accessible for all. One of their approaches has been to provide guidelines for what they call a "common look and feel for the Internet' (*Common look and feel for the Internet*, 2001). This standardization will help all users, in much the same way that standardized procedures at banks and gas stations do. (If you have ever travelled in a country with different standards for these sorts of things, you know what an adventure some of the basic elements of daily living can be.)

HOW PEOPLE PROCESS INFORMATION FROM THE INTERNET

We have learned that the Internet provides efficient access to incredible amounts of information, and that there are criteria available to help us assess the quality of that information. But how do people *process* this information? After all, it is not presented in tangible form as in a book, or even on the radio or television. It arrives on a computer screen, complete with text, images, and perhaps sound.

When you work on your computer, can you read and edit easily off the screen? In all likelihood, there are individual differences in this regard. Some people will like to print text and then read it off the page. Sometimes this is easily done from the Internet; however, some information does not print out well. Whatever the case, Internet information is first encountered on the computer screen, which means its layout matters, as does the text's font and the nature of the images. Research has used information-processing models to help understand how people consume information in this format.

One such model is the limited capacity model (Lang, 2000), which, as the name implies, works on the assumption that the viewer has finite attentional resources and must decide where to deploy them when confronted with a busy computer screen. A series of studies by Annie Lang and colleagues (Lang, Borse, Wise, & Prabu, 2002) measured people's **orienting responses** to various stimuli presented on a computer screen. For these studies, an orienting response was defined by a slowing of the viewer's heart rate. Stimuli included single-line text messages, either alone or in a box, and what are called ad banners, which typically appear toward the top of the screen. These can be either animated or non-animated.

Contrary to what was hypothesized, text messages, boxed or otherwise, did not elicit an orienting response from people looking at an otherwise blank computer screen. However, when the messages contained warnings of personal relevance, heart rate did slow, though the response was not very strong. In fact, the only stimuli that consistently elicited a fairly strong orienting response were the animated ad banners. Thus, many Internet sites, health-related or otherwise, feature these banners, and they do provide a distraction for the person trying to process the information on the site. Interestingly, this orienting response did not increase the likelihood that viewers would recognize the ad at a later time unless the viewer had controlled the original onset of the ad banner (by hitting the space bar).

In summary, models of information processing tell us that information presented on a computer screen feature distractions that we don't find on the printed page. Sites that use advertising will have more of these distractions, and people will orient their attention to animated advertisements rather than headlines. Even with all this competition for attention, people do not take away much screen-based information in memory. This is probably because they are scanning the screen in ways that don't include deep processing of the information. Rather than take notes in one's own words when reading a web site (as we might from a book), we might be more likely to read passively or "cut and paste" the information into another electronic file without giving it the attention it needs in order to be remembered.

IMPLICATIONS OF INTERNET USE FOR INDIVIDUAL AND PUBLIC HEALTH

It could be expected that such vast amounts of information available to large groups of people, and unavailable to other large groups of people, would have an effect on health and health care. Indeed, it has been predicted that people will soon be expecting to consume health services in the form of real-time consultations readily on the Internet (Christiansen & Nohr, 2003; Grover, Wu, Blanford, Holcomb, & Tidler, 2002).

Patient-Physician Relationships

When you read through Case 12-1, did you wonder if Wayne's use of the Internet was a help or a hindrance? Certainly, he took control of his own situation by seeking out information that he considered to be relevant to it. However, it may well have resulted in unnecessary worry. For Wayne's physician, when his patient went to the Internet, the result was one more e-mail message to answer, a worried patient to work with, and probably more time spent with Wayne during the upcoming visit than would otherwise have been the case.

But the physician did not simply dismiss Wayne's concerns. Rather, he respected Wayne's desire to be informed, regardless of the time costs to both people. Of course, skillful physicians know better than to offhandedly dismiss patients' concerns, no matter what their source. In this case, though, the Internet has affected the relationship between patient and practitioner.

CASE 12-1	Learning about Bones

Wayne has spent most of his adult life working as a carpet layer. Now, at age 48, his left knee is giving him trouble. It started when he was out jogging. He had to stop running and limp home. When he visited his doctor, he sent him for a bone scan, suspecting that he might have a bruise on the distal end of his femur. He explained to Wayne that the femur was the large bone in his thigh, and that the distal end was where his pain was originating, close to his knee. He told Wayne that this injury was not uncommon for people in Wayne's line of work, given that they are on their knees a lot.

The bone scan confirmed the doctor's diagnosis. However, in the time between going for the bone scan and returning to get the test results, Wayne went on the Internet to learn more about bone pain. He came across something called Paget's disease, which causes abnormal bone growth and leaves bones weak and brittle. Wayne learned that Paget's disease occurred most commonly in people about his age.

Wayne began to worry that he might have Paget's disease, so he sent his doctor an e-mail message asking about it. By then, his doctor had his bone scan results and knew Wayne had a bone bruise. However, rather than dismiss Wayne's concern, he e-mailed back and asked him for the URL of the web site where Wayne had learned about Paget's disease. In his e-mail reply, he told Wayne he was quite sure he had a bone bruise, but he would visit the web site and they could talk about it when Wayne came in to go over the results.

In chapter 4, we looked at communication between patients and practitioners. In this current section, we will explore ways in which that communication is affected by the Internet. Though one survey of almost 9 000 people found that 90 percent of the respondents stated Internet use had not affected physician visits or telephone contacts (Baker, Wagner, Singer, & Bundorf, 2003), other research provides a convincing case for the likelihood that patients' use of the Internet is affecting the way they consume face-to-face services.

For example, a study of 266 oncologists found that 98 percent of them felt they were spending increasing amounts of time discussing information patients derived from the Internet. The oncologists estimated that this has added about ten minutes to each patient consultation, compared to five years ago (Helft, Hlubocky, & Daugherty, 2003).

A study in the United States found that 12 percent of patients receiving radiation for cancer had purchased complementary therapies over the Internet (Metz et al., 2003). That same study recommended that radiation oncologists familiarize themselves with Internet-based resources available to their patients.

Patients' increased usage of the Internet is also affecting their expectations of the health care system. A study at Princess Margaret Hospital in Toronto (Chen & Siu, 2001) discovered a gap between the number of people who wanted as much information as possible about their cancer (86 percent) and the number who believed they were getting enough information from health care professionals (54 percent). The Internet provides one way to close this information gap. Of the 191 cancer patients surveyed in the Toronto study, 88 percent felt their doctors were willing to discuss information the patients found on the Internet.

While it was the case that patients in the Toronto study felt their doctors were receptive to discussions of Internet information, there were differences in patients' and physicians' views about that information. For example, of the 410 oncologists who took part in the study, only 6 percent thought their patients used Internet information correctly. Perhaps this helps explain differences in opinion regarding the helpfulness and potential negative impact of this information. Figure 12-1 shows that patients found Internet information to be more helpful and to have potentially less negative impact than did oncologists.

Another study of 266 oncologists found that 57 percent of them thought the information their cancer patients gleaned from the Internet made the patients more hopeful (Helft et al., 2003). Interestingly, of these 57 percent, half thought this was a good thing and half thought it wasn't. This difference of opinion was explained, in part, by written comments supplied by these oncologists. Just over half of these comments featured negative opinions about what they saw to be the fostering of false hopes or unwarranted anxiety when patients consulted the Internet. Other studies have shown that physicians' opinions of their patients' health-related Internet use is somewhat varied, but generally positive (Potts & Wyatt, 2002).

Sarah Maulden (Maulden, 2003) has presented a comprehensive analysis of the benefits and problems of Internet use as applied to the practice of neurology. Many of her con-

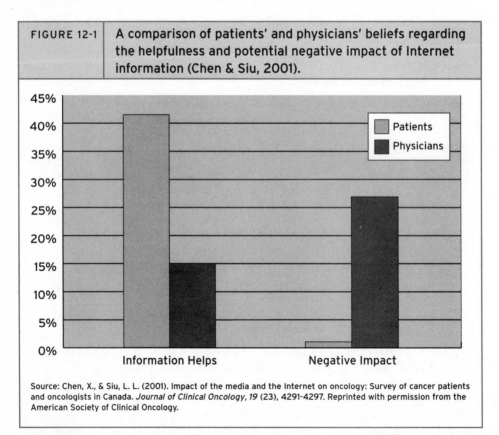

FIGURE 12-1 | A comparison of patients' and physicians' beliefs regarding the helpfulness and potential negative impact of Internet information (Chen & Siu, 2001).

Source: Chen, X., & Siu, L. L. (2001). Impact of the media and the Internet on oncology: Survey of cancer patients and oncologists in Canada. *Journal of Clinical Oncology, 19* (23), 4291-4297. Reprinted with permission from the American Society of Clinical Oncology.

A higher percentage of patients believed Internet information to be helpful, whereas a higher percentage of physicians thought it had the potential to have negative impact.

clusions apply well to other health care contexts and they remind us that the Internet involves more than the world wide web. For example, e-mail is the most widely used Internet activity among neurologists (Beresford & Brooke, 1999). In one year, the number of physicians using e-mail to communicate with patients increased by 200 percent.

There are a number of reasons for e-mail's popularity. Physicians report that they spend less time on patient phone calls when they have instituted e-mail communication. Furthermore, e-mail communication is *asynchronous*, meaning that the physician can reply when convenient and not necessarily at the moment the patient asks a question. This allows for more efficient time management. Physicians can also keep a permanent record of their communication with patients. For example, the exact wording of instructions and explanations can be placed in a patient's file (physical or electronic).

It is also possible that patients formulate clearer questions when they have the time to write them out in an e-mail message. (Have you ever felt that way when sending a question to an instructor?) Patients might also be more comfortable dealing with sensitive topics via e-mail rather than face-to-face.

Maulden also points out some of the possible problems with e-mail communication. Perhaps paramount among these is the concern for security. The security of e-mail communication simply cannot be guaranteed. Many people can read messages not intended for them. For this reason, confidentiality cannot be guaranteed either. A patient can have confidence that what he or she says to a practitioner behind the closed door of a consultation room will not become public knowledge. E-mail does not yield the same confidence. Also, the same asynchronicity that makes e-mail convenient makes it inappropriate for time-sensitive matters.

It is easy to send e-mail messages once one knows how. While this sounds like a distinct advantage, it can also be a disadvantage, as witnessed by the swelling number of messages many people now receive on a daily basis. A physician, who possesses so much valuable knowledge, could be flooded with more e-mail messages than he or she could possibly keep up with. This same ease of use has caused some to suggest that e-mail enables and reinforces the obsession with disease and dysfunction typical of hypochondria.

Maulden provides some helpful advice for practitioners. First and foremost, physicians should talk with their patients about the pros and cons of e-mail communication. Second, physicians might consider using **encryption**, which allows for message access to be restricted to those with passwords. This helps reduce problems of security and confidentiality. (For a comprehensive review of security issues and technological solutions, see Kelly & McKenzie, 2002.) In terms of managing the volume of messages, software is available that will route messages to the appropriate person in the office. For example, if someone sends a message in order to book an appointment, that message can be routed to the medical office assistant.

We have talked about health-related web sites designed for the general public. Many physicians are also creating their own web sites intended for their patients and prospective patients. Survey data from the year 2000 indicated that approximately 50 percent of physicians have their own web sites (Hsih, 2000). In Canada, 57 percent of physicians access the web from their offices (Martin, 2003). These numbers are surely growing. These sites might provide information regarding the background and qualification of the practitioner (or of a group working in a clinic). It might also provide details about the office such as location, parking, hours of operation, phone numbers, e-mail addresses and so on.

Physicians are also starting to include links to trusted web sites, which provides some reassurance to the patient that the web information they collect is credible.

Practitioners' Use of the Internet

In addition to having the potential to enhance communication with patients, Maulden (2003) points out that practitioners are using the Internet in other ways that improves the care they provide. For example, physicians are communicating with each other via mailing lists and newsgroups. Information about recent discoveries can now be sent to practitioners automatically. Discussions can take place online regarding best practice.

Just as you may have done for a recent assignment, practitioners are now doing targeted literature searches on a need-to-know basis. Extensive data bases like *Medline* are very valuable. Also, many of the journals found in a *Medline* search are now available in full text online. If practitioners don't have the time to read entire articles in these e-journals, they can access electronic sources that summarize the literature on a given topic. One excellent source for these summaries is the Cochrane Library, which is also available online. Sources like these make it much easier for health care professionals to practise evidence-based medicine.

The Internet also provides practitioners with decision-making aids for such things as medication and dose decisions. At present, most of the advice in this area is of a general nature and needs to be considered carefully before being applied to a specific patient. However, advances in this area now allow practitioners to enter specific characteristics of a patient before receiving advice regarding best practice.

Finally, and perhaps most relevant to Canada, health care professionals are practising **telemedicine**. This refers to the use of electronic media to practise medicine between physical sites. Radiologists refer to **filmless radiology** when they talk about sending diagnostic images electronically rather than processing film hard copies to be sent through the mail. The advantages of filmless radiology are numerous. Perhaps the most salient is the saving of time. In fact, a radiologist in Saskatoon can be looking at an image that has been sent from a northern community like Meadow Lake while the patient is still with the rural physician.

Maulden (2003) provides an example of a patient in a remote area who presents with the symptoms of a stroke. Fortunately, the area isn't so remote that it doesn't have a CT scanner. The CT image is relayed to a neurologist working in a large urban hospital and specializing in stroke cases of this type. She provides advice to the remote site regarding medication and immediate treatment. Though the patient was eventually flown to the urban centre, the communication in the first three hours of treatment proved vital to a successful outcome.

Examples like this one suggest that the Internet can be of benefit the world over. Indeed, one of the most exciting attributes of the Internet generally is its ubiquitous nature. Many students reading this book will have had the experience of travelling to some fairly remote corners of the world, and then to be reconnected with familiar things by walking into an Internet café and listening to a Montreal Canadiens game or having an e-mail chat with a friend at home. If the Internet is capable of shrinking the world in this way, then we might expect health-related Internet use to be worldwide. To explore this, we will look at some of the research on information technology use in other parts of the world.

A study of patients in Denmark with Internet access found that one-third of them had accessed the Internet in preparation for a visit with their doctor (Budtz & Witt, 2002). Regarding practitioners' use of information technology, a study of general practitioners along the east coast of Scotland revealed a high level of Internet connectivity (Moffat, Moffat, & Cano, 2001). Ninety-two percent of the practices had an available Internet connection and 67 percent of practitioners reported using the Internet in their practice for things like *Medline* searches and e-mail communication. Compare this to Switzerland, where 75 percent of the primary care practitioners surveyed in that country reported having Internet access. Of these only 14 percent said they found useful information on the Internet (Koller, Grutter, Peltenburg, Fischer, & Steurer, 2001). In Germany, where practitioners report acquiring 60 percent of their knowledge after medical school, continuing medical education is very important (as it is the world over). One study indicated that practitioners in that country are *not* relying extensively on information technologies for this education; preferring hard copy journals and interactions with colleagues (Butzlaff et al., 2002). By contrast, Australian practitioners in rural Queensland are characterized as extensive and sophisticated users of information technology, using the Internet for prescribing, conveying patient information, determining pathology, and pursuing education (White, Sheedy, & Lawrence, 2002).

These studies indicate considerable differences in the health-related use of the Internet, yet all these countries are relatively affluent. What about Internet use in developing countries? It has been observed that New York has more Internet users than does the entire continent of Africa (Fraser & McGrath, 2000). Dissemination of health information to these parts of the world could be very important (Parent, Coppieters, & Parent, 2001; Rodrigues & Risk, 2003).

Medical students at the University of Lagos, Nigeria were surveyed regarding their use of *Medline* in the CD-ROM version (Ogunyade & Oyibo, 2003). It was discovered that usage of this resource was low—only 24 percent of the students surveyed had used *Medline*. Only 52 percent were aware of *Medline* on CD ROM as a way of gathering medical information. This lack of awareness and usage was attributed to a number of factors, including an insufficient number of personal computers and little training in this area.

In Sri Lanka, a well-known medical web site exists; however, a study of the patterns of access over a 20-month period spanning 1997 and 1998 found that considerably more of the visits to the site were from people in developed countries than in Sri Lanka (Dissanayake & Jayasekara, 1999). Similar to the conclusions drawn from the Nigerian study, these authors recommend that computer technology be made more affordable and available in developing countries.

One way to close the gap between countries in their use of information technology is to create partnerships between developing nations and those with advanced technology usage. One such partnership, between Japan and Malaysia, featured the use of digital technology to share diagnostic images (Houkin et al., 1999). The results of this partnership were very encouraging.

This brief look at use of health-related information technology indicates considerable differences from one country to the next. In some cases, these differences are due to availability of resources, in others to prevailing attitudes about the usefulness of the technology.

Studies in the late 1990s showed that Internet use was leading to improved health care outcomes. Qualitative assessment provided by practitioners indicated that the use of

Medline led to more positive outcomes (Lindberg & Humphreys, 1998). The introduction of a computer-based physician ordering system has been shown to significantly reduce errors in prescription ordering (Bates et al., 1998) and other computer-based systems have improved decision making regarding drug dosing and the implementation of prevention strategies (Hunt, Haynes, Hanna, & Smith, 1998).

As you can see, the potential benefits of Internet use for practitioners are numerous. There are some downsides, though. One is the time it can take to learn how to use the computer technology. The other is that current telecommunication capabilities, specifically the bandwidth available, restrict the quality of images in some cases. However, these problems can be overcome, given the speed at which technology improves, and the fact that physicians are used to having to learn new things through continuing medical education (CME) (see for example, Kronick et al., 2003).

Hospital Web Sites

Just as practitioners are developing web sites, so are hospitals. In the United States, the web is seen as a potential marketing tool for hospitals (Romano, 2003). This potential has led to the development of web sites that go beyond "brochureware" (Romano, 2003) to include a wide range of information for patients and prospective patients. In Canada, where hospitals are less concerned about market competition, hospital web sites are nevertheless developing in valuable directions. The home page for the Vancouver Hospital and Health Sciences Centre (www.vanhosp.bc.ca, accessed July 2, 2003) provides health information, specific information for patients and practitioners using the hospital, career information, and information about making financial donations to the hospital. Other hospitals, such as Toronto's Hospital for Sick Children (www.sickkids.on.ca, accessed July 2, 2003) provides similar information.

Equality of Access

One of the real concerns about the explosive development of Internet use is equal access. Not everyone has access to the computers, much less the Internet. It is also very possible that those who have the least access are those in most need of health services. Remember that equity is an important focus of Canada's health promotion strategies; thus the Internet can pose challenges to the attainment of this fundamental goal. In our opening vignette, we met George, a recently diagnosed diabetes patient who did not own a computer. However, George was lucky in that he had a daughter who was computer-savvy. Also, he was able to visit a local library and access Internet-based information from there. Not everyone is as lucky.

This problem of unequal access to computer-based technology has been called the **digital divide**. The divide is based primarily on demographic and socioeconomic variables. For example, in Canada, most households with a combined income of $10 000 or more have a television set and a telephone (Sciadas, 2002). However, the percent of households with Internet access in Canada goes up in a near-linear fashion with income. In the year 2000, about 10 percent of households with incomes between $10 000 and $15 000 had Internet access, compared to almost 70 percent of homes with incomes over $70 000 per year (Sciadas, 2002). In Canada, Internet use is inversely related to age. Over

90 percent of people between the ages of 15 and 17 use the Internet, compared to about 10 percent between the ages of 70 and 74 (Sciadas, 2002). Generally, males are more likely to use the Internet, except when it comes to accessing health information. For this purpose, women use the Internet more frequently than do men (*How Canadians find health information on the Internet*, 2003).

A study in the United States investigated the possibility that the digital divide might extend to physicians' offices (Bell, Daly, & Robinson, 2003). These researchers found no evidence for this, however. Offices from what were called high-minority and high-poverty areas were just as likely to have Internet-capable technology as offices in other areas of the country.

The Challenges of Using the Internet Effectively

In our discussion of ways in which the Internet is used in health care, we have mentioned some of the pros and cons associated with this use. Here, we will summarize the main issues. We have already highlighted challenges associated with equal access and with potential misinterpretation of Internet-based information by patients. In addition, it is always possible that information taken from the Internet may be either inaccurate or out-of-date (Brann & Anderson, 2002). Brann and Anderson cite an example of a web site that recommends the treatment of childhood fever with Aspirin, a practice that physicians would not recommend because of the increased risk of Reye's Syndrome associated with this practice. Reye's Syndrome is a potentially fatal disease that attacks the liver, brain, and other organs (*What is Reye's Syndrome?* 2000).

We have also talked about the difficulties that can be encountered in trying to identify the *source* of the information provided on an Internet site. One study of English-language health sites found that the distinction between advertising and professional medical information was unclear in about half of the sites (Berland et al., 2001).

Source identification is important for assessing credibility and for the related issue of conflict of interest (Brann & Anderson, 2002). For example, it would be important to know whether a web site advocating the use of hormone replacement therapy over other treatments for prostate cancer was being sponsored by a pharmaceutical company. Anderson (1999) cited the example of a web site listing America's most innovative health care institutions. It was then discovered that each institution had paid $40 000 to be listed on the site.

Another important challenge concerns the security of information provided via the Internet. One real threat to this security is **data mining** (Brann & Anderson, 2002). As the term implies, this refers to the process of digging deeply into the information available on a given site. The deeper one digs, the closer one gets to confidential, patient-based information. Brann and Anderson cite examples of pharmacies in the United States providing prescription data to marketing firms. For the average person visiting health-related web sites, caution must be taken when entrance to the site is allowed only after the person has provided personal information. Brann and Anderson point out that this personal information can and has been sold to marketers, not only as general demographic data, but also to allow for individualized sales pitches.

One final, important challenge involves the creation of an effective balance between patient autonomy and practitioner involvement where patients' use of the Internet is concerned. Remember that the World Health Organization and others advise that the Internet can augment patients' interactions with physicians, but it cannot and should not replace those interactions. The importance of this is underscored by the reporting of a tragic case in which a 20-year-old woman with a history of anorexia unintentionally overdosed on a drug she had ordered off the Internet (Takeshita, 2003). She had had no contact with a physician in the ordering or consuming of the drug (phentermine).

HEALTH-RELATED USES OF THE INTERNET IN THE FUTURE

Given the great likelihood that Internet use by patients and practitioners will only increase in the future, what can we expect and what should we demand regarding that use? Certainly, we must continue to develop even more uniform measures for evaluating the information presented on the Internet. There are at least four ways this can be achieved in the future (Brann & Anderson, 2002). First, consumers must be educated regarding the consumption of Internet information. Checklists like the one provided by Health on the Net (HON) are very helpful in this regard. Second, those who are responsible for the sites must be encouraged to self-regulate. Standards of practice need to become industry norms, like seatbelts in automobiles. Third, because self-regulation is fraught with problems, we need to support the development of third-party evaluators, like the HON Code. More sites need to take part in that evaluation process. As it currently stands, there are many very good sites that do not bear the HON Code symbol because they have not engaged in the process. This means that, while the symbol can provide consumers with confidence, the *lack* of a HON Code symbol does not meant the site should be ignored. Finally, there must be ways in which sanctions can be enforced. Remember that there are monitoring organizations that field complaints about web sites, check them out, and maintain lists of sites and the number of verified complaints levied against them. However, we need to go beyond "black lists." For sites that truly violate well-established codes of conduct, there must be fines and access restrictions imposed.

Brann and Anderson conclude by making the point that, in all of these future steps, consumers must be more fully involved in all facets of web-based information development, dissemination, and evaluation.

KEY TERMS

data mining (p. 343)	FTP (p. 327)	search engine (p. 327)
digital divide (p. 342)	filmless radiology (p. 340)	telemedicine (p. 340)
e-journal (p. 326)	links (p. 326)	URL (p. 326)
encryption (p. 339)	orienting responses (p. 335)	Usability (p. 333)

Focused Module A

Conducting Research

in Health Psychology

Health psychology is an **applied discipline**. This means that psychologists working in this field spend more time using theories to explain real-world phenomena than they do developing the theories. This doesn't mean that health psychologists don't ever develop theories. The applied focus in health psychology means that much of the research conducted in the field is applied research, which is designed to solve real-world problems.

Applied research comes with its own set of challenges. Primary among these is that applied research must be *relevant*. While basic researchers can study a phenomenon for its own sake, applied researchers usually need some practical outcome for their work. For example, program improvement, improved coping, and wellness are goals of applied research. This is not to imply that one kind of research is better or more virtuous than the other.

In addition to requiring practical outcomes, applied research is challenging because it often takes place in the actual settings in which the application is to be made. In health psychology, this means doing a great deal of research in hospitals and clinics. These field experiments, which are conducted in real-life settings, can be difficult to carry out. Hospitals are very busy places with mandates that do not always include cooperation with research projects. The primary focus of the professionals working in hospitals is the care of the patient, not the completion of someone's research.

Psychosocial research in hospitals can be very intrusive. Imagine conducting a study in which nurses were asked to follow a script that differed from what they were used to. Now, in addition to concentrating on the patient, the nurses must also pay attention to this new protocol. Through all of this, patient care cannot be compromised. This means that close consultation must take place between practitioners and researchers before conducting hospital research in which routine is altered. To complicate matters, this consultation is time consuming, and practitioners usually don't have the luxury of spare time.

The intrusions of this research are not restricted to the practitioners. There are the patients to consider as well. For example, just trying to enlist the participation of patients in hospital settings can be problematic. Patients might not be at their most receptive immediately before undergoing a nuclear medicine test in which they may find that they have cancer, or before cardiac catheterization, in which a probe is going to be inserted into one of their coronary arteries. All the same, it is vital that we learn about the psychological factors relevant to patients undergoing such tests and procedures to help patients cope and to guide practitioners (see chapter 5, Hospital Stays and Medical Procedures).

Perhaps the greatest challenge is that field research is never "tidy," in that there are always going to be numerous variables that a researcher cannot control. Imagine being the researcher in the following example:

A patient arrives 30 minutes early for her CT scan so that she can fill out your questionnaires. However, the clinic is running a bit ahead of schedule on this day and the patient is asked to come in for her scan before she has finished completing the questionnaires. She offers to finish them after the scan. Other patients in the study completed all the questionnaires before the scan, but you don't want to lose valuable data, since so few patients fit the inclusion criteria for the study. So you take her up on her offer to complete them afterwards. The patient returns from her scan 45 minutes later, willing to complete the questionnaires. Unfortunately, she was feeling a bit anxious just before her scan and so she was given a mild tranquillizer. Will her data still be of value?

In spite of challenges like these, good psychological research can still be conducted in hospitals or other field settings. Indeed, we believe that a person trained in psychological principles can hardly walk through a hospital without generating important hypotheses about its workings.

OBSERVATIONAL METHODS: LEARNING BY LOOKING

One of the most fundamental ways to learn about phenomena in health psychology is to observe them. Observational research is almost always descriptive in its purpose. This method might seem straightforward on the surface, but there are many challenges inherent in this form of research. We'll explore some of these challenges in the following example.

Imagine that you wanted to study communication between physicians and their patients. You might decide that the best place to start would be with an observational design. To be of value, your observations would have to be made in real-life settings; by observing actual consultations between physicians and their patients. Your first challenge presents itself—how do you make your observations without getting in the way? In the language of observational methodology, how can you be unobtrusive? Just your being there would change the nature of the interaction you were hoping to observe. Will you hide behind a screen? A one-way mirror? Not likely. These solutions are both awkward and unethical. The patients and physicians must consent to being observed, and so they will know their behaviour is being monitored.

Maybe technology can help. There is audio tape. This method is much less obtrusive but you would lose valuable visual information that might help you understand non-verbal behaviour. There is videotape. The camera is more obtrusive, but perhaps if you set it up inconspicuously enough people will forget it is there and you will get to observe some fairly natural behaviour.

If you do get good tapes, what are you going to do with them? When you begin to view them, you will realize that there is a great deal going on in them. Body positions are shifting, words are zipping back and forth between patient and practitioner, other non-linguistic sounds like "uh" and "mmm" are coming out, and it's all happening so fast. This is another challenge of observational research; knowing what to observe. You're lucky. You have videotape that you can replay and even slow down if necessary. Those making real-time observations with the naked eye don't have these luxuries.

CASE STUDIES: CLOSE LOOKS AT ONE PERSON AT A TIME

Case studies are usually narrative in nature, providing details about one person's life (or in some cases, comparing two or more individuals) that help us learn about some aspect of health psychology. **Case studies** present such things as individual histories, symptoms, specific reactions, or treatment outcomes (Cozby, 1993). They can also be used at a more sociological level. As such, they would present descriptions of programs or institutions.

A research group may want to trace the life of a prostate cancer patient to discover what role, if any, social support plays in his story. How does he describe his relationship with his wife? Did attending a support group represent some sort of turning point for him in his ability to cope with his prostate cancer?

Case studies such as these can be very valuable because they provide rich sources of data that are rarely obtainable using other methods featuring large groups. Also, the data become "personalized" rather than "dehumanized," which is important in a discipline like health psychology that prides itself on its human focus. However, findings from case studies cannot always be generalized to other people.

SURVEY METHODS: TAKING SNAPSHOTS OF LARGE SAMPLES

Much of the data collected by social scientists working in health-related fields comes in the form of surveys. A well-designed survey can produce a wealth of information about a large group of people. It is particularly good for assessing trends in health behaviours and in the use of a health care system. For these reasons, you will find that much of the data available from sources like Statistics Canada has been collected through surveys.

In British Columbia, the Adolescent Health Survey (McCreary Centre, 1993, 1998) has collected data on adolescent health and risk behaviours on three occasions from large numbers of youth in high schools throughout the province. By "large numbers" we mean over 25 000, making it one of the largest surveys of its kind in the world.

There are two fundamental questions that have to be answered at the outset of planning survey research. What do you want to know and who do you want to ask? It's amazing how often a research group goes over survey results only to have one of the group say, "If only we had asked _____!" This happens, in part, because it can be difficult to anticipate all the important questions the first time you administer a survey. For example, the second administration of the Adolescent Health Survey in 1998 included most of the questions from the initial survey in 1992, although a few items were deleted and some new questions were added. This was done to reflect current issues among youth.

Of concern here is striking a balance between keeping the survey relevant, allowing for comparisons across different administrations of the survey, and keeping the administration within acceptable time limits—one high-school period in this case. Items that are deleted from one administration of the survey are lost for purposes of comparison, yet it is not possible to continuously add new items without deleting others. It can be a difficult tradeoff.

CORRELATIONAL METHODS: LOOKING FOR THINGS THAT CHANGE TOGETHER

For men with prostate cancer, it is possible that their ability to cope with the disease is related to their satisfaction with their social support. We might hypothesize that coping is *positively correlated* with social support. This means simply that as social support satisfaction increases, so does coping ability. These two variables change together—they *covary*. To test this hypothesis, we would conduct **correlational research**. This means that we would use statistical analyses to determine if these variables did, in fact, covary. Of course, the main statistic we would rely on would be correlation. Not surprisingly, correlational research is very common in health psychology.

Conceptually, correlations are not particularly complicated. For example, you need three things to do correlational analysis in our prostate cancer study. First, you need pairs of scores for a given individual. In this case, each man has a social support satisfaction score and a coping score. It would make no sense to correlate one man's satisfaction score with another man's coping score. Second, you need a large sample of these men and it would be best if they varied on these scores. Third, you need variables with multiple levels, preferably measured on a continuum. For example, age works well in correlational analysis because you can measure it right down to the day if necessary.

Once you have your pairs of scores on appropriate variables, you can calculate your correlation. There are three possibilities: 1) As one variable increases (or decreases), so does another. This would result in a **positive correlation**. For example, we would hypothesize a positive correlation between social support satisfaction and coping; 2) As one variable increases, the other might decrease. This would result in a **negative correlation**. For example, we might hypothesize a negative correlation between social support satisfaction and illness progression. The better the support, the slower the illness progression (as measured by some biomedical indicator in which higher scores meant more progression of illness); 3) Social support satisfaction and coping might be unrelated. One man might be very satisfied with social support but be coping poorly. Another could be satisfied and coping well. Others may be coping well without any social support.

It is very important to realize that correlational research does not allow us to draw conclusions regarding the cause–effect relationship between variables. For example, if satisfaction with support and coping are positively correlated, we cannot jump to the conclusion that support *caused* improved coping. There are at least two reasons why we can't draw cause–effect conclusions from correlations. The first of these is that both causal directions are possible. While it is possible that good social support causes better coping, it is also possible that those people who are coping better are more able to seek social support. If this is the case, then coping could affect social support scores. The point is that the correlation does not give us any definitive data regarding the direction of this relationship.

The second reason we can't draw cause–effect conclusions from correlations involves the possibility of third-variable explanations. It is entirely possible that social support and coping aren't causally related at all. Instead, there might be a third variable that explains both of them and, in so doing, results in a correlation. For example, it is possible that one's income could be related to both social support and coping. People who can afford cars go to support groups and get more support than people who can't. Also, that income might be affecting coping by allowing for the purchase of other things that make life more comfortable. In other words, income is a *third variable* that may be causally related to both support and coping.

In chapters 1 and 2, we discussed the Type A behaviour pattern. When it was first identified, the claim was that competitive, time-urgent, hostile people were at greater risk for heart disease. Further research has shown that it is hostility that is the truly toxic factor in this list. *Factor analysis* can be used in research that identifies such patterns. **Factor analysis** uses correlations among variables to group them into "factors," or variables that may be tapping into one over-arching phenomenon.

EXPERIMENTAL METHOD: DRAWING CONCLUSIONS REGARDING CAUSE

Correlational methods provide a number of powerful tools for furthering our understanding of the relationship between psychology and health. Besides their inability to identify cause, there are other things that these methods can't do. Perhaps the most obvious is that researchers using these methods have no control over the variables they are studying. The researchers trying to learn about social support and prostate cancer cannot control the amount of support the patients receive. They can only measure it. Similarly, they could not control the type of medical treatment the men received. If we want to learn anything definitive about the extent to which variables cause certain health outcomes, we must be able to control those variables. When we control a variable and then observe changes in a specific health outcome, we can be much more confident when drawing conclusions about that variable causing the change. This is known as the experimental method.

The language of experimental design is somewhat different from that used in correlational research. The variables researchers manipulate are called **independent variables**. The outcome variables that are measured to determine the effects of the manipulation are called **dependent variables**. In its most basic form, then, the experimental method involves manipulating independent variables to determine their effect on dependent variables.

Independent variables most often take the form of categories. In the simplest version, one group gets the manipulation (the independent variable) and another group doesn't. The group that receives the manipulation is called the **experimental group** and the group that doesn't is called the **control group**. The control group is used as a source of comparison to measure changes that can be attributable to the independent variable because, in theory, the independent variable is the only difference between the two groups. We say "in theory" because it is practically impossible to create groups that differ in only one way.

Individuals vary in many ways. Researchers using the experimental method take these individual differences into account by using **random assignment** to determine who will be in the experimental group and who will be in the control group. In this way, individual differences in such variables as intelligence and medical history, which might not be independent variables in a given study, should be evenly divided between the two groups because people have been placed randomly in the groups.

Main Effects and Interactions

A variable has a **main effect** if it alone causes a significant change in a dependent variable. Main effects certainly do occur in health psychology research, but it is much more common to find that variables *combine* to produce an effect. For example, the effects of a person's social support may combine with the amount of stress that person is experiencing to have an effect on how well the person is coping with an illness, an effect that is different from the effect of either independent variable alone. We call this combined effect an **interaction**.

In chapter 1, we introduced a number of prominent theories in health psychology. Most of these theories assume an interactional model. For example, remember that the two main elements of the theory of reasoned action are a person's attitudes toward a behaviour and his or her beliefs about what other people would do or would want him or her to do. To test this theory, we might want to manipulate these attitudes and beliefs to determine their effect on behaviour. Our assumption would be that these variables *interact*. In other words, the effect of a person's attitude toward the behaviour should depend on their beliefs about other people's thoughts regarding the behaviour.

QUASIEXPERIMENTAL DESIGNS: TAKING OUR EXPERIMENTS INTO THE FIELD

Experimental methods using laboratory settings have the advantage of control, but the disadvantage of artificiality. A method that allowed for control, yet was conducted in real-life settings would increase the ability to generalize results to applied settings. This is the objective of **quasiexperimental designs**. They are called "quasi" because researchers do relinquish some control by moving to real-life settings, but since they are still manipulating variables, they are using experimental methods. These studies are sometimes called **field research**, because they are conducted in real-life settings. Correlational studies can also fit into this broad category.

Because they attempt to strike a balance between realism and control, quasiexperimental studies can be difficult to carry out. Researchers talk about "noise" that enters into the data when they move to real-life settings. By "noise", they mean uncontrollable factors that can affect the results. For example, imagine asking an elderly patient to complete a questionnaire while in a waiting room at a hospital. She is accompanied by her daughter, who feels obliged to help her mother complete the questionnaire. As the researcher, you can urge her to let her mother complete the questionnaire alone. The daughter might even agree. Still, it is difficult to ensure that she will have no influence over her mother's responses. As a more extreme example, imagine you are having patients complete a measure of anxiety before going through a medical procedure. On one day, another patient has a heart attack in the waiting room. How would this affect the results on that day?

These examples illustrate the conundrum of field work. There are a number of inherent challenges in the enterprise. Life happens. On the one hand, these events get in the way of tidy data collection. On the other, it is *life* that researchers are trying to understand.

Matching Groups

Remember that, in a proper experiment, participants are randomly assigned to groups to ensure that extraneous variables such as age and IQ are equally distributed among the groups. In this way, the groups can be closely matched on most variables so researchers can attribute the cause of changes in the dependent variable to their manipulation (the independent variable). In quasiexperimental designs, researchers don't usually have the opportunity to randomly assign people to groups.

For example, researchers wanted to assess the effects of relaxation training on children's respiratory health (Reid, Mackinnon, & Drummond, 2001). At first glance, this seems like a straightforward study. Create two groups—one that gets the relaxation training and one that doesn't—and make upper respiratory infection scores the dependent variable. However, these researchers weren't just interested in the effects of relaxation on infection-prone children. They also wanted to know if it could benefit healthy children as well. This introduced another variable—health status. Because of this, they now had an interactional design with four groups: 1) a group of healthy children getting the relaxation training; 2) a group of infection-prone children getting the training; 3) a group of healthy children not getting the training; and 4) a group of infection-prone children not getting the training. Even this isn't particularly difficult. However, there is the problem of matching groups. The researchers cannot randomly assign children to the healthy or infection-prone groups. Therefore, they must be sure that the healthy and infection-prone children are similar in as many ways as possible. They must be matched for numerous variables such as age, family income, family structure, and other health indicators, to name just a few. This matching procedure is logistically challenging for a number of obvious reasons. One is that it can be hard to get a large enough sample size if you need to find a matching control for every experimental group participant. Another is that it can be difficult to decide how many variables need to be taken into account as matching criteria, given that the list is potentially endless. The researchers need to know which variables might be potential confounds and try to match control and experimental group participants on those.

RANDOM CLINICAL TRIAL STUDIES: ASSIGNING PARTICIPANTS TO GROUPS RANDOMLY

There are times when it is possible to randomly assign participants to groups even though the study is being conducted "in the field." In the study we just described, the health status of the children wasn't manipulated and randomly assigned, but the relaxation training variable was. In **random clinical trial studies**, participants are randomly assigned to treatment conditions. This eliminates the possibility that the treatment might work only because it attracted a certain type of person to it. In chapter 3, we introduce the early work of David Spiegel and colleagues. They randomly assigned women with breast cancer to either a support group condition or a control condition and discovered that the women in the support group condition significantly outlived the women in the control condition (Spiegel et al., 1989). This is an example of a random clinical trial study in health psychology.

Spiegel and colleagues' study did not control the medical condition. Instead, like most quasiexperimental designs, they used participants who fit within their inclusion criteria. **Inclusion criteria** are those characteristics that make a person eligible for a study. These criteria represent another challenge for people doing field research. On one hand, it is important to establish narrow enough inclusion criteria that a minimum number of confounding variables are introduced. On the other, if the inclusion criteria are too narrow the researchers could be waiting a long time before they find enough people who fit them. Also, it is important to note that results of a study cannot be generalized beyond the inclusion criteria. For example, if your inclusion criteria stipulate that children between the ages of 10 and 12 without a history of other illness are to be included, then you cannot draw conclusions about younger or older children, or children who have a host of medical conditions.

LONGITUDINAL VERSUS CROSS-SECTIONAL RESEARCH

Researchers must decide whether they are going to follow one group of people for a long period of time, or if they are going to look at a number of groups of people, each one being at a different stage of life. In the first approach, they must decide on the basic order of their work. Will they measure the variables they are interested in then monitor people to see how these variables affect their lives? Or will they find people in varying degrees of good and ill health and look back to see what variables might have brought them to this state?

The first issue we identified concerned following one group over time versus looking at different groups who were at different stages. Following one group over time is called **longitudinal research**. Using numerous groups that differ according to stage is called **cross-sectional research**. For example, if a research group was interested in the ways the needs of prostate cancer patients changed over time, they could conduct longitudinal research, in which they collected data from a group of newly diagnosed men and then continued to collect data from that same group every six months. Alternatively, they could test a wide variety of men who varied in terms of their time-since-diagnosis. They would then group these men according to stage (in six-month intervals) and compare groups in terms of their social support needs. This would be a cross-sectional approach.

The relative advantages and disadvantages of each approach are fairly obvious. Longitudinal research features fewer confounding variables than does cross-sectional research. This is because, in cross-sectional designs, there will be more differences between the groups than just time-since-diagnosis. Since it is impossible to randomly assign people to these groups, researchers have to do their best to keep track of these other differences such as age, severity of disease, marital status, and so on by either matching their groups carefully or perhaps taking these variables out of their analysis. On the other hand, researchers using a longitudinal approach will compare the same group of men at six months, one year, etc. While there will be some changes within the group in terms of severity of disease, marital status, and other variables, the differences across time will be fewer than would be expected between groups in the cross-sectional design. Also, in the longitudinal study the group will *age together*. This means that historical events, medical breakthroughs, and so on will occur at the same time for all participants.

On the other hand, longitudinal research is much more time consuming, logistically difficult and, therefore, more expensive. It is time consuming, of course, because many health problems take a long time to develop. This is good for our health but not so good for our research. Also, people don't live their lives for the convenience of longitudinal studies. They move from one city to another, they marry and change their names, they may even go to jail. For these and many other reasons, keeping a cohort together can be difficult. Just ask someone who has tried to organize a high school reunion.

Of course, one major reason for attrition in longitudinal cohorts is that people die. Researchers doing longitudinal research need to know the circumstances of these deaths. Exactly when did they occur and what were the official causes? If you were trying to answer these questions, you would need access to death certificates and, possibly, other medical records. You can just imagine trying to contact one of your participants for his six-month data collection in the prostate cancer study only to find that he had died; when you ask his wife for the cause of death and she says, "old age," or "He lost his will to live." When pressing these individuals for further details, such as whether the cancer had metastasized (spread), there is no guarantee that they will be forthcoming. And this lack of information can come after monitoring the patient for years. Certainly, you wouldn't give up at this point, but you can see that data collection can become very labour intensive.

If we wish to monitor people's health over long periods of time, longitudinal research is the ideal, though it requires rather extensive resources. However, there is a shortcut that can save time and effort. What if we started at the *end* of the timeline and moved *backward*? In other words, we could take people who have developed medical conditions, or who have died from them, and trace back in their history to find variables that would possibly explain how they came to have that condition. This is called **retrospective research**. Its advantages are clear in terms of convenience. Unfortunately, though, like so many shortcuts in research, there is a tradeoff between convenience and scientific rigour.

A classic example of this tradeoff surfaces when researchers attempt to determine a possible causal relationship between mood and cancer (some of these attempts are explored in chapter 3). If it were discovered that cancer patients are more likely to be depressed, who would be surprised? The most likely assumption is that having cancer makes people more depressed. If this work is to provide evidence for the opposite causal direction—that mood increases risk for cancer or makes cancer progress more quickly—it simply cannot be retrospective. Instead, it must be *prospective*. This means that the researchers must conduct a longitudinal study in which participants begin disease free or, at least, newly diagnosed.

COMMON FLAWS IN HEALTH PSYCHOLOGY RESEARCH

It is entirely possible that people change their behaviour when they know they are in a psychology study. They try to assess what is expected of them and either comply with that expectation or violate it. These implicit expectations that participants hold are called **demand characteristics** (Whitehouse, Orne, & Dinges, 2002; Orne, 1962). They refer to participants' beliefs regarding how they are "supposed" to respond. For example, what might be the demand characteristics when measuring patients' anxiety in a waiting room before they go in for a procedure in nuclear medicine? Possibly, a patient might think that a strong and mature person doesn't experience anxiety. Then, when you ask this patient to complete an anxiety questionnaire that features direct-item questions like, "Do you feel tense?" he or she may say, "No", because that is consistent with the perceived demands of the situation. On the other hand, the person might think, "This is obviously a study about anxiety in waiting rooms and this nice person who has asked me to complete this questionnaire is looking for anxiety, so I'll cooperate and say that I am experiencing it." Either way, the *validity* of the measure is compromised, because it is not measuring anxiety any more. Now it is measuring people's perceptions of what is expected. Demand characteristics are reduced by creating less direct measures and by assuring the participant that a wide range of responses is expected and that their responses will be kept confidential.

It is possible that simply *receiving attention* is medicinal. If this is true, then it poses some problems for researchers, since every experimental group in health psychology research receives attention. To account for the extent to which the effect of an intervention is due to the *placebo effect* of attention, researchers often include a placebo condition. In this condition, people are given general attention but not the specific intervention that constitutes the independent variable.

The potential for **experimenter bias** exists when a person who knows the hypothesis interacts with participants or interprets qualitative data. It means simply that this knowledge affects participants' responses or qualitative data interpretation. It is especially problematic when the researcher has a *vested interest* in the outcome of the study. If a researcher believes that anxiety is a problem for people about to go through medical procedures, then he or she can interact with the participant in such a way that anxiety is either induced or at least expected. This won't necessarily be done consciously, but it can have a powerful effect all the same.

Some of the most extensive longitudinal, prospective research investigating cancer-prone personality types has been criticized because the principal investigators did much of the interviewing that yielded the personality types (Amelang, 1997). Attempts to replicate studies substantiating the claim that there is a cancer-prone personality have often been unsuccessful. The original investigators have countered by claiming that the collection of personality data at the outset of the study must be done in a particular way for it to yield information on the cancer-prone type (Grossarth-Maticek, Eysenck, & Vetter, 1997). The reply to this claim, of course, is that the personality typing is the result of experimenter bias rather than of interviewer skill. The way to avoid experimenter bias is to, whenever possible, use people to collect data who are *blind* to the hypothesis or at least to which group a participant has been placed into. In this case, "blind" simply means unaware. Research on the cancer-prone personality is discussed in chapter 3.

People who take part in health psychology research must consent to do so. This is essential for ethical reasons. Nonetheless, it can result in a problem called **sampling bias**. This means that some variable or factor is shared by the people who take part in the study, which makes them somehow different from the population the researchers are studying. One form of sampling bias is quite straightforward—a researcher simply selects participants whom he or she expects to behave in ways consistent with the hypothesis (the researcher's prediction regarding results). This blatant form of bias isn't common, however. Instead, the most common form occurs because there is a certain type of person who is more likely to volunteer for a particular study, making a certain amount of sampling bias unavoidable. The best that can be done is to have a large sample of participants and hope that the sample is representative. People conducting survey research can at least use random sampling procedures in the way they send out their surveys or approach people to complete them. Still, there is the potential for bias in the sample that chooses to complete and return the surveys.

Focused Module B

Epidemiology: What Can Be Learned from the SARS Outbreak in Canada?

On February 23, 2003, a 78-year-old woman took a flight from Hong Kong to Toronto. What would normally have been an everyday occurrence changed the lives of many people living in Canada. This was because the woman was suffering from Severe Acute Respiratory Syndrome (SARS). When she arrived in Toronto, she became the first case of SARS in Canada. What followed was an outbreak of this infectious disease that, in Canada, resulted in 250 probable cases and 40 deaths by mid-June of 2003.[1]

An outbreak such as this, featuring an illness that is new to the country and virtually new to the world, demands fast and decisive action. Before cures can be found, the nature of the disease itself must be determined. The detective work on this falls primarily to epidemiologists who are trained to trace disease patterns and draw conclusions regarding the cause of the disease and how it is spread.

Epidemiology literally means the study of epidemics. More specifically, it is the study of incidence rates, prevalence rates, and locations of health-related phenomena. Epidemiologists chart *patterns* of health and disease (primarily disease) across populations and geographic areas, studying the origin and distribution of health problems (Cockerham, 1998). It is truly biopsychosocial in nature. People working in the field include everyone from sociologists to physicians to meteorologists (for such things as air pollution data). Psychologists also work with epidemiological data. As we will see in this Module, a basic understanding of illness patterns is very helpful to health psychologists.

THE LANGUAGE OF EPIDEMIOLOGY

To do their work, epidemiologists often start with a single case, then trace back to its starting point. From there, they determine how widespread the problem has become. They then

---

1 Details regarding the SARS outbreak in Toronto have been taken from a Health Canada Report entitled "Epi-Update: Interim Report on the SARS outbreak in the Greater Toronto Area, Ontario, Canada, April 24, 2003." Accessed on July 29, 2003 from: http://www.hc-sc.gc.ca/pphb-dgspsp/sars-sras/pef-dep/gta-20030424_e.html

try to identify factors shared by all people with the problem. The goal is to identify causes so the problem can be eliminated or at least controlled. In doing this work, epidemiologists use terminology that health psychologists need to be familiar with.

For example, a **case** is one instance of the problem. The **index case** is the first identified case. In the SARS outbreak, the 78-year-old woman who arrived from Hong Kong was the index case. When she was admitted to hospital, she was visited by her family. As a result, six of them contracted SARS. Three of these family members visited their physician, who was then infected as well. One of the family members (Case B) went to a hospital emergency department on March 7, 2003. During his treatment in ER, the disease spread to two other patients (Cases C and D) who were nearby. One of these patients (Case C) was admitted to intensive care on March 16, 2003 and, in the process, transmitted the disease to two paramedics, a firefighter, and four hospital staff. Three members of Case C's family also contracted SARS.

Soon, other hospitals became involved, as did groups of people who were believed to have been exposed to probable cases outside hospital settings. As a result, the number of cases in Toronto increased dramatically over a short period of time. In the language of epidemiology, this meant an increase in the **incidence rate**, which is the number of new cases of the problem in a set period of time. For example, if an epidemiologist says that there were 30 cases of X reported in the past two weeks, that would be its incidence rate. Epidemiologists use incidence rates to determine whether a problem is on the rise or if it is waning. The word "outbreak," as in "SARS outbreak," often refers to incidence rates. On the other hand, **prevalence** refers to the total number of cases that exist at any given time, including existing and new cases. **Point prevalence** refers to prevalence at a given point in time. **Lifetime prevalence** refers to the total number of people who have ever had the problem, even if the problem went away or if they died from it. Cancer rates are often reported in terms of lifetime prevalence, which presents the proportion of people who have ever had the disease. Cancer rates are often reported as proportions of the population, for example, the number of cases found per 100 000 people. We reported cases this way in chapter 11 when we talked about chronic and life-threatening illness.

There are many important psychological issues related to outbreaks. For example, it is often the case that the general public exaggerates the danger, creating a certain degree of hysteria. For the SARS outbreak, Canada decided to report both *probable* and *suspect* cases. The former refers to people who are showing all the defining symptoms and have been exposed to the disease. The latter refers to people who are displaying some of the symptoms but very possibly have not been exposed. Suspect cases rarely become probable cases. In British Columbia, there were 4 probable cases and 46 suspect cases. Because of this reporting strategy, the general public is presented with numbers that inaccurately reflect the risk of the disease. Also, the media might report lifetime prevalence numbers. These numbers would include people who had SARS and are recovered. This also results in an inflation of the magnitude of the problem.

This is not to say that SARS was not serious. It just hasn't been as serious as some members of the general public have come to believe. Some people began wearing surgical masks to protect themselves from a disease they had very little chance of being exposed to, and despite the fact that the masks probably did nothing to protect the wearer.

As we learned in chapter 7, on Health Promotion, fear does not always motivate people to engage in healthy behaviours. In the case of outbreak-induced panic, there is no guarantee that people will report symptoms promptly. Instead, they may try to carry on with their normal lives, and risk the health of others by riding public transit and coming into contact with many other people.

THE STEPS INVOLVED IN EPIDEMIOLOGICAL RESEARCH

The first step in epidemiological research is to establish a pattern of the problem and identify **agents** (Cockerham, 1998). These are the means by which the problem spreads. There are five types of agent: biological, nutritional, chemical, physical, and social/behavioural. For SARS, the agent was biological (coronavirus).

After an agent has been identified, epidemiologists look for **hosts**. These are the carriers of the agents. In human disease, human hosts are those people who are most susceptible to a given agent. Epidemiologists can determine if a given agent is travelling through a certain age group, or perhaps through people who have been in a certain area. For SARS, older people were most vulnerable. The 78-year-old woman who represented the index case, had come recently from the Metropole Hotel in the Kowloon district of Hong Kong. This hotel was the site of many cases of SARS.

There are other ways that agents are transmitted in addition to using hosts. For example, there are **vectors**. These are living organisms that can transfer an agent from one host to another (Prescott, Harley, and Klein, 1999). A good example of a vector is the *Anopheles* mosquito, which carries malaria. Also, there are **vehicles**. These are non-living media involved in the transmission of an agent (Prescott, Harley, and Klein, 1999). Biologists and epidemiologists describe transmission by way of vehicles as being water-borne, food-borne, or air-borne, depending upon the vehicle. For example, tuberculosis adheres to dust and then becomes air-borne (Prescott, Harley, and Klein, 1999). SARS could be transmitted through air-borne droplets.

The final step epidemiologists take is to propose strategies for control of the agent. Quarantine is a common step. After the final step, the process starts again to see if there are other agents and hosts or if the control measures have worked.

TRACING THE SPREAD OF AIDS

We have looked at some of the epidemiology of SARS. AIDS is another disease that epidemiologists have played an important role in attempting to control. The first known cases of AIDS began emerging in New York, San Francisco, and Los Angeles in 1979 (Cockerham, 1998). These cases attracted attention, in part, because they were defined by rare forms of cancer, such as Kaposi's sarcoma, and a particular type of pneumonia called *Pneumocystis carinii*. By 1981, physicians' reports about the disease were coming into the Centers for Disease Control in Atlanta, Georgia, and epidemiologists went to work identifying hosts and agents (Cockerham, 1998). At this time, the **prevalence** was about 50 cases. However, through the early 1980s, the **incidence** rate began to skyrocket. Within three years, the number of cases went from 50 to over 4900 in the United States. By 1995, the number had risen to over 500 000 (Cockerham, 1998).

At first, it was thought that the *agent* was a drug used by some gay men to enhance sexual experience, but interview data ruled this out when it revealed that men who used the drug were not infected with AIDS (Cockerham, 1998). Then, when a number of intravenous drug users and one transfusion patient (a baby in San Francisco) contracted AIDS, the search for an agent became biological; that is epidemiologists started suspecting a virus. The tracing of sexual partners as hosts supported this hypothesis.

This tracing of sexual partners of those first showing symptoms of AIDS in North America led back, eventually, to one person. This was the so-called "patient zero," a flight attendant from Canada named Gaetan Dugas (Taylor, 1999). After being located, Dugas estimated that he had had 2500 sexual partners in the 10 years prior to being identified (Taylor, 1999).

An analysis of the dramatic spread of the AIDS epidemic in sub-Saharan Africa, where nine percent of adults are infected (*AIDS epidemic update*, 2002), illustrates how sociological and anthropological factors can help to explain epidemiological data. In Africa, unlike North America, AIDS is spread primarily through sexual intercourse among heterosexuals. The economy of central Africa is such that there are many male migrant workers (Cockerham, 1998). Their movement from place to place facilitates the spread of the virus. In general, women in central Africa do not have the power to demand condom use or abstinence. From this analysis, we can see that economic, geographic, social, and cultural factors explain the proliferation of AIDS in central Africa (Cockerham, 1998).

Focused Module C

Complementary and

Alternative Medicine

Tyrell Dueck was a boy from Saskatchewan who died of cancer when he was 13 years old. For religious reasons, Tyrell's parents refused the treatment prescribed by oncologists, which would have involved chemotherapy and possible leg amputation. A Saskatchewan court ordered them to follow the oncologist's treatment but they refused. Instead, they took Tyrell to a clinic in Tijuana, Mexico, where he received treatments using laetrile and shark cartilage. Unfortunately, the treatments were unsuccessful and Tyrell returned to Canada, where he died in a Saskatchewan hospital.

The story of Tyrell Dueck reminds us that not everyone embraces the Western medical establishment. The use of medical treatments that are not the product of what has been called conventional medical science continues to grow in popularity. For this reason, health psychologists must develop an understanding of the many issues associated with the use of complementary and alternative therapies.

THE LANGUAGE OF CAM

Defining what is meant by "complementary" and "alternative" is no easy task. At one point, these were defined as therapies that were not normally part of medical school curricula, but these curricula have changed enough to make the definition obsolete (Thorne, Paterson, Russell, & Schultz, 2002). More comprehensive definitions contrast complementary and alternative medicine (CAM) with that which is dominant within a health care system or culture (Achilles, 2000). Such definitions say more about what CAM is *not* than what it is.

A number of different terms have been used to identify treatments that fall outside normative Western medical practice. Each carries its own set of connotations and implied set of values. As such, the terminology of the area makes for a good starting point.

We have used the terms *complementary* and *alternative* in the heading to this module. They are a pair of terms that are commonly used to describe the field. Although the terms are used together, they do not mean the same thing. **Complementary treatment** is used in conjunction with so-called allopathic treatments. **Allopathic treatment** features biomedical attempts to cure sickness by creating conditions in the body that oppose the disease (Clarke, 1996). This definition of complementary treatment implies that patients must be aware of potential interactions between the allopathic treatment and the complementary one, since they are being used simultaneously.

Alternative treatment is the term given to treatments that are not allopathic. Its use implies that the patient has either rejected allopathic treatment, given up on it, or perhaps is ignorant of it. Some may infer that the term "alternative" carries a certain attractive value, as in "viable alternative," or even "better alternative." In keeping with this, it has been suggested that proponents of such treatments were the ones to coin the term (Beyerstein, 1997). In contrast, others may consider the term to be pejorative, implying that such treatments are not mainstream and, as such, are marginalized. In other words, the implication is that they are not your best choice, but are an "alternative."

Others make the distinction between *traditional* and *non-traditional* treatments. However, this distinction is usually rejected by anthropologists because it implies that there is a single tradition, that being allopathic medicine. This contradicts the fact that many remedies called "alternative" have been around for centuries. Still others distinguish between "conventional" and "unconventional therapy" (UT). Some authors have argued that *unconventional* is the least pejorative of all the terms used to describe these treatments (Fitch et al., 1999). Not everyone interprets the word *unconventional* in neutral terms, however.

Finally, it has been suggested that the most useful dichotomy is between treatments that work and those that don't. From this point of view, other terms such as *alternative*, *unconventional*, *traditional*, or the less-often used term *frontier*, are unnecessary.

The conclusion that we can draw from this dilemma is that there is probably no single term that everyone is going to be comfortable with regarding such therapies. We have chosen the CAM terminology because, at the very least, those terms draw a useful distinction between treatment followed in conjunction with, and that used instead of allopathic regimens.

HOW PREVALENT IS THE USE OF COMPLEMENTARY AND ALTERNATIVE MEDICINE?

If complementary and alternative therapies were rarely used, they would not be such an important topic of discussion. However, this certainly isn't the case. A study conducted in 1999 revealed that 70 percent of Canadians had used one or more natural health products in the past six months (de Bruyn, 2000). Forty-six percent of patients with inflammatory bowel disease reported using CAM (Hilsden, Verhoef, Best, & Pocobelli, 2003). There is a discrepancy, though, between the number of people pursuing CAM and the number consulting a CAM practitioner. Only 24 percent of Canadians did the latter in 1999 (de Bruyn, 2000). For serious illnesses, such as head and neck cancer, it has been shown that 23 percent of patients had sought CAM for their cancer and 39 percent had used CAM more generally (Warrick et al., 1999). Another study found that 46 percent of parents whose children had cancer were using CAM for their child (Gagnon & Recklitis, 2003).

A study of brain tumour patients in southern Alberta found that 24 percent of them were using complementary therapy (Verhoef et al., 1999). Interestingly, these researchers in this study became interested in CAM when they discovered that some of their patients had a distinctive orange colour on their hands. It turned out that these patients were using beta carotene as a complementary treatment.

From all these studies, we can conclude that CAM is anything but rare. Indeed, it is likely that these figures represent an under-reporting of CAM use. A study in the United

States estimated that just under 39 percent of alternative therapy use was being disclosed by patients to their physicians (Eisenberg et al., 1998, cited in Wong, 1999). In the southern Alberta study, 45 percent of the patients said their doctors were aware of their alternative therapy use. This means that practitioners and health psychologists need to know more about CAM in terms of its perceived effectiveness and the reasons why patients pursue it. This need is underscored by evidence that the use of CAM is increasing steadily (de Bruyn, 2000). Also, CAM is big business. In Canada, it has been estimated that $3.8 billion was spent on CAM in 1996 and 1997 (de Bruyn, 2000).

SOME EXAMPLES OF COMPLEMENTARY AND ALTERNATIVE MEDICINE

It is important to realize that CAM covers a very wide and diverse collection of treatments. These range from the conservative, such as certain lifestyle changes (exercise and relaxation training), to what Beyerstein (1997) has called the "patently absurd" (p. 149), such as crystal healing. Of the many substances that may be prescribed as part of CAM regimens, some are herbal (such as echinacea), some animal or vegetable derivative (such as shark cartilage or mushrooms), some macrobiotic, and others vitamin (as in the beta carotene used by brain tumour patients). Some other CAM procedures do not require the ingestion of substances. These include such treatments as acupuncture and various forms of homeopathy (Verhoef et al., 1999).

HOW EFFECTIVE IS CAM?

Research on the effectiveness of complementary and alternative therapies varies considerably in its rigour and comprehensiveness from one therapy to the next. In general, these therapies are not well researched in terms of methodology or number of studies. This is gradually changing, however. The "gold standard" by which therapies of any type tend to be judged is the random clinical trial (RCT), and we are now seeing more RCT studies published assessing complementary and alternative therapies (Holdcraft, Assefi, & Buchwald, 2003; Weiger et al., 2002). See Focused Module B, Research Methods in Health Psychology, for a review of RCT logic.

There are those, however, who argue that RCT methodology does not always provide a valid assessment of the potential benefits of CAM (Verhoef, Casebeer, & Hilsden, 2002). For example, there has been a great deal of research on the vitamins A, C, and E and their potential role in the prevention and treatment of cancer (though considerably more on prevention than on treatment) (Kaegi, 1998a). Since it is widely accepted that a diet rich in fresh fruits and vegetables reduces the risk of some cancers and that these foods contain vitamins A, C, and E, it seems reasonable to investigate the potential of supplements of these vitamins as cancer treatments. Further indirect support for their use in cancer treatment comes from studies that have reported an enhancement in immune functioning associated with them. These effects are more common for vitamins A and C than for E. It also must be noted, however, that the dosages required to bring about real therapeutic effects, as opposed to measurable immune system enhancement, might be too high to be practical or even safe (Weiger et al., 2002). It appears that more research is required in this area.

For practitioners, some helpful literature reviews have been produced (Weiger et al., 2002). Also, resources such as the Cochrane library produce many useful reviews (http://www.update-software.com/cochrane/, accessed August 2, 2003). The conclusions from these reviews can be placed generally into one of three categories: 1) a therapy has been proven beneficial and, therefore should be encouraged or prescribed; 2) a therapy has been proven harmful and should be discouraged; or 3) a therapy has not been proven beneficial or harmful. Among the harmful therapies are those that interact poorly or even dangerously with other therapies. For example, high dose vitamin therapy can cause problems when taken concurrently with radiation or chemotherapy (Weiger et al., 2002).

The last conclusion, that a therapy is neither harmful nor beneficial, is a very common one in CAM studies. In these cases, the practitioner is left to decide if there are non-medical benefits to the patient's use of the therapy. We will discuss these in a moment when we talk about reasons why people choose CAM. Often, there are such benefits, in terms of the patient's sense of control and optimism, though false hopes can be a justified concern for practitioners.

A paper in the *Canadian Medical Association Journal* entitled, "A Patient's Guide to Choosing Unconventional Therapies" (Kaegi, 1998b) generated debate among its readers. In it, Kaegi provided detailed advice for the potential consumer of what she called "unconventional therapies." For example, she cautioned people to do the research before choosing, to ask practitioners for their credentials, to check for possible interactions with conventional therapy before committing to unconventional therapy, and to know one's comfort level regarding such therapy. This all seems like sound advice except that, for patients, doing the research isn't as easy as it sounds. Kaegi herself generally concluded that the research on the treatments she reviewed was still inconclusive. Others have argued that patients usually aren't assertive enough to ask for a practitioner's credentials or, if shown them, don't have the expertise to evaluate them (Tannock & Warr, 1998).

WHO USES COMPLEMENTARY AND ALTERNATIVE MEDICINE AND WHY

You may draw the conclusion that, given the paucity of current research proving the effectiveness of CAM, the only people who would use it would be those who aren't in a position to make educated choices. If you drew this general conclusion, however, you would be wrong. Warrick and colleagues' (1999) analysis of head and neck cancer patients found more use in patients who were younger, had postsecondary education, and were in upper income brackets. These findings are consistent with other similar analyses. In their study of brain tumour patients in southern Alberta, Verhoef and colleagues (1999) found that alternative therapy was more commonly used among younger patients.

Why do patients pursue alternative therapies? The reasons for using alternative therapies will, of course, vary considerably from person to person and from condition to condition. The Alberta brain tumour patients tended to talk about needing to take charge of their treatment, and pursuing alternative therapies provided them with the feeling they were doing that (Verhoef et al., 1999). Other studies have also found that increasing one's sense of personal control is a motivating factor in alternative treatment choice (e.g., Seidl & Stewart, 1998). Menopausal patients have said that some alternative therapies are more natural and holistic. On a related theme, these same patients expressed concerns with possible side effects and risks of allopathic methods. Still others reported that they have found CAM to be a more user-friendly approach to health (Seidl & Stewart, 1998).

Taken collectively, these reasons depict a patient who is interested in self-care and wants to manage it. As such, the use of CAM is not merely the result of rejection of conventional medicine (Thorne et al., 2002; Verhoef & White, 2002). This is an important point for practitioners to keep in mind.

Other research (Nam et al., 1999) indicates that people who attend support groups may be more likely to use complementary or alternative therapy. The study looked at men who either had prostate cancer or were considered at high risk for the disease, as defined by family history and abnormal prostate specific-antigen (PSA) scores. Among the high-risk men, 80 percent of those attending support groups were using complementary therapies, compared to 26 percent who were interviewed in a clinic. Of all the patients using CAM, 24 percent did not tell their urologist they were doing so.

One explanation for the effect of support group attendance on CAM usage might be that information about CAM is more available to support group attenders. Consistent with this possibility, another study of prostate cancer patients discovered that attenders of support groups were significantly more likely to cite fellow patients as their main source of informational support; whereas, non-attenders cited medical staff in this category (Poole et al., 2001).

Focused Module D

Medical Sociology

Psychology is not the only social science that has made a significant contribution to our understanding of health and health care. Anthropology, economics, geography, and sociology, just to name a few, have also done so. In this module, we look at medical sociology, which dovetails well with psychology to help us understand the forces that shape our health.

Sociology is "the study of social causes and consequences of behaviour" (Cockerham, 1998, p. 1). Sociologists study groups, institutions, and society. According to Clarke (2000), medical sociology is "the study of the ways the institutionalized medical system constructs what it deems to be illness out of what is recognized as signs and symptoms, and constitutes its response to such 'illness' through the treatments it prescribes" (p. 4).

Health psychologists, who tend to study health-related phenomena on a more individual level, can work well with medical sociologists. For example, in Chapter 3 we explored psychoneuroimmunology (PNI), which is the study of the ways in which our psychological states might affect our health. Research in PNI reveals physiological reasons why stress can be unhealthy. It focuses on the cellular level; specifically, the workings of the immune system. But what about some of the causes of that stress? Knowing what you know about PNI, would it surprise you to learn that illness tends to follow unemployment trends? Probably not. However, as soon as we introduce trends of this type into the analysis, we are no longer working at a microscopic level. Now we are working at the level of medical sociology.

Clarke (2000) asks why there is a moratorium on silicone breast implants in the United States and Canada (Holmich et al., 2003; Muller, 1996)? Is it because of a biomedical discovery or because of mass social action? Medical sociologists would say that this development is due more to the latter than the former.

THE SICK ROLE

Roles are sets of behaviours, attributes, and expectations that are institutionally defined. For example, the institution of family yields roles of father, mother, daughter, son, and so on. According to well-known sociologist Talcott Parsons (1951), the medical institution has created something called the **sick role**. People who legitimately adopt the sick role are temporarily exempt from their other roles. Because sick people can no longer perform their other roles adequately, the sick role was created to prevent social breakdown. We say that people adopting the sick role are *temporarily* exempt because the role is defined in such a way that people can't opt out of their other roles permanently and still keep the social organization functioning. Therefore, one defining characteristic of the sick role is that it can't be assumed indefinitely. Anyone who tries to do so will be given a different label, like malingerer, for example.

Roles carry with them certain rights and duties. People adopting the sick role have two duties. First, they must be trying to get well. Second, they should be seeking technically competent help and cooperating with the prescribed regimen. If someone were to shirk one of these duties, he or she would lose the rights of the sick role. There are two of these. First, as we have said, a person adopting the sick role is temporarily exempt from other responsibilities. Second, the person is not responsible for his or her condition, and so can't be blamed for his or her incapacitation.

Parsons' notion of the sick role has come under some criticism. For example, the reality is that the extent to which a person is held responsible for his or her incapacitation varies by condition. Also, with today's emphasis on health promotion and healthy lifestyles, people are being held more personally responsible for their health. This should mean that fewer people can legitimately adopt the sick role. Also, some people associate certain diseases with a person's moral worth; thus people with such diseases might have a more difficult time adopting the sick role. Indeed, it is generally the case that people with socially stigmatized diseases (such as sexually transmitted diseases) are not afforded sick-role status (Clarke, 2000).

You will remember that people must be trying to get well to be given sick-role status. But what about those people who may want to get well but cannot? These people must make long-term adaptations and in so doing come to take on another role, such as "disabled," or "impaired," or "chronically ill."

Sociologists refer to a person's *master status*. This is the status that reflects the person's most prominent position in society. This may stem from such things as his or her occupation, family role, or position in the community. A person's disease status should not become his or her master status, because the sick-role status normally intervenes. However, because AIDS is stigmatizing and chronic, people with this disease often find that their disease status does become their master status. Disease status overwhelms other aspects of their identity, and this can make coping with the disease all the more difficult.

Criticism of the sick role construct has also been levelled at the duty to cooperate with technically competent help. This duty is often interpreted in such a way that to be granted sick-role status, a person must accept the biomedical model. According to this interpretation, people seeking what are currently called complementary or alternative treatments would not be afforded the sick role. If the Western medical establishment is the gatekeeper of sick-role status, then this institution becomes even more powerful and dominant.

Indeed, from the perspective of medical sociologists, the medical establishment is seen as an agent of social control. There are at least two forms that this control takes. First, it dictates the conferring of sick-role status. Second, from this perspective, sickness is viewed as a form of deviation from the norm, and sick people need to be brought back to that norm. In what is often called Western society, the medical establishment holds the responsibility for doing this. As an indication of this, think of conditions that are viewed today as illnesses that were once considered to be religious or legal transgressions (hint: some of the best examples come from psychiatry).

CONFLICT THEORY AND THE RIGHTING OF INJUSTICES

Another school of thought in sociology argues that structures do not simply exist; rather, they exist in *conflict*. This is an important assumption of **conflict theory**. This theory has a long history in medical sociology. As early as 1845, Fredrich Engels, a collaborator with Karl Marx, made the point that inequality in living conditions and the emergence of capitalism in England had negative effects on people's health. To maximize profits, companies paid their workers poorly, forcing them to live in slums. These living conditions became breeding grounds for infectious diseases such as typhoid. Conflict theory, then, can be very useful when trying to understand socioeconomic differences in health status.

Modern multinational corporations have been accused of exploitation that is not dissimilar to that practised by their nineteenth century counterparts. Clarke (2000) points out that the Great Lakes, which supply drinking water for over 40 million people in Canada and the United States, also serve as a dumping site for industrial and municipal waste. Clarke also reminds us that it is the poor, those who cannot afford to drink bottled water or move to affluent suburbs well removed from toxic locations, who suffer the worst health effects of this pollution.

Proponents of conflict theory might also argue that the state tends to deflect responsibility for ill health away from governmental responsibility and focus it on the individual. Health then becomes a "commodity with a certain value in the marketplace" (Clarke, 2000, p. 28). These theorists would argue that research conducted by and funded by institutions within that marketplace, like pharmaceutical companies, cannot be expected to produce findings that are self-critical, hence the need for health-related research from the social sciences and humanities.

SYMBOLIC INTERACTIONISM: UNCOVERING SUBJECTIVE MEANING IN HEALTH AND HEALTH CARE

Sociologists also take a more microscopic look at social factors by analyzing the interactions between people and by interviewing people to determine the meaning they attach to events. When these researchers adopt the perspective of **symbolic interactionism**, they are assuming that people's interpretations of their interactions and the events of their lives go well beyond the actual words used or, in the case of health-related events, the diagnosis they are given. As is the case with much of sociology, another assumption here is that reality is *socially constructed* rather than objective. In other words, we piece together our version of the world by interacting with others and construing our own interpretation of that world.

Medical sociologists using symbolic interactionism often use **transcript analysis** in their research. As the term implies, they record interactions with patients then transcribe them to paper. They are particularly interested in the pauses between turns in a conversation, which can be very meaningful in an interaction between a physician and a patient. Another research method is the in-depth interview. For example, a person with arthritis may be interviewed at length to determine the meaning the person attaches to having that illness. It may be associated with aging, frustration, loss of control, or being pitied by others. The possibilities are numerous. The point is that it is the *person with the illness* who determines the meaning.

Researchers adopting this approach make a distinction between disease and illness. **Disease** refers to the physical pathology. **Illness** refers to the subjective experience of having that pathology. From this perspective, it is possible for two people to have the same disease but different illnesses. This distinction is rarely made in medical settings. It is the *illness* that sociologists try to understand. For example, two people with very similar tissue damage from a heart attack may have very different subjective experiences as a result. One may be motivated to re-prioritize his or her life and make the most of each day; another might live each successive day in fear and become an invalid unnecessarily.

Psychologists who use the theory of reasoned action, introduced in chapter 1, may do well to consider the tenets of symbolic interaction. You may remember that one important component of the theory of reasoned action is social norms—that collection of beliefs regarding what other people would do and would want us to do. Sociologists would remind us that, by interacting with others to establish these social norms, we are also constructing a social reality. The person then decides on a course of action based on this constructed meaning of the illness.

FEMINIST THEORY AS APPLIED TO HEALTH AND HEALTH CARE

In chapter 6, we discussed gender issues related to health care, specifically from the perspective of the practitioner. We could have adopted a more sociological perspective on those issues by applying feminist theory. In terms of health care, feminist theory focuses on at least three important topics. First, it makes salient the fact that women's health concerns are both biologically and socially different from men's. For example, stress-related medical conditions are different for women because the causes of their stress can be different. Women's stress is more likely to stem from **role strain**, in which a woman is expected to perform two or more roles that compete for her time and, in addition, may be in conflict with one another. This is compounded by the social fact that women still find themselves in subdominant positions, with little control compared to men.

A second topic concerns the fact that socially constructed meanings of health experiences have historically been male dominated. For example, one measure of the seriousness of an illness is the number of days a person misses from work. This is fairly easy to assess if that work takes place outside the home and is salaried. On the other hand, "days missed" are harder to quantify when the work is being done in the home. Traditionally, this situation has applied to women more than to men. More to the point, women may well argue that, when it comes to tasks like child-rearing, there is no such thing as a "day missed," regardless of one's health.

Third, we know that the health care system has been male dominated. This can make it more difficult for women to find practitioners who can empathize with and legitimize their health concerns. Feminists have been vocal in their attempts to raise awareness regarding these three issues and to change the health care system accordingly. As a result, feminist theory has had a tangible impact on health care and, indeed, on health psychology.

SUMMARY

Now that you have been introduced to medical sociology, think of the ways in which health psychologists and medical sociologists can collaborate. In what ways are the two fields similar? In what ways are they different? Clearly, they share a mutual concern for the improvement of health, as the World Health Organization defines health—not just the absence of disease, but the ability to live a life of reasonable quality. We hope that you can appreciate how sociologists and psychologists differ in their **unit of analysis**. For psychologists, it is the individual; for sociologists, it is people in groups, organizations, and societies. This isn't to say, of course, that psychologists aren't interested in social phenomena. However, the "bottom line" for psychologists tends to be how these phenomena affect the individual.

Focused Module E

Aboriginal Health

In chapter 11, on chronic and life-threatening illnesses, we made specific reference to Aboriginal health issues as they pertained to diabetes and HIV/AIDS. In this module, we will explore a wider range of issues related to Aboriginal health. There are many inequities and serious challenges that are revealed by this exploration; indeed, far more than we could adequately cover here.

WHO ARE CANADA'S ABORIGINAL PEOPLES?

Canada's Aboriginal population is not homogeneous. In fact, the term *Aboriginal* refers to a variety of groups in Canada. The language that is used, both officially and colloquially, to describe these groups carries its own collection of connotations. Our language is derived from documents produced by Health Canada. These documents make reference to four groups under the general heading "Aboriginal." These are: First Nations people, who include North American Indians registered under the Indian Act; North American Indians not registered; Métis people; and Inuit people (*The need for an Aboriginal Health Institute in Canada*, 2003). Some of the issues discussed under the heading of "Aboriginal Health" apply to all these groups. Some, however, do not.

The population of Aboriginal groups is growing faster than the general population in Canada. The Aboriginal population is generally younger as a result. Thirty-eight percent of that population is under the age of 15, compared to 21 percent of Canada's general population. Many of the health challenges faced by our Aboriginal peoples, therefore, relate to youth.

HEALTH CHALLENGES

For reasons that we will discuss in the next section, the health of our Aboriginal population is considerably poorer than that of other segments. Figures from the mid-1990s reveal that life expectancy for First Nations people is seven to eight years shorter than for the non-Aboriginal population. General violence, physical abuse, and sexual abuse are more common in Aboriginal communities, as are accidental deaths and injury among children. Add to this list infectious diseases, such as tuberculosis and AIDS, which are also more prevalent among Aboriginal peoples (*The need for an Aboriginal Health Institute in Canada*, 2003). Further challenges are presented in the form of substance abuse, which is recognized by members of Aboriginal communities as a serious problem (*Literature Review: Evaluation Strategies in Aboriginal Substance Abuse Programs: A Discussion*, 2002).

All of these challenges are significant, though two have received increased attention because of their severity. These are children's health and diabetes. We looked at diabetes in the Aboriginal population in chapter 11 (see box 11.1). Add to those statistics a University of Manitoba study showing that Type II diabetes is four times as prevalent among First Nations people in that province (Martens et al., 2002).

Children's health is a particular concern in Aboriginal communities, where 50 percent of children live in poverty (*The need for an Aboriginal Health Institute in Canada*, 2003). The good news is that infant mortality rates are declining in these communities, though they are still double the Canadian average (*The need for an Aboriginal Health Institute in Canada*, 2003). Injury and accident-related death rates are four times greater than for non-Aboriginal children. And suicide rates are significantly higher.

As we have mentioned, substance abuse is another major problem, though this varies depending upon which Aboriginal population is being studied. In some cases, general consumption of alcohol might be lower for a given group compared to the non-Aboriginal population; however, a concentrated percentage of that Aboriginal group might be drinking to excess (*Literature Review: Evaluation Strategies in Aboriginal Substance Abuse Programs: A Discussion*, 2002). Solvent use is a problem particular to youth. Recent data on solvent use is hard to come by, though studies in the mid-80s conducted in Manitoba and Québec revealed that two to three percent of Aboriginal youth were using solvents beyond an experimental level and their median age was 12 to 13 years (Layne, 1987). Reliable figures for other substances, such as drugs, are difficult to find. However, studies from the 1980s and 1990s in Saskatchewan (*Alcohol and drug abuse among treaty Indians in Saskatchewan: Needs assessment and recommendations for change*, 1984) and Manitoba (Gfellner & Hundleby, 1995) report higher-than-average drug use for Aboriginal persons.

SOME CAUSES

Many explanations have been proposed for the health problems documented in this module. These cover the full range of the biopsychosocial model. We agree with the belief that all Canadians, regardless of background, experience similar health problems when living in conditions similar to those of our Aboriginal peoples (*The need for an Aboriginal Health Institute in Canada*, 2003). These conditions feature poverty, poor education, poor recreational and social opportunities, a loss of cultural identity, and poverty and unemployment (Scott, 1994). In this context, substance abuse becomes a coping strategy, albeit an unsuccessful one.

SOLVING THE PROBLEMS

What is being done to help our Aboriginal population meet their health challenges? This is not a problem that governments can simply "throw money at," though funding is certainly necessary. Rather, solutions will be found by building partnerships among government, our Aboriginal peoples, and Canada's population at large. These partnerships must work at the community level because the Aboriginal tradition is such that well-being of the individual is rooted in the health of the community (*Volume III: Gathering strength*, 1996).

Many programs focused at the community level have been called for and initiated by such national organizations as the First Nations and Inuit Health Branch (FNIHB) and the Assembly of First Nations Health Secretariat.

When you peruse table E.1, you will find that women's and children's health is one of the priorities identified by the Assembly of First Nations. Programs addressing this priority could provide information regarding fetal alcohol syndrome (FAS) and fetal alcohol effect (FAE). This problem stems directly from the substance abuse problems we discussed earlier. FAS can result from alcohol consumption during pregnancy. It is manifest in a number of ways, including pre-or postnatal growth retardation, central nervous system abnormalities, and facial abnormalities (Robinson, Armstrong, Brendle-Moczuk, & Loock, 1992). FAE is typically less severe, featuring behavioural problems such as hyperactivity, social problems, and learning disabilities. In fact, prenatal exposure to alcohol is now thought to be associated with more subtle problems in judgment and reasoning in people of otherwise normal intelligence (Robinson et al., 1992).

TABLE E-1	Assembly of First Nations Health Secretariat Health Priorities

- Building and sustaining First Nations health and health care systems
- Creating a comprehensive First Nations health research and info-structure
- Resolving outstanding jurisdictional issues between the federal and provincial governments
- Establishing a national First Nations mental health program
- Developing comprehensive First Nations children's and gender-related health policy frameworks
- Obtaining the resources for smoking prevention, cessation and treatment programs
- Providing an infrastructure to address environmental health problems such as poor drinking water.

Adapted from the Assembly of First Nations Health Secretariat (http://www.afn.ca/Programs/health%20secretariat/health.htm, Accessed November 15, 2003)

Another priority of the Assembly of First Nations is the building of a sustainable First Nations health and health care system. This could be supported by trained paraprofessionals within these communities, and it must be assured that their roles are clear and valued by other health professionals (Minore & Boone, 2002). Bruce Minore and Margaret Boone, from the Centre for Rural and Northern Health Research at Lakehead University, have studied the work of Aboriginal paraprofessionals working in the communities of Northern Ontario.

A study of these communities reminds us that our Aboriginal population lives in every possible setting within the country. Unlike their urban counterparts, Inuit and First Nations people in Northern Ontario often live in very remote and small communities. Some might have one nurse, with physicians and others flying in once a month or so. Other communities share one nurse, who works with paraprofessionals within these communities. These are local people who have received training at institutions such as Nunavut Arctic College. They fulfill a variety of roles, including community health representative, mental health worker, and addiction and alcohol program worker (Minore & Boone, 2002).

According to Minore and Boone, the success of the paraprofessional model depends upon the establishment of role clarity and consistency for these workers. It also depends upon the attitudes of the health professionals who work in these communities. While training programs seem quite good, the reality is that, when paraprofessionals enter their jobs, they are often unsure of their exact roles. A good example concerns patient confidentiality. In some cases, in an attempt to adhere strictly to confidentiality, paraprofessionals not only do not discuss a case informally with members of the community, but they might fail to share important information with a health care professional (Minore & Boone, 2002). One of the keys here is the education of rural health care workers. They must be helped to develop an awareness of the roles played by Aboriginal paraprofessionals in order to appreciate their contributions and to make them contributing members of the team.

SUMMARY

This brief exploration of Aboriginal health cannot do justice to the scope of the problems and the efforts being taken to address them. However, we hope that you can develop some appreciation for each, and for the reasons we must continue our commitment to helping Canada's Aboriginal peoples improve their health and general well-being.

Focused Module F

A Sampling of Canadian Research

in Health Psychology

One of the objectives of this book has been to show you that there is considerable health psychology research being conducted in Canada. If you have read through the book, you will know that it is full of examples of this research.

In this module, we list some of that research so that you can get a sense of its scope, both conceptually and geographically. It is meant only as a sample. As such, this list is far from exhaustive. We cannot provide a comprehensive database of all the Canadian research in health psychology. Indeed, there are Canadian references found in this text that are not in this Module, though the vast majority of the references listed here appear somewhere in the text. Nor is this a historical list. If it were, you would find Hans Selye, Ron Melzack, and others here. Instead, we have tried to make this reasonably up-to-date, so that you can develop an appreciation for some of the work that has been done recently in the country. The sites listed are those of the first authors.

ALBERTA
Foothills Hospital Addiction Centre, Calgary, Alberta

Hodgins, DC., Ungar, J., el-Guebaly, N. and Armstrong, S. (1997). Getting back on the wagon: Reasons and strategies for terminating alcoholic relapses. *Psychology of Addictive Behaviors, 11*, 174–181. **Chapter 1**

University of Alberta

Dunn, J.G.H., Dunn, J.C., & Syrotuik, D.G. (2002). Relationship between multidimensional perfectionism and goal orientations in sport. *Journal of Sport and Exercise Psychology, 24,* 376–395. **Chapter 8**

Faculty of Physical Education, University of Alberta

Jones, L.W., Sinclair, R.C., and Courneya, K.S., (2003). The effects of source credibility and message framing on exercise intentions, behaviors and attitudes: An integration of the elaboration likelihood model and prospect theory. *Journal of Applied Social Psychology, 33,* 179–196. **Chapter 7**

Courneya, K. S., Friedenreich, C. M., Sela, R. A., Quinney, H. A., Rhodes, R. E., & Handman, M. (2003). The group psychotherapy and home-based physical exercise (group-hope) trial in cancer survivors: Physical fitness and quality of life outcomes. *Psycho-Oncology, 12*(4), 357–374. **Chapter 11**

The Centre for Health Promotion Studies, University of Alberta

http://www.chps.ualberta.ca/ **Chapter 7**

Faculty of Nursing, University of Alberta

Cummings, G. G., Fraser, K., & Tarlier, D. S. (2003). Implementing advanced nurse practitioner roles in acute care: an evaluation of organizational change. *J Nurs Adm 33*(3), 139–145. **Chapter 6**

Department of Medicine, University of Calgary

Hilsden, R. J., Verhoef, M. J., Best, A., & Pocobelli, G. (2003). Complementary and alternative medicine use by Canadian patients with inflammatory bowel disease: results from a national survey. *Am J Gastroenterol, 98*(7), 1563–1568. **Module C**

Department of Community Health Sciences, University of Calgary

Verhoef, M. J., Casebeer, A. L., & Hilsden, R. J. (2002). Assessing efficacy of complementary medicine: adding qualitative research methods to the "Gold Standard". *J Altern Complement Med, 8*(3), 275–281 **Module C**

Verhoef, M. J., & White, M. A. (2002). Factors in making the decision to forgo conventional cancer treatment. *Cancer Pract, 10*(4), 201–207. **Module C**

BRITISH COLUMBIA

The Institute for Health Promotion Research, University of British Columbia

http://www.ihpr.ubc.ca/ **Chapter 7**

Department of Psychology, University of British Columbia

McIsaac, H.K., Thordarson, D.S., Shafran, R., Rachman, S., & Poole, G. (1998). Claustrophobia and the magnetic imaging procedure. *Journal of Behavioral Medicine, 21*, 255–268. **Chapter 5**

School of Nursing, University of British Columbia

Bottorff, JL., Johnson, JL., Venables, LJ., Grewal, S., Popatia, N., Hilton, B.A., Clarke, H., Sumel, P., Bilkhu, S., Sandhu, G. (2001). Voices of immigrant South Asian women: Expressions of health concerns. *Journal of Health Care for the Poor & Underserved, 12*, 392–403. **Chapter 1**

Joachim, G., & Acorn, S. (2000). Stigma of visible and invisible chronic conditions. *J Adv Nurs, 32*(1), 243–248. **Chapter 11**

Thorne, S. E., & Paterson, B. L. (2000). Two decades of insider research: what we know and don't know about chronic illness experience. *Annu Rev Nurs Res, 18*, 3–25. **Chapter 11**

Thorne, S., Paterson, B., Russell, C., & Schultz, A. (2002). Complementary/alternative medicine in chronic illness as informed self-care decision making. *International Journal of Nursing Studies, 39*(7), 671–683, **Module C**

Faculty of Medicine, UBC

Robinson, G. C., Armstrong, R. W., Moczuk, I. B., & Loock, C. A. (1992). Knowledge of fetal alcohol syndrome among native Indians. *Canadian Journal of Public Health, 83*(5), 337–338. **Module E**

Simon Fraser University

Hart, I., & Poole, G.D. (1995). Individualism and collectivism and considerations in cross-cultural health research. *Journal of Social Psychology, 135*, 97–99. **Module D**

Poole, G. D., & Kallhood, L. (1996). Technologists' perceptions of patient stress and technologists' helping strategies: Survey results. *Radiaction*, April, pp. 19–20. **Chapter 5**

Poole, G.D., Poon, C., Achille, M., White, K., Franz, N., Jittler, S., Watt, K., Cox, D.N., Doll, R. (2001). Social Support for Prostate Cancer Patients: The Effect of Support Groups. *Journal of Psychosocial Oncology*, 1–19. **Chapter 7**

Victoria, B.C.

Hutchings, D. (2002). Parallels in practice: Palliative nursing practice and Parse's theory of human becoming. *American Journal of Hospice & Palliative Care, 19*(6), 408–414. **Chapter 5**

MANITOBA

Faculty of Nursing, University of Manitoba

Sawatzky, J.V. and Naimark, B.J. (2002). Physical activity and cardiovascular health in aging women: A health-promotion perspective. *Journal of Aging & Physical Activity, 10*, 396–412. **Chapter 7**

Centre for Health Policy, University of Manitoba

Martens, P., Bond, R., Jebamani, L., Brurchill, C., Noralou, R., Derksen, S., Beaulieu, M., Steinbach, C., MacWilliam, L., Walld, R., Dik, N., Sanders, D., Tanner-Spence, M., Leader, A., Elias, B., & O-Neil, J. (2002). *The Health and Health Care Use of Registered First Nations People Living in Manitoba: A Population-Based Study.* **Module E**

PsycHealth Centre, Winnipeg

Enns, M. W., Cox, B. J., Sareen, J., & Freeman, P. (2001). Adaptive and maladaptive perfectionism in medical students: A longitudinal investigation. *Medical Education, 35*(11), 1034–1042. **Chapter 6**

Dept of Psychology, Brandon University, Brandon

Gfellner, B. M., & Hundleby, J. D. (1995). Patterns of drug use among native and white adolescents: 1990–1993. *Canadian Journal of Public Health* (March-April), 95–97. **Module E**

University of Winnipeg

Botterill, C., & Brown, M. (2002). Emotion and perspective in sport. *International Journal of Sport Psychology, 33,* 38–60. **Chapter 8**

NEW BRUNSWICK

Dept of Psychology, U New Brunswick

Weaver, A.D. Byers, E.S., Sears, H.A., Cohen, J.N., & Randall, H.E.S. (2002). Sexual health education at school and at home: Attitudes and experiences of New Brunswick parents. *Canadian Journal of Human Sexuality, 11*(1), 19–31. **Chapter 7**

Faculty of Nursing, University of New Brunswick, Fredericton

Wuest, J., Ford-Gilboe, M., Merritt-Gray, M., & Berman, H. (2003). Intrusion: the central problem for family health promotion among children and single mothers after leaving an abusive partner. *Qual Health Res, 13*(5), 597–622. **Chapter 7**

Macintosh, J. (2002). Gender-related influences in nursing education. *J Prof Nurs, 18*(3), 170–175. **Chapter 6**

Doiron-Maillet, N., & Meagher-Stewart, D. (2003). The uncertain journey: women's experiences following a myocardial infarction. *Can J Cardiovasc Nurs, 13*(2), 14–23. **Chapter 11**

NEWFOUNDLAND

Centre for Rural Health Studies, Memorial University, Whitbourne, NF

Worrall, G., Elgar, F. J., & Knight, J. C. (2001). Predictive value of support systems in a long-term care program. *Home Care Provid, 6*(1), 32–36. **Chapter 7**

Centre for Nursing Studies, St. John's, NF

Murray, C. L., Gien, L., & Solberg, S. M. (2003). A comparison of the mental health of employed and unemployed women in the context of a massive layoff. *Women Health, 37*(2), 55–72. **Module D**

Division of Community Health, Medicine, Memorial University, St. John's

Hanrahan, M. C. (2002). Identifying the needs of Innu and Inuit patients in urban health settings in Newfoundland and Labrador. *Can J Public Health, 93*(2), 149–152. **Module E**

NOVA SCOTIA

Acadia University, Wolfville, Nova Scotia

Leiter, M., Harvie, P., & Frizzel, C. (1998). The correspondence of patient satisfaction and nurse burnout. *Social Science and Medicine, 47*, 1611–1617. **Chapter 5**

Dalhousie University

McGrath, P. A., & Gillespie, J. (2001). Pain assessment in children and adolescents. In D. C. Turk & R. Melzack (Eds.), *Handbook of pain assessment* (pp. 97–118, 2nd ed). New York: Guilford. **Chapter 10**

McGrath, P. A. (1987). An assessment of children's pain: A review of behavioral, physiological and direct scaling techniques. *Pain*, 31, 147–176. **Chapter 10**

McIntyre, L., Glanville, N. T., Raine, K. D., Dayle, J. B., Anderson, B., & Battaglia, N. (2003). Do low-income lone mothers compromise their nutrition to feed their children? *Cmaj, 168*(6), 686–691. **Module D**

Poulin, C., & Graham, L. (2001). The association between substance use, unplanned sexual intercourse and other sexual behaviours among adolescent students. *Addiction, 96*(4), 607–621. **Module D**

ONTARIO

Centre for Addiction & Mental Health, London

Ogborne, AC., Smart, RG. (2001). Public opinion on the health benefits of moderate drinking: Results from a Canadian National Population Health Survey. *Addiction, 96*, 641–649. **Chapter 1**

Ottawa Hospital

Balfour, L., Silverman, A., Tasca, G., Kowal, J., Seatter, R., and Cameron, W. (2003). Stress and depression related to lower immune system functioning among people with HIV (PHAS). Presentation to the 64th Annual Conference of the Canadian Psychological Association, June 12, Hamilton, Ontario. **Chapter 3**

School of Human Kinetics, University of Ottawa

Taylor, G.M., & Ste-Marie, D.M. (2001). Eating disorders symptoms in Canadian female pair and dance figure skaters. *International Journal of Sport Psychology, 32*, 21–28. **Chapter 9**

The Centre for Health Promotion, University of Toronto

http://www.utoronto.ca/chp/ **Chapter 7**

Faculty of Nursing, University of Toronto

Wells, D. (1997). A critical ethnography of the process of discharge decision-making for elderly patients. *Canadian Journal on Aging, 16*, 682–699. **Chapter 5**

University Health Network, Toronto General Hospital

Bergman, B., Ahmad, F., & Stewart, D. E. (2003). Physician health, stress and gender at a university hospital. *Journal of Psychosomatic Research, 54*(2), 171–178. **Chapter 6**

Musclow, S. L., Sawhney, M., & Watt-Watson, J. (2002). The emerging role of advanced nursing practice in acute pain management throughout Canada. *Clin Nurse Spec, 16*(2), 63–67. **Chapter 6**

Robinson, G. E. (2003). Stresses on women physicians: Consequences and coping techniques. *Depress Anxiety, 17*(3), 180–189. **Chapter 6**

Department of Psychology, University of Toronto

Polivy, J. & Herman, C.P. (2002). Causes of eating disorders. *Annual Review of Psychology, 53*, 187–213. **Chapter 9**

Hospital for Sick Children, Toronto

McVey, G. L., Pepler, D., Davis, R., Flett, G. L., & Abdolell, M. (2002). Risk and protective factors associated with disordered eating during early adolescence. *Journal of Early Adolescence, 22*(1), 75–95. **Chapter 9**

The Performing Edge, Toronto

Hays K.F. (2002). The enhancement of performing excellence among performing artists. *Journal of Applied Sport Psychology, 14,* 299–312. **Chapter 8**

Faculty of Medicine and Dentistry, The University of Western Ontario

Kronick, J., Blake, C., Munoz, E., Heilbrunn, L., Dunikowski, L., & Milne, W. K. (2003). Improving on-line skills and knowledge. A randomized trial of teaching rural physicians to use on-line medical information. *Canadian Family Physician, 49,* 312–317. **Chapter 12**

Centre for Studies in Family Medicine & Faculty of Health Sciences, University of Western Ontario

McWilliam, C.L., Brown, J.B., & Stewart, M. (2000). Breast cancer patients' experiences of patient–doctor communication: A working relationship. *Patient Education and Counseling, 39,* 191–204. **Chapter 4**

Stewart, M., Brown, J.B., Donner, A., McWhinney, I.R., Oates, J., Weston, W.W., & Jordan, J. (2000). The impact of patient-centered care on outcomes. *The Journal of Family Practice, 49,* 796–804. **Chapter 4**

Stewart, M., Brown, J.B., Weston, W.W., McWhinney, I.R., McWilliam, C.L., & Freeman, T.R. (1995). *Patient-centered medicine: Transforming the clinical method.* Thousand Oaks: Sage. **Chapter 4**

Roter, D.L., Stewart, M., Putnam, S.M., Lipkins, M., Jr., et al. (1997). Communication patterns of primary care physicians. *Journal of the American Medical Association, 277,* 350–356. **Chapter 4**

University of Western Ontario

Wong, E. (2003). Fostering interest in family medicine. Focusing on patient–physician relationships. *Can Fam Physician, 49,* 630–631, 637–638. **Chapter 6**

Merskey, H., & Teasell, R. W. (2000). The disparagement of pain: Social influences on medical thinking. *Pain Research & Management, 5,* 259–270. **Chapter 10**

Merskey, H. & Teasell, R. W. (2002). A troubling story: Insurance and medical research in Saskatchewan. *Pain Research & Management, 7,* 65–67. **Chapter 10**

Hamilton Health Sciences Centre, Hamilton, ON

Alvarado, K., Keatings, M., & Dorsay, J. P. (2003). Cultivating APNs for the future: a hospital-based advanced practice nursing internship program. *Can J Nurs Leadersh, 16*(1), 91–98. **Chapter 6**

McMaster University, Hamilton

Porteous, A. & Tyndall, J. (1994). Yes, I want to walk to the OR. *Canadian Operating Room Nursing Journal, 12,* 15–25. **Chapter 5**

Dept. Of Clinical Epidemiology and Health Biostatistics, McMaster University

Haynes, R. B., McDonald, H. P., & Garg, A. X. (2002). Helping patients follow prescribed treatment. *Journal of the American Medical Association, 288,* 2880–2883. **Chapter 4**

McDonald, H. P., Garg, A. X., Haynes, R. B. (2002). Interventions to enhance patient adherence to medication prescriptions: Scientific review. *Journal of the American Medical Association, 288,* 2868–2879. **Chapter 4**

Saint Paul U, Faculty of Human Sciences, Ottawa

Gall, T. L., & Cornblat, M. W. (2002). Breast cancer survivors give voice: A qualitative analysis of spiritual factors in long-term adjustment. *Psycho-Oncology, 11*(6), 524–535. **Chapter 11**

Renfrew Victoria Hospital, Renfrew

McLennan, C. (1999). Breast cancer: so much more than just a perioperative experience. *Can Oper Room Nurs J, 17*(3), 30–41. **Chapter 11**

Centre for Addiction and Mental Health, Toronto

Bisihop, S.R., & Warr, D. (2003). Coping, catastrophizing and chronic pain in breast cancer. *J Behav Med, 26*(3), 265–281. **Chapter 11**

Princess Margaret Hospital, Toronto

Chen, X., & Siu, L. L. (2001). Impact of the media and the Internet on oncology: Survey of cancer patients and oncologists in Canada. *Journal of Clinical Oncology, 19*(23), 4291–4297. **Chapter 12**

StatsCanada, Science, Innovation and Electronic Information Division, Ottawa

Sciadas, G. (2002, October 01). *The digital divide in Canada,* [Internet]. Statistics Canada [2003, July 4]. **Chapter 12**

Faculty of Nursing, University of Windsor

Thomas, B., Goldsmith, S. B., Forrest, A., & Marshall, R. (2002). Web site development: applying aesthetics to promote breast health education and awareness. *Comput Inform Nurs, 20*(5), 184–190. **Chapter 12**

Dept of Sociology & Anthropology, University of Windsor

Maticka-Tyndale, E. (2001). Sexual Health and Canadian youth: How do we measure up? *Canadian Journal of Human Sexuality, 10*, 1–17. **Chapter 7**

First Nations and Inuit Health Branch, Ottawa

Conn, K. (2000). *CP's role in First Nations and Inuit health care.* **Module E**

Centre for Rural & Northern Health Research, Lakehead University, Thunder Bay, ON

Minore, B., & Boone, M. (2002). Realizing potential: Improving interdisciplinary professional/paraprofessional health care teams in Canada's northern aboriginal communities through education. *Journal of Interprofessional Care, 16*(2), 139–147. **Module E**

PRINCE EDWARD ISLAND
School of Nursing, University of Prince Edward Island

Munro, M., Gallant, M., MacKinnon, M., Dell, G., Herbert, R., MacNutt, G., McCarthy, M. J., Murnaghan, D., & Robertson, K. (2000). The Prince Edward Island Conceptual Model for Nursing: a nursing perspective of primary health care. *Can J Nurs Res, 32*(1), 39–55. **Chapter 6**

Queen Elizabeth Hospital, Charlottetown

Robertson, K. A., Kayhko, K., & Kekki, P. (2003). Re-hospitalizations after myocardial infarction on Prince Edward Island: analysis of the reasons. *Can J Cardiovasc Nurs, 13*(1), 16–20. **Chapter 11**

QUEBEC
Montreal Children's Hospital, McGill University Health Centre School of Nursing

Rennick, J. E., Johnston, C.C., Dougherty, G., Platt, R., & Ritchie, J.A. (2002). Children's psychological responses after critical illness and exposure to invasive technology. *Journal of Developmental & Behavioral Pediatrics, 23*(3), 133–144. **Chapter 5**

Montreal General Hospital

Keefler, J., Duder, S., & Lechman, C. (2001). Predicting length of stay in an acute care hospital: The role of psychosocial problems. *Social Work in Health Care, 33*(2), 1–16. **Chapter 5**

Department of Social Work, Montreal General Hospital

Tennier, L. D. (1997). Discharge planning: An examination of the perceptions and recommendations for improved discharge planning at the Montreal General Hospital. *Social Work in Health Care, 26*(1), 41–60. **Chapter 5**

McGill University

Bloom, G.A., Stevens, D.E., & Wickwire, T.L. (2003). Expert coaches perceptions of team building. *Journal of Applied Sport Psychology, 15,* 129–143. **Chapter 8**

Malkin, L. (2003). Teaching family medicine. *Can Fam Physician, 49,* 630, 637. **Chapter 6**

Melzack, R. (1998). Pain and stress: Clues toward understanding chronic pain. In M. Sabourin, F. Craik, and M. Robert (Eds.), *Advances in psychological science: Vol. 2. Biological and cognitive aspects.* Hove: Psychology Press Limited. **Chapter 10**

Melzack, R. (1999). Pain–an overview. *Acta Anaesthesiologica Scandinavica, 43,* 880–884. **Chapter 10**

Melzack, R. (2001). Pain and the neuromatrix in the brain. *Journal of Dental Education, 65,* 1378–1382. **Chapter 10**

Montreal Heart Inst Research Centre, McGill University

Frasure-Smith, N., & Lesperance, F. (2003). Depression and other psychological risks following myocardial infarction. *Archives of General Psychiatry, 60*(6), 627–636. **Chapter 11**

SASKATCHEWAN

College of Nursing, University of Saskatchewan, Saskatoon

Donnelly, G. (2003). Clinical expertise in advanced practice nursing: a Canadian perspective. *Nurse Educ Today, 23*(3), 168–173. **Chapter 6**

Department of Psychology, University of Saskatchewan

von Baeyer, C. L., Baskerville, S., & McGrath, P. J. (1998). Everyday pain in three- to five-year-old children in day care. *Pain Research and Management, 3(2),* 111–116. **Chapter 10**

Department of Psychology, University of Regina

Hadjistavropolous, T., von Baeyer, C. & Craig, K. D. (2001). Pain assessment in persons with limited ability to communicate. In D. C. Turk & R. Melzack (Eds.), *Handbook of pain assessment* (pp. 134–152, 2nd ed). New York: Guilford. **Chapter 10**

Hadjistavropoulos, T. (1999). Chronic pain on trial: The influence of litigation and compensation on chronic pain syndromes. In A. R. Block, E. G. Kremer, & E. Fernandez (Eds.), *Handbook of pain syndromes* (pp. 59–76). Mahwah, NJ: Erlbaum. **Chapter 10**

Hadjistavropoulos, H. D., Craig, K. D., Grunau, R. E., & Whitfield, M. F. (1997). Judging pain in infants: Behavioural, contextual, and developmental determinants. *Pain, 73,* 319–324. **Chapter 10**

Glossary

A-Delta Fibres The afferent peripheral fibres that are associated with transmitting sharp, distinct pain.

Acceleration-Deceleration Injury A type of concussion that occurs when an immobile head is hit by a moving object or a moving head hits an immobile object.

Acceptance The final stage of Kübler-Ross' theory of death and dying in which the person achieves a peaceful acceptance of his or her own death.

Acquired Immune Deficiency Syndrome (AIDS) A disease that develops as a result of the human immunodeficiency virus (HIV). The body's compromised immune system makes it susceptible to a host of other infections.

Acquired Immunity Protection against an antigen as a result of prior exposure to the antigen, either by having contracted the disease or by receiving an inoculation that presents the body with a non-toxic dose of the antigen.

Active Coping Coping style that is problem-focused.

Active Leisure A positive experience that is associated with activities such as hobbies, playing a musical instrument, and exercise.

Active-Passive Model Situation in which a patient is unable to participate in his or her care or to make decisions because of his or her medical condition.

Acupuncture An ancient Chinese pain control technique that involves the insertion of fine needles to create stimulation to the peripheral nerves.

Acute Illness An illness with a defined beginning and end.

Acute Pain Pain that lasts less than six months and serves to warn of impending tissue damage or the need for convalescent rest.

Acute Stressor A stressor that is immediate in its duration and proximity.

Addiction The state of being physically or psychologically dependent on a substance.

Addictive Smokers Smokers who develop a psychological dependence on smoking and are keenly aware when they are not smoking.

Adherence The degree to which patients carry out the behaviours and treatments that physicians and other health professionals recommend.

Adjuvant Therapy Therapy used in conjunction with other therapy.

Adrenal Cortex The outer portion of the adrenal gland that provides hormones to the body at times of stress. These hormones provide energy and increase blood pressure, but they can adversely affect the body's ability to resist disease and recover.

Adrenal Medulla The central portion of the adrenal gland that secretes catecholamines (containing both adrenaline and noradrenaline) when the hypothalamus initiates the stress response.

Advanced Illness Stage of illness at which death is imminent.

Advanced Practice Nursing Nursing that includes teaching, consultation, and research within a specialty area where superior clinical skills and judgment are acquired through a combination of experience and education.

Aerobic Exercise Exercise that involves the increased consumption of oxygen over an extended period of time, such as jogging.

Affect   Psychological term for emotion.

Afferent (Sensory) Neurons   Nerve cells that conduct impulses from a sense organ to the central nervous system, or from lower to higher levels in the spinal cord and brain.

Agency-Provided Support   Social support provided by agencies and organizations that have been formed to fill the void when naturally occurring support is either lacking or unavailable.

Agent   In epidemiology, the means by which a disease spreads.

Alarm   The initial phase of Selye's General Adaptation Syndrome in which the body mobilizes its defences against a stressor.

Alcohol Dependency Syndrome Model A theory that suggests that for a variety of reasons people do not exercise control over their drinking and this leads to problem drinking.

Alcohol Myopia   A drinker's decreased ability to engage in insightful cognitive processing.

Allopathic Medicine   A form of medicine that attempts to cure sickness by creating conditions in the body that oppose the disease.

Alternative Treatment   Any intervention or treatment that is not allopathic.

Anaerobic Exercise   Exercise such as sprinting in which intense effort is expended over a short period of time, resulting in an oxygen debt.

Anger   A reaction that often follows denial when we are confronted with novel and severe trauma as identified by Kübler-Ross.

Angioplasty   A procedure in which a bubble-like device is inserted into the artery at the point of the blockage, thus expanding the artery and allowing for better blood flow.

Anorexia Nervosa   An eating disorder that is characterized by a dramatic reduction in food intake and extreme weight loss due to an extreme fear of gaining weight.

Anticipatory Nausea   Nausea that is felt before a chemotherapy treatment begins, explained in terms of classical conditioning.

Antiemetic Medication   Medication intended to reduce nausea and vomiting.

Antigens   Microorganisms that are foreign to our physiology.

Antimicrobial Substances   Chemicals created by the immune system that kill antigens.

Applied Discipline   Any field in which researchers spend more time using theories to explain real-world phenomena than they do developing the theories.

Applied Research   An area of research designed to solve real-world problems.

Appraisal Delay   The time it takes a person to decide that a symptom is a sign of illness.

Asymptomatic   Conditions that are not accompanied by palpable symptoms or sensations.

Attitude   A cognition in which a person evaluates some object or idea.

Attributions   The explanations people give for events such as their successes and failures.

Autonomic Activity Consciously uncontrollable physiological processes such as heart rate, respiration rate, blood pressure, hand surface temperature, and skin conductance.

Aversion Therapy   Therapy that includes the pairing of a behaviour that one is attempting to eliminate with some unpleasant stimulus so that the undesired behaviour will elicit negative sensations.

B Lymphocyte Cells   Cells that, when re-encountering a specific pathogen, produce an antibody designed to eliminate the pathogen.

Bargaining   A response, identified by Kübler-Ross, that may occur when a person is confronted with novel and severe trauma; includes trying to do things that will buy more time.

Behavioural Delay   The elapsed time between the decision to seek medical care and acting on this decision by making an appointment.

Behavioural Medicine   A branch of medicine concerned with the relationship between health and behaviour. The focus is usually on remediation.

Behaviourist   One who believes that most behaviour is learned as opposed to innate.

Beliefs as Person Variables   Pre-existing notions, both personal and cultural, that influence appraisal, and thus stress, by determining the meaning given to the environment.

Benefit Finding   Attitude or technique often referred to as finding the "silver lining in the cloud," that appears to aid in posttraumatic growth.

Benign Breast Biopsy   A false positive result based on which women with abnormal mammograms are called back for a biopsy procedure and the results show no evidence of malignancy.

Benign-Positive Appraisal   A cognitive process by which an event is appraised to involve outcomes that are positive and may enhance well-being.

Bereavement   Emotions attendant upon the loss of a close friend or loved one.

Biobehavioural Model   A model of smoking behaviour that maintains that people use and come to depend on the effects of nicotine to regulate cognitive performance and emotional affect.

Biofeedback   The recording of physiological measures through electronic instruments that provide immediate feedback concerning physiological state in an attempt to modify physiological processes.

Biomedical Model   An approach suggesting that health is best understood in terms of biology.

Biopsychosocial Approach   A model that suggests that biological, psychological and social factors are all involved in any given state of health or illness.

Biopsychosocial Communication Pattern   Communication patterns between a physician and patient that include a balance of psychosocial and biomedical topics.

Blind Procedure   Experimental design aimed at eliminating experimenter bias by ensuring that the people who collect data are unaware of the hypothesis or at least unaware of the group into which a participant has been placed.

Blunters   People who avoid information in their attempt to cope with illness and its accompanying challenges.

Body Dysmorphic Disorder   Condition in which individuals who suffer from eating disorders do not perceive their bodies accurately.

Body-Mass Index (BMI).   Measure of obesity calculated by dividing one's weight in kilograms by height in metres squared:

Box Scale   A scale on which people rate and report their pain by choosing the number that best indicates the degree of pain that they are experiencing from a series of numbers in boxes ranging from "no pain" to "worst pain imaginable."

Bulimia Nervosa   An eating disorder that involves recurrent episodes of binge eating followed by purging.

Burnout   A condition that is similar to compassion fatigue and includes symptoms of physical exhaustion, depersonalization of patients, and feelings of discouragement and low accomplishment.

C-Fibres   The afferent peripheral fibres that are associated with transmitting diffuse, dull, or aching pain.

Carcinogenic   Cancer-causing.

Cardiac Invalidism   The curtailing of activity levels far more than required by disease status because of anxiety related to a possible subsequent attack.

Caring   The role that most lay people think is the primary task of nurses.

Case   One instance of a medical problem.

Case Studies   Narrative accounts of one person's health, including individual histories, symptoms, specific reactions, or treatment outcomes that help us learn about some aspect of health psychology.

Central Control Trigger   In the gate control theory of pain, a specialized system of large-diameter, rapidly conducting fibres that activate selective cognitive processes that then influence, by way of descending fibres, the opening and closing of the gate.

Central Nervous System   The division of the nervous system that is composed of the brain and the spinal cord.

Central Route to Persuasion   The use of logic, facts, and reason to affect someone's attitude.

Centrally Acting Analgesics   Pain-killing medications that operate on the central nervous system by imitating the effects of the body's endogenous pain relief system.

Challenge Appraisal   Appraisal in which, though an event is perceived to be stressful, the focus is one of positive excitement and the potential for growth.

Chemotherapy   Treatment used in addition to surgery and/or radiation therapy when it is suspected that cancer has metastasized, or to help prevent it from doing so.

Chronic Condition   A condition that doesn't go away or get better.

Chronic Intractable Benign Pain Continuous pain that varies in intensity.

Chronic Pain   Pain lasting for longer than six months.

Chronic Progressive Pain   Continuous pain that gradually intensifies as a person's condition worsens.

Chronic Recurrent Pain   Intermittent intense episodes of acute pain followed by relief.

Claustrophobia   An intense fear of enclosed spaces that is a psychological concern for those undergoing MRI procedures.

Clinical Nurse Specialist   A nurse with a master's or doctoral degree in nursing and extensive experience in a given clinical specialty.

Coercive Power   The mediation of punishment by the physician in the form of withholding praise or services to promote patient adherence to medical recommendations.

Cognitive Appraisals   Assessments of whether or not an event is stressful.

Cognitive Reappraisal and Restructuring Therapy, sometimes used with cardiac patients, in which they learn to think differently about the things that make them angry and to make behavioural changes such as learning to control their breathing.

Cognitive Restructuring   A technique whereby maladaptive, stress-producing cognitions are identified and replaced with ones that are more appropriate.

Cognitive Transactional Models   Models that emphasize the relationship that exists between a person and his or her environment and the appraisal that the individual makes of the situation.

Collectivist   One who considers him- or herself to be part of a greater whole and who considers individualism to be less important than allegiance to the group.

Commitments as Person Variables   Values that influence appraisal by determining the importance of a particular encounter and that affect the choices made to achieve a desired outcome.

Compassion Fatigue   A lack of energy among health care professionals, particularly nurses, who are constantly working in an environment in which suffering is common.

Complementary Treatment   Treatment that is used in conjunction with allopathic treatment.

Compliance   The degree to which patients carry out the behaviours and treatments that physicians and other health professionals recommend.

Concussion (Closed Head Injury)   A bruising of the brain that can result in severe neurocognitive deficits, permanent disability, and even death.

Conflict Theory School of thought in sociology that claims that structures do not simply exist; rather, they exist in *conflict*.

Consumerist Communication Pattern The use of the physician as a consultant who answers questions rather than being the one who asks them.

Continuing Medical Education (CME) Ongoing education for practitioners.

Continuity of Care Arrangement in which a designated staff person, usually a nurse, takes primary responsibility for a patient during his or her hospital stay.

Control Group Participants in a study who don't receive the manipulation (the dependent variable).

Coping Strategies that an individual employs to deal with stresses caused by ever-changing demands of the environment.

Coping Goal The objective of a coping response (which is usually to reduce the impact of stress).

Coping Outcomes The specific outcomes of a coping response.

Coping Response An intentional physical or mental act that is initiated in response to a stressor.

Coping Styles Patterns in the way people deal with difficult situations.

Coronary Artery Bypass Graft (CABG, commonly called bypass surgery) A procedure in which healthy arteries from other parts of the body, often the legs, are grafted into the coronary artery system to bypass blocked arteries.

Correlational Research Studies including statistical analyses to determine whether two variables change together, or *covary*.

Creative Non-Adherence The intentional modification or supplementing of a recommended treatment regimen by the patient.

Cross-Sectional Research Comparison of two or more groups that differ according to stage of life.

Curing The role that most lay people think is the primary task of physicians.

Danger Control Constructive behavioural change focused on problem solving, which can proceed without fear when the danger is health-related.

Data Mining The process of digging deeply into the information available on a given site with the object of gaining access to confidential information.

Day Care Patient A person who goes to the hospital for a procedure or test that is more involved than, for example, routine radiography, but does not stay overnight.

Day Care Surgery Surgery that does not require the patient to stay in the hospital overnight.

Dehumanization The tendency to see people as objects or body parts rather than human beings.

Delayed Gratification Term used by behaviourists to describe a situation in which there is a time lag between a behaviour and its reinforcement.

Demand Characteristics Beliefs held by people when they know that they are in a psychology study as to what is expected of them or how they are "supposed" to respond.

Demographic Relating to personal variables such as age, culture, socioeconomic status, employment status, marital status, and gender.

Denial A coping strategy in which people deny that distressing events exist or that negative emotions are being felt.

Dependent Variable In an experiment, the variable that is hypothesized to be measurably affected by the manipulation of the independent variable.

Depersonalization The taking away of one's sense of individuality.

Diathesis-Stress Model A model that suggests that illness results from an interaction between certain personality characteristics and environmental stressors.

Digital Divide   Unequal access to computer-based technology based on demographic and socioeconomic variables.

Discharge Planning   A process in which post-hospital care is organized and risks, such as social problems and lack of support, are assessed.

Disease   Physical pathology.

Disease Model (of problem drinking)
A theory that suggests that alcoholism is a disease resulting from the physical properties of alcohol.

Diseases of Adaptation   Health problems that are the result of the impact of long-term neurological and hormonal changes present because of ongoing stress.

Disempowering Care   Patient care that yields dependence and can result in learned helplessness.

Disfigurement   A potential physical result of cancer surgery that can have serious psychological consequences.

Distraction   A pain management technique in which the patient focuses attention on something other than the sensation of pain.

Do Not Resuscitate Order   An order given by a physician indicating that CPR and other interventions are not to be used if the patient stops breathing.

Doctor-Centred Consultations
Consultations in which physicians tend to ask questions that require only very brief answers.

Drive Reduction Theory   A theory that suggests we are driven to reduce the tension brought about by deprivation or other negative states.

Duration   Temporal situational factor involved in stress appraisal.

E-journal   A journal that is accessible through the Internet.

Efficacy Belief   The extent to which one thinks a course of action (e.g., a preventive behaviour or treatment) will actually work.

Ego Orientation   A goal perspective that focuses on success and failure with success often coming at other people's expense.

Electroencephalograph (EEG)   An instrument that assesses pain by measuring electrical activity in the brain.

Electromyograph (EMG)   An instrument that assesses pain by measuring electrical activity in muscles.

Electromyographic Biofeedback
Biofeedback that measures muscle tension.

Emotion-Focused Coping   Coping by focusing on ways to reduce the emotional impact of a disease without trying to cure it.

Emotional Arousal   A source of efficacy expectation by which individuals assess their emotional level and evaluate their capabilities accordingly; for example, high levels of emotion may be thought to be debilitating and predictive of failure.

Emotional Support   Support provided by people who take the time to understand our fears and frustrations, who help calm us during anxious times, who help bring our moods up, or distract us from our worries.

Empowering Care   Patient care that yields independence and results in learned mastery.

Encryption   Means by which email message access can be restricted to those with passwords in order to reduce problems of security and confidentiality.

Endocrine System   A system of the body that controls glandular responses to stress, albeit more slowly than the nervous system but whose effects can persist for weeks.

Endogenous Opioids   Opiate-like substances produced within the body that regulate pain.

Enumerative Assay   A lab test done to count cells (typically white blood cells) as they exist in the bloodstream.

Environmental Tobacco Smoke (secondhand smoke)   Smoke that is in the air we breathe because of others smoking.

Epidemiologists Those who study patterns of illness across populations and geographic areas, focusing on the interrelationship of the status of health and demographic factors.

Ethanol (ethyl alcohol) The alcohol used in beverages.

Eustress A positive, yet stressful experience.

Euthanasia The deliberate ending of a patient's life to relieve suffering.

Event Uncertainty The inability to predict the probability of an event which, as a result, increases the stress response.

Evoked Potentials Electrical responses produced by stimuli.

Exercise Psychology The study of the influence that sport and exercise have on one's psychology and behaviour.

Exhaustion An end point identified by Selye in his General Adaptation Syndrome in which the body experiences fatigue and immuno-compromise because of the severity or duration of a stressor.

Expanded Biomedical Communication Patterns Communication patterns that include numerous closed-ended medical questions and moderate levels of biomedical and psychosocial exchange between the physician and patient.

Experimental Group Participants in a study who receive the manipulation (the independent variable).

Experimenter Bias An experimental construct flaw in which the person who interacts with participants or interprets qualitative data has knowledge that affects participants' responses or qualitative data interpretation.

Expert Power The power inherent in the role of physician that increases the likelihood that a patient will adhere to medical recommendations.

Expertise Model Model in which the physician and the intensive care team are assumed to be best informed and most objective, and therefore best equipped to make end-of-life decisions.

Extended Parallel Process Model A model that suggests that low fear messages stimulate neither fear nor danger control, whereas high fear messages stimulate fear control and control if the message is accompanied by an effective behavioural recommendation.

External Imagery A technique in which an individual becomes a third-person, passive, external observer of his or her own actions.

External Reinforcement The encouragement and praise needed by rehabilitation patients from physiotherapists, friends, family, and other practitioners for their successes.

Factor Analysis Grouping of variables based on discovered correlations to turn them into "factors," or variables that may be tapping into one over-arching phenomenon.

False Positive Result that indicates abnormality when none exists.

Family Oriented Care In comprehensive cancer care, the family becomes the patient because for virtually every cancer patient there is a family and a collection of close friends who are also affected by the disease.

Fear Appeals The attempt to change people's behaviour by presenting frightening accounts of what could happen to them if they continue a given behaviour or if they don't adopt a behaviour.

Fear Control Reducing the discomfort of a situation without addressing the source of danger.

Fear of Restriction Anxiety experienced due to the inability to move because of being in a small enclosed space.

Fear of Suffocation Anxiety experienced due to the belief that one might die from the inability to breathe.

Feminization of Medicine The trend toward increased proportions of female physicians in the profession.

Field Research Research conducted in real-life settings.

Fight-or-Flight Response The body's complex autonomic reaction when faced with a perceived threat.

Filmless Radiology   Technology that allows diagnostic images to be sent electronically rather than processing film copies to be sent through the mail.

Focal Infection   An infection that remains in one area of the body but sends toxins to other parts of the body.

FTP (File Transfer Protocol)   Means by which the Internet allows for the sharing of complex files that contain large data sets, graphics, or other media.

Functional Tests of Immunity   Tests done to assess the immune system at work.

Gastric Bypass   Radical surgical intervention to control extreme obesity in which a small pouch is created at the bottom of the esophagus to limit food intake.

Gate Control Theory   A theory that suggests that a neural mechanism in the dorsal horns of the spinal cord acts like a gate that can increase or decrease the flow of nerve impulses from peripheral fibres to the central nervous system thereby influencing the sensation of pain.

General Adaptation Syndrome   The three-stage response of the body to stressors as identified by Selye, which include alarm, resistance, and exhaustion.

Global Measures of Quality of Life   A general or overall assessment of quality of life without focusing on specific aspects.

Glucocorticoids   Substances released by the adrenal glands upon stimulation from the sympathetic division when one is under stress.

Grade-One Concussion   A concussion that does not involve a loss of consciousness, although the athlete may display transient confusion.

Grade-Two Concussion   A concussion in which the symptoms persist beyond the 15-minute period but does not involve a loss of consciousness.

Grade-Three Concussion   Any concussion that involves a loss of consciousness whether it is extremely brief or prolonged.

Gradient of Reinforcement   The lag time between a behaviour and a reinforcer; the greater the lag time, the weaker the behaviour.

Grief   Deep sorrow, usually in response to bereavement.

Guidance–Cooperation Model   Communication in which the patient seeks advice from the physician and answers the questions that are asked but the physician is responsible for determining the diagnosis and treatment.

Guided Imagery   A form of relaxation that relies on distraction in which the participant is told to imagine a calm, peaceful, and pleasant image.

Habitual Smokers   Smokers who smoke without the awareness that they are doing so.

Hallucinogens   Drugs that dramatically affect perception, emotions, and mental processes and can result in hallucinations.

Harm/Loss Appraisal   A type of stressful appraisal at the time of the initial evaluation of a situation (primary appraisal) that involves significant physical or psychological loss.

Health and Social Outcomes   Quality of life, ability to function independently, and reduced morbidity and morality.

Health Belief Model   A model that analyzes health behaviour in terms of the belief that a health threat exists and the belief that a given course of action will affect the threat.

Health Promotion   Strategies intended to maintain or improve the health of large populations.

Health Promotion Actions   Processes of health promotion, such as health education programs and political lobbying.

Health Promotion Mechanisms   Encouragement to make the environment healthier by reducing pollution, improving safety, and so on.

Health Promotion Outcomes   Results of health promotion such as changes in literacy rates, community capacity, and health policy.

Health Psychology The compilation of all that psychology has to offer to the diagnosis and treatment of illness as well as people's attempts to maintain health and well-being.

Help-Intended Communication Communication that includes support, especially emotional support.

Helper T Cells (T lymphocytes) Cells that produce substances called interleukins that speed the division of B lymphocyte cells.

Highly Active Antiretroviral Treatment (HAART) A treatment for AIDS that has been shown to significantly increase life expectancy.

Homeostasis The dynamic physiological response on the part of the body to maintain a stable internal state in spite of the demands of the environment.

Hospital Separation A measure of hospital usage calculated as an overnight hospital stay for one person.

Host In epidemiology, the carrier of an agent of disease.

Human Immunodeficiency Virus (HIV) A virus that gradually breaks down the body's immune system, making it susceptible to a host of other infections and eventually resulting in AIDS.

Hypnosis An altered state of consciousness.

Hypoglycemia Low blood sugar.

Hypometabolic State A state of the body in which the heart slows, blood pressure drops, breathing is slow and easy, muscle tension decreases, and blood flow shifts.

Hypothalamus A portion of the brain that initiates the stress response in both the nervous system and the endocrine system.

Illness The subjective experience of having a disease.

Illness Delay The time taken between recognizing that one is ill and deciding to seek medical care.

Imminence Interval during which an event is being anticipated; the more imminent an event, the more intense the appraisal.

Immune System Memory The ability of certain immune system cells to adapt to an antigen, to remember the antigen when it encounters it again, and to work to eliminate it.

Immunocompetence The extent to which our immune system is functioning properly to ward off microorganisms.

Incidence The number of new cases of a health problem in a set period of time.

Inclusion criteria Those characteristics that make a person eligible for a study.

Incommunication Stage A period in ICU during which a patient is either unconscious or barely conscious.

Individualist One who focuses on independence and self-reliance rather than placing group needs above his or her own.

Information–Motivation–Behavioural Skills Model A theory that maintains that there are a number of steps that one must go through to successfully achieve safe sex practices.

Informational Power The presentation of information or knowledge by a physician to promote patient adherence to medical recommendations.

Informational Support The provision of information that might include such things as treatment options or typical recovery times from a treatment or injury.

Insulin-Dependent Diabetes (Type I) A condition in which a person produces very little or no insulin and as a result is required to take insulin on a daily basis, usually by way of self-administered injection.

Interaction The phenomenon of variables combining to produce an effect that is different from the effect of either variable alone.

Interleukins Substances produced by T lymphocytes that speed the division of B lymphocyte cells.

Intermediate Health Outcomes Health promotion emphasis on lifestyle, provision of health services, and environmental factors.

Internal Imagery Technique in which an individual imagines being inside his or her body experiencing a given situation.

Internality–Externality Hypothesis Assertion that in people of normal weight, feelings of hunger and satiety come from within, in the form of internal stimuli (e.g., hunger pangs or feelings of fullness).

Internalization The changing of one's pattern of beliefs to accommodate the beliefs advocated by the health care practitioner.

Internship A labour-intensive training period the first year after a person graduates from medical school.

Interpersonal Small Talk Talk engaged in by a technologist during a procedure that has nothing to do with the procedure but passes the time and establishes rapport.

Intrusive Memories Unwanted thoughts, often visual in nature, that are related to memories that the patient has about cancer and death.

Invasiveness A measure of the extent to which hospital procedures, in a physical sense, involve piercing the skin or entering the body with instruments or, in a psychological sense, have the potential to cause embarrassment.

Irrelevant Appraisal A cognitive process by which an event is appraised to have no implications for the individual's well-being.

Isokinetic Exercise Exercise that involves placing tension on a muscle group through a complete range of motion.

Isometric Exercise Exercise that involves the contraction of a muscle group against an immovable object without movement in the body.

Isotonic Exercise Exercise that involves using weights or calisthenics to place tension on the muscle through the shortening or lengthening of the muscle group.

Job Strain Model A model that suggests a job with high strain is one that includes high demands and low control.

Lay Referral System An informal network of non-practitioners who offer their interpretation of symptoms well before any medical treatment is sought.

Learned Helplessness A state in which a person, because of experience with previously uncontrollable stressful situations, learns to do nothing about a new stressor, rather than trying to cope constructively with it.

Legitimate Power Power derived by virtue of the appointed position a person holds in a system.

Leptin Hormone that responds to weight loss by increasing hunger levels until the person's weight returns to its ideal or target level.

Limbic System A system of the brain that is responsible, in part, for emotion in the stress response.

Link Text or graphic on an Internet-based site that allows the user to click on the link and be taken quickly to another related site or another portion of the site being explored.

Local Anesthetics Pain-relieving chemicals that can be applied topically but are much more effective when injected at the site where the pain originates.

Localized Infection An infection that is confined to a defined site.

Lock-Out Interval The time period between allowable dosages, when patient controlled analgesia is used. A device is set by a practitioner to control this period.

Locus of Control The extent to which we believe that the events of our lives are controlled internally by ourselves, or externally by outside forces.

Longitudinal Research Experimental design in which researchers follow one group over time to chart their changes.

Main Effects Model Any scientific explanation that assumes an outcome is the result of the effects of one variable only.

Malignant Neoplasms Cancerous growths that may be treated by radiation and chemical therapy.

Medical Anthropologists Those who study the interrelationship of health and cultural factors.

Medical Delay The time between someone making an appointment and first receiving medical care.

Medical Geography The study of the health-related impact of differences in environments.

Medical Jargon Technical language used by a physician that is sometimes unintelligible to the patient.

Medical Level (of health promotion) Promotion in which the orientation is disease-based and the goal is disease treatment.

Medical Sociologists Those who study the interrelationship of health and demographic factors as well as the relationship between social systems and health.

Meditation A form of relaxation in which one attempts to focus attention fully on a single thought or image.

Memory B Cells A particular kind of B lymphocyte cell that develops a "memory" for a specific antigen after being exposed to it and acts only on that antigen by producing antibodies and immunoglobulins.

Metastasized Spread (frequently used to denote the spread of cancer).

Microorganisms In terms of the immune system, the relevant forms include bacteria, viruses, parasites, and fungi.

Mitogen A relatively harmless substance that stimulates immune cell activity as though the immune cell were acting against an invading cell or antigen.

Mixed Management Model of Care The preparation of a patient for eventual death while at the same time providing life-sustaining treatments.

Modelling A technique used to reduce stress associated with fear-provoking situations, in which observing a model coping well with a situation facilitates a similar response by the observer in a similar situation.

Monitors People who seek information in their attempt to cope with illness and its accompanying challenges.

Mood State A transient or short-term experience of emotion.

Motion Artifacts Distortions to an MRI image caused by a patient's movement.

Multilevel Explanations Explanations that use medical jargon followed by further explanation using everyday language.

Multidimensional Measures of Quality of Life Assessment that includes specific aspects of quality of life, such as physical, emotional, and social functioning.

Multidimensional Health Locus of Control Scale (MHLC) A scale that measures health-specific control beliefs.

Multidisciplinary Pain Management Program A program to manage pain that involves an interdisciplinary team often including physicians, psychologists or psychiatrists, physical therapists, and occupational therapists.

Multiple Regulation Model A theory that maintains that the physiological effects of nicotine interact with the psychological functions of smoking to produce addiction.

Muscle Dysmorphia Condition characterized by: belief that one's body is not sufficiently lean and muscular; clinically significant distress or impairment in social, occupational, or other areas of functioning; and a primary focus on being too small or inadequately muscular.

Mutual Aid Responsibility to family, friends, loved ones, and even society as a whole when it comes to health and safety.

Mutual Participation Model Healthcare model in which the physician and patient make joint decisions about every aspect of care.

Myocardial Infarction (MI) Heart attack caused by lack of blood flow to the heart.

Myocardial Ischemia A lack of blood flow to the heart muscle.

Narcotics Pain-killing drugs that work by binding to opiate receptors in the central nervous system.

Narrowly Biomedical Communication Pattern Communication pattern characterized mainly by biomedical talk, closed-ended medical questions, and very little discussion of psychosocial issues.

Natural-Killer (NK) Cells Cells that have the specific job of "seeking and destroying" cells that are infected, cancerous, or altered in some other way.

Naturally Occurring Support The support we obtain from friends, relatives, coworkers, and others in our own social networks.

Navigator Someone, often a nurse, community health worker, or social worker, who helps patients diagnosed with serious illnesses find their way through the sometimes complicated world of hospitals and treatment.

Negative-Affect Smoker A smoker who smokes to reduce negative affect such as anxiety, distress, fear, or guilt.

Negative Correlation Situation in which one variable decreases as another increases.

Negotiated Model Decision-making model that allows decision making to be shared between the practitioners, patient, and family.

Nervous System One of the two major components of the physical response to stress; made up of the central nervous system and the peripheral nervous system.

Neuromatrix Theory An extension to the gate control theory, with greater emphasis placed on the brain's role in pain perception.

Nicotine Fixed Effect Model A theory that maintains that nicotine produces addiction because of its paradoxical capacity to simultaneously produce feelings of mental alertness and relaxation.

Nicotine-Regulation Model A theory that proposes that smokers develop an optimal level of nicotine in their bodies and then smoke to maintain this level and avoid withdrawal symptoms.

Nicotine-Replacement Therapy A technique to help one stop smoking that provides some form of nicotine to replace that previously obtained through smoking.

NK-Cell Cytotoxic Activity Assay A test in which the proliferation and effectiveness of NK cells is measured after they have been exposed to diseased cells.

NK-Cell Lysis The destroying of tumour cells by exposing them to NK cells.

Nociceptors The afferent nerve endings that respond to pain stimuli.

Non-Adherence Failure to follow the advice of the health professional; the inability to stay with an exercise program.

Non-Discrepant Responses Responses by the physician to the patient's questions using the same sophistication of vocabulary that the patient used.

Non-Insulin-Dependent Diabetes (Type II) A condition in which a person does not produce enough insulin or is not able to use the insulin effectively.

Non-Invasive A term to describe any procedure that does not include piercing the skin or entering the body with an instrument.

Non-Specific Immunity General protection against antigens, rather than against one specific antigen.

Novelty   The extent to which an individual's previous experience with a situation influences the appraisal process.

Nurse Practitioner   A nurse who often works in rural, remote settings frequently performing functions that would be performed by a physician if available.

Obesity   Condition characterized by having an excess of body fat; Health Canada and the World Health Organization define obesity as a BMI of 30.0 or greater.

Observational Research   Method in research by which data about phenomena are collected by observing those phenomena without trying to manipulate them. It is usually descriptive in its purpose.

Occupational Rituals   Behaviours that indicate one has been socialized into a profession. For nurses, these are communicated through interaction with other nurses.

Oncology   The study and treatment of cancer.

Onset Control   The belief that the onset of an illness can be controlled or avoided. The greater this belief, the greater the depression when an illness recurs.

Operant Pain   Pain that is reinforced by a person's environment.

Orienting Responses   Reactions (such as the slowing of the viewer's heart rate) to various stimuli presented on a computer screen.

Outpatient   A person who goes to the hospital for a procedure or test but does not stay overnight.

Outcome Goals   Goals that are concerned with the results or outcomes of events and usually involve comparisons to others.

Pain Behaviours   Alterations in behaviour by a person experiencing pain to either reduce the pain or to prevent it from getting worse.

Pain Threshold   The point at which the intensity of a stimulus is perceived as painful.

Pain Tolerance   The duration of time or intensity at which a person is willing to endure a stimulus beyond the point where it began to hurt.

Palliative Care   Care intended to maintain quality of life as best as possible for a patient who is in the advanced stage of an illness. The focus is the control of pain and other symptoms as opposed to the cure of the illness.

Palliative Treatment   Treatment designed to relieve suffering but that is not expected to lead to a cure or remission.

Pancreas   A gland that secretes insulin and glucagon as a function of blood sugar levels.

Pap Test or Pap Smear   A test done to screen for cervical cancer.

Parallel-Response Model   A model that suggests that recipients of fear-arousing messages focus on either fear control or danger control or some combination of the two.

Parasympathetic   The component of the autonomic system that reestablishes homeostasis in the system and promotes the reconstructive process following a stressful experience.

Participant Modelling   A technique used to reduce stress in which, subsequent to an individual observing a model coping with an anxiety evoking situation, the person is encouraged to engage in the behaviour while receiving reassurance from the model.

Passive Coping   Coping style that places the responsibility for coping in the hands of others.

Passive Leisure   A positive experience that is associated with lack of activity (e.g., listening to music, daydreaming).

Passive Smoking   The breathing of environmental tobacco smoke.

Pathogens   Antigens that have the potential to create disease.

Patient-Centred Consultations   Consultations in which physicians tend to ask open-ended questions that allow patients to elaborate.

Patient-Controlled Analgesia (PCA)   Analgesic administration that is independently controlled by the patient.

Patient Delay   The period between an individual's first awareness of a symptom and treatment for that symptom.

Patient-Centred Care   Approach in which patients and families become active members of the treatment team.

Patient-Centred Consultations   Consultations with physicians that include open-ended questions by the physician.

Perceived Behavioural Control   The belief that a specific behaviour is within one's control.

Performance Accomplishments   Actual experiences of mastery, considered to be the most influential source of self-efficacy.

Performance Goals   Goals that describe an outcome that can be achieved independently of others' performances.

Periaqueductal Gray Area   An area of the midbrain that is involved in pain reception.

Peripheral Nervous System   The division of the nervous system that is made up of the somatic nervous system and the autonomic nervous system (which is further divided into the sympathetic and the parasympathetic nervous systems).

Peripheral Route to Persuasion   Attempts to affect attitude by appealing to emotion and general impression.

Peripherally Acting Analgesics   Non-narcotic medications that decrease pain by reducing inflammation at the site of tissue damage. They also inhibit the synthesis of neuro-chemicals in the peripheral nervous system that facilitate the transmission of pain impulses.

Person Variables   Variables, most importantly commitments and belief, that interact with situation variables to affect the appraisal of a situation in terms of its stressfulness.

Personal Control   A factor that influences a person's ability to cope with stress; personal control can be achieved either behaviourally or cognitively.

Personal Efficacy   The belief that we are able to succeed at a given task.

Personal Factors in Stress   Personal characteristics, such as high self-esteem and a clear sense of control, that make some people better able to cope with the stressors of their job.

Personal Resources   Resources that are available to people in their own lives to help them reduce the potential for stressful events and cope with stressful situations as they occur.

Personality   A person's collection of attributes and behavioural tendencies that are consistent over time and across a variety of situations.

Persuasion   The attempt to change people's attitudes and beliefs.

Phantom Limb Pain   The experience of pain in an absent body part.

Phenomenological   According to a person's own report on the phenomenon.

Physical Activity   The expenditure of energy, either purposely or without intention, as a result of bodily movements produced by skeletal muscles as part of leisure or work activities.

Physical Therapy   Therapy involved in the rehabilitation of muscle, bone, joint, or nerve disease.

Physical Fitness   Physiological functioning (including cardiorespiratory endurance, muscular endurance, muscular strength, body composition, and flexibility) that influences the ability to perform physical activity.

Physician Impairment   A state in which stress-related symptoms interfere with the physician's ability to perform his or her job.

Pituitary Gland   A gland located in the brain that is described as the master gland because of its control of other glands through the hormones it secretes. Most of these hormones have an indirect impact on stress.

Positive-Affect Smoker   A smoker who smokes to attain positive affect (e.g., increased stimulation, relaxation, or gratification of sensorimotor needs).

Positive Correlation.   Situation in which when one variable increases (or decreases), so does another.

Positive Psychology   Approach that encourages psychologists to use fewer negative or problem-focused frameworks and to focus more on effective human functioning.

Post-Concussion Syndrome Symptoms experienced subsequent to a concussion, such as memory problems, difficulties in concentration, headaches, dizziness, and irritability.

Posttraumatic Growth Positive psychological or lifestyle outcome from an experience with a life-threatening illness.

Practical Support (tangible support) Help with the demands of daily living, such as getting meals and rides to the doctor.

Predictability A characteristic of the environment that allows an individual to prepare for an event and therefore reduce the stress involved.

Prevalence In epidemiology, the total number of cases that exist at any given time.

Primary Appraisal The initial evaluation of a situation.

Primary Care Physicians Those physicians in general and family practice.

Problem-Focused Coping Coping by actively addressing the stressors associated with a disease such as cancer and its treatment.

Problem-Based Learning (PBL) Learning in which students work in groups to solve the problems posed by actual cases.

Problem-Focused Coping The altering of a situation or the creating of conditions in which stress and danger are reduced; a rational approach that involves changing the situation by defining the problem, looking at alternative solutions, evaluating the implications of the alternatives, and choosing the best one to act on.

Procedure-Based Information Information given by a technologist at the time of a procedure that addresses what will be done and why it will be done.

Process Goals Goals that focus on specific processes that a performer will be concerned with during a performance.

Prognosis A prediction of how a medical condition will change in the future.

Progressive Illness A condition that will continue to worsen in spite of treatment.

Progressive Muscle Relaxation (PMR) A technique in which a person achieves relaxation by flexing and gradually relaxing muscle groups.

Protease Inhibitors Medication that can significantly prolong the lives of people living with AIDS.

Psychoeducational Care When applied to the postoperative period, the provision of information regarding self-care practices, further procedures, and typical patterns of recovery.

Psychological Methods (in sport) Techniques such as relaxation, goal-setting, and imagery, which are used to develop psychological skills.

Psychological Skills (in sport) Arousal or attentional control implemented to enhance performance.

Psychoneuroimmunology (PNI) The study of the relationship between psychological states and the functioning of the immune system.

Psychosocial Communication Pattern A communication pattern that includes a substantial amount of psychosocial exchange between the physician and patient.

Psychosomatic Medicine Approach in which a particular medical complaint is viewed as being the result of an underlying chronic emotional conflict that ultimately surfaces in the form of physiological symptoms.

Public Health Level (of health promotion) Promotion in which the orientation is behaviour-based and the goal is disease prevention.

Quality of Life The extent to which symptoms and treatment affect a person's physical, social, cognitive, and emotional functioning.

Quasiexperimental designs Research done in real-life settings, but in which experimental methods (manipulation of variables) are used.

Radiation Therapy   A form of cancer treatment in which radiation is used to shrink or destroy tumours.

Radical Surgery   Cancer surgery that requires the removal of a considerable amount of normal tissue.

Random Assignment   Determining who will be in a experimental group and who will be in a control group randomly so that individual differences should be evenly divided between the two groups.

Random Clinical Trial Studies   Research in which participants are randomly assigned to treatment conditions.

Reactance   Behaving counter to recommendations in response to feeling that one has lost personal control over health behaviours; the non-compliant behaviours and attitudes of patients who perceive hospital rules and regiments to be unacceptable challenges to their freedom.

Reactivity Hypothesis   The hypothesis that people whose sympathetic divisions are more reactive would be more likely to experience immunosuppression when under stress.

Readaptation Stage   A period in ICU when a patient can sense a struggle to recover and recognizes his or her dependence on machines.

Reality Shock   The reaction to the discrepancy between a training environment and an actual work environment.

Reappraisal   A continuous experience in which existing appraisals of situations are changed or modified on the basis of new information.

Referent Power   Power that stems from a particular person or group with whom the patient desires to identify.

Reflexion Stage   A period during which a patient who was in ICU tries to piece together his or her recent experience.

Relaxation Skills   Techniques to reduce anxiety to manageable levels so that the energy can be used to positively influence performance;

based on the principle that we cannot be relaxed and tense at the same time.

Residency   A period of further training after internship, in which physicians encounter a rather sudden increase in accountability.

Resilience   Concept in positive psychology that describes "good outcomes in spite of serious threats to adaptation or development"

Resistance   A set of physiological responses that allow a person to deal with a stressor; the second phase of Selye's General Adaptation Syndrome in which the body mobilizes its resources if the source of stress moves from acute to chronic.

Respondent Pain   Pain that occurs in response to noxious stimulation or tissue damage.

Response Efficacy   The perception that a threat-reducing strategy will work.

Restraint Theory   An explanation for eating behaviour that claims that external sensitivity is linked to *restrained eating* (or strict dieting), rather than to body weight, and that overeating is more likely in people who restrain their eating.

Reticular Formation   Complex system running through the middle of the brain stem that serves as a communication network to filter messages between the brain and the body.

Retrospective Research.   Design in which researchers study people who have developed medical conditions, or who have died from them, and trace back in their history to find variables that would possibly explain how they came to have that condition.

Reward Power   The mediation of rewards, either tangible or intangible, by a physician to promote patient adherence to medical recommendations.

Role Strain   Stress as a result of the demands of multiple social roles, such as health care practitioner and mother.

Rotational Injury   A type of concussion resulting from a blow to the side of the head.

Sampling Bias   Situation in which the people who take part in a study are different somehow from the population that the researchers are studying.

Search Engine   Internet service that scans the web with remarkable speed and thoroughness to find locations where desired information is stored.

Second Impact Syndrome   The result when an athlete who has suffered a concussion returns to activity too soon and receives another blow to the head that can result in much greater trauma to the brain than that initially experienced.

Secondary Appraisal   A person's evaluation of his or her ability to cope with a situation subsequent to the initial evaluation of the nature of the event.

Sedatives   Medications, such as barbiturates, that affect pain indirectly by reducing anxiety and helping the patient to sleep.

Self-Awareness Model   A theory that suggests that drinking inhibits the use of normal complex information-processing strategies, such as memory and information acquisition, making people less self-aware.

Self-Care   Behaviours such as exercise, diet, voluntary screening, and regular medical check-ups that one engages in to promote one's health.

Self-Efficacy   An individual's perception of his or her ability to succeed at a particular task at a specific time.

Self-Management Strategies   Strategies used to help people overcome the environmental conditions that perpetuate smoking.

Self-Reinforcement   Praising oneself or rewarding oneself for accomplishments.

Self-Talk   Sport psychology concept to describe one of the methods athletes use to correct bad habits, focus attention, modify activation, increase self-confidence and efficacy, and maintain exercise behaviour.

Sensation-Based Information   Information given by a technologist at the time of a procedure that includes what a procedure will feel like or sound like and how long it will last.

Sensitivity (of medical tests) The ability of a test to identify correctly those who have a particular disease.

Seroconversion   The production of antibodies by memory B cells when exposed to a specific previously encountered and remembered antigen.

Set-Point Theory   The idea that the body contains a set-point that works like a thermostat. When one gains weight, biological control mechanisms diminish caloric intake. When one loses weight, similar mechanisms increase hunger levels until the weight returns to its ideal or target level.

Shiatsu Massage   A deep massage conducted with movements such as friction, percussion, and pettrisage to release the flow of energy blockages according to the underlying belief of this treatment.

Sick Role   A status that, when temporarily and legitimately adopted, exempts people from their other roles.

Sites of Cancer   Types of cancer as defined by the location of the tumour.

Situation Variables   Variables that interact with person variables to influence the appraisal of a situation.

Social Comparison   Monitoring of the opinions and experiences of others to determine what is right and wrong, normal and abnormal, and subsequent use of this information to help with decision making.

Social Dominance   A risk factor for coronary disease that is independent of hostility; social dominance is described as "a set of controlling behaviours, including the tendency to cut off and talk over the interviewer."

Social Factors in Stress   The elements of a person's social network, such as family, friends, and coworkers, that affect ability to cope with job stressors.

Social Learning Model   This theory, when applied to drinking behaviour, proposes that people drink because they experience positive reinforcement for doing so or because they observe others drinking and model the behaviour.

Social Support A collection of interpersonal resources that we have at our disposal to help us avoid or cope with difficult times in our lives.

Socioemotional Care Interactions that help patients maintain a sense of optimism and psychological well-being.

Socioenvironmental Level (of health promotion) Promotion in which the orientation is toward social change and public health policy.

Specific Immunity Protection against a particular antigen.

Specificity The ability of a test to identify correctly those who do not have a particular disease.

Specificity (of immune system cells) Ability of certain immune system cells to remember an antigen and respond only to the remembered antigen.

Sport An activity that involves rules or limits, a sense of history, an aspect of winning and losing, and an emphasis on physical exertion in the context of competition.

Sport Psychology The study of the influence of psychological factors on sport behaviour.

Stages of Change Model Model in which change is broken down into six stages: precontemplation, contemplation, action, maintenance, termination, and relapse.

States and Traits Psychological concept that distinguishes between short-term conditions (states) and enduring characteristics (traits).

Stimulant A drug that increases alertness, decreases appetite and the need for sleep, and may produce intense feelings of euphoria and a strong sense of well-being.

Stimulation-Produced Analgesia (SPA) Freedom from pain as a result of electrical stimulation.

Stress The non-specific mental or somatic result of any demand upon the body.

Stress-Buffering Hypothesis A theory that posits that social support has an indirect effect and acts as a buffer to protect individuals from the negative effects of stress.

Stress-Diathesis Model Model that examines the interaction between the environment and heredity, often referred to as *nature versus nurture*. This model proposes that predisposing factors in an individual may determine whether or not a physical effect is experienced in the presence of stressful events.

Stress Inoculation Training A technique designed to help people cope effectively with stressful events. It includes reconceptualizing events in less stressful ways, improving coping strategies, and applying the reconceptualized cognitive and behavioural approach to relevant stressors.

Stress Intrusion Scores A measure of the impact a stressful event has on a person's life.

Stress Literacy The degree to which an individual (or community) is knowledgeable about the effects of stress.

Stress Management Techniques Techniques that have been developed specifically to help people cope with stress either directly or indirectly.

Stress Response A response that reflects a spontaneous emotional or behavioural reaction to stress, rather than a deliberate attempt to cope.

Stressful Appraisal A cognitive process by which an event is appraised to involve harm/loss, threat, or challenge at the time of the primary appraisal.

Subjective Norms Beliefs regarding what others think we should do and the extent to which we are motivated to go along with these people.

Suppressor T Cells (CD8) Cells that stop the production of antibodies after the antigen has been destroyed.

Swedish Massage Slow, gentle stroking movements to warm and relax tissue and stimulate blood circulation.

Symbolic Interactionism Sociological theory that people's interpretations of their interactions and the events of their lives go well beyond the actual words used or, in the case of health-related events, the diagnosis they are given.

Sympathetic (nervous system) The system responsible for the "fight or flight" response when triggered by the hypothalamus (e.g., faster heart beat, increased blood pressure).

Systematic Desensitization A technique to help people cope with fear and anxiety by combining relaxation with gradual exposure to the fear-inducing stimulus.

Systemic Infection An infection that spreads to affect a number of areas of the body at once.

T Lymphocytes (helper T cells) Cells that produce substances called interleukins that speed the division of B lymphocyte cells.

Task Orientation A goal perspective in which individuals derive satisfaction from the sense of competence experienced as they improve. The focus is on effort and their own performance rather that that of others.

Technical Care Activities involving prescribed medical procedures, independent of the psychological needs of the patient.

Telemedicine The use of electronic media to practise medicine between physical sites.

Temporal Uncertainty Lack of knowledge as to when an event will occur, which can result in stress.

Tension Reduction Hypothesis A hypothesis that maintains that people drink alcohol because of its tension-reducing properties.

Theory of Planned Behaviour A theory that posits that behaviour is preceded by intention and that our intention is influenced, not only by subjective norms and beliefs about the efficacy of the behaviour, but also by the belief that one is actually capable of performing the behaviour.

Theory of Reasoned Action A theory that posits that behaviour is preceded by intention and that our intention is influenced by beliefs about the behaviour and subjective norms.

Therapeutic Rituals In nursing practice, primarily activities that deal with patient-nurse interactions, for example, the administration of medication and bathing of patients.

Thermal Biofeedback Biofeedback that measures temperature and blood flow.

Threat Appraisal An appraisal at the time of the initial evaluation of a potentially stressful situation (primary appraisal) that involves the anticipation of harm or loss.

Threat Perception The belief that a threat is real and that we are vulnerable to it.

Thyroid Gland A gland that is important in the stress response because of its production of thyroxine, which increases blood pressure and respiration rate and affects mental processes.

Tolerance (of immune system cells) The ability of immune system cells to remember and respond to a remembered antigen while not reacting to the body's own cells.

Total Institution Any institution, such as a hospital, that takes control of virtually every aspect of a person's day-to-day life.

Tranquillizers Medications such as diazepam (Valium) that affect pain indirectly by reducing patient anxiety.

Transcendental Meditation (TM) A technique of meditation to reduce stress introduced by Maharishi Mahesh Yogi in the late 1950s.

Transcript Analysis The recording of interactions with patients followed by transcribing them to paper; often used by medical sociologists adopting a symbolic interactionist perspective.

Transcutaneous Electrical Nerve Stimulation (TENS) A pain control technique that involves placing an electrode on the surface of the skin and applying electrical stimulation.

Triage The sorting and classifying of patients to determine priority of need and proper location and means of treatment.

Type A Behaviour Pattern Behaviours include impatience, time urgency, aggressiveness, hostility, and competitiveness; originally believed to be predictive of coronary heart disease.

Type C Personality   A cancer-prone personality typified by passivity.

Uncertainty   A significant source of stress for physicians resulting from the fact that the consequences of medical decisions are uncertain.

Uniformity Myth   Belief that all patients should receive the same amount of information in their preparation for a hospital stay regardless of their personal styles of coping with stress.

Unit of Analysis   The nature of a discipline's ultimate focus (in psychology, the individual; in sociology, the group).

Upper Respiratory Infection (URI)   One of a collection of illnesses such as colds, coughs, and bronchitis.

URL (Uniform Resource Locators)
Locations where desired information is stored and can be accessed from a computer.

Usability   The quality of a user's experience when interacting with a product or system; an important criterion in assessing Internet sites.

Verbal Rating Scale (VRS)   A rating scale in which people are asked to describe their pain by choosing the phrase that most closely resembles the pain that they are experiencing.

Vicarious Experience   Experience that is gained through observing or visualizing others perform a skill, which can alert one to one's own capabilities and raise one's sense of self-efficacy.

Viral Challenge Studies   Studies in which volunteer subjects are intentionally exposed to controlled dosages of upper respiratory infection viruses and to environmental stressors to measure the clinical progression of the virus and the response of the immune system.

Visual Analog Scale (VAS)   A scale on which people rate and report their pain by marking a point on a line anchored by the phrase "no pain" and by a phrase like "worst pain imaginable."

Vulnerability   Physically, the adequacy of an individual's resources; psychologically, when that which is valued by the individual is threatened.

Withdrawal   The unpleasant symptoms people experience when they stop using a substance on which they have become dependent.

References

Abbott, B., Ippoliti, C., Bruton, J., Neumann, J., Whaley, R., & Champlin, R. (1999). Antiemetic efficacy of granisetron plus dexamethasone in bone marrow transplant patients receiving chemotherapy and total body irradiation. *Bone Marrow Transplant, 23(3)*, 265–269.

Abbott, R.D., Rodriguez, B.L., Burfiel, C.M., & Curb, J.D. (1994). Physical activity in older middle-aged man and reduced risk of stroke: The Honolulu Heart Program. *American Journal of Epidemiology, 139*, 881–893.

Abrahm, J.L. (2003). Update in palliative medicine and end-of-life care. *Annu Rev Med, 54*, 53–72.

Abramson, L., Garber, J., & Seligman, M.E.P. (1980). Learned helplessness in humans: An attributional analysis. In J. Garber & M.E.P. Seligman (Eds.), *Human helplessness: Theory and applications* (pp. 3–34). New York: Academic Press.

Absetz, P., Aro, A.R., & Sutton, S.R. (2003). Experience with breast cancer, pre-screening perceived susceptibility and the psychological impact of screening. *Psychooncology, 12*(4), 305–318.

Achilles, R. (2000). *Defining complementary and alternative health care*. Ottawa: Strategies and Systems Health Directorate, Health Promotions and Programs Branch, Health Canada.

Achterberg, J., Kenner, C., & Lawlis, G.F. (1988). Severe burn injuries: A comparison of relaxation imagery and biofeedback for pain management. *Journal of Mental Imagery, 1*, 71–87.

Ader, R. (Ed.) (1981). *Psychoneuroimmunology*. New York: Academic Press.

Agras, S., Hammer, L., & McNicholas, F. (1999). A prospective study of the influence of eating-disordered mothers on their children. *International Journal of Eating Disorders, 25*, 253–263.

Agras, W.S., Schneider, J.A., Arnow, B., Raeburn, S.D., & Telch, C.F. (1989). Cognitive– behavioral and response-prevention treatments for bulimia nervosa. *Journal of Consulting and Clinical Psychology, 57*, 215–221.

AIDS. (2003). Ottawa: Health Canada.

AIDS epidemic update. (2002). Geneva, Switzerland: UN AIDS/ WHO.

AIDS: The AIDS/ HIV Files. (2002). Health Canada. Available: www.hc-sc.gc.ca/english/feature/aids/symptoms_main.html [2003, July 25].

Ajzen, I. (1985). From intentions to actions: A theory of planned behaviour. In J. Kuhland & J. Beckman (Eds.), *Action-control: From cognitions to behavior* (pp. 11–39). Heidelberg, Germany: Springer.

Ajzen, I. (1991). The theory of planned behavior. *Organizational Behavior and Human Decision Processes, 50*, 179–211.

Ajzen, I., & Fishbein, M. (1980). *Understanding attitudes and predicting social behaviour*. Englewood Cliffs, NJ: Prentice-Hall.

Akil, H., Watson, S.J., Young, E., Lewis, M.E., et al. (1984). Endogenous opioids: Biology and function. *Annual Review of Neuroscience, 7*, 223–255.

Alaranta, H., Rytökoski, U., Rissanen, A., Talo, S., et al. (1994). Intensive physical and psychosocial training program for patients with chronic low back pain: A controlled clinical trial. *Spine, 19*, 1339–1349.

Alberta Alcohol and Drug Abuse Commission (1999, December 31). Beyond the ABCs: Information for professionals. Http://www.gov.ab.ca/aadac/addictions/beyond/beyond

Albertsen, P. (1998, November). A competing risk analysis of outcomes associated with men treated conservatively for clinically localized prostate cancer. Paper presented at the *Cancer Care: Quality of Life and Outcomes Symposium*, Chicago, Illinois.

Alcohol and drug abuse among treaty Indians in Saskatchewan: Needs assessment and recommendations for change. (1984). Federation of Saskatchewan Indian Nations.

Aldwin, C.M. (1994). *Stress, coping and development: An integrative perspective.* New York: Guilford Press.

Alexander, C.N., Robinson, P., Orme-Johnson, D.W., Schneider, R.H., & Walton, K.G. (1994). The effects of transcendental meditation compared to other methods of relaxation and meditation in reducing risk factors, morbidity, & mortality. *Homeostasis, 35*, 243–263.

Allison, D.B., Kaprio, J., Korkeila, M., Koskenvuo, M., Neale, M.C., & Hayakawa, K. (1996). The heritability of body mass index among an international sample of monozygotic twins reared apart. *International Journal of Obesity and Related Metabolic Disorders, 20,* 501–506.

Allumbaugh, D.L., & Hoyt, W.T. (1999). Effectiveness of grief therapy: A meta-analysis. *Journal of Counseling Psychology, 46*, 370–380.

Aloise-Young, P.A., Hennigan, K.M., & Graham, J.W. (1996). Role of the self-image and smoker stereotype in smoking onset during early adolescence: A longitudinal study. *Health Psychology, 15*, 494–497.

Alon, E., Jaquenod, M., & Schaeppi, B. (2003). Post-operative epidural versus intravenous patient-controlled analgesia. *Minerva Anestesiol, 69*(5), 443–437.

Alonso, J., Black, C., Norregaard, J.C., Dunn, E., et al. (1998). *Medical Care, 36*, 868–878.

Amelang, M. (1997). Using personality variables to predict cancer and heart disease. *European Journal of Personality, 11*, 319–342.

American Psychiatric Association (n.d.). Practice guideline for the treatment of patients with eating disorders. http://www.psych.org/clin_res/guide.bk-4.cfm [July 21, 2003].

American Psychiatric Association (APA). (1997). *Diagnostic and statistical manual of mental disorders* (4th ed.). Washington, DC: Author.

Anand, B.K., & Chhina, G.S. (1961). Investigations on yogis claiming to stop their heart beats. *Indian Journal of Medical Research, 49*, 90–94.

Anand, B.K., Chhina, G.S., & Singh, B. (1961a). Studies on Shri Ramand Yogi during his stay in an air-tight box. Indian *Journal of Medical Research, 49*, 82–89.

Anand, B.K., Chhina, G.S., & Singh, B. (1961b). Some aspects of electroencephalographic studies in yogis. *EEG and Clinical Neurophysiology, 13*, 452–456.

Andersen, B.L., Cacioppo, J.T., & Roberts, D.C. (1995). Delay in seeking a cancer diagnosis: Delay stages and psychophysiological comparison processes. *British Journal of Social Psychology, 34*, 33–52.

Andersen, B.L., Farrar, W.B., Golden-Kreutz, D., Kutz, L.A., MacCallum, R., Courtney, E., and Glaser, R. (1998). Stress and immune responses after surgical treatment for regional breast cancer. *Journal of the National Cancer Institute, 90*, 30–36.

Andersen, M.R., & Urban, N. (1997). Physician gender and screening: Do patient differences account for differences in mammography use? *Women and Health, 26(1)*, 29–39.

Anderson, D.F., & Cychosz, C.M. (1994). Development of an Exercise Identity Scale. *Perceptual and Motor Skills, 78,* 747–751.

Anderson, E.A. (1987). Preoperative preparation for cardiac surgery facilitates recovery, reduces psychological distress, and reduces the incidence of acute postoperative hypertension. *Journal of Consulting and Clinical Psychology, 55,* 513–520.

Anderson, K.O., Bradley, L.A., Young, L.D., McDaniel, L.K., & Wise, C.M. (1985). Rheumatoid arthritis: Review of psycholgical factors related to etiology, effects, and treatment. *Psychological Bulletin, 98,* 358–387.

Anderson, J. G. (1999). The business of cyberhealthcare. *MD Computing, 16*(6), 23–25.

Anderson, P. (2000). The evidence of health promotion effectiveness: Shaping Public Health in a New Europe: Part Two. A report for the European Commission by the International Union for Health Promotion and Education. Brussels.

Anderson, R., Freedland, K., Clouse, R., & Lustman, P. (2001). Prevalence of comorbid depression in adults with diabetes. A meta-analysis. *Diabetes Care, 24,* 1069–1078.

Andersson, A., & Holmgren, E. (1975). On acupuncture analgesia and the mechanism of pain. *American Journal of Chinese Medicine, 3,* 311–334.

Antepohl, W., & Herzig, S. (1999). Problem-based learning versus lecture-based learning in a course of basic pharmacology: A controlled randomized study. *Medical Education, 33,* 106–113.

Antoni, M.H., August, S. LaPerriere, A., Baggett, H.L., Klimas, N., et al., (1990). Psychological and neuroendocrine measures related to functional immune changes in anticipation of HIV-1 serostatus notification. *Psychosomatic Medicine, 52,* 496–510.

Antoni, M.H., Kumar, M., Ironson, G., Cruess, D.G., Cruess, S., Lutgendorf, S., Klimas, N., Fletcher, M., and Schneiderman, N. (2000). Cognitive-behavioral stress management intervention effects on anxiety, 24-hr urinary norepinephrine output, and T-cytotoxic/suppressor cells over time among symptomatic HIV-infected gay men. *Journal of Consulting and Clinical Psychology, 68,* 31–45.

Arborelius, E., & Bremberg, S. (1992). What can doctors do to achieve a successful consultation? Videotaped interviews analyzed by the 'consultation map' method. *Family Practice, 9,* 61–66.

Arborelius, E., & Thakker, K.D. (1995). Why is it so difficult for general practitioners to discuss alcohol with patients? *Family Practice, 4,* 199–422.

Armitage, C.J., Norman, P. and Conner, M. (2002). Can the Theory of Planned Behaviour mediate the effects of age, gender and multidimensional health locus of control? *British Journal of Health Psychology, 7,* 299–316.

Arnow, B., Kenardy, J., & Agraw, S.W. (1992). Binge eating among the obese: A descriptive study. *Journal of Behavioral Medicine, 15,* 155–170.

Aronoff, G.M. (2000). Opioids in chronic pain management: Is there a significant risk of addiction? *Current review of Pain, 4,* 112–121.

Aronoff, G.M., Wagner, J.M., & Spangler, A.S. (1986). Chemical interventions for pain. *Journal of Consulting and Clinical Psychology, 54,* 769–775.

Arouni, A.J., & Rich, E.C. (2003). Physician gender and patient care. *J Gend Specif Med, 6*(1), 24–30.

Ary, D.V., & Biglan, A. (1988). Longitudinal changes in adolescent cigarette smoking behavior: Onset and cessation. *Journal of Behavioral Medicine, 11,* 361–382.

Asmundson, G.J.G., Norton, G.R., Allerdings, M.D., Norton, P.J., & Larsen, D.K. (1998). Posttraumatic stress disorder and work-related injury. *Journal of Anxiety Disorders, 12*, 57–69.

Aspinwall, L.G. 7 Taylor, S.E. (1997). A stitch in time: Self-regulation and proactive coping. *Psychological Bulletin, 121*, 417–436.

Astle, S.J. (1996). The experience of loss in athletes. *Journal of Sports Medicine and Physical Fitness, 26*, 279–284.

Atkinson, J.M. (1993). The patient as sufferer. *British Journal of Medical Psychology, 66(2)*, 113–120.

Auslander, G.K., Netzer, D., & Arad, I. (2003). Parental anxiety following discharge from hospital of their very low birth weight infants. *Family Relations: Interdisciplinary Journal of Applied Family Studies, 52*(1), 12–21.

Ayanian, J.Z., & Cleary, P.D. (1999). Perceived risks of heart disease and cancer among cigarette smokers. *Journal of the American Medical Association, 281*, 1019–1021.

Azar, B. (1999, February). Sex differences in pain reports may be smaller than previously thought. *APA Monitor*, p. 7.

Badgley, R.F. (1994). Health promotion and social change in the health of Canadians. In Pederson, A., O'Neill, M., & Rootman, I. (Eds.), *Health promotion in Canada: Provincial, national and international perspectives*. (pp. 200–239). Toronto, ON: Saunders.

Bahrke, M.S., & Morgan, W.P. (1978). Anxiety reduction following exercise and meditation. *Cognitive Therapy and Research, 2*, 323–334.

Baider, L., Cooper, C.L., & Kaplan De Nour, A. (Eds.) (1996). *Cancer and the family*. Chichester, England: Wiley.

Bain, D.J.G. (1979). The relationship between time and clinical management in family practice. *Journal of Family Practice, 8*, 551–559.

Baker, C., & Melby, V. (1996). An investigation into the attitudes and practices of intensive care nurses toward verbal communication with unconscious patients. *Journal of Clinical Nursing, 5*, 185–192.

Baker, L., Wagner, T.H., Singer, S., & Bundorf, M.K. (2003). Use of the Internet and e-mail for health care information: Results from a national survey. *JAMA: Journal of the American Medical Association, 289*(18), 2400–2406.

Baker, L.H., Cooney, N.L., & Pomerleau, O.F. (1987). Craving for alcohol: *Theoretical processes and treatment procedures. In Treatment and prevention of alcohol problems: A resource manual* (pp. 183–202).

Balfour, L., Silverman, A., Tasca, G., Kowal, J., Seatter, R., and Cameron, W. (2003). Stress and depression related to lower immune system functioning among people with HIV (PHAS). Presentation to the 64th Annual Conference of the Canadian Psychological Association, June 12, Hamilton, Ontario.

Ball, G.D.C., & McCargar, L.J. (2003). Childhood obesity in Canada: A review of prevalence estimates and risk factors for cardiovascular diseases and type 2 diabetes. *Canadian Journal of Applied Physiology, 28*, 117–140.

Balla, J.I. (1982). The late whiplash syndrome: A study of an illness in Australia and Singapore. *Culture, Medicine and Psychiatry, 6*, 191–210.

Bandura, A. (1977). Self-efficacy: Toward a unifying theory of behavior change. *Psychological Review, 84*, 191–215.

Bandura, A. (1986). *Social foundations of thought and action: A social cognitive theory*. Inglewood Cliffs, New Jersey: Prentice-Hall.

Bandura, A. (1990). Perceived self-efficacy in the exercise of personal agency. *Journal of Applied Sport Psychology, 2*, 128–163.

Bandura, A. (1991). Self-efficacy mechanism in physiological activation and health-promotion behavior. In J. Madden IV (Ed.), *Neurobiology of learning, emotion, and affect* (pp. 229–269). New York: Raven Press.

Bandura, A. (1997) *Self-efficacy: The exercise of control*. New York: Freeman.

Bannister, R (l955) *The four-minute mile*. New York: Dodd, Mead.

Barber, J. (1986). Hypnotic analgesia. In A.D. Holzman & D.C. Turk (Eds.), *Pain management: A handbook of psychological treatment approaches*. New York: Pergamon Press.

Barbounis, V., Koumakis, G., Hatzichristou, H., Vassilomanolakis, M., Tsoussis, S., & Efremidis, A. (1999). The anti-emetic efficacy of tropisotron plus dexamethasone in patients treated with high-dose chemotherapy and stem cell transplantation. *Support Care Cancer, 7(2)*, 79–83.

Barling, N.R., & Moore, S.M. (1996). Prediction of cervical cancer screening using the theory of reasoned action. *Psychological Reports, 79*, 77–78.

Baron, R.S., Cutrona, C.E., Hicklin, D., Russell, D.W., & Lubaroff, D.M. (1990). Social support and immune function among spouses of cancer patients. *Journal of Personality and Social Psychology, 59*, 344–352.

Barraclough, J., Pinder, P., Cruddas, M., Osmond, C., Taylor, I., & Perry, M. (1992). Life events and breast cancer prognosis. *British Medical Journal, 304*, 1078–1081.

Barton, J., Chassin, L., Presson, C.C., & Sherman, S.J. (1982). Social image factors as motivators of smoking initiation in early and middle adolescence. *Child Development, 53*, 1499–1511.

Bates, D.W., Leape, L.L., Cullen, D.J., Laird, N., Petersen, L.A., Teich, J.M., Burdick, E., Hickey, M., Kleefield, S., Shea, B., Vliet, M.V., & Seger, D.L. (1998). Effect of computerized physician order entry and a team intervention on prevention of serious medication errors. *Journal of the American Medical Association, 280*(15), 1311–1316.

Battle, E.K., & Brownell, K.D. (1996). Confronting a rising tide of eating disorders and obesity: Treatment vs. prevention and policy. *Addictive Behaviors, 21*, 755–765.

Bauchner, H., Vinci, R., Bak, S., Pearson, C., & Corwin, M.J. (1996). Parents and procedures: A randomized controlled trial. *Pediatrics, 98*, 861–867.

Baum, A., & Posluszny, D.M. (1999). Health psychology: Mapping biobehavioral contributions to health and illness. *Annual Review of Psychology, 50*, 137–163.

Baxter, N., Cohen, R., & McLeod, R. (1996). The impact of gender on the choice of surgery as a career. *American Journal of Surgery, 172*, 373–376.

Beck, A. (1963). Thinking and depression: 1. Idiosyncratic content and cognitive distortions. *Archives of General Psychiatry, 9*, 324–333.

Beck, A. (1976). *Cognitive therapy and the emotional disorders*. New York: International Universities Press.

Becker, M.H. (1974). The health belief model and sick role behavior. *Health Education Monographs, 2*, 409–419.

Becker, M.H. (1979). Understanding patient compliance: The contributions of attitudes and other psychosocial factors. In S.J. Cohen (Ed.), *New directs in patient compliance*. Lexington, MA: Heath.

Becker, M.H., & Janz, N.K. (1987). On the effectiveness and utility of health hazard/health risk appraisal in clinical and nonclinical settings. *Health Services Research, 22*, 537–551.

Becker, M.H., & Maiman, L.A. (1975). Sociobehavioral determinants of compliance with health care and medical care recommendations. *Medical Care, 13*, 10–24.

Beckman, H.B., & Frankel, R.M. (1984). The effect of physician behavior on the collection of data. *Annals of Internal Medicine, 101*, 692–696.

Beecher, H.K. (1959). *Measurement of subjective responses*. New York: Oxford University Press.

Begun, F.P. (1993). Epidemiology and natural history of prostate cancer. In Lepor, H, & Lawson, R.K. (Eds.), *Prostate disease* (pp. 257–268). Philadelphia: W.B. Saunders.

Beisecker, A. & Beisecker, T. (1990). Patient information-seeking behaviors when communicating with doctors. *Medical Care, 28*, 19–28.

Bell, D.S., Daly, D.M., & Robinson, P. (2003). Is there a Digital Divide Among Physicians? A geographic analysis of information technology in Southern California physician offices. *Journal of the American Medical InformaticsAssociation, 10*, 484–493.

Bender, R., Trautner, C., Spraul, M., & Berger, M. (1998). Assessment of excess mortality in obesity. American *Journal of Epidemiology, 147*, 42–48.

Benesh, L.R., Szigeti, E., Feraro, F.R., & Gullicks, J.N. (1997). Tools for assessing chronic pain in rural elderly women. *Home Healthcare Nurse, 15*, 207–211.

Bennenbroek, F.T.C., Buunk, B.P., van der Zee, K.I., & Grol, B. (2002). Social comparison and patient information: What do cancer patients want? *Patient Education & Counseling, 47*, 5–12.

Ben-Sira, Z. (1980). Affective and instrumental components in the physician-patient relationship: An additional dimension of interaction theory. *Journal of Health and Social Behavior, 21*, 180–180.

Benson, H. (1975). *The relaxation response*. New York: William Morrow.

Benson, H., Beary, J.F., & Carol, M.P. (1974). The relaxation response. *Psychiatry, 37*, 37–46.

Ben-Zur, H. (2002). Monitoring/blunting and social support: Associations with coping and affect. *International Journal of Stress Management, 9*(4), 357–373.

Beresford, H.R., & Brooke, M.H. (1999). The Webster's Dictionary: Neurologists on the Internet. *Neurology, 52*, 1730–1731.

Bergh, K.D. (1998). The patient's differential diagnosis. Unpredictable concerns in visits for acute cough. *Journal of Family Practice, 46, 153–158.*

Bergman, B., Ahmad, F., & Stewart, D.E. (2003). Physician health, stress and gender at a university hospital. *Journal of Psychosomatic Research, 54*(2), 171–178

Berkley, K.J. (1997). Sex differences in pain. *Behavioral and Brain Sciences, 20*, 371–380.

Berkman, L.F., Breslow, L., & Wingard, D. (1983). Health practices and mortality risk. In L.F. Berkman & L. Breslow (Eds.), *Health and ways of living: The Alameda county study*. New York: Oxford University Press.

Berkman, L.F., & Syme, S.L. (1979). Social networks, host resistance, and mortality: A nine-year follow-up study of Alameda County residents. *American Journal of Epidemiology, 109*, 186–204.

Berkowitz, R.I., Agras, W.S., Korner, A.F., Kraemer, H.C., & Zeanah, C.H. (1985). Physical activity and adiposity: A longitudinal study from birth to childhood. *Journal of Pediatrics, 106, 734–738.*

Berland, G.K., Elliott, M.N., Morales, L.S., Algazy, J.I., Kravitz, R.L., Broder, M.S., Kanouse, D.E., Muñoz, J.A., Puyol, J.-A., Lara, M., Watkins, K.E., Yang, H., & McGlynn, E.A. (2001). Health information on the Internet: Accessibility, quality, and readability in English and Spanish. *Journal of the American Medical Association, 285*(20), 2612–2621.

Bernstein, D.A., & Borkovec, T.D. (1978) *Progressive relaxation training: A manual for the helping professions*. Champaign, Illinois: Research Press.

Bernstein, D.A., & Given, B.A. (1984). Progressive relaxation: Abbreviated methods. In R. Woolfolk and P. Lehrer (Eds.), *Principles and practice of stress management*. New York: Guilford Press.

Beyer, J.E., & Wells, N. (1989). The assessment of pain in children. *Pediatric Clinics of North America, 36*, 837–855.

Beyerstein, B. (1997). Alternative medicine: Where's the evidence? *Canadian Journal of Public Health, 88*, 149–152.

Bezak, J.E., & Lee, J.W. (1990). Relationship of self-efficacy and locus of control constructs in predicting college students' physical fitness behaviors. *Perceptual and Motor Skills, 71*, 499–508.

Bilney, C. & D'Ardenne, P. (2001). The truth is rarely pure and never simple: A study of some factors affecting history-sharing in the GUM clinic setting. *Sexual and Relationship Therapy, 16*, 349–374.

Bhatnagar, D. Anand, I.S., Durrington, P.N., Patel, D.J., Wander, G.S., Mackness, M. I., et al. (1995). Coronary risk factors in people from the Indian subcontinent living in west London and their siblings in India. *Lancet, 345*, 405–409.

Biddle, S.J.H. & Mutrie, N. (2001). *Psychology of physical activity: Determinants, well-being and interventions*. New York: Routledge.

Biglan, A., Duncan, T.E., Ary, D.V., & Smolkowski, K. (1995). Peer and parental influences on adolescent tobacco use. *Journal of Behavioral Medicine, 18*, 315–330.

Biglan, A., McConnell, S., Severson, H.H., Bavry, J., & Ary, D. (1984). A situational analysis of adolescent smoking. *Journal of Behavioral Medicine, 7*, 109–114.

Birk, L. (Ed.) (1973). *Biofeedback: Behavioral medicine*. New York: Grune and Stratton.

Bishop, S.R., & Warr, D. (2003). Coping, catastrophizing and chronic pain in breast cancer. *J Behav Med, 26*(3), 265–281.

Birmingham, C.L., Muller, J.L., Palepu, A., Spinella, J.J., & Anis, A.H. (1999). The cost of obesity in Canada. *Canadian Medical Association Journal, 160*, 483–488.

Birnbaum, M.H., Wong, R., & Wong, L.K. (1976). Combining information from sources that vary in credibility. *Memory and Cognition, 4*, 330–336.

Blackwell, B. (1997). From compliance to alliance: A quarter century of research. In B. Blackwell (Ed.), *Treatment compliance and the therapeutic alliance* (pp. 1–15). Amsterdam: Harwood Academic Publishers.

Blair, S.N., Kohl, H.W., Paffenberger, R.S., Clark, D.G., Cooper, K.H., & Gibbons, L.W. (1989). Physical fitness and all-cause mortality: A prospective study of healthy men and women. *Journal of the American Medical Association, 262*, 2395–2401.

Blanchard, C.G., Albrecht, T.L., Ruckdceschel, J.C., Grant, C.H., Hemmick, R.M. (1995). The role of social support in adaptation to cancer and to survival. *Journal of Psychosocial Oncology, 13*, 75–95.

Blanchard, E.B. (1977). Behavioral medicine: A perspective. In R.B. Williams and W.D. Gentry (Eds.), *Behavioral approaches to medical treatment*. Cambridge, Massachusetts: Ballinger.

Blanchard, E.B. (1987). Long-term effects of behavioral treatment of chronic headache. *Behavior Therapy, 18*, 375–385.

Blanchard, E.B., & Andrasik, F. (1985). *Management of chronic headaches: A psychological approach*. New York: Pergamon Press.

Blanchard, E.B., & Haynes, M.R. (1975). Biofeedback treatment of a case of Raynaud's disease. *Journal of Behavior Therapy and Experimental Psychiatry, 6*, 230–234.

Blanchard, E.B., & Young, L.B. (1973). Self-control of cardiac functioning: A promise as yet unfulfilled. *Psychological Bulletin, 79*, 145–163.

Blanchard, E.B., Andrasik, F., Guarnieri, P., Neff, D.F., & Rodichok, L.D. (1987). Two-, three-, and four-year follow-up on the self-regulatory treatment of chronic headache. *Journal of Consulting and Clinical Psychology, 55*, 257–259.

Blanchard, E.B., Appelbaum, K.A., Guarnieri, P., Morrill, B., & Dentinger, M.P. (1987). Five year prospective follow-up on the treatment of chronic headache with biofeedback and/or relaxation. *Headache, 27*, 580–583.

Block, A. (1997). Controlling the costs of pain-related disability. *Journal of Pain and Symptom Management, 13*, 1–3.

Block, S.D., & Billings, J.A. (1995). Patient requests for euthanasia and assisted suicide in terminal illness: The role of the psychiatrist. *Psychosomatics, 36*, 445–457.

Bloom, F.E., Lazerson, A., & Hofstadter, L. (1985). *Brain, mind, and behavior*. New York: Freeman.

Bloom, G.A., Stevens, D.E., & Wickwire, T.L. (2003). Expert coaches perceptions of team building. *Journal of Applied Sport Psychology, 15*, 129–143.

Bloom, J.R., & Kessler, L. (1994). Emotional support following cancer: A test of the stigma and social activity hypothesis. *Journal of Health and Social Behavior, 35*, 118–133.

Boey, K.W. (1999). Distressed and stress resistant nurses. *Issues in Mental Health Nursing, 20*, 33–54.

Bogart, L.M., & Helgeson, V.S. (2000). Social comparisons among women with breast cancer: A longitudinal investigation. *Journal of Applied Social Psychology, 30*(3), 547–575.

Boldt, J., Thaler, E., Lehmann, A., Papsdorf, M., & Isgro, F. (1998). Pain management in cardiac surgery patients: Comparison between standard therapy and patient-controlled analgesia regimen. *Journal of Cardiothoracic and Vascular Anesthesiology, 12*, 654–658.

Booth, M.J. (1998). Nurse anesthetist reaction to the unexpected or untimely death of patients in the operating room. *Holistic Nursing Practice, 13*, 51–58.

Borland, R. (1997). Tobacco health warnings and smoking related cognitions and behaviours. *Addiction, 92*, 1427–1435.

Boroditsky, R., Fisher, W., & Sand, M. (1996). The 1995 Canadian contraception study. *Journal SOGC, 18 Supplement*, 1–31.

Boscarino, J.A. (1997). Diseases among men 20 years after exposure to severe stress; Implications for clinical research and medical care. *Psychosomatic Medicine, 59*, 605–614.

Botterill, C., & Brown, M. (2002). Emotion and perspective in sport. *International Journal of Sport Psychology, 33*, 38–60.

Bottomley, A., Hunton, S., Roberts, G., Jones, et al., (1996). A pilot study of cognitive behavioral therapy and social support group interventions with newly diagnosed cancer patients. *Journal of Psychosocial Oncology, 14*, 65–83.

Botvin, G.J., & Willis, T.A. (1985). Personal and social skills training: cognitive-behavioral approaches to substance abuse prevention. In C.S. Bell & R. Batties (eds.), *Prevention research: Deterring drug abuse among children and adolescents (NIDA Research Monograph 63)*. Washington, DC: U.S. Government Printing Office.

Botvin, G.J., Baker, E., Dusenbury, L., Tortu, S., & Botvin, E.M. (1990). Preventing adolescent drug abuse through a multimodal cognitive-behavioral approach: Results of a 3-year study. *Journal of Consulting and Clinical Psychology, 58*, 437–446.

Bouchard, C.B. (1994). Genetics of obesity: Overview and research direction. In C.B. Bouchard (Ed.), *The genetics of obesity* (pp. 223–233). Boca Raton, FL: CRC Press.

Bouchard, L., & Renaud, M. (1997). Female and male physicians' attitudes toward prenatal diagnosis: A Pan-Canadian survey. *Social Science and Medicine, 44*, 381–392.

Bower, J. E., Kemeny, M. E., Taylor, S. E., and Fahey, J. L. (1998). Cognitive processing, discovery of meaning, CD4 decline, and AIDS-related mortality among bereaved HIV- seropositive men. *Journal of Consulting and Clinical Psychology, 66*, 979–986.

Bowler, D.F. (2001). "It's all in your mind": The final common pathway. *Work: Journal of Prevention, Assessment & Rehabilitation, 17*, 167–174.

Bozoin, S., Rejeski, W.J., & McAuley, E. (1994). Self-efficacy influences feeling states associated with acute exercise. *Journal of Sport and Exercise Psychology, 16*, 326–333.

Bracegirdle, H. (1995). Children's stereotypes of visibly physically impaired targets: An empirical study. *British Journal of Occupational Therapy, 58*, 25–27.

Bradley, L.A. (1983). Coping with chronic pain. In T.G. Burish & L.A. Bradley (Eds.), *Coping with chronic disease: Research and applications*. New York: Academic Press.

Brady, J.V., Porter, R.W., Conrad, D.G., & Mason, J.W. (1958). Avoidance behavior and the development of duodenal ulcers. *Journal of the Experimental Analysis of Behavior, 1*, 69–72.

Brand, R.J., Paffenberger, R.S., Scholtz, R.I., & Kampert, J.B. (1979). Work activity and fatal heart attack studied by multiple logistic risk analysis. *American Journal of Epidemiology, 110*, 52–56.

Brandsma, J.M., Maultsby, M.C., & Welsh, R.J. (1980). *The outpatient treatment of alcoholism: A review and comparative study*. Baltimore: University Park Press.

Brann, M., & Anderson, J.G. (2002). E-medicine and health care consumers: recognizing current problems and possible resolutions for a safer environment. *Health Care Analysis, 10*(4), 403–415.

Brannon, L., & Feist, J. (2000) *Health psychology: An introduction to behavior and health*. Belmount, California: Wadsworth/Thompson Learning.

Braun, B.L., Murray, D., & Sidney, S. (1997). Lifetime cocaine use and cardiovascular characteristics among young adults: the CARDIA study. *American Journal of Public Health, 87*, 629–634.

Bray, G.A. (1998). *Contemporary diagnosis and management of obesity*. Newton: PA: Handbooks in Health Care.

Bray, G.A., & Tartaglia, L.A. (2000). Medicinal strategies in the treatment of obesity. *Nature, 404*, 672–67.

Brehm, J.W. (1966). *A theory of psychological reactance*. New York: Academic Press.

Brewer, B.W. (2001). Psychology of sport injury rehabilitation. In R.N. Singer, H.A. Hausenblas & C.M. Janelle (Eds.), *Handbook of Sport Psychology,* (2nd ed. pp. 767–809). New York Wiley.

Brewer, B.W., Van Raalte, J.L., & Linder, D.E. (1991). Peak performance and the perils of retrospective introspection. *Journal of Sport and Exercise Psychology, 10*, 45–61.

Brewer, J. (2001, January 4, 2001). *How people with disabilities use the web*, [web site]. W3C. Available: http://www.w3org/WAI/EO/Drafts/ PWD-Use-Web/ [2003, July 6].

Brewin, C.R., Watson, M., McCarthy, S., Hyman, P., & Dayson, D. (1998). Intrusive memories and depression in cancer patients. *Behaviour Research and Therapy, 36*, 1131–1142.

Brewster, J.M. (2001). Helping physicians with alcohol problems. *Cmaj, 164*(2), 179.

Brinchmann, B.S., Forde, R., & Nortvedt, P. (2002). What matters to the parents? A qualitative study of parents' experiences with life-and-death decisions concerning their premature infants. *Nursing ethics, 9*(4), 388–404.

British Columbia Eating Disorder Association (1998). *School outreach program training manual*. Victoria, BC.

Brody, D.S., Miller, S.M., Leman, C.E., Smith, D.G., & Caputo, G.C. (1989). Patient perception on involvement in medical care: Relationship to illness attitudes and outcomes. *Journal of General Internal Medicine, 4,* 506–511.

Brousse, T. (1946). A psycho-physiological study. *Main Currents in Modern Thought, 4,* 77–84.

Brown, D.L. (1988). No pretending not to know. *Journal of the American Medical Association, 260,* 2720.

Brown, M.A., & Stetz, K. (1999). The labor of caregiving: A theoretical model of caregiving during potentially fatal illness. *Qualitative Health Research, 9,* 182–197.

Bruch, H. (1973). Eating disorders. *Obesity, anorexia nervosa and the person within*. New York: Basic Books.

Bruch, H. (1978). *The golden cage: The enigma of anorexia nervosa*. Cambridge. MA: Harvard University Press.

Bruch, H. (1982). Anorexia nervosa: Therapy and theory. *American Journal of Psychiatry, 139,* 1531–1538.

Brunton, P. (1972). *A search in secret India*. New York: Samuel Weiser.

Bryant, J. (1999). Social determinants of participation in preventive screening services in Prince George, British Columbia. Unpublished Masters Thesis, The University of Northern British Columbia.

Buckalew, L.W. (1991). Patients' compliance: The problem and directions for psychological research. *Psychological Reports, 68,* 348–350.

Budtz, S., & Witt, K. (2002). Consulting the Internet before visit to general practice. Patients' use of the Internet and other sources of health information. *Scand J Prim Health Care, 20*(3), 174–176.

Bulik, C.M., Sullivan, P.F., & Kendler, K.S. (2003). Genetic and environmental contributions to obesity and binge eating. *International Journal of Eating Disorders, 33,* 293–298.

Buller, M.K., & Buller, D.B. (1987). Physicians' communication style and patient satisfaction. *Journal of Health and Social Behavior, 28,* 375–388.

Burack, J.H., Young, L.D., Anderson, K.O., Turner, R.A., Agudelo, C.A., et al. (1993). Depressive symptoms and CD4 lymphocyte decline among HIV-infected men. *Journal of the American Medical Association, 270,* 2568–2573.

Burack, R.C., & Carpenter, R.R. (1983). The predictive value of the presenting complaint. *Journal of Family Practice, 16,* 749–754.

Burgoon, M. Callister, M., & Hunsaker, F.G. (1994). Patients who deceive: An empirical investigation of patient–physician communication. *Journal of Language and Social Psychology, 13,* 443–468.

Burke, R.J., & Richardsen, A.M. (1990). Sources of satisfaction and stress among Canadian Physicians. *Psychological Reports, 67,* 1335–1344.

Burns, J.W., Sherman, M.L., Devine, J., Mahoney, N., & Pawl, R. (1995). Association between workers' compensation and outcome following multidisciplinary treatment of chronic pain: Roles of mediators and moderators. *Clinical Journal of Pain, 11,* 94–102.

Burnum, M.A., Timbers, D.M., & Hough, R.L. (1984). *Journal of Health and Social Behavior, 25*, 24–33.

Burton, D., Naylor, S., & Holliday, B (2001). Goal setting in sports: Investigating the goal effectiveness paradox. In R.N. Singer, H.A. Hausenblas & C.M. Janelle (Eds.), *Handbook of Sport Psychology* (2nd ed. pp., 497–528). New York: Wiley.

Butzlaff, M., Koneczny, N., Floer, B., Vollmar, H.C., Lange, S., Kunstmann, W., & Kock, C. (2002). [Family physicians, the internet and new knowledge. Utilization and judgment of efficiency of continuing education media by general physicians and internists in family practice]. *Med Klin, 97*(7), 383–388.

Byrne, A., Ellershaw, J., Holcombe, C., & Salmon, P. (2002). Patients' experience of cancer: Evidence of the role of "fighting' in collusive clinical communication. *Patient Education & Counseling, 48*(1), 15–21.

Byrne, D. (1977). Social psychology and the study of sexual behavior. *Personality and Social Psychology Bulletin, 3*, 3–30.

Calderone, K. (1990). The influence of gender on the frequency of pain and sedative medication administered to post-operative patients. *Sex Roles, 23*, 713–725.

Calhoun, E. (1998, November). Reimbursement dilemmas for patients with refractory ovarian cancer. Paper presented at the *Cancer Care: Quality of Life and Outcomes Symposium*, Chicago, Illinois.

Calle, E.E., Thun, M.J., Petrelli, J.M., Rodriguez, C., & Heath, C.W. (1999). Body-mass index and mortality in a prospective cohort of U.S. adults. *The New England Journal of Medicine, 341,* 1097–1105.

Calzavara, L.M., Bullock, S.L., Myers, T. Marshall, V.W., Cockerill, R. (1999). Sexual partnering and risk of HIV/STD among Aboriginals. *Canadian Journal of Public Health, 90,* 186–191.

Cameron, L. (1997). Screening for cancer: Illness perceptions and illness worry. In Petrie, K.J. and J.A. Weinman (Eds). *Perceptions of health and illness: Current research and applications.* pp. 291–322.

Cameron, L., Leventhal, E.A., & Leventhal, H. (1995). Seeking medical care in response to symptoms and life stress. *Psychosomatic Medicine, 57,* 1–11.

Campbell-Heider, N., & Knapp, T.R. (1993). Toward a hierarchy of adaptation to biomedical technology. *Crit Care Nurs Q, 16*(3), 42–50.

Canadian Cancer Society (2003, April 8). Cigarette package warning labels. http://www.mb.cancer.ca/ccs/internet/standard/0,2939,3172_334419_436451_langId-en,00.htm [July 10, 2003].

Canadian cancer statistics: Current incidence and mortality. (2001). Toronto: National Cancer Institute of Canada.

Canadian Centre on Substance Abuse. (1999). Http://www.ccsa.ca/ [August 25, 2003].

Canadian Institute for Health Information. (1998). *National health expenditure trends, 1975–1998.* Ottawa.

Canadian Medical Protective Association (August 1, 2001). *2001 Annual Report.* http://www.cmpa-acpm.ca/portal/pub_index.cfm [June 24, 2003].

Canadian Nurses Association. (1997a). Out in front—advanced nursing practice. *Nursing Now: Issues and Trends in Canadian Nursing,* January, 1997.

Canadian Nurses Association. (1997b) *The future supply of registered nurses: A discussion paper*, Ottawa, October, 1997.

Carlsson, C.P.O. & Sjolund, B.H. (2001). Acupuncture for chronic low back pain: A randomized placebo-controlled study with long-term follow-up. *Clinical Journal of Pain, 17,* 296–305.

Cannon, W.B. (1939). *The Wisdom of the Body.* New York: Norton.

Carlat, D.J., Camargo, C.A., Herzog, D.D. (1997). Eating disorders in males: A report on 135 patients. *American Journal of Psychiatry, 154*, 1127–1132.

Carlson, C.R., & Hoyle, R.H. (1993). Efficacy of abbreviated progressive muscle relaxation training: A quantitative review of behavioral medicine research. *Journal of Consulting and Clinical Psychology, 61*, 1059–1067.

Carlsson, C.P.O., & Sjolund, B.H. (1994). Acupuncture and subtypes of chronic pain: Assessment of long-term results. *Clinical Journal of Pain, 10*, 290–295.

Carney, R.M., Freedland, K.E., Veith, R.C., Cryer, P.E., Skala, J.A., Lynch, T., & Jaffe, A.S. (1999). Major depression, heart rate, and plasma norepinephrine in patients with coronary heart disease. *Biological Psychiatry, 45*, 458–463.

Carney, R.M., & Jaffe, A. S. (2002). Treatment of depression following acute myocardial infarction. *JAMA: Journal of the American Medical Association, 288*(6), 750–751.

Carpenter, D.J., Gatchel, R.J., & Hasegawa, T. (1994). Effectiveness of a video-taped behavioral intervention for dental anxiety: The role of gender and need for information. *Behavioral Medicine, 20*, 123–132.

Carpenter, K.M., Hasin, D.S., Allison, D.B., & Faith, M.S. (2000). Relationships between obesity and DSM-IV major depressive disorder, suicide ideation, and suicide attempts: Results from a general population study. *American Journal of Public Health, 90,* 251–257.

Carron, H., DeGood, D.E., & Tait, R.A. (1985). A comparison of low back pain patients in the United States and New Zealand: Psychosocial and economic factors affecting severity of disability. *Pain, 21*, 77–89.

Carter, B.S., & Leuthner, S.R. (2002). Decision making in the NICU—strategies, statistics, and "satisficing". *Bioethics Forum, 18*(3–4), 7–15.

Carter, M. (2003). *On the Art of Being a Very Successful Patient Navigator for Breast Cancer Patients*. The Snowmass Institute. Available: http://www.snowinst.com/articles/Lexington%20Medical%20Center.htm [2003, July 21].

Casperson, C.J. Powell, K.E., & Christenson, G.M. (1985). Physical activity, exercise, and physical fitness: Definitions and distinctions for health-related research. *Public Health Reports, 100*, 126–131.

Cassidy, K., Reid, G.J., McGrath, P.J., Finely, G.A., Smith, D.J., Morley, C., et al. (2002). Watch needle, watch tv: Audiovisual distraction in preschool immunization. *Pain Medicine, 3,* 108–118.

Catania, J.A., Kegeles, S.M., & Coates, T.J. (1990). Towards an understanding of risk behavior: An AIDS risk reduction model (ARRM). *Health Education Quarterly, 17*, 53–72.

Catchlove, R. & Cohen, K. (1982). Effects of a directive return to work approach in the treatment of workman's compensation patients with chronic pain. *Pain, 14*, 181–191.

Cella, D. F., Tulsky, D. S., Gray, G., Saraflan, B., Linn, E., Bonomi, A., Silberman, M., Yellen, et al. (1993). The Functional Assessment of Cancer Therapy Scale: Development and validation of the general measure. *Journal of Clinical Oncology, 11*, 570–579.

Centers for Disease Control and Prevention (CDC). (1993). Cigarette smoking—attributable mortality and years of potential life lost—United States, 1990. *Morbidity and Mortality Weekly Report, 42,* 645–649.

Chamberlain, J., Clifford, R.E., Nathan, B.E., Price, J.L., & Burn, I. Repeated screening for breast cancer. *Journal of Epidemiology and Community Health, 38*, 54–57.

Chan, B. (2002). *From perceived surplus to perceived shortage:*. Ottawa, Ontario: Canadian Institute for Health Information.

Chapman, C.R. (1984). New directions in the understanding and management of pain. *Social Science and Medicine, 19,* 1261–1277.

Chapman, C.R., & Syrjala, K.L. (1990). Measurement of pain. In J.J. Bonica (Ed.), *The management of pain* (2nd ed., pp. 580–594). Malvern, PA: Lea & Febiger.

Chapman, C.R., Casey, K.L., Dubner, R., Foley, K.M., et al. (1985). Pain measurement: An overview. *Pain, 22,* 1–31.

Chapman, S.L. (1991). Chronic pain: Psychological assessment and treatment. In J.J. Sweet, R.H. Rozensky, & S.M. Tovian (Eds.), *Handbook of clinical psychology in medical settings.* New York: Plenum.

Charlton, A., Minagawa, K.E., & While, D. (1999). Saying "no" to cigarettes: A reappraisal of adolescent refusal skills. *Journal of Adolescents, 22,* 695–707.

Charnley, F. (1999). Occupational stress in the newly qualified staff nurse. *Nursing Standard, 13(29),* 33–36.

Chassin, L., Presson, C.C., Pitts, S.C., & Sherman, S.J. (2000). The natural history of cigarette smoking from adolescence t o adulthood in a Midwestern community sample. Multiple trajectories and their psychosocial correlates. *Health Psychology, 19,* 223–231.

Chaves, I.F., & Barber, T.X. (1976). Hypnotism and surgical pain. In D. Mostofsky (Ed.), *Behavioral control and modification of physiological activity.* Englewood Cliffs, NJ: Prentice-Hall.

Chen, J., & Millar, W.J. (1998). Age of smoking initiation: Implications for quitting. *Health Reports, 9(4),* 39–46.

Chen, J., Fair, M, Wilkins, R., Cyr, M. (1998). Maternal education and fetal and infant mortality in Quebec. *Health Reports, 10(2),* 53–64.

Chen, J., Ng, E., & Wilkins, R. (1996). The health of Canada's immigrants in 1994–1995. *Health Reports, 7,* 42.

Chen, J., & Wilkins, R. (1998). Seniors' needs for health-related personal assistance. *Health Reports, 10(1),* 39–50.

Chen, X., & Siu, L.L. (2001). Impact of the media and the Internet on oncology: Survey of cancer patients and oncologists in Canada. *Journal of Clinical Oncology, 19(23),* 4291–4297.

Cherny, N.I. (1996). The problem of inadequately relieved suffering. *Journal of Social Issues, 52,* 13–30.

Chilcoat, H.D., Dishion, T.J., & Anthony, J.C. (1995). Parent monitoring and the incidence of drug sampling in urban elementary school children. *American Journal of Epidemiology, 141,* 25–31.

Christiansen, E.K., & Nohr, L.E. (2003). [Professionally adequate health care on the Internet.]. *Tidsskr Nor Laegeforen, 123(13–14),* 1854–1855.

Christianson, S. (1992). Emotional stress and eyewitness memory: A critical review. *Psychological Bulletin, 112,* 284–309.

Cinciripini, P.M., & Floreen, A. (1982). An evaluation of a behavioral program for chronic pain. *Journal of Behavioral Medicine, 5,* 375–389.

Cinciripini, P.M., Cinciripini, L.G., Wallfisch, A., Haque, W., & Van Vunakis, H. (1996). Behavior therapy and the transdermal nicotine patch: Effects on cessation outcome, affect, and coping. *Journal of Consulting and Clinical Psychology, 64,* 314–323.

Chung, B. (2001). Muscle dysmorphia: A critical review of the proposed criteria. *Perspectives in Biology and Medicine, 44(4),* 565–574.

Clack, G.B., & Head, J.O. (1999). Gender differences in medical graduates' assessment of their personal attributes. *Medical Education, 33,* 101–105.

Clark, J. (1998, November). Prostate cancer quality of life: Patient centered measures of health outcomes. Paper presented at the

Cancer Care: Quality of Life and Outcomes Symposium, Chicago, Illinois.

Clark, N.M., Gong, M., Schork, M.A., Evans, D., et al. (1998). Impact of education for physicians on patient outcomes. *Pediatrics, 101*, 831.

Clarke, J.N. (2000). *Health, illness, and medicine in Canada*. Don Mills, ON: Oxford University Press.

Clowers, M. (2002). Young women describe the ideal physician. *Adolescence, 37,* 695–704.

Coambs, R.B., Jensen, P., Her, M.H., Ferguson, B.S., et al. (1995). *Review of the scientific literature on the prevalence, consequences, and health costs of noncompliance and inappropriate use of prescription medication in Canada*. Ottawa, ON: Pharmaceutical Manufacturers Association of Canada (University of Toronto Press).

Coambs, R.B., Li, S., & Kozlowski, L.T. (1992). Age interacts with heaviness of smoking in predicting success in cessation of smoking. *American Journal of Epidemiology, 135*, 240–246.

Cockerham, W.M. (1998). *Medical sociology, 7th ed*. Upper Saddle River, NJ: Prentice Hall.

Cohen, H.J. (2000). Editorial: In search of the underlying mechanisms of frailty. *Journals of Gerontology Series A-Biological Sciences & Medical Sciences. 55*, M706–708.

Cohen, S., Doyle, W. J., and Skoner, D. P. (1999). Psychological stress, cytokine production, and severity of upper respiratory illness. *Psychosomatic Medicine, 61*, 171–180.

Cohen, S., Doyle, W.J., Skoner, D.P., Fireman, P., Gwaltner, J.M. Jr., & Newsom, J.T. (1995). State and trait negative affect as predictors of objective and subjective symptoms of respiratory viral infections. *Journal of Personality and Social Psychology, 68*, 139–169.

Cohen, S., Doyle, W. J., Skoner, D. P., Rabin, B. S., and Gwaltney, J. M. (1997). Social ties and susceptibility to the common cold.

Journal of the American Medical Association, 277, 1940–1944.

Cohen, S., & Herbert, T.B. (1996). Health psychology: Psychological factors and physical disease from the perspective of human psychoneuroimmunology. *Annual Review of Psychology, 47*, 113–142.

Cohen, S., Lichtenstein, E., Prochaska, J.O., Rossi, J.S., et al. (1989). Debunking myths about self-quitting. Evidence from 10 prospective studies of persons who attempt to quit smoking by themselves. *American Psychologist, 44*, 1355–1365.

Cohen, S., Rodriguez, M.S., Feldman, P.J., Rabin, B.S., and Manuck, SB. (2002). Reactivity and vulnerability to stress-associated risk for upper respiratory illness. *Psychosomatic Medicine, 64*, 302–310.

Cohen, S. Tyrrell, D.A.J., & Smith, A.P. (1993). Negative life events, perceived stress, negative affect, and susceptibility to the common cold. *Journal of Personality and Social Psychology, 64*, 131–140.

Cohen, S., & Wills, T.A. (1985). Stress, social support, and the buffering hypothesis. *Psychological Bulletin, 98*, 310–357.

Cole, B. (1998, November). An overview of the Q-Twist method for evaluating trade-offs in clinical trials.. Paper presented at the *Cancer Care: Quality of Life and Outcomes Symposium*, Chicago, Illinois.

COMMIT Research Group. (1995a). Community intervention trial for smoking cessation (COMMIT): I. Cohort results from a four-year community intervention. *American Journal of Public Health, 85*, 183–192.

COMMIT Research Group. (1995b). Community intervention trial for smoking cessation (COMMIT): II. Changes in adult cigarette smoking prevalence. *American Journal of Public Health, 85*, 193–200.

Common look and feel for the Internet. (2001, June 27, 2003). [web site]. Treasury Board of Canada Secretariat. Available:

http://www.cio-dpi.gc.ca/clf-upe/index_e.asp [2003, July 6].

Compas, B.E., Haaga, D.A., Keefe, F.J., Leitenberg, H., & Williams, D.A. (1998). Sampling of empirically supported psychological treatments from health psychology: Smoking, chronic pain, cancer, and bulimia nervosa. *Journal of Consulting and Clinical Psychology, 66,* 89–112.

Concheiro, A., Diaz, E., Luaces, C., Pou, J., & Garcia, J. (2001). [Triage criteria in an emergency department]. *An Esp Pediatr, 54*(3), 233–237.

Conn, K. (2000). *CP's role in First Nations and Inuit health care.* Ottawa: First nations and Inuit Health Branch.

Conrad, K.M., Flay, B.R., & Hill, D. (1992). Why children start smoking cigarettes: Predictors of onset. *British Journal of Addiction, 87,* 1711–1724.

Considine, R.V., & Carol, J.F. (1996). Leptin in humans: Current progress and future directions. *Clinical Chemistry, 6,* 843–844.

Constable, R.T. (2003). MR physics of body MR imaging. *Radiol Clin North Am, 41*(1), 1–15,

Cooke, M.W., Arora, P., & Mason, S. (2003). Discharge from triage: modelling the potential in different types of emergency department. *Emerg Med J, 20*(2), 131–133.

Coombs, R.H. (1998). *Surviving medical school.* Thousand Oaks, CA: Sage.

Coombs, R.H., & Fawzy, F.I. (1993). Surgeons' personalities: The influence of medical school. *Medical Education, 27,* 337–343.

Cooper, C.L., & Baglioni, A.J. (1988). A structural model approach toward the development of a theory of the link between stress and mental health. *British Journal of Medical Psychology, 61,* 87–102.

Cordova, M.J., Cunningham, L.L.C., Carlson, C.R., & Andrykowski, M.A. (2001). Posttraumatic growth following breast cancer: A controlled comparison study. *Health Psychology, 20*(3), 176–185.

Coulter, A. (2002). Patients' views of the good doctor. *British Medical Journal, 325,* 668–669.

Courneya, K.S., Friedenreich, C.M., Sela, R.A., Quinney, H.A., Rhodes, R.E., & Handman, M. (2003). The group psycho-therapy and home-based physical exercise (group-hope) trial in cancer survivors: Physical fitness and quality of life outcomes. *Psycho-Oncology, 12*(4), 357–374.

Cousins, N. (1988). Intangibles in medicine: An attempt at a balancing perspective. *Journal of the American Medical Association, 260,* 1610–1612.

Coyne, J. Aldwin, C., & Lazarus, R.S. (1981). Depression and coping in stressful episodes. *Journal of Abnormal Psychology, 90,* 439–447.

Cox, H. (1973). *The Seduction of the Spirit.* New York: Simon and Schuster.

Cox, R.H. (2002). *Sport psychology: Concepts and applications* (5th Ed.). New York: McGaw-Hill.

Cozby, P.C. (1993). *Methods in behavioral research, 5th ed.* Mountain View CA: Mayfield.

Craig, K.D. (1996). The back pain controversy—Reply. *Pain Research Management, 1,* 183.

Cramer, J.A., Mattson, R.H., Prevey, M.L., Scheyer, R.D., & Ouellette, V.L. (1989). How often is medication taken as prescribed? *Journal of the American Medical Association, 261,* 3273–3277

Crepaz, N. and Marks, G. (2002). Towards an understanding of sexual risk behavior in people living with HIV: A review of social, psychological, and medical findings. *AIDS, 16,* 135–149.

Crisp, A., Sedgwick, P., Halek, C., Joughin, N., & Humphrey, H. (1999). Why may teenage girls persist in smoking? *Journal of Adolescence, 22,* 657–672.

Critchley, J. A., & Capewell, S. (2003). Mortality risk reduction associated with smoking cessation in patients with coronary heart disease. *Journal of the American Medical Association, 2*90, 86–97.

Crook, J. (1982). Women and chronic pain. In R. Roy & E. Tunks (Eds.), *Chronic pain: Psychosocial factors in rehabilitation* (pp. 68–78). Baltimore: Williams and Williams.

Crook, J. (1993). Comparative experiences of men and women who have sustained a work related musculoskeletal injury. (Abstracts) 7th World Congress on Pain. Seattle: IASP Press.

Crossley, M.L., & Mubarik, A. (2002). A comparative investigation of dental and medical student's motivation towards career choice. *Br Dent J, 193*(8), 471–473.

Croyle, R.T., & Ditto, P.H. (1990). Illness cognition and behavior: An experimental approach. *Journal of Behavioral Medicine, 13*, 31–52.

Croyle, R.T., & Hunt, J.R. (1991). Coping with health threat: Social influence processes in reactions to medical test results. *Journal of Personality and Social Psychology, 60*, 382–389.

Croyle, R.T., & Uretsky, M.B. (1987). Effects of mood on self-appraisal of health status. *Health Psychology, 6*, 239–253.

Csikzentmihalyi, M. (1997). *Finding flow.* New York: Basic Books.

Cullinane, C.A., Chu, D.Z.J., & Mamelak, A.N. (2002). Current surgical options in the control of cancer pain. *Cancer Practice, 10,* s21–s26.

Cummings, G.G., Fraser, K., & Tarlier, D.S. (2003). Implementing advanced nurse practitioner roles in acute care: an evaluation of organizational change. *J Nurs Adm, 33*(3), 139–145.

Cunningham, J.A. (1999). Resolving alcohol-related problems with and without treatment: The effects of different problem criteria. *Journal of Studies on Alcohol.*

Cutler, R.B., Fishbain, D.A., Rosomoff, H.L., Abdel-Moty, E., et al. (1994). Does nonsurgical pain center treatment of chronic pain return patients to work? A review and meta-analysis of the literature. *Spine, 19*, 643–652.

Dalal, S. & Melzack, R. (1998). Potentiation of opioid analgesia by psychostimulant drugs: A review. *Journal of Pain and Symptom Management.*

Danish, S.J., Nellon, V.C., & Owens, S.S. (1996). Teaching life skills through sport: Community-based programs for adolescents. In J.L. Van Raalte and B. Brewer (Eds.), *Exploring sport and exercise psychology* (pp. 205–225). New York: American Psychological Association.

Danish, S.J., Pettipas, A.J., & Hale, B.D. (1993). Life development intervention for athletes: Life skills through sports. *The Counseling Psychologist, 21*, 352–385.

Dare, C. & Eisner, I. (1995). Family therapy and eating disorders. In K. Brownell & C. Fairburn (Eds.), *Eating disorders and obesity: A comprehensive handbook* (pp. 318–323). New York: The Guilford Press.

Dantendorfer, K., Amering, M., Bankier, A., Helbich, T., Prayer, D., Youssefzadeh, S., Alexandrowicz, R., Imhof, H., & Katschnig, H. (1997). A study of the effects of patient anxiety, perceptions and equipment on motion artifacts in magnetic resonance imaging. *Magnetic Resonance Imaging, 15*, 301–306.

de Bruyn, T. (2000). *Taking stock: Policy issues associated with complementary and alternative health care.* Ottawa: Health Systems Division, Health Promotion and Programs Branch, Health Canada.

Deinzer, R., & Schüller, N. (1998). Dynamics of stress-related decrease of salivary immunoglobulin A (sIgA): Relationship to symptoms of the common cold and studying behavior. *Behavioral Medicine, 23*, 161–169.

De Koninck, M., Bergeron, P., & Bourbonnais, R. (1997). Women physicians in Québec. *Social Science and Medicine, 44,* 1825–1832.

Dembroski, T.M., & Costa, P.T. (1988). Assessment of coronary-prone behavior: A current overview. *Annals of Behavioral Medicine, 10,* 60–63.

Denis, M.A., Ecochard, R., Bernadet, A., Forissier, M.F., Porst, J.M., Robert, O., Volckmann, C., & Bergeret, A. (2003). Risk of occupational blood exposure in a cohort of 24,000 hospital healthcare workers: position and environment analysis over three years. *J Occup Environ Med, 45*(3), 283–288.

Desbiens, N.A., Mueller-Rizner, N., Haniel, M.B., & Connors, A.F., Jr. (1998). Preference for comfort care does not affect the pain experience of seriously ill patients. The SUPPORT Investigators. Study to Understand Prognoses and Preferences for Outcomes and Risks of Treatment. *Journal of Pain and Symptom Management, 16,* 281–289.

Devine, E.C. (2003). Meta-analysis of the effect of psychoeducational interventions on pain in adults with cancer. *Oncol Nurs Forum, 30*(1), 75–89.

Diabetes among aboriginal (First Nations, Inuit and Metis) people in Canada: The evidence. (2002). Ottawa: Health Canada.

Diabetes in Canada, 2nd Edition. (2003). Ottawa: Health Canada.

Dialogue on Health Reform. (1996). Ontario Nurses Association.

DiFranceisco, W., Kelly, J.A., Sikkema, K.J., Somlai, A.M., Murphy, D.A., & Stevenson, L.Y. (1998). Differences between completers and early dropouts from 2 HIV intervention trials: A health belief approach to understanding prevention program attrition. *American Journal of Public Health, 88,* 1068–1073.

Dillbeck, M.C., & Orme-Johnson, D.W. (1987). Physiological differences between transcendental meditation and rest. *American Psychologist, 42,* 879–880.

Diltmar, S.S., Haughey, B., O'Shea, R.M., & Brasure, J. (1989). Health practices of nursing students: A survey. *Health Values, 13(2),* 24–31.

DiMatteo, M.R. (1979). A social-psychological analysis of physician–patient rapport: Toward a science of the art of medicine. *Journal of Social Issues, 35,* 12–33.

DiMatteo, M.R. (1995). Health psychology research: The interpersonal challenges. In Brannigan, G.G. & Merrens, M.R. (Eds.) *The social psychologists: Research adventures.* New York: McGraw-Hill, pp. 207–221.

DiMatteo, M.R. (1994). Enhancing patient adherence to medical recommendations. *Journal of the American Medical Association, 271,* 79–83.

DiMatteo, M.R., & DiNicola, D.D. (1982). *Achieving patient compliance: The psychology of the medical practitioner's role.* New York: Pergamon.

DiMatteo, M.R., Hays, R.D., & Prince, L.M. (1986). Relationship of physicians' nonverbal communication skill to patient satisfaction, appointment noncompliance and physician workload. *Health Psychology, 5,* 581–594.

DiMatteo, M.R., Linn, L.S., Chang, B.L., & Cope, D.W. (1985). Affect and neutrality in physician behavior: A study of patients' values and satisfaction. *Journal of Behavioral Medicine, 8,* 397–409.

DiMatteo, M.R. & Martin, L.R. (2002). *Health psychology.* Boston: Allyn & Bacon.

Dimeo, F. (2002). Radiotherapy-related fatigue and exercise for cancer patients: a review of the literature and suggestions for future research. *Front Radiat Ther Oncol, 37,* 49–56.

Dimeo, F. C. (2001). Effects of exercise on cancer-related fatigue. *Cancer, 92*(6 Suppl), 1689–1693.

Dimeo, F.C., Stieglitz, R.D., Novelli-Fischer, U., Fetscher, S., & Keul, J. (1999). Effects of physical activity on the fatigue and psychologic status of cancer patients during chemotherapy. *Cancer, 85*, 2273–2277.

Dinh, K.T., Sarason, I.G., Peterson, A.V., & Onstad, L.E. (1995). Children's perception of smokers and nonsmokers: A longitudinal study. *Health Psychology, 14*, 32–40.

DiNicola, D.D., & DiMatteo, M.R. (1984). Practitioners, patients, and compliance with medical regimens: A social psychological perspective. In A. Baum, S.E. Taylor, & J.E. Singer (Eds.), *Handbook of psychology and health: Vol. 4. Social psychological aspects of health* (pp. 55–84). Hillsdale, NJ: Erlbaum.

Dishman, R. K. (Ed.). (1988). *Exercise adherence: Its impact on public health.* Champaign, Illinois: Human Kinetics.

Dishman, R.K., & Buckworth, J. (1997). Adherence to physical activity. In W.P. Morgan (Ed.), *Physical activity and mental health* (pp. 63–80). Washington, DC: Taylor and Francis.

Dissanayake, V.H., & Jayasekara, R.W. (1999). Pattern of use of medical information made available via an Internet website. *Ceylon Med J, 44*(1), 14–17.

DiTomasso, R.A., & Kovnat, K.D. (1994). Medical patients. In F.D. Dattilio and A. Freeman. (Eds.), *Cognitive-behavioral strategies in crisis intervention* (pp.325–344). New York: Guilford Press.

Diverty, B. & Pérez, C. (1998). The health of Northern residents. *Health Reports, 9*(4), 49–58.

Dlin, B.M. (1980). The experience of surviving almost certain death. *Advances in Psychosomatic Medicine, 10*, 111–118.

Donaldson, S.I., Graham, J.W., Piccinin, A.M. & Hansen, W.B. (1995). Resistance-skills training and onset of alcohol use: Evidence for beneficial and potentially harmful effects in public schools and in private Catholic schools. *Health Psychology, 14*, 291–300.

Donnelly, G. (2003). Clinical expertise in advanced practice nursing: a Canadian perspective. *Nurse Educ Today, 23*(3), 168–173.

Doucet, M.D., Purdy, R.A., Kaufman, D.M., & Langille, D.B. (1998). Comparison of problem-based learning and lecture format in continuing medical education on headache diagnosis and management. *Medical Education, 32*, 590–596.

Drisckell, J.E., Copper, C., Moran, A. (1994). Does mental practice enhance performance? *Journal of Applied Psychology, 79*, 481–492.

Drozda, D.J., Allen, S.R., Standiford, D.A., Turner, A.M., & McCain, G.C. (1997). Personal illness models of diabetes: Parents of preadolescents and adolescents. *Diabetes Education, 23*, 550–557.

Dubbert, S. (2002). Physical activity and exercise: Recent advances and current challenges. *Journal of Consulting and Clinical Psychology, 70*, 526–536.

Duda, J.L. (1992). Motivation in sport settings: A goal perspective approach. In G. Roberts (Ed.), *Motivation in Sport and Exercise* (pp. 57–91). Champaign, Illinois: Human Kinetics.

Duda, J.L. & Hall, H. (2001). Achievement goal theory in sport: Recent extensions and future directions. In R.N. Singer, H.A. Hausenblas & C.M. Janelle (Eds.), *Handbook of Sport Psychology* (2nd ed. pp., 417–443) New York: Wiley.

Dudgeon, D., Raubertas, R.F., & Rosenthal, S.M. (1993). The Short-Form McGill Pain Questionnaire in chronic cancer pain. *Journal of Pain and Symptom Management, 8*, 191–195.

Dugan, J., Lauer, E., Bouquot, Z., Dutro, B.K., Smith, M., & Widmeyer, G. (1996). Stressful nurses: The effect on patient outcomes. *Journal of Nursing Care Quality, 10*(3), 46–58.

Dumont, C., St. Onge, M., Fougeyrollas, P., & Renaud, L.A. (1998). Perceived burden in family caregivers with physical disabilities. *Canadian Journal of Occupational Therapy, 65*, 258–270.

Dunkel-Schetter, C. (1984). Social support and cancer: Findings based on patient interviews and their implications. *Journal of Social Issues, 40*(4), 77–98.

Dunn, J., Steginga, S.K. Occhipinti, S., & Wilson, K. (1999). Evaluation of a peer support program for women with breast cancer—lessons for practitioners. *Journal of Community and Applied Social Psychology, 9*, 13–22.

Dunn, J.G.H., Dunn, J.C., & Syrotuik, D.G. (2002). Relationship between multidimensional perfectionism and goal orientations in sport. *Journal of Sport and Exercise Psychology, 24*, 376–395.

Eagly, A.H., & Chaiken, S. (1993). *The psychology of attitudes.* New York: Harcourt Brace Jovanovich.

Edwards, C.L., Fillingim, R.B., & Keefe, F. (2001). Race, ethnicity and pain. *Pain, 94*, 133–137.

Edwards, G., & Gross, M.M. (1976). Alcohol dependence: Provisional description of a clinical syndrome. *British Medical Journal*, 1058–1061.

Edwards, R.R., & Fillingim, R.B. (2003). Ethnic differences in thermal pain responses. *Psychosomatic Medicine, 61*, 346–354.

Egbert, LD., Battet, G.E., Welch, C.E., & Bartlett, M.K. (1964). Reduction of postoperative pain by encouragement and instruction of patients. *New England Journal of Medicine, 270*, 825–827.

Eifert, G.H., Hodson, S.E., Tracey, D.R., Seville, J.L., & Gunawardane, K. (1996). Heart-focused anxiety, illness beliefs, and behavioral impairment: Comparing healthy heart-anxious patients with cardiac and surgical inpatients. *Journal of Behavioral Medicine, 19*, 385–400.

Eisenberg, D.M., Davis, R.B., Eltner, S.L., Appel, S., Wilkey, S., Van Rompay, M., et al. (1998). Trends in alternative medicine use in the United States 1990–1997. *Journal of the American Medical Association, 280*, 1569–1575.

Eisenberg, J.M., Kitz, D.S., & Webber, R.A. (1983). Development of attitudes about sharing decision-making: A comparison of medical and surgical residents. *Journal of Health and Social Behavior, 24*, 85–90.

Eisler, I., Dare, C., Russell, G.F., Szmukler, G., le Grange, D., & Dodge, E. (1997). Family and individual therapy in anorexia nervosa. A 5-year follow-up. *Archives of General Psychiatry, 54*, 1025–1030.

Eller, L.S. (1999). Guided imagery interventions for symptom management. *Annual Review of Nursing Research, 17*, 57–84.

Ellingson, L.A., & Yarber, W.L. (1997). Breast self-examination, the health belief model and sexual orientation in women. *Journal of Sex Education and Therapy, 22*, 29–24.

Elliot, J., & White, H. (1990). Patients are patients [letter]. *New Zealand Medical Journal, 103*, 593.

Elliott, A.J., Russo, J., Bergam, K., Claypoole, K., Uldall, K.K., & Roy-Byrne, P.P. (1999). *Journal of Clinical Psychiatry, 60*, 226–231.

Ellis, A. (1962). *Reason and emotion in psychotherapy.* New York: Lyle Stuart.

Ellis, A. (1975). *How to live with a "neurotic".* (rev. ed.). New York: Crown.

Ellis, A. (1977). The basic clinical theory of rational-emotive therapy. In A. Ellis & R. Grieger (Eds.), *Handbook of rational-emotive therapy.* New York: Springer.

Ellis, A. (1994). The sport of avoiding sports and exercise: A rational emotive behavior therapy perspective. *The Sport Psychologist, 8*, 248–261.

Ellis, A. and Harper, B.A. (1975). *A new guide to rational living*. North Hollywood, California: Wilshire.

Ellison, L.F., Mao, Y., & Gibbons. (1995). Projected smoking-attributable mortality in Canada, 1991–2000. *Chronic Diseases in Canada, 16*, 84–89.

Ellison, L.F., Morrison, H.I., de Groh, M., & Villeneuve, P.J. (1999). Health consequences of smoking among Canadian smokers: An update. *Chronic Diseases in Canada, 20*, 36–39.

Emanuel, E.J., & Emanuel, L.L. (1992). Four models of the physician–patient relationship. *Journal of the American Medical Association, 267*, 2221–2226.

Emergy, Hauck, E.R., Blumethal, J.A. (1992). Exercise adherence or maintenance among older adults: 1-year follow-up study. *Psychology and Aging, 7*, 466–470.

Emmanouilides, C., & Hammond, K. (2000). Internet usage: Predictors of active users and frequency of use. *Journal of Interactive Marketing, 14*(2), 17–32.

Emmons, K.M., Wechsler, H., Dowdall, G., & Abraham, M. (1998). Predictors of smoking among U.S. college students. *American Journal of Public Health, 88*, 104–107.

Engebretson, T.O., Clark, M.M., Niaura, R.S., Phillips, T., Albrecht, A., & Tilkemeier, P. (1999). Quality of life and anxiety in a phase II cardiac rehabilitation program. *Medical Science in Sports Exercise, 31*, 216–223.

Engel, G.L. (1977). The need for a new medical model: A challenge for biomedicine. *Science, 196*, 129–136.

Ennett, S.T., & Bauman, K.E. (1993). Peer group structure and adolescent cigarette smoking: A social network analysis. *Journal of Health and Social Behavior, 34*, 226–236.

Enns, M.W., Cox, B.J., Sareen, J., & Freeman, P. (2001). Adaptive and maladaptive perfectionism in medical students: A longitudinal investigation. *Medical Education, 35*(11), 1034–1042.

Epp, J. (1986). Achieving health for all: A framework for health promotion. *Canadian Journal of Public Health, 77*, 393–430.

Epstein, L.H., & Cluss, P.A. (1982). A behavioral medicine perspective on adherence to long-term medical regimens. *Journal of consulting and Clinical Psychology, 50*, 950–971.

e-Quarterly Report on Transplant, Waiting List and Donor Statistics: 2002 Summary Statistics. (2003). Canadian Institute for Health information. Available: http://secure.cihi.ca/cihiweb/en/reports_corrstats2002c_f1_e.html [2003, July 8].

Erickson, M.H. (1967). An introduction to the study and application of hypnosis for pain control. In J. Lassner (Ed.), *Hypnosis and psychosomatic medicine* (p. 83). New York: Springer.

Estabrooks, P.A. (2000). Sustaining exercise participation through group cohesion. *Sport Science Reviews, 28*, 63–67.

Esterling, B.A., Kiecolt-Glaser, J.K., Bodnar, J.C., & Glaser, R. (1994). Chronic stress, social support, and persistent alterations in the natural killer cell response to cytokines in older adults. *Health Psychology, 13*, 291–298.

Etnier, J.L., Salazar, W., Landers, D.M., Petruzzello, S.J., Han, M., & Nowell, P. (1997). The influence of physical fitness and exercise upon cognitive functioning: A meta-analysis. *Journal of Sport and Exercise Psychology, 19*, 249–277.

Evans, B., Duggan, W., Baker, J., Ramsay, M., & Abiteboul, D. (2001). Exposure of healthcare workers in England, Wales, and Northern Ireland to bloodborne viruses between July 1997 and June 2000: analysis of surveillance data. *British Medical Journal, 322*, 397–398.

Evans, D.L., Staab, J.P., Petitto, J.M., Morrison, M.F., Szuba,M.P., Ward, H.E., Wingate, B., Luber, M.P., & O'Reardon, J.P. (1999). Depression in medical settings: Biopsychological interventions and treatment considerations. *Journal of Clinical Psychiatry, 60 (Suppl 4)*, 40–55.

Evans, P.D., Doyle, A., Hucklebridge, F., & Clow, A. (1997). Positive but not negative life-events predict vulnerability to upper respiratory illness. *British Journal of Health Psychology, 2*, 339–348.

Evans, R.L., & Connis, R.T. (1995). Comparison of brief group therapy for depressed cancer patients receiving radiation treatment. *Public Health Reports, 110*, 306–311.

Evans, R.L., & Hendricks, R.D. (1993). Evaluating hospital discharge planning: A randomized clinical trial. *Medical Care, 31*, 358–370.

Eysenck, H.J. (1996). Personality and cancer. In C.L. Cooper (Ed.), *Stress, medicine and coping*. (pp. 193–215). Boca Raton, FL: CRC Press.

Facione, N.C. (1993). Delay versus help seeking for breast cancer symptoms: A critical review of the literature on patient and provider delay. *Social Science and Medicine, 36*, 1521–1534.

Facione, N.C., & Giancarlo, C.A., & Ingram, C. (1999). Women's decisions to seek help for breast symptoms occur in a complex social context. *Western Journal of Medicine, 171*, 164.

Farooqui, I.S., Matarese, G., Lord, G.M., Keogh, J.M., Lawrence, E., Agwu, C. et al. (2002). Beneficial effects of leptin on obesity, T cell hyporesponsiveness, and neuroendocrine/metabolic dysfunction of human congenital leptin deficiency. *The Journal of Clinical Investigation, 110*, 1093–1103.

Farrell, G.A. (1999). Aggression in clinical settings: Nurses' views—a follow-up study. *Journal of Advanced Nursing, 29*, 532–541.

Faulkner, M. (2001). The onset and alleviation of learned helplessness in older hospitalized people. *Aging & Mental Health, 5*(4), 379–386.

Fawcett, S.B., Paine-Andrews, A., Francisco, V.T., Schultz, J., Richter, K.P., Berkley-Patton, J., Fisher, J.L., Lewis, R.K., Lopez, C.M., Russos, S., Williams, E.L., Harris, K.J., and Evansen, P. (2001). Evaluating community initiatives for health and development. In Rootman, I., Goodstadt, M., Hyndman, B., McQueen, D.V., Potvin, L., Springett, J., and Ziglio (Eds.). *Evaluation in health promotion: Principles and perspectives*. World Health Organization Regional Publications, European Series, No. 92.

Fawzy, F.I., & Fawzy, N.W. (1998). Group therapy in cancer settings. *Journal of Psychosomatic Research, 45*, 191–200.

Federoff, I.C., Polivy, J. Herman, C.P. (1997). The effect of pre-exposure to food cues on the eating behavior of restrained and unrestrained eaters. *Appetite, 28,* 33–47.

Federoff, I.C., Polivy, J. Herman, C.P. (1997). The specificity of restrained versus unrestrained eaters' responses to food cues: General desire to eat, or craving for the cued food? *Appetite, 41*, 7–13.

Felton, G.M., Parsons, M., & Bartoces, M.G. (1997). Demographic factors: Interaction effects on health promoting behavior and health related factors. *Public Health Nursing, 14,* 361–367.

Felton, J.S. (1998). Burnout as a clinical entity—its importance in health care workers. *Occupational Medicine, 48*, 237–250.

Feltz, D.L. (1988). Self-confidence and sports performance. In K.B. Pandolf (Ed.), *Exercise and sport sciences reviews* (pp. 423–457). New York: MacMillan.

Feltz, D.L., & Landers, D.M. (1983). The effects of mental practice on motor skill learning and performance: A meta-analysis. *Journal of Sport Psychology, 5*, 25–57.

Feltz, D.L. & Lirgg, C.D. (2001). Self-efficacy beliefs in athletes, teams, and coaches. In R.N. Singer, H.A. Hausenblas & C.M. Janelle (Eds.), *Handbook of Sport Psychology* (2nd ed., pp.340–361). New York: Wiley.

Ferguson, E., & Cassaday, H.J. (1999). The Gulf War and illness by association. *British Journal of Psychology, 90*, 459–475.

Ferguson, E., James, D., & Madeley, L. (2002). Factors associated with success in medical school: Systematic review of the literature. *BMJ: British Medical Journal, 324*(7343), 952–957.

Ferguson, E., James, D., O'Hehir, F., & Sanders, A. (2003). Pilot study of the roles of personality, references, and personal statements in relation to performance over the five years of a medical degree. *BMJ: British Medical Journal, 326*(7386), 429–431.

Ferrell, B., Smith, S., Cullinane, C., & Melancon, C. (2003). Symptom concerns of women with ovarian cancer. *J Pain Symptom Manage, 25*(6), 528–538.

Ferraro, D.P. (1980). Acute effects of marijuana on human memory and cognition. In R.C. Peterson (Ed.), *Marijuana research findings*. National Institute on Drug Abuse. Washington, DC: U.S. Government Printing Office.

Festinger, L. (1954). A theory of social comparison processes. *Human Relations, 7*, 117–140.

Finkelstein, P. (1986). Studies in the anatomy laboratory: A portrait of individual and collective defense. In R.H. Coombs, D.S. May, and G.W. Small (Eds.), *Inside doctoring: Stages and outcomes in the professional development of physicians* (pp. 22–42). New York: Praeger.

Finley, A., Chambers, C.T., McGrath, P.J., & Walsh, T. (1999, October). Further validation of the Parents' Postoperative Pain Measure. Poster session presented at the annual meeting of the American Pain Society, Fort Lauderdale, FL.

Finsen, V., Persen, L., Lovlien, M., Veslegaard, E., et al. (1988). Transcutaneous electrical nerve stimulation after major amputation. *British Journal of Bone and Joint Surgery, 70(B)*, 109–112.

Fisch, M.J., Loehrer, P.J., Kristeller, J., Passik, S., Jung, S.H., Shen, J., Arquette, M.A., Brames, M.J., & Einhorn, L.H. (2003). Fluoxetine versus placebo in advanced cancer outpatients: a double-blinded trial of the Hoosier Oncology Group. *J Clin Oncol, 21*(10), 1937–1943.

Fischer, S., Smith, G.T., & Anderson, K.G. (2003). Clarifying the role of impulsivity in bulimia nervosa. *International Journal of Eating Disorders, 33*(4), 406–411.

Fishbein, M., & Ajzen, I. (1975). *Belief, attitude, intention, and behavior: An introduction to theory and research*. Reading, MA: Addison-Wesley.

Fisher, J.D., & Fisher, W.A. (1992). Changing AIDS risk behavior. *Psychological Bulletin, 111*, 455–474.

Fisher, J.D., & Fisher, W.A. (1998). Theoretical approaches to individual level change in HIV risk behavior. In J. Peterson & R. Diclemente (Eds.), *HIV prevention handbook*. New York: Plenum.

Flaherty, J.A., & Richman, J.A. (1993). Substance use and addiction among medical students, residents, and physicians. *Psychiatric Clinics of North America, 16*, 189–197.

Flakus, B.J. (1998). Stress relief for critical care nurses. *Nursing Management, 29*, 48D, 48H–48J.

Fletcher, A.B. (1988). Pain in the neonate. *The New England Journal of Medicine, 317*, 1347–1348.

Flor, H., Fydrich, T., & Turk, D.C. (1992). Efficacy of multidisciplinary pain treatment centers: A meta-analytic review. *Pain, 49*, 221–230.

Flor, H., Kerns, R.D., & Turk, D.C. (1987). The role of spouse reinforcement, perceived pain, and activity levels of chronic pain patients. *Journal of Psychosomatic Research, 31*, 251–259.

Folkins, C.H., & Syme, W.E. (1981) Physical fitness training and mental health. *American Psychologist*, 373–389.

Folkman, S., & Lazarus, R.S. (1985). If it changes it must be a process: Study of emotion and coping during three stages of a college examination. *Journal of Personality and Social Psychology, 48,* 150–170.

Folkman, S., Lazarus, R.S., Dunkel-Schetter, C., DeLongis, A., & Gruen, R.J. (1986). Dynamics of a stressful encounter: Cognitive appraisal, coping and encounter outcomes. *Journal of Personality and Social Psychology, 50,* 992–1003.

Follick, M.J., Ahern, D. K, Attanasio, V., & Riley, J.F. (1985). Chronic pain programs: Current aims, strategies, and needs. *Annals of Behavioral Medicine, 7(3)*, 17–20.

Fontaine, K.R., Redden, D.., Wang, C., Westfall, A.O. & Allison, D.B. (2003). Years of life lost due to obesity. *Journal of the American Medical Association, 289* (2), 187–193.

Fordyce, W.E. (1976). *Behavioral methods for chronic pain and illness*. St. Louis: C.V. Mosby.

Fordyce, W.E. (1978). Learning processes in pain. In R.A. Sternbach (Ed.), *The psychology of pain*. New York: Raven Press.

Fordyce, W.E. (1995). *Back pain in the workplace*. Seattle: IASP Press.

Fordyce, W.E. (1996). Response to Thompson/Merskey/Teasell. *Pain, 65*, 112–114.

Forester, B., Kornfeld, D.S., Fleiss, J.L., & Thompson S. (1993). Group psychotherapy during radiotherapy: Effects on emotional and physical distress. *American Journal of Psychiatry, 150*, 1700–1706.

Fox, E.J., & Melzack, R. (1976). Transcutaneous electrical stimulation and acupuncture: Comparison of treatment for low-back pain. *Pain, 2*, 141–148.

Fox, K.R. (2000). The effects of exercise on physical self-perceptions and self-esteem. In S.J.H. Biddle, K.R. Fox & S.H. Boutcher (Eds.), *Physical activity and psychological well-being* (pp.88-117). London: Routledge & Kegan Paul.

Fox, R., & Gourlay, Y.J. (2000). The impact of highly active antiretroviral combination therapy in HIV infected patients in Glasgow. *Health Bull (Edinb), 58*(4), 309–315.

Fraley, S.S., Altmaier, E.M. (2002). Correlates of patient satisfaction among menopausal women. *Journal of Clinical Psychology in Medical Settings, 9,* 235–243.

Franco-Bronson, K. (1996). The management of treatment-resistant depression in the medically ill. *Psychiatric Clinics of North America, 19*, 329–350.

Frankel, R., & Beckman, H. (1989). Evaluating the patient's primary problem(s). In M. Stewart and D. Roter (Eds.), *Communicating with medical patients* (pp. 86–98). Newbury Park, Calif: Sage Publications.

Frankish, C.J., Milligan, C. D., & Reid, C. (1998). A review of relationships between active living and determinants of health. *Social Science and Medicine, 47*, 287–301.

Fraser, H.S., & McGrath, S.J. (2000). Information technology and telemedicine in sub-Saharan Africa. *British Medical Journal, 321*, 465–466.

Frasure-Smith, N., & Lesperance, F. (2003). Depression and other psychological risks following myocardial infarction. *Archives of General Psychiatry, 60*(6), 627–636.

Frasure-Smith, N., Lesperance, F., Juneau, M., Talajic, M., & Bourassa, M.G. (1999). Gender, depression, and one-year prognosis after myocardial infarction. *Psychosomatic Medicine, 61*, 26–37.

Frasure-Smith, N., Lesperance, F., & Talajic, M. (1993). Depression following myocardial infarction: Impact on 6-month survival. *Journal of the American Medical Association, 270*, 1860–1861.

Fredericks, L.E. & Evans, F.J. (2001). *The use of hypnosis in surgery and anesthesiology: Psychological preparation of the surgical patient.* Springfield, Ill: Charles C. Thomas.

Fredrickson, B.L. (2001). The role of positive emotions in positive psychology: The broaden-and-build theory of positive emotions. *American Psychologist, 56,* 218–226.

French, J.R.P., Jr., & Raven, B. (1959). The bases of social power. In D. Cartwright (Ed.), *Studies in social power* (pp. 150–167). Ann Arbor: University of Michigan, Institute for Social Research.

Friedman, J. M. (2000). Obesity in the new millennium. *Nature, 404,* 632–634.

Friedman, J. M. (2003). A war on obesity, not the obese. *Science, 299,* 856–858.

Friedman, L.A., & Kimball, A.W. (1986). Coronary heart disease mortality and alcohol consumption in Framingham. *American Journal of Epidemiology, 124,* 481–489.

Friedman, M., & Rosenman, R.H. (1959). Association of specific overt behavior pattern with blood and cardiovascular findings—blood cholesterol level, blood clotting time, incidence of arcus senilis, and clinical coronary artery disease. *Journal of the American Medical Association, 162,* 1286–1296.

Friedman, M., & Rosenman, R.H. (1974). *Type A behavior and your heart.* New York: Knopf.

Frisoni, G.B., Fedi, V., Geroldi, C., Trabucchi, M. (1999). Cognition and perception of physical symptoms in the community-dwelling elderly. *Behavioral Medicine, 25,* 5–12.

Fuchs, C.S., Stampfer, M.J., Colditz, G.A., Giovannucci, E.L., et al. (1995). Alcohol consumption and mortality among women. *New England Journal of Medicine, 332,* 1245–1250.

Fulton, T.R. (1996). Nurses' adoption of patient-controlled analgesia approach. *Western Journal of Nursing Research, 18,* 383–396.

Gagliese, L. & Katz, J. (2003). Age differences in postoperative pain are scale dependent: A comparison of measures of pain intensity and quality in younger and older surgical patients. *Pain, 103,* 11–20.

Gagliese, L., & Melzack, R. (1997). Age differences in the quality of chronic pain: A preliminary study. *Pain Research and Management, 2,* 157–162.

Gagnon, E.M., & Recklitis, C.J. (2003). Parents' decision-making preferences in pediatric oncology: the relationship to health care involvement and complementary therapy use. *Psychooncology, 12*(5), 442–452.

Gall, T.L., & Cornblat, M.W. (2002). Breast cancer survivors give voice: A qualitative analysis of spiritual factors in long-term adjustment. *Psycho-Oncology, 11*(6), 524–535.

Gallagher, E.J., Viscoli, C.M., & Horwitz, R.I. (1993). The relationship of treatment adherence to the risk of death after myocardial infarction in women. *Journal of the American Medical Association, 270,* 742–743.

Gard, M.C.E., & Freeman, C.P. (1996). Dismantling of a myth: Review of eating disorders and socioeconomic status. International *Journal of Eating Disorders, 20,* 1–12.

Gareis, K.C., & Barnett, R.C. (2002). Under what conditions do long work hours affect psychological distress: A study of full-time and reduced-hours female doctor. *Work & Occupations, 29*(4), 483–497.

Gathchel, R.J., & Oordt, M.S. (2003). Coping with chronic or terminal illness. In R.J. O. Gatchel, Mark S. Oordt (Ed.), *Clinical health psychology and primary care: Practical advice and clinical guidance for successful collaboration.* (pp. 213–233). Washington, DC, US: American Psychological Association.

Gaudette, L.A., Richardson, A., & Huang, S. (1998). Which workers smoke? *Health Reports, 10(3),* 35–45.

Gauvin, L. (1990). An experiential perspective on the motivational features of exercise and lifestyle. *Canadian Journal of Sport Sciences, 15,* 51–58.

Gauvin, L., Levesque, L. & Richard, L. (2001). Helping people initiate and maintain a more active lifestyle: A public health framework for physical activity promotion research In R.N. Singer, H.A. Hausenblas & C.M. Janelle (Eds.), *Handbook of Sport Psychology* (2nd ed.pp.718–739). New York. Wiley.

Gauvin, L. and Spence, J.C. (1995). Psychological research on exercise and fitness: Current research trends and future challenges. *The Sport Psychologist, 9,* 434–448.

Gay, M., Philippot, P., and Luminet, O. (2002). Differential effectiveness of psychological interventions for reducing osteoarthritis pain: A comparison of Erickson hypnosis and Jacobson relaxation. *European Journal of Pain, 6,* 1–16.

Gaziano, J.M., Buring, J.E., Breslow, J.L., Goldhaber, S.Z., et al. (1993). Moderate alcohol intake, increased levels of high-density lipoprotein and its subfractions, and decreased risk of myocardial infarction. *New England Journal of Medicine, 329,* 1829–1834.

Geist, R., Heinmaa, M., Katzman, D., & Stephens, D. (1999). A comparison of male and female adolescents referred to an eating disorder program. *Canadian Journal of Psychiatry, 44,* 374–378.

Gentry, W.D. (1979). Preadmission behavior. In W.D. Gentry & R.B. Williams (Eds.), *Psychological aspects of myocardial infarction and coronary care* (2nd ed., pp. 67–77). St. Louis: C.V. Mosby.

George, T.R. (1994). Self-confidence and baseball performance: A causal examination. *Journal of Sport and Exercise Psychology,* 16, 3181–399.

Geyer, S. (1991). Life events prior to manifestation of breast cancer: A limited prospective study covering eight years before diagnosis. *Journal of Psychosomatic Research, 35,* 335–363.

Gfellner, B.M., & Hundleby, J.D. (1995). Patterns of drug use among native and white adolescents: 1990–1993. *Canadian Journal of Public Health*(March–April), 95–97.

Gilbar, O. (1989). Who refuses chemotherapy: A profile. *Psychological Reports, 64,* 1291–1297.

Giles, B.E., & Walker, J.S. (2000). Sex differences in pain and analgesia. *Pain Reviews, 7,* 181–193.

Gilpin, E.A., Pierce, J.P. and Parkas, A.J. (1997). Duration of smoking abstinence and success in quitting. *Journal of the National Cancer Institute, 89,* 572–576.

Glaser, R., Kiecolt-Glaser, J.K., Bonneau, R., Malarkey, W., & Hughes, J. (1992). Stress-induced modulation of the immune response to recombinant hepatitis B vaccine. *Psychosomatic Medicine, 54,* 22–29.

Glaser, R., Kiecolt-Glaser, J.K., Speicher, C.E., & Holliday, J.E. (1985). Stress, loneliness, and changes in herpesvirus latency. *Journal of Behavioral Medicine, 8,* 249–260.

Glaser, R., Pearson, G.R., Bonneau, R.H., Esterling, B.A., et al. (1993). Stress and memory T-cell response to the Epstein-Barr virus in healthy medical students. *Health Psychology, 12,* 435–442.

Glaser, R., Sheridan, J.F., Malarkey, W.B., MacCallum, R.C., and Kiecolt-Glaser, J.K. (2000). Chronic stress modulates the immune response to a pneumococcal pneumonia vaccine. *Psychosomatic Medicine, 62,* 804–807.

Glassman, A.H., and Shapiro, P.A. (1998). Depression and the course of coronary artery disease. *American Journal of Psychiatry, 155,* 4–11.

Godin, G., Maticka-Tyndale, E, Adrien, A., Manson-Singer, S., et al. (1996). Cross-cultural testing of three social cognitive theories: An application to condom use. *Journal of Applied Social Psychology, 26,* 1556–1586.

Goffman, E. (1961). *Asylums.* New York: Anchor.

Goldner, E.M., & Birmingham, C.L. (1994). Anorexia nervosa: Methods of treatment. In L. Alexander-Mott & D.B. Lumsden (Eds.), *Understanding eating disorders: Anorexia nervosa, bulimia nervosa, and obesity* (pp. 135–157). Washington, DC: Taylor & Francis.

Goodheart, C.D., & Lansing, M.H. (1997). *Treating people with chronic disease: A psychological guide.* Washington, DC: American Psychological Association.

Goodkin, K., Blaney, N.T., Feaster, D., Fletcher, M., Baum, M.K., Mantero-Atienza, E., Klimas, N.G., Millon, C., Szapocznic, J., & Eisdorfer, C. (1992). Active coping style is associated with natural killer cell cytoxicity in asymptomatic HIV-1 seropositive homosexual men. *Journal of Psychosomatic Research, 36,* 535–650.

Goodman, G., & Dooley, D. (1976). A framework for help-intended communication. *Psychotherapy: Theory, Research and Practice, 13,* 106–117.

Goodwin, J.S., Hunt, W.C., Key, C.R., & Samet, J.M. (1987). The effect of marital status on stage, treatment, and survival of cancer patients. *Journal of the American Medical Association, 258,* 3125–3130.

Gotham, A.M., Brown, R.G., Marsden, C.D. (1986). Depression in Parkinson's disease: a quantitiative and qualitiative analysis. *Journal of Neurology, Neurosurgery and Psychiatry, 49,* 381–389.

Gott, C.M, Rogstad, K.E., Riley, V., & Ahmed-Jushuf, I. (1999). Delay in symptom presentation among a sample of older GUM clinic attenders. *International Journal of STD & AIDS, 10,* 43–46.

Gould, D., & Damarjian, N. (1996). Imagery training for peak performance. In J.L. Van Raaalte and B.W. Brewer (Eds.), *Exploring sport and exercise psychology* (pp. 25–50). Washington, D.C.: American Psychological Association.

Graham, N.M.H., Douglas, R.M., & Ryan, P. (1986). Stress and acute respiratory infection. *American Journal of Epidemiology, 124,* 389–401.

Grams, G.D., Herbert, C., Heffernan, C., Calam, B., Wilson, M.A., Grzybowski, S., & Brown, D. (1996). Haida perspectives on living with non-insulin-dependent diabetes. *Canadian Medical Association Journal, 155,* 1563–1568.

Gray, F., Chretien, F., Vallat-Decouvelaere, A.V., & Scaravilli, F. (2003). The changing pattern of HIV neuropathology in the HAART era. *J Neuropathol Exp Neurol, 62*(5), 429–440.

Gray, R.E., Fitch, M., Davis, C., & Phillips, C. (1997). Interviews with men with prostate cancer about their self-help group experiences. *Journal of Palliative Care, 13,* 15–21.

Green, E.E., Green, A.M., & Walters, E.D. (1972). Biofeedback for mind-body self-regulation: Healing and creativity. *Fields...Within Fields, 5,* n131–144.

Green, L., & Kreuter, M. (1991). *Health promotion planning: An educational and environmental approach.* Mountain View, CA: Mayfield Publishing.

Greenwald, A.G. (1968). Cognitive learning, cognitive response to persuasion, and attitude change. In Greenwald, A.G., Brock, T.C., & Ostrom, T.M. (Eds.), *Psychological foundations of attitudes* (pp. 147–170). San Diego, CA: Academic Press.

Greenwood, J. (1998). Meeting the needs of patients' relatives. *Professional Nurse, 14,* 156–158.

Greer, S., & Moorey, S. (1997). Adjuvant psychological therapy for cancer patients. *Palliative Medicine, 11,* 240–244.

Gregoire, I., Kalogeropoulos, D., & Corcos, J. (1997). The effectiveness of a professionally led support group for men with prostate cancer. *Urological Nursing, 17*, 58–66.

Greist, J.H. (1984). *Exercise in the treatment of depression. Coping with mental stress: The potential and limits of exercise intervention.* Washington, DC: National Institute of Mental Health.

Griffin, M.J., Brennan, L., & McShane, A.J. (1998). Preoperative education and outcome of patient controlled analgesia. *Canadian Journal of Anaesthiology, 45* , 943–948.

Grippo, A.J., & Johnson, A.K. (2002). Biological mechanisms in the relationship between depression and heart disease. *Neuroscience & Biobehavioral Reviews, 26*(8), 941–962.

Grinspoon, L., & Bakalar, J.B. (1995). Marijuana as medicine: A plea for reconsideration. *Journal of the American Medical Association, 273*, 1875–1876.

Grohol, J.M. (1999). *The insider's guide to mental health resources online.* New York: Guilford Press.

Gross, R., Bilker, W.B., Friedman, H.M., Coyne, J.C., & Strom, B.L. (2002). Provider inaccuracy in assessing adherence and outcomes with newly initiated antiretroviral therapy. *AIDS, 16,* 1835–1837.

Grossarth-Maticek, R., Eysenck, H.J., & Boyle, G.J. (1994). An empirical study of the diathesis-stress theory of disease. *International Journal of Stress Management, 1*, 3–18.

Grossarth-Maticek, R., Eysenck, H. J., Pfeifer, A., Schmidt, P., & Koppel, G. (1997). The specific action of different personality risk factors on cancer of the breast, cervix, corpus uteri and other types of cancer: A prospective investigation. *Personality & Individual Differences, 23*(6), 949–960.

Grunau, R V.E. & Craig, K.D. (1987). Pain expression in neonates: Facial action and cry. *Pain, 28*, 395–410.

Grover, F.J., Wu, H.D., Blanford, C., Holcomb, S., & Tidler, D. (2002). Computer-using patients want internet services from family physicians. *Journal of Family Practice, 51*(6), 570–572.

Grunberg, N.E., & Straub, R.O. (1992). The role of gender and taste class in the effects of stress on eating. *Health Psychology, 11,* 97–100.

Gruzelier, J., Smith, F., Nagy, A., and Henderson, D. (2001). Cellular and humoral immunity, mood and exam stress: The influences of self-hypnosis and personality predictors. *International Journal of Psychophysiology, 42*, 55–71.

Gura, T. (2003). Cellular warriors at the battle of the bulge. *Science, 299*, 846–849.

Gushue, G.V., & Brazaitis, S.J. (2003). Lazarus and group psychotherapy: AIDS in the era of protease inhibitors. *Counseling Psychologist, 31*(3), 314–342.

Gutkin, C. (2003). Medical schools' accountability for physician resources. *Canadian Family Physician, 49*, 263.

GVU's WWW user surveys: Frequency of use. (1997). Georgia Tech's Graphic, Visualization, & Usability Center. Available: http://www.gvu.gatech.edu/user_surveys/survey-1998-04/; [2003, June 30].

Haan, N. (1993). The assessment of coping, defense, and stress. In L. Goldberger & S. Breznitz (Eds.) *Handbook of stress: Theoretical and clinical aspects* (2nd ed., pp 258–273). New York: Free Press.

Hadjistavropoulos, H.D., Craig, K.D., Grunau, R.E., & Johnston, C.C. (1994). Judging pain in newborns: Facial and cry determinants. *Journal of Pediatric Psychology, 19*, 485–491.

Hadjistavropoulos, H.D., Craig, K.D., Grunau, R.E., & Whitfield, M.F. (1997). Judging pain in infants: Behavioural, contextual, and developmental determinants. *Pain, 73*, 319–324.

Hadjistavropoulos, T. (1999). Chronic pain on trial: The influence of litigation and compensation on chronic pain syndromes. In A.R. Block, E.G. Kremer, & E. Fernandez (Eds.), *Handbook of pain syndromes* (pp. 59–76). Mahwah, NJ: Erlbaum.

Hadjistavropolous, T., von Baeyer, C. & Craig, K.D. (2001). Pain assessment in persons with limited ability to communicate. In D. C. Turk & R. Melzack (Eds*.), Handbook of pain assessment* (pp. 134–152, 2nd ed). New York: Guilford.

Hadlow, J., & Pitts, M. (1991). The understanding of common terms by doctors, nurses and patients. *Social Science and Medicine, 32*, 193–196.

Halfens, R.G. (1995). Effect of hospital stay on health locus-of-control beliefs. *Western Journal of Nursing Research, 17*, 156–167.

Hall, C.R. (2001) Imagery in sport and exercise. In R.N. Singer, H.A. Hausenblaus & C.M. Janelle (Eds.), *Handbook of Sport Psychology* (2nd ed. pp. 529–549). New York: Wiley

Hall, R.A., Rappaport, M., Hopkins, H.K., & Griffin, R. (1973). Tobacco and evoked potential. *Science, 180*, 212–214.

Hall, S., & Smith, A. (1996). Investigation of the effects and aftereffects of naturally occurring upper respiratory tract illness on mood and performance. *Physiology and Behavior, 59*, 569–577.

Hamm, R.M., & Smith, S.L. (1998). The accuracy of patients' judgments of disease probability and test sensitivity and specificity. *Journal of Family Practice, 47*, 44–52.

Haney, C., Banks, C., & Zimbardo, P. (1973). Interpersonal dynamics in a simulated prison. *International Journal of Criminology and Penology, 1*, 69–97.

Hansen, R.G. (1986). *The joy of stress*. Fairway, Kansas: Andrews, McMeel and Parker.

Hansen, W.B., Graham, J.W., Sobel, J.L., Shelton, D.R., Flay, B.R., & Johnson, C.A. (1987). The consistency of peer and parent influences on tobacco, alcohol, and marijuana use among young adolescents. *Journal of Behavioral Medicine, 10*, 559–579.

Hardy, L., Jones, G., Gould, D. (1996). *Understanding psychological preparation for sport: Theory and practice of elite performers*. Chichester, England: John Wiley and Sons.

Hare, B.D., & Milano, R.A. (1985). Chronic pain: Perspectives on physical assessment and treatment. *Annals of Behavioral Medicine, 7*(3), 6–10.

Harper, D.C. (1999). Presidential address: Social psychology of difference: Stigma, spread, and stereotypes in childhood. *Rehabilitation Psychology, 44*, 131–144.

Harris, L.M., Robinson, J., & Menzies, R.G. (1999). Evidence for fear of restriction and fear of suffocation as components of claustrophobia. *Behaviour Research and Therapy, 37*, 155–159.

Harrison, A. (1999). All change? *British Medical Journal, 319*, 793.

Harrison, D., & Chick, J. (1994). Trends in alcoholism among make doctors in Scotland. *Addiction, 89*, 1613–1617.

Harrison, M.J., Kushner, K.E., Benzies, K., Rempel, G., & Kimak, C. (2003). Women's satisfaction with their involvement in health care decisions during a high-risk pregnancy. *Birth, 30*(2), 109–115.

Hart, I., & Poole, G.D. (1995). Individualism and collectivism and considerations in cross-cultural health research. *Journal of Social Psychology, 135*, 97–99.

Harvey, O.J. (1997). Beliefs, knowledge, and meaning from the perspective of the perceiver: Need for structure-order. In McGarty, C., S.A. Haslam. (Eds). *The message of social psychology: Perspectives on mind in society.* pp. 146–165.

Haskell, W.L., Alderman, E.L., Fair, J.M., et al. (1994). Effects of intensive multiple risk factor reduction on coronary atherosclerosis and clinical cardiac events in men and women with coronary artery disease: The Stanford Coronary Risk Intervention Project (SCRIPT). *Circulation, 89*, 975–990.

Haug, M.R., Musil, C.M., Warner, C.D., & Morris, D.L. (1997). Elderly persons' interpretation of a bodily change as an illness symptom. *Journal of Aging Research, 9*, 529–552.

Haupt, E., Herrmann, R., Benecke-Timp, A., Vogel, H., Haupt, A., & Walter, C. (1996). The KID Study II: Socioeconomic baseline characteristics, psycho-social strain, standard of current medical care education of the Federal Insurance for Salaried Employees' Institution (BfA) diabetic patients in inpatient rehabilitation. Kissingen Diabetes Intervention Study. *Experimental Clinics in Endocrinology and Diabetes, 104*, 378–386.

Hawton, K., Clements, A., Sakarovitch, C., Simkin, S., & Deeks, J.J. (2001). Suicide in doctors: A study of risk according to gender, seniority and specialty in medical practitioners in England and Wales, 1979–1995. *Journal of Epidemiology & Community Health, 55*(5), 296–300.

Haynes, R.B., McDonald, H.P., & Garg, A.X. (2002). Helping patients follow prescribed treatment. *Journal of the American Medical Association, 288*, 2880–2883.

Haynes, R.B., McKibbon, K.A., & Kanani, R. (1996). Systematic review of randomized trials of interventions to assist patients to follow prescriptions for medications. *Lancet, 348*, 383–386.

Haynes, S.G., Feinleib, M., & Kannel, W.B. (1980). The relationship of psychosocial factors to coronary heart disease in the Framingham Study: I. Methods and risk factors. *American Journal of Epidemiology, 107*, 362–383.

Hays, K. (1999). *Working it out: Using exercise in psychotherapy*. Washington, D.C: American Psychological Association.

Hays, K.F. (2002). The enhancement of performing excellence among performing artists. *Journal of Applied Sport Psychology, 14*, 299–312.

Health Canada. (1995). *Horizon three: Young Canadians' alcohol and other drug use: Increasing our understanding*. Hewitt, D., Vinje, G., & MacNeil, P. (Eds.). Catalogue no. H39–307/3–1996E.

Health Canada. (1996). *Aids in Canada: Annual report on AIDS in Canada*. Division of HIV/AIDS Surveillance.

Health Canada. (1997). *AIDS and Aboriginal People: National AIDS Strategy, Phase II*. National AIDS Clearinghouse, Ottawa, Canada.

Health Canada (1999). *Toward a healthy future: Second report on the health of Canadians*. Ottawa: Health Canada Publications.

Health Canada (2000a). *Preventing substance use problems among young people: A compendium of best practices*. Ottawa, ON: Health Canada Publications.

Health Canada. (2000b). *Straight facts about drugs and drug abuse*. Ottawa, ON: Health Canada Publications.

Health Canada. (2001). *Canadian Tobacco Use Monitoring Survey, 2001,* http://www.hc-sc.gc.ca/hecs-sesc/tobacco/research/ctums/2001.

Health Canada. (2003) *Body Mass Index (BMI) Nomogram*. http://www.hc-sc.gc.ca/hpfb-dgpsa/onpp-bppn/bmi_chart_java_e.html. [July 6, 2003].

Health Canada (2003). *Canadian Tobacco Use Monitoring Survey 2002: Environmental tobacco smoke: At home, at work and in public places*. http://www.hc-sc.gc.ca/hecs-sesc/tobacco/research/ctums/2001/2001ets.html [July 17, 2003].

Health Care in Canada. Canadian Institute for Health Information, Ottawa, Canada, 2002.

Hearn, J., & Higginson, T.J. (1998). Do specialist palliative care teams improve outcomes for cancer patients? A systematic literature review. *Palliative Medicine, 12,* 317–332.

Heart disease information: Incidence of cardiovascular disease. (2003). Ottawa: Heart and Stroke Foundation.

Heatherton, T.F., Herman, C.P., & Polivy, J. (1992). Effects of distress on eating: The importance of ego-involvement. *Journal of Personality and Social Psychology 62,* 81–803

Helft, P.R., Hlubocky, F., & Daugherty, C.K. (2003). American Oncologists' vies of Internet use by cancer patients: A mail survey of American Society of Clinical Oncology members. *Journal of Clinical Oncology, 21*(5), 942–947.

Henbest, R.J., & Fehrsen, G.S. (1992). Patient-centredness: Is it applicable outside the west? Its measurement and effect on outcomes. *Family Practice, 9,* 311–317.

Hendler, N.H., & Kozikowski, J.G. (1993). Overlooked physical diagnoses in chronic pain patients involved in litigation. *Psychosomatics, 34,* 494–501.

Hendricks, L.E., & Hendricks, R.T. (1998). Greatest fears of type 1 and type 2 patients about having diabetes: Implications for diabetes educators. *Diabetes Education, 24,* 168–173.

Henningfield, J.E., Cohen, C., & Pickworth, W.B. (1993). Psychopharmacology of nicotine. In C.T. Orleans & J. Slade (Eds.), *Nicotine addiction: Principles and management.* New York: Oxford University Press.

Henthorne, T.L., LaTour, M.S., & Nataraajan, R. (1993). Fear appeals in print advertising: An analysis of arousal and ad response. *Journal of Advertising, 22,* 59–69.

Herbert, T.B., & Cohen, S. (1993). Stress and immunity in humans: A meta-analytic review. *Psychosomatic Medicine, 55,* 364–379.

Herbert, T.B., Cohen, S., Marsland, A.L., Bachen, E.A., Rabin, B.S., et al. (1994). Cardiovascular reactivity and the course of immune response to an acute psychological stressor. *Psychosomatic Medicine, 56,* 337–344.

Herman, C.P., Fitzgerald, N.E., & Polivy, J. (2003). The influence of social norms on hunger ratings and eating. *Appetite, 41,* 15–20.

Herman, C.P., & Polivy, J. (1975). Anxiety, restraint, and eating behavior. *Journal of Abnormal Psychology, 84,* 666–672.

Herman, C.P., & Polivy, J. (1980). *Restrained eating.* In A. J. Stunkard (Ed.), Obesity (pp. 593–606. Philadelphia: Saunders.

Herrmann, C.K., Brand-Driehorst, S., Kaminsky, B., Leibing, E., Staats, H., & Rüger, U. (1998). Diagnostic groups and depressed mood as predictors of 22-month mortality in medical inpatients. *Psychosomatic Medicine, 60,* 570–577.

Hickok, J.T., Roscoe, J.A., Morrow, G.R., King, D.K., Atkins, J.N., & Fitch, T.R. (2003). Nausea and emesis remain significant problems of chemotherapy despite prophylaxis with 5-hydroxytryptamine-3 antiemetics: a University of Rochester James P. Wilmot Cancer Center Community Clinical Oncology Program Study of 360 cancer patients treated in the community. *Cancer, 97*(11), 2880–2886.

Hicks, C.L., von Baeyer, C.L., Spafford, P.A., van Korlaar, I., & Goodenough, B. (2001). The Faces Pain Scale—revised: Toward a common metric in pediatric pain measurement. *Pain, 93*(2), 173–183.

Hickson, G.B., Clayton, E.W., Entmman, S.S., Miller, C.S., et al. (1994). Obstetricians' prior malpractice experience and patients' satisfaction with care. *Journal of the American Medical Association, 272,* 1583–1587.

Hickson, G.B., Clayton, E.W., Githens, P.B., & Sloan, F.A. (1992). Factors that prompted families to file medical malpractice claims following perinatal injuries. *Journal of the American Medical Association, 267,* 1359–1363.

Hilgard, E.R., & Hilgard, J.R. (1975). *Hypnosis in the relief of pain.* Los Altos, CA: Kaufman.

Hill, J.O., Wyatt, H.R., Reed, G.W., & Peters, J.C. (2003). Obesity and the environment: Where do we go from here? *Science, 299,* 853–855.

Hilsden, R.J., Verhoef, M.J., Best, A., & Pocobelli, G. (2003). Complementary and alternative medicine use by Canadian patients with inflammatory bowel disease: results from a national survey. *Am J Gastroenterol, 98*(7), 1563–1568.

Hinds, P.S., Sanders, C.B., Srivastava, D.K., Hickey, S., Jayawardene, D., Milligan, M., Olson, M.S., Puckett, P., Quargnenti, A., Randall, E.A., & Tye, V. (1998). Testing the stress-response sequence model in paediatric oncology nursing. *Journal of Advanced Nursing, 28,* 1146–1157.

Hines, D., Saris, R.N., Throckmorton-Belzer, L. (2000). Cigarette smoking in popular films: Does it increase viewers' likelihood to smoke? *Journal of Applied Social Psychology, 30,* 2246–2269.

Hirai, T. (1974). *The Psychophysiology of Zen.* Tokyo: Igaku Shoin Ltd.

Hislop, T.G., Waxler, N.E., Coldman, A.J., Elwood, J.M., & Kan, L. (1987). The prognostic significance of psychosocial factors in women with breast cancer. *Journal of Chronic Disease, 40,* 729–735.

HIV/AIDS among Aboriginal persons in Canada: A continuing concern. (2003). Ottawa: Health Canada, Centre for Infectious Disease Prevention and Control.

Hoffman, A.J., & Scott, L.D. (2003). Role stress and career satisfaction among registered nurses by work shift patterns. *J Nurs Adm, 33*(6), 337–342.

Holdcraft, L.C., Assefi, N., & Buchwald, D. (2003). Complementary and alternative medicine in fibromyalgia and related

syndromes. *Best Pract Res Clin Rheumatol, 17*(4), 667–683.

Holland, C.K. (1993). An ethnographic study of nursing culture as an exploration for determining the existence of a system of ritual. *Journal of Advances in Nursing, 18,* 1461–1470.

Holland, J.C., Romano, S.J., Heiligenstein, J.H., Tepner, R.G., & Wilson, M.G. (1998). A controlled trial of fluoxetine and desipramine in depressed women with advanced cancer. *Psychooncology, 7,* 291–300.

Holland, K.D., Holahan, C.K. (2003). The relation of social support and coping to positive adaptation to breast cancer. *Psychology & Health, 18,* 15–29.

Holmes, D.S. (1981). The use of biofeedback for treating patients with migraine headaches, Raynaud's disease, and hypertension: A critical evaluation. In C.K. Prokop & L.A. Bradley (Eds.), *Medical psychology: Contributions to behavioral medicine* (pp. 423–441). New York: Academic Press.

Holmich, L.R., Friis, S., Fryzek, J.P., Vejborg, I.M., Conrad, C., Sletting, S., Kjoller, K., McLaughlin, J.K., & Olsen, J. H.(2003). Incidence of silicone breast implant rupture. *Arch Surg, 138*(7), 801–806.

Homo-Delarche, F., Fitzpatrick, F., Christeff, N., Nunez, E.A., Bach, J.F., & Dardenne, M. (1991). Sex steroids, glucocorticoids, stress and autoimmunity. *Journal of Steroid Biochemistry and Molecular Biology, 40,* 619–637.

HON Code of Conduct for medical and health Web sites. (2003, April 23, 2003). [Web site]. Health on the Net Foundation. Available: http://www.hon.ch/ [2003, July 1].

Hope, A., Kelleher, C.C., & O'Connor, M. (1998). Lifestyle practices and the health promotion environment of hospital nurses. *Journal of Advanced Nursing, 28,* 438–447.

Hopkins, E.J., Pye, A.M., Solomon, M., & Solomon, S. (1967). A study of patient choice of doctor in an urban area. *Journal of the Royal College of the General Practitioners, 6,* 282.

Hornberger, J., Thom, D., & MacCurdy, T. (1997). Effects of a self-administered previsit questionnaire to enhance awareness of patients' concerns in primary care. *Journal of General Internal Medicine, 12,* 597–606.

Horwitz, R.I., Viscoli, C.M., Berkman, L., Donaldson, R.M., et al. (1990). Treatment adherence and risk of death after myocardial infarction. *Lancet, 336,* 5420–545.

Hoskins, C.N., Baker, S., Sherman, D., & Bohlander, J. (1996). Social support and patterns of adjustment to breast cancer. *Scholarly Inquiry For Nursing Practice, 10,* 99–123.

Hospital days and average length of stay for Canada, Provinces and Territories, 1994/95 to 1999/00. (2001, Sept 26, 2001). [web site]. Hospital Morbidity Database, Canadian Institute for Health Information. Available: http://secure.cihi.ca/chihweb/en/media_26sep2001_tab3_e.html [2003, July 8].

Houkin, K., Fukuhara, S., Selladurai, B.M., Zurin, A.A., Ishak, M., Kuroda, S., & Abe, H. (1999). Telemedicine in neurosurgery using international digital telephone services between Japan and Malaysia—technical note. *Neurol Med Chir (Tokyo), 39*(11), 773–777; discussion 777–778.

House, J.S. (1981). *Work stress and social support.* Reading, MA: Addison-Wesley.

House, J.S., Landis, K.R., & Umberson, D. (1988). Social relationships and health. *Science, 241,* 540–545.

Hovland, C.I., Janis, I.L., & Kelley, H.H. (1953). *Communication and persuasion: Psychological studies of opinion change.* New Haven, CT: Yale University Press.

How Canadians find health information on the Internet. (2003, March 15, 2003). [web site]. Canadian Health Network. Available: http://www.canadian-health-network.ca/html/newnotable/mar15a_2003e.html [2003, June 29].

Howard, G., Wagenknecht, L.E., Burk, G.L., Diez-Roux, A., et al. (1998). Cigarette smoking and progression of atherosclerosis: The Atherosclerosis Risk in Communities (ARIC) Study. *Journal of the American Medical Society, 279,* 119–124.

Howard, V.A. & Thurber. (1998). The interpretation of infant pain: Physiological and behavioral indicators. *Pediatric Nursing, 13(3),* 164–174.

Howie, J.G., Porter, A.M., Heaney, D.J., & Hopton, J.L. (1991). Long to short consultation ratio: A proxy measure of quality of care for general practice. *British Journal of General Practice, 41(343),* 48–54.

Hsih, C. (2000). *Use of the Internet.* American Medical Association. Available: http://www.medem.com [2003, July 3].

Hunt, D.L., Haynes, R.B., Hanna, S.E., & Smith, K. (1998). Effects of Computer-based clinical decision support systems on physician performance and patient outcomes: A systematic review. *Journal of the American Medical Association, 280*(15), 1339–1346.

Hunter, M. & Philips, C. (1981). The experience of headache: An assessment of the qualities of tension headache pain. *Pain, 10,* 209–219.

Hurley, A.D., Tomasulo, D.J. & Pfadt, A.G. (1998). Individual and group psychotherapy approaches for persons with mental retardation and developmental disabilities. *Journal of Developmental and Physical Disabilities, 10,* 365–386.

Hyland, M., & Birrell, J. (1979). Government health warning and the "boomerang" effect. *Psychological Reports, 44,* 643–647.

Ikard, F.F., & Tomkins, S. (1973). The experience of affect as a determinant of smoking behavior: A series of validity studies. *Journal of Abnormal Psychology, 81*, 172–181.

Ilacqua, G.E. (1994). Migraine headaches: Coping efficacy of guided imagery training. *Headache, 34*, 99–102.

Imrie, D.D. (1994). "Client" versus "patient" [letter]. *Canadian Medical Association Journal, 150*, 123.

Irwin, M., Daniels, M., Smith, T.L., Bloom, E., & Weiner, H. 1987). Impaired natural killer cell activity during bereavement. *Brain, Behavior, and Immunity, 1*, 98–104.

Iserson, K.V. (1999). Hypnosis for pediatric fracture reduction. *Journal of Emergency Medicine, 17(1)*, 53–56.

Iverson, G. (1998). Mild head trauma: Epidemic in nature. *Recovery, 9*, 4–7.

Iwai, K. (1996). 1: The self-image of muscular dystrophy inpatients and the psychological effects of their disease. *Japanese Journal of Special Education, 33*(5), 1–6.

Jackson, S.A., & Csikszentmihalyi. M. (1999). *Flow in sports*. Champaign, Illinois: Human Kinetics.

Jacobson, A.M., & Weinger, K. (1998). Treating depression in diabetic patients; Is there an alternative to medications? *Annals of Internal Medicine, 129*, 656–657.

Jacobson, E. (1938). *Progressive relaxation: A physiological and clinical investigation of muscle states and their significance in psychology and medical practice (2nd ed.)*. Chicago: University of Chicago Press.

Jacobson, L.D., Wilkinson, C., & Owen, P.A. (1994). Is the potential of teenage consultations being missed? A study of consultation times in primary care. *Family Practice, 11*, 296–299.

Jacobson, P.D., Bovbjerg, D.H., Schwartz, M.D., Hudis, C.A., Gilewski, T.A., & Norton, L. (1995). Conditioned emotional distress in women receiving chemotherapy for breast cancer. *Journal of Consulting and Clinical Psychology, 63*, 108–114.

JAMA. (1998). NIH Consensus Conference. Acupuncture. *Journal of the American Medical Association, 280*(17), 1518–1524.

Jamsa, K., & Jamsa, T. (1998). Technology in neonatal intensive care—a study on parents' experiences. *Technology and Health Care, 6*, 225–230.

Jarvik, M.E. (1973). Further observations on nicotine as the reinforcing agent in smoking. In W.L. Dunn, Jr. (Ed.), *Smoking behavior: Motives and incentives* (pp. 33–50). Washington, DC: Winston.

Jasnowski, M.L., Holmes, D.S., & Banks, D.L. (1988). Changes in personality associated with changes in aerobic and anaerobic fitness in women and men. *Journal of Psychosomatic Research, 32*, 273–276.

Jed, E. (1999). Reflections on the NICU. A mother's perspective. *American Journal of Nursing, 99*(3), 22.

Jellinek, E.M. (1960). *The disease concept of alcoholism*. New Haven, CT: College and University Press.

Jemmott, JB III, Borysenko, M., Chapman, R., et al., (1983). Academic stress, power motivation,a n decrease in secretion rate of salivary secretory Immunoglobulin A. *Lancet*, 1400–1402.

Jenkins, C., Carmody, T.J., & Rush, A.J. (1998). Depression in radiation oncology patients: A preliminary evaluation. *Journal of Affective Disorders, 50*, 17–21.

Jenkins, C.D. (1996). Where there's hope, there's life. *Psychosomatic Medicine, 58*, 122–124.

Jenner, B. (1976). It was too easy. *Sport, 63*. 67–78.

Jensen, M.P., & Karoly, P. (2001). Self-report scales and procedures for assessing pain in adults. In D. C. Turk & R. Melzack (Eds.), *Handbook of pain assessment* (2nd ed., pp. 15–34). New York: Guildford.

Jensen, M.P., & McFarland, C.A. (1993). Increasing the reliability and validity of pain intensity measurement in chronic pain patients. *Pain, 55*, 195–203.

Jensen, M.P., Turner, J.A., Romano, J.M., & Strom, S.E. (1995). The Chronic Pain Coping Inventory: Development and preliminary validation. *Pain, 60,* 203–216.

Jensen, T.S., Krebs, B., Nielsen, J. & Rasmussen, P. (1985). Immediate and long-term phantom limb pain in amputees; incidence, clinical characteristics and relationship to preamputation limb pain. *Pain, 21,* 267–278.

Joachim, G., & Acorn, S. (2000). Stigma of visible and invisible chronic conditions. *J Adv Nurs, 32*(1), 243–248.

Job, E. (2003) *Learning to show "it hurts": The role of developmental factors in predicting young children's use of self-report scales for pain.* Unpublished master's thesis, University of British Columbia, Vancouver, British Columbia, Canada.

Johnson, B.G. (1984). Biofeedback, trans-cutaneous electrical nerve stimulation, acupuncture, and hypnosis. In G.K. Riggs & E.P. Gall (Eds.), *Rheumatic diseases: Rehabilitation and management.* Boston: Butterworth.

Johnson, C.G., Levenkron, J.C., Suchman, A.L., & Manchester, R. (1988). Does physician uncertainty affect patient satisfaction? *Journal of General Internal Medicine, 3,* 144–149.

Johnson, J.L. (1991). Learning to live again: The process of adjustment following a heart attack. In J.M. Morse & J.L. Johnson (Eds.), *The illness experience: Dimensions of suffering* (pp. 13–87). Newbury Park: Sage.

Johnson, M., & Vögele, C. (1993). Benefits of psychological preparation for surgery: A meta-analysis. *Annals of Behavioral Medicine, 15,* 245–256.

Johnston, K.L. and White, K.M. (2003). Binge–drinking: A test of the role of group norms in the theory of planned behaviour. *Psychology and Health, 18,* 63–77.

Jolly, A.M., Orr, P.H., Hammond, G., & Young, T.K. (1995). Risk factors for infection in women undergoing testing for Chlamydia trachomatis and Neisseria gonorrhoeae in Manitoba, Canada. *Sexually Transmitted Diseases, 22,* 289–295.

Jonasson, G., Carlsen, K.H., Sodal, A., Jonasson, C., & Mowinckel, P. (1999). Patient compliance in a clinical trial with inhaled budesonide in children with mild asthma. *European Respiratory Journal, 14,* 150–154.

Jones, G.(2002). Performance excellence: A personal perspective on the link between sport and business. *Journal of Applied Sport Psychology, 14,* 268–281.

Jones, L.W., Sinclair, R.C., and Courneya, K.S., (2003). The effects of source credibility and message framing on exercise intentions, behaviors and attitudes: An integration of the elaboration likelihood model and prospect theory. *Journal of Applied Social Psychology, 33,* 179–196.

Jones, S. (1996). Demographic distributions of literacy in Canada. In *Reading the future: A portrait of literacy in Canada.* Ottawa: Ministry of Industry.

Jorenby, D.E., Leischow, S.J., Nides, M.A., Rennard, S.I., et al. (1999). A controlled trial of sustained-release bupropion, a nicotine patch, or both for smoking cessation. *New England Journal of Medicine, 340,* 685–691.

Kaasa, S., & Loge, J.H. (2003). Quality of life in palliative care: principles and practice. *Palliat Med, 17*(1), 11–20.

Kabat-Zinn, J. (1993). Mindfulness meditation: Health benefits of an ancient Buddhist practice. In D. Goleman & J. Gurin (eds.), *Mind/body medicine: How to use your mind for better health* (pp. 259–275). Yonkers, NY: Consumer Reports Books.

Kaegi, E. (1998a). Unconventional therapies for cancer: 5. Vitamins A, C and E. Task Force on Alternative Therapies of the Canadian Breast Cancer Research Initiative. *Canadian Medical Association Journal, 158,* 1483–1488.

Kaegi, E. (1998b). A patient's guide to choosing unconventional therapies. *Canadian Medical Association Journal, 158*, 1161–1165.

Kahneman, D. & Miller, D.T. (1986). Norm theory: Comparing reality to its alternatives. *Psychological Review, 80*, 136–153.

Kahneman, D., & Tversky, A. (1973). On the psychology of prediction, *Psychological Review, 80*, 237–251.

Kalisch, P.A., & Kalisch, B.J. (1987). *The changing image of the nurse*. Menlo Park, CA: Addison-Wesley.

Kanerva, M., Tarkkila, P., & Pitkaranta, A. (2003). Day-case tonsillectomy in children: parental attitudes and consultation rates. *Int J Pediatr Otorhinolaryngol, 67*(7), 777–784.

Kang, D., Coe, C.L.; Karaszewski, J., and McCarthy, D.O. (1998). Relationship of social support to stress responses and immune function in healthy and asthmatic adolescents. *Research in Nursing & Health, 21*, 117–128.

Kaplan, R.M. (1990). Behavior as the central outcome in health care. *American Psychologist, 45*, 1211–1220.

Kaplan, R.M., Sallis, J.F. and Patterson, T.L. (1993). *Health and human behavior*. New York: McGraw-Hill.

Kaplan, S.H., Gandek, B., Greenfield, S., Rogers, W. & Ware, J.E. (1995). Patient and visit characteristics related to physicians' participatory decision-making style: Results from the Medical Outcomes Study. *Medical Care, 33*, 1176–1187.

Kaps, E.C. (1994). The role of the support group, "Us Too". *Cancer, 74*, 2188–2189.

Karaca, I., Ilkay, E., Akbulut, M., & Yavuzkir, M. (2003). Treatment of in-stent restenosis with excimer laser coronary angioplasty. *Jpn Heart J, 44*(2), 179–186.

Karasek, R. (1979). Job demands, job decision latitude, and mental strain: Implications for job design. *Administrative Science Quarterly, 24*, 285–310.

Karoly, P., & Ruehlman, L.S. (1996). Motivational implications of pain: Chronicity, psychological distress, and work global construal in a national sample of adults. *Health Psychology, 15*, 383–390.

Kasamatsu, A., & Hirai, T. (1966). An electroencephalographic study on the zen meditation (Zazen). *Folia psychiatrica et neurological Japonica, 20*, 315–336.

Kasamatsu, A., & Hirai, T. (1963). Science of Zazen. *Psychologia, 6*, 86–91.

Kashani, J., & Hakami, N. (1982). Depression in children and adolescents with malignancy. *Canadian Journal of Psychiatry, 27*, 474–477.

Katz, J., Wowk, A., Culp, D., & Wakeling, H. (1999). A randomized, controlled study of the pain- and tension-reducing effects of 15 minute workplace massage treatments versus seated rest for nurses in a large teaching hospital. *Pain Research and Management, 4*(2), 81–88.

Katz, R.C., Flasher, L., Cacciapaglia, H., & Nelson, S. (2001). The psychosocial impact of cancer and lupus: A cross validation study that extends the generality of "benefit finding" in patients with chronic disease. *Journal of Behavioral Medicine, 24*(6), 561–571.

Katz, R.C., Wilson, L., & Frazer, N. (1994). Anxiety and its determinants in patients undergoing magnetic resonance imaging. *Journal of Behavior Therapy and Experimental Psychiatry, 25*, 131–134.

Kaufman, D.M., & Mann, K.V. (1998). Comparing achievement on the Medical Council of Canada Qualifying Examination Part I of students in conventional and problem-based learning curricula. *Academic Medicine, 73*, 1211–1213.

Kavussanu, M. and McAuley, E. (1996). Exercise and optimism: Are highly active individuals more optimistic? *Journal of Sport and Exercise Psychology, 18*, 264–280.

Kawachi, I., Colditz, G.A., Stampfer, M.J., Willett, W.C., et al. (1993). Smoking cessation and decreased risk of stroke in women. *Journal of the American Medical Association, 269*, 232–236.

Keefe, F.J., Williams, D.A., & Smith, S.J. (2001). Assessment of pain behaviors. In D.C. Turk & R. Melzack (Eds.), *Handbook of pain assessment* (2nd ed., pp. 170–189). New York: Guildford.

Keefler, J., Duder, S., & Lechman, C. (2001). Predicting length of stay in an acute care hospital: The role of psychosocial problems. *Social Work in Health Care, 33*(2), 1–16.

Kelly, B., Raphael, B., Judd, F., Perdices, M., Kernutt, G., Burnett, P., Dunne, M., & Burrows, G. (1998). Posttraumatic stress disorder in response to HIV infection. *General Hospital Psychiatry, 20*, 345–352.

Kelly, G., & McKenzie, B. (2002). Security, privacy, and confidentiality issues on the Internet. *J Med Internet Res, 4*(2), E12.

Kelly, J.A. (1998). Group psychotherapy for persons with HIV and AIDS-related illnesses. *International Journal of Group Psychotherapy, 48*, 143–162.

Kelner, K. & Helmuth, L. (2003). Obesity— What is to be done? *Science, 299*, 845.

Kelner, M. (1995). Activists and delegators: Elderly patients' preferences about control at the end of life. *Social Science & Medicine, 41*(4), 537–545.

Kendall, C., & Hailey, B.J. (1993). The relative effectiveness of three reminder letters on making and keeping mammogram appointments. *Behavioral Medicine, 19*, 29–34.

Kendler, K.S., Kessler, R.C., Heath, A.C., Neale, M.C., & Eaves, L.J. (1991). Coping: A genetic epidemiological investigation. *Psychological Medicine, 21*, 337–346.

Kerns, R.D., Turk, D.C., & Rudy, T.E. (1985). The West Haven–Yale Multidimensional Pain Inventory. *Pain, 23*, 345–356.

Kerssens, J.J., Bensing, J.M., & Andela, M.G. (1997). Patient preference for genders of health professionals. *Social Science and Medicine, 44*, 1531–1540.

Kessler, M., Kronstorfer, R., & Traue, H.C. (1996). Depressive symptoms and disability in acute and chronic back pain patients. *International Journal of Behavioral Medicine, 3*, 91–104.

Kettunen, T.P., Marita Gerlander, M. (2002). Nurse–patient power relationship: Preliminary evidence of patients' power messages. *Patient Education & Counseling, 47*(2), 101–113.

Kiecolt-Glaser, J.K., Cacioppo, J.T., Malarkey, W.B., & Glaser, R. (1992). Acute psychological stressors and short-term immune changes: What, why, for whom, and to what extent? *Psychosomatic Medicine, 54*, 680–685.

Kiecolt-Glaser, J.K., Dura, J.R., Speicher, C.E., Trask, O.J., & Glaser, R.G. (1991). Spousal caregivers of dementia victims: Longitudinal changes in immunity and health. *Psychosomatic Medicine, 53*, 345–362.

Kiecolt-Glaser, J.K., Fisher, J.D., Ogrocki, P., Stout, J.C., Speicher, C.E., Glaser, R. (1987a). Marital quality, marital disruption, and immune function. *Psychosomatic Medicine, 49*, 13–34.

Kiecolt-Glaser, J.K., Garner, W., Speicher, C., Penn, G.M., Holliday, J., & Glaser, R. (1984). Psychosocial modifiers of immunocompetence in medical students. *Psychosomatic Medicine, 46*, 7–14.

Kiecolt-Glaser, J.K., & Glaser, R. (1995). Psychoneuroimmunology and health consequences: Data and shared mechanisms. *Psychosomatic Medicine, 57*, 269–274.

Kiecolt-Glaser, J. K., & Glaser, R. (2001). Stress and immunity: Age enhances the risks. *Current Directions in Psychological Science, 10*, 18–21.

Kiecolt-Glaser, J.K., Glaser, R., Shuttleworth, E.C. Dyers, C.S., Ogroki, P., & Speicher, C.E. (1987b). Chronic stress and immunity in family caregivers of Alzheimer's disease victims. *Psychosomatic Medicine, 49,* 523–535.

Kiecolt-Glaser, J.K., Kennedy, S., Malkoff, S., Fisher, L., Speicher, C.E., & Glaser, R. (1988). Marital discord and immunity in males. *Psychosomatic Medicine, 50,* 213–229.

Kiecolt-Glaser, J.K., Marucha, P.T., Atkinson, C., and Glaser, R. (2001). Hypnosis as a modulator of cellular immune dysregulation during acute stress. *Journal of Consulting & Clinical Psychology, 69,* 674–682.

Kiecolt-Glaser, J.K., McGuire, L., Robles, T.F., and Glaser, R. (2002a). Psychoneuro-immunology: Psychological influences on immune function and health. *Journal of Consulting and Clinical Psychology, 70,* 537–547.

Kiecolt-Glaser, J.K., McGuire, L., Robles, T.F., and Glaser, R. (2002b). Emotions, morbidity, and mortality: new perspectives from psychoneuroimmunology. *Annual Review of Psychology, 53,* 83–107.

Kiesler, D.J. (1966). Some myths of psycotherapy research and the search for a paradigm. *Psychological Bulletin, 65,* 110–136.

Kilborn, L.C., & Labbe, E.E. (1990). Magnetic resonance imaging scanning procedures: Development of phobic response during scan and at one-month follow-up. *Journal of Behavioral Medicine, 13,* 391–401.

Kim, J., & Dellon, A.L. (2001). Pain at the site of tarsal tunnel incision due to neuroma of the posterior branch of the saphenous nerve. *Journal of the American Podiatric Medical Association, 91,* 109–114.

King, A.J.C., Boyce, W.F., & King, M.A. (1999). Trends in the health of Canadian youth. Health Behaviors in School-Aged Children, a World Health Organization Cross-National Study. Canada: Health Canada.

King, K.M., & Teo, K.K. (1998). Cardiac rehabilitation referral and attendance: Not one and the same. *Rehabilitation Nursing, 23,* 246–251.

Kingston, G. (1999). Concussion leaves a gap in Long's memory. *Vancouver Sun,* October 18.

Kinsey, A.C., Pomeroy, W.B., & Martin, C.C. (1948). *Sexual behavior in the human male.* Philadelphia: Saunders.

Kinsey, A.C., Pomeroy, W.B., Martin, C.C., & Gebhard, P.H. (1953). *Sexual behavior in the human female.* Philadelphia: Saunders.

Kirby, S.D.; Ureda, J.R. (1998). Peripheral cues and involvement level: influences on acceptance of a mammography message. *Journal of Health Communication, 3,* 119–135.

Kircaldy, B.D, & Shephard, R.J. (1990). Therapeutic implications of exercise. *International Journal of Sport Psychology, 21,* 165–184.

Kirkley, B.G., Schneider, J.A., Agras, W.J., Bachman, J.A. (1985). Comparison of two group treatments for bulimia. *Journal of Consulting and Clinical Psychology, 53,* 43–48.

Kirschenbaum, D. (1998). Using sport psychology interventions to improve health psychology outcomes. *The Health Psychologist, 20,* 16–23.

Kirschenbaum, K.S. (1997). Prevention of sedentary lifestyles: Rationale and methods. In W.P. Morgan (Ed.) *Physical activity and mental health* (pp.33–48). Washington, DC: Taylor and Francis.

Kitamura, A., Hiroyasu, I., Sankai, T., Naito, Y., et al. (1998). Alcohol intake and premature coronary heart disease in urban Japanese men. *American Journal of Epidemiology, 147,* 59–65.

Kivlahan, D.R., Marlatt, G.A., Fromme, K., Coppel, D.B., & Williams, E. (1990). Secondary prevention with college drinkers: Evaluation of an alcohol skills training program. *Journal of Consulting and Clinical Psychology, 58*, 805–810.

Kleinke, C.L., & Spangler, A.S. (1988). Psychometric analysis of the audiovisual taxonomy for assessing pain behavior in chronic back-pain patients. *Journal of Behavioral Medicine, 11*, 83–94.

Klesges, R.C., Eck, L.H., Hanson, C.L., Haddock, C.K., & Klesges, L.M. (1990). Effects of obesity, social interactions, and physical environment on physical activity in preschoolers. *Health Psychology, 9,* 435–559.

Klepp, K.I., Kelder, S.H., & Perry, C.L. (1995). Alcohol and marijuana use among adolescents: Long-term outcomes of the Class of 1989 Study. *Annals of Behavioral Medicine, 17*, 19–24U : D. Klonoff, E.A., & Landrine, H. (1994). Culture and gender diversity in commonsense beliefs about the causes of six illnesses. *Journal of Behavioral Medicine, 17*, 407–418.

Klump, K., McGue, M., & Iacono, W.G. (2000). Age differences in genetic and environmental influences on eating attitudes and behaviors in preadolescent and adolescent female twins. *Journal of Abnormal Psychology, 109*, 239–251.

Knoerl, D.V., Faut-Callahan, M., Paice, J., & Shoot, S. (1999). Preoperative PCA teaching program to manage postoperative pain. *Medsurgical Nursing, 8*, 25–33,36.

Kohen, D., Burgess, A.P., Catalán, J., & Lant, A. (1998). The role of anxiety and depression in quality of life and symptom reporting in people with diabetes mellitus. *Quality of Life Research, 7*, 197–204.

Koller, M., Grutter, R., Peltenburg, M., Fischer, J.E., & Steurer, J. (2001). Use of the Internet by medical doctors in Switzerland. *Swiss Med Wkly, 131*(17–18), 251–254.

Koltyn, K.F. & Vaughn, A.C. (1999, October) Pain responses in men and women exposed to three different noxious stimuli. Poster session presented at the annual meeting of the American Pain Society, Fort Lauderdale, FL.

Komaroff, A.L. (March 7, 2003). *An update on the obesity problem*. Journal Watch (General). http://general-medicine.jwatch.org/cgi/content/full/2003/307/8 [July 9, 2003].

Komproe, I.H., Rijken, M., Ros, W.J.G., Winnubst, J.A.M., & Harm't H. (1997). Available support and received support: Different effects under stressful circumstances. *Journal of Social and Personal Relationships, 14*, 59–77.

Kools, S., Tong, E.M., Hughes, R., Jayne, R., Scheibly, K., Laughlin, J., & Gilliss, C. L. (2002). Hospital experiences of young adults with congenital heart disease: Divergence in expectations and dissonance in care. *American Journal of Critical Care, 11*(2), 115–127.

Korsch, B.M., Gozzi, E.K., & Francis, V. (1968). Gaps in doctor–patient communication. *Pediatrics, 42*, 855–871.

Kowalcek, I., Muhlhoff, A., Bachmann, S., & Gembruch, U. (2002). Depressive reactions and stress related to prenatal medicine procedures. *Ultrasound Obstet Gynecol, 19*(1), 18–23.

Kozlowski, L.T. (1979). Psychosocial influences on cigarette smoking. In *Smoking and health: A report of the surgeon general. DHEW Publ. No. 79–40066. Washington, DC: GPA.*

Kozlowski, L.T., Herman, C.P. (1984). The interaction of psychosocial and biological determinants of tobacco use: More on the boundary model. *Journal of Applied Social Psychology, 14, 244–256.*

Kramer, M. (1974). *Reality shock—Why nurses leave nursing.* St. Louis, MO: CV Mosby.

Krantz, D.S., Baum, A., & Wideman, M.V. (1980). Assessment for preferences for self-treatment and information in health care. *Journal of Personality and Social Psychology, 39*, 977–990

Krantz, D.S., Grunberg, N.E., & Baum, A. (1985). Health psychology. *Annual Review of Psychology, 36*, 349–383.

Krause, J.S., Stanwyck, C.A., & Maides, J. (1998). Locus of control and life adjustment: Relationship among people with spinal cord injury. *Rehabilitation Counseling Bulletin, 4*, 162–172.

Krebs, B., Jensen, T.S., Kroner, K., Nielsen, J., & Jorgenssen, H.S. (1984). *Phantom limb phenomena in amputees 7 years after limb amputation. Pain (Suppl.), 2*, S85.

Krebs, L.U., Myers, J., Decker, G., Kinzler, J., Asfahani, P., & Jackson, J. (1996). The oncology nursing image: Lifting the mist. *Oncology Nursing Forum, 23*, 1297–1304.

Kroner-Herwig, B., Jakle, C., Frettloh, J., Peters, K., et al. (1996). Predicting subjective disability in chronic pain patients. International *Journal of Behavioral Medicine, 3*, 30–41.

Kronick, J., Blake, C., Munoz, E., Heilbrunn, L., Dunikowski, L., & Milne, W.K. (2003). Improving on-line skills and knowledge. A randomized trial of teaching rural physicians to use on-line medical information. *Canadian Family Physician, 49*, 312–317.

Krüger, S. McVey, G., & Kennedy, S.H. (1998). The changing profile of anorexia nervosa at the Toronto Programme for eating disorders. *Journal of Psychosomatic Research, 45*, 533–547.

Krupat, E., Fancey, M., & Cleary, P.D. (2000). Information and its impact on satisfaction among surgical patients. *Social Science & Medicine, 51*(12), 1817–1825.

Kübler-Ross, E. (1969). *On death and dying.* New York: Macmillan.

Kuttner, L. (1997). Mind body methods of pain management. *Child and Adolescent Psychiatric Clinics of North America, 6*, 783–796.

Kuuppelomäki, M., & Lauri, S. (1998). Cancer patients' reported experiences of suffering. *Cancer Nursing, 21*, 364–369.

La Greca, A.M., & Stone, W.L. (1985). Behavioral pediatrics. In N. Schneiderman & J.T. Tapp (Eds.), *Behavioral medicine: The biopsychosocial approach.* Hillsdale, NJ: Erlbaum.

La Via, M.F., Munno, I., Lydiard, R.B., Workman, E.W., Hubbard, J.R., Michel, Y., & Paulling, E. (1996). The influence of stress intrusion on immunodepression in generalized anxiety disorder patients and controls. *Psychosomatic Medicine, 58*, 138–142.

Labonte, R. (1987). Community health promotion strategies. *Health Promotion, 16*, 5–10, 32.

Labonte, R. (1990). Health promotion: From concepts to strategies. In Eikenberg, G. (ed.), *The seeds of health: Promoting wellness in the '90s.* (pp. 129–146). Ottawa: Canadian College of Health Service Executives.

Laboratory Centre for Disease Control, Bureau of HIV/AIDS and STD, Health Canada (May, 1997), Ottawa.

Laboratory Centre for Disease Control, Division of HIV/AIDS Surveillance, Bureau of HIV/AIDS and STD, Health Canada (May, 1997). *Epi update: HIV/AIDS epidemiology among Aboriginal people in Canada.* Ottawa: Health Canada. Ottawa.

Laboratory Centre for Disease Control (LCDC) (1998). Diabetes.

Lacroix, J.M., Martin, B., Avendano, M., & Goldstein, R. (1991). Symptom schemata in chronic respiratory patients. *Health Psychology, 10*, 268–273.

Ladwig, K.-H., & Dammann, G. (1997). Psychological adaptation after successful out-of-hospital resuscitation. *Journal of Psychosomatic Research, 43*(6), 559–564.

Ladwig, K.H., Schoefinius, A., Dammaun, G., Danner, R., Gurtler, R., & Herrmann, R. (1999). Long-acting psychotraumatic properties of a cardiac arrest experience. *American Journal of Psychiatry, 156*, 912–919.

Laforge, R.G., Greene, G.W., & Prochaska, J.O. (1994). Psychosocial factors influencing low fruit and vegetable consumption. *Journal of Behavioral Medicine, 17*, 361–374.

Laitinen, J. (1976). Acupuncture and transcutaneous electric stimulation in the treatment of chronic sacrolumbalgia and ischialgia. *American Journal of Chinese Medicine, 4*, 169–175.

Lalonde, M. (1974). *New perspectives on the health of Canadians.* Ottawa: Information Canada.

Lambert, S.A. (1996). The effects of hypnosis/guided imagery on the postoperative course of children. *Journal of Developmental and Behavioral Pediatrics, 17*, 307–310.

Lamping, D.L., Abrahamowicz, M., Gilmore, N., Edgar, L., Grover, S.A., Tsoukas, C., Falutz, J., Lalonde, R., Hamel, M., & Darsigny, R. (1993, June). *A randomized controlled trial to evaluate a psychosocial intervention to improve quality of life in HIV infection.* Paper presented to the IX International Conference on AIDS, Berlin, Germany.

Landers, D.M. & Arent, S.M. (2001) In R.N. Singer, H.A. Hausenblas & C.M. Janelle (Eds.), *Handbook of Sport Psychology* (2nd ed., pp. 740–765). New York: Wiley.

Landers, D.M., & Peruzzello, S.J. (1994). Physical activity, fitness, and anxiety. In C. Bouchard, R.J. Shephard, & T. Stephens (Eds.), *Physical activity, fitness, and health: International proceedings and consensus statement* (pp. 868–882). Champaign, Illinois: Human Kinetics.

Lang, A. (2000). The information processing of mediated messages: A framework for communication research. *Journal of Communication, 50*, 46–70.

Lang, A., Borse, J., Wise, K., & Prabu, D. (2002). Captured by the World Wide Web: Orienting to structural and content features of computer-presented information. *Communication Research, 29*(3), 215–245.

Larocque, D. (1996). Absenteeism. *Canadian Nurse, 92*(9), 42–46.

Larson, P.J., & Ferketich, S.L. (1993). Patients' satisfaction with nurses' caring during hospitalization. *Western Journal of Nursing Research, 15*, 690–707.

Larson, R., & Sutker, S. (1966). Value differences and value consensus by socioeconomic levels. *Social Forces, 44*, 563–569.

Larsson, U.S., Johanson, M., & Svardsudd, K. (1994). Sensitive patient–doctor communications relating to the breasts and prostate. *Journal of Cancer Education, 9*, 19–25.

Lau, R.R., Hartman, K.A., & Ware, J.E. Jr. (1986). Health as a value: Methodological and theoretical considerations. *Health Psychology, 5*, 25–43.

Lautenbacher, S., & Rollman, G.B. (1993). Sex differences in responsiveness to painful and non-painful stimuli are dependent upon the stimulation method. *Pain, 53*, 255–264.

Lauver, D., Coyle, M., & Panchmatia, B. (1995). Women's reasons for and barriers to seeking care for breast cancer symptoms. *Women's Health Issues, 5*, 27–35.

Lavie, C.J., Milani, R.V., Cassidy, M.M., & Gilliland, Y.E. (1999). Effects of cardiac rehabilitation and exercise training programs in women with depression, *American Journal of Cardiology, 83*, 1480–1483.

Layne, N. (1987). *Solvent use/abuse among the Canadian Registered Indian and Inuit population. An overview paper. Unpublished report.* Ottawa: National Native Alcohol and Drug Abuse Program.

Lazurus, R.S. (1999). *Fifty years of the research and theory of R.S. Lazurus: An analysis of historical and perennial issues.* Mahwah, NJ: Erlbaum.

Lazarus, R.S., & Folkman, S. (1984). *Stress, appraisal, and coping.* New York: Springer.

Leathart, A. (1994). Communication and socialisation (1): An exploratory study and explanation for nurse–patient communication in ITU. *Intensive and Critical Care Nursing, 10*, 93–104.

Lee, I-M., Paffenberger, R.S., & Hsieh, C-C. (1992). Physical activity and risk of prostatic cancer among college alumni. *American Journal of Epidemiology, 146*, 413–417.

Lee, J., Parsons, G.F., & Gentleman, J.F. (1998). Falling short of the Pap test guidelines. *Health Reports, 10*(1), 9–19.

Lee, M. R., Cohen, L., Hadley, S. W., & Goodwin, F. K. (1999). Cognitive-behavioral group therapy with medication for depressed gay men with AIDS or symptomatic HIV infection. *Psychiatric Services, 50*(7), 948–952.

Lee, R. S., Kochman, A., & Sikkema, K. J. (2002). Internalized stigma among people living with HIV-AIDS. *AIDS & Behavior, 6*(4), 309–319.

Leit, R.A., Gray, J.J., & Pope, H.G., Jr. (2002). The media's representation of the ideal male body: A cause for muscle dysmorphia? *International Journal of Eating Disorders, 13*(3), 334–338.

Leit, R.A., Pope, H.G., Jr., & Gray, J.J. (2000). Cultural expectations of muscularity in men: The evolution of playgirl centerfolds. *International Journal of Eating Disorders, 29*(1), 90-93.

Leiter, M., Harvie, P., & Frizzel, C. (1998). The correspondence of patient satisfaction and nurse burnout. *Social Science and Medicine, 47*, 1611–1617.

Lemos, K., Suls, J., Jenson, M., Lounsbury, P., & Gordon, E.E.I. (2003). How do female and male cardiac patients and their spouses share responsibilities after discharge from the hospital? *Annals of Behavioral Medicine, 25*(1), 8–15.

Lenz, E.R., & Perkins, S. (2000). Coronary artery bypass graft surgery patients and their family member caregivers: outcomes of a family-focused staged psychoeducational intervention. *Appl Nurs Res, 13*(3), 142–150.

LeResche, L. (2000). Epidemiologic perspectives on sex differences in pain. In R. B. Fillingim (Ed.), *Sex, gender, and pain* (pp. 233–249). Seattle, WA: IASP Press.

Le Scanff, C. & Taugis, T. (2002). Stress management for police special forces. *Journal of Applied Sport Psychology, 14*, 330–343.

Lester, N., Lefebvre, J.C., & Keefe, F.J. (1994). Pain in young adults: 1. Relationship to gender and family pain history. *Clinical Journal of Pain, 19*, 282–289.

Leszcz, M., & Goodwin, P.J. (1998). The rationale and foundations of group psychotherapy for women with metastatic breast cancer. *International Journal of Group Psychotherapy, 48*, 245–273.

LeUnes, A. & Nation, J.R. (2002). *Sport Psychology (3rd Ed.)*. Pacific Grove, CA: Wadsworth.

LeUnes, A.D. and Nation, J.R. (1989). *Sport psychology: An introduction*. Chicago, Illinois: Nelson-Hall.

Leuthner, S.R. (2001). Decisions regarding resuscitation of the extremely premature infant and models of best interest. *Journal of Perinatology, 21*(3), 193–198.

Leventhal, E.A., Hansell, S., Diefenbach, M., Leventhal, H., & Glass, D.C. (1996). Negative affect and self-report of physical symptoms: Two longitudinal studies of older adults. *Health Psychology, 15*, 193–199.

Leventhal, H. (1970). Findings and theory in the study of fear communications. In Berkowitz L., (Ed.), *Advances in experimental social psychology, 5*, (pp. 119–186). San Diego, CA: Academic Press.

Leventhal, H., & Cleary, P.D. (1980). The smoking problem: A review of the research and theory in behavioral risk modification. *Psychological Bulletin, 88*, 370–405.

Leventhal, H., Prochaska T.R., & Hirschman, R.S. (1985). Public attitudes toward cancer pain. *Cancer, 56,* 2337–2339.

Levin, J.S., & Puchalski, C.M. (1997). Religion and spirituality in medicine: Research and education. JAMA. *Journal of the American Medical Association, 278,* 792–793.

Levinson, W. (1994). Physician–patient communication. A key to malpractice prevention. *Journal of the American Medical Association, 272,* 1619–1620.

Levinson, W. Roter, D.L., Mullooly, J.P., Dull, V.T., & Frankel, R.M. (1997). Physician–patient communication. The relationship with malpractice claims among primary care physicians and surgeons. *Journal of the American Medical Association, 277,* 553–559.

Levy, S.M., Herberman, R.B., Whiteside, T., Sanzo, K., Lee, J., & Kirkwood, J. (1990). Perceived social support and tumor estrogen/progesterone receptor status as predictors of natural killer cell activity in breast cancer patients. *Psychosomatic Medicine, 52,* 73–85.

Lewis, C.C., Brimacombe, C.A.E., & Matheson, D.H. (2003). *Patient honesty in birth control clinics: The truth about lies.* Unpublished honours thesis, University of Victoria, Victoria, British Columbia, Canada.

Ley, P. (1977). Psychological studies of doctor–patient communication. In Rachman, S., (Ed.) *Contributions to medical psychology, 1.* Oxford: Pergamon.

Ley, P. (1982). Satisfaction, compliance, and communication. *British Journal of Clinical Psychology, 21,* 241–254.

Li, C., Unger, J.B., Schuster, D. Rohrbach, L.A., Howard-Pitney, B., Norman, G. (2003). Youths' exposure to environmental tobacco smoke(ETS) associations with health beliefs and social pressure. *Addictive Behaviors, 28,* 39–53.

Lindberg, D.A.B., & Humphreys, B.L. (1998). Medicine and health on the Internet: The good, the bad, and the ugly. *Journal of the American Medical Association, 280,* 1303–13004.

Lindsted, K.D., & Singh, P.N. (1997). Body mass and 26-year risk of mortality among women who never smoked: Findings from the Adventist Mortality Study. *American Journal of Epidemiology, 146,* 1–11.

Lindsay, E., Cameron, R., Walker, R., & Ferster, D. (1996). Planning and implementing the commit protocol in Brantford. *Health and Canadian Society, 2,* 237–267

Linn, B.S., Linn, M.W., & Jensen, J. (1981). Anxiety and immune responsiveness. *Psychological Reports, 49,* 969–970.

Liossi, C., & Hatira, P. (1999). Clinical hypnosis versus cognitive behavioral training for pain management with pediatric cancer patients undergoing bone marrow aspirations. *International Journal of Clinical and Experimental Hypnosis, 47*(2), 104–116.

Liossi, C., & Hatira, P. (2003). Clinical hypnosis in the alleviation of procedure-related pain in pediatric oncology patients. *International Journal of Clinical and Experimental Hypnosis, 51*(1), 4–28.

Lipkus, I.M., Barefoot, J.C., Williams, R.B., & Siegler, I.C. (1994). Personality measures as predictors of smoking initiation and cessation in the UNC Alumni Heart Study. *Health Psychology, 13,* 149–155.

Literature Review: Evaluation Strategies in Aboriginal Substance Abuse Programs: A Discussion. (2002). Ottawa: Health Canada.

Litt, M.D., Nye, C., & Shafer, D. (1995). Preparation for oral surgery: Evaluating elements of coping. *Journal of Behavioral Medicine, 18,* 435–459.

Lloyd, E.C., Mathews, K.A., Wing, R.R., & Orchard, T.I. (1992). Psychosocial factors and complications of IDDM. The Pittsburgh Epidemiology of Diabetes Complications Study VIII. *Diabetes Care, 15,* 166–172.

Locke, E.A., & Latham, G.P. (1985). The application of goal setting to sports. *Journal of Sports Psychology, 7*, 205–222.

Locke, E.A., & Latham, G.P. (1990) *A theory of goal-setting and task performance*. Englewood Cliffs, New Jersey: Prentice-Hall.

Locke, E.A., (1968). Toward a theory of task motivation and incentives. Organizational Behaviour and Human *Performance, 3,* 157–189.

Loeser, J.D. (1996). The IASP report on back pain in the work place. *Pain Research and Management, 1*, 180.

Lollis, C.M., Johnson, E.H., & Antoni, M.H. (1997). The efficacy of the health belief model for predicting condom usage and risky sexual practices in university students. *AIDS Education and Prevention, 9*, 551–563.

Lorber, J. (1975). Good patients and problem patients: Conformity and deviance in a general hospital. *Journal of Health and Social Behavior, 16,* 213–225.

Lower, J. S., Bonsack, C., & Guion, J. (2003). Peace and quiet. *Nurs Manage, 34*(4), 40A–40D.

Lowery, D., Fillingim, R.B., & Wright, R.A. (2003). Sex differences and incentive effects on perceptual and cardiovascular responses to cold pressor pain. *Psychosomatic Medicine, 65*, 284–291.

Lu, D.P., Lu, G.P., & Kleinman, L. (2001). Acupuncture and clinical hypnosis for facial and head and neck pain: A single crossover comparison. *The American Journal of Clinical Hypnosis, 44,* 141–148.

Luce, G. and Peper, E. (1971). Mind over body, mind over mind. *New York Times Magazine*, September.

Ludwick,-Rosenthal, R., & Neufeld, R.W.J. (1988). Stress management during noxious medical procedures: An evaluative review of outcome studies. *Psychological Bulletin, 104,* 326–342.

Lukins, R., Davan, I.G.P., & Drummond, P.D. (1997). A cognitive behavioural approach to preventing anxiety during magnetic resonance imaging. *Journal of Behavior Therapy and Experimental Psychiatry, 28,* 97–104.

Lurie, J.D., & Sox, H.C. (1999). Principles of medical decision making. *Spine, 24,* 493–498.

Lurie, N., Rank, B., Parenti, C., Woolley, T., & Snoke, W. (1989). How do house officers spend their nights? A time study of internal medicine staff on call. *New England Journal of Medicine, 320, 1673–1677.*

Lurie, N., Slater, J., McGovern, P., Ekstrum, J., Quam, L., & Margolis, K. (1993). Preventive care for women: Does the sex of the physician matter? *New England Journal of Medicine, 329,* 478–482.

Luschen, G., Cockerham, W., & Kunz, G. (1996). The sociocultural context of sport and health problems of causal relations and structural interdependence. *Sociology of Sport Journal, 13*, 197–213.

Lustman, P.J., Freedland, K.E., Griffith, L.S., & Clouse, R.E. (1998). Predicting response to cognitive behavior therapy of depression in type 2 diabetes. *General Hospital Psychiatry, 20*, 302–306.

Lustman, P.J., Griffith, L.S., Freedland, K.E., & Clouse, R.E. (1998). Cognitive behavior therapy for depression in type 2 diabetes mellitus. A randomized, controlled trial. *Annals of Internal Medicine, 129,* 613–621.

Lutsky, I., Hopwood, M., Abram, S.E., Jacobson, G.R., Haddox, J.D., & Kampine, J.P. (1993). Psychoactive substances use among American anesthesiologists: A 30-year retrospective study. *Canadian Journal of Anaesthesiology, 40*, 915–921.

Lyketsos, C.G., Hoover, D.R., Guccione, M., et al., (1993). Depressive symptoms as predictors of medical outcomes in HIV infection. *Journal of the American Medical Association, 270,* 2563–2567.

Lynch, M.E., Clark, A.J., & Sawynok, J. (2003). Intravenous adenosine alleviates neuropathic pain: A double blind placebo controlled crossover trial using an enriched enrolment design. *Pain, 103,* 111–117.

Lykken, D.T. (1987). Psychophysiology. In R.J. Corsini (Ed.), *Concise encyclopedia of psychology.* New York: Wiley.

Lynch, G.P. (1988). Athletic injuries and the practicing sport psychologist: Practical guidelines for assisting athletes. *The Sport Psychologist, 2,* 161–167.

Lynge, E., Olsen, A.H., Fracheboud, J., & Patnick, J. (2003). Reporting of performance indicators of mammography screening in Europe. *Eur J Cancer Prev, 12*(3), 213–222.

Lyubomirsky, S. (2001). Why are some people happier than others? The role of cognitive and motivational processes in well-being. *American Psychologist, 56,* 239–249.

Macciocchi, S.N., Barth, J.T., Alves, W.A., Rimel, R.W., & Jane, J.J. (1996). Neuro-psychological functioning and and recovery after mild head injury in collegiate athletes. *Neurosurgery, 39,* 510–514.

MacDonald, N.E., Wells, G.A., Fisher, W.A., Warren, W.K., et al. (1990). High-risk STD/HIV behavior among college students. *Journal of the American Medical Association, 263,* 3155–3159.

MacDonald, T.K., MacDonald, N.E., Zanna, M.P., & Fong, G.T. (2000). Alcohol, sexual arousal, and intentions to use condoms: applying alcohol myopia to risky sexual behavior. Manuscript submitted for publication.

MacDonald, T.K., Zanna, M.P., & Fong, G.T. (1996). Why common sense goes out the window: Effects of alcohol on intentions to use condoms. *Personality and Social Psychology Bulletin, 22,* 763–775.

MacDonald, T.K., Zanna, M.P., & Fong, G.T. (1998). Alcohol and intentions to engage in risky behaviors: Experimental evidence for a causal relationship. In J.G. Adair, D. Belanger, & K. Dion (Eds.), *Advances in Psychological Science: Vol. 1. Social, personal, and cultural aspects* (pp. 407–428). East Sussex, UK: Psychology Press.

MacDonald, T.K., Zanna, M.P., & Fong, G.T. (1995). Decision making in altered states: Effects of alcohol on attitudes toward drinking and driving. *Journal of Personality and Social Psychology, 68,* 973–985.

MacKean, P., & Gutkin, C. (2003). Fewer medical students selecting family medicine. Can family practice survive? *Can Fam Physician, 49,* 408–409, 415–407.

MacLeod, S. (September 23, 2002). Research, education, and the impact of prescription compliance on better medicine. Paper presented at the 2003 Conference entitled Toward a National Strategy on Drug Insurance: Challenges and Priorities. http://www.irpp.org/events/archive/sep02/macleod.pdf [June 9, 2003].

Maclure, M. (1993). Demonstration of deductive meta-analysis: Ethanol intake and risk of myocardial infarction. *Epidemiology Review, 15,* 328–351.

Magni, G., Rossi, M.R., Rigatti-Luchini, S., & Merskey, H. (1992). Chronic abdominal pain and depression. Epidemiologic findings in the United States. Hispanic Health and Nutrition Examination Survey. *Pain, 49,* 549–559.

Maguire, P. & Pitceathly, C. (2002). Key communication skills and how to acquire them. *British Medical Journal, 325,* 697–700.

Mahler, H.I.M., & Kulik, J.A. (1991). Health care involvement preferences and social-emotional recovery of male coronary-artery-bypass patients. *Health Psychology, 10,* 399–408.

Mahoney, M. (1996). Foreward. In J.L. Van Raalte and B.W. Brewer (Eds.), *Exploring sport and exercise psychology.* Washington, D.C.: American Psychological Association.

Mahoney, M.J., Gabriel, T.J., & Perkins, T.S. (1987). Psychological skills and exceptional athletic performance. *The Sport Psychologist, 1*, 181–199.

Maier, S.F., Watkins, L.R., Fleshner, M. (1994). Psychoneuroimmunology: The interface between behavior, brain, and immunity. *American Psychologist, 49*, 1004–1017.

Main, C.J., & Spanswick, C.C. (1995). "Functional overlay", and illness behaviour in chronic pain: Distress or malingering? Conceptual difficulties in medicolegal assessment of personal injury claims. *Journal of Psychosomatic Research, 39*, 737–753.

Malcarne, V.L., Compas, B.E., Epping-Jordan, J.E., & Howell, D.C. (1995). Cognitive factors in adjustment to cancer: Attributions of self-blame and perceptions of control. *Journal of Behavioral Medicine, 18*, 401–417.

Malkin, L. (2003). Teaching family medicine. *Can Fam Physician, 49*, 630, 637.

Malouff, J., Schutte, N., Wiener, K., Brancazio, C., & Fish, D. (1993). Important characteristics of warning displays on alcohol containers. *Journal of Studies on Alcohol, 54*, 457–461.

Mangelli, L., Gribbin, N., Buchi, S., Allard, S., & Sensky, T. (2002). Psychological well-being in rheumatoid arthritis: relationship to 'disease' variables and affective disturbance. *Psychother Psychosom, 71*(2), 112–116.

Mann, T., Nolen-Hoeksema, S., Huang, K., Burgard, D., et al. (1997). Are two interventions worse than none? Joint primary and secondary prevention of eating disorders in college females. *Health Psychology, 16*, 215–225.

Manne, S.L., Jacobsen, P.B., Gorfinkle, K., Gerstein, F., & Redd, W.H. (1993). Treatment adherence difficulties among children with cancer: The role of parenting style. *Journal of Pediatric Psychology, 18*, 47–62.

Manuck, S.B., Cohen, S., Rabin, B.S., Muldoon, M.F., & Bachen, E.A. (1991). Individual differences in cellular immune response to stress. *Psychological Science, 2*, 111–115.

Marcoux, B.C., & Shope, J.T. (1997). Application of the theory of planned behavior to adolescent use and misuse of alcohol. *Health Education Research, 12*, 323–331.

Marlatt, G.A., & Gordon, J.R. (1980). Determinants of relapse: Implications for the maintenance of behavior change. In P.O. Davidson and S.M. Davidson (Eds.), *Behavioral medicine: Changing health lifestyles.* (pp. 410–452). New York: Brunner/Mazel.

Marrero, D.G., Guare, J.C., Vandagriff, J.L., & Fineberg, N.S. (1997). Fear of hypoglycemia in the parents of children and adolescents with diabetes; Maladaptive or health response? *Diabetes Education, 23*, 281–286.

Marsh, H.W., Hey, J., Johnson, S., & Perry, C. (1997). Elite Athlete Self Description Questionnaire: Hierarchical confirmatory factor analysis of responses by two distinct groups of elite athletes. *International Journal of Sport Psychology, 3*, 237–252.

Marsh, H.W., Richards, G.E. Johnson, S., Roche, L., & Tremayne, P. (1994). Physical Self-Description Questionnaire: Psychometric properties and a multitrait-multimethod analysis of relations to existing instruments. *Journal of Sport and Exercise Psychology, 16*, 270–305.

Marshall, S.P., Smith, M.S., & Weinberger, E. (1995). Perceived anxiety of pediatric patients to magnetic resonance. *Clinical Pediatrics, 34*, 59–60.

Marsland, A.L., Manuck, S.B., Fazzari, T.V., Steward, C.J., & Rabin, B.S. (1995). Stability of individual differences in cellular immune responses to acute psychological stress. *Psychosomatic Medicine, 57*, 295–298.

Martelli, M.F., Auerbach, S.M., Alexander, J., & Mercuri, L.G. (1987). Stress management in the health care setting: Matching interventions with patient coping styles. *Journal of Consulting and Clinical Psychology, 56*, 856–872.

Martens, P., Bond, R., Jebamani, L., Brurchill, C., Noralou, R., Derksen, S., Beaulieu, M., Steinbach, C., MacWilliam, L., Walld, R., Dik, N., Sanders, D., Tanner-Spence, M., Leader, A., Elias, B., & O-Neil, J. (2002). *The Health and Health Care Use of Registered First Nations People Living in Manitoba: A Population-Based Study*. Winnipeg: Manitoba Centre for Health Policy, University of Manitoba.

Martin, D.P., Diehr, P., Conrad, D.A., Davis, J.H., Leickly, R., & Perrin, E.B. (1998). Randomized trial of a patient-centered hospital unit. *Patient Education and Counseling, 34*, 125–133.

Martin, J.J. & Cutler, K. (2002). An exploratory study of flow and motivation in theater actors. *Journal of Applied Sport Psychology, 14,* 344–352.

Martin, S. (2003). MDs' office Internet use hits 57%. *Canadian Medical Association Journal, 168*(4), 475.

Martinsen, E.W. (1990). Benefits of exercise for the treatment of depression. *Sports Medicine, 9*, 380–389.

Martinsen, E.W. (1993). Therapeutic implications of exercise for clinically anxious and depressed patients. *International Journal of Sport Psychology, 24*, 185–199.

Martinsen, E.W. (1994). Physical activity and depression: Clinical experience. *Actua Psychiatrca Scandinavica, 377,* 23–27.

Martinson, E.W., & Morgan, W.P. (1997). Antidepressant effects of physical activity. In W.P. Morgan (Ed.), *Physical activity and mental status* (pp.93–106). Washington, DC: Taylor and Francis.

Marvel, M.K. (1993). Involvement with the psychosocial concerns of patients. *Archives of Family Medicine, 2,* 629–633.

Marvel, M.K., Epstein, R.M., Flowers, K., & Beckman, H.B. (1999). Soliciting the patient's agenda: Have we improved? *Journal of the American Medical Association, 281*, 283–287.

Maslach, C. (1979). The burn-out syndrome and patient care. In C. Garfield (Ed.), *The emotional realities of life-threatening illness* (pp. 111–120). St. Louis, MO: CV Mosby.

Maslach, C., & Leiter, M. P. (1997). *The truth about burnout*. San Francisco: Jossey-Bass.

Mason, E. (1970). Obesity in pet dogs. *Veterinary Record, 86,* 612–616.

Masten, A.S. (2001). Ordinary magic: Resilience processes in development. *American Psychologist, 56,* 227–238.

Masur, F.T., III. (1981). Adherence to health care regimens. In C.K. Prokop & L.A. Bradley (Eds.), *Medical psychology: Contributions to behavioral medicine.* New York: Academic Press.

Matarazzo, J.D. (1980). Behavioral health and behavioral medicine. American *Psychologist, 35*, 807–817.

Matarazzo, J.D., Weiss, S.M., Herd, J.A., Miller, N.E., Weiss, S., (Eds.) (1984). *Behavioral Health: A handbook of health enhancement and disease prevention*. New York: Wiley.

Matheson, D.H. (1997). The painful truth: Interpretation of facial expressions of pain in older adults. *Journal of Nonverbal Behaviour, 21,* 223–238.

Maticka-Tyndale, E. (2001). Sexual Health and Canadian youth: How do we measure up? *Canadian Journal of Human Sexuality, 10*, 1–17.

Matrunola, P. (1996). Is there a relationship between job satisfaction and absenteeism? *Journal of Advanced Nursing, 23*, 827–834.

Matsunaga, H., Kiriike, N., Iwasaki, Y., Miyata, A., & Matsui, T. (2000). Multi-impulsivity among bulimic patients in Japan. *International Journal of Eating Disorders, 27,* 348–352.

Mattila-Lindy, S., Hemminki, E., Malin, M., Makkonen, K., Topo, P., Maentyranta, T., & Kangas, I. (1998). Physicians' gender and clinical opinions of reproductive health matters. *Women and Health, 26*(3), 15–26.

Maulden, S.A. (2003). Information technology, the Internet, and the future of neurology. *Neurologist, 9*(3), 149–159.

Mauer, M.H., Burnett, K.F., Ouellette, E.A., Ironson, G.H., & Dandes, H.M. (1999). Medical hypnosis and orthopedic hand: pain perception, postoperative recovery, and therapeutic comfort. *International Journal of Clinical and Experimental Hypnosis, 47*(2), 144–161.

Maunsell, E., Jacques, B., & Deschenes, L. (1995). Social support and survival among women with breast cancer. *Cancer, 76*, 631–637.

Mayled, A. (1998). Medical admissions units: The role of the nurse practitioner. *Nursing Standard, 12*, 44–47.

Mayne, T.J., & Ambrose, T.K. (1999). Research review on anger in psychotherapy. *Journal of Clinical psychology, 55*, 353–363.

Mazullo, J.M., Lasagna, L., Griner, P.F. (1974). Variations in interpretation of prescription instructions. *Journal of the American Medical Association, 227*, 929–931.

McAuley, E. (1991). Efficacy, attributional and affective responses to exercise participation. *Journal of Sport and Exercise Psychology, 13*, 382–393.

McAuley, E. and Corneya, K.S. (1992). Self-efficacy relationships with affective and exertion responses to exercise. *Journal of Applied Social Psychology, 22*, 312–326.

McAuley, Schaffer, & Rudolph. (1995). Affective responses to acute exercise in elderly impaired males: The moderating effects of self-efficacy and age. *International Journal of Aging and Human Development, 41*, 13–35.

McCain, G.C., & Morwessel, N.J. (1995). Pediatric nurses' knowledge and practice related to infant pain. *Issues in Comprehensive Pediatric Nursing, 18*, 277–286.

McCaul, K.D., Schroeder, D.M., & Reid, P.A. (1996). Breast cancer worry and screening. Some prospective data. *Health Psychology, 15*, 430–433.

McCool, J.P., Cameron, L.D., & Petrie, K.J. (2001). Adolescent perceptions of smoking imagery in film. *Social Science & Medicine, 52*, 1577–1587.

McCracken, L.M., Zayfert, C., & Gross, R.T. (1993). The pain anxiety symptoms scale (PASS): A multi-modal measure of pain specific anxiety symptoms. *Behaviour Research and Therapy, 31*, 647–652.

McCreary Centre Society (1993). Adolescent Health Survey: Province of British Columbia. Richmond, BC: New Leaf Computer.

McCreary Centre Society (1999). *Healthy Connections: Listening to BC Youth.* Burnaby, BC: The McCreary Centre Society.

McDaniel, J.S. (1996). Stressful life events and psychoneuroimmunology. In T.W. Miller (Ed.), *Theory and assessment of stressful life events*, pp. 3–36. Madison, CT: International Universities Press.

McDonald, D.D. (1994). Gender and ethnic stereotyping and narcotic analgesic administration. Res. *Nurs. Health, 17*, 45–49.

McDonald, H.P., Garg, A.X., Haynes, R.B. (2002). Interventions to enhance patient adherence to medication prescriptions: Scientific review. *Journal of the American Medical Association, 288*, 2868–2879.

McFarland, K.F., & Rhoades, D.R. (1998). Gender-related values and medical specialty choice. *Academic Psychiatry, 22*, 236–239.

McFarlane, T., Polivy, J., & Herman, C.P. (1998). Effects of false weight feedback on mood, self-evaluation, and food intake in restrained and unrestrained eaters. *Journal of Abnormal Psychology, 107,* 312–318.

McFarlane, T., Polivy, J., & McCabe, R.E. (1999). Help, not harm: Psychological foundation for a nondieting approach toward health. *Journal of Social Issues, 55,* 261–276.

McGovern, R.J., Heyman, E.N., & Resnick, M.I. (2002). An examination of coping style and quality of life of cancer patients who attend a prostate cancer support group. *Journal of Psychosocial Oncology, 20*(3), 57–68.

McGehee, D.S., Heath, M.J.S., Gelber, S., Devay, P., & Role, L.W. (1995). Nicotine enhancement of fast excitatory transmission in CNS by presynaptic receptors. *Science, 269,* 1692–1696.

McGinnis, J.M., Shopland, D., & Brown, C. (1987). Tobacco and health: Trends in smoking and smokeless tobacco consumption in the United States. In L. Breslow, J.E. Fielding, & L.B. Lave (Eds.). *Annual review of public health (Vol. 8).* Palo Alto, CA: Annual Reviews.

McGrath, P.A. (1987). An assessment of children's pain: A review of behavioral, physiological and direct scaling techniques. *Pain, 31,* 147–176.

McGrath, P.A., & Gillespie, J. (2001). Pain assessment in children and adolescents. In D.C. Turk & R. Melzack (Eds.), *Handbook of pain assessment* (pp. 97–118, 2nd ed). New York: Guilford.

McGuire, W.J. (1985). Attitudes and attitude change. In G. Lindzey, & E. Aronson, (Eds.), *Handbook of social psychology* (3rd ed.), Vol. 2, pp. 233–346. New York: Random House.

McIsaac, H.K., Thordarson, D.S., Shafran, R., Rachman, S., & Poole, G. (1998). Claustrophobia and the magnetic imaging procedure. *Journal of Behavioral Medicine, 21,* 255–268.

McKinlay, J.B., Burns, R.B., Feldman, H.A., Freund, K.M., Irish, J.T., Kasten, L.E., Moskowitz, M.A., Potter, D.A., & Woodman, K. (1998). Physician variability and uncertainty in the management of breast cancer. Results from a factorial experiment. *Medical Care, 36,* 385–396.

McLennon, B., & Gauthier, (1998). Presentation to The Standing Committee on Finance Roundtable on Research. October, 1999, Ottawa

McMurran, M. (1994). *The psychology of addiction.* London: Taylor & Francis.

McWilliam, C.L., Brown, J.B., & Stewart, M. (2000). Breast cancer patients' experiences of patient–doctor communication: A working relationship. *Patient Education and Counseling, 39,* 191–204.

Meechan, G., Colins, J., & Petrie, K. J. (2003). The relationship of symptoms and psychological factors to delay in seeking medical care for breast symptoms. *Preventive Medicine, 36,* 374–378.

Mehler, P.S. (2003). Osteoporosis in anorexia nervosa: Prevention and treatment. International *Journal of Eating Disorders, 33*(2), 113–126.

Meichenbaum, D. (1975). Enhancing creativity by modifying what subjects say to themselves. *American Educational Research Journal, 12,* 129–145.

Meichenbaum, D. (1977). *Cognitive-behavior modification: An integrative approach.* New York: Plenum Press.

Meichenbaum, D.H. (1985). *Stress inoculation training.* New York: Pergamon Press

Melamed, B.G., & Siegal, L, J. (1975). Reduction of anxiety in children facing surgery by modeling. *Journal of Consulting and Clinical Psychology, 43,* 511–521.

Melendez, J.C., & McCrank, E. (1993). Anxiety-related reactions associated with magnetic resonance imaging examinations. *Journal of the American Medical Association, 270,* 745–747.

Melzack, R. (1973). *The puzzle of pain*. New York: Basic Books.

Melzack, R. (1975). The McGill Pain Questionnaire: Major properties and scoring methods. *Pain, 1*, 277–299.

Melzack, R. (1987). The short-form McGill Pain Questionnaire. *Pain, 30*, 191–197.

Melzack, R. (1989). Folk medicine and the sensory modulation of pain. In P.D. Wall & R. Melzack (Eds.), *Textbook of pain (2nd ed.)*. Edinburgh: Churchill Livingstone.

Melzack, R. (1991). The gate control theory 25 years later: new perspectives on phantom limb pain. In M.R. Bond, J.E. Charloton, & C.J. Woolf (Eds.), *Proceedings of the VIth World Congress on Pain* (pp. 9–21). Amsterdam: Elsevier Science Publishers.

Melzack, R. (1992). Phantom limbs. *Scientific American, 266*, 120–126.

Melzack, R. (1993). Pain: Past, present and future. *Canadian Journal of Experimental Psychology, 47(4)*, 615–629.

Melzack, R. (1998). Pain and stress: Clues toward understanding chronic pain. In M. Sabourin, F. Craik, and M. Robert (Eds.), *Advances in psychological science: Vol. 2. Biological and Cognitive Aspects*. Hove: Psychology Press Limited.

Melzack, R. (1999). Pain—an overview. *Acta Anaesthesiologica Scandinavica, 43*, 880–884.

Melzack, R. (2001). Pain and the neuromatrix in the brain. *Journal of Dental Education, 65*, 1378–1382.

Melzack, R., Israel, R., Laxroix, R., & Schultz, G. (1997). Phantom limbs in people with congenital limb deficiency or amputation in early childhood. *Brain, 120*, 1603–1620.

Melzack, R. & Katz, J. (2001). The McGill pain questionnaire: Appraisal and current status. In D.C. Turk & R. Melzack (Eds.), *Handbook of pain assessment* (2nd ed., pp. 35–52). New York: Guildford

Melzack, R., & Wall, P.D. (1965). Pain mechanisms: A new theory. *Science, 150*, 971–979.

Mendes-de-Leon, C.F., Powell, L.H., & Kaplan, B.H. (1991). Change in coronary-prone behaviors in the Recurrent Coronary Prevention Project. *Psychosomatic Medicine, 53*, 407–419.

Merskey, H. (1970). On the development of pain. *Headache, 10*, 116–123.

Merskey, H. (1986). Psychiatry and pain. In R.A. Sternbach (Ed.), *The psychology of pain (2nd ed.)*. New York: Raven Press.

Merskey, H. (1996a). Back pain, psychology and money. *Pain Research and Management, 1*, 13.

Merskey, H. (1996b). Re: Back pain in the work place. *Pain, 65*, 111–112.

Merskey, H., & Teasell, R.W. (2000). The disparagement of pain: Social influences on medical thinking. *Pain Research & Management, 5*, 259–270.

Merskey, H. & Teasell, R.W. (2002). A troubling story: Insurance and medical research in Saskatchewan. *Pain Research & Management, 7*, 65–67.

Messing, K. (1998). Hospital trash: Cleaners speak of their role in disease prevention. *Medical Anthropology Quarterly, 12*, 168–187.

Metry, J.-M., & Meyer, U.A. (Eds.). (1999). *Drug regimen compliance: Issues in clinical trials and patient management*. NY: Wiley.

Metz, J. M., Devine, P., DeNittis, A., Jones, H., Hampshire, M., Goldwein, J., & Whittington, R. (2003). A multi-institutional study of Internet utilization by radiation oncology patients. *Int J Radiat Oncol Biol Phys, 56(4)*, 1201–1205.

Meyer, J.M., & Stunkard, A.J. (1994). Twin studies of human obesity. In C. Bouchard (Ed.), *The genetics of obesity* (pp. 63–78). Boca Raton, FL: CRC Press.

Michalko, S.L., McAuley, E., & Bane, S. (1996). Self-efficacy and affective responses to acute exercise in middle-aged adults. *Journal of Social Behavior and Personality, 11*, 375–385.

Miles, F., & Meehan, J.W. (1995). Visual discrimination of pigmented skin lesions. *Health Psychology, 14*, 171–177.

Millar, M.G. (1997). The effects of emotion on breast self-examination: Another look at the Health Belief Model. *Social Behavior and Personality, 25*, 223–232.

Miller, D.L., & Stark, L.J. (1994). Contingency contracting for improving adherence in pediatric populations. Journal of the *American Medical Association, 271*, 81–83.

Miller, N.E. (1969). Learning of visceral and glandular responses. *Science, 163*, 434–445.

Miller, N.E. (1983). Behavioral medicine: Symbiosis between laboratory and clinic. *Annual Review of Psychology, 34*, 1–31.

Miller, N.E., & DiCara, L.V., (1967). Instrumental learning of heart rate changes in curarized rats: Shaping, and specificity to discriminate stimulus. *Journal of Comparative and Physiological Psychology, 63*, 1–6.

Miller, S.M. (1980). When is a little information a dangerous thing? Coping with stressful life-events by monitoring vs. blunting. In Levine, S., & Ursin, H. (Eds.) *Coping and health*. New York: Plenum Press.

Miller, S.M. (1996). Monitoring/blunting of threatening information: Cognitive interference and facilitation in the coping process. In I.G. Sarison & G.R. Pierce & S. B.R. (Eds.), *Cognitive interference: Theories, methods and findings* (pp. 175–190). Hillsdale, NJ: Lawrence Erlbaum.

Miller, S.M., & Mangan, C.E. (1983). Interacting effects of information and coping style in adapting to gynecologic stress: Should the doctor tell all? *Journal of Personality and Social Psychology, 45*, 223–236.

Miller, T.D., Balady, G.J., & Fletcher, G.F. (1997). Exercise and its role in the prevention and rehabilitation of cardiovascular disease. *Annals of Behavioral Medicine, 19*, 220–229.

Miller, W.R., & Hester, R.K. (1980). Treating the problem drinker: Modern approaches. In W.R. Miller (Ed.), *The addictive behaviors* (pp. 11–141). Oxford, England: Pergamon Press.

Millstein, S.G. (1996). Utility of the theories of reasoned action and planned behavior for predicting physician behavior: A prospective analysis. *Health Psychology, 15*, 398–402.

Minor, M.A., & Sanford, M.K. (1993). Physical interventions in the management of pain in arthritis. *Arthritis Care and Research, 6*, 197–206.

Minore, B., & Boone, M. (2002). Realizing potential: Improving interdisciplinary professional/paraprofessional health care teams in Canada's northern aboriginal communities through education. *Journal of Interprofessional Care, 16*(2), 139–147.

Miró, J., Turk, D.C., & Rudy, T.E. (1991). *Chronic pain management. Against the uniformity myth.* Paper presented at the II congr´s Internacional Latini Dies, Sitges, Spain.

Miró, J.R., & Rosa M. (1999). Preoperative preparation for surgery: An analysis of the effects of relaxation and information provision. *Clinical Psychology & Psychotherapy, 6*(3), 202–209.

Misovich, S.J., Fisher, J.D., & Fisher, W.A. (1996). The perceived AIDS-preventive utility of knowing one's partner well: A public health dictum and individuals' risky sexual behaviour. *The Canadian Journal of Human Sexuality, 5*, 83–90.

Mitchell, A., & Kumar, M. (2003). Search strategy used is inadequate. *BMJ: British Medical Journal, 326*(7389), 599.

Mitchell, J.E., & de Zwaan, M. (1993). Pharmacological treatments of binge eating. In C.G. Fairburn & G.T. Wilson

(Eds.), *Binge eating: Nature, assessment, and treatment* (pp. 250–269). New York: Guilford Press.

Miyazaki, T., Ishikawa, T., Iimori, H., Miki, A., Wenner, M., Fukunishi, I., & Kawamura, N. (2003). Relationship between perceived social support and immune function. *Stress & Health: Journal of the International Society for the Investigation of Stress, 19*, 3-7.

Moffat, M.O., Moffat, K.J., & Cano, V. (2001). General practitioners and the Internet—a questionnaire survey of Internet connectivity and use in Lothian. *Health Bull (Edinb), 59*(2), 120–126.

Moffett, J.K., Torgerson, D., Bell-Syer, S., Jackson, D., Llewlyn-Phillips, H., Farrin, A., & Barber, J. (1999). Randomized controlled trial of exercises for low back pain: Clinical outcomes, costs, and preferences. *British Medical Journal, 319*, 279–283.

Mollema, E.D., Snoek, F.J., Ader, H.J., Heine, R.J., & van der Ploeg, H.M. (2001). Insulin-treated diabetes patients with fear of self-injecting or fear of self-testing: Psychological comorbidity and general well-being. *Journal of Psychosomatic Research, 51*(5), 665–672.

Monane, M. Bohn, R.L., Gurwitz, J.H., Glynn, R.J., Levin, R., & Avorn, J. (1996). Compliance with antihypertensive therapy among elderly Medicaid enrollees: The rates of age, gender, and race. *American Journal of Public Health, 86*, 1805–1808.

Montgomery, C., Pocock, M., Titley, K., & Lloyd, K. (2003). Predicting psychological distress in patients with leukaemia and lymphoma. *Journal of Psychosomatic Research, 54*(4), 289–292.

Moore, S.M., Barling, N.R., & Hood, B. (1998). Predicting testicular and breast self-examination behaviour: A test of the theory of reasoned action. *Behaviour Change, 15*, 41–49.

Morgan, W.P. (Ed.). (1997). *Physical activity in mental health*. Washington, D.C.: Taylor and Francis.

Morgan, W.P., & Ellickson, K.A. (1989). Health, anxiety and physical exercise. In D. Hackfort & Spielberger, C. (Eds.) *Anxiety in sports: An international perspective*. New York: Hemisphere Publishing.

Morley, J.E. (1998). The elderly Type 2 diabetic patient: Special considerations. *Diabetes Medicine, 15 (Suppl 4)*, S41–S46.

Morris, E. (1999). Reflections on the NICU. A nurse's perspective. *American Journal of Nursing, 99*(3), 23.

Morrison, D.M., Baker, S.A. and Gillmore, M.R. (2000). Using the Theory of Reasoned Action to predict condom use among high-risk heterosexual teens. In Norman, P. and C. Abraham, (Eds.). *Understanding and changing health behaviour: From health beliefs to self-regulation.* pp. 27–49.

Moulin, D.W., Clark, A.H., Speechley, M., & Morley-Forster, P.K. (2002). Chronic pain in Canada—Prevalence, treatment, impact and the role of opioid analgesia. *Pain Research and Management, 7,* 179–184.

Moyer, A. (1997). Psychosocial outcomes of breast-conserving surgery versus mastectomy: A meta-analytic review. *Health Psychology, 16*, 284–298.

Mpofu, E., & Houston, E. (1998). Assessment of value change in persons with acquired physical disabilities: Current and prospective applications for rehabilitation counselors. *Canadian Journal of Rehabilitation, 12*, 53–61.

Muller, G. H. (1996). Breast implants and their history. *Ann Chir Plast Esthet, 41*(6), 666–675.

Mulvihill, C.K. (1996). AIDS education for college students: Review and proposal for a research-based curriculum. *AIDS Education and Prevention, 8*, 11–25.

Munro, L., Rodwell, J., & Harding, L. (1998). Assessing occupational stress in psychiatric nurses using the full job strain model: The value of social support to nurses. *International Journal of Nursing Studies, 35,* 339–345.

Murphy, H., Dickens, C., Creed, F., & Bernstein, R. (1999). Depression, illness perception and coping in rheumatoid arthritis. *Journal of Psychosomatic Research, 46,* 155–164.

Murphy, K.J., & Brunberg, J.A. (1997). Adult claustrophobia, anxiety and sedation in MRI. *Magnetic Resonance Imaging, 15,* 51–54.

Murphy, L.R. (1996). Stress management in work settings: A critical review of the health effects. *American Journal of Health Promotion, 11,* 112–135.

Murry, M. (1980). *Seeking the master.* London: Neville Spearman.

Musclow, S.L., Sawhney, M., & Watt-Watson, J. (2002). The emerging role of advanced nursing practice in acute pain management throughout Canada. *Clin Nurse Spec, 16*(2), 63–67.

Muscroft, J., & Hicks, C. (1998). A comparison of psychiatric nurses' and general nurses' reported stress and counselling needs; A case study approach. *Journal of Advanced Nursing, 27,* 1317–1325.

Mushlin, A.I., Kouides, R.W., & Shapiro, D.E. (1998). Estimating the accuracy of screening mammography: A meta-analysis. *American Journal of Preventative Medicine, 14,* 143–153.

Musselman, D.L., Evans, D.L., & Nemeroff, C.B. (1998). The relationship of depression to cardiovascular disease. *Archives of General Psychiatry, 55,* 580–592.

Muustedt, K., Muller, H., Blauth-Eckmeyer, E., Stenger, K., Zygmunt, M., & Vahrson, H. (1999). Role of dexamethoasone dosage in combination with 5-HT3 antagonists for prophylaxis of acute chemotherapy-induced nausea and vomiting. *British Journal of Cancer, 79,* 637–639.

Nakamura, M., Tanaka, M., Kinukawa, N., Abe, S., Itoh, K., Imai, K., et al. (2000). Association between basal serum and leptin levels and changes in abdominal fat distribution during weight loss. *Journal of Atherosclerosis and Thrombosis, 6,* 28–32.

Nair, B.R. (1998). Patient, client or customer? *Medical Journal of Australia, 169,* 593.

Nam, R.K., Fleshner, N., Rakovitch, E., Klotz, L., Trachtenberg, J., Choo, R., Morton, G., & Danjoux, C. (1999). Prevalence and patterns of the use of complementary therapies among prostate cancer patients: An epidemiological analysis. *Journal of Urology, 161,* 1521–1524.

Naranjo, C. (1971). *On the Psychology of Meditation.* New York: The Viking Press.

National Cancer Institute of Canada, Canadian Cancer Statistics 1998, Toronto, 1998.

National Highway Traffic Safety Administration. (1993–1996). Fatality analysis reporting system, 1992–1995. Washington, DC: U.S. Department of Transportation.

National Institute on Alcohol Abuse and Alcoholism (NIAAA). (1988). Alcohol and aging. *Alcohol Alert, 2,* 1–4.

National Institute on Alcohol Abuse and Alcoholism (October, 2000) Alcohol alert: New advances in alcoholism treatment. Bethesda, MD. http://www.niaaa.nih.gov [August 25, 2003].

The need for an Aboriginal Health Institute in Canada. (2003). Ottawa: Health Canada.

Neittaanmäki, L., Gross, E.B., Virjo, I, Hyppölä, H., Kumpusalo, E. (1999). Personal values of male and female doctors: Gender aspects. *Social Science and Medicine, 48,* 559–568.

Nerenz, D.R., & Leventhal, H. (1983). Self-regulation theory in chronic illness. In T.G. Burish & L.A. Bradley (Eds.), *Coping with chronic disease: Research and applications* (pp. 13–87). New York: Academic Press.

Neumarker, K.J. (1997). Mortality and sudden death in anorexia nervosa. *International Journal of Eating Disorders, 21*, 202–212.

Newport, D.J., & Nemeroff, C.B. (1998). Assessment and treatment of depression in the cancer patient. *Journal of Psychosomatic Research, 45*, 215–237.

Newsom, J.T., Knapp, J.E., & Schulz, R. (1996). Longitudinal analysis of specific domains of internal control and depressive symptoms in patients with recurrent cancer. *Health Psychology, 15*, 323–331.

Nezu, A.M.,Nezu, C.M., Fridman, S.H., Faddis, S., & Houts, P.S. (1998). Helping cancer patients cope: A problem-solving approach. Washington, D.C.: American Psychological Association.

Ng, E., Wilkins, R., Pole, J., & Adams, O.B. (1997). How far to the nearest physician? *Health Reports, 8*(4), 19–31.

Ng, K., & von Gunten, C.F. (1998). Symptoms and attitudes of 100 consecutive patients admitted to an acute hospice/palliative care unit. *Journal of Pain and Symptom Management, 16*, 307–316.

Niaura R., & Abrams, D. B. (2002). Smoking cessation: Progress, priorities, and prospectus. *Journal of Consulting and Clincial Psychology, 70*, 494–509.

Nicholas, D.R. (2000). Men, masculinity, and cancer: Risk-factor behaviors, early detection, and psychosocial adaptation. *Journal of American College Health, 49*, 27–33.

Nideffer, R.M. (1985). *Athlete's guide to mental training.* Champaign, Illinois: Human Kinetics.

North, T.C., McCullagh, P., & Tran, Z.V. (1990). Effects of exercise on depression. *Exercise and Sport Science Reviews, 18*, 379–415.

Norton, G.R., Norton, P.J., Asmundson, G.J.G., Thompson, L.A., & Larsen, M.A. (in press). Neurotic butterflies in my stomach: The role of anxiety, anxiety sensitivity and depression in functional gastrointestinal disorders. *Journal of Psychosomatic Research.*

Ockene, J.K., Emmons, K.M., Mermelstein, R.J., Perkins, K.A. Bonollo, D.S., Voorhees, C.C., & Hollis, J.F. (2000). Relapse and maintenance issues for smoking cessation. *Health Psychology, 19,* 17–31.

Ockene, J.K., Kuller, L.H., Svendsen, K.H., & Meilahn, E. (1990). The relationship of smoking cessation to coronary heart disease and lung cancer in the Multiple Risk Factor Intervention Trial (MRFIT). *American Journal of Public Health, 80,* 954–958.

O'Connor, P.G., & Spickard, A. Jr. (1997). Physician impairment by substance abuse. *Medical Clinics of North America, 81,* 1037–1052.

Ogunyade, T.O., & Oyibo, W.A. (2003). Use of CD-ROM MEDLINE by medical students of the College of Medicine, University of Lagos, Nigeria. *J Med Internet Res, 5*(1), e7.

Olivardia, R. (2001). Mirror, mirror on the wall, who's the largest of them all? The features and phenomenology of muscle dysmorphia. *Harvard Review of Psychiatry, 9,* 254–259.

Olivardia, R., Pope, H.G., Jr., Hudson, J.I. (2000). Muscle dysmorphia in male weightlifters: A case-control study. *American Journal of Psychiatry, 157*(8), 1291–1296.

Olson, J.M., and Maio, G.R. (2003). Attitudes in social behavior. In Millon, T. and Lerner, M.J. (Eds.). *Handbook of psychology: Personality and social psychology, Vol. 5.* New York: Wiley & Sons, pp. 299–325.

Olson, J.M., & Zanna, M. (1987). Understanding and promoting exercise: A social psychological perspective. *Canadian Journal of Public Health, 78,* S1–S7.

O'Neill, M., Rootman, I., & Pederson, A. (1994). Beyond Lalonde: Two decades of Canadian health. In Pederson, A., O'Neill, M., & Rootman, I. (Eds.), *Health promotion in Canada: Provincial, national and international perspectives*. (pp. 374–386). Toronto, ON: Saunders.

Onions, C.T. (Ed.). (1986). *Shorter Oxford English dictionary on historical principles (3rd ed.)*. Oxford: Oxford University Press.

Orlick, T., & Partington, J. (1988). Mental links to excellence. *The Sport Psychologist, 2*, 105–130.

Orne, M.T. (1962). On the social psychology of the psychological experiment: With particular reference to demand characteristics and their implications. *American Psychologist, 17*, 776–783.

Orne, M.T. (1989). On the construct of hypnosis: How its definition affects research and its clinical application. In G.D. Burrows & L. Dennerstein (Eds.), *Handbook of hypnosis and psychosomatic medicine*. Amsterdam: Elsevier.

Orne, M.T., & Dinges, D.F. (1989). Hypnosis. In P.D. Wall & R. Melzack (Eds.), *Textbook of pain (2nd ed.)*. Edinburgh: Churchill Livingstone.

Osowiecki, D., & Compas, B.E. (1998). Psychological adjustment to cancer: Control beliefs and coping in adult cancer patients. *Cognitive Therapy and Research, 22*, 483–499.

Osterhouse, R.A., & Brock, T.C. (1970). Distraction increases yielding to propaganda by inhibiting counterarguing. *Journal of Personality and Social Psychology, 15*, 344–358.

Ostrow, A.C. (Ed.). (1996). *Directory of psychological tests in the sport and exercise sciences (2nd ed.)*. Morgantown, West Virginia: Fitness Information Technology.

Owen, H., & Plummer, J. (1997). Patient-controlled analgesia: Current concepts in acute pain management. *CNS Drugs, 8*, 203–218.

Paffenberger, R.S., Wing, A.L., & Hyde, R.T. (1978). Physical activity as an index of heart attack risk in college alumni. *American Journal of Epidemiology, 108*, 161–175.

Paice, J.A., Toy, C., & Shott, S. (1998). Barriers to cancer pain relief: Fear of tolerance and addiction. *Journal of Pain Symptom Management, 16*, 1–9.

Pallavicini-Gonzalez, J., Venegas-Ramirez, L., & Espinoza, M.A. (1995). The experience of intensive care patients of J.J. Aguirre Hospital: 1989–1992. *Revista de Psiquiatria Clinica, 32(1–2)*, 25–36.

Parboosingh, E.J., Anderson, G., Clark, E.A., et al. (1996). Cervical cancer screening: Are the 1989 recommendations still valid? *Canadian Medical Association Journal, 154*, 1867–1869.

Parent, F., Coppieters, Y., & Parent, M. (2001). Information technologies, health, and "globalization": anyone excluded? *J Med Internet Res, 3*(1), E11.

Pargman, D. (1998). *Understanding sport behavior*. Upper Saddle River, New Jersey: Prentice –Hall.

Park, D.C., Hertzog, C., Leventhal, H., Morrell, R.W., et al. (1999). Medication adherence in rheumatoid arthritis patients: Older is wiser. *Journal of the American Geriatric Society, 47*(2), 172–183.

Parker, D.R., McPhillips, J.V., Derby, C.A., Gans, K.M., et al. (1996). High-density-lipoprotein cholesterol and types of alcoholic beverages consumed among men and women. *American Journal of Public Health, 86*, 1022–1027.

Parker, P.A., & Kulik, J.A. (1995). Burnout, self- and supervisor-related job performance, and absenteeism among nurses. *Journal of Behavioral Medicine, 18*, 581–599.

Parrish, J.M. (1986). Parent compliance with medical and behavioral recommendations.

In N.A. Krasnegor, J.D. Arasteh, & M.F. Cataldo (Eds.), *Child health behavior: A behavioral pediatrics perspectiv*e. New York: Wiley.

Parsons, T. (1951). *The social system.* Glencoe, IL: Free Press.

Paskett, E.D., & Rimer, B.K. (1995). Psychosocial effects of abnormal Pap tests and mammograms: A review. *Journal of Women's Health, 4,* 73–82.

Passik, S.D., & Weinreb, H.J. (2000). Managing chronic nonmalignant pain: Overcoming obstacles to the use of opioids. *Advances in Therapy, 17,* 70–83.

Pate, R.R., Pratt, M., Blair, S.N., Haskell, W.L., et al. (l995). Physical activity and public health: A recommendation from the Centers for Disease Control and Prevention and the American College of Sports Medicine. *Journal of the American Medical Association, 273,* 402–407.

Patton, G.C., Selzer, R., Coffey, C., Carlin, J.B., & Wolfe, R. (1999). Onset of adolescent eating disorders: Population based cohort study over 3 years. *British Medical Journal, 318,* 765–768.

Payne, D.K., Hoffman, R.G., Theodoulou, M., Dosik, M., & Massie, M.J. (1999). Screening for anxiety and depression in women with breast cancer; Psychiatric and medical oncology gear up for managed care. *Psychosomatics, 40,* 64–69.

Payne, S.A., Dean, S.J., & Kalus, C. (1998). A comparative study of death anxiety in hospice and emergency nurses. *Journal of Advanced Nursing, 28,* 700–706.

Pearlin, L.I. (1993). The social contexts of stress. In L. Goldberger and S. Breznitz (Eds.) *Handbook of stress: Theoretical and clinical aspects* (2nd ed., pp. 303–315). New York: Free Press.

Peay, M.Y. & Peay, E.R. (1998). The evaluation of medical symptoms by patients and doctors. *Journal of Behavioral Medicine, 21,* 57–81.

Peck, C.L., & King, N.J. (1985). Compliance and the doctor–patient relationship. *Drugs, 30,* 78–84.

Pederson, L.L. (1982). Compliance with physician advice to quit smoking: A review of the literature. *Preventive Medicine, 11,* 71–84.

Pennebaker, J.W. (1983). Accuracy of symptom perception. In A. Baum, S.E. Taylor, & J. Singer (Eds.), *Handbook of psychology and health (Vol. 4).* Hillsdale, NJ: Erlbaum.

Pennebaker, J.W. (1994). Psychological bases of symptom reporting: Perceptual and emotional aspects of chemical sensitivity. *Toxicology and Industrial Health, 10,* 497–511.

Penninx, B.W., Guralnik, J.M., Mendes de Leon, C.F., Pahor, M., Visser, M., Corti, M.C., & Wallace, R.B. (1998). Cardiovascular events and mortality in newly and chronically depressed persons > 70 years of age. *American Journal of Cardiology, 81,* 988–94.

Pereles, L., & Russell, M.L. (1996). Needs for CME in geriatrics. Part 2: Physician priorities and perceptions of community representatives. *Canadian Family Medicine, 42,* 632–640.

Perna, R.B., Durgin, D.L., & Geller, S.E. (1999, October). Patient ratings of modalities in multidisciplinary pain management. Poster session presented at the annual meeting of the American Pain Society, Fort Lauderdale, FL.

Persky, V.W., Kempthorne,Rawson, J., & Shekelle, R.B. (1987). Personality and risk of cancer: 20-year follow-up of the Western Electric Study. *Psychosomatic Medicine, 49,* 435–449.

Peterkin, A.D. (1998). *Staying human during residency training.* Toronto, ON: University of Toronto Press.

Petersen, I., Bhagwanjee, A., and Makhaba, L. (2001). Understanding HIV transmission dynamics in a university student population in South Africa: A qualitative systemic approach. *Journal of Psychology in Africa; South of the Sahara, the Caribbean & Afro-Latin America, 11,* 144–164.

Petticrew, M., Bell, R., & Hunter, D. (2002). Influence of psychological coping on survival and recurrence in people with cancer: Systematic review. *BMJ: British Medical Journal, 325*(7372), 1066–1069.

Petty, R.E., & Cacioppo, J.T. (1981). *Attitudes and persuasion: Classic and contemporary approaches.* Dubuque, IA: Brown.

Phares, F. (1957). Expectancy changes in skill and chance situations. *Journal of Abnormal and Social Psychology, 54,* 339–342.

Philips, S.P. (1997). Problem-based learning in medicine: New curriculum, old stereotypes. *Social Science and Medicine, 45,* 497–499.

Phillips, D. (1996). Medical professional dominance and client dissatisfaction: A study of doctor–patient interaction and reported dissatisfaction with medical care among female patients at four hospitals in Trinidad and Tobago. *Social Science and Medicine, 42,* 1419–1425.

Phillips, K.D., & Morrow, J.H. (1998). Nursing management of anxiety in HIV infection. *Issues in Mental Health Nursing, 19,* 375–397.

Phillips, S. (1996). Sexual harassment of female physicians by patients. What is to be done? *Canadian Family Physician, 42,* 73–76.

Pierce, J.P., Choi, W.S., Gilpin, E.A., Farkas, A.J., & Berry, C.C. (1998). Tobacco industry promotion of cigarettes and adolescent smoking. *Journal of the American Medical Association, 279,* 511–515.

Pinder, R. (1990). *The management of chronic disease: patient and doctor perspectives on Parkinson's disease.* London: MacMillan Press.

Pinckney, R.G., Geller, B.M., Burman, M., & Littenberg, B. (2003). Effect of false-positive mammograms on return for subsequent screening mammography. *The American Journal of Medicine, 114*(2), 120–125.

Piotrowski, C. (1998). Assessment of pain: A survey of practicing clinicians. *Perceptual and Motor Skills, 86,* 181–182.

Pistrang, N., Barker, C., & Rutter, C. (1997). Social support as conversation: Analysing breast cancer patients' interactions with their partners. *Social Science and Medicine, 45,* 773–782.

Pi-Sunyer, X. (2003). A clinical view of the obesity problem. *Science, 299,* 859–860.

Pitts, M.K., Wooliscroft, J., Cannon, S., Johnson, I., & Singh, G. (2000). Factors influencing delay in treatment seeking by first-time attenders at a genitourinary clinic. *International Journal of STD & AIDS, 11,* 375–378.

Plomin, R., DeFries, J.C., McClearn, G.E., & McGuffin, P. (2001). *Behavioral genetics* (4th ed.). New York: Worth.

Poczwarsdowski, A. & Conroy, D.E. (2002). Coping responses to failure and success among elite athletes and performing artists. *Journal of Applied Sport Psychology, 14,* 313–329.

Polatin, P.B., & Mayer, T.G. (2001). Quantification of function in chronic low back pain. In D.C. Turk & R. Melzack (Eds.), *Handbook of pain assessment* (2nd ed., pp. 191–203). New York: Guildford.

Polimeni, A.-M., & Moore, S. (2002). Insights into women's experiences of hospital stays: Perceived control, powerlessness and satisfaction. *Behaviour Change, 19*(1), 52–64.

Polivy, J. (1996). Psychological consequences of food restriction. *Journal of the American Dietetic Association, 96,* 859–592.

Polivy, J., & Herman, C.P. (1987). Diagnosis and treatment of normal eating. *Journal of*

Consulting and Clinical Psychology, 55, 635–644.

Polivy, J. & Herman, C.P. (2002). Causes of eating disorders. *Annual Review of Psychology, 53,* 187–213.

Pomerleau, O.F. (1979). Behavioral factors in the establishment, maintenance, and cessation of smoking. In *Smoking and health: A report of the Surgeon General,* pp. 16–31. Washington, D.C.: GPO.

Pomerleau, O.F., & Pomerleau, C.S. (1989). A biobehavioral perspective on smoking. In T. Ney & A. Gale (Eds.), *Smoking and human behavior.* New York: Wiley.

Pomerleau, O.F., Collins, A.C., Shiffman, S., & Pomerleau, C.S. (1993). Why some people smoke and others do not: New perspectives. *Journal of Consulting and Clinical Psychology, 61,* 723–731.

Pomeroy, W.B. (1972). *Dr. Kinsey and the institute for sex research.* New York: Harper & Row.

Ponte, P.R., Conlin, G., Conway, J.B., Grant, S., Medeiros, C., Nies, J., Shulman, L., Branowicki, P., & Conley, K. (2003). Making patient-centered care come alive: achieving full integration of the patient's perspective. *J Nurs Adm, 33*(2), 82–90.

Poole, G.D., & Craig, K.D. (1992). Judgments of genuine, suppressed, and faked facial expressions of pain. *Journal of Personality and Social Psychology, 63,* 797–805.

Poole, G. D., & Kallhood, L. (1996). Technologists' perceptions of patient stress and technologists' helping strategies: Survey results. *Radiaction,* April, pp. 19–20.

Poole, G.D., Poon, C., Achille, M., White, K., Franz, N., Jittler, S., Watt, K., Cox, D. N., & Doll, R. (2001). Social Support for Prostate Cancer Patients: The Effect of Support Groups. *Journal of Psychosocial Oncology, 19*(2), 1–16.

Poole, G.D., & Ting, K. (1995). Cultural differences between Euro-Canadian and Indo-Canadian maternity patients. *Journal of Social Psychology, 135,* 631–644.

Pope, H.G., Jr. (2001). Unraveling the Adonis complex. *Psychiatric Times, 18*(3), 22–26.

Pope, H.G., Jr., Olivardia, R., Gruber, A.J., & Borowiecki, J. (1999). Evolving ideals of male body image as seen through action toys. *International Journal of Eating Disorders, 26,* 65–72.

Portenoy, R.K., & Lesage, P. (1999). Management of cancer pain. *Lancet, 353*(9165), 1695–1700.

Porteous, A. & Tyndall, J. (1994). Yes, I want to walk to the OR. *Canadian Operating Room Nursing Journal, 12,* 15–25.

Potts, H.W., & Wyatt, J.C. (2002). Survey of doctors' experience of patients using the Internet. *J Med Internet Res, 4*(1), e5.

Pratt, J.P., Overfield, T., & Hilton, H.G. (1994). Health behaviours of nurses and general population women. *Health Values, 18*(5), 41–46.

Prescott, L.M., Harley, J.P., & Klein, D.A. (1999). *Microbiology, 4th ed.* Boston: WCB/McGraw-Hill.

Price, R.A. (2002). Genetics and common obesities: Background, current status, strategies and future prospects. In T. A. Wadden & A. J. Stunkard (Eds.), *Handbook of obesity treatment* (pp. 73–94). New York: Guilford Press.

Prochaska, J.O., & DiClemente, C.C. (1983). Stages and processes of self-change of smoking: Toward an integrative model of change. *Journal of Consulting and Clinical Psychology, 51,* 390–395.

Prochaska, J.O., & DiClemente, C.C. (1986). Toward a comprehensive model of change. In Miller, W.R., Heather, N. et al., (Eds.) *Treating addictive behaviors: Processes of change. Applied clinical psychology.* (pp. 3–27). New York: Plenum Press.

Prochaska, J.O., & Velicer, W.F. (1997). The transtheoretical model of health behavior change. *American Journal of Health Promotion, 12*, 38–48.

Pryse-Phillips, W., Findlay, H., Tugwell, P., Edmeads, J., et al. (1992). A Canadian population survey on the clinical, epidemiological and societal impact of migraine and tension-type headache. *Canadian Journal of Neurol Sci, 19*, 333–339.

Ptacek, J.T., Fries, E.A., Eberhardt, T.L., & Ptacek, J.J. (1999). Breaking bad news to patients: Physicians' perceptions of the process. *Support and Care for Cancer, 7(3)*, 113–120.

Public and Population Health Branch of Health Canada (http://www.hc-sc.gc.ca/pphb)

Quirk, M., & Wapner, S. (1995). Environmental psychology and health. *Environment and Behavior, 27*, 90–99.

Rachman, S., & Taylor, S. (1993). Analysis of claustrophobia. *Journal of Anxiety Disorders, 7*, 1–11.

Raglan, J.S., & Morgan, W.P. (1987). Influence of exercise and "distraction therapy" on state anxiety and blood pressure. *Medicine and Science in Sport and Exercise, 19*, 456–463.

Rains, J.C., Penzien, D.B., & Jamison, R.N. (1992). A structured approach to the management of chronic pain. In L. VandeCreek, S. Knapp, & T.L. Jackson (Eds.), *Innovations in clinical practice: A source book. Vol. 11* (pp. 521–539). Sarasota, FL: Professional Resource Press.

Ramachandran, V.S. (1993). Behavioral and magnetoencephalographic correlates of plasticity in the adult human brain. *Proceedings of the National Academy of Science USA, 90*, 10413–10420.

Ramirez, A.J., Craig, T.K., Watson, J.P., Fentiman, I.S., North, W.R., & Rubens, R.D. (1989). Stress and relapse of breast cancer. *British Medical Journal, 298*, 291–293.

Ramirez, A.J., Westcombe, A.M., Burgess, C.C., Sutton, S., Littlejohns, P. &

Richards, M.A. (1999). Factors predicting delayed presentation of symptomatic breast cancer: A systematic review. *The Lancet, 353*, 1127–1131.

Raphael, B., & Emmerson B. (1991). Are patients clients or people? *Medical Journal of Australia, 154*, 183–184.

Raven, B.H., Freeman, H.E., & Haley, R.W. (1982). Social science perspectives in hospital infection control. In A.W. Johnson, O. Grusky, & B. Raven (Eds.), *Contemporary health services: Social science perspectives* (pp. 139–176). Boston, MA: Auburn House.

Raps, C.S., Peterson, C., Jonas, M., & Seligman, M.E.P. (1982). Patient behavior in hospitals: Helplessness, reactance, or both? *Journal of Personality and Social Psychology, 42*, 1036–1041.

Raven, B.H. (1974). The comparative analysis of power and influence. In J.T. Tedeschi (Ed.), *Perspectives on social power*. Chicago: Aldine.

Ravussin, E., Valencia, M.E., Esparza, J., Bennett, P.H., & Schulz, L.O. (1994). Effects of a traditional lifestyle on obesity in Pima Indians. *Diabetes Care, 17*, 1067-1074.

Reading, J. (1997). The tobacco report. First Nations and Inuit Regional Health Survey. Ottawa, ON: Health Canada.

Rehm, J.T., Bondy, S.J., Sempos, C.T., & Vuong, C.V. (1997). Alcohol consumption and coronary heart disease morbidity and mortality. *American Journal of Epidemiology, 146*, 495–501.

Reid, M.R., Mackinnon, L.T., & Drummond, P.D. (2001). The effects of stress management on symptoms of upper respiratory tract infection, secretory immunoglobulin A, and mood in young adults. *Journal of Psychosomatic Research, 51*, 721–728.

Rejeski, W.J., Hardy, C.H., & Shaw, J. (1991). Psychometric confounds of assessing state anxiety in conjunction with acute bouts of vigorous exercise. *Journal of Sport and Exercise Psychology, 13,* 65–74.

Rennick, J.E., Johnston, C.C., Dougherty, G., Platt, R., & Ritchie, J.A. (2002). Children's psychological responses after critical illness and exposure to invasive technology. *Journal of Developmental & Behavioral Pediatrics, 23*(3), 133–144.

Rentsch, D., Luthy, C., Perneger, T.V., & Allaz, A.F. (2003). Hospitalisation process seen by patients and health care professionals. *Soc Sci Med, 57*(3), 571–576.

Report on the health of Canadians. Prepared by the Federal, Provincial, and Territorial Advisory Committee on Population Health for the meeting of Ministers of Health, Toronto, Canada, September 10–11, 1996

Research-based web design & usability guidelines. (2002, May 8, 2002). [web site]. National Cancer Institute. Available: http://www.usability.gov/guidelines/index.html [2003, July 6].

Research Quarterly for Exercise and Sport (1995). Physical Activity, Health and Well-being. *Research Quarterly for Exercise and Sport Science,* special issue: Proceedings of the International Scientific Consensus Conference, 66, (4): whole.

Resident Duty Hours Language: Final Requirements. (2003, February 13, 2003). Accreditation Council for Graduate Medical Education Board of Directors. Available: www.acgme.org/new/ [2003, July 11].

Resnick, B. (1996). Motivation in geriatric rehabilitation. *IMAGE: Journal of Nursing Scholarship, 28,* 41–45.

Reynolds, D.V. (1969). Surgery in the rat during electrical anesthesia induced by focal brain stimulation. *Science, 164,* 444–445.

Reynolds, F. (2001). Strategies for facilitating physical activity and wellbeing: A health promotion perspective. *British Journal of Occupational Therapy, 64,* 330–336.

Reynolds, P., & Kaplan, G.A. (1990). Social connections and risk for cancer: Prospective evidence from the Alameda County Study. *Behavioral Medicine, 16,* 101–110.

Rice, P.R. *Stress and health (3rd ed.).* Pacific Grove, California: Brooks/Cole.

Richards, J.S., Nepomuceno, C., Riles, M., & Suer, Z. (1982). Assessing pain behavior: The UAB Pain Behavior Scale. *Pain, 14,* 393–398.

Richards, M.A., Westcombe, A.M., Love, S.B., Littlejohns, P., & Ramirez, A.J. (1999). Influence of delay on survival in patients with breast cancer: A systematic review. *The Lancet, 353,* 1119–1126.

Richards, T. (1990). Chasms in communication. *British Medical Journal, 301,* 1407–1408.

Richardsen, A.M., & Burke, R.J. (1991). Occupational stress and job satisfaction among Canadian physicians. *Work and Stress, 5,* 301–313.

Riegel, B.J., Dracup, K.A., & Glaser, D. (1998). A longitudinal causal model of cardiac invalidism following myocardial infarction. *Nurs Res, 47*(5), 285–292.

Rieger, E., Touyz, S.W., & Wain, G.V. (1998). *Journal of Psychosomatic Research, 45,* 201–214.

Riley, J.L. III., Robinson, M.E., Wise, E.A., Myers, C.D., & Fillingim, R.B. (1998). Sex differences in the perception of noxious experimental stimuli: A meta-analysis. *Pain, 74,* 181–187.

Riley, J.L., III, Wade, J.B., Myers, C.D., Sheffield, D., Papas, R.K., & Price, DD. (2002). Racial/ethnic differences in the experience of chronic pain. *Pain, 100,* 291–298.

Rithotz, M.D., & Jacobson, A.M. (1998). Living with hypoglycemia. *Journal of General Internal Medicine, 13,* 799–804.

Robins, L.N. (1995). Editorial: the natural history of substance use as a guide to setting drug policy. *American Journal of Public Health, 85,* 12–13.

Robinson, D. (1973, July 15). Ten noted doctors answer ten tough questions. Parade.

Robinson, G.C., Armstrong, R.W., Brendle-Moczuk, & Loock, C.A. (1992). Knowledge of fetal alcohol syndrome among native Indians. *Canadian Journal of Public Health, 83*(5), 337–338.

Robinson, G.E. (2003). Stresses on women physicians: Consequences and coping techniques. *Depress Anxiety, 17*(3), 180–189.

Robinson, L. (2000). *Statistical information related to medical schools and teaching hospitals*: Association of American Medical Colleges Data Book.

Robinson, T.N., & Killen, J.D. (1997). Do cigarette warning labels reduce smoking? Paradoxical effects among adolescents. *Archives of Pediatrics and Adolescent Medicine,151,* 267–272.

Rodin, J. (1981). Current status of the internal–external hypothesis for obesity: What went wrong? *American Psychologist, 36,* 361–372.

Rodin, J. & Janis, I.L. (1982). In H.S. Friedman & M.R. DiMatteo (Eds.), *Interpersonal Issues in Health Care* (pp. 33–49). New York: Academic Press.

Rodin, J., & Salovey, P. (1989). Health psychology. *Annual Review of Psychology, 40,* 533–579.

Rodrigue, J.R., & Hoffman, R.G. (1994). Caregivers of adults with cancer: multi-dimensional correlates of psychological distress. *Journal of Clinical Psychology in Medical Settings, 1,* 231–244.

Rodrigues, R.J., & Risk, A. (2003). eHealth in Latin America and the Caribbean: development and policy issues. *J Med Internet Res, 5*(1), e4.

Romano, M. (2003). Not just a Web site. In response to consumers as well as competitors, hospitals are getting more sophisticated with their Internet presence. *Modern Healthcare, 33*(21), 22–26.

Rootman, I., Goodstadt, M., Potvin., and Springett, J. (2001). A framework for health promotion evaluation. In Rootman, I., Goodstadt, M., Hyndman, B., McQueen, D.V., Potvin, L., Springett, J., and Ziglio (Eds.). *Evaluation in health promotion: Principles and perspectives.* World Health Organization Regional Publications, European Series, No. 92.

Rose, J.S., Chassin, L., Presson, C.C., & Sherman, S.J. (1996). Prospective predictors of quit attempts and smoking cessation in young adults. *Health Psychology, 15,* 261–268.

Rosen, D.M., Lam, A.M., Carlton, M.A., Cario, G.M., & McGride, L. (1998). Analgesia following major gynecological laparoscopic surgery—PCA versus intermittent intramuscular injection. *Journal of the Society of Laparoendoscopic Surgery, 2*(1), 25–29.

Rosengard, C., Chambers, D.B., Tulsky, J.P., Long, H.L., and Chesney, M. (2001). Value on health, health concerns and practices of women who are homeless. *Women & Health, 34,* 29–44.

Rosenstock, I.M. (1974). Historical origins of the health belief model. *Health Education Monographs, 2,* 328–335.

Rosenstock, I.M., Strecher, V.J., & Becker, M.H. (1994). The Health Belief Model and HIV risk behavior change. In R.J. DiClemente & J.L. Peterson (Eds.), *Preventing AIDS: Theories and methods of behavioral interventions* (pp. 5–25). New York: Plenum.

Roseveare, C., Seavell, C., Patel, P., Criswell, J., Kimble, J., Jones, C., & Shepherd, H. (1998). Patient-controlled sedation and analgesia, using propofol and alfentanil, during colonoscopy: A prospective randomized controlled trail. *Endoscopy, 30,* 768–773.

Ross, C.E., & Duff, R.S. (1982). The effects of client characteristics, type of practice and experiences with care. *Journal of Health and Social Behavior, 23*, 119–131.

Ross, C.E. and Mirowsky, J. (2002). Family relationships, social support and subjective life expectancy. *Journal of Health & Social Behavior, 43,* 469–489.

Rosser, W.W. (1996). Approach to diagnosis by primary care clinicians and specialists: Is there a difference? *Journal of Family Practice, 42*, 139–144.

Roter, D.L., & Hall, J.A. (1998). Why physician gender matters in shaping the physician–patient relationship. *Journal of Women's Health, 7*, 1093–1097.

Roter, D.L., Hall, J.A., Merisca, R., Nordstrom, B., et al. (1998). Effectiveness of interventions to improve patient compliance: A meta-analysis. *Medical Care, 36*, 1138–1161.

Rotter, J. (1996). Generalized expectancies for internal versus external control of reinforcement. *Psychological Monographs, 80*, (Whole issue).

Rotton, J., and Dubitsky, S.S.. (2002). Immune function and affective states following a natural disaster. *Psychological Reports, 90*, 521–524.

Rouse, B.A. (Ed.). (1998). Substance abuse and mental health statistics source book. Rockville, MD: Department of Health and Human Services: Substance Abuse and Mental Health Services Administration.

Roux, S., Markle, L., & Diamond, A. (1998). False positive rate for screening mammography. *New England Journal of Medicine, 339*, 561.

Rowbotham, M.C., & Lowenstien, D.H. (1990). Neurolgic consequences of cocaine use. In W.P. Creger, C.H. Coggins, & E.W. Hancock (Eds.), *Annual review of medicine (Vol. 41)*. Palo Alto, CA: Annual Reviews.

Rowley, B.B., Baldwin, D.C., & McGuire, M.B. (1991). Selected characteristics of graduate medical education in the Unites States. *Journal of the American Medical Association, 266*, 933–943.

Rozanski, A., Blumenthal, J.A., & Kaplan, J. (1999). Impact of psychological factors on the pathogenesis of cardiovascular disease and implications for therapy. *Circulation, 99*, 2192–2217.

Rudolph, D.L., & Butki, B.D. (1998). Self-efficacy and affective responses to short bouts of exercise. *Journal of Applied Sport Psychology, 10*, 268–280.

Rudolph, K.D., Dennig, M.D., & Weisz, J. R. (1995). Determinants and consequences of children's coping in the medical setting: Conceptualization, review and critique. *Psychological Bulletin, 118*, 328–357.

Rugulies, R. (2002). Depression as a predictor for coronary heart disease: A review and meta-analysis. *American Journal of Preventive Medicine, 23*(1), 51–61.

Ruiter, R.A.C., Abraham, C., and Kok, G. (2001). Scary warnings and rational precautions: A review of the psychology of fear appeals. *Psychology and Health, 16*, 613–630.

Rushall, B.S., (1984). The content of competition thinking. In W.F. Straub and J.M. Williams (Eds.), *Cognitive Sport Psychology*. Lansing, Michigan: Sport Science Associates.

Russell, N.K., & Roter, D.L. (1993). Health promotion counseling of chronic-disease patients during primary care visits. *American Journal of Public Health, 83*, 979–982.

Russell, S. (1999). An exploratory study of patients' perceptions, memories and experiences in an intensive care unit. *Journal of Advanced Nursing, 29*, 783–791.

Rutledge, P. C. & Sher, K. J. (2001). Heavy drinking from the freshman year into early young adulthood: The roles of stress, tension-reduction drinking motives, gender and personality. *Journal of Studies on Alcohol, 62,* 457–466.

Saarinen-Rahiika, H., & Binkley, J.M. (1998). Problem-based learning in physical therapy: A review of the literature and overview of the McMaster University experience. *Physical Therapy, 78*, 195–207.

Sabir, S., Godwin, M., & Birtwhistle, R. (1997). Men and women residents' experiences with women's health care in a family medicine center. *Academic Medicine, 72*, 293–295.

Sacco, R.L., Elkind, M., Boden-Albala, B.I., Feng, L., et al. (1999). The protective effect of moderate alcohol consumption on ischemic stroke. *Journal of the American Medical Association, 281*, 53–60.

Sachs, B.C. (1992). Coping with cancer. *Stress Medicine, 8*, 167–170.

Safer, M.A., Tharps, Q.J., Jackson, T.C., & Leventhal, H. (1979). Determinants of three stages of delay in seeking care at a medical care clinic. *Medical Care, 17*, 11–29.

Sainsbury, R., Johnston, C., & Haward, B. (1999). Effect on survival of delays in referral of patients with breast-cancer symptoms: A retrospective analysis. *The Lancet, 353*, 1132–1135.

Salmela, J.H. (1992). *The World Sport Psychology Sourcebook* (2nd ed.). Champaign, Illinois: Human Kinetics.

Salmon, P. (2000). Effects of physical exercise on anxiety, depression, and sensitivity to stress: A unifying theory. *Clinical Exercise Review, 21*, 33–61.

Salovey, P., O'Leary, A., Stretton, M.S., Fishkin, S.A., & Drake, C.A. (1991). Influence of mood on judgments about health and illness. In J.P. Firgas (Ed.), *Emotion and social judgments* (pp. 241–262).

Sanderson, B.K., Raczynski, J.M., Cornell, C.E., Hardin, M., & Taylor, H.A., Jr. (1998). *American Journal of Epidemiology, 149*, 489.

Sands, L. P., Yaffe, K., Covinsky, K., Chren, M.-M., Counsell, S., Palmer, R., Fortinsky, R., & Landefeld, C. S. (2003). Cognitive screening predicts magnitude of functional recovery from admission to 3 months after discharge in hospitalized elders. *Journals of Gerontology: Series A: Biological Sciences & Medical Sciences, 58*(1), 37–45.

Santavirta, N., Bjorvell, H., Solovieva, S., Alaranta, H. Hurskainen, K., & Konttinen, Y.T. (2001). Coping strategies, pain and disability in patients with hemophilia and related disorders. *Arthritis and Rheumatism, 45,* 48–55.

Santos, S.R., Carroll, C.A., Cox, K.S., Teasley, S.L., Simon, S.D., Bainbridge, L., Cunningham, M., & Ott, L. (2003). Baby boomer nurses bearing the burden of care: A four-site study of stress, strain, and coping for inpatient registered nurses. *J Nurs Adm, 33*(4), 243–250.

Sarafino, E.P. (1998). *Health psychology: Biopsychosocial interactions*. New York: John Wiley and Sons.

Sarafino, E.P., & Goehring, P. (2000). Age comparisons in acquiring biofeedback control and success in reducing headache pain. *Annals of Behavioral Medicine, 22,* 10–16.

Sasieni, P., Adams, J., & Cuzick, J. (2003). Benefit of cervical screening at different ages: evidence from the UK audit of screening histories. *Br J Cancer, 89*(1), 88–93.

Sawatzky, J.V. and Naimark, B.J. (2002). Physical activity and cardiovascular health in aging women: A health-promotion perspective. *Journal of Aging & Physical Activity, 10*, 396–412.

Schacter, S. (1971). Some extraordinary facts about obese humans and rats. *American Psychologist, 26,* 129–144.

Schacter, S. (1982). Recidivism and self-cure of smoking and obesity. *American Psychologist, 37*, 436–444.

Scheifer, S.J., Keller, S.E., Camerino, M., Thornton, J.C., & Stein, M. (1983). Suppression of lymphocyte stimulation following bereavement. *Journal of the American Medical Association, 250*, 374–377.

Scheifer, S.J., Keller, S.E., Meyerson, A.T., Raskin, M.J., Davis, K.L., & Stein, M. (1984). Lymphocyte function in major depressive disorder. *Archives of General Psychiatry, 41*, 484–486.

Schilling, L.M., Scatena, L., Steiner, J.F., Albertson, G.A., Lin, C.T., Cyran, L., Ware, L., & Anderson, R.J. (2002). The third person in the room: Frequency, role, and influence of companions during primary medical care encounters. *Journal of Family Practice, 51*(8), 685–690.

Schmale, A.H., Jr., & Engel, G.L. (1967). The giving up–given up complex illustrated on film. *Archives of General Psychiatry, 17*, 135–145.

Schmittdiel, J., Selby, J.V., Grumbach, K., & Quesenberry, C.P. (2000). Effect of physician and patient gender concordance on patient satisfaction and preventive care practices. *Journal of General Internal Medicine, 15*, 761–769.

Schmitz, M.F., & Crystal, S. (2000). Social relations, coping, and psychological distress among persons with HIV/AIDS. *Journal of Applied Social Psychology, 30*(4), 665–683.

Schneiderman, N., Antoni, M., Saab, P.G., and Ironson, G. (2001). Health psychology: Psychosocial and biobehavioral aspects of chronic disease management. *Annual Review of Psychology, 52*, 555–580.

Schroder, I.M. (1971). Conceptual complexity and personality organization. In Schroder, H.M. & Suedfeld, P. (Eds.), *Personality theory and information processing* (pp. 240–273). New York: Ronald Press.

Schubert, D., Burns, Paras, W., & Sioson, E. (1992). Increase of medical hospital length of stay by depression in stroke and amputation patients: A pilot study. *Psychotherapy and Psychosomatics, 57*, 61–66.

Schuckit, M.A. (1996). Recent developments in the pharmacotherapy of alcohol dependence. *Journal of Consulting and Clinical Psychology, 64*, 669–676.

Schulz, R., Bookwalla, J., Knapp, J.E., Scheier, & Williamson, G.M. (1996). Pessimism, age, and cancer mortality. *Psychology and Aging, 11*, 304–309.

Schutz, J., & Luthe, W. (1959). *Autogenic training: A psychophysiological approach to psychotherapy.* New York: Grune and Stratton.

Schwam, K. (1998). The phenomenon of compassion fatigue in perioperative nursing. *AORN Journal, 68*, 642–645, 647–648.

Schwartz, G.E., & Weiss, S.M. (1978). Behavioral medicine revisited: An amended definition. *Journal of Behavioral Medicine, 1*, 249–251.

Schwitzer, G. (2002). A review of features in Internet consumer health decision–support tools. *J Med Internet Res, 4*(2), E11.

Sciadas, G. (2002, October 01). *The digital divide in Canada*, [Internet]. Statistics Canada [2003, July 4].

Scott, C.G., & Ambroson, D.L. (1994). The rocky road to change: Implications for substance abuse programs on college campuses. *Journal of American College Health, 42*, 291–296.

Scott, K. (1994). *Substance abuse among Indigenous Canadians.* Paper presented at the Joint Research Advisory Meeting, Ottawa.

Segall, A., & Roberts, L.W. (1980). A comparative analysis of physician estimates and levels of medical knowledge among patients. *Sociology of Health and Illness, 2*(3), 317–334.

Seligman, M.E.P. (1975). *Helplessness.* San Francisco: Freeman.

Sellick, S.M., & Zaza, C. (1998). Critical review of 5 nonpharmacologic strategies for managing cancer pain. *Cancer Prevention and Control, 2*(1), 7–14.

Sellwood, W., & Tarrier, N. (1994). Demographic factors associated with extreme non-compliance in schizophrenia. *Social Psychiatry and Psychiatric Epidemiology, 29*, 172–177.

Selye, H. (1974). *Stress without distress.* Philadelphia: Lippincott.

Selye, H. (1976). *Stress in health and disease.* Woburn, MA: Butterworth.

Selye, H. (l956). *The stress of life.* New York: McGraw-Hill.

Selye, H. (l993). History of the stress concept. In L. Goldenberger and S. Breznitz (Eds.), *Handbook of stress: Theoretical and clinical aspects* (pp. 7–17). New York: Free Press.

Serdula, M.K., Mokdad, A.H., Williamson, D.F., Galuska, D.A., Mendelein, J.M., & Heath, G.W. (1999). Prevalence of attempting weight loss and strategies for controlling weight. *Journal of the American Medical Association, 282*, 1353–1358.

Serprell, L., & Tresure, J. (2002). Bulimia nervosa: Friend or foe? The pros and cons of bulimia nervosa. *International Journal of Eating Disorders, 32*(2), 164–170.

Sexton, M.M. (1979). Behavioral epidemiology. In O.F. Pomerleau & J.P. Brady (Eds.), *Behavioral medicine: Theory and practice* (pp. 3–22). Baltimore MD: Williams & Wilkins.

Seymour, G.J., Savage, N.W., & Walsh, L.J. (1995). *Immunology: An introduction for the health sciences.* Roseville, NSW: McGraw-Hill Australia.

Sgoutas-Emch, S.A., Cacioppo, J.T., Uchino, B.N., Malarkey, W., Pearl, D., Kiecolt-Glaser, J.K., & Glaser, R. (1994). The effects of an acute psychological stressor on cardiovascular, endocrine, and cellular immune response: A prospective study of individuals high and low in heart reactivity. *Psychophysiology, 31*, 264–271.

Shadel, W.G., Shiffman, S., Niaura, R., Nichter, R., Nichter, M., & Abrams, D.B. (2000). Current models of nicotine

dependence: What is known and what is needed to advance understanding of tobacco etiology among youth. *Drug and Alcohol Dependence, 59* (Suppl.), S9–S22.

Shapiro, S. (1977). Evidence on screening for breast cancer from randomised trial. *Cancer, 39*, 2772–2782.

Shekelle, R.B., Raynor, W.J., Ostfeld, A.M., Garron, D.C., Bieliauskas, L.A., Liu, S.C., Maliza, C., & Paul, O. (1981). Psychological depression and 17-year risk of death from cancer. *Psychosomatic Medicine, 43*, 117–125.

Sheldon, K.M. & Laura, K. (2001). Why positive psychology is necessary. *American Psychologist, 56*, 216–217.

Sheperd, T.M. (2003). Effective management of obesity. *The Journal of Family Practice, 52*, 34–42.

Sheridan, M. (1992). *Pain in America.* Tuscaloosa: University of Alabama Press.

Shields-Poe, D., & Pinelli, J. (1997). Variables associated with parental stress in neonatal intensive care units. *Neonatal Network, 16*, 29–37

Shiffman, S., Paty, J.A., Gnys, M., Kassel, J.D., & Elash, C. (1995). Nicotine withdrawal in chippers and regular smokers: Subjective and cognitive effects. *Health Psychology, 14*, 301–309.

Shifren, K., Bauserman, R., & Carter, D.B. (1993). Gender role orientation and physical health: A study among young adults. *Sex Roles, 29*, 421–432.

Shlain, L. (1979). Cancer is not a four-letter word. In C.A. Garfield, (Ed.), *Stress and survival: The emotional realities of life-threatening illness.* St. Louis: C.V. Mosby.

Shopland, D.R., & Burns, D.M. (1993). Medical and public health implications of tobacco addiction. In C.T. Orleans & J. Slade (Eds.) *Nicotine addiction: Principles and management.* New York: Oxford University Press.

Silverman, J., Kurtz, S. & Draper, J. (1998). *Skills for communicating with patients.* Radcliffe Medical Press: Abingdon, Oxon, UK.

Silver Wallace, L. (2002). Osteoporosis prevention in college women: Application of the expanded health belief model. *American Journal of Health Behavior, 26,* 163–172.

Simon, E.P. (1999). Hypnosis using a communication device to increase magnetic resonance imaging tolerance with a claustrophobic patient. *Military Medicine, 164*(1), 71–72.

Simpson, M., Buckman, R., Stewart, M., Maguire, P., et al. (1991). Doctor–patient communication: The Toronto consensus statement. *British Medical Journal, 303,* 1385–1367.

Sinclair, S. (1997). *Making doctors: An institutional apprenticeship.* Oxford: Berg.

Sist, T.C., Florio, G.A., Miner, M.F., Lema, M.J., & Zevon, M.A. (1998). The relationship between depression and pain language in cancer and chronic non-cancer pain patients. *Journal of Pain and Symptom Management, 15,* 350–358.

Sluijs, E.M., Kerssens, J.J., van der Zee, J., & Myers, L.B. (1998). Adherence to physiotherapy. In L.B. Meyers, Midence, K., et al., (Eds.), *Adherence to treatment in medical conditions.* Amsterdam: Harwood Academic.

Smart, G. (1997). Helping children relax during magnetic resonance imaging. *American Journal of Maternity and Child Nursing, 22,* 236–241.

Smith, B.N. and Stasson, M.F. (2000). A comparison of health behavior constructs: Social psychological predictors of AIDS-preventive behavioral intentions. *Journal of Applied Social Psychology, 30,* 443–462.

Smith, J.C. (l993). *Understanding stress and coping.* New York: MacMillan.

Smith, R.E. (1980). Development of an integrated coping response through cognitive-affective stress management training. In I.G. Sarason and C.D. Spielberger (Eds.), *Stress and anxiety (Vol. 7).* Washington, D.C.: Hemisphere Publishing Corporation.

Smith, R.E. (1999). Generalization effects in coping skills training. *Journal of Sport and Exercise Psychology, 21,* 189–204.

Smith, T.W., Kendall, P.C., & Keefe, F.J. (2002). Behavioral medicine and clinical health psychology: Introduction to the special issue: A view from the Decade of Behavior. *Journal of Consulting and Clinical Psychology, 70,* 459–462.

Smith, T.W. & Ruiz, J.M. (2002). Psychosocial influences on the development and course of coronary heart disease: Current status and implications for Research and practice. *Journal of Consulting and Clinical Psychology, 70,* 548–568.

Sobel, L.C., Sobel, M.B., Toneatto, T., & Leo, G.I. (1993). What triggers the resolution of alcohol problems without treatment? *Alcoholism: Clinical and Experimental Research, 17,* 217–224.

Sohara, N., Takagi, H., Abe. T., Hashimoto, Y., Kojiina, A., Takahashi, H., Nagamine, T., & Mori, M. (1999). Nausea and vomitting by arterial chemo-embolization in patients with hepatocellular carcinoma and the antiemetic effect of ondansetron hydrochloride. *Support Care Cancer, 7*(2), 84–88.

Solomon, G.F., & Moos, R.H. (1964). Emotions, immunity and disease: A speculative theoretical integration. *Archives of General Psychiatry, 11,* 657–674.

Solomon, G.F. Segerstrom, S.C., Grohr, P., Kemeny, M., and Fahey, J. (1997). Shaking up immunity: Psychological and immuno-logic changes after a natural disaster. *Psychosomatic Medicine, 59,* 114–127.

Sonstroem, R.J. (1997). Physical activity and self-esteem. In W.P. Morgan (Ed.), *Physical activity and mental health* (pp. 127–143). Washington, DC: Taylor and Francis.

Spencer, J., Young, M.E., Rintala, D., & Bates, S. (1995). Socialization to the culture of a rehabilitation hospital: an ethnographic study. *Journal of Occupational Therapy, 49*, 53–62.

Spickard, A., Gabbe, S.G., & Christensen, J.F. (2002). Mid-career burnout in generalist and specialist physicians. *JAMA: Journal of the American Medical Association, 288*(12), 1447–1450.

Spiegel, D. & Bloom, J.R. (1983). Group therapy and hypnosis reduce metastatic breast carcinoma pain. *Psychosomatic Medicine, 45*, 333–339.

Spiegel, D., Bloom, J.R., Kraemer, H.C., & Gottheil, E. (1989). Psychological support for cancer patients. *Lancet, 2*, 1447.

Spiegel, D., Sephton, S.E., Terr, A.I., & Stites, D.P. (1998). Effects of psychosocial treatment in prolonging cancer survival may be mediated by neuroimmune pathways. *Annals of the New York Academy of Sciences, 840*, 674–683.

Stainer, U.M., Grond, S., & Maier, C. (1999). Responders and non-responders to post-operative pain treatment: The loading dose predicts analgesic needs. *European Journal of Anaesthesiology, 16*, 103–110.

Standl, T., Burmeister, M.A., Ohnesorge, H., Wilhelm, S., Striepke, M., Gottschalk, A., Horn, E.P., & Schulte Am Esch, J. (2003). Patient-controlled epidural analgesia reduces analgesic requirements compared to continuous epidural infusion after major abdominal surgery. *Can J Anaesth, 50*(3), 258–264.

Stanton, W.R., Mahalski, P.A., McGee, R., & Silva, P.A. (1993). Reasons for smoking or not smoking in early adolescence. *Addictive Behaviors, 18*, 321–329.

Starfield, B. (1994) Is primary care essential?, *Lancet, 344*, 1129.

Starfield, B., Wray, C., Hess, K., Gross, R., et al. (1981). The influence of patient-practitioner agreement on outcome of care. *American Journal of Public Health, 71*, 127–131.

Starkes, J.L., Helson, W., & Jack, R. (2001). In R.N. Singer, H.A. Hausenblas & C.M. Janelle (Eds.), *Handbook of Sport Psychology* (2nd ed. pp.174–204). New York: Wiley.

Statistics Canada (1999). *Toward a Healthy Future: Second Report on the Health of Canadians*. Ottawa, Ontario.

Statistics Canada. (2002). *The Daily: Household Internet use survey* (56F0003XIE).

Statistics Canada (2002, May 8). Canadian community health survey: A first look. *The Daily,* http://www.statcan.ca/Daily/English/020508/d020508a.htm [July 9, 2003].

Statistics Canada (2003). *Selected leading causes of death by sex.* htttp://www.statcan.ca/english/Pgdb/health36.htm [July 11, 2003].

Steele, C.M., & Josephs, R.A. (1990). Alcohol myopia: Its prized and dangerous effects. *American Psychologist, 45*, 921–933.

Steffens, D.C., O'Connor, C.M., Jiang, W.J., Pieper, C.F., Kuchibhatia, M.N., Arias, R.M., Look, A., Davenport, C., Gonzalez, M.B., & Krishnan, K.R. (1999). The effect of major depression on functional status in patients with coronary artery disease. *Journal of the American Geriatric Society, 47*, 319–322.

Stegen, K., Neujens, A., Crombez, G., Hermans, D., et al. Negative affect, respiratory reactivity, and somatic complaints in a CO_2 enriched air inhalation paradigm. *Biological Psychology, 49*, 109–122.

Stein, P.N., & Motta, R.W. (1992). Effects of aerobic and nonaerobic exercise on depression and self-concept. *Perceptual Motor Skills, 74*, 79–89.

Steinhausen, H.C., Winkler, C., & Meier, M. (1997). Eating disorders in adolescence in a Swiss epidemiological study. *International Journal of Eating Disorders, 22*, 247–251.

Sternbach, R.A. (1968). *Pain: A psychophysio-logical analysis.* New York: Academic Press.

Sternbach, R.A. (1986). Clinical aspects of pain. In R.A. Sternbach (Ed.), *The psychology of pain (2nd ed.).* New York: Raven Press.

Sternbach, R.A. (1989). Acute versus chronic pain. In P.D. Wall & R. Melzack (Eds.), *Textbook of pain (2nd ed.).* Edinburgh: Churchill Livingstone.

Stevens, B. (1997). Pain assessment in children: Birth through adolescence. *Child and Adolescent Psychiatric Clinics of North America, 6,* 725–743.

Stevens, B. (2001). Acute pain management in infants in the neonatal intensive care unit. In G. A. Finley & P. J. McGrath (Eds.) Acute and procedure pain in infants and children. *Progress in pain research and management, 20,* 101–128. Seattle: IASP Press.

Stevenson, K. (2002). Health information on the Net. *Canadian Social Trends*(Autumn), 7–9.

Stewart, M., Brown, J.B., Donner, A., McWhinney, I.R., Oates, J., Weston, W.W., & Jordan, J. (2000). The impact of patient-centered care on outcomes. *The Journal of Family Practice, 49,* 796–804.

Stewart, M. A, Brown, J. B, Levenstein, J.H., McCracken, E., & McWhinney, I.R. (1986). The patient-centered clinical method: Changes in residents' performance over two months of training. *Family Practice, 3,* 164–167.

Stewart, M.A., Brown, J.B., Weston, W.W., McWhinney, I.R., et al. (1999). *Patient–centred medicine: Transforming the clinical method.* Thousand Oaks: Sage.

Stewart, M.A., McWhinney, I.R., & Buck, C.W. (1979). The doctor–patient relationship and its effect upon outcome. *Journal of the Royal College of General Practice, 29,* 77–82.

Stice, E. (1994). Relation of media exposure to eating disorder symptomology: An examination of mediating mechanisms.

Journal of Abnormal Psychology, 103, 836–840.

Stice, E., Cameron, R.P., Killen, J.D., Hayward, C., & Taylor, C.B. (1999). Naturalistic weight-reduction efforts prospectively predict growth in relative weight and onset of obesity among female adolescents. *Journal of Consulting and Clinical Psychology, 67,* 967–974.

Stilwell, N.A., Wallick, M.M., Thal, S.E., & Burleson, J.A. (2000). Myers-Briggs type and medical specialty choice: A new look at an old question. *Teaching & Learning in Medicine, 12*(1), 14–20.

Stoller, E.P. (1984). Self-assessments of health by the elderly: The impact of informal assistance. *Journal of Health and Social Behavior, 25,* 260–270.

Stone, A.A., Cox, D.S., Valdimarsdottir, H., Jandorf, L., & Neale, J.M. (1987). Evidence that secretory IgA antibody is associated with daily mood. *Journal of Personality and Social Psychology, 52,* 988–993.

Stone, A.A., Mezzacappa, E.S., donaatone, B.A., and Gonder, M. (1999). Psychosocial stress and social support are associated with prostate-specific antigen levels in men: Results from a community screening program. *Health Psychology, 18,* 482–486.

Story, M., French, S.A., Resnick, M.D., et al. (1995). Ethnic/racial and socioeconomic differences in dieting behaviors and body image perceptions in adolescents. International *Journal of Eating Disorders, 18,* 173–179.

Straub, R.O. (2002). *Health psychology.* New York: Worth.

Strauss, G.J. (1996). Psychological factors in intensive management of insulin dependent diabetes mellitus. *Nursing Clinics of North America, 31,* 737–745.

Strecher, V.J., Champion, V.L., & Rosenstock, I.M. (1997). The health belief model and health behavior. In Gochman, D.S. et al.

(Eds.). *Handbook of health behaviour research 1: Personal and social determinants* (pp. 71–91). New York: Plenum Press.

Struckman-Johnson, C., Struckman-Johnson, D., Gilliland, R.C., & Ausman, A. (1994). Effective persuasive appeals in AIDS PSAs and condom commercials on intentions to use condoms. *Journal of Applied Social Psychology, 24*, 2223–2244.

Stuber, M.L. (1995). Stress responses to pediatric cancer: A family phenomenon. *Family Systems Medicine, 13*, 163–172.

Stuijs, E.M., Kerssens, J.J., van der Zee, J., Myers, L.B. (1998). Adherence to physiotherapy. In L.B. Myers, K. Midence et al. (Eds.), *Adherence to treatment in medical conditions* (pp. 363–382). Amsterdam: Harwood Academic Publishers.

Suinn, R. (1972). Behavioral rehearsal training for ski racers. *Behavior Therapy, 3*, 519.

Sullivan, M.D., LaCroix, A.Z., Spertus, J.A., Hecht, J., & Russo, J. (2003). Depression predicts revascularization for 5 years after coronary angiography. *Psychosomatic Medicine, 65*(2), 229–236.

Sullivan, M.J.L., Tripp, D.A., & Santor, D. (2000). Gender differences in pain and pain behavior: The role of catastrophizing. *Cognitive Therapy and Research, 24,* 121–134.

Sullivan, P. (1990). Women close in on 50% share of places in Canada's medical schools. *Canadian Medical Association Journal, 143*, 781–783.

Sullivan, P. (2003). Famiily medicine crisis? Field attracts smallest-ever share of residency applicants. *Canadian Medical Association Journal, 168*(7), 881–882.

Sullivan, P., & Buske, L. (1998). Results from CMA's huge 1998 physician survey point to a dispirited profession. *Canadian Medical Association Journal, 159*(5), 525–528.

Suls, J., Martin, R., & Leventhal, H. (1997). Social comparison, lay referral, and the decision to seek medical care. In B. P.

Buunk & F. X. Gibbons (Eds.), *Health, coping, and well-being: Perspectives from social comparison theory,* (195–226). Mahwah, NJ: Erlbaum.

Sunshine, A., & Olson, N.Z. (1989). Non-narcotic analgesics. In P.D. Wall & R. Melzack (Eds.), *Textbook of pain (2nd ed.).* Edinburgh: Churchill Livingstone.

Surgenor, L.J., Horn, J., Hudson, S.M. Lunt, H. and Tennent, J. (2000). Metabolic control and psychological sense of control in women with diabetes mellitus: Alternative considerations of the relationship. *Journal of Psychosomatic Research, 49*, 267–273.

Sutton, S.R., & Eiser, J.R. (1984). The effect of fear-arousing communications on cigarette smoking: An expectancy-value approach. *Journal of Behavioral Medicine, 7*, 13–34.

Szasz, T.S., & Hollender, M.H. (1956). A contribution to the philosophy of medicine. The basic models of the doctor–patient relationship. *Archives of Internal Medicine, 97*, 585–592.

Tabar, L., Fagerberg, G., Duffy, S., & Day, N. (1989). The Swedish two-country trial of mammographic screening for breast cancer: Recent results and calculations of benefit. *Journal of Epidemiology and Community Health, 43*, 107–114.

Takeshita, J. (2003). Internet pharmacy prescription and phentermine overdose. *Journal of Clinical Psychiatry, 64*(2), 215.

Tagliacozzo, D.L., & Mauksch, H.O. (1972). The patient's view of the patient's role. In E.G. Jaco (Ed.), *Patients, physicians, and illness* (2nd ed., pp. 172–185).

Tannock, I.F., & Warr, D.G. (1998). Unconventional therapies for cancer: A refuge from the rules of evidence? *Canadian Medical Association Journal, 159*, 801–802.

Tate, A.K., & Petruzzello, S.J. (1995). Varying the intensity of acute exercise: Implications for changes in affect. *Journal of Sports Medicine and Physical Fitness, 35*, 1–8.

Taylor, J. (1994). On exercise and sport avoidance: A reply to Dr. Albert Ellis. *The Sport Psychologist, 8*, 262–271.

Taylor, J. (1996). Intensity regulation and athletic performance. In J.L. Van Raalte and B.W. Brewer (Eds.), *Exploring sport and exercise psychology* (pp. 75–106). Washington, D.C.: American Psychological Association.

Taylor, J., & Taylor, S. (1997). *Psychological approaches to sports injury rehabilitation.* Gaithersburg, MD: Aspen Publishers.

Taylor, N., Hall, G.M., & Salmon, P. (1996). Is patient–controlled analgesia controlled by the patient? *Social Science and Medicine, 43*, 1137–1143.

Taylor, S.E. (1979). Hospital patient behavior: Reactance, helplessness, or control? *Journal of Social Issues, 35*, 156–184.

Taylor, S.E., Klein, L.C., Lewis, B.P., Gruenewald, T.L., Gurung, R.A.R., & Updegraff, J.A.. (2000). Biobehavioral responses to stress in females: Tend-and-befriend, not fight-or-flight. *Psychological Review, 107,* 411–429.

Taylor, S.M., Goldsmith, C.H., & Best, J.A. (1996). The community intervention trial for smoking cessation (COMMIT). *Health and Canadian Society, 2,* 179–195.

Taylor, S.M., Ross, N.A., Cummings, K.M., Glasgow, R.E., et al. (1998). Community intervention trial for smoking cessation (COMMIT): Changes in community attitudes toward cigarette smoking. *Health Education Research, 13*, 109–122.

Taylor, V.M., Anderson, G.M., McNeney, B., Diehr, P., Lavis, J.N., Deyo, R.A., Bombardier, K C. Malter, A., & Axcell, T. (1998). Hospitalizations for back and neck problems: a comparison between the Province of Ontario and Washington State. *Health Services Research, 33*, 929–945.

Tedeschi, R.G., & Calhoun, L.G. (1995). *Trauma and transformation: Growing in the aftermath of suffering.* Thousand Oaks, CA: Sage.

Tell, G.S., Polak, J.F., Ward, B.J., Kittner, S.J., et al., (1994). Relation of smoking with carotid artery wall thickness and stenosis in older adults.: The Cardiovascular Health Study. *Circulation, 90*, 2905–2908.

Tennier, L.D. (1997). Discharge planning: An examination of the perceptions and recommendations for improved discharge planning at the Montreal General Hospital. *Social Work in Health Care, 26*(1), 41–60.

Teno, J.M., & Coppola, K.M. (1999). For every numerator, you need a denominator: A simple statement but key to measuring the quality of care of the "dying". *Journal of Pain and Symptom Management, 17*, 109–113.

Thackwray, D.E., Smith, M.C., Bodfish, J.W., & Meyers, A.W. (1993). A comparison of behavioral and cognitive–behavioral intervention for bulimia nervosa. *Journal of Consulting and Clinical Psychology, 61*, 639–645.

Theorell, T., Blomkvist, V., Jonsson, H., Schulman, S., Berntorp, E., & Stigendel, L. (1995). Social support and the development of immune function in human immunodeficiency virus infection. *Psychosomatic Medicine, 57*, 32–36.

Thomas, D.B., Gao, D.L., Ray, R.M., Wang, W.W., Allison, C.J., Chen, F.L., Porter, P., Hu, Y.W., Zhao, G.L., Pan, L.D., Li, W., Wu, C., Coriaty, Z., Evans, I., Lin, M.G., Stalsberg, H., Self, S.G. (2002). Randomized trial of breast self-examination in Shanghai: Final results. *Journal of the National Cancer Institute, 94*,1420–1421.

Thomas, K.B. (1987). General practice consultations: Is there any point in being positive? *British Medical Journal, 294*, 1200–1202.

Thomas, P.D., Goodwin, J.M., & Goodwin, J.S. (1985). Effects of social support on stress-related changes in cholesterol level, urine acid level, and immune function in an elderly sample. *American Journal of Psychiatry, 142*, 735–737.

Thomas, R.E. (1997). Problem-based learning: measurable outcomes. *Medical Education, 31*, 320–329.

Thomas, W., White, C.M., Mah, J., Geisser, M.S., et al. (1995). Longitudinal compliance with annual screening for fecal occult blood. *American Journal of Epidemiology, 142*, 176–182.

Thomason, T.E., McCune, J.S., Bernard, S.A., Winer, E.P., Tremont, S., & Lindley C.M. (1998). Cancer pain survey: Patient-centered issues in control. *Journal of Pain Symptom Management, 15*, 275–284.

Thompson, C.L., & Pledger, L.M. (1993). Doctor–patient communication: Is patient knowledge of medical terminology improving? *Health communication, 5*, 89–97

Thompson, D.S., & Shear, M.K. (1998). Psychiatric disorders and gynecological oncology: A review of the literature. *General Hospital Psychiatry, 20*, 241–247.

Thompson, J.K. (1986, April). Larger than life. *Psychology Today*, pp. 38–44.

Thompson, R.A., & Sherman, R.T. (1993). *Helping athletes with eating disorders.* Champaign, IL: Human Kinetics Publishers.

Thompson, S. (1999). Perceptions of health risks by cigarette smokers. *Journal of the American Medical Association, 282,* 1722–1723.

Thorne, S., Paterson, B., Russell, C., & Schultz, A. (2002). Complementary/alternative medicine in chronic illness as informed self-care decision making. *International Journal of Nursing Studies, 39*(7), 671–683.

Thun, M.J., Day-Lally, C.A., Calle, E.E., Flanders, W.D., & Heath, C.W., Jr. (1995). Excess mortality among cigarette smokers: Changes in a 20-year interval. *American Journal of Public Health, 85*, 1223–1230.

Tierney, A.J., Taylor, J., Closs, S.J. (1992). Knowledge, expectations and experiences of patients receiving chemotherapy for breast cancer. *Scandinavian Journal of Caring Sciences, 6*(2), 75–80.

Timko, C. (1987). Seeking medical care for a breast cancer symptom: Determinants of intentions to engage in prompt or delay behavior. *Health Psychology, 6*, 305–328.

Tinsley, J.A. (1998). Reverse gender bias—a caution to women faculty. *Academic Medicine, 73*, 1130–1131.

Tjepkema, M. (2002). The health of the off-reserve Aboriginal population. *Health Reports: How Health Are Canadians*, Supplement to Volume 13, 73–88.

Tomasi, T.B., Jr. (1971). *The immune system of secretions.* Englewood Cliffs, NJ: Prentice-Hall.

Tomkins, S.S. (1966). Psychological model for smoking behavior. *American Journal of Public Health, 56 (Suppl. 12)*, 17–20.

Tomkins, S.S. (1968). A modified model of smoking behavior. In E.F. Borgatta & R.R. Evans (Eds.), *Smoking, health and behavior* (pp. 165–188). Chicago: Aldine.

Tomporowski, P.D., & Ellis, N.R. (1986). Effects of exercise on cognitive process: A review. *Psychological Bulletin, 99*, 338–346.

Topaz, O., Minisi, A.J., Bernardo, N., Alimar, R., Ereso, A., & Shah, R. (2003). Comparison of effectiveness of excimer laser angioplasty in patients with acute coronary syndromes in those with versus those without normal left ventricular function. *Am J Cardiol, 91*(7), 797–802.

Toynbee, P. (1977). *Patients.* New York: Harcourt Brace.

Tremblay, S., Ross, N.A., and Berthelot, J-M. (2002). Regional socio-economic context and health. *Health Reports: How Healthy Are Canadians*, Supplement to Volume 13, 33–44.

Triandis, H.C., Bontempo, R., Villareal, M.J., Asai, M., & Lucca, N. (1998). Individualism and collectivism: Cross-cultural perspectives on self-ingroup relationships. *Journal of Personality and Social Psychology, 54*, 323–338.

Trotter, R.T., II. (1991). Ethnographic research methods for applied medical anthropology. In Hill, C.E. (Ed.), *Training manual in applied medical anthropology.* (pp. 180–212). Washington, D.C.: American Anthropological Association.

Tsoh, J.Y., McClure, J.B., Skaar, K.L., Wetter, D.W., et al. (1997). Smoking cessation 2: Components of effective intervention. *Behavioral Medicine, 23*, 15–27.

Turk, D.C. (1997). The role of demographic and psychosocial factos in transition from acute to chronic pain. In T.S. Jensen, J.A. Turner, & Z. Wiesenfeld-Hallin (Eds.), *Proceedings of the 8th World Congress on Pain: Progress in pain research and management* (pp. 185–213). Seattle: International Association for the Study of Pain Press.

Turk, D.C., Kerns, R.D., & Rosenberg, R. (1992). Effects of marital interaction on chronic pain and disability: Examining the downside of social support. *Rehabilitation Psychology, 37*, 259–274.

Turk, D.C., Litt, M.D., Salovey, P., & Walker, J. (1985). Seeking urgent pediatric treatment: Factors contributing to frequency, delay, and appropriateness. *Health Psychology, 4*, 43–59.

Turk, D.C., & Meichenbaum, D. (1991). Adherence to self-care regimens: the patient's perspective. In R.H. Rozensky, J.J. Sweet, & S.M. Tovian (Eds.), *Handbook of clinical psychology.I. Medical settings* (pp. 249–266). New York: Plenum.

Turk, D.C., Meichenbaum, D., & Genest, M. (1983). *Pain and behavioral medicine: A cognitive-behavioral perspective.* New York: Guilford Press.

Turk, D.C., & Melzack, R. (2001). The measurement of pain and the assessment of people experiencing pain. In D.C. Turk & R. Melzack (Eds.), *Handbook of pain assessment* (2nd ed., pp. 1–11). New York: Guilford.

Turk, D.C., & Melzack, R. (Eds.). (2001). *Handbook of pain assessment.* (2nd ed.) New York: Guilford.

Turk, D.C., & Okifuji, A. (1996). Perception of traumatic onset, compensation status, and physical findings: Impact on pain severity, emotional distress, and disability in chronic pain patients. *Journal of Behavioral Medicine, 19*, 435–454.

Turk, D.C., & Stacey, B.R. (2000). Multidisciplinary pain centers in the treatment of chronic back pain. In J. W. Frymoyer, T. B. Ducker, N. M. Hadler, J. P. Kostuik, J. N. Weinstein, & T. S. Whitcloud (Eds.), *The adult spine: Principles and practice* (2nd ed). Philadelphia: Lippincott Williams & Wilkins.

Turk, D.C., Wack, J.T., & Kerns, R.D. (1985). An empirical examination of the "pain-behavior" construct. *Journal of Behavioral Medicine, 8*, 119–130.

Turk, D.C., Zacki, H.S., & Rudy, T.E. (1993). Effects of intraoral appliance and biofeedback/stress management alone and in combination in treating pain and depression in TMD patients. *Journal of Prosthetic Dentistry, 70*, 158–164.

Turk, M. (1993). High anxiety. *The New Physician*, September, pp. 16–22.

Turncock, C. (1991). Communicating with patients in the ICU. *Nursing Standard, 5(15)*, 38–40.

Turner Cobb, J.M., & Steptoe, A. (1998). Psychosocial influences on upper respiratory infectious illness in children. *Journal of Psychosomatic Research, 45*, 319–330.

Twycross, R.G. & McQuay, H.J. (1989). Opioids. In P.D. Wall & R. Melzack (Eds.), *Textbook of pain (2nd ed.).* Edinburgh: Churchill Livingstone.

Tyc, V.L., Fairclough, D., Fletcher, B., Leigh, L., et al. (1995). Children's distress during magnetic resonance imaging procedures. *Children's Health Care, 24*, 5–19.

Unruh, A.M. (1996). Gender variations in clinical pain experience. *Pain, 65,* 123–167.

Unruh, A.M., Ritchie, J., & Merskey, H. (1999). Does gender affect appraisal of pain and pain coping strategies? *Clinical Journal of Pain, 15(1),* 31–40.

Urbszat, D., Herman, C.P., & Polivy, J. (2002). Eat, drink, and be merry, for tomorrow we diet: Effects of anticipated deprivation on food intake in restrained and unrestrained eaters. *Journal of Abnormal Psychology, 111,* 396–401.

Usability basics. (2002, May 8, 2002). [web site]. National Cancer Institute. Available: http://www.usability.gov/ [2003, June 29].

U.S. Department of Health and Human Services (USDHHS). (1998). Preliminary results from the 1997 National Household Survey on Drug Abuse (DHHS Publication No. SMA 98–3251). Washington, DC: U.S. Government Printing Office.

Vallerand, R.J. & Rousseau, F.L. (2001). Intrinsic and extrinsic motivation in sport and exercise: A review using the hierarchical model of intrinsic and extrinsic motivation. In R.N. Singer, H.A. Hausenblas & C.M. Janelle (Eds.), *Handbook of Sport Psychology* (2nd ed. pp. 389–416).New York: Wiley.

Vaillant, G.E., Sobowale, N.C., & McArthur, C. (1972). Some psychologic vulnerabilities of physicians. *New England Journal of Medicine, 287,* 372–375.

Van Elderen, T., Maes, S., Rouneau, C., & Seegers, G. (1998). Perceived gender differences in physician consulting behaviour during internal examination. *Family Practice, 15,* 147–152.

Van Wel, F., & Knobbout, J. (1998). Adolescents and fear appeals. *International Journal of Adolescence and Youth, 7,* 121–135.

VanIneveld, C.H., Cook, D.J., Kane, S.L., & King, D. (1996). Discrimination and abuse in internal medicine residency. The Internal Medicine Program Directors of Canada. *Journal of General Internal Medicine, 11,* 401–405.

Varni, J.W., & Thompson, K.L. (1986). Biobehavioral assessment and management of pediatric pain. In N.A. Krasnegor, J.D. Arasteh, & M.F. Cataldo (Eds.), *Child health behavior: A behavioral pediatrics perspective.* New York: Wiley.

Varni, J.W., Thompson, K.L., & Hanson, V. (1987). The Varni/Thompson Pediatric Pain Questionnaire I: Chronic musculoskeletal pain in juvenile rheumatic arthritis. *Pain, 28,* 27–38.

Vealey, R. (1988). Future directions in psychological skills training. *The Sports Psychologist, 2,* 318–336.

Verberne, T.J.P. (2002). Suicide in doctors. *Journal of Epidemiology & Community Health, 56(3),* 237.

Verhoef, M.J., Casebeer, A.L., & Hilsden, R.J. (2002). Assessing efficacy of complementary medicine: adding qualitative research methods to the "Gold Standard". *J Altern Complement Med, 8(3),* 275–281.

Verhoef, M.J., Hagen, N., Pelletier, G., & Forsyth, P. (1999). Alternative therapy use in neurologic diseases: Use in brain tumor patients. *Neurology, 52,* 617–622.

Verhoef, M.J., & White, M.A. (2002). Factors in making the decision to forgo conventional cancer treatment. *Cancer Pract, 10(4),* 201–207.

Veronin, M. A. (2002). Where are they now? A case study of health-related Web site attrition. *J Med Internet Res, 4(2),* E10.

Viemeroe, V., & Krause, C. (1998). Quality of life in individuals with physical disabilities. *Psychotherapy and Psychosomatics, 67,* 317–322.

Villareal, M.C., Brown, C.M., & Lawson, K.A. (1998). Differences in morphine consumption administered by PCA and traditional IV methods in a pediatric population. *Journal of Pharmaceutical Care in Pain and Symptom Control, 6,* 75–94.

Volume III: Gathering strength. (1996). Ottawa: Royal Commission on Aboriginal Peoples.

von Baeyer, C.L., Baskerville, S., & McGrath, P.J. (1998). Everyday pain in three- to five-year-old children in day care. *Pain Research and Management, 3(2)*, 111–116.

von Baeyer, C.L., Johnson, M.E., & McMillan, M.J. (1984). Consequences of nonverbal expression of pain: Patient distress and observer concern. *Social Science and Medicine, 19*, 1319–1324.

Von Koch, L., Wottrich, A. W., & Holmqvist, L.W. (1998). Rehabilitation in the home versus the hospital: The importance of context. *Disability and Rehabilitation: An International Multidisciplinary Journal, 20*, 367–372.

Vuckovic, N. (1999). Fast relief: Buying time with medications. *Medical Anthropology Quarterly, 13*, 51–68.

Wadden, T.A., Brownell, K.D., & Foster, G.D. (2002). Obesity: Responding to the global epidemic. *Journal of Consulting and Clinical Psychology, 70,* 510–525.

Wadden, T.A., Womble, L.G., Stunkard, A.J., & Anderson, D.A. (2002). Psychosocial consequences of obesity and weight loss. In T. A. Wadden & A. J. Stunkard (Eds.) *Handbook of obesity treatment* (pp. 144–169). New York: Guilford Press.

Wadee, A.A., Kuschke, R.H., Kometz, S., and Berk, M. (2001). Personality factors, stress and immunity. *Stress & Health: Journal of the International Society for the Investigation of Stress, 17*, 25–40.

Waite, B.T., Gansneder, B., & Rotella, R.J. (1990). A sport-specific measure of self-acceptance. *Journal of Sport and Exercise Psychology, 12*, 264–279.

Waitzkin, H. (1984). Doctor–patient communication: Clinical implications of social scientific research. *Journal of the American Medical Association, 252*, 2441–2446.

Waitzkin, H. (1985). Information giving in medical care. *Journal of health and Social Behavior, 26*, 81–101.

Walsh, B.T., & Devlin, M.. (1998). Eating disorders: Progress and problems. *Science, 280,* 1387–1390.

Walsh, J.D., Blanchard, E.B., Kremer, J.M., & Blancard, C.G. (1999). The psychosocial effects of rheumatoid arthritis on the patient and the well partner. *Behaviour Research and Therapy, 37*, 259–271.

Walsh, N.E., & Dimitru, D. (1988). The influence of compensation on recovery from low back pain. *Occupational Medicine: State of the Art Reviews, 3*, 109–120.

Walsh-Burke, K. (2000). Matching bereavement services to level of need. *Hospice Journal, 15*(1), 77–86.

Walston, K.A., Wallston, B.S., & DeVellis, R. (1978). Development of the Multi-dimensional Health Locus of Control (MHLC) scale. *Health Education Monographs, 6*, 161–170.

Wann, D.L. (1997). *Sport psychology.* Upper Saddle River, New Jersey: Wadsworth.

Ward, A., Ramsay, R., & Treasure, J.L. (2000a). Attachment research in eating disorders. *British Journal of Medical Psychology, 73,* 35–51.

Walters, E.E., & Kendler, K.S. (1995). Anorexia nervosa and anorexic-like syndromes in a population-based female twin sample. *American Journal of Psychiatry, 152*, 64–71.

Ward, A., Ramsay, R., & Turnbull, S., Benedettini, M., & Treasure, J. (2000b). Attachment patterns in eating disorders: Past in the present. *International Journal of Eating Disorders, 28,* 370–376.

Ward, H.E., Tueth, M., & Sheps, D. (2003). Depression and cardiovascular disease. *Current Opinion in Psychiatry, 16*(2), 221–225.

Ward, K.G. (1999). A TEAM approach to NICU care. *RN, 62*(2), 47–49.

Wardle, J., & Pope, R. (1992). The psychological costs of screening for cancer. *Journal of Psychosomatic Research, 36*, 609–624.

Ware, M. A., Doyle, C. R., Woods, R., Lynch, M. E., & Clark, A. J. (2003). Cannabis use for chronic non-cancer pain: Results of a prospective study. *Pain, 102*, 211–216.

Warrick, P.D., Irish, J.C., Morningstar, M., Gilbert, R., Brown, D., & Gullane, P. (1999). Use of alternative medicine among patients with head and neck cancer. *Archives of Otolaryngolical Head and Neck Surgery, 125*, 573–579.

Watkins, L.L., & Grossman, P. (1999). Association of depressive symptoms with reduced baroreflex cardiac control in coronary artery disease. *American Heart Journal, 137*, 453–457.

Watkins, L.R., & Maier, S.F. (2000). The pain of being sick: Implications of immune-to-brain communication for understanding pain. *Annual Review of Psychology, 51*, 29–57.

Watson, D., Roos, N., Katz, A., & Bogdanovic, B. (2003). Is a 5% decline in physician supply significant? *Canadian Family Physician, 49*(5), 566–567.

Watson, M., Davidson-Homewood, J., Haviland, J., & Bliss, J. (2003). Psychological coping and cancer. *BMJ: British Medical Journal, 326*(7389), 598.

Watson, J. (1988). New dimensions in human caring theory. *Nursing Science Quarterly, 4*, 175–181.

Waxler-Morrison, N., Hislop, T.G., Mears, B., & Kan, L. (1991). Effects of social relationships on survival for women with breast cancer: A prospective study. *Social Science and Medicine, 33*, 177–183.

Weiger, W.A., Smith, M., Boon, H., Richardson, M.A., Kaptchuk, T.J., & Eisenberg, D.M. (2002). Advising patients who seek complementary and alternative medical therapies for cancer. *Ann Intern Med, 137*(11), 889–903.

Weinberg, R. & McDermott, M.. (2002). A comparative analysis of sport and business organizations: Factors perceived critical for organizational success. *Journal of Applied Sport Psychology, 14,* 282–298.

Weinberg, R.S. (1996). Goal setting in sport and exercise: Research to practice. In J.L. Van Raalte and B.W. Brewer (Eds.), *Exploring sport and exercise psychology* (pp. 3–24). Washington, D.C.: American Psychological Association.

Weinberg, R.S. & Gould, D. (2003). *Foundations of sport and exercise psychology (3rd Ed.).* Champaign, Illinois: Human Kinetics.

Weiner, D., Peiper, C., McConnell, E., Martinez, S., & Keefe, F. J. (1996). Pain measurement in elders with chronic low back pain: Traditional and alternative approaches. *Pain, 67,* 461–467.

Weiner, E.L., Swain, G.R., Wolf, B., & Gottleib, M. (2001). A qualitative study of physician's own wellness promotion practices. *Western Journal of Medicine, 174*, 19–23.

Weir, E. (2000). Substance abuse among physicians. *Cmaj, 162*(12), 1730.

Weiss, M.R., Wiese, D.M., & Klint, K.A. (1989). Head over heels with success: The relationship between self-efficacy and performance in competitive youth gymnastics. *Journal of Sport and Exercise Psychology, 11*, 444–451.

Weiss, S.R., McFarland, B.H., Burkhart, G.A., & Ho, P.T. (1998). Cancer recurrences and secondary primary cancers after us of antihistamines or antidepressants. *Clinical Pharmacology Therapy, 63*, 594–599.

Weller, A., & Hener, T. (1993). Invasiveness of medical procedures and state anxiety in women. *Behavioral Medicine, 19*, 60–65.

Weller, S.C. (1983). New data on intracultural variability: The hot–cold concept of medicine and illness. *Human Organization, 42*, 341–351.

Wells, D. (1997). A critical ethnography of the process of discharge decision-making for elderly patients. *Canadian Journal on Aging, 16*, 682–699.

Wenger, M., Bagchi, B., & Anand, B. (1961). Experiments in India on "voluntary" control of the heart and pulse. *Circulation, 24,* 1319–1325.

West C. (1993). Reconceptualizing gender in physician–patient relationships. *Social Science and Medicine, 36*, 57–66.

Weston, W.W., & Brown, J.B. (1995). In M. Stewart, J.B. Brown, W.W. Weston, I.R. McWhinney, C.L. McWilliam, & T.R. Freeman. *Patient-centered medicine: Transforming the clinical method.* Thousand Oaks: Sage.

What is Reye's Syndrome? (2000). [Web site]. National Reye's Syndrome Foundation. Available: http://www.reyessyndrome.org [2003, July 4].

What is the Internet, the World Wide Web, and Netscape? (2002, Sept. 27). [Web site]. UC Berkeley Library. Available: http://www.lib.berkeley.edu/TeachingLib/Guides/Internet [2003, June 29].

Whatley, S. (2003). Avoiding the family physician path. *Can Fam Physician, 49*, 565; author reply 565–566.

Whelan, F., & Cooper, P. (2000). The association between childhood feeding problems and maternal eating disorder: A community study. *Psychological Medicine, 30,* 69–77.

While, A.E., & Wilcox, V.K. (1994). Paediatric day surgery: day-case unit admission compared with general paediatric ward admission. *Journal of Advances in Nursing, 19*, 52–57.

White, C., Sheedy, V., & Lawrence, N. (2002). Patterns of computer usage among medical practitioners in rural and remote Queensland. *Aust J Rural Health, 10*(3), 137–146.

White, S.A., & Duda, J.L. (1991, October). The interdependence between goal perspectives, psychological skill, and cognitive interference among elite skiers. Paper presented at the annual meeting of the Association for the Advancement of Applied Sport Psychology, Savannah, Georgia.

Whitehouse, W.G., Orne, E.C., and Dinges, D.F. (2002). Demand characteristics: Toward an understanding of their meaning and application in clinical practice. *Prevention & Treatment*, 5, Article 34.

Whitemore, A.S., Perlin, S.A., & DiCiccio, Y. (1995). Chronic obstructive pulmonary disease in lifetime nonsmokers: Results from NHANES. *American Journal of Public Health, 85*, 702–706.

WHO. (1999). *Medical products and the internet: A guide to finding reliable information* (WHO/EDM/QSM/99.4). Geneva: World Health Organization.

Wiegmann, S.M., & Berven, N.L. (1998). Health locus-of-control beliefs and improvement in physical functioning in a work-hardening, return-to-work program. *Rehabilitation Psychology, 43*, 83–100.

Wilkins, K. (1995). Causes of death: How the sexes differ. *Health Reports, 7*(2), 33–43.

Wilkins, K., & Beaudet, M.P. (1998). Work stress and health. *Health Reports, 10*(3), 47–62.

Wilkins, R., Berthelot, J-M., and Ng, E. (2002). Trends in mortality by neighbourhood income in urban Canada from 1971 to 1996. *Health Reports: How Health Are Canadians*, Supplement to Volume 13, 45–71.

Wilkins, K., & Park, E. (1997). Characteristics of hospital users. *Health Reports, 9*(3), 27–36.

Wilkins, R. (1993). The use of postal codes and addresses in the analysis of health data. *Health Reports, 5*(2), 157–177.

Willenbring, M.L., Levine, A.S., & Morley, J.E. (1986). Stress induced eating and food preference in humans: A pilot study. *International Journal of Eating Disorders, 5,* 855–864.

Williams, J. (2001). Psychology of injury risk and prevention. In R.N. Singer, H.A. Hausenblas & C.M. Janelle (Eds.), *Handbook of Sport Psychology* (2nd ed. pp. 766–786).

Williams, J.E., Paton, C.C., Siegler, I.C. Eigenbrot, M. I., Nieto, F.J., & Tyroler, H.A. (2000). Clinical investigation and reports: Anger proneness predicts coronary heart disease risk: Prospective analysis from the Atherosclerosis Risk in Communities (ARIC) Study. *Circulation, 101,* 2034–2039.

Williams, J.M., & Leffingwell, T.R. (1996). Cognitive strategies in sport and exercise psychology. In J.L. Van Raalte and B.W. Brewer (Eds.), *Exploring sport and exercise psychology* (pp. 51–74). Washington, D.C.: American Psychological Association.

Williams, P.A., Dominick-Pierre, K., Vayda, E., Stevenson, M., & Burke, M. (1990). Women in medicine: Practice patterns and attitudes. *Canadian Medical Association Journal, 143,* 194–201.

Williams, S., Weinman, J., Dale, J., & Newman, S. (1995). Patient expectations: What do primary care patients want from the GP and how far does meeting expectations affect patient satisfaction? *Family Practice, 12*(2), 193–201.

Wing, P.C. (1997). Patient or client? If in doubt, ask. *Canadian Medical Association Journal, 157*(3), 287–289.

Wing, R.R. (2002). Behavioral weight control. In T.A. Wadden & A.J. Stunkard (Eds.), *Handbook of obesity treatment* (pp. 301–316). New York: Guilford Press.

Wing, R.R., Jeffery, R.W., Burton, L.R., Thorson, C., Nissinoff, K. S., & Baxter, J. E. (1996). Food provision versus meal plans in the behavioral treatment of obesity. *International Journal of Obesity, 20,* 56–62.

Winters, R. (1985). Behavioral approaches to pain. In N. Schneiderman & J.T. Tapp (Eds.), *Behavioral medicine: The biopsychosocial approach.* Hillsdale, NJ: Erlbaum.

Witte, K. (1992). Putting fear back into fear appeals; The extended parallel process model. *Communication Monographs, 59,* 329–349.

Witte, K. (1994). Fear control and danger control: A test of the extended parallel process model (EPPM). *Communication Monographs, 61,* 113–134.

Wolf, A.M., & Colditz, G.A. (1998). Current estimates of the economic costs of obesity in the United States. *Obesity Research, 6,* 97–106.

Wolf, Z.R. (1993). Nursing rituals: doing ethnography. *NLN Publications,* August, 269–310.

Wolpe, J. (1958). *Psychotherapy by reciprocal inhibition.* Stanford, California: Stanford University Press.

Wong, H.C. (1999). Educating medical students about alternative therapies. *Canadian Medical Association Journal, 161,* 128–129.

Wood, B.S., & McGlynn, F.D. (2000). Research on posttreatment return of claustrophobic fear, arousal, and avoidance using mock diagnostic imaging. *Behavior Modification, 24*(3), 379–394.

Woods, J.H. (1966). *The yoga-system of Patanjali.* Delhi, India: Motilal Banarsidass.

Woodward, N.J., & Wallston, B.S. (1987). Age and health care beliefs: Self-efficacy as a mediator of low desire for control. *Psychology and Aging, 2,* 3–8.

World Health Organization. (1986). Ottawa Charter for Health Promotion, Ottawa, Canada. Canadian Public Health Association.

World Health Organization. (1998). *Malaria, Fact Sheet No. 94.*

World Health Organization. (1998). *Obesity. Preventing and managing the global epidemic. Report of a WHO consultation on obesity*. Geneva: World Health Organization.

Wright, K.B., & Bell, S.B. (2003). Health-related support groups on the Internet: Linking empirical findings to social support and computer-mediated communication theory. *Journal of Health Psychology, 8*(1), 39–54.

Wright, L. (1988). The Type A behavior pattern and coronary heart disease. *American Psychologist, 43*, 2–14.

Wu, Z. H., Freeman, J. L., Greer, A. L., Freeman, D. H., & Goodwin, J. S. (2001). The influence of patients' concerns on surgeons' recommendations for early breast cancer. *European Journal of Cancer Care, 10*(2), 100–106.

Ye, Z.Q., Lan, R.Z., Du, G.H., Yuan, X.Y., Chen, Z., Ma, Y.Z., et al. (2003). Biofeedback therapy for chronic pelvic pain syndrome. *Asian Journal of Andrology, 5,* 155–158.

Yogananda, P. (1969). *Autobiography of a yogi*. Bombay, India: Jaico Publishing House.Z

Zabora, J., Brintzenhofeszoc, K., Curbow, B., Hooker, C., & Piantadosi, S. (2001). The prevalence of psychological distress by cancer site. *Psycho-Oncology, 10*(1), 19–28.

Zachariae, R., Pedersen, C.G., Jensen, A.B., Ehrnrooth, E., Rossen, P.B., & von der Maase, H. (2003). Association of perceived physician communication style with patient satisfaction, distress, cancer-related self-efficacy, and perceived control over the disease. *British Journal of Cancer, 88,* 658–665.

Zajonc, R.B. (1968). Attitudinal effects of mere exposure. *Journal of Personality and Social Psychology Monograph Supplements, 9*, 1–27.

Zalewski, C., Keller, B., Bowers, C., Miske, P. et al. (1994). Depressive symptomatology and post-stroke rehabilitation outcome. *Clinical Gerontologist, 14*, 62–67.

Zhang, Y., Proenca, R., Maffei, M., Barone, M., Leopold, L., & Friedman, J.M. (1994). Positional cloning of the mouse obese gene and its human homologue. *Nature, 372*, 425–432.

Zanna, M., Cameron, R., Goldsmith, C.H., Poland, B., et al. (1996). Critique of the COMMIT study based on the Brantford experience. *Health and Canadian Society, 2*, 319–336.

Zatzick, d.F., & Dimsdale, J.E. (1990). Cultural variations in response to painful stimuli. *Psychosomatic Medicine, 52*, 544–557.

Zeitlin, D., Keller, S.E., Shiflett, SC., Schleifer, S.J., and Bartlett, J.A. (2000). Immunological effects of massage therapy during acute academic stress. *Psychosomatic Medicine, 62*, 83–84.

Zeltzer, L.R., Tsao, J.C.I., Stelling, C., Powers, M., Levy, S., & Waterhouse, M. (2002). A phase I study on the feasibility and acceptability of an acupuncture/hypnosis intervention for chronic pediatric pain. *Journal of Pain & Symptom Management, 24*, 437–446.

Zifferblatt, S.M. (1975). Increasing patient compliance through applied analysis of behavior. *Preventive Medicine, 4*, 173–182.

Zimbardo, P.G. (1970). The human choice: Individuation, reason, and order versus deindividuation, impulse, and chaos. In W.J. Arnold & D. Levine (Eds.), *Nebraska symposium on motivation, 1969*. Lincoln, NE: University of Nebraska Press.

Zucker, T.P., Flesche, C.W., Germing, U., Schroeter, S., Willers, R., Wolf, H.H., & Hevil, A. (1998). Patient-controlled versus staff-controlled analgesia with pethidine after allogeneic bone marrow transplantation. *Pain, 75*, 305–312.

Zussman, R. (1993). Life in the hospital: A review. *Milbank Quarterly, 71*, 167–185.

Zyzanski, S.J., Strange, K.C., Langa, D., & Flocke, S.A. (1998). Trade-offs in high-volume primary care practice. *Journal of Family Practice, 46*, 397–402.

Index

A

Aboriginal peoples
    diabetes, 309
    health inequities, 177
    HIV/AIDS, 315
    sexual behaviour, 241
    smoking rates, 224
acceleration-deceleration injury, 218
acceptance, reaction to impending death, 322
accessibility, of web sites, 334–335
acquired immunity, 58
active leisure, 200
active-passive model, 96
acupuncture, 283–285
acute condition, 295
acute pain, 266
addictive smokers, 228
A-delta fibres, 262
adherence/compliance, 108–115
    assessing, 108–109
    behavioural strategies, 114
    educational strategies, 114
    health outcomes, 115–116
    internalization and, 113–114
    methods of increasing, 115
    personal characteristics of patient, 110–111
    to physical activity, 211–212
    to physical rehabilitation program, 169
    physician characteristics and, 111
    physician-patient interaction and, 111–112
    social support and, 114–115
    treatment regimen and, 110
    See also non-adherence/non-compliance
adjuvant therapy, 302
adrenal cortex, 37
adrenaline, 36
adrenal medulla, 36
adrenocorticotropic hormone(ACTH), 37
advance practice nursing, 161–162
advertising, online, 336
aerobic exercise, 202
afferent (sensory) neurons, 262
age
    and adherence, 110–111
    and alcohol use, 235
    and experience of symptoms, 88
    and patient delay, 93–94
    and smoking, 224
agency-provided support, 181

agents, 357
AIDS. *See* HIV/AIDS
alarm stage, of General Adaptation Syndrome, 37
alcohol abuse, prevention and treatment
    of, 237–238
alcohol dependency syndrome model, 236
Alcoholics Anonymous (AA), 237
alcohol myopia, 237
alcohol use
    drinking behaviours, 236–237
    and driving, 238
    effects of, 235–236
aldosterone, 37
Aldwin, C.M., 33
allopathic treatment, 360
alternative medicine. *See* complementary and alternative medicine (CAM)
alternative treatment, 360
anaerobic exercise, 202
analgesics, 280
Anand, B. K., 46–47
anger
    and health risks, 42
    as reaction to impending death, 321, 322
    as risk factor of coronary heart disease, 41–42,
        313–314
angioplasty, 311
anorexia nervosa, 251–252, 254–255
antiemetic medication, 302
antigens, 57, 61–62
antimicrobial substances, 59
anxiety
    HIV/AIDS and, 316
    magnetic resonance imaging, 131–134
    myocardial infarction and, 311–312
applied discipline, 345
applied research, 345–346
appraisal delay, 91
arthritis, 318
asymptomatic conditions, 6
atherosclerosis, 230
Athletic performance, methods of enhancing,
    212–216
attitude, 183
autoimmune disease, 69
automatic nervous system, 35
autonomic activity, 273
autonomic nervous system, 35
aversion therapies, 232–233, 238

B

Bagchi, B., 46–47
Bandura, A., 39, 44–45, 50, 205, 206, 207, 287
Bannister, Roger, 205
bargaining, reaction to impending death, 321, 322
Barraclough, J., 70
Baum, A., 5, 7, 8
Beck, A., 50
behavioural alternative to fight-or-flight
    response, 35
behavioural delay, 94
behavioural medicine, 3–4, 5–7
behavioural treatment
    of obesity, 249–250
behaviour therapy, 49–50
beliefs, 40, 183
benefit finding, 306
benign appraisals, 39
benign breast biopsy, 130–131
bereavement, and grief, 322–323
Bernstein, D.A., 51
biobehavioural model, of smoking, 229
biofeedback, 48–49, 288
biomedical model, 14
biopsychosocial approach, 8
    interdisciplinary approach, 12–13, 15
biopsychosocial communication patterns, 97
blunters, 8, 123
B lymphocytes, 58
body dysmorphic disorder, 252–253
    See also muscle dysmorphia
body mass index (BMI), 243
Bonica, John, 290
Borkovec, T.D., 51
Boscarino, J.A., 66
box scale, 275
Brannon, L., 31
Brousse, T., 46–47
Brunton, P., 46
bulimia nervosa, 251, 255
burnout, professional, 127, 128–129, 152, 154

C

Canada
    Internet usage for health information, 328
Canadian Health Network, 333
Canadian Institute for Health Information, 119, 330
Canadian Psychological Association, 10
cancer, 295–307
    biomedical perspective, 12
    and breast self-examination, 19
    as cause of death, 10
    characteristics of disease, 296
    lung cancer, 12
    mood and, 74–76
    physical effects of, 297–298

prostate cancer, 12
    and psychological distress, 298–300
    smoking and, 230
    social support and, 81
    treatment of, 300–302
cancer, stress and, 69–70
cancer screening, health belief model and, 19
cannabis, 239
Cannon, W.B., 34–35
cardiac invalidism, 311
cardiovascular disease, 311–314
    coping with, 313–314
    and psychological distress, 311–313
    types of conditions, 311
cardiovascular health
    behaviour and, 7
    exercise and, 210
    smoking and, 230
caring, *vs.* curing, 161
case, in epidemiological research, 356
case method, 347
catecholamines, 36
Centers for Disease Control, 357
central control trigger, 262–263
centrally acting analgesics, 280–281
central nervous system, 35, 262
central route, of persuasion, 184, 189
Centre for Health Evidence, 330
cerebrovascular disease, smoking and, 230
C fibres, 262
challenge appraisals, 39
chemotherapy, 302
Chhina, G.S., 47
Children's Comprehensive Pain Questionnaire, 279
chronic condition, 294–295, 317–321
    See also cancer; cardiovascular disease; diabetes;
        HIV/AIDS
chronic intractable benign pain, 267
chronic obstructive pulmonary diseases, 230
chronic pain, 267
Chronic Pain Coping Inventory, 278
chronic progressive pain, 267
chronic recurrent pain, 267
cigarette smoking. *See* smoking
claustrophobia, 132
clinical nurse specialist, 162
Clinical significance, 63–64
closed head injury. *See* concussion
cocaine, 240
coercive power, 112
cognitive appraisals, 39–41, 219
cognitive behaviour therapy (CBT), 310
cognitive reappraisal, 39, 40, 313–314
cognitive restructuring, 7, 313–314
cognitive strategies, for coping, 43, 45
cognitive transaction models, 37–41

Cohen, S., 5, 68
commitments, 40
communication, in intensive-care unit, 139–140
Community Intervention Trial for Smoking
    Cessation, 233–234
community-oriented health promotion
    locus of responsibility, 179
    model, 176
    mutual aid, 180
    public policy, 175–176
    self-care, 179–180
    social support, 180–182
compassion fatigue, 152, 162
complementary and alternative medicine
    (CAM), 357–363
    effectiveness of, 361–362
    forms of, 361
    problem of definition, 359–360
    users of, 362–363
complementary treatment, 360
compliance studies, 6–7, 8
concussion, 218–219
conflict theory, 366
consultations, physician, 105–106
consumerist communication patterns, 97, 98
continuing medical education (CME), 165
continuity of care, 136
control group, 349
coping, 43–45
    with cancer, 304–307
    cognitive transaction models, 38–40
    coping response *vs.* stress response, 43
    emotional support, 44
    emotion-focused, 43, 187, 298–299
    goal, 43
    informational support, 44
    outcomes, 43
    and personal control, 44–45
    personal resources, 44
    problem-focused, 43, 187, 298–299
    with psychological loss of control, 123–124
    research on, 8
    social support, 44, 304–306
    styles of, 8, 298–300
    tangible support, 44
    See also stress
coping techniques
    behavioural therapy, 49–50
    cognitive therapy, 49–51
    relaxation skills, 51–53
    relaxation techniques, 45–48, 286–287
    stress management techniques, 45
coronary artery bypass graft (CABG), 311
correlational methods, 348–349
cost-gain belief, 17

Cox, Harvey, 46
creative non-adherence, 108
crisis, 51
cross-sectional research, 352
culture
    and adherence, 111
    and beliefs, 40
    and health, 13
    of hospital, 125–128
    and interpretation of symptoms, 89
    and muscle dysmorphia, 254
    and pain, 272
curing, *vs.* caring, 161
cytotoxic activity, 61

D
Dalhousie Everyday Pain Scale, 278, 279
danger control, 187
data mining, 343
day surgery, 134
death, and dying
    attitude of health professionals, 152
    end-of-life decisions, 141, 145
    stages of, 321–323
defensive reappraisal, 40
dehumanization. *See* depersonalization
delayed gratification, 6–7
demand characteristics, 353
denial
    reaction to impending death, 321, 322
    of uncertainty, 156
Dennig, M.D., 43
dependent variables, 349
depersonalization, 124–125, 139, 152, 154
depressant drugs, 235, 281
depression
    and cancer, 75
    cancer-related, 298–299
    and coping styles, 298–300
    diabetes and, 310
    exercise and, 209
    and heart disease, 71
    heart disease and, 312–313, 314
    and mortality, 71–72
    and pain, 267–268
    See also mood
desensitization, systematic, 49
developing nations
    and Internet access, 341
diabetes, 308–310
    and psychological distress, 308–310
    types of, 308
diathesis-stress model, 80
dieting, 249
digital divide, 342–343

DiMatteo, M.R., 33
direct-effect coping model, 44
discharge planning, 141, 142–143
disease model, of problem drinking, 236
disease of adaptation, 38
disease *vs.* illness, 367
disempowering care, 122
distraction techniques, 287–288
DiTomasso, R.A., 51
doctor-centred consultations, 106
doctors. *See* physicians
do not resuscitate order, 145
Doyle, W.J., 68
drive-reduction theory, 184–187
duration, and cognitive appraisal, 41

E
eating disorders, 8, 251–255
efficacy belief, 17, 185
ego orientation, 216
Eigenbrot, M.I., 42
e-journals, 326
elaboration likelihood model of persuasion, 183–184
electroencephalograph (EEG), 273
electromyograph (EMG), 273
Ellis, A., 50
e-mail, 327, 331, 339
emotional arousal, and efficacy expectations, 207
emotional support, 181
Emotion-focused coping, 298–299
emotion-focused coping, 43, 187
empowering care, 122–123
Empowerplus, 333
encryption, 339
endocrine system, 35, 37
endocrine system, stress and, 172
end-of-life decisions, in palliative care, 141, 145
endogenous opioids, 265
Engel, Fredrich, 367
enumerative assay, 60
environmental tobacco smoke (ETS), 230–231
epidemiologists, 13
epidemiology, 355–357
Epp, Jake, 175
eustress, 33
euthanasia, 145
event uncertainty, and cognitive appraisal, 41
exercise, 11
exercise psychology, 197
exhaustion stage, of General Adaptation Syndrome, 38
expanded biomedical communication patterns, 97
experimental group, 349
experimental method, 349

experimenter bias, 354
Expertise Model, 140
expert power, 113
extended parallel process model, 187–188
external imagery, 215
external reinforcement, 169
Eysenck, J.H., 70, 80

F
factor analysis, 349
false positive results, 130–131, 156
fear, and patient delay, 93
fear appeals, 184–188
fear control, 187
Feist, J., 31
feminism, 367
field research. *See* quasiexperimental designs
fight or flight response, 34–35, 82–83
filmless radiology, 340
focal infection, 57
Folkman, S., 33, 39, 40, 43
Frasure-Smith, N., 314
Friedman, M., 8, 42
FTP (file transfer protocol), 327
Functional Assessment of Cancer Therapy (FACT), 320

G
gastric bypass, 250
gate control theory, 262–263
gender
    and adherence, 111
    and alcohol use, 234
    and effect of alcohol use, 236
    and health values, 18
    and job status, 166
    and medical specialization, 149
    and pain, 270–272
    and physicians experience of stress, 155
    and provision of patient care, 159–161
    and response to stress, 34–35
    self-perception of physicians, 158–159
    and smoking, 224
General Adaptation Syndrome (GAS), 37–38
germ theory, 5
gestational diabetes, 308
Given, B.A., 51
global assessments, 321
glucocorticoids, 37, 83
goal-setting, 216
Goffman, E., 121
grades, of concussion, 219
grief. *See* bereavement, and grief
Grossarth-Maticek, R, 80
Gruenewald, T.L., 35

Grunberg, N.E., 5, 7, 8
guidance-cooperation (collaborative) model, 96, 98
guided imagery, 287
Gurung, R.A.R., 35

H
Haan, N., 32
habitual smokers, 228
Hadjistavropoulos, T., 268, 269–270
hallucinogens, 239–240
Hanson, R.G., 33
harm/loss appraisals, 39
head injuries. *See* concussion
health
    biopsychosocial approach, 12–13
    components of, 200
    and lifestyle, 11–12
    of nurses, 164
    WHO concept of, 4
health and social outcomes, 193
health belief model, 16–19, 182, 242
    usefulness of, 18–20
Health Canada, 328–330, 331, 333
health-care costs, 178
health care system
    inequities of, 177
    shortage of general practitioners, 148–149
    shortage of nurses, 162
health initiatives, online, 330–331
Health On the Net (HON), 333
health promotion
    in Canada, 175–177
    defined, 174
    evaluation of initiatives, 193–194
    goals of, 177–178
    implementation of initiatives, 191–192
    mechanisms, 179–182
    online, 330–331
    planning of initiatives, 191–192
    principles of health psychology and, 182–188
    public policy, 175–176
    social-psychological principles and, 183–189
    WHO and, 174, 175
health promotion actions, 193
health promotion campaigns, 183, 189–191
    credibility of message, 189
    nature of audience, 189–191
health promotion outcomes, 193
health psychology
    and beliefs about personal control, 23–24
    biological links, 64–83
    biopsychosocial approach, 13–15
    defined, 4
    development of, 5–9

emergence of, 3–5
    health belief model, 16–19
    stages of change model, 24–26
    theory of planned behaviour, 22–23
    theory of reasoned action, 20–22
    underlying growth factors, 10–13
health-related inequities, 177–178
health values, 18
heart attack, and patient delay, 91
helper T cells, 59
help-intended communication, 304–305
Herbert, T.B., 5
heredity
    and obesity, 244
    and smoking, 228
Herman, C.P., 247–248
herpesviruses, 61
Highly active antiretroviral treatment
    (HAART), 317
HIV/AIDS, 315–317
    AIDS risk reduction model, 242
    coping with, 316–317
    epidemiology, 358
    negative mood and, 106
    psychological distress, 316
    risk-related behaviours, 18
    social support and, 81–82
    stress and, 78
    symptoms, 315
homeostasis, 34
hormones, and food intake, 245
hospices, 144
hospital care
    and depersonalization, 124–125, 139
    patient adaptation to, 120–124, 125
hospital cleaners, 166–167
Hospital for Sick Children (Toronto), 342
hospitals
    admission procedure, 120
    emergency department, 135–136
    intensive-care unit, 138–141
    neonatal intensive care unit, 141–142
    palliative care, 143–145
    as total institution, 121
hospital separation, 135
hosts, 357
Human Becoming, Theory of, 144
humour, 152, 157
hypermetabolic response, 45
hypnosis, 288–289
hypnotherapy, 307
hypoglycemia, 308–309
hypometabolic response, 45
hypothalamus, 36

I

illicit drug use, 238–241
illness behaviour
    delaying medical care, 91–94
    seeking medical care, 90–91
illness delay, 91
illness vs. disease, 367
imagery, 215
imminence, and cognitive appraisal, 41
immune system, workings of, 57–59
immune-system memory, 58
immunity
    acquired, 58
    non-specific, 59
    specific, 58
immunocompetence, 56
    enumerative assay, 60
    functional tests of, 60–62
    measurement of, 59–63
    mood and, 70–77
    multiple measures, 63
    personality and, 70, 80
    short-term vs. long-term effects of stressors, 62–63
    social support and, 80–82
    statistical significance vs. clinical significance of measures, 63–64
    stress and, 64–70
incidence rate, 356
inclusion criteria, 351–352
incommunication stage, 138
independent variables, 349
index case, 356
infant mortality rates, 178
infections, 57–58
informational power, 112, 113–114
informational support, 181
information-motivation-behavioural skills model, 242
injuries, physical exercise, 216–220
intensive-care unit (ICU), 138–141
interaction, 350
interleukins, 59
intermediate health outcomes, 193
internal imagery, 215
internality-externality hypothesis, 246–247
internalization, 113–114
International Association for the Study of Pain (IASP), 269
Internet
    challenges of, 343–344
    computer networks, 326–327
    consumer information processing, 335–336
    developing nations and, 341
    equality of access, 342–343
    future health-related uses, 344

health-related resources, 327–331
    implications for individuals and public health, 336
    and patient-physician relationships, 336–340
    patterns of usage, 327–328
    physicians' use of, 340–342
    quality of online information, 331–335
    security, 339, 343
    web sites, 333–334, 335
Internet Trade Bureau, 331, 332
internship, 152
interviews, and assessment of pain, 275
intrusive memories, 298
invasiveness, of medical procedure, 129–130
in vitro tests, of immunocompetence, 60–62
irrelevant appraisals, 39
isokinetic exercise, 202
Isometric exercise, 202
isotonic exercise, 202

J

Jackson, T.C., 91–93
Jacobsen, E., 51
Jenner, Bruce, 205
Job Strain Model, 164

K

Kaplan, RM., 44
Kiecolt-Glaser, J.K., 64
Klein, L.R., 35
Kovnat, K.D., 51
Krantz, D.S., 5, 7, 8
Kübler-Ross, E., 321–322

L

Lalonde, Marc, 175
Landy, John, 205
La Via, M.F., 67
lay referral system, 89, 90
Lazarus, R.S., 33, 39, 40, 43
learned helplessness, 122
legitimate power, 113
leptin, 245, 249
Leventhal, H., 91–93
Lewis, B.P., 35
life skills, 212–213
lifestyle, and health, 11–12
lifetime prevalence, 356
limbic system, 36
links, 326
literacy, 190
local anesthetics, 281
localized infection, 57
longitudinal research, 353–354
loss of control, sense of, 120–124

LSD (lysergic acid diethylamide), 239–240
Luce, G., 47
Lyubomirsky, S., 45

M
magnetic resonance imaging, psychology
    of, 131–134
main effects, 350
malpractice claims, 101–102
mammography, psychology of, 129–131
Martin, L.R., 33
Marx, Karl, 366
Masten, A.S., 45
matching groups, 350–351
Maulden, S.A., 339, 340
McCreary Centre Society, 331
McGill Pain Questionaire (MPQ), 276–277, 278,
    279
MDMA (3,4-methylenedioxymethylamphetamine),
    239–240
medical anthropology, 13
medical articles and reports, online, 328–330
medical delay, 91
medical geography, 12
medical jargon, 103–105
medical school, 150–153
medical sociology, 13, 364
medicine
    as career choice, 149–150
    feminization of, 158–161
meditation, 46–48, 286–287
Medline, 340, 341, 342
Melamed, B.G., 50
Melzack, R., 260, 262–263, 264, 265, 276
memory, faulty, 107
memory B cells, 58
message, 285
metastasized cancer, 296
micoorganisms, 57
Miller, N.E., 5, 6, 7
Miller, S.M., 8
mind-body integration, of exercise, 203
mineralococorticoids, 37
Minnesota Multiphasic Personality Inventory
    (MMPI), 75
Mitchell, Weir, 263
mitogen, 61
mixed management of care, 145
Miyazaki, T., 69
modelling, 50
monitors, 8, 123
mood
    and cancer, 74–76
    and experience of symptoms, 88
    and heart health, 105–106

and immune functioning, 70–77
    pain and, 268
    physical activity and, 208–209
    state *vs.* trait (personality), 72–74
    and upper respiratory infection, 72–74
Moos, R.H., 65
mortality statistics, 10, 178
motion artefacts, 132
multidimensional questionnaires, 321
multilevel explanations, 105
multiple regulation model, of smoking, 229
multitasking, and stress, 163
muscle dysmorphia, 253–254
mutual aid, 180
mutual participation model, 95–97
myocardial ischemia, 311

N
Naranjo, C., 46
narcotics. *See* centrally acting analgesics
narrowly biomedical communication patterns, 97, 98
National Cancer Institute, 333
natural-killer (NK) cells, 59
naturally occurring support, 181
negative-affect smoker, 228
negative correlation, 348–352
Negotiated model, 140–141
neonatal intensive care unit (NICU), 141–142
nervous system, stress and, 35–37
neuromatrix theory, 264–265
neurosignature patterns, 265
nicotine fixed-effect model, of smoking, 229
nicotine regulated model, of smoking, 229
nicotine-replacement therapy, 232
Nieto, F.J., 42
NK cell cytotoxic activity assay, 61
NK cell lysis, 61
nociceptors, 261
non-adherence/non-compliance
    behaviours, 108
    cost of, 109–110
    frequency of, 109
    and gradient of reinforcement, 6–7
    health outcomes, 115–116
    to physical activity, 211–212
    reactance and, 113
non-discrepant responses, 105
non-invasive procedures, 119
non-narcotic analgesics. *See* peripherally acting
    analgesics
non-specific immunity, 59
"No Pretending Not to Know," 153
noradrenaline, 36
novelty, as variable in appraisal process, 41
nurse practitioner, 162

nurses
  burnout, 127, 128–129
  health of, 164
  in hospital culture, 125–128
  intensive-care unit, 139
  in palliative care, 145
nursing, 161–167
  nature of, 161–162
  rituals, 125–127
  stress in, 162–164

O

obesity, 242–250
  behavioural treatment of, 249–250
  biological factors, 244–245
  and health-care costs, 179
  and health risks, 243
  heredity and, 244
  measurement of, 243
  pharmacological treatment of, 249
  prevention of, 248–249
  psychosocial factors, 246
  sociocultural factors, 246
  surgical treatment of, 250
observational methods, 346–347
occupational rituals, 126, 127
oncology, 296
online health services, 330
operant pain, 267
orienting responses, 335–336
Oucher scale, 279–292
outcome goals, 216

P

pacreas, 37
pain
  acute *vs.* chronic, 265–270
  behavioural assessment of, 273–274
  behaviours, 267–268
  compensation for injury and, 268, 270
  cues of infants, 278–279
  endogenous opioids and, 265
  functions of, 260
  infants and children, 278–279
  measurement of, 273–280
  neurochemical basis of, 265
  older adults, 279–280
  perception of, 261–262
  phantom limb, 263–264
  psychosocial factors, 270–272
  self-reports, 274–278
  theories of, 262–265
  threshold, 270
  tolerance, 271
Pain Anxiety Symptoms Scale, 278

pain clinics, 290–292
pain management/control
  acupuncture, 283–285
  analgesics, 280
  depressants, 281
  distraction techniques, 287–288
  drug combinations, 281
  local anesthetics, 281
  message, 285
  multidisciplinary programs, 290–292
  narcotics, 280
  in palliative care, 144
  in physical rehabilitation, 170–171
  physical therapy, 285
  postoperative patients, 136–138
  surgery, 281
  transcutaneous electrical nerve stimulation
    (TENS), 282–283
  See also relaxation techniques
palliative care, 143–145
Pap test/Pap smear, 179
parasympathetic nervous system, 35, 37
Parents' Postoperative Pain Measure, 278
Parkinson's disease, 318
Parsons, Talcott, 364
participant modelling, 50
passive leisure, 200
passive smoking, 230
pathogens, 57
patient-centred approach, 128
  consultations, 105–106
  physician-patient interaction, 98–99
patient controlled analgesia (PCA), 137–138
patient deception, 106–107
patient delay, 91–94
patients
  consumption of Internet-based informa-
    tion, 337–338
  day care, 119
  intensive-care unit experience, 138–140
  lack of information-seeking behaviours, 107
  and loss of control, 120–124
  outpatients, 119
  problem of terminology, 95
  sick role, 364–365
Paton, C.C., 42
Patterson, T.L., 44
PCP (phycyclidine), 239–240
Pediatric Pain Questionnaire, 279
Peper, E., 47
performance accomplishments, and efficacy expec-
    tations, 206
performance goals, 216
periaqueductal grey area, 265
peripherally acting analgesics, 280

peripheral nervous system, 35, 262
peripheral route, of persuasion, 184, 189
    See also fear appeals
Perlin, L.I., 32
person, as variable in appraisal process, 40
personality, 41–42
    and cancer, 70, 80
    and coronary heart disease, 41–42
    and immune functioning, 80
    and medicine, 149–150
person variables, 40
persuasion, 183
phantom limb pain, 263–264, 265
pharmacological treatment
    of alcohol abuse, 237
    of obesity, 249
    of pain, 280–281
physical activity
    adherence to, 211–212
    characteristics of, 197
    and cognitive functioning, 207–208
    and components of health, 200
    and injuries, 216–220
    and mood, 208–209
    parameters of, 197
    physical benefits of, 209–211
    psychological benefits of, 202–203
    rates of, 200–202
    and sense of self, 203–207
    types, 197, 202
physical exercise
    definitions of, 197
physical fitness, 197
physical rehabilitation. See rehabilitation programs
physical therapy, 285
physician impairment, stress and, 157
physician-patient communication
    faulty communication, 102–103, 105, 106–107
    information-giving, 99
    and malpractice claims, 101–102
    participation in, 100
    patient behaviours in, 106–107
    patient expectations and preferences, 101–102
    patterns of, 95–98, 99–107
    physician behaviours in, 102–105
    time factor, 105–106
physician-patient interaction, 94–107
    models of, 95–99
    physician attitudes and behaviour, 95
    prognosis, 155–156
    social influence in, 112–114
physicians
    and e-mail, 339
    emotional involvement, 153–154
    and Internet-based information, 337, 338

patient delay, 94
    primary-care, 157
    self-perceptions, 158–159
    and stress, 154–157
    use of Internet, 340–342
    See also gender; medical school; medicine
pituitary gland, 37
placebo effect, 354
planned behaviour, theory of, 22–23, 182, 184
point prevalence, 356
Polivy, J., 247–248
positive-affect smoker, 228
positive appraisals, 39
positive correlation, 348
positive psychology, 45
post-concussion syndrome, 218
postoperative recovery, 136–138
posttraumatic growth, 306
post-traumatic stress disorder (PTSD), 66, 316
power. See social power
practical support, 181
Precede-Proceed model, for health promotion programs, 191–193
predictability, and cognitive appraisal, 41
pre-med syndrome, 122
prevalence, 356
primary appraisals, 39
problem-based learning, 164–166
problem-focused coping, 43, 187, 298–299
process goals, 216
prognosis, 155–156
progressive illnesses, 144
progressive muscular relaxation (PMR), 48, 214, 286
prospective studies, 70, 74–75, 353
protease inhibitor, 317
psychoeducational care, 136
psychoneuroimmunology (PNI), 9, 56
    biological links, 64–83
    components of, 56–57
    future research, 83–84
    and health psychology, 57
    See also immune system, workings of; immunocompetence
psychosocial communication pattern, 97
psychosomatic medicine, 4–5
psychotherapy, 4, 306–307, 316–317
psychotropic medication, 306, 316

Q
quality of life, 144, 318–321
quasiexperimental designs, 350

R
radiation therapy, 301–302

radical surgery, 301
random assignment, 349
random clinical trial studies, 351–352, 361
rational emotive behaviour therapy (REBT), 50, 214–215
reactance, 113, 122
reactivity hypothesis, 82–83
readaptation stage, 138, 139
reality shock, 163
reappraisal. *See* cognitive reappraisal
reasoned action, theory of, 20–22, 182, 242, 367
recurrent pain, 270
referent power, 113, 114
reflexion stage, 138
rehabilitation programs
 adherence, 169
 behavioural interventions, 169–170
 for cardiac patients, 313
 cognitive interventions, 170
 goal setting, 169
 pain management, 170–171
 physical, 169–171
reinforcement, 169–170
relaxation skills, 51–53, 213–214
relaxation techniques, 45–48, 286–287
 biofeedback, 48–49, 288
 Eastern philosophies and, 46–48
 guided imagery, 287
 meditation, 48, 286–287
 progressive muscular relaxation, 48, 286
research
 in epidemiology, 357–358
 flaws in, 353–354
 methods, 345–353
residency, 152
resilience, concept of, 45
resistance stage, of General Adaptation Syndrome, 38, 63
respondent pain, 267–268
restraint theory of eating behaviour, 247–248
reticular formation, 36–37
retrospective research, 353
reward power, 112
Rice, P.R., 35, 43
Rodin, J., 5, 8, 247
role strain, 159
Rosenman, R.H., 8, 42
rotational injury, 218
Rudolph, K.D., 43
Ruiz, J.M., 42

S
Safer, M.A., 91–93
Sallis, J.F., 44
Salovey, P., 5, 8

sampling bias, 354
Sarafino, E.P., 43
SARS (Severe Acute Respiratory Syndrome), 355, 356–357
Schacter,S., 246–247
search engines, 326, 327
secondary appraisals, 39, 40
second impact syndrome, 218
sedatives, 281
sedentary lifestyle, of Canadian adolescents, 201–202
self-awareness model, 237
self-care, 179–180
self-efficacy
 and fear appeal, 187–188
 theory of, 204–207
self-esteem, exercise and, 203–207
self-examination, health belief model and, 19, 20
self-reinforcement, 170
self-talk, 214–215
Selye, Hans, 33, 34, 37–38
sensitivity, of medical tests, 156
seroconversion, 58
set-point theory, 245
sexual behaviour sequence model, 242
Shiatsu, 285
sick role, 364–365
Siegal, L.J., 50
Siegler, I.C., 42
Singh, B., 47
sites of cancer, 296
situation, as variable in appraisal process, 40
situation variables, 40
Skoner, D.P., 68
sleep disturbances, chronic pain and, 268
Smith, J.C., 32
Smith, T.W., 42
smoking, 7, 12
 age and gender, 224
 health consequences of, 229–230
 income and, 234
 motivating factors to start, 225–226
 regular smokers, 228–229
 sociocultural factors, 224–225
smoking cessation, 231–234
 aversion therapies, 232–233
 health hazard warnings and, 180, 226–227
 nicotine-replacement therapy, 232
 on one's own, 232
 and self-care, 179–180
 self-management therapy, 233
social comparison processes, 305–306
social dominance, 42
socialization
 and eating behaviours, 246

and interpretation of symptoms, 89
social learning model, 237
social power, 112–114
social support, 7
    and adherence/compliance, 114–115
    and coping, 44
    coping with cancer, 304–306
    and health promotion, 180–182
    and immune functioning, 80–82
    moderating effect of, 69
socioemotional care, 127
sociology
    theoretical perspectives, 364–367
    See also medical sociology
Solomon, G.F., 65
somatic nervous system, 35
specific immunity, 58
specificity, 58
specificity, of medical tests, 156
Spiegel, D., 69, 70
sport, problem of definition, 198
sport psychology, 197
    and athletic performance, 212–216
    Canadian contributions to, 217
stages of change model, 24–26, 242
stages-of-reaction approaches, to athletic
    injuries, 219
Statistical significance, 63–64
stimulant drugs, 240, 249
stimulation-produced analgesia (SPA), 265
Stone, A.A., 70
stress
    and autoimmune disease, 69
    and cancer, 69–70
    cognitive transaction models, 38–41
    and eating behaviours, 246
    exercise and, 209
    and experience of symptoms, 87
    external causes, 35
    fight or flight response, 34–35
    General Adaptation Syndrome (GAS), 37–38
    of giving bad news, 154–155
    and HIV-positive immune system, 78
    and immunity, 64–70
    literacy, 31–32
    long-term effects of, 63, 66
    personality and, 7–8, 41
    and physicians, 154–157
    physiology of, 35–38
    pioneering work of Selye, 33–34
    problem of definition, 31–33, 34–35
    reality shock, 163
    and upper respiratory infection, 66–69
    See also coping

stress-buffering hypothesis, 44
stress-diathesis model, 38
stressful appraisals, 39
stress inoculation training, 50
stress-intrusion scores, 67
stress management techniques, 45
stressors, 35
substance abuse
    alcohol use, 234–238
    illicit drug use, 238–241
    smoking, 224–234
supressor T cells, 59
surgical control, of pain, 281
surgical treatment, of cancer, 301
survey methods, 347
surveys, 331
Swedish message, 285
symbolic interactionism, 366–367
sympathetic nervous system, stress and, 35–37
symptoms
    interpreting, 88–89, 90
    perceiving, 87–88
    seeking medical care, 90–91
systematic desensitization, 49
systemic infection, 57

T
task orientation, 216
Taylor, S.E., 35
technical care, 127
telemedicine, 340
temporal uncertainty, and cognitive appraisal, 41
tension reduction hypothesis, 237
Tharps, Q.J., 91–93
T-helper cells, 59, 77, 78, 82
therapeutic rituals, 126
threat appraisals, 39
threat perception, 184
thyroid gland, 37
T lymphocytes, 59
tolerance, 58
total institution, 121
total-person approach, to patient problems, 98–99
tranquillizers, 281
transcendent accomplishments, 205–206
transcript analysis, 366–367
transcutaneous electrical nerve stimulation
    (TENS), 282–283
triage, 135
tumours, 296
Type A behaviour pattern, 7
    and coronary heart disease, 41–42
Type A Coronary Prone Behaviour Pattern, 7–8
Type C personality, 80

Type I diabetes, 308, 309
Type II diabetes, 308
Type 1 personality, 70, 80

U
uncertainty, as source of stress, 155–157
uniformity myth, 123
unsafe sexual behaviours, 241–242
upper respiratory infection
    mood and, 72–74
    stress and, 66–69
URLs (uniform resource locators), 326
usability, of web site, 333–334

V
Valsalva manoeuver, 46
Vancouver Hospital and Health Sciences
    Centre, 342
vectors, 357
verbal persuasion, and efficacy expectations, 207
verbal rating scale (VRS), 275, 279
vicarious experience, and efficacy expectations, 206
viral challenge studies, 68
visual analog scale (VAS), 275, 279
vulnerability, concept of, 40

W
Waitzkin, H., 8
Wall, P.D., 260, 262–263
web sites
    hospital, 342
    physician-owned, 339–340
    usability of, 333–334
Weisz, J.R., 43
Wenger, M, 46–47
West Haven-Yale Multidimensional Pain Inventory
    (MPI), 277–278
Williams, J.E., 42
withdrawal, 231
Wolpe, J., 49
women
    interpretation of symptoms, 89
    patient delay, 93, 94
Woods, J.H., 46
workplace stress, nursing, 163
World Health Organization (WHO), 4, 174, 175,
    331, 333

Y
Yoga, 46
yo-yo dieting, 249

Photo Credits